PRODUCT SAFETY

AUSTRALIA

The Law Book Company
Brisbane • Sydney • Melbourne • Perth

CANADA

Carswell
Ottawa • Toronto • Calgary • Montreal • Vancouver

AGENTS

Steimatzky's Agency Ltd., Tel Aviv
N.M. Tripathi (Private) Ltd., Bombay
Eastern Law House (Private) Ltd., Calcutta
M.P.P. House, Bangalore
Universal Book Traders, Delhi
Aditya Books, Delhi
MacMillan Shuppan KK, Tokyo
Pakistan Law House, Karachi, Lahore

PRODUCT SAFETY

FIRST EDITION

EDITORS

Christopher J. S. Hodges M.A. (Oxon.)
Solicitor of the Supreme Court of England and Wales
Solicitor of the Supreme Court of Hong Kong
Partner, McKenna & Co., Solicitors, London

Mark Tyler M.A. (Oxon.) LL.M. (Lond.)
Solicitor of the Supreme Court of England & Wales
Partner, McKenna & Co., Solicitors

Howard Abbott
Product Risk Associates

LONDON
SWEET & MAXWELL
1996

Published in 1996 by
Sweet & Maxwell Limited of
South Quay Plaza, 183 Marsh Wall, London E14 9FT.
Computerset by LBJ Enterprises Ltd. Aldermaston and Chilcompton
Printed and Bound in Great Britain by Hartnolls Ltd, Bodmin

No natural forests were destroyed to make this product; only farmed timber was used and re-planted

The index was prepared by Robert Spicer, Barrister

A CIP catalogue record for this book
is available from the British Library

ISBN 0 421 50370 X

Foreword

Competitiveness is the key issue facing businesses today. It covers a wide range of factors which must be addressed if any company is to succeed. Not least of these is the safety of the products it supplies to consumers. Unsafe products risk a loss of competitiveness and market share, not to mention a damaged reputation, claims for compensation and, in some cases, prosecution.

We can justifiably claim that with the introduction in 1987 of a general safety requirement, the United Kingdom has been at the forefront of legislation designed to ensure the safety of consumer products. Indeed, the General Product Safety Directive takes the United Kingdom experience as its model in producing a Europe-wide general safety duty.

This Directive, which is implemented in the United Kingdom by the General Product Safety Regulations 1994, provides a framework for assessing the safety of consumer goods which is flexible and which makes use of commonly agreed standards wherever possible. This is clearly of benefit to consumers and of great importance to businesses selling their goods in the United Kingdom and the test of Europe.

This book deals with a wide range of product safety issues, including safety legislation, risk management, product recalls and product liability law. It is aimed at decision-takers in business and, I have no doubt, will be a valuable addition to the body of information and guidance in these very important areas.

Rt. Hon. Ian Lang M.P.
President of the Board of Trade

Making products which are safe, and are recognised as being safe, is a vital concern to British industry. From a householder buying kitchen equipment to a manufacturer buying production equipment, purchasers and users need to be able to rely upon the safety of their products. Safety should be taken for granted as much as the quality of British products.

British industry has an enviable record in making products to the highest safety and quality standards. As the statistics in Chapter 1 of this book demonstrate, the volume of prosecutions and enforcement actions taken against consumer and workplace products in this country in recent years is low, with most problems coming from imported products. Our concern for product safety has been reflected in a history of consumer protection and health and safety legislation which stretches back over thirty and twenty years respectively—far longer than most countries.

European harmonisation has now reached the product safety and health and safety fields. This comprehensive and timely book explains the intricacies of the new legislation in these areas and goes further in providing practical advice on how to design, manufacture and market safe products. The editors have all been closely involved with working parties of the Confederation of British Industry on these topics. I am pleased to be able to commend this book to designers, manufacturers, marketing and commercial managers, as well as to lawyers.

Adair Turner
Director-General
Confederation of British Industry

Preface

This book is addressed to the directors and managers within British industry who are responsible for the design, manufacture and marketing of products and to the lawyers, regulatory affairs and risk managers and insurers who advise them. It aims to describe the new regulatory controls over products, introduced largely as a result of new European measures. These rules are supposed to be the same throughout the countries of the European Union. We say "supposed to be" because they should be more or less the same but they certainly will not be. That makes things difficult for companies to do business with certainty and for company managers to know how they are exposed under the regulatory law. Such people are exposed. Make no mistake: if you are in industry — this means you!

Why have we written this book? There is basically a lot of new law. The stimulus is an important European Directive, which introduces a number of standard regulatory provisions across the European Union relating to the marketing of safe products. Directive 92/59/EEC on general product safety specifies that all consumer products must be safe and can only be marketed if they are safe. All Member States are to have extensive powers to control the marketing of products, including the power to order withdrawal. Many of these powers are not new in this country nor in some other Member States. Part II of the Consumer Protection Act 1987, following the Consumer Safety Act 1978, itself having origins in the Consumer Protection Act 1961, established both a general safety requirement for products and extensive regulatory powers. However, although at least the general framework of these provisions is to remain largely unaltered, it is now subject to the requirement of conformity with the Directive. Any aspect of the current legislation which is not in conformity may be challenged. Thus, the general product safety legislation in each State of the European Union should, as a matter of Community law, conform to the Directive.

This book is in two notional halves: the first is about law and the second addresses practical aspects. In reality, however, all the chapters are about different ways of looking at the same thing—the achievement of product safety. You will find some overlap between aspects discussed in different chapters: this is not only inevitable in considering product safety but deliberate.

In the first half of this book, Christopher Hodges and Mark Tyler examine a wide range of relevant law. The basic objective running through all this new law is to achieve a high level of product safety. In

Chapter 1 we examine why product safety is important and look at some revealing statistics. The UK General Product Safety Regulations 1994 which implement Directive 92/59/EEC are examined in Chapter 5 and the other provisions of the Directive, particularly the Community notification and monitoring schemes, are discussed in Chapter 4.

The Directive on general product safety is part of the extensive programme of Community provisions establishing a single Community market with no internal barriers to trade. Many products are becoming subject to legislation under a family of Directives called the "New Approach", under which, products are subject to a single assessment in order to be marketed in any Member State and may thereafter circulate freely within the Community market. The general rules of the new approach governing the assessment of products' conformity with the essential requirements for marketing can now be seen both in overview and in many product sectors in detail. There is a strong emphasis on standards. It is a fundamental aim and requirement of Community internal market legislation relating to health, safety, environmental protection and consumer protection that it should afford a high level of protection (Article 100a of the Treaty). These aspects are examined in Chapter 3.

Running in parallel with these provisions aimed at markets and commerce is an important concern with consumer protection. The Community background to this aspect is traced in Chapter 2.

Product safety issues arise not only once products are marketed and sold to consumers but also when they are being used in the workplace. Many of the laws relating to health and safety at work are also new and based on EC Directives. Mark Tyler examines them in Chapter 6.

Drawing all these legal strands together, we try to give an overview in Chapters 7, 9 and 10 of what all the new law means in practice to those who make and market products. We tackle the perennial questions of what safety information should be given about products, when should warnings be given, what action should be taken post-marketing when safety issues arise: for all these the issues we address not just "what" but also "how much", "when" and "where".

Product safety regulation is aimed at preventing dangerous products from reaching the market or consumers, informing users about how to use products safely and as intended, and at withdrawing or notifying users of products which are recognised as being unsafe. Product safety is complemented by product liability, for which a new harmonised European regime of strict liability was introduced with Directive 85/374/EEC, implemented in the United Kingdom by Part I of the Consumer Protection Act 1987. Chapter 8 outlines this legislation.

It is not enough for producers merely to design, make and sell products which are intended to be safe. The way in which a product is used may affect the safety of those who use it or are affected by it. The use to which a product can or may be put can be affected by advertising and promotion. Regulatory controls also exist on safety claims. In Chapter 11 Tim Hardy examines the whole area of advertising products.

PREFACE

In the second half of this book three contributors examine what to do about product safety in practice, followed by case histories which tell the story of what did happen to a wide range of products.

In *Managing the Producer's Risk* Howard Abbott tackles the general principles of product safety management. The ethical problems that can post a conflict between theory and practice are given a pragmatic review and realistic risk management is positioned against current expert thinking. The pressures on producers show that they can be caught between the new mandatory ordinances on the one hand and the threat of strict liability with unlimited damages on the other; both can be expensive for producers who are unprepared. The difficulties in managing design, manufacturing and other sensitive areas are put against the new General Product Safety Regulations. Every company will make a bad one sooner or later and some actions to reduce this risk are reviewed, with particular consideration of risk perception which has so far not received the exposure it demands. The final section, on product recall, includes examples of good and bad advertisements and a succinct flow chart with accompanying notes.

An overview of the management of quality is provided by Ian Hodgskinson in Chapter 14. Quality control, quality assurance and the set of standards in ISO 9000 are considered, as well as the differences between first, second and third party audits.

The challenge of communicating while under public scrutiny is the subject for Mike Seymour in Chapter 12. There is a number of diverse audiences to address in a product safety incident. The training of teams and the planning of procedures are crucial to managing a crisis.

The case histories by Howard Abbott range from a very large ship to a pot of yoghurt to recount real life product safety stories. They illustrate the part played by the human factor in product failures.

Achieving product safety is obviously an important objective: the risk of physical injury to consumers and users of products is equally a risk to the business of producers of products and their risk insurers. At the April 1995 conference of the Association of Insurance and Risk Managers, Peter Lerwill, the Chairman, said that risk management has finally come of age in Britain. "There is now an appreciation of the full range of risk management techniques and how they can benefit a company's bottom line." Around 80 per cent of firms surveyed by AIRMIC consider risk management to be important in reducing costs associated with both civil and criminal proceedings. We hope that this book will contribute to the proper assessment of reduction risk and to achieving product safety.

Christopher J.S. Hodges
Mark Tyler
Howard Abbott

September 1995

Contributors

Tim Hardy

Solicitor of the Supreme Court of England & Wales
Partner, McKenna & Co., Solicitors

Ian Hodgskinson

Director of Research & Marketing,
Lloyd's Register Quality Assurance Ltd

Mike Seymour

Executive Director,
Crisis and Issues Management, Burson-Marsteller

Kathleen M. Sanzo

Council with Morgan, Lewis & Bockius

CONTENTS

CONTENTS

CONTENTS

1 How Safe Are Our Products?

THE COMMUNITY PICTURE

In its Explanatory Memorandum introducing the draft of the GPS Directive in 1989, the Commission quoted some startling statistics. Around 80 per cent of all accidents occur in the private sphere: in the home, during leisure activities, sports and at school. In contrast, road accidents only represent 5–6 per cent and accidents at work between 10 and 15 per cent. In the pre-1993 Community of twelve States, then with a total population of some 321 million, this represented about 45 million "domestic" accidents which required medical attention, most frequently in hospital casualty departments, and between 50,000 and 80,000 fatal accidents. Approximately 40–50 per cent of these accidents involve children and adolescents up to 19 years old. Home accidents are the third biggest cause of hospitalisation in the EU. Washing machines, for example, accounted for 100,000 fires and 20 deaths in Community States around 1991. About three million workers in the Community are away from work following accidents in the private sphere, the average absence due to this being 17 working days per annum.

It should come as no surprise that the Community has devoted so much attention to safety. The occurrence of accidents and injuries was declared in 1993 to be one of the priority areas for future Community action.[1]

ACCIDENTS IN THE UNITED KINGDOM

The statistics set out below relate to accidents and deaths in the United Kingdom. Manufacturers would do well to ponder these and similar information in designing their products and labelling.

Accidents

In 1992, there were 4,546 fatal accidents and over three million people seeking medical attention for injuries caused by accidents. Figure 1.1 is

[1] Commission Communication on the framework for action in the field of public health, COM(93) 559.

the Government's estimate for 1994 of the source of accidents at home requiring medical attention (the accidents treated in hospital and by GPs are in very similar proportions).

Figure 1.1 Source of all medically treated home accidents in 1994

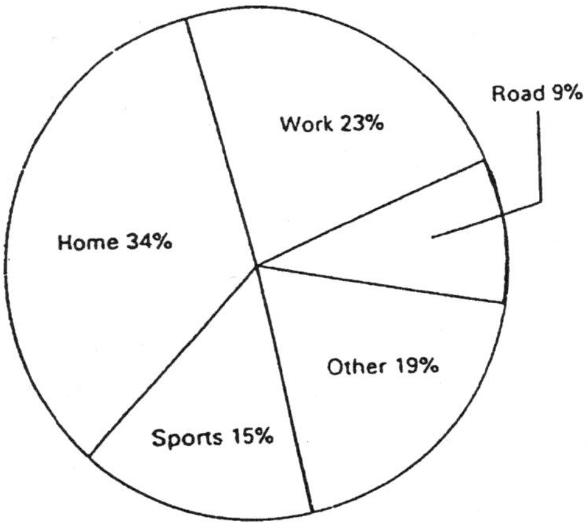

Source: Department of Trade and Industry

Tables 1.1 and **1.2** give the figures estimated by the Consumer Safety Unit of the Department of Trade and Industry for the national totals, extrapolated from figures recorded in the Home Accident Surveillance System (HASS) and Leisure Accident Surveillance System (LASS) databases, for accidents in the home and in leisure and sport activities respectively for 1989–92. The highest figures relating to products are recorded for DIY tools and equipment, household furnishings, personal items, vehicles and sports equipment.

Table 1.1 National estimate of accidents in the home from statistics recorded in the Home Accident Surveillance System (HASS)

	Categories	1992 (000s)	1991 (000s)	1990 (000s)	1989 (000s)
01	Baby and child furniture	15	15	14	14
02	Baby and child transport	12	13	13	14
03	Cleaning equipment	15	14	13	14
04	Cleaning products	13	14	14	13
05	Clothing and clothing accessories	15	14	14	14
06	Stereo, radio and telephone equipment	19	18	18	19
07	Constructional features of the house	530	527	510	533
08	Containers and wrappings	68	72	71	78
09	Cooking appliances	14	13	14	15
10	Do-it-yourself tools and equipment	199	209	214	237
11	Dust/dirt/particles	44	43	45	45

12	Electrical wiring and accessories	8	9	9	9
13	Flammable/corrosive liquids (other than domestic bleach)	6	6	6	7
14	Food and drink (other than hot liquids)	90	88	87	92
15	Footware	122	118	101	80
16	Freezing/refrigerating equipment	6	6	5	7
17	Garden equipment and tools	31	37	34	40
18	Imprecisely specified articles	548	93	88	108
19	Heating and ventilation equipment	34	33	30	33
20	Household fixtures	82	77	71	74
21	Household furnishings	95	86	78	78
22	Household furniture	297	292	282	290
23	Household linen	10	11	11	12
24	Hot liquids and vapours	31	37	38	42
25	Smoking implements and sources of ignition (including fuels and gases)	18	19	17	17
26	Kitchen utensils	110	109	105	115
27	Laundry equipment	19	18	18	21
28	Leisure/hobbies equipment – adults	3	2	2	3
29	Lighting equipment	6	6	6	6
30	Luggage/personal carrying equipment	5	5	5	5
31	Medicinal products	24	30	27	29
32	Miscellaneous household equipment	44	45	39	42
33	Features of the outside environment (other than plants and trees)	204	223	206	207
34	Personal items and personal hygiene	246	255	238	240
35	Pet's articles	6	8	7	7
36	Plants and trees	35	36	33	39
37	Playthings	52	52	50	53
38	Sewing and knitting equipment	10	10	10	13
39	Stationery, writing and drawing equipment	12	13	12	13
40	Vehicles (other than baby's transport)	62	69	67	71
41	Walking aids	8	8	7	8
42	Wall and floor furnishings and coverings	34	33	32	29
43	Waste disposal	8	9	8	8
44	Pets/insects	101	110	119	128
45	Sports equipment	32	34	34	38
No article specified			499	527	535
Total for table		3,345	3,437	3,353	3,494
Total accidents		2,547	2,634	2,596	2,750

Source: Department of Trade and Industry, Consumer Safety Unit, Annual Reports

Table 1.2 National estimate of accidents in leisure and sport activities from statistics collected in the Leisure Accident Surveillance System (LASS)

	Categories	1992 (000s)	1991 (000s)	1990 (000s)	1989 (000s)
01	Baby and child furniture	—	—	—	—
02	Baby and child transport	7	8	7	8
03	Cleaning equipment	—	—	—	—

04	Cleaning products	—	—	—	—
05	Clothing and clothing accessories	8	6	7	8
06	Stereo, radio and telephone equipment	—	—	—	—
07	Constructional features of the house	173	164	157	184
08	Containers and wrappings	21	21	21	29
09	Cooking appliances	—	—	—	—
10	Do-it-yourself tools and equipment	71	78	79	108
11	Dust/dirt/particles	26	29	31	35
12	Electrical wiring and accessories	—	—	—	—
13	Flammable/corrosive liquids (other than domestic bleach)	3	—	4	—
14	Food and drink (other than hot liquids)	46	49	45	52
15	Footware	178	188	150	148
16	Freezing/refrigerating equipment	—	—	—	—
17	Garden equipment and tools	5	5	5	7
18	Imprecisely specified articles	805	88	84	110
19	Heating and ventilation equipment	3	4	3	—
20	Household fixtures	10	8	8	8
21	Household furnishings	8	6	5	7
22	Household furniture	45	45	41	49
23	Household linen	—	—	—	—
24	Hot liquids and vapours	4	5	4	5
25	Smoking implements and sources of ignition (including fuels and gases)	3	4	4	4
26	Kitchen utensils	7	8	8	10
27	Laundry equipment	—	—	—	—
28	Leisure/hobbies equipment – adults	—	3	3	—
29	Lighting equipment	—	—	—	—
30	Luggage/personal carrying equipment	8	14	14	16
31	Medicinal products	—	—	—	—
32	Miscellaneous household equipment	10	9	8	9
33	Features of the outside environment (other than plants and trees)	430	438	367	512
34	Personal items and personal hygiene	462	510	470	563
35	Pet's articles	—	3	3	4
36	Plants and trees	38	41	39	43
37	Playthings	88	112	91	108
38	Sewing and knitting equipment	—	—	—	—
39	Stationery, writing and drawing equipment	7	7	7	8
40	Vehicles (other than baby's transport)	291	320	284	360
41	Walking aids (aids for the disabled)	5	4	3	4
42	Wall and floor furnishings and coverings	38	43	37	47
43	Waste disposal	—	3	3	4
44	Pets/insects	142	162	160	177
45	Sports equipment	485	611	555	591
46	Street features	294	329	264	273
47	Fairground equipment	12	11	8	10
No article specified			864	857	975
Total for table		3,751	4,216	3,849	4,496
Total accidents		2,877	3,231	2,991	3,492

Source: Department of Trade and Industry, Consumer Safety Unit, Annual Reports

In the past 15 years there has been a modest fall in the number of accidents and accident fatalities in the country. The pattern of accidents and injuries has also changed, with large reductions in numbers of accidents involving hedgetrimmers, lawnmowers and saws, and a corresponding increase in accidents involving millers, grinders and cement mixers. As more people have leisure time, the Consumer Safety Unit anticipates an increase in accidents involving such items as sports equipment, garden furniture, portable barbecues, garden vacuum cleaners, birchwood shredders, high pressure water hoses, home saunas and jacuzzis, and equipment to assist elderly people in the house. A campaign was recently launched to encourage safety awareness of those undertaking DIY — especially hiring DIY tools and equipment.

Death

Fatal accidents at home recorded in the Home Accidents Death Database (HADD) for 1987–92 are shown in **Table 1.3**. **Table 1.4** records the products, articles and features most frequently recorded as being involved in fatal accidents. Stairs, fire, food and drink, poisonous fumes, medicines and alcohol have the most associations. The main causes of accidental death are shown by sex in Figure 2. In descending order of severity they are road traffic and transport accidents, home accidents and occupational accidents.

Table 1.3 Fatal home accidents registered in England and Wales on the Home Accidents Death Database (HADD)

	Number of Accidents					
Categories	1992	1991	1990	1989	1988	1987
Baby and child furniture	8	5	14	8	12	4
Baby and child transport	1	1	2	1	0	2
Cleaning equipment	4	1	4	1	0	0
Cleaning products	5	2	2	3	4	6
Clothing and clothing acessories	65	23	64	69	67	68
Communication equipment	5	5	7	6	6	3
Constructional features of the house	604	612	639	603	596	617
Containers/wrappings	7	7	14	13	19	9
Cooking appliances	34	22	34	18	33	31
DIY/house maintenance	70	70	63	51	65	66
Dust/dirt/wood particles	0	1	2	2	1	2
Electric equipment	21	15	21	14	31	23
Flammable/corrosive liquids	12	7	18	15	13	15
Food and drink	359	373	364	382	343	394
Footware	0	1	0	0	0	0
Freezing/refrigerating equipment	1	1	6	0	1	1
Garden equipment/tools	5	6	6	8	5	7
Imprecisely specified articles	17	19	15	54	32	18
Heating and ventilation equipment	105	141	118	130	153	145
Household fixtures	49	47	66	66	55	50

Household furnishings	23	13	10	19	8	12
Household furniture	177	158	196	225	236	202
Household linen	26	53	25	29	27	24
Hot liquids	73	68	60	20	80	34
Ignition (source)	539	562	739	639	837	713
Kitchen utensils	23	15	25	20	23	16
Laundry equipment	7	6	7	1	6	4
Leisure activities (adults)	0	1	1	1	1	2
Lighting	13	18	17	17	19	7
Luggage	0	1	0	1	0	1
Medicines/tablets	378	324	320	270	281	273
Miscellaneous household equipment	9	9	11	16	14	7
Outside environment	32	37	48	28	31	28
Personal items	29	37	26	25	17	25
Pets' articles	0	1	0	3	1	1
Plants and trees	6	2	7	4	7	6
Playthings/toys	8	8	7	12	15	9
Sewing/knitting	0	0	0	0	0	0
Stationery/writing equipment	4	3	4	1	0	3
Vehicles	31	31	25	23	40	22
Walking aids	6	5	8	3	4	6
Wall and floor coverings	0	2	1	4	2	0
Waste disposal	3	2	3	3	4	0
Pets/insects	0	1	1	0	1	1
Sports equipment	4	6	7	14	12	6
Unspecified	1,595	1,658	1,632	1,741	1,799	1,741
Total	4,358	4,380	4,639	4,563	4,901	4,604
Total accidents	3,841	3,870	3,949	3,968	4,136	4,024

Source: Department of Trade and Industry, Consumer Safety Unit, Annual Reports

Table 1.4 Products, articles, and features of the home most frequently involved in fatal accidents, as recorded on HADD

	Number of Accidents			
Item	1990	1989	1988	1987
Stairs/steps In/Out	541	511	503	519
Fire – uncontrolled	306	306	372	318
Food and drink unspecified	243	276	248	284
Smoke and fumes (not CO)	154	110	192	162
Carbon monoxide	153	105	132	107
Aspirin/painkillers	135	104	109	106
Alcohol	117	100	109	106
Medicine	110	96	104	94
Bed	102	96	86	89
Sleeping pills	68	90	79	86
Fire – controlled	62	77	71	75
Bath and Fittings	55	60	69	63
Hot water – in bath/sink	55	57	60	60
Cigarettes	54	57	54	47
Chair (not folding)	50	43	45	44

Note: Only top 15 items have been presented.

1991		1992	
Stairs/steps In/Out	526	Stairs/steps In/Out	515
Fire – uncontrolled	295	Fire – uncontrolled	316
Food and drink – unspecified	239	Food and drink – unspecified	229
Aspirin/painkillers	146	Aspirin/painkillers	180
Alcohol	124	Medicine – specified	138
Medicine - specified	113	Alcohol	121
Carbon Monoxide	95	Bed	82
Fire – controlled	86	Carbon Monoxide	80
Bed	65	Hot water – in bath/sink	65
Hot water – in bath/sink	60	Cigarettes	63
Chair (not folding)	59	Fire – controlled	55
Smoke/fumes (not CO)	59	Chair (not folding)	55
Cigarettes	55	Steps/ladder (unspecified)	54
Sleeping pills	54	Sleeping pills	52
Steps/ladder – unspecified	42	Window whole (unspecified)	43

Source: Department of Trade and Industry, Consumer Safety Unit, Annual Reports

Figure 1.2 Deaths from accidents*

Males England and Wales 1990

100% = 7.182 deaths

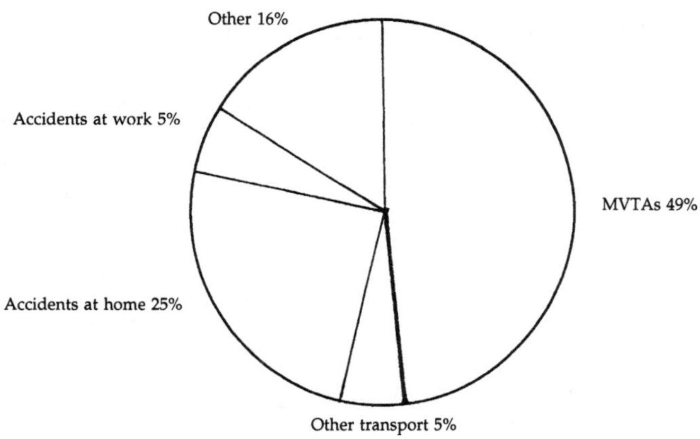

Source: OPCS

Females England and Wales 1990

100% = 4.554 deaths

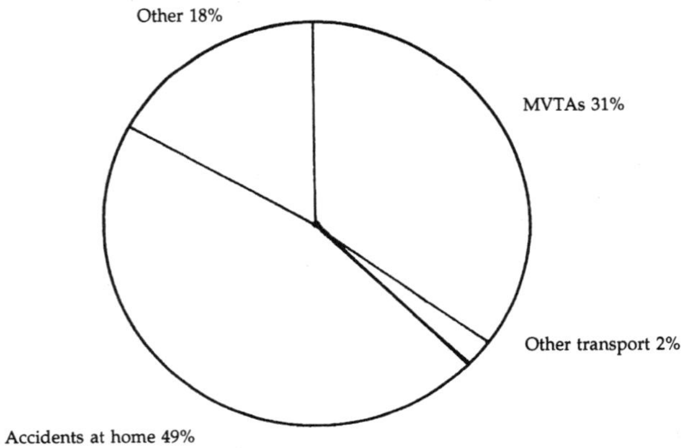

* Excludes deaths under 28 days

Source: OPCS

Most accidental deaths occur in the 15–24 age group and the elderly — **Table 1.5** gives the figures for 1991. In the young, many more boys die than girls as a result of accidents — see **Figures 1.3** and **1.4.** In 1991, 543 children under 15 in England died as a result of an accident, which

Table 1.5 Deaths caused by accidental injuries (ICD 800:949) England, 1991

	Males			Females		
Age group	Number	Rate per 100,000 population	Per cent of total deaths	Number	Rate per 100,000 population	Per cent of total deaths
Under 1*	34	10.0	1.2	27	8.3	1.3
1–4	105	8.0	21.1	53	4.2	13.3
5–14	225	7.4	35.4	99	3.4	23.1
15–24	1,234	35.5	45.2	310	9.3	30.5
25–34	879	23.2	25.4	171	4.6	10.8
35–44	675	20.3	11.8	186	5.6	5.4
45–54	573	20.8	4.6	229	8.3	2.9
55–64	494	20.9	1.5	273	11.1	1.4
65–74	625	32.9	0.9	509	21.9	1.0
75–84	752	77.4	0.8	1,129	68.4	1.2
85+	408	205.5	1.1	1,203	212.4	1.3
Total	6,004	—	2.3	4,189	—	1.5

* Excludes deaths under 28 days

Source: The Health of the Nation: ACCIDENTS Key Area Handbook (HMSO 1993)

was the most common cause of death in children over 1 year. The major causes of accidental death in children are road traffic accidents, burns and scalds, suffocation and drownings — see **Table 1.6**. Up to age four, most fatal accidents occur in the home: thereafter most are caused by road traffic accidents.

Figure 1.3 Death rates for accidents: England 1970–90*, by sex aged 0–14 years#

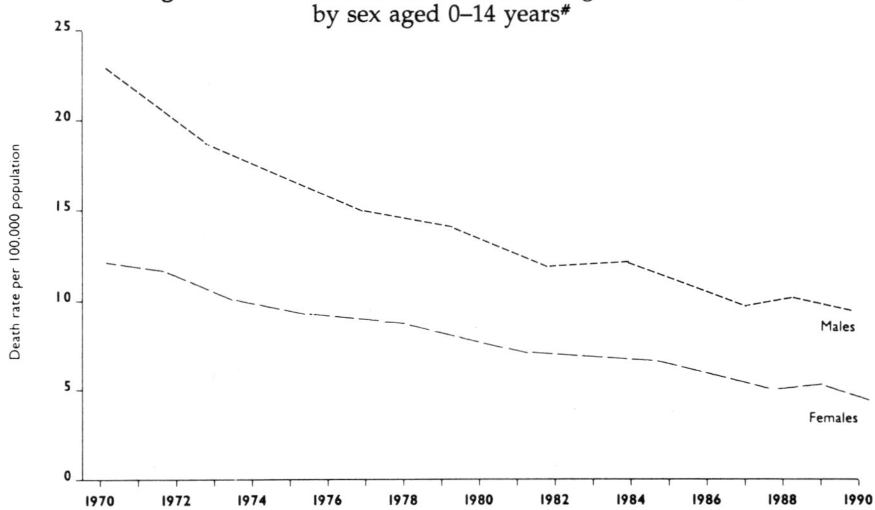

* Rates are calculated using a 3-year average plotted against the middle year of the average

Rates are calculated using the European Standard Population to take into account differences in age structure

Source: OPCS (ICD E800:E949)

Figure 1.4 Death rates for accidents: England 1970–90*, by sex aged 15–24 years

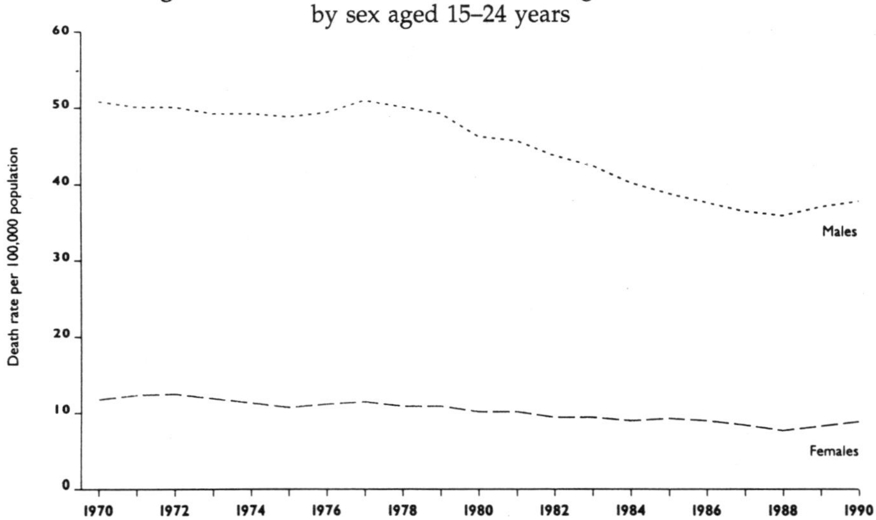

* Rates are calculated using 3-year average plotted against the middle year of the average.

Source: OPCS (ICD E800:E949)

Table 1.6 Accidental deaths in children under 15: England, 1991

Cause	*Number of male deaths*	*Number of female deaths*
Motor vehicle traffic accidents *ICD E810-E819*	187	96
Motor vehicle non-traffic accidents *ICD E820-E825*	1	1
Falls *ICD E880-E888*	20	5
Fire and Flames *ICD E890-E899*	40	29
Drowning and submersion *ICD E910*	29	8
Inhalation of food or other substances and suffocation *ICD E911-E914*	46	18

Source: OPCS

Accidents are not a major cause of death in people aged 65 and over, but many may be preventable. In 1991 4,626 people in that age group died accidentally in England — see **Figure 1.5**. In the over 75s the death rate from accidents is considerably higher than in any other age group. For them in 1991, falls (67 per cent female deaths, 53 per cent male deaths) and road traffic accidents (14 per cent female deaths, 24 per cent male deaths) were the most significant causes.

Figure 1.5 Death rates for accidents: England 1970–90*, by sex aged 65 & over#

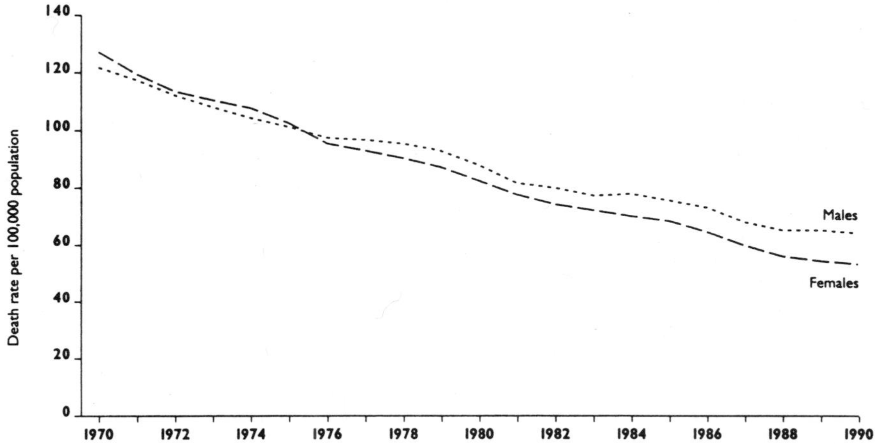

* Rates are calculated using a 3-year average plotted against the middle year of the average
# Rates are calculated using the European Standard Population to take into account differences in age structure

Source: OPCS (ICD E800:E949)

Accidents at work

It is interesting to compare home, leisure and sporting statistics with those for accidents at work. **Table 1.7** shows the dangerous occurrences at work reported to U.K. enforcement authorities for 1988–89 to 1993–94. **Table 1.8** shows the injuries to employees reported to enforcement authorities for 1988–89 to 1993–94. These indicate that falling, collapsing structures and being struck by moving vehicles or objects are particular hazards: implications for safe design can obviously be drawn. Finally, **Table 1.9** shows the number of notices issued and prosecutions and convictions under section 6 of the Health and Safety at Work etc. Act 1974 for 1990–91 to 1992–93. The average fine has doubled over that period.

Table 1.7 Dangerous occurrences, 1988–89–1993–94p
(as reported to all enforcement authorities)

Reported to HSE Inspectorates	1988–89	1989–90	1990–91	1991–92	1992–93	1993–94p
Part 1						
1 Failure, collapse or overturning of lifting machinery, excavator, pile driving frame or mobile powered access platform	888	911	782	709	723	675
2 Failure or collapse of passenger carrying amusement device or safety arrangement at a fair	23	15	13	13	20	13
3 Explosion, collapse or bursting of any closed vessel including boiler, above or below atmospheric pressure	178	165	170	149	157	161
4 Electrical fault causing fire or explosion and plant stoppage for over 24 hours	119	142	147	142	140	124
5 Explosion or fire due to ignition of process materials, waste or finished products and stoppage for over 24 hours	365	375	365	281	278	234
6 Uncontrolled release or escape of 1 tonne or more of highly flammable liquids or flammable gas	104	86	86	89	94	101
7 Collapse or part collapse of scaffold over 5 m high	104	115	79	77	75	99
8 Collapse or partial collapse of (a) any building or structure under construction involving over 5 tonnes of materials or (b) any floor or wall of a building used as a place of work	79	106	61	60	69	77
9 Uncontrolled or accidental release of potentially harmful substance or pathogen from certain equipment or sites	631	696	676	656	689	550
10 Unintentional ignition or explosion of explosives	137	137	184	151	97	27

11 Failure or collapse of a lifted freight container or part thereof	38	32	49	20	27	30
12 Bursting, explosion or collapse of a pipeline or any part thereof or the ignition of anything in a pipeline (excluding water pipes)	74	93	75	75	68	96
13 Overturning or serious damage to the tank while conveying by road prescribed dangerous substances, or the uncontrolled release or fire involving the substance being conveyed	71	107	91	89	65	35
14 Uncontrolled release or escape of a dangerous substance, or a fire involving the dangerous substance, when being conveyed by road in a vehicle	35	44	42	42	40	55
15 Failure of breathing apparatus in service	36	54	69	59	68	77
16 Plant or equipment coming into contact unintentionally with overhead electric cables or causing an electrical discharge	250	220	189	216	242	176
17 Accidental collision between locomotive or train and other vehicle causing a reportable injury	15	21	45	21	23	27
Part 1 (Notifiable in relation to any place of work) Total	**3,147**	**3,319**	**3,123**	**2,849**	**2,875**	**2,557**
Part 2 (Notifiable in relation to mines) Total	**268**	**255**	**198**	**106**	**71**	**47**
Part 3 (Notifiable in relation to quarries) Total	**25**	**25**	**18**	**9**	**18**	**22**
Part 4 (Notifiable in relation to railways) Total	–	–	–	–	–	–
Not elsewhere classified	**290**	**341**	**321**	**379**	**339**	**327**
	3,730	3,940	3,660	3,343	3,303	2,953
Reported to local authorities	420	210	292	333	344	n/a
Grand Total	4,150	4,150	3,952	3,676	3,647	n/a

Notes

[1] The table excludes occurences in the oil and gas industry reported under offshore safety legislation.

[2] The table excludes occurrences notified to the Railway Inspectorate under the Railway (Notice of Accidents) Order. Full details of occurrences notified under this order can be found in the Department of Transport annual report on the safety record of the railways in Great Britain.

n/a not available
p provisional

Source: Health and Safety Commission Health and Safety Statistics 1993–94 (Statistical Supplement to the 1993–94 Annual Report).

Table 1.8 Injuries to employees by kind of accident and severity of injury 1988–89 to 1993–94p
(as reported to all enforcing authorities (a))

	Fatal					
	1988–89	1989–90	1990–91	1991–92	1992–93	1993–94p
Kind of accident						
Contact with moving machinery	30	25	29	19	22	14
Struck by moving including flying/falling object	46	62	51	33	37	28
Struck by moving vehicle	70	50	53	52	47	42
Struck against something fixed or stationary	3	2	3	3	1	2
Injured while handling, lifting or carrying	–	2	–	2	–	2
Slip, trip or fall on same level	8	5	1	2	4	4
Fall from height	93	110	81	83	63	60
of which: Up to and including 2 m	*10*	*13*	*8*	*11*	*12*	–
Over 2m	*77*	*89*	*66*	*59*	*45*	*51*
Height not stated	*6*	*8*	*7*	*13*	*6*	*9*
Trapped by something collapsing/overturning	28	36	24	25	27	42
Drowning or asphyxiation	16	15	10	12	7	12
Exposure to or contact with harmful substance	8	9	14	2	11	8
Exposure to fire	2	8	5	6	9	2
Exposure to an explosion	7	8	8	11	6	4
Contact with electricity or electrical discharge	18	24	24	14	25	10
Injured by an animal	3	–	3	–	2	3
Other kind of accident	24	12	28	20	15	2
Injuries not classified by kind	173(b)	2	12	13		
Total	**529(b)**	**370**	**346**	**297**	**276**	**235**

	Non-fatal major					
	1988–89	1989–90	1990–91	1991–92	1992–93	1993–94p
Kind of accident						
Contact with moving machinery	2,118	2,003	1,738	1,472	1,366	1,266

Struck by moving including flying/falling object	2,541	2,752	2,371	2,157	2,013	1,953
Struck by moving vehicle	747	772	733	578	565	540
Struck against something fixed or stationary	808	763	781	642	604	648
Injured while handling, lifting or carrying	1,408	1,359	1,257	1,098	1,092	1,061
Slip, trip or fall on same level	5,563	5,852	6,396	5,628	5,513	5,826
Fall from height	4,340	4,551	4,274	3,994	3,741	3,421
of which: Up to and including 2 m	*1,958*	*2,060*	*1,964*	*1,911*	*1,768*	*1,642*
Over 2m	*1,447*	*1,532*	*1,337*	*1,192*	*1,004*	*949*
Height not stated	*935*	*959*	*973*	*891*	*969*	*830*
Trapped by something collapsing/overturning	247	220	204	191	180	151
Drowning or asphyxiation	28	19	22	28	34	19
Exposure to or contact with harmful substance	702	804	806	726	745	578
Exposure to fire	106	109	109	75	92	57
Exposure to an explosion	80	74	90	63	56	39
Contact with electricity or electrical discharge	276	305	298	308	286	269
Injured by an animal	75	75	72	66	81	73
Other kind of accident	812	657	651	535	569	423
Injuries not classified by kind	93	81	94	36	1	2
Total	**19,944**	**20,396**	**19,896**	**17,597**	**16,938**	**16,326**

	Over–3–day					
	1988–89	1989–90	1990–91	1991–92	1992–93	1993–94p
Kind of accident						
Contact with moving machinery	7,968	7,848	7,724	6,983	6,353	6,175
Struck by moving including flying/falling object	25,076	25,662	23,366	21,927	19,716	18,251
Struck by moving vehicle	4,254	4,146	3,845	3,792	3,427	3,358
Struck against something fixed or stationary	10,811	10,886	10,290	9,666	8,895	8,079
Injured while handling, lifting or carrying	53,373	55,513	54,220	53,109	49,664	45,832
Slip, trip or fall on same level	30,311	32,087	33,452	31,082	28,501	27,885
Fall from height	12,516	13,077	12,585	11,749	11,258	10,195
of which: Up to and including 2 m	*7,272*	*7,401*	*7,289*	*6,827*	*6,250*	*5,704*
Over 2m	*1,786*	*1,918*	*1,759*	*1,450*	*1,393*	*1,254*
Height not stated	*3,458*	*3,758*	*3,537*	*3,472*	*3,615*	*3,237*
Trapped by something collapsing/overturning	608	616	548	485	451	434
Drowning or asphyxiation	39	39	26	52	36	38
Exposure to or contact with harmful substance	4,123	4,586	4,516	4,180	3,798	3,697
Exposure to fire	536	631	576	519	483	466
Exposure to an explosion	231	256	220	233	164	140

Contact with electricity or electrical discharge	635	703	607	609	597	497
Injured by an animal	758	913	853	786	729	809
Other kind of accident	7,880	7,562	7,281	7,166	7,055	6,469
Injuries not classified by kind	4,000	719	702	168	20	18
Total	163,119	165,244	160,811	152,506	141,147	132,343

Notes
(a) Includes injuries in the offshore oil and gas industry collected under offshore legislation.
(b) Data include the 167 fatalities of the Piper Alpha disaster, July 6, 1988.
p provisional

Source: Health and Safety Commission Health and Safety Statistics 1993–94 (Statistical Supplement to the 1993–94 Annual Report)

Table 1.9 Notices and proceedings issued by HSE's Field Operations Inspectorates under section 6 of the Health and Safety at Work Act 1974

Number of Requirements

	Improvements	*Deferred prohibition*	*Immediate prohibition*	*Total*
1990–91	15	1	6	22
1991–92	75	–	4	79
1992–93	9	–	6	15

Proceedings instituted by HSE's Field Operations Division Inspectorates under section 6 of the Health and Safety at Work Act 1974

	Informations laid	*Convictions*	*Average penalty per conviction*
1990–91	38	34	£844
1991–92	47	39	£1,299
1992–93	27	19	£1,676

Source: HSE Statistical Information Department

Fires

In 1992, the Home Office recorded accidental fires in 54,000 dwellings and 27,200 other occupied buildings. Almost half of the former and one-fifth of the latter were caused by misuse of appliances, and around 20 per cent of the former and 30 per cent of the latter were caused by faults in appliances.[2] **Table 1.10** shows the main sources of ignition for accidental dwelling fires, and casualties, in the United Kingdom in 1992.

Of the 3,100 dwelling fires where the source of ignition was electrical distribution apparatus, 30 per cent were ignited in leads to appliances

[2] Fire Statistics 1992 (HMSO).

and a further 8 per cent were due to plugs, sockets and switches. The remainder were ignited by other wiring. Most fires ignited in leads to appliances are caused by faulty leads, whereas the majority of other fires igniting electrical distribution apparatus are caused by faulty fuel supplies. The fatal and non-fatal casualty incidence rate for such fires is highest in fires ignited by leads to appliances.

Table 1.10 Main sources of ignition for accidental dwelling fires, showing casualties, UK 1992

Source of ignition	Fires	Fatal casualties		Non-fatal	
		Total	*Per 1,000 fires*	Total	*Per 1,000 fires*
Total accidental	**54,000**	**526**	***10***	**9,700**	***180***
Cooking appliances—	25,500	58	*2*	4,300	*167*
Electric*	17,200	27	*2*	2,800	*160*
Gas	7,300	29	*4*	1,400	*193*
Other	1,000	2	..	100	*103*
Space heaters	3,400	7	*23*	800	*239*
Electric*	1,200	34	*29*	300	*260*
Gas	900	17	*19*	200	*251*
Other	1,300	26	*19*	300	*213*
Smokers' materials	6,100	213	*35*	1,900	*315*
Matches	3,200	39	*12*	800	*247*
Candle	700	17	*24*	200	*250*
Electric blanket*	1,000	17	*17*	240	*242*
Washing machine*	2,100	2	..	60	*31*
Electrical distribution*	3,100	8	..	370	*121*
Plugs, sockets switches	200	—	..	30	*129*
Leads to appliances	900	5	..	140	*146*
Other wiring[1]	1,900	3	..	200	*108*
Total electrical[2]	27,800	96	*3*	4,180	*150*

[1] may include connectors and terminals
[2] All electrical appliances as shown in table 31 (includes all*)
.. rates not calculated where fewer than 10 deaths

Source: Fire Statistics 1992 (HMSO)

Of the 6,100 dwelling fires ignited in other electrical appliances, about a third have a washing machine as the source of ignition (nearly always caused by a fault in the appliance). These fires resulted in two fatal and 66 non-fatal casualties.

A further one-sixth of electrical appliance fires had electric blankets or bedwarmers as the source of ignition, two-thirds of which were caused by faults in appliances; most of the rest were caused by misuse of equipment. Fires in electric blankets and bedwarmers caused nearly two-thirds of fatal and one-third of non-fatal casualties from fires ignited in other electrical appliances.

Enforcement action against unsafe products

How safe are consumer products? **Table 1.11** shows the enforcement action taken by Trading Standards Officers and others under Part II of the Consumer Protection Act 1987 in relation to unsafe consumer products between April 1988 and March 1993.

Table 1.11 Product Safety Enforcement Statistics 01.04.88 to 31.03.93

Forfeiture Orders	299
Prohibition Notices	18
Suspension Notices	1,702
Notices to Warn	0
Secretary of State's Notice to furnish information	0
Convictions	1,931
Written warnings and formal cautions	4,295

Source: Consumer Safety: Report by the Secretary of State for Trade and Industry for the period 1 April 1988–31 March 1993 (HMSO)

The 18 prohibition notices were issued in respect of only two product types: elastic sweet-like toys (four importers in August 1988) and imitation jelly balls and similar products (14 suppliers in December 1992) all of which presented a choking hazard to children.

No notices to warn were issued by the Secretary of State to suppliers in the period under consideration. The Secretary of State's Report notes that this was not found necessary because the Department was able to secure the necessary co-operation of suppliers without the necessity of exercising this power. In other words, the threat posed by the existence of this and other enforcement powers is sufficient to secure suppliers' conformity. On other occasions, the Report notes that the publication of a press notice was considered to be more effective.

Table 1.12 gives the breakdown of the Statutory Instruments under which the enforcement actions noted above were taken. This shows that the major risks encountered in practice clearly involve electricity and toys, with risk of fire in furniture and furnishings also being significant.

Given the vast number of products on the market during these five years considered in the Secretary of State's Report, it might be argued that the figures in which enforcement action was taken are not excessive and that the vast majority of consumer products are reasonably safe. However, it must be remembered in seeking to draw conclusions from enforcement statistics that it is widely recognised that the existence of enforcement powers operates as a coercive factor in influencing the actions and cooperation of businesses and the powers may not need to be used.

Table 1.12 Consumer safety: Quinquennial report to Parliament enforcement April 1, 1988–March 31, 1993

					OUTCOME		
Statutory instrument	Total No of Cases*	Written Warnings (inc Formal Cautions)	Suspension Notice	Forfeiture Order	Conviction	Dismissal	Voluntary Withdrawal
Regulations made under the Consumer Protection Act 1961							
Standards for Carry Cots (Safety) Regulations 1966	—	3	—	—	—	—	—
Electrical Appliances (Colour Code) Regulations 1969 (as amended)	132	490	—	2	71	4	57
Cooking Utensils (Safety) Regulations 1972	6	12	4	—	4	1	1
Heating Appliances Fireguards Regulations 1973	2	—	2	1	2	—	—
Pencils and Graphic Instruments (Safety) Regulations 1974	35	29	5	2	20	1	14
Toys (Safety) Regulations 1974	381	426	59	38	179	24	178
Glazed Ceramic Ware Regulations 1975	1	—	—	—	1	—	—
Filament Lamps for Vehicles (Safety) Regulations 1982	—	—	—	—	—	—	—
Pedal Bicycles (Safety) Regulations 1984 (as amended)	16	63	6	2	8	5	3
Food Imitations Regulations 1984	3	—	—	—	3	—	—
Motor Vehicle Tyres (Safety) Regulations 1984	17	33	81	3	6	1	10

Cosmetic Products (Safety) Regulations 1984 (as amended)	12	46	11	1	4	1	7
Gas Catalytic Heaters (Safety) Regulations 1984	—	9	—	—	—	—	—
Aerosol Dispensers (EEC) Requirement and the Cosmetic Products (Amendment) Regulations 1985	1	—	—	—	—	—	1
Asbestos Products (Safety) Regulations 1985 (as amended)	2	—	—	1	—	—	2
Nightwear (Safety) Regulations 1985 (as amended)	84	55	166	7	52	3	29
Pushchair (Safety) Regulations 1985	52	53	8	—	14	2	36
Ceramic Ware (Safety) Regulations 1985	13	1	4	—	5	—	8
Child Resistant Packaging (Safety) Regulations 1986 (as amended)	12	11	3	—	5	2	5
Fireworks (Safety) Regulations 1986	59	223	—	2	31	8	20
Plugs and Sockets (Safety) Regulations 1987	146	174	9	11	56	3	—
Bunk Beds (Entrapment Hazards) (Safety) Regulations 1987	30	33	9	—	11	—	19
Regulations made under the Consumer Protection Act 1987	6	98**					
Benzene in Toys (Safety) Regulations 1987	—	1	—	—	—	—	—

Furniture and Furnishings (Fire) (Safety) Regulations 1988 (as amended)	274	744	712	18	209	6	59
Gas Cooking Appliances (Safety) Regulations 1989	69	43	3	4	57	—	12
Low Voltage Electrical Equipment (Safety) Regulations 1989	515	459	77	85	one case 318	pending 11	185
Toys (Safety) Regulations 1989	487	577	277	47	two cases 234	pending 35	216
Food Imitations (Safety) Regulations 1989	51	53	19	—	24	1	26
Cosmetic Products (Safety) Regulations 1989	47	56	14	6	7	—	40
All-Terrain Motor Vehicles (Safety) Regulations 1989	1	5	9	—	—	—	1
Oral Snuff (Safety) Regulations 1989	—	—	—	—	—	—	—
Tobacco Products Labelling (Safety) Regulations 1991	—	8	—	—	—	—	—
Heating Appliances (Fireguards) (Safety) Regulations 1991	2	2	—	—	2	—	—
Imitation Dummies (Safety) Regulations 1992	—	9	4	—	—	—	—
Gas Appliances (Safety) Regulations 1992	—	—	—	—	—	—	—
Consumer Protection Act 1987, s.10	699	551	207	39	498	26	175
Regulations made under the Consumer Protection Act (Northern Ireland) 1965							
Stands for Carry Cots (Safety) Regulations 1978	—	—	—	—	—	—	—

Electrical Appliances (Colour Code) Regulations (NI) 1970 (as amended)	—	1	—	—	—	—	—
Cooking Utensils (Safety) Regulations (NI) 1971	—	1	—	—	—	—	—
Pencils and Graphic Instruments (Safety) Regulations (NI) 1975	—	1	—	—	—	—	—
Glazed Ceramic Ware (Safety) Regulations 1975	—	1	—	—	—	—	—
Toys (Safety) Regulations (NI) 1975	2	6	4	—	2	—	—
Children's Clothing (Hood Cords) Regulations (NI) 1976	—	10	10	—	—	—	—
Vitreous Enamel Ware (Safety) Regulations (NI) 1976	—	—	—	—	—	—	—
Oil Heater (Safety) Regulations (NI) 1977	—	3	—	—	—	—	—
Cosmetic Products Regulations (NI) 1978	—	3	—	—	—	—	—
Perambulators and Push-Chair (Safety) Regulations (NI) 1978	—	2	—	—	—	—	—

* Cases not informations *e.g.* two informations laid in respect of one item under the same Regulation will count as one case. If laid under separate Regulations they will count as more than one case.

Source: Department of Trade and Industry, Consumer Safety Report 1988–1993

On the other hand, the Consumers Association points to data such as that referred to above in relation to the high incidence of fires in domestic washing machines:

Year	1992	1991	1990	1989
Fires	2125	1872	1808	1725

Source: Fire Statistics 1984–1992 (HMSO)

Clearly, there is no room for complacency in product safety.

2 Product safety in Community consumer protection policy

> The General Product Safety Directive has the dual objective of establishing the E.C.'s internal market (a commercial matter) and providing a high level of protection of consumer citizens' safety and health (a consumer protection matter).
>
> It is one of the most significant in a sequence of E.C. consumer measures. This Chapter charts the growing importance of product safety in E.C. consumer policy.

The New Approach Technical Directives described in Chapter 3 came into existence as part of the creation of the single internal market for goods and services within the European Community. This Chapter outlines the development by the Community of matters of policy and action relating to consumer protection, which have taken place in parallel with the economic and industry based provisions relating to the internal market. The interests of industry and of consumers are often portrayed as being in conflict. Their interests in relation to the development or agreement of Community policy and legislation are, however, not as divergent as might be thought. A considerable divergence in understanding comes about through poor communication. At the macro-economic level of the Community as a whole, the removal of trading restrictions can be equally beneficial for both industry and consumers. The Commission therefore rightly describes the policy objectives of creation of the internal market and consumer protection as being complementary.

It is surprising given the frequent references to consumers in Community legislation that there is no definitive Community definition of a consumer. In the context of some legislation, a consumer of a product might include an economic operator (*i.e.* a commercial company) as well as the more normal meaning of a private individual. The Unfair Contract Terms Directive[1] includes the following definition but this measure is clearly directed at protection of individuals:

> "Consumer means any natural person who, in contracts covered by this Directive, is acting for purposes which are outside his trade, business or profession."

[1] Directive 93/13/EEC on unfair terms in consumer contracts. OJ No. L 95/29, 21.4.93.

International consumer policy

Recognition of the specific character and relevance of the interests of consumers has developed in the last three decades of the twentieth century. Important texts have been written by the Consumer Policy Committee of the Organisation for Economic Co-operation and Development, set up in 1969, the Council of Europe[2] and the United Nations.[3] Five categories of basic consumers' rights have been recognised: right to information and education; right to protection of health and safety; right to protection of financial interests; right to protection of legal interests; and rights to representation and participation.

Initial Community consumer policy

Consumer policy was not included in the EEC Treaty of 1957. However, references to consumer policy in the Community's basic documents have been growing in importance since the Heads of State and Government called on the Community on the eve of the Community's first enlargement in October 1972 to adopt a programme to augment and coordinate national measures in favour of the protection of consumers. This policy was formally inaugurated in April 1975 with the adoption of the first programme for consumer protection[4] which noted the increased abundance and complexity of goods and services on an ever-widening market. This set out to guarantee five basic consumer rights:

- protection of the consumer against health and safety risks;
- protection of consumers' economic interests;
- improvement of the consumers' legal position (help, advice, the right to seek legal remedy);
- improvement of consumer education and information;
- appropriate consultation and representation of consumers in the taking of decisions affecting their interests.

The Council laid down a number of principles in relation to the first of these rights, protection of the consumer against health and safety hazards, including:

1. goods and services offered to consumers must be such that, under normal or foreseeable conditions of use, they present no risk to the health or safety of consumers. There should be quick and simple procedures for withdrawing them from the market in the event of

[2] Council of Europe Recommendation 705 (1973) on consumer protection; the Council of Europe's report on the protection of the economic and social interests of consumers (Doc. 4920 of June 3, 1982).

[3] The guidelines for consumer protection adopted by the General Assembly of the United Nations on April 9, 1985 (Resolution No. 39/248).

[4] Council Resolution of April 14, 1975 on preliminary programme for a consumer protection and information policy. OJ No. C 92, 25.4.1975.

their presenting such risks; in general, consumers should be informed in an appropriate manner of any risk liable to result from a foreseeable use of goods and services, taking account of the nature of the goods and services and of the persons for whom they are intended;

2. the consumer must be protected against physical injury caused by defective products and services supplied by manufacturers of goods and providers of services;
3. particular regulated control of foodstuffs;
4. machines, appliances and electrical and electronic equipment and any other category of goods which may prejudicially affect the health and safety of consumers either in themselves or by their use, should be covered by special rules and be subject to a procedure recognised or approved by the public authorities (such as type approval or declaration of conformity with harmonised standards or rules) to ensure that they are safe for use;
5. certain categories of new products which may prejudicially affect the health or safety of consumers should be made subject to special authorisation procedures harmonised throughout the Community.

In this category, harmonisation was chiefly directed towards the types of products shown in **Table 2.1** (the references to legislation are as at the date of this book).

Table 2.1 E.C. measures included in the First Programme for Consumer Protection

foodstuffs:	Council Directive 79/112
cosmetics	Council Directive 76/768
medicinal products	
— for human use:	Council Directives 65/65, 75/318, 75/319 and numerous others
— for veterinary use:	Council Directives 81/851, 81/852 and numerous others
dangerous substances:	various directives on classification, labelling, packaging and use
textiles, toys, tobacco, alcohol and manufactured products, especially motor vehicle components and inflammability of materials used in manufacturing furniture or for fitting out buildings	

The Council also resolved that, to comply with the principles set out above, the fullest and most objective information possible must be available on the various aspects of product safety. As a general principle, sufficient information should be available to the purchaser of goods or services, and to the general public, to enable him to:

- assess the basic features of the goods and services offered, such as the nature, quality, quantity, energy consumption and price;

- make a rational choice between competing products and services;
- use these products and services safely and to his satisfaction;
- claim redress for any injury or damage resulting from the product supplied or service received.

The following legislative measures were amongst those proposed during this programme:

- safety of cosmetics: Directive 76/768 and numerous amendments;
- a framework for labelling food adequately, clearly and uniformly;
- rules to protect consumers who are the object of doorstep selling: Directive 85/577;
- defining and forbidding misleading advertising: Directive 84/450;
- liability for damage caused by defective products: Directive 85/374;
- regulating the provision of consumer credit: Directive 87/102.

A second programme affirmed the same rights in May 1981.[5] A study had been undertaken of the feasibility and value of drawing up general rules on labelling for all mass-consumption non-food products, but it was concluded that it was more useful to work out rules for each specific category of products. Accordingly, any proposals on specific products or services were to include special provisions to take account of their specific properties, with the aim of guaranteeing that the consumer receives proper information on the properties and the quality of the goods and services supplied. The Commission did, however, proceed to set up a Community system of information on accidents involving products, excluding occupational activities and road traffic,[6] and a Community system for rapid exchange of information on dangers arising from consumer products,[7] which are described in Chapter 2.

The new impetus

However, by 1985 it was accepted that for various reasons the achievements fell far short of the intentions of the consumer action programme. The Commission proposed a new impetus,[8] justified by the dual standpoint of citizens' welfare and efficiency of production. The principal proposed lines of action under the previous programmes were

[5] Council Resolution on a second programme of the European Economic Community for a consumer protection and information policy, OJ No. C 133/1, 3.6.81.

[6] Council Decision 86/138/EEC, OJ No. L 109, 26.4.86, as amended, now replaced by Council Decision No. 3092/94/EC of December 7, 1994 introducing a Community system of information on home and leisure accidents amended by Council Decision No. 95/184/EC of May 22, 1995.

[7] Council Decision 84/133 on a Community system for the rapid exchange of information on dangers arising from the use of consumer products, OJ No. L 70/18, 13.3.84, as extended by Decision 89/45/EEC of December 21, 1988, OJ No. L 17/51, 21.1.89, and Council Decision 90/352/EEC of June 29, 1990, OJ No. L 173/49, 6.7.90.

[8] A New Impetus for Consumer Protection Policy, Communication from the Commission to the Council, COM(85) 314 final, 27.6.85.

continued. The aims were stated as follows: "Consumers want to be sure that before products are put on the market they conform to acceptable health and safety standards. Once this is ensured, they want them to move freely and to be sold on fair terms throughout the Community." Three main objectives were identified:

- Products traded in the Community should conform to acceptable safety and health standards;
- Consumers must be able to benefit from the common market;
- Consumer interests should be taken more into account in other Community policies.

Paramount importance was therefore placed on product safety, which was stated to be a basic requirement and condition for the achievement of the internal market. The establishment of a comprehensive product safety policy was called for, the essential components of which were to be:

- a programme of legislation which was to set out clearly for manufacturers and suppliers the health and safety levels which their products must meet in order to ensure the protection of the consumer;
- a programme of cooperative action between national authorities responsible for the safety of consumer products designed to facilitate proper enforcement of safety laws;
- the creation of Community facilities for surveillance and control of health and safety risks posed by the use of consumer products;
- campaigns for the information and education of consumers concerning the safe use of products in the home and in leisure activities.

These points were aired by the Commission shortly after the adoption of the "New Approach" to technical harmonisation, described in the previous chapter. However, the new impetus towards consumer policy of 1985 specifically mentioned the need to assess the imposition at Community level of a general obligation on manufacturers to produce and market products which are safe. This was the origin of the General Product Safety Directive of 1992.

The Council welcomed the Commission's "new impetus" document and acknowledged the importance for consumer protection of producing and marketing only safe products and noted the Commission's intention to propose a general obligation on this topic.[9]

A new approach to consumer policy

In 1986, the Single European Act provided that measures intended to establish the internal market should be proposed by the Commission

[9] Council Resolution of June 23, 1986 concerning the future orientation of the policy of the European Economic Community for the protection and promotion of consumer interests, OJ No. C 167/1; Council Resolution of June 25, 1987 on consumer safety, OJ No. C 176/3.

and adopted by the Council. Any of these proposals which concern health, safety, environmental protection and consumer protection are to take as a base a high level of protection.

A new Commission took office in 1989 and quickly established an autonomous Consumer Policy Service, headed by a Director-General to take specific responsibility for the implementation of Community consumer policy, which had previously been one of the functions of Directorate-General XI (Environment and Consumer Protection). This led to the adoption of a Council Resolution on consumer policy protection in 1989 which set out priorities for re-launching consumer policy, particularly as regards consumer representation, the general safety of goods and services, access to legal redress and the integration of consumer protection policies in other Community policies. A Three-year Action Plan (1990–93) was then produced. This took account of the principle of subsidiarity and set objectives in the areas of representation, information, safety and transactions. Subsidiarity in this context meant that practical consumer policy must be effectively managed in the Member States on an ongoing basis with the management and control of safety, information and redress being adapted in each instance to local needs. It was recognised as being unrealistic to undertake such tasks continuously at a Community level.

Community legislation from the mid-1980s onwards which is of particular benefit to consumers includes the measures in **Table 2.**

Table 2 Important consumer measures from the mid-1980s

- Directive 86/653 on self-employed commercial agents
- Directive 88/378 on toy safety
- Directive 90/88 amending Directive 87/102, on consumer credit
- Directive 91/442 on dangerous preparations the packaging of which must be fitted with child-resistant fastenings
- Directive 91/689 on hazardous waste
- Directive 92/27 on labelling of medicinal products for human use and on package leaflets
- Directive 92/28 on advertising of medicinal products for human use
- Directive 92/59 on general product safety
- Several Directives on foodstuffs intended for the final consumer
- Directive 93/13 on unfair terms in consumer contracts

Consumer policy as an end in itself

The European Council meeting at Maastrict in 1992 amended the Treaty of Rome so that consumer protection was formally included as a matter of official and legal Community policy. Article 3(s) thus established as an objective of Community action "a contribution to the strengthening of consumer protection". A new Article 129A specified:

> "The Community shall contribute to the attainment of a high level of consumer protection through:
> (a) measures adopted pursuant to Article 100a in the context of the completion of the internal market;
> (b) specific action which supports and supplements the policy pursued by the Member States to protect the health, safety and economic interests of consumers and to provide adequate information to consumers."

By the target date for the creation of the internal market, January 1, 1993, a total of 42 Directives on consumer issues should have been transposed by Member States. The average transposition rate reported was 94 per cent but this concealed wide disparities. In July 1993 the Commission produced its Second Consumer Policy Action Plan, covering 1993–95. This established priorities in consumer information, consultation, access to justice and settlement of disputes, and adapting financial services to consumer needs.

The Council Resolution of July 1992[10] set out priorities in the areas of information and education, legal redress, safety and health, and representation of consumers' economic interests. In relation to legal redress, the Council encouraged Member States to facilitate simplification of procedures for settling consumer disputes, legal aid for consumers in respect of cases brought before the European courts, and access for consumer organisations which have, under national law, a legitimate interest in bringing the matter to the courts. In relation to safety and health priorities, the Council identified:

- development of any necessary harmonised systems to ensure that health and safety legislation is being effectively applied,
- fostering the levelling-up of scientific know-how and practices of consumer-product inspectors in the Member States,
- further harmonisation of the packaging, labelling and classification of products.

Developments on labelling

In furtherance of the above policy, the Council invited the Commission in April 1993[11] to examine the need and merits of a Community-wide solution to providing information on products by means of labelling and to study the possibility of establishing a Community framework for labelling requirements. A list of issues were specified:

[10] Council Resolution of July 13, 1992 on future priorities for the development of consumer protection policy, 92/C 186/01, OJ No. C 186/1.

[11] Council Resolution of April 5, 1993 on future action on the labelling of products in the interest of the consumer, 93/C 110/01, OJ No. C 110/1, 20.4.93.

1. The Commission should consider that labelling would in particular have to be:
   - comprehensible, *i.e.* legible and easy for the consumer to understand;
   - distinctive, *i.e.* make the necessary distinction between product labelling, on the one hand, and other information and advertising given on the product, on the other,
   - relevant, *i.e.* not be misleading and contain sufficient information enabling consumers to make purchase decisions based on the information they find important regarding a particular product,
   - transparent, *i.e.* enabling the consumer to compare different products within the same group of products in relation to quality and price,
   - verifiable, *i.e.* subject to appropriate supervision according to national legislation or practices, in order to ensure that the labelling complies with the agreed requirements,
   - practicable, *i.e.* easy for manufacturers, retailers and control services to implement.

2. The Commission should examine labelling requirements for all consumer products taking due account of products already covered by Community legislation and taking advantage of the experience gained from this legislation. In this context, the Commission should also examine the role of standardisation at Community level.

   The Commission should also reflect on the need to include guarantees and after-sales service.

3. The Commission should examine whether Community labelling requirements:
   - should follow a horizontal or a combined horizontal and vertical approach;
   - should aim at minimum provisions only or foresee full harmonisation;
   - would be more appropriate and efficient as an obligatory or as a voluntary scheme;
   - should be based on a modular, integrated system.

A problem with the development and certainly the implementation of a consumer policy on product labelling flows from its timing. The labelling requirements are already included in many directives covering consumer products, for example foodstuffs, medicinal products, toys, medical devices and so on. It is, therefore, somewhat late to develop an unified, general policy in relation to labelling of products where labelling requirements have already been considered from the point of view of the requirements of individual product types or sectors so as to ensure safety in use.

How effective has consumer safety policy been?

The point just made holds good in a wider context. This chapter has traced the development of consumer safety over 20 years from small and generalised beginnings to development of policies and measures with greater impact. A dedicated administration for consumer policy has now been in existence for five years at Commission level and in 1995 the Commission's Consumer Policy Service was elevated to the status of Directorate-General XXIV. This is supported by a reformed Consumer Committee,[12] replacing the Consumers' Consultative Council which had been created in 1990,[13] and may be consulted by the Commission on all problems relating to the protection of consumer interests at Community level. Undoubtedly, consumer policy is gathering focus and momentum and consumer interests will need to be taken into account in relevant legislation and policies.

However, many measures which have been claimed as being of benefit to consumers have been drafted and remain overseen by Directorates-General whose paramount concern is with the internal market and industrial policy, rather than with consumer affairs. Community measures relating to foodstuffs, medicinal products and all of the New Approach Directives are typically, of necessity, highly technical. It is difficult for consumers or even consumer representatives to understand or take part in the drafting, implementation or operation of such highly technical and scientific measures. This is merely to state the position: This is not the place to debate whether greater consumer involvement in such activities would be beneficial, necessary, counterproductive or adverse. All of these views can rationally be advanced.

Although there may be little consumer input into the drafting or forms of measures dealing with products, this is not to say that safety aspects are ignored in product measures. The policy requirement that New Approach Directives must be based on a high level of protection of health and safety will clearly have an important impact on the interpretation of the detail of such measures in the courts. An early example of this is the Court of Justice's decision rejecting Germany's challenge to the legal basis of the Commission's powers in Directive 92/59/EEC on general product safety, in which the Court's analysis was based on the importance of the policy of a high level protection of health and safety[14].

[12] Commission Directive 95/260/EEC of June 13, 1995 setting up a Consumer Committee, OJ No. L 162/37, 13.7.95.

[13] Commission Decision 90/55/EEC OJ No. L 38/40, 10.2.90, as amended.

[14] Case C–359/92.

3 Safety aspects of "New Approach" Technical Directives

Many Community Directives enacted since 1985 which harmonise the rules for placing products on the market conform to the same "blueprint", known as the "New Approach". Examples include Directives on machinery, construction products, medical devices, personal protective equipment, electromagnetic compatibility, pressure vessels, gas appliances, non-automatic weighing instruments, hot water boilers and toys. More will follow.

New Approach Directives set out the essential safety requirements to which products covered must conform in order to have CE marking and be placed on the Community market. Products which comply with national standards transposing harmonised Community technical standards are presumed to conform to the essential requirements.

Member States have residual powers under safeguard clauses to withdraw or restrict or prohibit the placing on the market of products which nevertheless might compromise safety.

The "New Approach" Directives

As stated in Chapter 2, the principal means by which the European Union sets out to achieve a high level of safety and health for its citizens, as well as the removal of barriers to trade within its internal market, is through an extensive programme of legislation which harmonises the conditions which must be met in order to authorise a product being placed on the market. These harmonised rules are contained in a growing series of Directives which are authorised under Article 100A of the EC Treaty.

The Directives all follow the same format and basic approach which was established in 1985 as part of the Community's "New Approach" to technical harmonisation and standards[1] and its "global approach" to conformity assessment.[2] A list of the current New Approach Directives is at **Table 3.1**.

[1] Council Resolution of May 7, 1985 on a new approach to technical harmonisation and standards, OJ 1985 No. C136/1, 4.6.85.

[2] Council Resolution of December 21, 1989 on a global approach to conformity assessment, OJ 1989 No. C10/1, 16.1.90.

Table 3.1 New Approach Directives

All Directives up to and including Directive 92/42/EEC have been amended by Directive 93/68/EEC.

Directive	U.K. implementing legislation
73/23/EEC Electrical Equipment designed for use within certain voltage limits ("Low Voltage")	Low Voltage Electrical Equipment (Safety) Regulations 1989 (S.I. 1989 No. 728), amended by the Electrical Equipment (Safety) Regulations S.I. 1994 No. 3260
87/404/EEC amended by 90/488/EEC Simple Pressure Vessels	Simple Pressure Vessels (Safety) Regulations 1991 (S.I. 1991 No. 2749) amended by the Simple Pressure Vessels (Safety) (Amendment) Regulations 1994 (S.I. 1994 No. 3098)
88/378/EEC Toy Safety	Toys (Safety) Regulations 1989 (S.I. 1989 No. 1275) amended by the Toys (Safety) (Amendment) Regulations 1993 (S.I. 1993 No. 1547)
89/106/EEC Construction Products[3]	Construction Products Regulations 1991 (S.I. 1991 No. 1620)
89/336/EEC amended by 92/31/EEC Electromagnetic Compatibility	Electromagnetic Compatibility Regulations 1992 (S.I. 1992 No. 2372) amended by the Electromagnetic Compatibility (Amendment) Regulations 1994 (S.I. 1994 No. 3080)
89/392/EEC Machinery (general health and safety requirements) amended by 91/368/EEC Mobile machinery and lifting appliances (specific risks) and 93/44/EEC Appliances for the lifting or moving of persons (specific risks); additional provisions for safety components placed on the market separately	Supply of Machinery (Safety) Regulations 1992 (S.I. 1992 No. 3073) amended by the Supply of Machinery (Safety) (Amendment) Regulations 1994 (S.I. 1994 No. 2063).
89/686/EEC Amended by 93/95/EEC Personal Protective Equipment	Personal Protective Equipment (E.C. Directive) Regulations 1992 (S.I. 1992 No. 3139) amended by the Personal Protective Equipment (EC Directive) Amendment Regulations 1994 (S.I. 1994 No. 2326)

[3] Amplified by Commission Decision 92/204/EC.

90/384/EEC Non-automatic Weighing Instruments	Non-automatic Weighing Instruments (EEC Requirements) Regulations 1992 (S.I. 1992 No. 1579) amended by the Non-automatic Weighing and Non-automatic Weighing Instruments (Amendment) Regulations 1995 (S.I. 1995 No. 428)
90/385/EEC amended by 93/42/EEC Active Implantable Medical Devices	Active Implantable Medical Devices Regulations 1992 (S.I. 1992 No. 3146) amended by the Active Implantable Medical Devices (Amendment and Transitional Provisions) Regulations 1995 (S.I. 1995 No. 1671)
90/396/EEC Appliances Burning Gaseous Fuels	Gas Appliances (Safety) Regulations 1992 (S.I. 1992 No. 711) and the Gas Appliances (Safety) Regulations 1995 (S.I. 1995 No. 1629)
91/263/EEC Telecommunications Terminal Equipment supplemented by 93/97/EEC Satellite Earth Station Equipment	Telecommunications Terminal Equipment Regulations 1992 (S.I. 1992 No. 2423) amended by the Telecommunications Terminal Equipment (Amendment and Extension) Regulations 1994 (S.I. 1994 No. 3129) and the Telecommunications Terminal Equipment (Amendment) Regulations 1995 (S.I. 1995 No. 144)
92/42/EEC New hot water boilers fired with liquid and gaseous fluids (efficiency requirements)	Boiler (Efficiency) Regulations 1993 (S.I. 1993 No. 3083)
93/15/EEC Explosives for civil uses	Placing on the Market and Supervision of Transfers of Explosives Regulations 1993 (S.I. 1993 No. 2714) (except Art. 10)
93/42/EEC Medical Devices	Medical Devices Regulations 1994 (S.I. 1994 No. 3017)
94/9/EC Equipment and protective systems intended for use in potentially explosive atmospheres	
94/25/EC Recreational craft	

The essence of the "New Approach" is that a product which is subject to one of the relevant Directives may be placed on the market and put into service only if:

(a) it does not endanger the health or safety of persons when properly installed, maintained and used for its intended purpose; and
(b) it satisfies the essential health and safety requirements which are set out in the Directive, invariably in Annex I.

Conformity assessment and CE marking

In order to be marketed, a product must therefore undergo assessment to ensure that it conforms to the relevant essential requirements. It may only be marketed if it conforms[4] to the essential requirements and bears the CE marking of conformity (**Figure 3.1**): the CE marking may only be applied to products which have satisfied the relevant conformity assessment procedure.

Figure 3.1 CE Mark of Conformity

Quality systems and type examination

Different products carry differing degrees of inherent risk. Toys or bandages generally carry little risk but more serious hazards may be associated with complex machinery, particularly if it uses electricity or radiation. For low risks, it may be appropriate merely for the manufacturer to self-certify that his product conforms to the essential requirements. In other cases, it may be appropriate for an independent testing house to be involved in the assessment and certification procedure. Testing houses approved for this purpose are known as "notified bodies", since their authorisation by the competent authority in their Member State has to be notified to the Commission and other Member States and is published in the Official Journal of the European Commu-

[4] Some Directives contain exceptions, such as for medical devices which are used solely for the purpose of clinical evaluation or are custom-made under Directive 93/42/EEC.

nities. Each notified body is given an unique identifying number which has to appear next to the CE marking on each product for which it has conformity assessment responsibility. Approval of a notified body is carried out by assessment of its own conformity to the EN 45000 series of standards.

The independent assessment of conformity to the essential requirements might be based on the quality management system of the manufacturer (to standard BS EN ISO 9000, formerly known as BS 5750) or the examination of a specimen of the product (type examination) together with examination for conformity to the approved type either of a sample of production or of all products produced of that type. There is, therefore, a range of possible options for approval of a product or production system and the New Approach Directives specify one or more of the options from nine possible approved modules.[5] A diagram of the approved modules is shown at **Figure 3.2**.

The conformity assessment modules cover both the design and production phases. Where possible, Directives specify as many modules as possible so that manufacturers have as much choice as possible over the method of conformity assessment which they wish to select as being appropriate for their product. There are also historical, political dimensions: the approach based on a system for quality management has been particularly favoured in the United Kingdom, where BS 5750 originated, whereas the type-testing approach has been favoured elsewhere, particularly in Germany. The quality management system is discussed further in Chapter 14.

Standards

There would be little point in a Directive specifying the essential requirements of health and safety for approval of a product in extensive detail. Technology evolves and not all detailed requirements may be appropriate to all products of the same type. A prescriptive approach may best be avoided. Accordingly, New Approach Directives generally provide that Member States shall presume that a product which complies with a national technical standard which transposes a harmonised European standard is in conformity with the essential requirements. Initial conformity assessment of a product may therefore be carried out as against such a standard, rather than against the essential requirements themselves.

A harmonised standard is one which has been approved by one of the three European standardisation bodies, pursuant to a mandate issued by

[5] Council Decision 90/683/EEC of December 13, 1990 replaced by Council Decision 93/465/EEC of July 22, 1993 concerning the modules for the various phases of the conformity assessment procedures and the rules for the affixing and use of the CE conformity marking, which are intended to be used in the technical harmonisation directives. OJ No. L220/23, 30.8.93.

Figure 3.2 Conformity assessment procedures in Community legislation

	A. *(Internal control of production)*	B. *(type examination)*	G. *(unit verification)*	H. *(full quality assurance*
D E S I G N	Manufacturer Keeps technical documentation at the disposal of national authorities Aa Intervention of notified body	Manufacturer submits to notified body —Technical documentation —Type Notified body —Ascertains conformity with essential requirements —Carries out tests, if necessary —Issues EC type-examination certificate	Manufacturer —submits technical documentation	EN 29001 Manufacturer —Operates an approved quality system (QS) for design Notified body —Carries out surveillance of the QS —Verifies conformity of the design[1] —Issues E.C. design examination certificate[1]

		C. *(conformity to type)*	D. *(production quality assurance)*	E. *(product quality assurance)*	F. *(product verification)*		
			EN 29002	EN 29003			
PRODUCTION	A. Manufacturer —Declares conformity with essential requirements —Affixes the CE marking	Manufacturer —Declares conformity with approved type —Affixes the CE marking	Manufacturer —Operates an approved quality system (QS) for production and testing —Declares conformity with approved type —Affixes the CE marking	Manufacturer —Operates an approved quality system (QS) for inspection and testing —Declares conformity with approved type, or to essential requirements —Affixes the CE marking	Manufacturer —Declares conformity with approved type, or with essential requirements —Affixes the CE marking	Manufacturer —Submits product —Declares conformity —Affixes the CE marking	Manufacturer —Operates an approved QS for production and testing —Declares conformity —Affixes the CE marking
	Aa Notified body —Tests on specific aspects of the product[1] —Product checks at random intervals[1]	Notified body —Tests on specific aspects of the product[1] —Product checks at random intervals[1]	Notified body —Approves the QS —Carries out surveillance of the QS	Notified body —Approves the QS —Carries out surveillance of the QS	Notified body —Verifies conformity —Issues certificate of conformity	Notified body —Verifies conformity with essential requirements —Issues certificate of conformity	Notified body —Carries out surveillance of the QS

[1] Supplementary requirements which may be used in specific Directives.

the European Commission, as itself conforming to the essential requirements. A standard affords the opportunity of being highly technical and may cover all or only one aspect of the essential requirements. It may also be amended relatively quickly to take account of technical and scientific developments. Many thousands of such harmonised standards are being prepared by the European standardisation bodies:

- CEN — the European Standards Organisation
- CENELEC — The European Electrotechnical Standards Organisation
- ETSI — the European Telecommunications Standards Institute

Examples of essential requirements relating to safety

Essential requirements are generally comprehensive and extensive. There is insufficient space to reproduce here the texts of all the essential requirements in New Approach Directives, still less to cover individual standards. Merely to list the current or proposed standards takes large volumes. As an example, **Table 3.2** lists the main headings of the essential health and safety requirements from Directive 89/392/EEC relating to the design and construction of machinery.

Table 3.2 Main headings from the essential health & safety requirements of Directive 89/392/EEC relating to the design and construction of machinery

1.	ESSENTIAL HEALTH & SAFETY REQUIREMENTS
1.1	**General Remarks**
1.1.1	*Definitions*
1.1.2	*Principles of safety integration*
1.1.3	*Materials and productions*
1.1.4	*Lighting*
1.1.5	*Design of machinery to facilitate its handling*
1.2	**Controls**
1.2.1	*Safety and reliability of control systems*
1.2.2	*Control devices*
1.2.3	*Starting*
1.2.4	*Stopping device*
	Normal stopping
	Emergency stop
	Complex installations
1.2.5	*Mode selection*
1.2.6	*Failure of the power supply*
1.2.7	*Failure of the control circuit*
1.2.8	*Software*
1.3	**Protection Against Mechanical Hazards**
1.3.1	*Stability*
1.3.2	*Risk of break-up during operation*
1.3.3	*Risks due to falling or ejected objects*
1.3.4	*Risks due to surfaces, edges or angles*

1.3.5 *Risks related to combined machinery*
1.3.6 *Risks relating to variations in the rotational speed of tools*
1.3.7 *Prevention of risks related to moving parts*
1.3.8 *Choice of protection against risks related to moving parts*
A. Moving transmission parts
B. Moving parts directly involved in the process

1.4 **Required Characteristics of Guards and Protection Devices**
1.4.1 *General requirement*
1.4.2 *Special requirements for guards*
1.4.2.1 Fixed guards
1.4.2.2 Moveable guards
1.4.2.3 Adjustable guards restricting access
1.4.3 *Special requirements for protection devices*

1.5 **Protection Against Other Hazards**
1.5.1 *Electricity supply*
1.5.2 *Static electricity*
1.5.3 *Energy supply other than electricity*
1.5.4 *Errors of fitting*
1.5.5 *Extreme temperatures*
1.5.6 *Fire*
1.5.7 *Explosion*
1.5.8 *Noise*
1.5.9 *Vibration*
1.5.10 *Radiation*
1.5.11 *External radiation*
1.5.12 *Laser equipment*
1.5.13 *Emissions of dust, gases, etc.*

1.6 **Maintenance**
1.6.1 *Machinery maintenance*
1.6.2 *Access to operating position and servicing points*
1.6.3 *Isolation of energy sources*
1.6.4 *Operator intervention*

1.7 **Indicators**
1.7.0 *Information devices*
1.7.1 *Warning devices*
1.7.2 *Warning of residual risks*
1.7.3 *Marking*
1.7.4 *Instructions*

2. [Additional essential health & safety requirements are given for certain categories of machinery: agri-foodstuffs machinery, portable hand-held and/or hand-guided machinery, and machinery for working wood and analagous materials]

3. [Further essential health & safety requirements were added to Directive 91/368/EEC to offset the particular hazards due to the mobility of machinery or to a lifting operation or for machinery intended solely for underground work. Further requirements were provided by Directive 89/392/EEC to offset the particular hazards due to the lifting or moving of persons]

Safeguard clauses

Member States are prohibited from setting up any system of control prior to placing on the market, except where they are specified in a Directive. However, national authorities are to exercise control on the market by way of spot checks. Where a Member State finds that a product might compromise the safety of individuals, domestic animals or property, it shall take all appropriate measures to withdraw or prohibit the placing on the market of the product in question or to restrict its free movement even if it is accompanied by one of the means of attestation. This standard power in New Approach Directives is known as the "safeguard clause". Where a Member State takes such a measure in relation to a product which is accompanied by one of the means of attestation, it must inform the Commission within a given period of time,[6] indicating the reasons for its decision and in particular whether the non-conformity results from:

(a) non-compliance with the general clause or essential safety requirements;
(b) incorrect application of the harmonised standards; or
(c) a shortcoming in the harmonised standards themselves.

The Commission must then consult the Member States and refer the matter to the Standing Committee which is concerned with the implementation of the Directives. The Standing Committee is chaired by a representative of the Commission and consists of representatives appointed by the Member States, who may avail themselves of the help of experts or advisers. Where, after consultation with the Committee, the Commission finds that the Member State's action is justified, it will inform all the Member States that, all else being equal, they are also obliged to prevent the product in question from being placed on the market. Where failure of the product to comply results from a shortcoming in the harmonised or national standards, the standards shall be examined by the Standing Committee. This examination may also take place where a Member State or the Commission considers that the harmonised standards do not fully satisfy the general clause or the essential safety requirements. In the light of the opinion of the Committee, the Commission notifies the Member States whether or not the standard in question should continue to enjoy the presumption of conformity. If it is inadequate, it will be withdrawn from the authorised list of published references.

Directives not of the "New Approach"

There are many other Directives which govern the placing of products on the EEA market which do not and need not involve reference to

[6] Between 1990 and 1992 the Commission received 63 notifications under safeguard clauses, OJ No. C202/14, 26.7.93.

technical standards and/or essential requirements in the way discussed here. Such Directives include those dealing with foodstuffs, human or veterinary medicinal products and cosmetics. These Directives do, of course, lay down requirements for the high level of protection of the health and safety of persons. The marketing of medicinal products, for example, is subject to the issue by a competent regulatory authority of a marketing authorisation, usually after scrutiny of extensive data obtained from physico-chemical, biological or microbiological tests, pharmacological and toxicological tests, and clinical trials. An authorisation to manufacture medicinal products is also required.

4 The General Product Safety Directive

This chapter describes the European Union legislation on general product safety: Directive 92/59/EEC which governs the United Kingdom's General Product Safety Regulations 1994. The Regulations are made pursuant to the United Kingdom's obligation, as a Member State of the European Community, to implement the Directive. This Chapter therefore covers the provisions of that Directive which arise as matters of Community Law: Chapter 5 covers the implementing Regulations.

It would be nice if all we needed to do was to read the General Product Safety Regulations and ignore the Directive. The legal system is unfortunately not that simple. In short, the Regulations must conform to the Directive and where they differ, important consequences may follow, as outlined below: it is important to be alive to this legal issue.

In the case of this particular Directive, there are further issues which arise at Community level. First, there is the difficult problem of overlap between the provisions of this Directive and other product regulatory directives. Secondly, the Directive gives important powers and duties to Member States in relation to enforcement, market surveillance and coordination of action. These matters are covered in this chapter.

THE NATURE OF DIRECTIVES AND THEIR ENFORCEMENT

The Community chose to legislate in the field of product safety by means of directive. This form of Community legislation is binding as to the result to be achieved upon each Member State to which it is addressed, but it is for national authorities to determine the means of implementation.[1] Directives have the inherent disadvantage that the detail of national implementation will differ according to the particular legal tradition of a Member State, even though core principles may be respected.

Difficulties can be compounded where Member States have a different understanding of the result to be achieved by a directive. Implementa-

[1] Art. 189 EC Treaty.

tion which departs from the terms of a directive can prompt an infringement action by the E.C. Commission against the Member State before the European Court of Justice (ECJ).[2]

Although it is always open for an individual to encourage the European Commission to bring an infringement action against a Member State, it is perhaps more likely for discrepancies between national implementing legislation and the Directive to be argued in domestic court litigation. The national judge wishing to clarify the meaning of the Directive can seek interpretative guidance through a preliminary ruling from the ECJ under the procedure in Article 177 EC Treaty. To do so the national judge would stay national proceedings and frame abstract questions of law for the ECJ to answer. The national judge would then apply the ECJ's reply to the particular facts. Preliminary rulings were conceived to ensure uniform interpretation of Community law in national courts.

The overlap and interplay of Community law and national law is governed by a series of further interpretative rules. Generally, where a directive and national law conflict, the provisions of the directive take precedence.[3] This means that inconsistent national rules should not be applied or that the national rules should be interpreted consistently with the directive.

Generally, a directive can be relied upon by private individuals before national courts where the Member State has implemented the directive erroneously or not at all, provided that the terms relied upon are clear, precise and unconditional. However, this right only applies "vertically", *i.e.* as between an individual and the State and not "horizontally" as between private individuals.[4] In most situations Directive 85/374 would be relied upon in actions between private parties rather than in actions between a private party and the State. The scope for direct reliance on the Directive in this way is therefore significantly reduced. Despite the apparent limiting effect of this rule an important secondary form of reliance can be available to individuals, which in practical terms could have a similar effect. This is an extension of the principle that national courts are bound to interpret national law consistently with a directive. The ECJ has gone further to say that if Community law has not been implemented national courts cannot apply inconsistent national law.[5] There will therefore be situations where national legislation has not been put in place or indeed where it contradicts the Directive. In those

[2] Under Art. 169 EC Treaty. So far no infringement actions concerning Directive 85/374 have been brought before the European Court of Justice although formal proceedings against the United Kingdom are anticipated.

[3] *e.g.* Case 51/76, *Verbond van Nederlandse Ondernemingen v. Inspecteur der Invoerrechten en Accijnzen* [1977] E.C.R. 113.

[4] Case 152/84, *Marshall v. Southampton and South West Hampshire Health Authority* [1986] E.C.R. 723.

[5] Case C-106/89, *Marleasing SA v. La Comercial Internacional de Alimentacion SA* [1990] E.C.R. I-4135; Case C-221/89, *Factortame Ltd v. Secretary of State for Transport (No. 3)* 3 C.M.L.R. 589.

situations a private party cannot assert the direct applicability of the Directive against another private party. However it can argue that the national court has the wider Community obligation not to apply inconsistent national law and achieve a similar result as if the direct effect of the Directive could have been relied upon.

The Member State can also be liable in damages to the individual. Where a Member State has not enacted legislation and this deprives the individual of a remedy, the individual can recover against the Member State in certain circumstances.[6] The Court's criteria for the recovery of damages were first, that the Directive involves rights granted to individuals; secondly, that the scope of those rights are clear from the face of the Directive; and thirdly, that there is a causal link between the failure of the Member State to fulfil its obligations and the loss suffered by the individual concerned. These criteria could in the future be applied to a number of provisions in the Directive.

The foregoing principles are important and emphasise the significance of reading the Directive and national legislation together. These principles also demonstrate the need to consider arguments and remedies which may be available through Community law as well as those at national law.

Overview of the Directive

The European Community's Directive 92/59/EEC ("GPS Directive") on General Product Safety was adopted by the Council of Ministers meeting in Lisbon on June 29, 1992.[7] The text of the Directive followed the draft of the Common Position which had been adopted on December 23, 1991, with two minor additions. The Directive was to be implemented into the national law of the Member States by the target date of June 29, 1994.

The GPS Directive is a measure with potentially far-reaching implications.[8] It establishes, at Community level, a "general safety requirement", under which all consumer products placed on the market must be safe. The measures are aimed at reducing the estimated 45 million accidents per year involving consumer products which occur across the Community. The way in which this is to be done is by imposing obligations on both producers and on Member States. Lesser obligations are also imposed on distributors and others, arguably even including consumers and users.

Producers must provide customers with the relevant information to enable them to assess the risks inherent in a product through the normal

[6] Joined cases C-6/70 and C-9/90, *Francovich and others v. Italian Republic*, judgment of November 19, 1991.

[7] The Directive was adopted by qualified majority, Germany voting against.

[8] It was referred to in the U.K. Parliament as "one of the most far-reaching pieces of consumer legislation that has been considered in this country". May 10, 1990, Hansard H.C., 493.

or reasonably foreseeable period of its use. They must also monitor in an appropriate manner the safety of products placed on the market. If necessary, producers must take appropriate action, including withdrawing the product from the market, to avoid safety problems.

The obligations on Member States are to make producers and distributors comply with their obligations and to monitor the compliance of products with the obligation to place only safe products on the market.[9] In order to fulfil these obligations, Member States are to adopt wide-ranging powers of regulatory control. In the event of different Member States adopting conflicting approaches, there is a Community procedure under which the Commission consults with a Committee on Product Safety Emergencies, at the conclusion of which the Council of Ministers, or the Commission as a last resort, is entitled to take a final decision. There is some controversy over the validity of this "policing" function that has been acquired by the Commission.

The Community objective of general product safety

The objects of the Directive[10] were to harmonise the different laws on consumer product safety regulation which Member States were in the course of adopting and also that:

> "A firm undertaking by manufacturers, traders and importers to supply safe goods will restore consumers' confidence, as soon as they have proof that a mechanism exists capable of dealing with dangerous or risky situations.
>
> Moreover, an obligation on the manufacturer to market only products which are safe will also increase the quality of European products and will thus improve the competitiveness of European firms vis-à-vis their competitors."

The Community's priority objective was completion of the internal market. This was to be done, in accordance with the "New Approach" to technical harmonisation and standards from 1985,[11] by harmonising laws on specific products or categories of products which define the essential safety requirements, while leaving the preparation of technical specifications to competent standards bodies. This vertical approach meant, however, that certain products would not be covered by vertical directives and would therefore be outside the ambit of any safety legislation. The GPS Directive was intended to fill this gap by introducing a horizontal general safety obligation. It was not intended to affect present or future sectoral directives.

[9] See also Council Regulation No. 339/93 of February 8, 1993 on checks for conformity with rules on product safety in the case of products imported from third countries.

[10] Commission Communication on safety of consumers in relation to consumer products, COM(87) 209 final, 8.5.87.

[11] Council Resolution of May 7, 1985 on a new approach to technical harmonisation and standards, O.J. 1985 No. C136/1, 4.6.85. See also Council Resolution of December 21, 1989 on a global approach to conformity assessment, O.J. 1989 No. C10/1, 16.1.90.

Achieving fair competition is at the heart of the internal market. Accordingly, the United Kingdom Minister for Consumer Affairs justified earlier national measures on the basis that: "Supplying unsafe goods is a form of unfair competition as it gives the supplier of unsafe goods an unfair advantage over a competitor who is prepared to incur the costs associated with ensuring that his goods are safe."[12]

Although this is not stated in the Directive, it also forms an important part of the Community's consumer protection policy as well as its internal market policy. The background to the consumer aspects are traced in Chapter 12.

The Directive undoubtedly increases the obligations on producers and distributors and extends the system of regulatory control. Nevertheless, the Commission presented the proposals in a low key:

> "Taken as a whole, the intention is not at all to build up a perfectionist regulatory machinery, but rather to summarise, in a general way, certain relatively simple principles, which anyway apply, in one way or the other, in the Member States and throughout the Community, and to give them a Community dimension."[13]

Similarly, the United Kingdom government, for example, stated that in its view compliance with pre-existing provisions of the Consumer Protection Act 1987 should mean that the GPS obligations were complied with.[14] The Directive was viewed as not entailing significant changes in either consumer safety policy or the prevailing practice of industry or enforcement authorities.

Legal Basis of the Directive

A Directive must have proper legal basis under the EEC Treaty. A challenge can be made to the validity of a Directive if it is not based correctly on an appropriate provision in the Treaty.[15]

The legal basis for the Directive is Article 100a of the Treaty of Rome: this means that it has been created as one of the measures to establish the internal market and to eliminate barriers to trade within the Community. Some Member States had previously adopted legislation on product safety which imposed, in particular, a general obligation on economic operators to market only safe products. However, these laws differed in the level of protection afforded to persons. It was concluded that these disparities and the absence of horizontal legislation in other Member States were liable to create barriers to trade and distortions of

[12] April 27, 1987, Hansard H.C., 51.
[13] Explanatory Note, COM (89) 162/6.
[14] Speech by Mr David Jones, Head of the Consumer Safety Unit, Department of Trade and Industry at the McKenna & Co/Confederation of British Industry Conference, March 15, 1994.
[15] Germany challenged the legal basis of the Directive: Case C-359/92.

competition within the internal market. Accordingly, this Directive was adopted.

The general policy and measures which the Community has adopted in establishing the internal market are discussed in Chapter 3. They include the legislative harmonisation (through the adoption of technical directives) of rules governing placing products on the market, on a sector-by-sector basis. Technical directives contain a general requirement that a product which they cover may be marketed only if it does not compromise the safety and health of the users and others when it is properly installed, maintained and used in accordance with its intended purpose. However, as the third recital to the GPS Directive states, it is very difficult to adopt Community legislation for every product which exists or may be developed. The Community therefore perceived a need for a broadly-based horizontal legislative framework to deal with all products and to cover lacunae in existing or forthcoming specific legislation. In short, the GPS Directive is intended to fill in the gaps left by other sectoral directives.

The European Commission's "Explanatory Note" of 1989, introducing the original proposals, referred to the complexities and fragmentation of E.C. and national laws and product standards and asserted that:

> "There is, indeed, despite the success of the idea of 'completing the internal market by 1992', its consecration under the European Single Act and the generally satisfactory progress of legislative work undertaken in this perspective, some residual uneasiness expressed by several quarters in Member States about what will be the practical consequences and results for everybody, once this target is reached . . . a general legal instrument, establishing rather simple basic principles, such as proposed here, should help to overcome certain feelings of insecurity and some reluctance not only on the part of final consumers but equally on the part of workers and of professionals who are all users and consumers of whatever products freely circulate throughout the Common Market. The proposal is, therefore, designed to *strengthen general confidence* in the proper functioning of the internal market." [emphasis added]

A high level of protection

It is a requirement under Article 100a.3 of the Treaty that all measures based on Article 100a which concern health, safety, environmental protection and consumer protection "will take as a base level a high level of protection" of health and safety. This phrase is repeated in the GPS Directive and all technical directives. It is an important aid to the interpretation of the standard of safety set in these directives and should be born in mind by manufacturers, notified bodies, competent authorities and the courts. However, the reference to "a high level of protection" in Article 100a has been criticised by the Economic and Social Committee on two particular grounds. First it only applies to Commission proposals and is not explicitly binding on the Council, the Court of Justice or the Member States. Accordingly, as defined, the criterion means weakening consumer protection in Member States where protection exceeds that specified by Community legislation. Secondly, it was argued that the best criterion for the consumer would be the highest degree of protection.[16] This was supported by the European Parliament.[17] It is therefore clear that "a high level of protection" is not necessarily the highest level which prevails or can be imagined, for example in that Member State which had made the most progress in adopting consumer protection or technical safety measures in a particular area.

Previous product safety legislation in Member States

Many Member States (such as France, Germany, Spain and the United Kingdom) had pre-existing product safety legislation and six others (Belgium, Denmark, Ireland, Italy, the Netherlands and Portugal) were preparing to legislate. These laws should now be amended so as to conform to the Directive. However, full amendment of pre-existing product safety legislation may not occur in all Member States. The relevant pre-existing United Kingdom legislation is Part II of the Consumer Protection Act 1987 (CPA). **Table 2.1** summarises the main regulatory provisions under the Directive (and the General Product Safety Regulations 1994) and the CPA. It will be seen that there are notable similarities between the two laws. For example, although a number of detailed differences could be highlighted, the products covered and the authorities' powers are broadly similar. Equally, both systems are backed by criminal sanctions. The most significant differences lie in the imposition by the Directive of specific, positive obligations on a supplier to provide information to consumers on any risks associated with products, to monitor safety in use and to take appropriate action from time to time, including withdrawal of a product if this is necessary.

As discussed in Chapter 5, the text of the CPA has not been re-written so as to conform to the Directive, as might have been expected. Instead, a new and parallel set of General Product Safety Regulations 1994 have been created. This produces a confusing duplication.

The Directive's precedence over national product safety legislation

What is the position where the Directive is implemented into the national law of a Member State in such a way that other product safety

[16] Opinion on Consumer Protection and Completion of the Internal Market, Economic and Social Committee, 91/C339/08, O.J. No. C339/16, 31.12.91.

[17] Resolution A3 — 0060/92.

Table 4.1 Comparison of GPS Directive and U.K. Law

	GPS Directive	CPA 1987, Pt. II
Products	• Any product intended for or likely to be used by consumers • Exceptions where product specific Community provisions exist and for antiques or repaired or reconditioned goods where supplier has notified consumer of nature of goods.	• Consumer goods ordinarily intended for private use or consumption; • exceptions for second hand goods
Sectoral Exclusions	• Products covered by specific provisions of Community Law, in so far as they govern safety aspects.	• Growing crops and food etc, gas, aircraft, motor vehicles, controlled drugs and licensed medicines, tobacco.
Test of safety	• Minimum risks compatible with the product's use, and considered acceptable and consistent with high level of protection for health and safety of persons. (The feasibility of obtaining higher levels of safety or availability of safer products not grounds for considering a product unsafe.) • Products are deemed safe where they comply with specific rules of national law.	• Not reasonably safe having regard to all the circumstances. (Existence of means by which it would have been reasonable to make goods safer a relevant factor.) • Compliance with safety regulations or approved standards meets the general safety requirement.

Supplier's obligations	• Producers to place only safe products on the market.
	  • Provide information and warnings to consumers
	  • Mark batches and test samples
	  • Monitor safety in use
	  • Investigate complaints
	  • Take appropriate action, including withdrawal
	• Distributors to act with due care to help ensure compliance with general safety requirement.
		• Supply only goods which meet the general safety requirement.
		-
		-
		-
		-
		• Comply with statutory notices etc
		• Supplying goods which meet the general safety requirement. [Due diligence and retailer defences]

State powers	• Suitable penalties for failure to comply • Checks on safety and sampling • Requiring information • Imposing marketing conditions • Requiring warnings and informing persons exposed • Temporary prohibition on marketing • Banning a dangerous batch • Organising effective and immediate withdrawal and destruction • Notify E.C. of action taken	• Contravention is an offence • Testing and inspection of goods, search and seizure powers • Requiring information • Safety regulations made by the Secretary of State • Notices to warn • Suspension notice • Prohibition on supplying goods/raw materials or component for goods • Prohibition notices against persons responsible, forfeiture orders -

provisions also continue in effect? This is, for example, the position in the United Kingdom where the pre-existing conditions of Part II of the Consumer Protection Act 1987 have not been repealed as a consequence of the introduction of the General Product Safety Regulations 1994 but the two systems, each with its unique terminology and approach, apparently continue in parallel effect. Regulation 5 of the General Product Safety Regulations 1994 merely states that the relevant provisions of Part II of the Consumer Protection Act 1987 shall be disapplied to the extent that they impose general safety requirements if products are to be placed on the market or supplied etc. It might seem, therefore, that an enforcement official might have a choice about whether to apply the provisions of the Consumer Protection Act or of the General Product Safety Regulations. Nevertheless, this result could not be right under Community law.

As a matter of Community law, the competent authorities of Member States must apply the GPS Directive in relation to the regulation of consumer products which it governs. Accordingly, if a Member State seeks to apply legislation which is inconsistent with the GPS provisions, it would be contravening Community law and the purported application could be resisted by the defendant.

It might also be argued that the application of any provisions of national law which fall outside the Directive would be illegal under Community law. This is a more difficult issue since certain directives are held merely to lay down minimum requirements which a Member State is entitled to exceed, whereas other Directives are held comprehensively to cover their field and a Member State may not impose provisions which are inconsistent with them. There is no authoritative statement on whether the GPS Directive is a "minimal approach" measure or a comprehensive measure, but it is certainly arguable that it should be considered to be the latter. If so, provisions of national law which are extraneous to the GPS Directive and which deal with aspects of substantive law rather than enforcement (the latter being generally a matter for individual States) might be contrary to Community law.

WHEN DOES THE GPS DIRECTIVE APPLY?

It is of fundamental importance to know when the GPS Directive applies and when it does not. The answer is not easy to find or to work out. One needs to consider:

- whether the person involved falls within the definitions of a *producer* or *distributor*;
- whether the product involved falls within the definition of a *product*;
- the extent to which particular provisions of the GPS Directive apply, whether in relation to the obligations on producers, or distributors or Member States. The answer to this question is surprisingly

complicated and involves a detailed comparison of the GPS Directive and any other relevant regulatory provisions.

These items are discussed in detail below.

Products subject to specific Community safety provisions

The principle of complementarity between directives

Many products are already subject to Community provisions governing their safety and the circumstances in which they may be placed on the market. Some safety provisions are always included in New Approach technical directives, although the obligations in certain directives are limited: for example the Cosmetics Directives do not cover all safety aspects, such as flammability and misuse (sniffing of aerosols is a problem with significant mortality and morbidity). The GPS Directive seeks to apply the principle of complementarity between itself and other Community provisions which govern the safety of products. The basic intention is that a product is considered safe when it conforms to specific Community provisions governing its safety. In particular, where a New Approach technical directive lays down obligations regarding product safety, the seventh recital to the GPS Directive confirms that further obligations should not be imposed on economic operators as regards the placing on the market of products covered by such rules. The details are set out in Article 1.2:

> "The provisions of this Directive shall apply in so far as there are no specific provisions in rules of Community law governing the safety of the products concerned.
>
> In particular, where specific rules of Community law contain provisions imposing safety requirements on the products which they govern, the provisions of Articles 2 to 4 of this Directive shall not, in any event, apply to those products.
>
> Where specific rules of Community law contain provisions governing only certain aspects of product safety or categories of risks for the products concerned, those are the provisions which shall apply to the products concerned with regard to the relevant safety aspects or risks."

These provisions should be read together with the sixth to eighth recitals to the Directive:

> "Whereas, in the absence of more specific safety provisions, within the framework of Community regulations, covering the products concerned, the provisions of this Directive are to apply;
>
> Whereas when there are specific rules of Community law, of the total harmonisation type, and in particular rules adopted on the basis of the new approach, which lay down obligations regarding product

safety, further obligations should not be imposed on economic operators as regards the placing on the market of products covered by such rules;

Whereas, when the provisions of specific Community regulations cover only certain aspects of safety or categories of risks in respect of the product concerned, the obligations of economic operators in respect of such aspects are determined solely by those provisions."

These provisions have caused considerable confusion. It can indeed be far from easy to state precisely which GPS obligations apply to a given product and which do not. The first point is that if a product is subject to any rules of Community law, but these do not impose *safety* requirements, the *whole* of the GPS Directive applies.

Where specific rules of Community law exist which contain provisions which impose safety requirements on the products which they govern, the second paragraph of Article 1.2 makes clear that Articles 2–4 of the GPS Directive do not apply. The seventh recital clarifies that the specific rules of Community law involved must be of the total harmonisation type such as, in particular, rules set out in new approach measures. Accordingly, where these rules lay down obligations regarding product safety, the obligations on producers and distributors which arise under Article 3 of the GPS Directive do not apply. However, the second paragraph of Article 1.2 does not exempt the operation of Articles 5–19 of the GPS Directive, which place particular obligations on, and grant powers to, Member States and the Commission.

The third paragraph of Article 1.2 makes clear that where specific rules of Community law (not in the GPS Directive) contain provisions which govern only *certain aspects* of product safety or categories of risks for the products concerned, those provisions do apply. The wording states that "those are the provisions which shall apply to the products concerned with regard to the relevant safety aspect or risks". This is open to possible argument. It might be said that those rules are the *only* rules of Community law which apply to the product. In other words where a sectoral Directive, such as the Machinery Directive, applies to a product, the GPS Directive does not apply at all. That approach would have the benefit of certainty and the United Kingdom government argued during negotiations on the GPS Directive for total sectoral exclusion of defined products.[18] However, it is suggested that that view is incorrect: the rules which relate only to certain aspects or risks apply to those "relevant" aspects or risks, but the first paragraph of Article 1.2 makes clear that any provisions of the GPS Directive which are not ousted by other applicable rules of Community law continue to apply as well. This interpretation is that of the European Commission[19] and of the

[18] May 10, 1990, Hansard H.C., 491.

[19] Explanatory Note, COM (89) 162/6; Communication from the Commission to the European Parliament, SEC (92) 11 final-SYN 192; R. Gielisse, "La nouvelle directive relative à la sécurité générale des produits", *Revue du Marché Unique Européen* 3/1992.

United Kingdom Government[20] and it is submitted that it is correct. Nevertheless, it is understood that some other Member States hold the view that the only rules of Community law which are relevant for these purposes are those of total harmonisation of a product sector which govern *all* aspects of safety.

What all this means is that if a product is subject to any rules of Community law which impose safety requirements (let us say Directive X), it will be subject to any of the provisions contained in the GPS Directive which are not contained in Directive X. A careful and detailed comparison must therefore be made to ascertain which of the individual provisions of any directive apply to a product, so as to determine the provisions it does not contain which *are* covered in the GPS Directive, and the latter provisons therefore apply to that extent. The overlap between the GPS directive and other product Directives may therefore vary in the case of each Product Directive. This approach to the integration of directives is, therefore, not based on specific sectoral exclusions, as was argued for, but on individual analysis. This approach inevitably leads to uncertainty as to whether the GPS Directive should apply or not in any individual case. There has been massive confusion in some sectors of industry. Even in cases in which the answer seems obvious, there will be no absolute certainty until the European Court has ruled on the point. It would be helpful if the Commission would clarify the extent to which the GPS Directive should apply in addition to specific directives, in an amendment to the GPS Directive or at least temporarily in sectoral Guidelines.

Two examples illustrate the problems faced by industry and commerce: the extent of obligations in relation to information supplied with products and post-marketing surveillance obligations. Many products are subject to specific labelling requirements set out in extensive detail in Community-based measures. For example, the lengthy requirements of Directive 92/27/EEC on labelling of medicinal products for human use and package leaflets presumably oust any labelling requirement at the time of marketing under the GPS Directive. The requirements of Directive 92/27/EEC strictly speaking only apply at the time of the assessment of the product for marketing, even though in practice if important further safety information comes to light about a product which is already in circulation, the competent authorities and marketing authorisation holders usually take appropriate steps to inform users. However, it is clear that a continuing obligation to take appropriate action to inform users of risks or to withdraw the product from the market arises under Article 3.2 of the GPS Directive after the product has been placed on the market and for as long it remains in use.

Some products might conform to what might initially seem to be extensive labelling requirements by the provision of only minimial

[20] *The General Product Safety Regulations 1994: Guidance for Businesses, Consumers and Enforcement Authorities*, paras. 13 and 14, Department of Trade and Industry 1995.

labelling information, on the basis that most of the requirements do not apply to a product or can be satisfied by giving minimal information. An example might be the relatively brief label for a bandage or other over-the-counter medical device labelled in accordance with the deceptively lengthy requirements of paragraph 13 of Annex I to Directive 92/43/EEC. It would seem that no purpose would be served by considering such a product to be subject to any more extensive requirements which might be thought to arise under Article 3.2 of the GPS Directive in addition to the product-specific requirements of Directive 92/43/EEC. Thus, it would seem pointless to interpret the GPS requirement to provide "the relevant information to enable [consumers] to assess the risks inherent in a product" as requiring anything further than the labelling requirements of a product-specific directive. Any other result would leave producers and distributors with massive uncertainty over product labelling.

The post-marketing situation illustrates another side of the problem. Directive 92/43/EEC on medical devices contains in each of the available procedures of conformity assessment the following obligation on the manufacturer:

> "An undertaking by the manufacturer to institute and keep up to date a systematic procedure to review experience gained from devices in the post-production phase and to implement appropriate means to apply any necessary corrective action. This undertaking must include an obligation for the manufacturer to notify the competent authorities of the following incidents immediately on learning of them:
>
> (i) any malfunction or deterioration in the characteristics and/or performance of a device, as well as any inadequacy in the instructions for use which might lead to or might have led to the death of a patient or user or to a serious deterioration in his state of health;
>
> (ii) any technical or medical reason connected with the characteristics or performance of a device leading for the reasons referred to in subparagraph (i) to systematic recall of devices of the same type by the manufacturer."

This clearly imposes a general post-marketing obligation similar to Article 3.2 of the GPS Directive but with two differences; first, the wording differs as, secondly, does the status and enforceability of the obligation. Firstly, therefore, do the differences in wording lead to the conclusion that certain aspects of the GPS obligations are not covered in the product-specific obligation and, to that extent, the former apply? For example, the basic obligations under this provision of Directive 92/43/EEC are to "keep up to date a systematic procedure to review experience," to "implement appropriate means to apply any necessary corrective action" and to "notify the competent authorities" of certain incidents. These obligations are not quite the same as providing consumers with information, adopting measutes to be informed of risks, and taking appropriate action to avoid these risks. Perhaps this is merely nit-picking, but a literal reading and comparison of the tests does give rise to questions of overlap and exclusion. Secondly, under Directive 92/43/EEC, the obligation is an undertaking by the manufacturer to a notified body which, in particular circumstances, might or might not form part of his contract with a notified body. Breach of the obligation would not, at least under United Kingdom law, be a criminal offence or entitle the competent or enforcement authorities to take direct action against the manufacturer under the medical device legislation, although there would be residual powers to take action against unsafe products under Part II of the CPA. There is, therefore, a difference in the legal and enforcement status of these two sets of requirements. It might be possible for the notified body to seek a court order for specific performance in relation to breach of contract. But it is far from clear whether the specific medical device requirements constitute provisions which "impose safety requirements on the products" as stated in Article 1.2 of the GPS Directive, in which case at least some of the GPS post-marketing obligations do not apply, or on the other hand, whether the provisions are not sufficiently "imposed," in which case the GPS post-marketing obligations apply in their entirety. The position is confused further by the fact that breach of Article 3.2 of the GPS Directive is not an offence in the United Kingdom under the GPS Regulations, although it will presumably be so in other Member States.

The Commission certainly did not intend that the GPS Directive should oust other provisions of Community law. The GPS Directive is colloquially described as "filling in the gaps" of other legislation: the third recital refers to this as covering lacunae in existing or forthcoming specific legislation. It:

> "is not meant to interfere, in any way, with such legislation nor, in principle, to replace it. Its purpose is only to establish, as a basic residual rule of law, a general common denominator to all more specific legislation on product safety in any area, to which recourse can be taken where there are loopholes or inadequacies in existing legislation which cannot be mended, in the short run, or where such legislation is just not existing.
>
> In areas already largely or, in principle, even totally covered by detailed regulatory rules, where, moreover, existing procedures allow for rapidly coping, in a consistent way, with emergency situations throughout the Community, the general safety requirement in itself may, indeed, hardly ever need to be brought into play."[21]

The United Kingdom Department of Trade and Industry issued with its consultation paper on the draft implementing legislation a non-binding list of product specific Regulations which it considers to be outside the scope of the GPS provisions, which are listed in **Table 2.2**. However, a

[21] Explanatory Note, COM (89) 162/6.

Table 4.2 Community product safety legislation implemented in the U.K. which the Department of Trade and Industry considers to be outside the scope of the General Product Safety Regulations

* These Directives are amended by Directive 93/68.
† Further amendments have been made to these Regulations, some of which are noted in Table 3.1.

Product	Directive	U.K. Regulations
Active Implantable Medical Devices*	90/385	Active Implantable Medical Devices Regulations 1992 (S.I. 1992 No. 3146)†
Aerosol Dispensers	75/324	Aerosol Dispensers (EEC Requirements) Regulations 1977 (S.I. 1977 No. 1140)
Asbestos	91/659	Asbestos (Prohibitions) Regulations 1992 (S.I. 1992 No. 3067)
Chemicals (See also the Marketing and Use Directive below)	88/379 91/155 92/32	Chemicals (Hazardous Information and Packaging) Regulations 1993 (S.I. 1993 No. 1746)
Classification, Packaging and Labelling of Dangerous Substances	91/410	Child Resistant Packaging (Safety)Regulations 1993 (S.I. 1993 No. 1546)
Cosmetics As amended (See also the Marketing and Use Directive)	76/768 80/1335 82/147 82/434 82/368 83/191 83/341 83/496 83/514 83/547 84/415 85/391 85/490 86/179 86/199 87/137 87/143 88/233 88/667 89/174 90/121 90/207 91/184 92/8 92/86	Cosmetic Products (Safety) Regulations: 1989 (S.I. 1989 No. 2233)† Cosmetic Products (Safety) (Amendment) Regulations 1991 (S.I. 1991 No. 447) Cosmetic Products (Safety) (Amendment) Regulations 1992 (S.I. 1992 No. 1525) Cosmetic Products (Safety) (Amendment) Regulations 1993 (S.I. 1993 No. 1539)
Electrical goods [low voltage]*	73/23	Low Voltage Electrical Equipment (Safety) Regulations 1989 (S.I. 1989 No. 728) Electrical Equipment (Safety) Regulations 1994 (S.I. 1994 No. 3)†

Product	Directive	U.K. Regulations
Explosives	93/15	Placing on the Market and Supervision of Explosives Regulations 1993 (S.I. 1993 No. 2714)
Food Imitations	87/357	Food Imitations (Safety) Regulations 1989 (S.I. 1989 No. 1291)
Foodstuffs	84/500	Ceramic Ware (Safety) Regulations 1988 (S.I. 1988 No. 1647)
Gas Appliances*	90/396	Gas Appliances (Safety) Regulations 1992 (S.I. 1992 No. 711)†
Machinery Directive* Amended	89/392 90/488	Supply of Machinery (Safety) Regulations 1992 (S.I. 1992 No. 3073) Supply of Machinery (Safety) (Amendment) Regulations 1994 (S.I. 1994 No. 2063)
Marketing and Use Directive First amendment Second amendment Fourth amendment Fifth Amendment Seventh amendment	76/769 79/663 82/806 83/264 83/478 85/610	Dangerous Substances and Preparations (Safety) Regulations 1980 (S.I. 1980 No. 136)† Benzene in Toys (Safety) Regulation 1987 (S.I. 1987 No. 2116) Dangerous Substances and Preparations (Safety) (Amendment) Regulations 1985 (S.I. 1985 No. 127) Novelties (Safety) (Amendment) Regulations 1985 (S.I. 1985 No. 128) Novelties (Safety) Regulations 1980 (S.I. 1980 No. 958) Asbestos (Prohibition) Regulations 1985 (S.I. 1985 No. 910) Control of Asbestos at Work Regulations 1987 (S.I. 1987 No. 2115) Asbestos Products (Safety) Regulations 1985 (S.I. 1985 No. 2042) Dangerous Substances and Preparations (Safety) Regulations 1980 (S.I. 1980 No. 136) Aerosol Dispensers (EEC Requirements) (Amendment) Regulations 1981 (S.I. 1981 No. 1549) Aerosol Dispensers (EEC Requirements) and the Cosmetic Products (Amendment) Regulations 1985 (S.I. 1985 No. 1279) Asbestos Products (Safety) Regulations (Amendment) Regulations 1987 (S.I. 1987 No. 1979)
Medicinal Products (for human use)	65/65 75/319 83/570 87/21 89/341 92/27	Medicines Act 1968† and numerous Statutory Instruments particularly the Medicines for Human Use (Marketing Authorisations Etc.) Regulations 1994 (S.I. 1994 No. 3144)

WHEN DOES THE GPS DIRECTIVE APPLY?

Product	Directive	U.K. Regulations
Testing of medicinal products	75/318 (new annex substituted by 91/507)	
Colouring in medicinal products	78/25	
Placing on the market of high technology medicinal products Immunological medicinal products Radiopharmaceuticals Medicinal products derived from human blood or plasma	87/22 89/342 89/343 89/381	
Good manufacturing practice for medicinal products Wholesale distribution of medicinal products Classification of medicinal products Labelling and package leaflets for medicinal products Advertising of medicinal products Homeopathic medicinal products	91/356 92/25 92/26 92/27 92/28 92/73	
Medicinal products (for veterinary use) Testing of veterinary medicines Amended by Placing on the market and use of medicated feedingstuffs Amended by Good manufacturing practice for veterinary products	81/851 90/676 90/677 81/852 92/18 70/524 84/587 92/412	The Medicines Act 1968† and numerous Statutory Instruments particularly the Medicines for Human Use (Marketing Authorisation Etc.) Regulation 1994 (S.I. 1994 No. 3144)
Personal protective equipment*	89/686	Personal Protective Equipment (E.C. Directive) Regulations 1992 (S.I. 1992 No. 3139) Personal Protective Equipment (E.C. Directive) Regulations 1993 (S.I. 1993 No. 3074) Personal Protective Equipment (E.C. Directive) Regulations 1994 (S.I. 1994 No. 2326)
Simple Pressure Vessels*	87/404 90/488	Simple Pressure Vessels (Safety) Regulations 1991 (S.I. 1991 No. 2749)†

Product	Directive	U.K. Regulations
Labelling of Tobacco products	89/622 90/239 92/41	Tobacco Products Labelling (Safety) Regulations 1991 (S.I. 1991 No. 1530) Cigarettes (Maximum Tar Yield) (Safety) Regulations 1992 (S.I. 1992 No. 2738) Tobacco for Oral Use (Safety) Regulations 1992 (S.I. 1992 No. 3134) and the Tobacco Products (Labelling) (Safety) Regulations 1993 (S.I. 1993 No. 1947)
Toy Safety* (See also Marketing and Use Directive)	88/378	Toys (Safety) Regulations 1989 (S.I. 1989 No. 1275) Toys (Safety) (Amendment) Regulations 1993 (S.I. 1993 No. 1547)

detailed individual comparison must be undertaken in each case as to whether the safety provisions covering the obligations on producers and distributors and the powers of Member States are covered in a specific provision and therefore the extent to which the GPS obligations remain. For example, the Toys Directive does not include requirements as to noise, the Cosmetics Directives do not cover flammability and the Food Directives do not cover various safety aspects.

The above list of products at Table 2.2, whilst of persuasive force, is not binding and was not repeated in the Department of Trade and Industry's Guidance document on the GPS Regulations.[22] However, the position in relation to medicines for human use has been clarified since The Medicines for Human Use (Marketing Authorisations Etc.) Regulations 1994[23] amends the GPS Regulations so as to specify that nothing in the GPS Regulations applies to a medicinal product for human use which is covered by those medicines Regulations.

A recipe for confusion

The result is a recipe for confusion and litigation. The overlap between product specific provisions and GPS provisions is impossible to state in general terms and far from clear in any individual case. Detailed comparison between the various provisions is necessary and there can be no certainty as to the correct answer in the absence of a court decision. This situation may encourage industrial sectors to press for the introduction of more technical directives, containing more extensive provisions, so as to attempt to remove uncertainty about the extent to which the GPS provisions apply. This result would be ironic in view of industry's usual emphasis on deregulation.

[22] *The General Product Safety Regulations 1994: Guidance for Business, Consumers and Enforcement Authorities*, Department of Trade and Industry, 1995.
[23] S.I. 1994 No. 3144, Sched. 7, para. 21, reproduced below.

There is an inconsistency in approach between the technical directives and the GPS Directive which is relevant. Technical directives lay down the *minimum* essential requirements for placing a product on the market, covering such matters as the composition, performance, packaging, labelling and instructions for use of a product. The GPS Directive sets a higher standard by imposing further requirements and controls in relation to consumer products.

New Approach sectoral directives, such as the Machinery Directive and the Medical Devices Directive, contain extensive provisions which regulate the circumstances in which a device may be placed on the market, namely where it does "not compromise the safety and health of patients, users" and others (Article 2 of these Directives) and where it satisfies their extensive essential requirements. These Directives clearly constitute rules of Community law, but do they "impose safety requirements on the products which they govern"? The official answer is that they are intended to do so. They contain the specific reference quoted above to "not compromising the safety of persons [patients, users]" etc. The recitals to these Directives specify, with only slight differences, their purpose as being to "give [patients], users and other persons a high level of protection and achieve the intended level of performance" and to achieve a harmonised level of safety amongst Member States. There are further references in the texts of the Directives to health and safety which also assist this interpretation. However, the matter is not established beyond all doubt or argument and only the European Court is ultimately competent to decide the matter.

No other Community safety rules

It is clear that if no specific rules of Community law exist which contain provisions which impose safety requirements on the products which they govern, then the GPS Directive applies in its entirety. In these circumstances, Article 4 sets out the approach to deciding whether a product is safe for the purposes of the Directive. This is discussed below under the heading "When is a product safe?"

Examples of products which are not governed by specific Community rules include furniture, general office equipment and stationery, narrow boats excluded from the Small Boats Directive, bicycles, skates and cots.

PRODUCTS IMPORTED INTO THE COMMUNITY

Applicability of the GPS Directive

The definition of a producer in Article 2(d) of the GPS Directive specifically includes an importer, where the manufacturer or his representative is not established within the Community. Measures adopted by national authorities to restrict or prohibit the marketing of a risky or dangerous product will also be applied at the Community's external frontiers. Restrictive measures are not applicable when the importer applies for a customs destination other than free circulation (inward processing arrangements, customs warehouse, free warehouse, free zone, processing in customs, temporary admission, external transit, export outside the Community customs territory). Clearly, if a consumer product has been declared for temporary admission, non-application of the measures will be subordinate to the condition that the product is excluded from all direct contact with the public (fairs, exhibitions, etc).

The European Parliament preferred to ban exports for dangerous products which have been withdrawn from the Community market, but this was not included in the GPS Directive. The main reason for this was that the Directive is concerned exclusively with the marketing of products within the Community; moreover, integration of this common commercial policy measure would implicate Article 113 of the Treaty. It was also thought that such a measure would have to be regulated at a general level rather than at a sectoral level. The Commission may make initiatives in this direction.

Checks for product safety on products imported into the Community

Products that are imported from third countries into the Community are subject to checks by the customs authorities of the Community states for conformity with the rules on product safety. Council Regulation 339/93 of February 8, 1993[24] specifies that the customs authorities have power to suspend release of a product or batch where it:

- displays certain characteristics which would give rise to a serious doubt as to the existence of a serious and immediate risk to health or safety in the event of that product's being used under normal and foreseeable conditions, and/or;
- it is not accompanied by a document which must physically accompany it when it is placed on the market in accordance with the Community or national legislation in force, or not marketed in accordance with the Community or national rules on product safety applicable in the Member State in which release for free circulation is sought. A list of specific products subject to this provision is drawn up by the Commission assisted by a committee of representatives of the Member States.[25] The list currently comprises toys, medicinal products for human use, veterinary medicinal products and foodstuffs.[26]

[24] Council Regulation No 339/93 of February 8, 1993 on checks for conformity with the rules on product safety in the case of products imported from third countries, OJ No L 40/1, 17.2.93.

[25] Regulation No. 339/93 *supra*, Arts. 8 and 9.

[26] Commission Decision of July 28, 1993 (93/583/EEC), OJ No. L279/39, 12.11.93.

The customs authorities shall immediately notify the national authority responsible for monitoring the market and the Member State shall inform the Commission, which shall inform the other Member States. The national authority responsible for monitoring the market must be in a position to make a decision and act in respect of any product the release of which has been suspended by the customs authorities in this way. Where the national authorities find that the product presents a serious and immediate risk, they shall take measures to prohibit it from being placed on the market and ask the customs authorities to include on the commercial invoice accompanying the product and on any other relevant accompanying document the endorsement "Dangerous product — release for free circulation not authorised — Regulation (EEC) No. 339/93" in the relevant Community language. Where the national authorities find that the product does not comply with the Community or national rules in force on product safety, they shall take appropriate action, which may, if necessary, include prohibiting the product from being placed on the market in accordance with the said rules. In cases where placing on the market is prohibited, they shall ask the customs authorities to include on the commercial invoice accompanying the product and on any other relevant accompanying document the endorsement "Product not in conformity — release for free circulation not authorised — Regulation (EEC) No 339/93" in the appropriate Community language.

Where the customs authorities suspend release of a product, the Member State shall inform the Commission, which shall inform the other Member States. Where the national authorities consider that the product does not present a serious and immediate risk to health and safety and/or cannot be regarded as being in breach of Community or national laws on product safety, the product in question shall be released for free circulation provided that all the other requirements and formalities pertaining to such release have been met. The product shall also be released, subject to the same proviso, within three working days where the customs authorities have not been notified of any action taken by the national authorities responsible for monitoring the market.

These provisions apply only in so far as Community rules do not contain specific provisions relating to the organisation of border controls on specific products. The Regulation does not in any event apply in cases covered by Community rules relating to plant-health, veterinary and zootechnical controls and to animal protection.

Member States were invited in November 1992 to make provision for taking steps necessary to check whether products notified through the rapid information exchange system (Decision 89/45/EEC) present a serious and immediate risk within their own jurisdictions, or whether imported products identified by their customs authorities might present a genuine serious and immediate risk to consumer health or safety and to take urgent appropriate steps.[27]

[27] Commission Recommendation 92/579/EEC of November 27, 1992 calling upon Member States to set up the infrastructures needed to identify dangerous products at the external frontiers.

OBLIGATIONS AND POWERS OF MEMBER STATES

Obligations of Member States

The GPS Directive places on Member States the responsibility for ensuring that a product safety policy is properly operated. This is in accordance with the principle of subsidiarity.[28] It is the Member States who are responsible for arranging for authorities to carry out the monitoring of the market, with powers to take appropriate measures to ensure that only safe products are placed on the market (recitals 11 and 12 and Articles 5 and 6). The effect of the Directive requires Member States to have a proper national infrastructure for regulatory monitoring and enforcement of the requirements on producers and distributors.

Enforcement of the General Safety Requirement

The basic obligation on Member States is to "adopt the necessary laws, regulations and administrative provisions to make producers and distributors comply with their obligations under this Directive in such a way that products placed on the market are safe".[29]

In order to achieve this safety objective, Member States are required to establish or nominate authorities with "the necessary powers . . . to take the appropriate measures" to monitor the market and enforce the general safety requirement. Prior to the Directive, there was considerable variation between the enforcement measures available in different Member States. The Directive therefore sets out a long and non-exhaustive list of particular measures set out in Article 6 which enforcement authorities must have power to take:

"(a) organising appropriate checks on the safety properties of products, even after their being placed on the market as being safe, on an adequate scale, up to the final stage of use or consumption[30];

(b) requiring all necessary information from the parties concerned;

(c) taking samples of a product or a product line and subjecting them to safety checks;

[28] This is defined in Article 3b of the Treaty on European Union:

"In areas which do not fall within its exclusive competence, the Community shall take action, in accordance with the principle of subsidiarity, only if and in so far as the objectives of the proposed action cannot be sufficiently achieved by the Member States and can therefore, by reason of the scale or effects of the proposed action, be better achieved by the Community."

[29] Directive, Art. 5.

[30] The Council Minutes noted the statement of the Council and the Commission that the characteristics to be checked include the way in which a product behaves when disposed of in so far as such disposal may present direct risks to the health and safety of consumers.

(d) subjecting product marketing to prior conditions designed to ensure product safety and requiring that suitable warnings be affixed regarding the risks which the product may present;
(e) making arrangements to ensure that persons who might be exposed to a risk from a product are informed in good time and in a suitable manner of the said risk by, *inter alia*, the publication of special warnings;
(f) temporarily prohibiting, for the period required to carry out the various checks, anyone from supplying offering to supply or exhibiting a product or product batch, whenever there are precise and consistent indications that they are dangerous:
(g) prohibiting the placing on the market of a product or product batch which has proved dangerous and establishing the accompanying measures needed to ensure that the ban is complied with[31];
(h) organising the effective and immediate withdrawal of a dangerous product or product batch already on the market and, if necessary, its destruction under appropriate conditions."

The Directive does not allow the Member States to use these powers with absolute discretion. The powers as listed in the above order represent a general escalation in the degree of intervention in the market and with the affairs of economic operators. Article 6 specifies that Member States shall use these powers "acting in accordance with the degree of risk and in conformity with the Treaty, and in particular with Articles 30 and 36 thereof, to adopt appropriate measures . . .".

A measure adopted by a Member State in a given case must therefore be appropriate, in proportion to the degree of risk involved and not out of proportion to it, and in conformity with the Treaty, in particular the requirements eliminating quantitative restrictions between Member States.

Any measures taken by competent authorities must be effective. Article 6.2 provides that the measures shall be addressed, as appropriate, to:

(a) the producer;
(b) distributors (within the limits of their respective activities) and in particular the party responsible for the first stage of distribution on the national market;
(c) any other person, where necessary, with regard to co-operation in action taken to avoid risks arising from a product.

The Directive says nothing about who is to bear the costs of taking any of these measures against a supposedly unsafe product in any given case. A personal view by an author of the Directive is that it would seem

[31] The Council minutes noted the statement of the Council and the Commission that this provision may lead to a decision to prohibit the manufacture of the product concerned if the health and safety of consumers so require.

logical that national measures accompanying the Directive's transposition should stipulate the general principle that the person responsible for a defect should assume the direct costs of remedying it.[32]

Table 4.1 contains brief comparisons between the existing powers available to the authorities under Part II of the Consumer Protection Act and this list of powers in the Directive. Probably the most important difference overall is the power to order withdrawal of products from the market.

It should not be forgotten that the mere existence of these regulatory powers can be a powerful encouragement for commercial enterprises to take voluntary action. In practice, regulatory powers may not formally be used. However, the threat of their use can act as indirect coercion. This is particularly true in an emergency situation. For example, a recalcitrant manufacturer may well find himself forced to publish a press release at his own expense about an unsafe product against the threat of more extensive and damaging regulatory action.

What measures are appropriate?

It is not at all clear what measure(s) will be appropriate for a company or a Member State to take — or not take — in any given situation. Failure by a company to take a measure which is subsequently considered by a court to have been appropriate in given circumstances may expose the company, and perhaps the directors and officers, to criminal sanctions. Similarly, a Member State which does not act appropriately might be in breach of Community law.

In accordance with the principle of subsidiarity, it is primarily up to Member States to take measures in relation to product safety. Proper communication between Member States should lead to a harmonised approach as to the measures which are appropriate in any given case. However, it is not difficult to imagine situations in which Member States' views will differ as to evaluation of a risk or what measures are appropriate.

The Commission undertakes an automatic review of all measures adopted by Member States which are not local in effect, whether or not they are emergency measures (Article 7). The Commission also retains a residual power to adopt its own decision in relation to serious and immediate risks in certain circumstances, which requires Member States to take temporary measures (Article 8). These are examined in more detail below.

The powers of the Commission to take direct action against products have been watered down considerably from earlier proposals. Nevertheless, the Commission still has a role of pivotal importance involving co-ordination, initiation and decision making on Community-wide action. At the very least the Commission will be highly influential.

[32] R. Gielisse, *supra.*

The fact is that there is a series of options of escalating severity which are open to a company which require safety information in relation to mass-produced products which are already being marketed. The voluntary options which are open to a producer, importer or distributor might include doing nothing, amending the instructions for use, altering the warnings, informing distributors, advertisements in trade or specialist press, general publicity campaign, modification of the design or manufacturing process, repackaging, temporary cessation of production, limited recall of particular batches or total recall. These options are discussed further in Chapter 10. The question is: what is the appropriate response in any given situation? Which criteria are to be applied by a manager to decide upon the appropriate response and by the authorities in measuring whether a given response is appropriate? There is some, but very little, guidance available under the civil law of negligence, where the basic proposition is that one must act reasonably[33] and make a clean breast of the problem. These generalised legal principles are of very little practical help and require considerable interpretation.[34]

Are distinctive criteria under the GPS Directive to be applied and, if so, how? It is admittedly extremely hard to devise any meaningful rules against which to measure the legal requirement to recall but as the Directive includes an obligation "to take appropriate action including, if necessary, withdrawing the product in question from the market to avoid [the risks which a product might present]" it should surely have also specified some criteria against which the criminal sanction is to be measured. The Directive does not even say that risks must be unreasonable, or sufficiently serious, in order to justify withdrawal: it merely says that they must exist. Some form of risk in fact exists with virtually every product: much depends in practice on the circumstances and duration of its use. In short, businesses now have an express duty to take "appropriate action" including withdrawal, but no legal criteria against which to define this duty. This therefore represents not only no improvement over the present position but, in fact, a deterioration.

In this context it is also worth noting that the powers of the authorities are not limited to action against producers and other suppliers. It is not inconceivable that the withdrawal process could involve a positive duty on users to return or dispose of dangerous products. (Article 14 has a somewhat enigmatic requirement for withdrawal measures to "take into consideration the need to encourage distributors, users and consumers to contribute to the implementation of such measures".)

The "safeguard clause"

As has already been noted, the principle behind the Directive is that unless non-conformity with the general safety requirement is estab-

[33] *Walton v. British Leyland* (1980) unreported.
[34] See H. Abbott, *Managing Product Recall* (1991).

lished, the product is enabled to circulate freely within the Community. Ensuring product safety does not cease with initial marketing and must include continued monitoring. Article 4(3) provides that a product's conformity with the general safety requirement:

> ". . . shall not bar the competent authorities of the Member States from taking appropriate measures to impose restrictions on its being placed on the market or to require its withdrawal from the market where there is evidence that, despite such conformity, it is dangerous to the health and safety of consumers".

This provision is at face value contradictory (how can a product that is accepted as being safe be dangerous?) and it attracted some criticism during the development of the Directive. It is, however, understandable that it survived given that equivalent so-called "safeguard clauses" appear in the New Approach Directives, and Article 100a(5) of the Treaty requires a safeguard clause to be included in harmonisation measures where appropriate: this clause is, essentially, the manifestation of a residual degree of national sovereignty reflecting matters of national interest set out in Article 36 of the Treaty as justifying restrictions on trade between Member States. Article 4(3) of the GPS Directive is the basis in Community law for enforcement powers against products contained in section 11 of the Consumer Protection Act 1987, or similar powers in various Regulations. Whilst the provision may be valuable (*e.g.* in enabling action to be taken against mis-use of an intrinsically safe product) there is undoubtedly scope for the unscrupulous imposition of restrictions on exports into other countries in the Community and the clause gives rise to a considerable degree of uncertainty as to how effective the Directive will ultimately be in its stated aim of eliminating barriers to trade and distortions of competition. The exercise of the power will, however, be subject to scrutiny at Commission level (see below).

Powers under the GPS Directive and technical directives

It has been said above that it is necessary to compare the powers which are available to Member States under the GPS Directive with their powers which arise under other provisions of Community law governing the safety of the products concerned, such as technical Directives, so as to obtain a complete picture of the powers which exist. To the extent to which powers exist under a technical Directive, a power under the GPS Directive is ousted.

To what extent are the powers which Member States are to have under the GPS Directive included in technical directives? **Table 2.3** shows a general comparison. The wording of the eight powers in the GPS Directive does not directly match most of the wording or format used in technical directives, so this exercise cannot be carried out with total confidence. However, it can be seen that the inter-relation of the two systems does give rise to confusion:

TABLE 2.3 General comparison of Member States' powers under Article 6 of the GPS Directive and under New Approach Technical Directives

GPS Directive	New Approach Directives
(a) Checking products for safety at any stage up to use or consumption	During the production stage this strictly arises only with notified body verification under modules F and G, although tests on specific aspects or random samples of products may arise under modified modules Aa and C, and some opportunity for checking products implicitly arises with surveillance of the quality system under modules D, E and H. After production, same as for (c) below.
(b) Requiring all necessary information from the parties concerned	Implicit in all conformity assessment. After a product is assessed as conforming, this only arises under surveillance of the quality system, not directly in relation to individual products.
(c) Taking samples and checking them for safety	During production, as for (a) above. After production, general power under Arts. 2 and 3.
(d) Imposing prior conditions on product marketing and requiring warnings to be affixed	Conditions and warnings relevant to specific products are set out in the essential requirements. No conditions or warnings other than the essential requirements may be imposed.
(e) Making arrangements to ensure that persons who might be exposed to risk from a product are informed in a good time and in a suitable manner of the said risk, *inter alia*, the publication of special warnings.	No specific power other than as provided for in those parts of the essential requirements dealing with labelling and information.
(f) Temporarily prohibiting the supplying, offering to supply or exhibiting of a product or batch	Power under the Safeguard Clause re a product bearing the CE marking. Otherwise, general prohibition power under Arts. 2 and 3.
(g) Prohibiting the marketing of a dangerous product or batch	Power under the Safeguard Clause re a product bearing the CE marking. Otherwise, general prohibition power under Arts. 2 and 3.
(h) Organising the withdrawal and destruction of a dangerous product or batch	Power under the Safeguard Clause re a product bearing the CE marking. Otherwise, general prohibition power under Arts. 2 and 3.

- It may be that where certain conformity assessment modules (particularly modules A and C) are used, Member States have no explicit power, in the absence of other specific provisions, to check or sample products for safety.
- The essential requirements to which a product must conform are set out in Annex I to each technical directive. For example, the essential requirements stipulate, to the extent appropriate in relation to given

products, the extent to which products must be accompanied by appropriate labelling and information on the intended use and appropriate method of use.[35] However, no requirements other than the essential requirements may be imposed, since Article 4 in technical directives specifies that Member States shall not prohibit, restrict or impede the placing on the market or putting into service in their territory of products which comply with the provisions of the Directive. If a product conforms to the essential requirements, there are no further powers in technical directives for Member States to impose further obligations or conditions on products which conform to the essential requirements. If so, a number of the powers in Article 6 of the GPS Directive would apply.

- Member States do appear to have residual powers which arise under Articles 2 and 3 of technical directives, which generally state that:

  "2. Member States shall take *all appropriate measures* to ensure that products covered by this Directive may be placed on the market and put into service only if they do not endanger the health or safety of persons . . . when properly installed and maintained and used for their intended purpose . . .

  3. Products covered by this Directive shall satisfy the essential health and safety requirements set out in Annex I" [emphasis added]

- The power to take all appropriate measures is wide and apparently unfettered. However, this power may only be exercised in relation to products which do not endanger health and safety, *i.e.* which do not satisfy the essential requirements.
- The only explicit power which Member States have in relation to products which bear the CE marking but which are nevertheless liable to endanger the safety of persons when used in accordance with the intended purpose is under the Safeguard Clause (Article 7). However, this power does not arise in relation to products which:

  (a) do not bear the CE marking; or

  (b) are not liable to endanger the safety of persons when used in accordance with the intended purpose.

  The power extends only to certain actions, namely to take all appropriate measures to:

  — *withdraw* the products from the market,[36]

  — *prohibit* their being placed on the market or put into service or use, or

[35] The Medical Devices Directive contains a requirement that, where appropriate, instructions for use must accompany a product, and contain specified information on risks to be avoided (Annex I, para. 13). The Machinery Directive (Annex I, paras. 1.7.2 and 1.7.4) provides that "where risks remain . . . the manufacturer must provide warnings" and specifies that "All machinery must be accompanied by instructions including . . . instructions for safe . . . use, handling . . ."

[36] See later for the meaning of this power.

— *restrict* their free movement.

It is not all clear whether the power to restrict free movement extends to imposing further conditions on marketing products or to imposing further obligations to inform or warn consumers or user. In any event, Article 5 of the GPS Directive goes further than the Safeguard Clause provisions in specifying that there should be penalties in the event of failing to comply with its obligations.

The above analysis is between different instruments of Community law—the GPS Directive and New Approach Directives. This is, of course, only part of the picture since none of these Directives, in fact, include *specific* enforcement powers of Member States, which are left to the discretion of Member States to adopt under national law and differ from Member State to Member State. Thus, in the United Kingdom, Regulations implementing New Approach Directives (see Table 3.1) generally either themselves contain specific enforcement powers similar to, or expressly cross-refer to, the powers existing under Part II of the Consumer Protection Act 1987, such as the power to require information, or to issue suspension or prohibition notices (referred to in more detail in Chapter 5).

Accordingly, a comparison between the powers of the GPS Directive and UK Regulations would conclude that there are considerable, if not often total, areas of overlap in the powers of Member States for which they provide. Article 1.2 of the GPS Directive specifies that the correct analysis is between "rules of Community law". It is probably right to consider as rules of Community law powers which are contained in the UK Regulations implementing Community Directives which contain, as New Approach Directives do, a requirement for Member States first to take all necessary steps to ensure that products which they cover do not compromise the safety and health of users and others when properly used in accordance with their intended purpose and, secondly, to take appropriate action to remove unsafe products from the market.

The point of this perhaps rather abstruse analysis is to decide whether enforcement action should be taken under, on the one hand, powers such as the CPA or Safety Regulations implementing New Approach Directives or similar provisions or, on the other hand, under GPS powers. The *vires* question should be examined in each case but the general conclusion seems to be that any product-specific powers apply and oust the GPS powers. The position is further complicated since, as analysed in Chapter 5, the UK's GPS Regulations do not themselves provide for enforcement powers against individual products since it was thought that the pre-existing powers under Part II of the Consumer Protection Act 1987 were satisfactory and should continue to apply to consumer products. (It is thought to be acceptable for pre-existing national law to be taken as "implementing" a Community obligation: it would be pointless to insist on re-enacting the same legislation.) Thus, in the case of the UK at least, the question of whether powers do or do not arise under GPS provisions or under product specific provisions is sometimes academic, since a number of roads lead to the CPA powers (or at least to almost identical powers under product-specific Regulations).

Variations in sanctions between Member States

A further point follows from the fact that, like other Community law based regulatory legislation, sanctions for breaches of the GPS Directive are to be imposed under the criminal law of Member States. However, the Directive does not specify the offences, sanctions and penalties which are to apply.[37] Accordingly, no attempt has been made to harmonise such matters. This may give rise to considerable variation between the law in different Member States and the practice of their courts. It will be important for commercial operators to have clear information on such matters. Not only will directors of a company need to inform consumers about any risks which are associated with the company's products but, ironically, the directors will themselves need to be warned of any risks which are associated with marketing to consumers in particular locations! Furthermore, certain Member States may impose criminal liability not only on the company but on directors and officers personally. This is an area which will need to be studied very carefully.[38]

Member States' discretion on implementation

When a Community regulation does not provide any specific penalty in case of breach but refers to national provisions, the Member States retain a discretion as to the choice of penalties.[39]

Article 5 of the EC Treaty requires the Member States to take all measures necessary to guarantee the application and effectiveness of Community law. They must ensure that infringements of a Community regulation are penalised under conditions, both procedural and substantive, which are analogous to those applicable to infringements of national law of a similar nature and importance and which, in any event, make the penalty effective, proportionate and dissuasive.

It has been held that neither Article 5 of the Treaty nor a provision in Regulation 3820/85 requiring Member States to adopt the provisions necessary for the implementation of the Regulation, relating to rest periods for road transport drivers, requires a Member State to introduce

[37] ECOSOC took the view that Community law does not allow the imposition by the Commission of criminal proceedings. ECOSOC and the Commission were influenced by the pre-existing United Kingdom legislation, the Consumer Protection Act 1987, which is based on criminal offences relating to the *supply*, offer or agreeing to supply, or exposing or possessing for supply, of any goods which fail to comply with a general safety requirement. ECOSOC Opinion on the general safety requirement for products, OJ No. C175/12, 4.7.88.

[38] At the time of writing, some Member States are far from implementing the Directive.

[39] Case C-326/88, *Anklagemyndighedem v. Hansen & Sons I/S*, [1990] I E.C.R. 2911.

into its national law a specific system of criminal liability, such as the criminal liability of legal persons, in order to ensure compliance with obligations imposed under the Regulation on the undertaking (*i.e.* road transport operator or company) to make periodic checks to ensure rest periods were being observed and to take appropriate steps to prevent repetition of breaches.[40]

Standards and consistency of enforcement

Considerable concern has been expressed by industry that enforcement action in different Member States will be inconsistent. Certain countries have no (or only recent) experience of operating product safety laws. The high standards and common sense approach expected of, for example, United Kingdom Trading Standards Officers may not prevail elsewhere. Since so many product "defects" are related not to their intrinsic quality (as occurs in the case of contamination) but rather to the conditions in which a product is actually used, one might speculate whether the use of significant powers against a producer might be triggered on the basis of a purely "local" mis-use by a consumer which has perhaps not been properly investigated by the local governmental agencies. Thus, the implications of the GPS Directive are serious not only for industry and those involved in commerce but also for governments and the Commission.

In a Community without internal frontiers, defective products manufactured in one country will find their way to another by an infinite number of routes, often passing through other Member States. Only if information concerning such products is made available to all authorities can effective action be taken to protect the interests of all Community citizens. Similarly, the conclusions arrived at by two or more Member States in relation to interpretation or application of Community legislation will be of interest to all Member States.

The Community authorities recognised the need to develop administrative co-operation in the implementation and enforcement of Communitity legislation in the internal market and in February 1994 proposed a policy framework for co-operation between Member States' administrations and the Commission[41] which was accepted by the Council.[42] The Council recognised that it is essential for the proper functioning of the Community to increase mutual confidence and transparency between administrations and thereby ensure that Community legislation is enforced effectively, efficiently and uniformly in all Member States. The creation of stable, economically viable framework

[40] Case C–7/90, *Belgium v. Vandevenne and others* [1993] 3 C.M.L.R. 608.

[41] Communication from the Commission to the Council and the European Parliament on the development of administrative co-operation in the implementation and enforcement of Community legislation in the internal market. Com (94) 29 final, 16.2.1994.

[42] Council Resolution of June 16, 1994 on the development of administrative cooperation in the implementation and enforcement of Community legislation in the internal market. OJ No. C179/1, 1.7.94.

conditions especially by, amongst other matters, limiting the financial and non-financial burdens on the business, and eliminating unnecessary bureaucratic burdens for enterprises, are amongst the matters which the Community considers to be particularly urgent in relation to strengthening the competitiveness of Community industry.[43]

The policy framework proposed by the Commission adopted the following guiding principles:

- all administrative services in the Member States responsible for the enforcement of Community law must, taking into account Article 5 of the Treaty, provide one another with mutual assistance in the exercise of their functions, and in particular reply as soon as possible to requests for co-operation originating from one of them, and exchange the information required for this purpose;
- these exchanges of information should be performed under conditions of:
  - *confidentiality, i.e.* they should be covered by professional secrecy and the requirements of the services from which the information originates;
  - *proportionality* between the nature of information requested and the objective of the check to be carried out;
- to this effect, each Member State needs to take appropriate measures for providing the most effective possible interface between its own services and those of other Member States and the Commission;
- each Member State should ensure the transparency of these measures and of its control mechanisms and their modalities of operation, in particular by notifying them to the Commission and the other Member States. Each Member State was called upon to notify to the Commission by the end of 1994 contact points and essential information on their administrative structures in relation to 18 areas including technical harmonisation (directives on the elimination on barriers to trade), public procurement, the general product safety directive, foodstuffs and notification of technical regulations.

Accordingly, the Commission embarked on a programme of discussions with the authorities of the Member States by area of activity in:

- setting up or strengthening the practical organisation of co-operation between the competent administrations of the Member States and the Commission.
- developing Community support measures for the development and strengthening of these co-operation systems, such as the publication of guidelines for implementation, the setting up and subsequent operation of telematic networks, the collection and analysis of data, the promotion of exchanges of civil servants, training activities, and so on;

[43] Council Resolution of November 21, 1994 on the strengthening of the competitiveness of Community industry. OJ No. C 343/1, 6.12.94.

- proposing adjustments to Community legislation in which shortcomings have come to light as a result of experience gleaned from administrative co-operation;
- reporting on developments in administrative co-operation in the Commission's annual report on the internal market.

When this matter was considered by the Council, it was noted that it was necessary to ensure that systems for communication and information exchange between administrations involved in administrative co-operation within the Community are efficient and interoperable, as well as to avoid duplication and to ensure optimum use of available resources. Accordingly, the Council called on the Commission and Member States to take appropriate measures to ensure efficient coordination and to encourage and facilitate communication and good co-operation between all parties involved in setting up and operating communication and information exchange systems.[44] The Council specified the following objectives in this respect:

- co-ordination of all activities relating to the introduction and operation of communications and information exchange systems between administrations, at both Community and national levels;
- setting up of a common framework for the future development of systems for communication and information exchange between administrations;
- progressive introduction, in appropriate areas corresponding to identified needs of operational communication and information exchange systems between the administrations involved in the Community's operation.

Under the Treaties, the Member States retain responsibility for the implementation and enforcement of Community law within their jurisdiction. Article 5 of the Treaty requires Member States to take all appropriate measures to ensure fulfilment of the obligations arising from the Treaty and to abstain from any measure which could jeopardise the objectives of the Treaty. In some fields (for example, customs, indirect taxation, agriculture, foodstuffs and pharmaceuticals) the Council has adopted detailed secondary legislation in respect of the enforcement of the Community law which requires Member States to take specific measures.

The Commission specifically noted that co-operation between two or more authorities may be necessary in order to ensure that a product found to be unsafe in one area is no longer manufactured in another area or marketed in a third.

In its review of current practice, the Commission noted that in those areas where the Community has not yet agreed on detailed rules for the enforcement of Community law, national enforcement authorities are

[44] Council Resolution of June 20, 1994 on co-ordination with regard to information exchange between administrations. OJ No. C 181/1, 2.7.94.

sometimes reluctant to contemplate the establishment of such rules, often assuming that co-operation between enforcement authorities in different Member States will occur wherever necessary as a matter of course. Similarly, the Commission noted that the participation of Member States in existing co-operation systems is often unequal. For instance, some Member States never notified problems or emergencies under the systems in place or, where the system provides for Member States to react to the information circulated, never react or do so with considerable delay. This situation can hardly engender confidence as to the future workings of the internal market and a consistency and coordination of decisions and enforcement measures relating to product safety.

The need to adopt a consistent and mutually-recognised approach to official product testing had been recognised by 1992. It was noted that tests carried out by laboratories used by any market control authority in surveillance of the market should be conducted in such a way that the results are acceptable to all authorities so that similar action can be taken across the Community market as a whole.[45] It was suggested that such laboratories, whether operated by public authority or contracted to it, should:

(a) respect the same criteria as testing and certification bodies notified under New Approach directives (EN 45000 series); and
(b) carry out product tests which are recognised across the Community. In principle they should be the same as those with which manufacturers or suppliers are required to comply.

In addition, while it was noted that laboratories need to be capable of devising extra tests where existing ones are not sufficiently demanding, a mechanism needs to be established to enable effective intercomparison of test methods or, at least, to provide for the circulation of information concerning test methods.

In June 1995 the Council confirmed[46] that administrative co-operation between national authorities must be strengthened and that it was essential to ensure the effective, uniform and efficient enforcement of Community legislation in all Member States. It recognised a need for a soundly based pragmatic and sectoral approach to the question of penalties. National arrangements must be transparent, proportionate and disuasive. If there prove to be serious difficulties for the smooth operation of the internal market due to disparities in national penalty arrangements, the Council agreed to seek solutions, so that penalties are such as to ensure that legislation is applied equally effectively throughout the Union. The Council expressed support for the Commission's on-going studies on penalties and their future extension. It also

[45] Provisional working document "New Approach Directives: Official Market Control" Doc. Certif 92/2, 4.3.92.

[46] Council Resolution of June 29, 1995 on the effective uniform application of Community law and on the penalties applicable for breaches of Community law in the internal market, 95/C 188/01, OJ No. C 188/1, 22.07.95.

encouraged the Commission to include provisions on penalties in proposals for future Community legislation.

Karolus

It had been recognised before the 1994 framework policy just referred to that the functioning of all the Community's internal market legislation requires uniform application in the Member States. The Council concluded in 1992 that uniform application cannot be achieved without closer co-operation and the building of mutual confidence between national administrations. Accordingly, it established an action plan for the exchange of 1900 national officials engaged in the implementation of Community internal market legislation.[47] This is known as the Karolus programme. It is funded jointly by the Commission and by participating Member States. It is open to all those involved in the enforcement of Community law, whether they are employed by national or local administrations or by private bodies engaged to carry out enforcement tasks. General product safety was one of the priority areas selected for 1994.

PROSAFE

The European Consumer Safety Association (ECOSA) launched the Product Safety Enforcement Forum of Europe (PROSAFE) in 1991. This is an initiative aimed specifically at promoting co-ordination and uniform enforcement action between enforcement agents in relation to non-food product safety control throughout the European Economic Area. Membership of PROSAFE is restricted to representatives of European enforcement practitioners: all EU states except Greece and Liechtenstein are currently members. Co-ordinated activities include the provision, collection and exchange of information, encouragement of liaison, provision of a forum for discussion and exchange of ideas, development of closer understanding, trust and working relations, and the promotion of computerised and other links. PROSAFE also aims to consider and recommend solutions to harmonised enforcement problems. It provides language training and translation facilities, assistance with legal interpretation, identification of deficiencies in legislation and technical standards, and promotes exchange visits. Its secretariat is provided by the Institute of Trading Standards Administration in Edinburgh. PROSAFE claims to have an increasing and high level of influence on enforcement practice within the EU.

United Kingdom Code for Enforcement Agencies

In July 1993, the Department of Trade and Industry published *Working with Business: a Code for Enforcement Agencies* as part of the Deregulation

[47] Council Decision 92/481/EEC of September 22, 1992 on the adoption of an action plan for the exchange between Member State administrations of national officials who are engaged in the implementation of Community legislation required to achieve the internal market, OJ No. L 286/65, 1.10.92 amended by Commission Decision 94/818/EC of December 16, 1994 OJ No. L 337/89, 24.12.94.

Initiative and the Citizens' Charter. The Code included the following points:

1. Publication of clear statements of standards, setting out the level of service business people should be able to receive. Such standards are to include the time taken to respond to queries and the effectiveness of complaints procedures. Performance against the standards will be published annually.
2. Provision of information and advice in plain language on the rules that are enforced. Advice should distinguish between practices which set out the obligatory requirements on business and those improvements which are not mandatory. Charges for advice and enforcement should be set out sufficiently in advance to allow for consultation. Enforcement bodies shall be open about how they set about their work.
3. Consultation with business to discuss compliance failures or difficulties.
4. Provision of a courteous and efficient service. Enforcement staff should identify themselves by name.
5. Establishment of well publicised, swift and effective complaints systems that are easily accessible to business. An element of independence should be included so that business can complain without fear and enforcement agencies carry out their duties impartially.
6. Costs of compliance imposed on business by enforcement to be minimised. As far as possible, enforcers should aim to ensure that compliance costs are proportionate to the risk and take account of the particular circumstances of small firms.

The Code was expressed to apply to 72 enforcement agencies in the United Kingdom, including the Engineering Inspectorate, Gas Examiners and Gas Meter Examiners, Health & Safety Executive, HM Inspectorate of Pollution, Medical Devices Agency, Medicines Control Agency, National Weights and Measures Laboratory, Good Laboratory Practice Monitoring Authority, and the Vehicle Inspectorate. Each enforcement agency should have published its own code of practice by January 1, 1994 stating how it was putting the general principles established by the Code into practice.

COMMUNITY PROCEDURES ON UNSAFE PRODUCTS

The Directive specifies three procedures for notification of measures, exchange of information and adopting emergency measures between Member States and the Commission. These are:

1. Notification of measures taken by a Member State — Article 7.
2. Notification of emergency measures adopted by a Member State in relation to products presenting a serious and immediate risk and co-ordination by the Commission of appropriate measures in all Member States — Article 8.

3. Adoption of a decision by the Commission, in the case of a serious and immediate risk, which requires Member States to take temporary measures — Article 9.

These will now be examined in more detail.

Notification procedure for non-conforming products

Member States are obliged to notify the Commission as specified in Article 7 where they take restrictive measures against a product. The obligation to notify arises where a Member State takes measures which restrict the placing of a product or a product batch on the market or require the withdrawal from the market, such as provided for in Article 6(1)(d)–(h). Notification is not required in two situations, first to the extent that it is specified separately under any specific Community legislation. This provision is intended to cover all products which conform, products presenting a serious and immediate risk (see below) and products covered by specific provisions (in particular agriculture and under Directive 89/377/EEC on the control of foodstuffs, which introduced co-ordination of inspection services and a system for the exchange of information on products which are non-conforming or dangerous and which have been placed on the market). Secondly, notification is not required where the measures taken by the Member State relate to an event which is local in effect and in any case limited to the territory of the Member States concerned. This local exclusion is not at all clearly worded. It contrasts with wording in Article 8 where the notification obligation is disapplied if the effects of the risk do not, or cannot, go beyond the territory of the Member State concerned. This might be where a product is only marketed in one territory (although there is no way of knowing this for certain) or where the hazard arises because of a particular local problem, such as unusual damage in transit or storage.

The Member State's notification to the Commission of the measures which it has adopted must specify the reasons for adopting them. The Directive is silent on whether the Member State has to inform the producer of the product or anyone else involved of either the reasons for the measures or the notification to the Commission. However, the Commission is obliged to enter into consultations with the parties concerned as quickly as possible. There is no definition of who might constitute a party concerned but the policy consideration of ensuring public safety and health would indicate that everyone with a reasonable interest should be consulted. The producer or his representative or importer and, where relevant, the distributor should be given all relevant information and opportunity to comment. No formalities are specified for the consultations, which may be bilateral or multilateral meetings. The consultations take place outside the framework of the

Committee on Product Safety Emergencies established under Article 10 or any other institutionalised committee. There is no explicit provision for trade associations or medical authorities or consumer bodies to be consulted but any of these might be relevant in certain circumstances.

The purpose of the procedure is to enable the Commission to monitor and review measures taken by national authorities. It is, in effect, an automatic review or appeal procedure. After its consultations, the Commission should conclude whether the measure adopted by the Member State is justified or not. If it concludes that the measure is justified, it has immediately to inform the notifying Member State and all the other Member States. Where the Commission concludes that the measure is not justified, it has immediately to inform the notifying Member State. The Directive does not specify what action, if any, either the other Member States are to take in the former case, or the notifying Member State is to take in the latter case. There may, at least, be political and moral pressure to adopt the Commission's conclusion. However, it may be that the Commission's conclusion will be considered to be a decision under Article 189 of the Treaty, which is therefore binding on the person to whom it is addressed. A decision contrasts with a recommendation or opinion, which are not binding. A decision is subject to review by the Court of Justice, not only by the Member State(s) concerned but also by the individual directly affected, such as the producer (Article 173 of the Treaty).

Community system for the exchange of information on products which may jeopardise consumers' health or safety

From October 25, 1993 until June 29, 1994, the Community instituted a temporary system of exchange of information on products which might jeopardise consumers' health or safety, prior to the introduction of the Directive on general product safety. This specified a format under which appropriate information was to be forwarded to the Commission in relation to all products intended for use by consumers except products intended exclusively for professional use and in so far as notification of the Commission was not already prescribed in a specific instrument of Community legislations.[48]

Community home and leisure accidents surveillance system (EHLASS)

The above Community level notification system under Article 7 of the GPS Directive supplements a Community system which has been developed over some years for obtaining and publishing information on

[48] Council Decision 93/580/EEC of October 25, 1993 concerning the institution of a Community system for the exchange of information in respect of certain products which may jeopardise consumers' health or safety, OJ No. L 278/64, 11.11.93.

European home and leisure accidents (EHLASS).[49] The current system applies for four years from January 1, 1994. This began as a demonstration project set up from December 1, 1985 for six years.[50] The project was not considered to be a statistical instrument, at least not at Community level. However, it was regarded as a key indicator for planning safety measures. In reports covering 1990 and 1991, many Member States reported on the number of domestic and leisure accidents involving children (of particular concern to Portugal and Denmark), including toys, playing areas, child care articles, the elderly, sports injuries and equipment (in particular paragliding, physical training equipment, aquaparks and swimming pool covers), fireworks (noted by the Netherlands, Denmark and Portugal), bleach (50 per cent of domestic poisoning cases in France were caused by bleach), portable ladders and electrical products (focused on by the Netherlands, France and the United Kingdom), in particular garden implements (especially lawn-mowers and hedge-cutters), kitchen equipment and DIY tools (in particular circular saws).[51]

The management of consumer safety is primarily the responsibility of each Member State. However, there was felt to be a need for co-ordination in order to ensure the overall quality of data by the use of homogeneous methods of collection, so that the conclusions of one Member State can, where appropriate, be used for other Member States as well as at Community level.

The system's objectives are to collect data on home and leisure accidents with a view to promoting accident prevention, improving the safety of consumer products and informing and educating consumers so that they make better use of products. The system does not apply to industrial accidents, nor to road,[52] rail, sea or air traffic accidents. Its technical aims are to promote compatibility of the methodologies applied in the Member States, paying particular attention to improving the homogeneity of the data definitions and classifications as well as the data-collection basis and national reports on the processing of data.

The system applies to home and leisure accidents which are followed by medical treatment and which occur in the home or its immediate surroundings, such as gardens, yards and garages, or during leisure, sports or school activities.

The basic information is obtained from the casualty departments of certain hospitals selected by the member states so as to be propor-

[49] Council Decision 93/683/EEC of October 29, 1993 introducing a Community system of information on home and leisure accidents for one year. Council Decision 3092/94/EC of May 1994, OJ No. L331/1, extended this until 1997.

[50] Council Decision 86/138/EEC, OJ No. L 109, 26.4.86, as amended by Decision 90/534/EEC, OJ No. L 296, 27.10.90.

[51] Communication from the Commission to the Council on home and leisure accidents, COM(93) 18 final, January 26, 1993; Proposal for a European Parliament and Council Decision introducing a Community system of information on home and leisure accidents, COM (44) 17 final, 8.2.94.

[52] Council Decision 93/704/EEC of November 30, 1993 created a Community database on road accidents.

tionally representative of rural and urban communities. Fifty-four hospitals are to be involved in nine Member States, of which 11 are in the United Kingdom. For administrative and technical reasons, collection of data from Germany, Spain and Luxembourg is obtained from household surveys rather than hospitals. Member States also take into account additional information including that obtained from poison-antidote centres, death certificates, family doctors, burns treatment centres, fire services and first-aid systems. The Member States process the data collected and submit a report to the Commission containing summaries and evaluations of the results and conclusions. The Commission may also request Member States to supply available data on the safety of certain products or specific categories of products involved in home and leisure accidents and the circumstances surrounding such accidents. The Commission processes, summarises and publishes the data received from the Member States. The reports of both Member States and of the Commission are made public. However, the details are anonymised so that the identities of victims remain confidential.

It is specifically provided that any data from the system is published on the basis that it provides only general indications and cannot be regarded as statistical proof of the safety or lack of safety of a given product.

The data collected includes information on the aspects set out in **Table 4.4.**

Table 4.4: Data collected under EHLASS
• the place where an accident occurred • the date of the accident • the place of treatment • the activity of the victim at the time of the accident • the type of accident • the type of product involved in the accident • the age of the victim • the sex of the victim • the type of injury • the parts of the body injured • the treatment of the injury • hospitalisation • a brief description of the accident and its causes (including, where possible, the main features and identifying details of the product involved)

The United Kingdom component of EHLASS is called HASS. These systems only report on products *involved* in accidents: no assessment of causation is undertaken. It is possible for manufacturers to obtain raw data from HASS on their products in order to study product safety. In the USA there is the National Electronic Injury Surveillance System (NEISS).

Emergency procedures : The Rapid Exchange of Information System

The Rapid Exchange of Information System for emergency situations (known as RAPEX, SER and CONSOM ALERT) is intended to inform Member States and the Commission of measures taken by Member States in relation to serious and immediate dangers posed by consumer products. It was first established in 1985[53] and was incorporated into the GPS Directive with some new features to enhance its effectiveness. Its purpose is to enable the Member States to take necessary measures promptly to ensure public safety.

There is no definition of what constitutes a serious and immediate risk, nor any criteria for its assessment. It is for the national authorities to assess risks on a case by case basis. The Commission considered that it was preferable to avoid a precise definition of "serious" and "immediate" but to proceed by means of guidelines issued by the Consultative Committee, which could be modified in the light of experience.[54]

Two Rapid Information Exchange Systems in fact exist. The first concerns food products coordinated by Directorate-General III responsible for food products, and the second concerning non-food products, operated by the Consumer Policy Service of the Commission which become Directorate-General XXIV in 1995. Common information forms have been developed which are designed to serve as a model for the exchange of information particulars. It has been made clear, however, that the rapid exchange of information should not be hindered by an excessive exactitude in supplying all the particulars specified in the forms.[55] Detailed information is above all envisaged to facilitate the identification of dangerous products: Marking and description; trade name; derivation, the established or presumed origin; details of the producer; packer, importer, exporter; the total numbers concerned; information on the transport or the marketing status of the dangerous product; whether the product has already been sold in other Member States; whether the producer, distributor or importer has already been consulted and whether particular measures have already been taken or particular information has already been released; more exact details on the nature, gravity, immediacy and extent of the dangers arising from the use of the products in question, and on the specific measures which have already been taken or are planned. Since it is often the case that all such information is not immediately available, the practice has evolved of sending a photograph of the product in question by fax.[56]

It will be seen that the Rapid Information Exchange System does not envisage direct horizontal exchange of information between the compe-

[53] Council Decision 84/133/EEC on a Community system for the rapid exchange of information on dangers arising from the use of consumer products, OJ No L 17/9, 21.1.84, as extended by Council Decision 89/45/EEC of December 21, 1988 and Council Decision 90/352/EEC of June 29, 1990.

[54] *cf.* OJ C 146/13, 3.6.88.

[55] COM(86) 562 final, Annex II, no. 5.

[56] COM(90), 172 final, 9ff.

tent authorities in each Member State. Instead, the specified information channels are exclusively vertical, from local authorities through national authorities to the Commission and back again. At any stage in the chain, the information might be filtered or altered. This system may lead to incorrect or inefficient communication. The design of the system owes more to consideration of the political expediency of observing the principle of solidarity than being a custom-designed system.[57]

The contact point at governmental level required under the Rapid Information Exchange System for the United Kingdom is the Consumer Safety Unit (CSU) at the Department of Trade and Industry. With the international links being developed by local enforcement officials through PROSAFE and the HAZPROD database (discussed in Chapter 5) it seems that the official system provided for in the Directive may be by-passed. LACOTS and HAZPROD have been described in a study for the Commission of the operation of national product safety systems as constituting the leading position on information exchange systems and consultation procedures, unaffected by constitutional or status problems which exist in other Member States, notably Germany.[58]

The system covers products placed on the market, as defined in Article 2(a) of the Directive. The procedure is set out in Article 8 and the Annex and is outlined in **Figure 2.1**. There are certain differences between these two as to when the notification obligation is triggered. The steps are as follows:

1. As soon as a serious and immediate risk is detected, the national authority shall consult, in so far as possible and appropriate, the producer or distributor of the product concerned. Their point of view and the details which they supply may be useful both to the administrations of the Member States and to the Commission in determining what action should be taken to ensure that the consumer is protected with a minimum of commercial disruption. To these ends the Member States should endeavour to obtain the maximum of information on the products and the nature of the danger, without compromising the need for rapidity.
2. When a Member State adopts or decides to adopt emergency measures to prevent, restrict or impose specific conditions on the possible marketing or use, within its own territory, of a product or batch because of a serious and immediate risk presented by that product or batch to the health and safety of consumers, the Member State must forthwith inform the Commission. As discussed above in relation to the standard notification procedure, the Member State has no obligation to notify the Commission under this emergency procedure either where a similar notification obligation arises under other Community instruments or if the effects of the risk do not, or cannot, go beyond the territory of the Member State concerned.

[57] Hans-W. Micklitz, T. Roethe, S. Weatherill (eds) *Federalism and Responsibility: A study on product safety law and practice in the European Community* (1994).
[58] *Ibid.*

Figure 4.1 Outline of Rapid Exchange of Information System

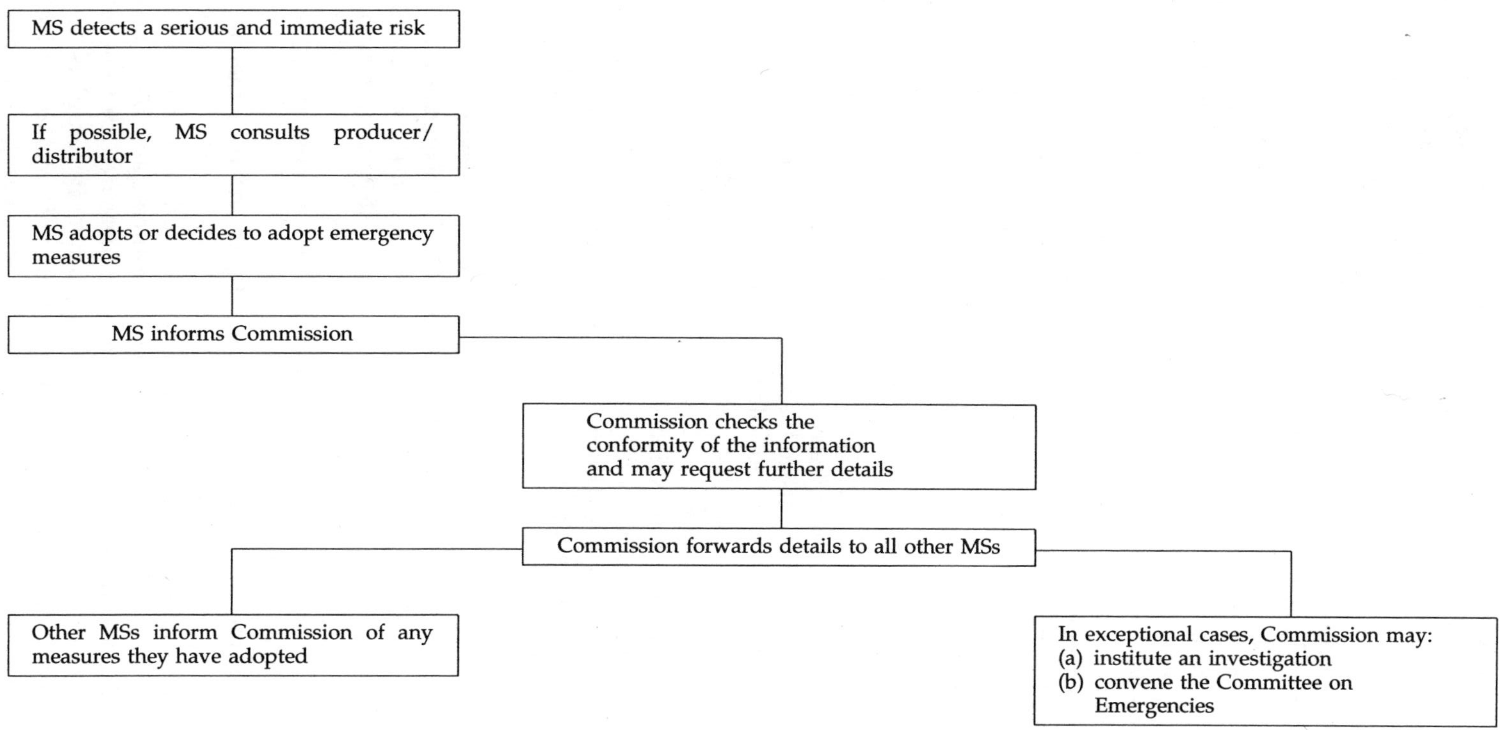

3. The Annex stipulates that a Member State must immediately inform the Commission as soon as it has detected a serious and immediate risk, the effects of which extend or could extend beyond its territory, and measures have been taken or decided on. All available details shall be given, in particular on:
   (a) information to identify the product;
   (b) the danger involved, including the results of any tests/analyses which are relevant to assessing the level of risk;
   (c) the nature of the measures taken or decided on;
   (d) information on supply chains where such information is possible.
4. Member States need not wait to notify the Commission before deciding to adopt any measures but may pass on to the Commission any information regarding the existence of a serious and immediate risk. In this case, it is not clear whether the Commission must pass it on. Immediate contact, as soon as a risk is discovered or suspected, can of course facilitate preventative action.
5. If the Member State considers certain information to be confidential, it should specify this and justify its request for confidentiality, bearing in mind that the need to take effective measures to protect consumers normally outweighs considerations of confidentiality. It should also be remembered that precautions are taken in all cases, both by the Commission and by the members of the network responsible in the various Member States, to avoid any unnecessary disclosure of information likely to harm the reputation of a product or series of products.
6. On receiving a notification, the Commission checks the conformity of the information with the Directive, requesting further details where necessary, and forwards it to all other Member States, who immediately inform the Commission of any measures they have adopted.
7. The other Member States are requested, wherever possible, to inform the Commission without delay of the following:
   (a) whether the product has been marketed in its territory;
   (b) supplementary information it has obtained on the danger involved, including the results of any tests/analyses carried out to assess the level of risk;

   and in any case they must inform the Commission as soon as possible of the following:
   (c) the measures taken or decided on, of the type mentioned in Article 8(1) of the Directive;
   (d) when the product mentioned in this information has been found within their territory but no measures have been taken or decided on and the reasons why no measures are to be taken.
8. At the same time the Commission, when it considers it to be necessary, and in order to supplement the information received, can in exceptional circumstances institute an investigation of its own

motion and/or convene the Committee on Emergencies provided for in Article 10(1) of the Directive.[59] In the case of such an investigation Member States shall supply the Commission with the requested information to the best of their ability.

9. The Commission may,[60] in the light of the evolution of a case and the information received from Member States, convene the Committee on Emergencies in order to exchange views on the results obtained and to evaluate the measures taken. The Committee on Emergencies may also be convened at the request of a representative of a Member State.

   The Commission shall, by means of its internal co-ordination procedures, endeavour to:
   (a) avoid unnecessary duplication in dealing with notifications;
   (b) make full use of the expertise available within the Commission;
   (c) keep the other services concerned fully informed;
   (d) ensure that discussions in the various relevant committees are held in accordance with Article 10 of the Directive.

10. When a Member State intends, apart from any specific measures taken because of serious and immediate risks, to modify its legislation by adopting technical specifications, the latter must be notified to the Commission at the draft stage, in accordance with Directive 83/189/EEC, if necessary, quoting the urgent reasons set out in Article 9(3) of that Directive.

11. To allow it to have an overview of the situation, the Committee on Emergencies shall be periodically informed of all the notifications received and of the follow-up. Where the Commission originates its own investigation or convenes the Committee on Emergencies, and in those cases which fall within the scope of procedures and/or committees provided for by Community legislation governing specific products or product sectors, those committees shall be involved. In cases where the Committee on Emergencies is not involved and no provisions are made with other relevant committees, the contact points shall be informed of any exchange of views within other committees.

Experience with the RAPEX system

The RAPEX system operated from March 1985, and supplemented a Rapid Exchange System for foodstuffs which began in 1978. The new

[59] The Committee was created by Council Decision 84/133 as a Consultative Committee to assist the Commission in the implementation and management of the previous system. The Consultative Committee's field of activity was enlarged by the adoption of the Directive on dangerous imitations, under which it may be consulted at the request of the Commission or of a Member State.

[60] It was originally proposed that the Commission could directly take appropriate temporary measures to prevent the risk (see OJ No. C 193/1, 31.7.89). Objections were raised (notably by Germany, The Netherlands, the United Kingdom and Ireland) that this gave the Commission excessive decision-making power, inconsistent with the principle of subsidiarity (see Internal Market No. 1624).

system covered all products intended for use by consumers except those intended exclusively for professional use and those which were subject to equivalent notification procedures under other Community instruments, including pharmaceutical products[61] and under the Animal Diseases Notification System[62] and other measures.[63] Member States notified to the Commission and to each other measures taken by them to prevent, restrict or attach particular conditions to the marketing or use, or possible marketing or use, on their territory of products because of the serious risk which those products presented for the health or safety of consumers when used in normal and foreseeable conditions.

There have been considerable variations between Member States in the way notifications have been dealt with but in general the following steps have been taken. Each Member State nominates a contact point in a national authority which decides whether other Ministries are competent to deal with any individual case. The national authorities carry out a check on the market to ascertain whether the product is on sale. If it is found, most countries have it tested for the reported danger in an official laboratory. In 1988, certain countries (Denmark, Germany, Greece, Spain, France, Ireland, Italy, Luxembourg, Portugal, United Kingdom) had power to temporarily block or ban any consumer product, whereas in others (Belgium, Netherlands) this power extended only to certain categories of products.

A number of problems were experienced with the operation of the system,[64] including failure to report cases by Member States and their failure to provide sufficient information in notifications. However, by 1988 the Commission felt that although there was much room for improvement, the system had proved its usefulness as a warning system and an instrument of crisis management and was improving. It was also expected to provide a valuable instrument for the prevention of accidents involving consumer products by focusing attention on those products or categories of products which had been the subject of frequent measures in Member States and, as a result, by establishing priorities for action.

Between March 1985 and December 31, 1987:

- of the non-food cases, 50 per cent were electrical goods, but of 18 notifications received only one directly concerned children. However, the predominance of electrical goods might have been

[61] Originally pursuant to Art. 30 of Council Directive 75/319/EEC, as amended by Directive 83/570/EEC for human medicines. Directive 81/851/EEC as amended for veterinary medicines.

[62] Directive 64/432/EEC, Art. 9, OJ No. 121, 29.7.64.

[63] Animals to which Directive 82/894/EEC applies OJ No. L 378/58, 31.12.82; products of animal origin to the extent covered by Directive 89/662/EEC OJ No. L 347/33, 28.11.89; the radiological emergency system established by Council Decision 87/600/Euratom concerning large-scale contamination of products, OJ No. L 371/76, 30.12.87.

[64] Interim report COM(86) 562 final approved by the Commission on October 24, 1986 and presented to the Council on October 29, 1986; Report from the Commission on the system for the rapid exchange of information on dangers arising from the use of consumer products in accordance with Art. 8(2) of Council Decision 84/133/EEC, OJ No. C 146/8, 3.6.88.

due to the existence of a specific requirement to test imported electrical goods to assess conformity with the "low voltage" directive.

- of the non-food notifications, about 50 per cent originated in non-Community countries.

A problem with the system was to achieve uniform understanding of what was meant by serious and immediate danger. The Commission noted that the concept of safety is a changing one and products which were considered safe ten years before were now deemed to be unsafe. It was decided not to attempt to give a more precise definition but to tackle the issue by means of guidelines issued by the Consultative Committee.

In 1990 there were only 16 notifications, but this rose to 96 in 1991 (Belgium 49, Spain 11, United Kingdom 19 but none from other States).

Serious and immediate risks — the Commission's powers

Although the power and obligation to ensure that only safe products are put on the market rests with Member States, the Commission has a residual power to take action itself where there is a serious and immediate risk from a product to the health and safety of consumers in various Member States. The procedure is illustrated in **Figure 2.2**. Article 9 states the following further conditions:

(a) one or more Member States have adopted measures entailing restrictions on the marketing of the product or requiring its withdrawal from the market, such as those provided for in Article 6(1)(d)–(h);
(b) Member States differ on the adoption of measures to deal with the risk in question;
(c) the risk cannot be dealt with, in view of the nature of the safety issue posed by the product and in a manner compatible with the urgency of the case, under the other procedures laid down by the specific Community legislation applicable to the product or category of products concerned; and
(d) the risk can be eliminated effectively only by adopting appropriate measures applicable at Community level, in order to ensure the protection of the health and safety of consumers and the proper functioning of the common market.

Article 11 specifies the following procedure[65]:

1. The Commission must consult the Member States.
2. At least one Member State must request the Commission to adopt a decision.

[65] This is variant III(b) of the template provision provided in Council Decision 87/373/EEC, OJ No. L 197/33, 18.7.87. The Commission favoured the type IIa procedure.

Figure 4.2 Outline of emergency procedure for a Commission Decision

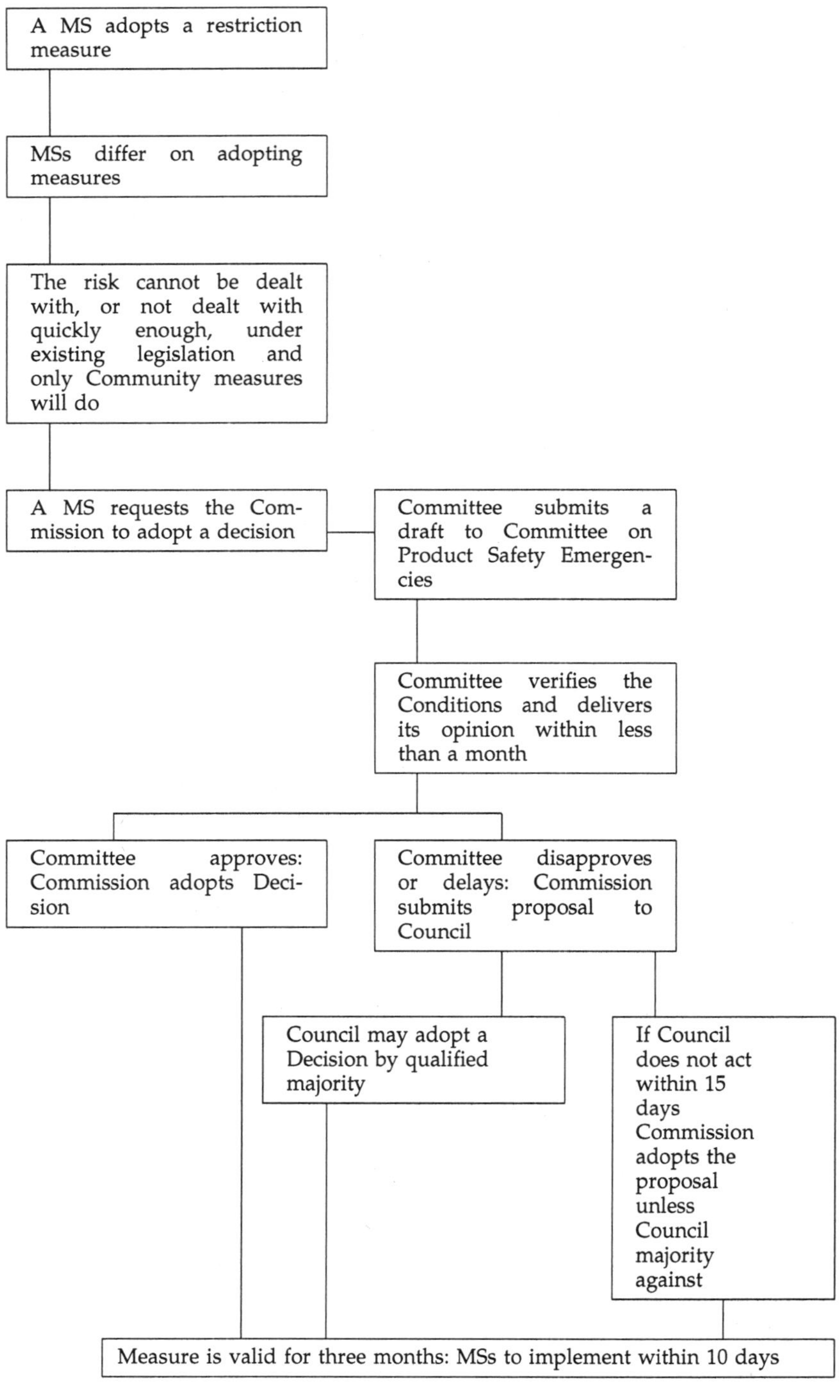

3. The Commission submits a draft of the proposed measures to the Committee on Product Safety Emergencies, which is composed of the representatives of the Member States and chaired by a representative of the Commission.
4. The Committee verifies that the conditions listed in Article 9 are fulfilled and delivers its opinion on the draft within a time limit which the Chairman may lay down according to the urgency of the matter but not exceeding one month. The opinion is adopted on a qualified majority, as specified in Article 148(2) of the Treaty.
5. If the Committee opinion is in accordance with the proposed measures, the Commission adopts its decision.
6. If the Committee opinion is not in accordance with the proposed measures, or in the absence of an opinion, the Commission forthwith submits a proposal (not necessarily the same as the previous proposal) to the Council.
7. The Council may adopt a decision by qualified majority.
8. If the Council has not acted within 15 days of the proposal being submitted, the Commission shall adopt the proposal unless the Council has decided against it by a simple majority.
9. Any measure adopted under this procedure is valid for no longer than three months. The period may be prolonged under the same procedure.
10. Member States are to implement decisions adopted under this procedure within less than 10 days. The Council minuted the statement of itself and the Commission that the period must be reduced to the minimum in the case of highly perishable products.
11. The competent authorities of the Member States responsible for carrying out measures adopted under this procedure shall, within one month, give the parties concerned an opportunity to submit their views and shall inform the Commission accordingly.

This procedure is cumbersome. It was reached as a compromise within the Council in order to overcome objections by some Member States that the Commission would otherwise have had too much power.

Germany unsuccessfully challenged the validity of the power in Article 9 of the Directive enabling the Commission to adopt a decision on the grounds of absence of a legal basis and infringement of the principle of proportionality.[66] The Court of Justice said:

> "The free movement of goods could be secured only if product safety requirements did not differ significantly from one Member State to another. A high level of protection could be achieved only if dangerous products were subject to appropriate measures in all the Member States."

The Court noted the restrictions imposed on the Commission by the Directive when it sought to require action. The Commission can only act

[66] Case C–359/92.

after a request to do so by a Member State and after consulting the Member States. The Commission's action must be in accordance with the opinion of the Committee. Decisions taken would be addressed only to the Member States and a decision will not be of direct application to traders in the Community but must instead be incorporated into a national measure. The Court concluded that action by Community authorities is justified by the fact that the risk arising from particular dangerous goods could be eliminated effectively only by adopting appropriate measures at Community level in order to ensure the protection of the health and safety of consumers and the proper functioning of the Common Market. Accordingly, such action is not contrary to the EEC Treaty. In certain fields, particularly that of product safety, the Court stated that the approximation of general laws alone might not be enough to ensure the unity of the market. Consequently the concept of "measures for the approximation" of legislation is to be read as encompassing the power of the Council to lay down measures relating to a specific product or class of products and, if necessary, individual measures concerning those products.

The Court also held that this aspect of the Directive does not breach the principle of proportionality. The powers conferred on the Commission by the Directive are: "appropriate for the purpose of attaining the objectives pursued by the Directive, that is to say, ensuring a high level of protection for the health and safety of consumers, whilst eliminating barriers to trade and distortions of competition arising as a result of disparities between national measures taken in relation to consumer products". The alternative of bringing infringement provisions under the Treaty against any Member States which had not taken appropriate measures would inevitably render the procedure more cumbersome. Even supposing that such proceedings were initiated and upheld by the Court, "it is not certain that a declaration . . . would enable the objective set out in the Directive to be achieved as effectively as would be the case by Community harmonisation measure. In particular the infringement procedure would not enable consumer protection to be secured in the shortest possible time." This approach is "scarcely compatible with urgency".

Confidentiality

Member States and the Commission may obtain information of considerable commercial value in performing their functions, whether provided voluntarily or otherwise by producers and distributors, or obtained from third parties, such as results of tests or about market conditions. Article 12 specifies that the Member States and the Commission shall take the steps necessary to ensure that their officials and agents are required not to disclose information obtained for the purposes of this Directive which, by its nature, is covered by professional secrecy, except for information relating to the safety properties of a given product which must be made public if circumstances so require, in order to protect the health and safety of persons. There is a similar confidentiality provision under the emergency notification procedure.[67]

Consultation and reasons for decisions

Certain provisions of natural justice are included in Article 14 of the Directive.

"1. Any decision adopted under this Directive and involving restrictions on the placing of a product on the market, or requiring its withdrawal from the market, must state the appropriate reasons on which it is based. It shall be notified as soon as possible to the party concerned and shall indicate the remedies available under the provisions in force in the Member State in question and the time limits applying to such remedies.

The parties concerned shall, whenever feasible, be given an opportunity to submit their views before the adoption of the measure. If this has not been done in advance because of the urgency of the measures to be taken, such opportunity shall be given in due course after the measure has been implemented.

Measures requiring the withdrawal of a product from the market shall take into consideration the need to encourage distributors, users and consumers to contribute to the implementation of such measures.

2. Member States shall ensure that any measure taken by the competent authorities involving restrictions on the placing of a product on the market or requiring its withdrawal from the market can be challenged before the competent courts.

3. Any decision taken by virtue of this Directive and involving restrictions on the placing of a product on the market or requiring its withdrawal from the market shall be entirely without prejudice to assessment of the liability of the party concerned, in the light of the national criminal law applying in the case in question."

FINAL COMMENTS

Review of the Directive

The Commission is to submit a report on the implementation of the Directive to the European Parliament and the Council every two years.[68]

[67] Directive, Art. 8 and point 6 of the Annex.
[68] Directive, Art. 15.

In 1998, the Commission is to report to the Council on the experience acquired, together with appropriate proposals. The Council is to decide whether to adjust the Directive, in particular to extend its scope to all products (Article 2(a)) and to alter the emergency procedures in Articles 8 to 12.

Product safety and product liability

The General Product Safety Directive and the Product Liability Directive 85/374/EEC are intended to be complementary.[69] Article 13 of the GPS Directive specifies that it is without prejudice to the Product Liability Directive 85/374/EEC. This provision was added to clarify that the GPS Directive does not affect injured persons' rights under the Product Liability Directive.[70] Both Directives are aimed at harmonising the rules for marketing products within the Community and at achieving a high level of consumer protection. The aim of the first is to prevent injury by preventing the marketing of dangerous products which might cause injury, whereas the aim of the latter Directive is to provide compensation for people who are injured by defective products. The former is a regulatory provision with intervention powers backed by criminal sanctions, the latter provides for a claim for compensatory damages in civil law. It is not surprising to note the similarities between the two Directives, for example in the concept and definition of "producer" and in the definitions of a dangerous product and a defective product.

The Product Liability Directive was intended to harmonise national laws in relation to product injury. It did not, of course, do so in so far as it left pre-existing remedies which were not based on strict product liability, such as fault liability, entirely unharmonised. The issue which now arises is the extent to which the tort of breach of statutory duty can be based on the GPS Directive. This is not entirely clear under English law, as discussed in the section on breach of statutory duty in Chapter 8. However, it is conceivable that *different* results may occur in the other Member States: if breach of statutory duty is allowed to found a civil action at all elsewhere on the continent this would completely undermine the provisions of the Product Liability Directive. Strict liability with no development risk, component or other defences and no 10–year long stop on claims might sneak in by the back door!

[69] Explanatory Note, COM (89) 162/6.

[70] Communication from the Commission to the European Parliament, SEC (92) 11 final-SYN 192.

5 U.K. Consumer Safety Legislation

This chapter is primarily concerned with how the safety of consumer products is regulated by the authorities of the United Kingdom: the statutory framework governing the supply of products, the notion of a "safe product", powers which are available to inspectors to enforce the law against suppliers, and, in particular, the impact of the General Product Safety Regulations 1994 which implemented Council Directive 92/59/EEC.

REGULATORY CONTROL

The principal statute governing consumer safety is the Consumer Protection Act 1987 (Part II). This Act is largely a consolidation of measures contained in earlier statutes.[1] The Act is the basis for three main groups of regulatory controls:

1. The Secretary of State is empowered to make regulations for product safety.
2. The Secretary of State is empowered to serve notices prohibiting the recipient from supplying goods which he considers to be unsafe. In addition the Secretary of State is able to require a supplier to publish warnings about unsafe goods.
3. The enforcement authorities are empowered to issue suspension notices prohibiting supply of goods contravening safety provisions for up to six months; to apply to the Court for an Order for forfeiture of any goods on the grounds that there has been a contravention of the safety provision. (There are also various ancillary powers authorising the enforcement authorities to bring prosecutions for offences under the Act or the Regulations and making provision for searches, seizure, inspection of goods and documents, and other means of obtaining information.)

The Consumer Protection Act 1987 also introduced for the first time in consumer protection the concept of a "general safety requirement"

[1] The Consumer Protection Acts 1961 and 1971, the Consumer Safety Act 1978 and Consumer Safety (Amendment) Act 1986, all repealed with effect from October 1, 1987. (Consumer Protection Act 1987, s.48(3) and Sched. 5).

making it an offence to supply consumer goods failing to meet the statutory criteria for safety. This offence was not, however, for general application to all products, since the term *consumer goods* for these particular — meant "any goods ordinarily intended for private use or consumption" specifically not extend to six categories of products, namely[2]:

(a) growing crops or things comprised in land by virtue of being attached to it;
(b) water, food, feeding stuff or fertiliser;
(c) gas supplied under the Gas Act 1986;
(d) aircraft (other than hang-gliders) or motor vehicles;
(e) controlled drugs or licensed medicinal products;
(f) tobacco.

The rationale for these sectoral exclusions was in most cases the existence of distinct regulatory regimes.[3] In addition, two more classes of products were effectively outside the scope of the 1987 Act's general safety requirement by virtue of defences available to suppliers of second-hand[4] goods and goods for export outside the U.K.[5]

Finally, many supplies of unsafe goods would not give rise to the offence of supplying goods in breach of the 1987 Act's general safety requirement. A retailer could rely upon a defence under the Act if the following conditions were satisfied:

1. that he supplied the goods, offered or agreed to supply them or, as the case may be, exposed or possessed them for supply in the course of carrying on a retail business; and
2. that at the time he supplied the goods or offered or agreed to supply them or exposed or possessed them for supply he neither knew nor had reasonable grounds for believing that the goods failed to comply with the general safety requirement.[6]

The European Directive on General Product Safety[7] ("the GPS Directive") represented a Community blueprint of a regulatory system for consumer safety, requiring producers and distributors to be fully responsible for the safety of their products and to monitor their performance once they are on the market. The General Product Safety Regulations 1994 ("GPS" Regulations) came into force on October 3, 1994. These regulations effectively superimpose the provisions of the GPS Directive on to the pre-existing U.K. consumer safety legislation and were intended to be more a restatement of the existing law than a

[2] s.10(7).
[3] See the Water Act 1989, the Food Safety Act 1990, the Gas Act 1986, the Medicines Act 1968, and numerous statutory instruments regulating the supply of tobacco products.
[4] s.10(4)(c), Consumer Protection Act 1987.
[5] s.10(a), Consumer Protection Act 1987.
[6] s.10(4)(b).
[7] Council Directive 92/59/EEC of June 29, 1992 on General Product Safety (OJ No. L 228/24, 11.08.92).

substantive change to the standards of safety, manufacturers and other suppliers are to meet. The roles of enforcement bodies and the powers available to them under the 1987 Act are unaffected but a new version of the general safety requirement has been created, along with a number of more specific obligations on producers and others who form part of the chain of supply to the ultimate consumer to undertake certain steps. The result is a complex arrangement of new provisions interwoven with the old legislation. The GPS Regulations adopt the approach, and much of the language, of the GPS Directive. The regulations do not go so far as to repeal fully the general safety requirement under the 1987 Act. Instead they put in parallel with the 1987 Act a new general safety requirement complementing Community product safety rules, so there are two discrete general safety requirements in U.K. law, with different definitions of key terms, different criteria and different scope. The 1987 Act general safety requirement is however "disapplied" in cases where the GPS Regulations apply and the GPS Regulations have therefore become the relevant requirements governing most supplies of consumer goods.[8] Not surprisingly, the result is a complex fusion of two sets of rules.

As can be seen from the discussion of the GPS Directive in Chapter 2 the general safety requirement under the Directive is more comprehensive than that of the 1987 Act. Its application extends to "any product intended for consumers or likely to be used by consumers, supplied whether for consideration or not in the course of a commercial activity and whether new, used or reconditioned". Its requirements extend to retailers as well as others in the supply chain. The only exceptions are in relation to second-hand products sold as antiques or for the purposes of repair or reconditioning. The approach to sectoral exclusions is different to the 1987 Act: under the Directive the exclusions are based not on the nature of the products themselves but on the existence of specific European laws governing the safety of products concerned.

THE BODIES RESPONSIBLE FOR CONSUMER PROTECTION

There is no single institution with responsibility for enforcing consumer safety requirements within the United Kingdom. The primary duty to enforce legislative safety provisions lies at local level with the Weights and Measures Authorities[9] in England, Wales and Scotland, and with District Councils in Northern Ireland.[10] For practical purposes these responsibilities lie with local councils who administer them through their Trading Standards Departments, Consumer Protection Depart-

[8] Reg. 5, GPS Regulations.
[9] As defined in the Weights and Measures Act 1985, s.69.
[10] s.27(1), Consumer Protection Act 1987.

ments or some other similarly named department under their auspices. These authorities are under an obligation to carry out enforcement within their area.

A variety of statutory powers are available to authorities in support of their enforcement functions which they can exercise to obtain information about unsafe products and, should it be necessary, prevent their supply or prosecute those responsible. These powers are examined at the end of this chapter. Although the local enforcement authorities operate on an area-by-area basis in practice they do not do so in isolation. The Local Authority Co-ordinating Body on Food and Trading Standards (LACOTS) enables Trading Standards Departments to liaise with one another on operational issues such as interpretation of legislation, uniform approaches to enforcement action and technical examination of products. LACOTS promotes the "home authority" principle which applies to all trading standards, food hygiene, product safety and consumer protection laws. The objectives of the principle are to ensure that:

- local authorities place special emphasis on surveillance in their areas;
- businesses are able to depend on a specific home authority for preventative guidance and advice;
- enforcing authorities liaise with a "home authority";
- machinery exists for monitoring and resolving disputes.[11]

The principle is not enshrined in statute and is based wholly on voluntary co-operation between local authoriities and individual trading standards officers. It is essentially an advisory and co-ordination mechanism which operates alongside, rather than, replacing formal enforcement and the duty to comply with statutory requirements. Under the principle, responsibility for enforcement is designated at three levels:

The home authority This is the authority where the relevant decision making base of a busines is located. It could be the head office, or a main factory or place of importation. Where a business has no distinct base various authorities may need to resolve which will take this role. There may be circumstances such as resource constraints or the need for specialised officers to operate which will mean that the home authority might have to be appointed somewhere other than the main base of the business concerned.

The originating authority This is an authority in whose area goods are produced or packaged. The originating authority will commonly be the same as the home authority where a business has its headquarters at its main production facility.

The enforcing authority This can be any authority which deals with complaints, enquiries or which detects contraventions of statutory requirements.

[11] See *Home Authority Principle*, LACOTS, April 1994.

The role of the home authority

The home authority is meant to take the lead role in providing guidance on compliance issues, standards, codes of practice and remedial action. It will be the first port of call for the business for any queries or guidance on policy issues, and it is meant to liaise with the other authorities, and in particular an originating authority if this is separate. The corollary of this is that businesses are expected to co-operate fully with home authority in providing information when requested. The home authority is encouraged to maintain a record of incidents, company policy, due diligence systems and any enforcement action taken by other authorities. The home authority will not, however, have power to dictate to other authorities, nor can it give a definitive statement of a manufacturers or suppliers legal duties. LACOTS guidance states that in offering advice it may be appropriate for home authorities to give the following caveat:

> "That whilst this authority would not institute proceedings in respect of this product you must be aware that this does not preclude any other authority from taking legal action."

The role of the originating authority

The main role of the originating authority is in relation to surveillance of production and packaging operations, and liaising with the home authority in relation to any enquiries that are needed. The demarcation between the home and originating authority will not necessarily be rigidly adhered to when for practical purposes an originating authority can carry out the functions. This will be a matter for the officers of the respective authorities to agree among themselves. LACOTS guidelines envisage that originating authority will acquire practical and first hand experience of manufacturing procedures including quality assurance.

The role of the enforcing authority

Enforcing authorities (unless they also happen to be the originating or home authority) will generally have no established relationship with a manufacturer or supplier whose products are subject to complaint or investigation in their area, and the rationale for the home authority principle is that enforcing authorities should always operate in conjunction with the home or originating authority. This is meant to avoid duplication of work, but also to maintain a consistent approach to the interpretation of product safety law and standards and to ensure that an enforcing authority is aware of any history problems or arrangements that are in place to rectify the matters which have come to the enforcing authorities attention. Enforcing authorities are meant to ensure that any cautions that are issued when enforcement action is taken (including prosecution) are notified to the home authority, and generally speaking enforcing authorities should, in taking such action, take into account the advice of the home authority.

LACOTS itself may play a role in assisting to resolve differences of opinion where this cannot be dealt with between the authorities informally themselves and specialist panels may offer national guidance. However, the findings of such powers are not binding. These arrangements do not extend to a dispute resolution facility between enforcing authorities and individual businesses, nor will LACOTS panels become involved in cases which are proceeding before the Courts. LACOTS also sponsors various European product safety co-ordination initiatives.[12] The formal community arrangements for community-wide notification of enforcement action are discussed separately in Chapter 2.

There are other enforcement powers which can be exercised centrally by the Secretary of State.[13] Within the Department of Trade and Industry there is a Consumer Safety Unit which is responsible for developing product safety regulations, undertaking research and authorising testing bodies for the purposes of certifying compliance with standards. It also maintains contact with the local enforcement authorities, monitoring the effectiveness of their functions.

The Secretary of State retains power to make regulations transferring the functions of the existing enforcement authority in part or in whole to other bodies which could include another central Government department, or even an entirely new body such as a consumer protection authority if the Government were to create one.[14] Specific examples contemplated at the time of introducing the legislation were non-prescription medicinal products, where it might be appropriate in some circumstances to hand responsibility for enforcement over to the Secretary of State. The GPS Regulations now specify that licensed medicinal products fall within the enforcement powers of the Medicines Control Agency. Foods are subject to the enforcement regime of the Food Safety Act 1990.

Sectoral legislation: medicines[15]

Medicines for both human and animal use are regulated in almost every detail by the Medicines Act 1968 and subordinate legislation and, at European level, by E.C. Regulations and Directives which have since 1965 directed the development of the regulations of medicines in Europe. By way of a licensing system, the manufacture, distribution, (importation) and marketing of medicines are strictly controlled. The

[12] See *Home Authority Principle*, para. 9.

[13] The powers are exercised nominally by the Secretary of State for Trade and Industry but usually in practice by the Under Secretary of State for Consumer Affairs.

[14] s.27(2).

[15] For a fuller explanation of the law relating to medicinal products see Dale & Applebe's *Pharmacy Law and Ethics* (1993) and C. Bendall, *European Pharmaceutical Law* due to be published in 1996.

licensing system is the responsibility of government ministers (the Secretary of State for Health and the Secretary of State for Agriculture: acting together, the ministers comprise the "licensing authority"). They exercise their power with the advice of the Medicines Commission and expert committees established under the Act. It is, however, the Medicines Control Agency (MCA) of the Department of Health who operate and "police" the licensing system on behalf of Ministers in relation to human medicines and the Veterinary Medicines Directorate (VMD) that undertakes these functions in respect of medicines for veterinary use and medicated feeding stuffs.

The licensing system applies to all *medicinal products* which are defined as being products used "wholly or mainly . . . for a medicinal purpose". Medicinal purposes are further defined as including:

"(a) Treating or preventing disease [including any injury, ailment or adverse condition, whether of body or mind]; . . .

(e) Otherwise preventing or interfering with the normal operation of the physiological function, whether permanently or temporarily, and whether by way of terminating, reducing or postponing, or increasing or accelerating the operation of that function or in any other way".[16]

A product licence, or marketing authorisation, covers all the main activities associated with the marketing of a medicinal product. With limited and very specific exceptions, an authorisation must be held before any such activities may legally be undertaken. Applications are lodged together with relevant supporting data relating to pharmaceutical quality, safety and efficacy for the proposed indications. Licenses are issued for five years, or shorter if specified in the licence. Applications can be granted, refused, reviewed, suspended, revoked or varied as the licensing authority sees fit if for any reason quality, safety or efficacy is questioned after it is granted.

In order to manufacture a medicinal product, a manufacturer's licence must be obtained. This will only be granted after one of the licensing authority inspectors have inspected the manufacturer's premises, equipment, the qualifications of the supervisors and the safety arrangements. The manufacturer must meet the high standards set by legislative provisons and known as "Good Manufacturing Practice".

A wholesale dealer's license is required by any person who in the course of his business sells, offers for sale or distributes any medicinal product. (This does not apply to whole human blood, plasma, or blood cells of human origin, or certain radio-pharmaceuticals or homoeopathic products.)

Detailed regulations have been issued setting out the requirements relating to containers and packaging of medicinal products including, in relation to human medicines, the need to include a patent information

[16] s.131(1), Medicines Act 1968. See also Directive 65/65/EEC, Art. 2.

leaflet.[17] Medicinal products must be correctly described, readily identifiable and give accurate and correct information which is important for safe and proper use.

The Act provides extensive enforcement powers exercised by the licensing authority through the enforcement branch of the MCA and the Ministry of Agriculture, Fisheries and Food (MAFF) (for veterinary products). Inspectors have wide powers to enter premises, to take samples and to investigate breaches of the law. It is an offence for any person in the course of business carried on by him to sell, supply or have in his possession for the purpose of sale and supply medicinal products in contravention of the Act. The Act and its subordinate legislation clearly specify the contraventions of its varied requirements that will amount to criminal offences. For example, on contravention of labelling regulations, a person will be liable on summary conviction to a fine of up to £5,000 and upon indictment, to a fine (unlimited) or imprisonment to a term not exceeding two years, or both.

Part VI of the Medicines Act 1968, together with specific Regulations issued in 1994,[18] provide wide powers to control the advertising of medicinal products. Adverts are strictly controlled requirements differing depending upon whether the intended recipients are doctors, health care professionals or member of the public. Any person who issues or causes another person to issue an advert which do not conform to the above, or makes false or misleading representations, will be guilty of an offence, the penalty upon conviction being the same as above.

Sectoral legislation: food and drink

The legislation governing the sale or supply of food is complex.[19] In the U.K. the principal legal restrictions are contained in the Food Safety Act 1990 which requires that all food (including drink and ingredients used in the preparation of food) must meet the basic food safety requirements, *i.e.* it must not be contaminated, or rendered injurious to health or be generally unfit for human consumption. The Act also governs the general presentation and labelling of foods and makes it an offence to sell food which is not of the nature or substance or quality demanded or to falsely describe or present a food. Liability under the Act is generally strict. However traders may be able to rely on the "due diligence" defence to escape liability if they can show that the offence arose because of another's mistake and they took all reasonable precautions and exercised all due diligence to avoid committing the offence.

In addition there is a whole raft of extremely detailed regulations made under the Act governing different aspects of the composition,

[17] The Medicines for Human Use (Marketing Authorisation, etc) Regulations 1994.

[18] ss.92–93, Medicines Act 1968 and the Medicines (Advertising) Regulations 1994 and the Medicines (Monitoring of Advertising) Regulations 1994.

[19] For a more detailed introduction to food legislation see A.A. Painter, *Butterworths Food Law* (1992) and Lister, *Regulation of Food Products by the European Community* (1992).

labelling, hygienic preparation and sale or display of foods, which take the form of both general regulations such as the Food Labelling Regulations 1984 and specific rules relating to particular foods (for example the Ice Cream Regulations 1967). There is no requirement for positive approval of foods by the authorities to ensure compliance with the legislation, akin to the U.K.'s licensing system for medicines. The obligation is on food suppliers, importers and manufacturers to meet the legislative requirements or risk prosecution or other enforcement action.

The powers to enforce both breaches of the 1990 Act and the food regulations are contained in the 1990 Act. This gives enforcing officers (generally Trading Standards Officers) a whole range of powers including the power to inspect and seize suspected food, to enter premises and to take samples for analysis. Officers have power to issue improvement or prohibition orders requiring measures to be taken to rectify breaches of food legislation and in certain circumstances emergency powers. Alternatively inspectors may decide to prosecute a proprietor for breach of the legislation. Under the 1990 Act most of the offences are "either way", and can be tried in either the magistrates' court or if the breach is considered to be particularly serious in the Crown Court. Where the case is tried on indictment in the Crown Court an unlimited fine may be imposed, or in certain circumstances up to two years' imprisonment. The maximum penalties for breaches of the principal requirements of the 1990 Act following conviction in the magistrates' court have recently been increased and exceed the maximum penalties for equivalent offences under general consumer product safety legislation: fines of up to £20,000 can now be imposed, or in certain circumstances up to six months' imprisonment. Other offences under the 1990 Act carry the statutory maximum penalty for cases brought in the magistrates' court, which is currently £5,000.

PRODUCT SAFETY REGULATIONS

There are at present some 50 sets of safety regulations made, and in force under section 11 of the Consumer Protection Act 1987 and the earlier consumer safety statutes. These cover a wide range of products and the list is contained in Appendix 4. Notwithstanding the GPS Regulations, almost all these Regulations remain in force and continue to apply to the categories of products concerned.[20] Such products must also meet the general safety requirement under the GPS Regulations, but there is a presumption of compliance if the regulations relevant to the product are adhered to:

> "Where in relation to any product such product conforms to the specific rules of the law of the United Kingdom laying down the

[20] The Approval of Standards Regulations 1987 (S.I. 1987 No. 1911) were revoked by reg. 6(2) of the GPS Regulations. See below p.110.

> health and safety requirements which the product must satisfy in order to be marketed there shall be a presumption that, until the contrary is proved, the product is a safe product".[21]

It is important to remember that this notion of compliance with these national regulatory requirements is not conclusive in terms of compliance with the general safety requirements. The GPS Regulations (reg. 10) anticipate circumstances in which a product may meet the detailed requirements of specific regulations but nevertheless is unsafe in a more general sense.[22] In such circumstances, the producer would have breached the general safety requirement, and the full range of enforcement measures could be applied to prevent further supply.

Procedures for implementing safety regulations under Part II of the Consumer Protection Act 1987

Section 11 of the 1987 Act empowers the Secretary of State to make safety regulations for three purposes. These are[23]:

1. that goods are safe;
2. that goods which are unsafe, or would be unsafe in the hands of persons of a particular description, are not made available to persons generally or, as the case may be, to persons of that description; and
3. that appropriate information is, and inappropriate information is not, provided in relation to goods.

The definition of "safe" is contained in section 19 of the Act:

> "'Safe' in relation to any goods, means such that there is no risk, or no risk apart from one reduced to a minimum, that any of the following will (whether immediately or after a definite or indefinite period) cause the death of, or any personal injury to, any person whatsoever, that is to say:
> (a) the goods;
> (b) the keeping, use or consumption of the goods;
> (c) the assembly of any of the goods which are, or are to be, supplied unassembled;

[21] reg. 10, GPS Regulations.

[22] Art. 4(3) of the GPS Directive (which has not been reproduced in the GPS Regulations 1994) also provides that:

> "conformity of a product with the provisions mentioned in paragraphs 1 or 2 [which includes specific rules of national law] shall not bar the competent authorities of the Member States from taking appropriate measures to impose restrictions on its being placed on the market or to require its withdrawal from the market where there is evidence that, despite such conformity, it is dangerous to the health and safety of consumers."

Thus regulatory controls can still be imposed in relation to hazards not anticipated by existing specific regulations. See further discussion below in the context of the criteria for evaluation of conformity with the general safety requirements.

[23] s.11(1)(a)–(c), CPA 1987.

(d) any emission or leakage from the goods or, as a result of the keeping, use or consumption of the goods, from anything else; or

(e) reliance on the accuracy of any measurement, calculation or other reading made by or by means of the goods,

and 'safer' and 'unsafe' shall be construed accordingly."

Safety in this context is confined to consideration of risks of injury to the person. This contrasts with the civil liability provisions of Part I of the 1987 Act in which risks of property damage are material.[24]

The power to make safety regulations is exercisable by statutory instruments subject to annulment in pursuance of a resolution of either House of Parliament. The Secretary of State is, however, subject to limitations with regard to the type of goods to which regulations can be made pursuant to these powers: regulations cannot be made in respect of growing crops and things comprised in land by virtue of being attached to it; water, food feeding stuff and fertiliser; gas supplied under the Gas Act 1986; controlled drugs and licensed medical products.[25]

Section 11(2) goes on to give a (non-exhaustive) list of the provisions that safety regulations may contain with respect to the following matters:

(a) the composition or contents, design, construction, finish or packing of goods to which this section applies, with respect to standards for such goods and with respect to other matters relating to such goods;

(b) the giving, refusal, alteration or cancellation of approvals of such goods, of descriptions of such goods or of standards for such goods;

(c) the conditions that may be attached to any approval given under the regulations;

(d) fees to be paid on the giving or alteration of any approval under the regulations and on the making of an application for such an approval or alteration;

(e) appeals against refusals, alterations and cancellations of approvals given under the regulations and against the conditions contained in such approvals;

(f) rules for goods to be approved under the regulations or to conform to the requirements of the regulations or to descriptions or standards specified in or approved by or under the regulations;

(g) testing or inspection of goods (including provision for determining the standards to be applied in carrying out any test or inspection);

(h) the ways of dealing with goods of which some or all do not satisfy a test required by or under the regulations or a standard connected with a procedure so required;

(i) requiring a mark, warning or instruction or any other information relating to goods to be put on or to accompany the goods or to be used or provided in some other manner in relation to the goods, and

[24] s.3 CPA 1957.

[25] s.11(7).

for securing that inappropriate information is not given in relation to goods either by means of misleading marks or otherwise;

(j) prohibiting persons from supplying, or from offering to supply, agreeing to supply, exposing for supply or possessing for supply, goods and component parts and raw materials for such goods:

(k) requiring information to be given to any such person as may be determined by or under the regulations for the purpose of enabling that person to exercise any function conferred on him by the regulations.

Section 11(5) imposes a duty on the Secretary of State to enter into consultations before making safety regulations. The consultees are not defined, except in respect of the Health and Safety Commission in relation to goods suitable for use at work.[26] In practice the consultation is carried out by the DTI who typically consult organisations such as trade associations, consumer safety bodies, the CBI and representatives of the enforcement authorities. The Secretary of State is, however, able to act without consultation where he is of the view that "the need to protect the public requires that the Regulations should be made without delay".[27] In such cases the regulations could only apply for a limited duration of not more than 12 months.[28] Restrictions on the supply of products, whether they be outright bans, mandatory warnings or imposition of other conditions will trigger the operation of provisions for notification to the European Commission exchange of information arrangements under Articles 7 and 8 of the GPS Directive or other product-specific Community legislation, possibly leading to action being taken against the product in question across the Community.[29]

Contravention of safety regulations is an offence by virtue of section 12 of the 1987 Act. (The regulations cannot themselves make provision for specific offences of their own requirements.[30]) The requirements contained in the Safety Regulations are also deemed to be "safety provisions" for the purposes of other enforcement measures under the Act in the form of statutory notices and forfeiture of products. The subject of enforcement is considered in more detail later in this chapter.

Examples of safety regulations

There is no standard approach taken to the way in which safety regulations are formulated, and a variety of approaches has been taken.

[26] s.11(5), CPA 1987.

[27] s.11(5), CPA 1987.

[28] An example is the Three-Wheeled All-Terrain Vehicles (Safety) Regulations 1988 (SI 1988 No. 2122) which were subsequently replaced by the All-Terrain Motor Vehicles (Safety) Regulations 1989 (SI 1989 No. 2288) the year after their implementation after the Secretary of State had in the meantime used the consultation procedure.

[29] See Chap. 4.

[30] s.11(4).

Regulations may have a narrow focus on a particular hazard, for example entrapment of children within parts of bunk beds, for which the Bunk Beds (Entrapment Hazards) (Safety) Regulations 1987 contain very descriptive details for the design and manufacture of bunk beds and their components. Regulations may also be targeted specifically at certain products which are inherently dangerous prohibiting their sale as, for example, with certain novelty toys specified in the Dangerous Substances and Preparations (Safety) (Consolidation) Regulations 1994. These Regulations also adopt an approach commonly seen in product safety regulations which is to prohibit the use of materials as a component or ingredient for certain limited classes of products (*e.g.* benzene in toys). A more significant example of this latter approach is found in the Asbestos Products (Safety) Regulations 1985 which restrict the supply of asbestos, not entirely but by reference to certain types of asbestos compounds and in relation to specified application only. These Regulations also contain requirements for labelling for products containing asbestos, another common approach found also, for example, in the Nightwear (Safety) Regulations 1985.

The Nightwear (Safety) Regulations 1985 provided an example of another approach taken in regulations which is to lay down criteria for safety (in this case flammability performance requirements) the criteria for which are contained in a British Standard; the standard is effectively incorporated by reference and made a statutory requirement. A similar approach it taken in the Pushchair (Safety) Regulations 1985 whereby it is an offence to supply a pushchair failing to comply with the requisite British Standard. These regulations are short and straightforward, but a variation on this approach is found in the Plugs and Sockets, etc. (Safety) Regulations 1994 which incorporate a number of standards for plugs, fuses and socket outlets, but which go on to require type approval or an equivalent level of safety by using alternative methods of construction because these implement the European Low Voltage Directive.[31] Provisions are laid down for appointment of notified bodies and procedures where notified bodies refuse, cancel or impose conditions on approvals. There are also requirements laid down in relation to the provision and information on labelling. There is a general prohibition on supplying any appliances unless correctly fitted with a standard plug meeting the requirements of the regulations.

The approach taken in the Plugs and Sockets, etc. (Safety) Regulations 1994 demonstrates the way in which wide-ranging regulatory requirements may be imposed, but this approach is developed further in regulations implementing the European New Approach Directives; these Regulations are meant to provide a comprehensive code under which the products in question meet the defined *essential requirements* as has been discussed earlier in Chapter 3. There is an important distinc-

[31] Council Directive 73/23/EEC on harmonisation of the laws of the member states of the European Economic Community relating to electrical equipment designed for use with certain voltage limits as amended by Council Directive 93/68/EEC.

tion to be made here, however, in legal basis for the regulations implementing new approach directives which is that they are not made pursuant to section 11 of the Consumer Protection Act 1987 but rather under section 2(2) of the European Communities Act 1972. The practical differences that this might entail are reduced by virtue of the fact that the enforcement provisions generally incorporate by reference powers which are available to trading standards officers in relation to consumer products generally, but there is not exact equivalence and the enforcement powers need to be checked.[32]

The role of standards

The CPA 1987 contained provisions whereby safety standards could be approved formally.[33] Once approved such standards were not mandatory for producers but became the yardstick for determining whether relevant products complied with the general safety requirements, and more importantly compliance with the standards afforded a complete defence against prosecution under the Act as regards relevant features of the product concerned. Sixty-five British Standards were so approved between 1987 and 1993, but the enabling provisions have those repealed[34] and the previous approvals cancelled. The automatic defence for producers complying with standards has therefore now gone. The standards themselves still exist and more will continue to be made. They retain an extremely important role in product safety for their *evidential* value in relation to proof of compliance or non-compliance with general safety requirements on account of the fact that published safety standards are relevant criteria under the GPS Regulations for the statutory tests for compliance with the general safety requirement.[35]

THE OBLIGATIONS OF PRODUCERS AND GENERAL SAFETY REQUIREMENT

The GPS Directive has, as its basic proposition, a requirement that *producers shall be required to place only safe products on the market*, and this is termed the general safety requirement. There is a clear connection with the pre-existing U.K. law which contained the offence of supplying

[32] See Chap. 6 with regard to enforcement of New Approach Directives, and in particular the distinctions that have to be made between situations where products concerned are consumer products or products for use at work because the enforcement rules may differ accordingly.

[33] s.10(3)(b)(ii) and s.11(2)(f), (g) and (h), CPA 1987 and the Approval of Safety Standards Regulations 1987 (S.I. 1987 No. 1911).

[34] reg. 6(1) of the GPS Regulations.

[35] See reg. 10(2), GPS Regulations. The role of standards in evidencing compliance with the general safety requirement is considered further below, p.128.

consumer goods *which fail to comply with the general safety requirement*,[36] although in implementing the directive a fresh approach has been taken. The European language has been adopted, but the duty is expressed differently: regulation 7 of the GPS Regulations defines the general safety requirement in prohibitionary terms that *no producer shall place a product on the market unless the product is a safe product*.

This apparently simple and straightforward imperative does, however, require quite detailed examination; the terms used are subject to definitions which are based on those contained in the directive. The first issue for consideration is that of the identity of a producer for these purposes.

Who is a producer?

The GPS Regulations differ from Part II of the 1987 Act in that producers are defined as a class. This definition has similarities with the extended liability of persons other than producers in Part I of the 1987 Act,[37] so that it is possible to have two or more persons subject to producers' duties. Three main categories of people are deemed to be producers for the purposes of the GPS Regulations:

> "(a) the manufacturer of the product, when he is established in the Community, and includes any person presenting himself as the manufacturer by affixing to the product his name, trade mark or other distinctive mark, or the person who reconditions the product,
>
> (b) when the manufacturer is not established in the Community -
>
> (i) if the manufacturer does not have a representative established in the Community, the importer of the product;
>
> (ii) in all other cases, the manufacturer's representative; and
>
> (c) other professionals in the supply chain, insofar as their activities may affect the safety properties of a product placed on the market."[38]

Manufacturers within the U.K., or importers or representatives of foreign manufacturers placing a product on the market were previously covered by the general safety requirements applicable to suppliers under Part II of the 1987 Act. The GPS Regulations however extend the concept of producer into three new areas. First, as is the case with civil liability under Part I of the 1987 Act, the use of trade marks and brand names, and in particular own-brand names, can made the person applying such a mark or label into a producer, irrespective of the fact that such a person does not actually make the goods themselves. In such

[36] Consumer Protection Act 1987, s.10(1)(a). s.10(2) sets out the criteria against which compliance with the general safety criteria is to be measured.
[37] s.2(2), CPA 1987.
[38] reg. 2, GPS Regulations.

circumstances it may be necessary to ensure contractual arrangements are in place in order to exercise a degree of control over the actual manufacturer in order to protect against liability.[39] For a person to be treated as a producer for these purposes it is necessary however for there to be an element of holding himself out as a producer, so that merely endorsing a product or giving it some kind of "seal of approval" will not necessarily cause the legislation to apply. Where products are sold under franchise agreemets it will be necessary to examine the exact nature of the arrangements between the parties to determine if the franchisor is presenting himself as the manufacturer under the licensing arrangements for the brand name.

A person who carries out work to recondition a product will also be classed as a manufacturer which is a departure from the previous position under the 1987 Act where a specific defence was included for suppliers of secondhand goods to a charge of supplying products in contravention of the general safety requirements. A reconditioner could now in some circumstances face liability under the GPS Regulations for supplying a product which was faulty or of intrinsically unsafe design when first made or for defects which have arisen in prior use since he is effectively deemed a producer *ab initio*. However, where products are supplied with a view to being reconditioned they will not be covered by the regulations, as will be seen below when used and secondhand products are considered in more detail.

The last category of producer contained in the GPS Regulations definition is the most difficult to deal with. The term "other professionals in the supply chain" refers not to persons with recognised vocational qualifications as might be assumed by use the word "professional", but to any person carrying on a commercial activity in the broadest sense.[40] It is meant to restrict the ambit of the rules to a commercial supplier or retailer as opposed to a private seller or a volunteer giving products away.[41] The provision that such persons are producers "in so far as their activities may affect the safety properties of a product . . ." has been taken straight from the directive where there is no explanation of how the provision should operate. It would seem that such a person is not meant to have all the same obligations that a manufacturer would have since the phrase must be interpreted as qualifying their position as producer as being one limited to the extent of the possible effect on safety. What makes the interpretation par-

[39] Contractual arrangements will be a material consideration in relation to producers' duties under reg. 8 which are qualified to the extent that the matters concerned are "within the limits oof his activity". Contractual arrangements would not however protect an own-brander or a person whose name or mark is being used in relation to a contravention of the general safety requirement contained in reg. 7 which would appear to be absolute offence. For discussion of liability in relation to the use of marks and brands see M.L. Tyler, "Brands and Product Liability", *The Journal of Brand Management*, Vol. 1, No. 6, 1994.

[40] See the definition of "professional" in the DTI's Guidance (Appendix 7).

[41] The point is reinforced by the requirement for a supplier of products for the purposes of the regulations to be in the course of a commercial activity. See below, p.117.

ticularly uncertain however is that it refers to activities which *may* rather than *do* affect the safety of a product, which could mean that it will not always be possible to determine at a point of time anterior to the happening of an incident that a particular person was a producer for these purposes; this may be a question that can only be resolved *post hoc* when it has become clear that a person's activities did in fact affect safety of a product notwithstanding that there was no anticipation beforehand that they would do so.

The upshot is that it might be possible for someone having a contractual relationship with the actual manufacturer, such as a designer or someone supplying packaging materials, or even a consultant advising on labelling, to fall within the producer category on account of the potential for endangering consumers that would exist in relation to their work. On a strict interpretation, however, the regulations should not apply to service activities as such, since the person is not "in the supply chain" as this phrase is normally understood. It appears to be the case that in this limited sense a retailer, distributor or other intermediary (such as a carrier) might in the course of their activities affect the safety properties of a product, for example by storage at the wrong temperature, proximity to other goods which might taint or damage the product, or might simply damage it through mishandling or cause it to become separated from important safety instructions that are meant to accompany it. It does not appear to be within the overall scheme of the GPS Regulations that such a person should be deemed to have all the same responsibilitiies as the original manufacturer[42] but the responsibilities of such persons in relation to compliance with the general safety requirement are problematical and may require the Courts to rule on the interpretation of the legislation in order to be clarified. This may be so, for example, to resolve beyond any doubt whether arrangements such as commercial hiring make the hirer a producer for these purposes, and thus responsible as a principal for the safety of products and accompanying instructions for safe use. Under the 1987 Act various financing arrangements such as hire purchase and credit sale were subject to specific rules whereby the finance company would not be treated as the effective supplier of the goods concerned. There are no provisions in the GPS Regulations providing the same degree of certainty.[43]

What products are covered?

The definition of "product" in Regulation 2 of the GPS Regulations is:

> "any product intended for consumers or likely to be used by consumers, supplied whether for consideration or not in the course of a commercial activity and whether new, used or reconditioned

[42] The qualification in reg. 8 as to the duty being "within the limits of his activity".
[43] s.46(2), CPA 1987. See also the discussion on "distributors" below, p.138.

provided, however, a product which is used exclusively in the context of a commercial activity even if it is used by a consumer shall not be regarded as a product for the purposes of these Regulations provided always and for the avoidance of doubt this exception shall not extend to the supply of any such product to a consumer."

This definition involves some circularity by itself using the word "product", although it is unlikely that there would be much confusion over what is meant.[44] The important point about the definition of a product for the purposes of the Regulations is that it is restricted to consumer products. The term "consumer" is defined (again with circularity) in regulation 2 as meaning: "A consumer acting otherwise than in the course of a commercial activity".

Products purely for private use by individual consumers are obviously covered. The regulations can apply to the full range of such products, without distinguishing in any way between them in terms of product-type, or whether or not they have been subject to processing. This contrasts with Parts I and II of the 1987 Act which both contain exclusionary provisions. As will be seen below, exclusions of products are made in less explicit manner by reference to other safety directives.

There are nevertheless a number of grey areas where an element of consumer involvement in use may exist. Two tests are given in the regulations: (a) products which are *intended* for consumers; or (b) products which are *likely to be* used by consumers. The intention test, test (a), appears to revolve around the subjective intention of the manufacturer, or possibly the person who places the product on the market. Did that person intend the product for use by consumers? Even so, a manufacturer's denial that the product was intended for consumers is unlikely to be conclusive of the issue, certainly after the event. An element of objectivity based on the evidence of what ought to have been expected to be the ultimate destination of the product in question is likely to sway the court's decision.[45] Evidence in marketing materials or information in the written instructions for use that the product was intended for consumers (*e.g.* advertisements directed at consumers) will obviously be relevant. Accordingly, manufacturers may consider whether they want their product to be intended for or used by consumers, or not, and look more closely at the implications of drawing up express statements of the intended purpose and use of this product (as they are usually required to do anyway in order to comply with the essential requirements of product-specific technical directives).

The likelihood test (b) (is the product likely to be used by consumers?) involves a more ostensible objective assessment by the court than the first test, although the evidence of the subjective expectations of the

[44] It may be of some assistance that "product" is defined in standard EN 29001, adopting the definition in ISO 8402, the international standard of definitions, as "the result of activities or processes (tangible product; intangible product, such as a service, a computer program, a design, directions for use), . . ."

[45] See *Ross v. Moss* [1965] 3 All E.R. 145.

manufacturer that he (reasonably) did not expect the product to be used by consumers will be relevant. The manufacturer might escape under test (a) because "intent" cannot be proven, but fail under test (b) because he suspected or connived in marketing to consumers.

There are difficulties with the notion of consumer products in the scheme of these regulations. One relates to products that are used in the course of a business but which are available for use by the members of the public if they choose such as lifts in department stores and public transport vehicles. Another is in relation to products which have dual uses — in business as well as for consumers — for example tins of paints, light bulbs, lawmowers or computers. Components and spare parts are also problematical.

The fifth recital to the Directive addressed these issues in general terms:

> "Whereas production equipment, capital goods and other products used exclusively in the context of a trade or business are not covered by this Directive".

The intention to exclude products which consumers never encounter is clear enough. This clearly covers much industrial machinery. This recital was inserted after insistence by the United Kingdom in order to narrow the scope of the Directive and give more legal certainty. The GPS Regulations seek to clarify the position further by the inclusion in the definition of product qualification (not expressly written in the Directive) that excludes a product used "exclusively in the course of a commercial activity even if used by a consumer". The approach in the U.K. therefore is to confine these new safety rules to products meant for private use or consumption — precisely the same position as under the pre-existing law.[46] Products used commercially in supplying a *service* to consumers — for example, buses, trains, aircraft, lifts and escalators, are therefore not included. This does not rule out the application of the GPS Regulations to "dual use" products such as the personal computer or tins of paint. While suppliers to business users will be subject to control under separate work product safety legislation[47] suppliers to consumers will fall inside the ambit of the GPS Regulations. An example given in the DTI guidance is a car cleaning product supplied to a customer to take home for private use. Use by a car valet service of the same would not be within the GPS Regulations.[48]

The status of products which are supplied as components for incorportion into a finished consumer product, or which are supplied as spares or accessories is rather less clear. Such products which are

[46] s.10(7), Consumer Protection Act 1987 provides that ". . . 'consumer goods' means any goods which are ordinarily intended for private use or consumption . . .".

[47] See Chap. 6.

[48] See Appendix 7. This example demonstrates the producers possible difficulty in knowing if his products are "likely to be used by consumers" for the purposes of defining a "consumer product", as there will often be no control over the ultimate use of the product.

available in the market place for consumers to purchase and fit "consumer products" are within the meaning of the GPS Regulations. It is also arguable that a component for manufacture or assembly of a new product or for repair or maintenance of an existing product (*e.g.* a replacement gearbox for a car) is itself "intended for consumers"; the definition refers to *any* product which would suggest this broad interpretation is correct. When applied to raw materials and certain high volume components (*e.g.* timber, screws, or computer chips) which may be used in very many types of production processes which the manufacturers do not control this analysis seems unsatisfactory. In principle, however, manufacturers of such products should be subject to the same basic duties of safety as other producers,[49] albeit a duty qualified by what it is reasonable for them to foresee and to do in relation to risks the products may give rise to.[50]

Products subject to specific Community safety provision

Having established that a product is subject to the GPS Regulations on account of its nature and purpose, the other critical question is whether it is already subject to safety requirements contained in E.C. law. The GPS Directive is intended to complement rather than duplicate other existing product safety rules made at the level of European law. This has to be considered in two stages. First, is there Community law with specific provisions governing *all* aspects of the safety of the product?[51] If so, then result is that the GPS Regulations are wholly inapplicable, and reference need be made only to whatever U.K. Act or Regulation implements the relevant E.C. provisions. The difficulty here is determining whether safety aspects are dealt with *in toto* by the sectoral directives; it would seem to be the case with the New Approach Directives for products such as for machinery, medical devices, and Personal Protective Equipment. If, however, these directives have not anticipated a particular safety issue or type of risk, or if certain products are excluded from their scope or are subject to transitional provisions that exclude second-hand goods, the GPS Regulations are meant to fill the gap that would exist by applying the general safety requirement.

This is achieved by the second stage of the analysis, when the question is whether there are provisions of Community law which apply to the product even though they are not exhaustive of the safety requirements. The GPS Regulations apply to such a product only *in so far as those provisions do not make specific provision governing an aspect of the safety of the product*.[52] The operation of these provisions has been

[49] See regulation 8.

[50] The definition of a product for Pt. I of the CPA 1987 avoids these difficulties by including within the meaning "a product which is comprised in another product, whether by virtue of being a component part or raw material or otherwise" (s.1(2)).

[51] reg. 3(c).

[52] reg. 4.

examined more fully in Chapter 2, and it should be emphasised that there is no single test or method for determining whether or not the GPS Regulations are ousted by more product-specific rules: a detailed analysis of the rules and the risks the products may have is needed. Reference may be made to **Table 4.2** in Chapter 4 listing the main E.C. Directives which deal with specific risks, but this cannot be taken as conclusive of whether or not the GPS Regulations will have some bearing on any given product. The GPS Regulations were however subject to an amendment made soon after they were made, by virtue of which medicinal products for human use (to which the Medicines for Human Use Marketing Authorisations Etc Regulations 1994 apply) are wholly excluded from the scope of the GPS Regulations.[53] This is a unique class of product the safety of which has been formally identified in legislation as being covered fully by the E.C. legislation on medicines.

Supply in the course of commercial activity

It is clear from the wording of the Directive that it only applies to a product which is supplied in the course of commercial activity. It is irrelevant for these purposes whether or not the product is supplied for consideration, *i.e.* in exchange for money or money's worth. A free gift supplied with a product or a promotional sample given by a sales representative to a potential customer would both be covered as they were supplied in the course of a commercial activity.

It would seem at first sight that the product must actually have been supplied in order to come under the GPS Regulations. This result would conflict with the policy objective of keeping unsafe products off the market in the first place but is is dealt with by regulation 13 which makes it an offence to expose or possess a dangerous product for placing on the market or supply or to offer or agree to supply or place on the market such a product. It would not however be an offence merely to possess with a view to display only as samples or at exhibitions or trade fairs (as long as they are not made available to consumers),[54] store indefinitely or to dispose of a dangerous product, subject to any specific regulatory requirements being met for storage or disposal.

The need for there to be a commercial activity raises the question of charities, supplies made by voluntary organisations, or one-off fund-

[53] See reg. 1(2), which was introduced by the Medicines for Human Use (Marketing Authorisations) Etc Regulations 1994, Sched. 7, para. 21. The Marketing Authorisations for Veterinary Medicinal Products Regulations 1994 do not wholly exclude the GPS Regulations but apply the enforcement provisions of the Medicines Act 1968 instead of those under the CPA 1987.

[54] See para. 15 of the DTI Guidance for Business, Consumers and Enforcement Authorities, Appendix 7, an interpretation derived from the European Commission's Guide to the implementation of Community harmonisation directives based on the new approach and global approach (First Revision, 1994).

raising events. The fact that the activity may be for charitable purposes is unlikely to be decisive since it may still be of a business nature.[55] It will be a question of degree in each case as to what constitutes commercial activity; jam-making for a church fete is unlikely to be covered, but products supplied through a charity shop probably are subject to the regulations. The position of companies making donations of new products or giving away unwanted equipment is also not clear. Supplying products for such purposes at a discounted price would still be a supply. In the broadest sense pure gifts made for benevolent purposes would still appear to be supplied in the course of a commercial activity, even if they are made as an alternative to scrapping or destroying the products.

Second-hand products and products for repair/re-conditioning

The definition or product expressly states that the product may be new, used or reconditioned when it is supplied. However, the GPS Regulations do not apply to:

(a) second-hand products supplied as antiques;
(b) products supplied for the purpose of repair or reconditioning before use, provided the supplier clearly informs the person to whom he supplies the product to that effect.[56]

For antiques to be exempt they must be second-hand. Under the wording of the directive it is not entirely clear whether, as an additional requirement for the exclusion of antiques, the supplier must positively indicate that the product supplied is in fact a second-hand antique, or whether the information requirement only applies to the repair situation. The GPS Regulations wording does not have the requirement. It seems also that if supplied *as* antique the exemption may apply even if in reality the product is of more recent origin, or even fake. The regulations are unambiguous in these respects.[57]

The exclusion of products (whether or not second-hand) supplied as products to be repaired or reconditioned prior to being used is contingent upon the supplier *clearly* informing the person to whom he supplies the product that they are supplied second-hand to be repaired or reconditioned prior to being used. The intention is that suppliers should specify clearly on commercial invoices that the product cannot be used in its present state. A notice at the point of sale or in an advert might serve well enough to exempt the supply but the DTI's guidance

[55] A similar difficulty has arisen in interpreting the meaning of 'business' for the purposes of statutory security of tenure under the Landlord and Tenant Act 1954. See, *e.g. Parkes v. Westminster Roman Catholic Diocese Trustee* (1978) P. & C.R. 22, C.A.

[56] reg. 3(a) and (b).

[57] The DTI's guidance suggests that "working definition" of antique is a product which is 100 years old, or which is of a type which has long gone out of circulation and as such is unlikely to be used by a consumer for its original purpose (see Appendix 7.).

advises cautiously that consumers should be informed specifically on each transaction (see Appendix 7, para. 16). Some concern has been expressed that suppliers of, for example, dangerous second-hand cars, may be able to avoid regulatory action by stating that the car is not roadworthy and is to be repaired prior to use, when the reality is that they will be used with no or minimal repair. (A number of types of products are subject to specific regulations which cover second-hand as well as new supplies, and so cannot be sold unless they meet the relevant safety requirements (*e.g.* toys, electrical and gas appliances).[58])

Where the exemption applies, whatever faults may have existed at the time of supply will not be the responsibility of the supplier. Where does the general safety requirement lie in the case of the ultimate supply of these products after repair or reconditioning? The manufacturer or other producer will be responsible for any original defects. The definition of producer expressly covers someone who, if he is not the manufacturer, reconditions the product. The mere "repairer" only provides a service to the owner and is arguably not within the producer definition as he can be said to be "a professional in the supply chain".[59]

Safe and dangerous products

The basic requirement of the GPS Regulations is that producers observe what the general safety requirement.[60] The general safety requirement is supplemented by regulation 8 and a number of specific requirements on the way producers carry on business but before examining that it is necessary to examine the basic concepts involved, namely the definitions of safety and risk.

The concept of risk

For these purposes, a product is either safe or dangerous, since a dangerous product is defined as meaning any product which does not meet the definition of "safe product". In reality, safety is a relative concept, not an absolute and there is no such thing as a safe product. The ISO/IEC guidelines for the inclusion of safety aspects in standards state:

> "Safety is a balance between freedom from risks of harm and other demands to be met by a product, process or service among which such items as utility, suitability for purpose, and the like are included.
>
> There can be no absolute safety. Even at the highest level of safety, a product, process or service can only be relatively safe. The conven-

[58] See DTI Guidance, Appendix 7, paragraph 18.

[59] A person repairing in the course of a business would, however be subject to s.3 of the Health and Safety at Work Act 1974 insofar as his undertaking creates risks to the safety of persons not in his employment.

[60] reg. 7.

> tions of society, including levels of safety or degrees of risk, are subject to changes. In this respect decision-making is based on two interrelated considerations: evaluating the risk and judging the safety.
>
> ***Evaluating risk*** — assessing the probability of harm, the magnitude of the consequent injury by identifying the characteristics and the likely conditions of use relevant to safety and means of quantifying them — is an empirical scientific activity.
>
> ***Judging safety*** — assessing the acceptability of risks — is an activity associated with such factors as the socio-economic and educational background of the society concerned, and whether design, or manufacturing processes, could play a role in increasing safety.
>
> As safety will pose different problems it is impossible to provide a set of precise provisions and recommendations that will apply in every case."[61]

Consistent with this approach, the Directive defines the safety of a product by adopting the terminology of risk. The Commission believed that the concept of risk was "sufficiently flexible to cover any product, without unreasonably restricting its marketing and further development — including those products which are said to bear an inherent risk".[62] It is therefore surprising that such a fundamental concept as that of risk was not defined in the legislation. A definition is given in ISO 8402 as:

> "the chance, in quantitative terms of a defined hazard occurring. It therefore combines a probabilistic measure of the occurrence of the primary event(s) with a measure of the consequences of that/those event(s). Criteria for acceptability of some predicted risk or measured risk can be set voluntarily by the organisation responsible and/or subjected to the hazard, or be set mandatorily by some regulatory organisation".

Accordingly, risk is defined in that standards as:

> "A combination of the probability, or frequency, of occurrence of a defined hazard and the magnitude of the consequences of the occurrence."

Another definition of risk is given in the ISO/IEC guidelines:

> "The probable rate of occurrence of a hazard causing harm and the degree of the severity of the harm."

Both these definitions of risk refer to hazard and these two concepts should not be confused.[63] The definition of hazard in ISO 8402 refers to a situation or "the potential for adverse consequences of some primary

[61] Ref. No. ISO/IEC Guide 51: 1990 E.
[62] Explanatory Note COM (89) 162/6.
[63] See also Chap. 6 where risk is discussed further in the light of the Courts' interpretation of the use of the word in the Health and Safety at Work Act 1974.

event, sequence of events or combination of circumstances". The ISO/IEC Guide 51 defines hazard simply as "A potential source of harm".

The GPS Regulations criteria for safety

The GPS Regulations mirror the Directive, and adopt — without definition — the term risk:

> "'Safe product' means any product which under normal or reasonably foreseeable conditions of use, including duration, does not present any risk or only the minimum risks compatible with the product's use, considered as acceptable and consistent with a high level of protection for the safety and health of persons, taking into account in particular—
>
> (a) the characteristics of the product, including its composition, packaging, instructions for assembly and maintenance;
>
> (b) the effect on other products, where it is reasonably foreseeable that it will be used with other products;
>
> (c) the presentation of the product, the labelling, any instructions for its use and disposal and any other indication or information provided by the producer; and
>
> (d) the categories of consumers at serious risk when using the product, in particular children.
>
> and the fact that higher levels of safety may be obtained or other products presenting a lesser degree of risk may be available shall not of itself cause the product to be considered other than a safe product."[64]

A product must, therefore, present either no risk or the "minimum risks" as defined. The relevant risks are of personal injury, since the risk of damage to property or economic loss which are coupled with personal injury were outside the purposes of the GPS Regulations.[65]

Acceptable risk

The test to be applied in deciding whether the risks are acceptable should be an objective one. The opinions of consumers or of producers will not be decisive in any individual case but might be persuasive evidence of the prevailing standards of safety. Standards and perceptions of safety do vary over time. For example, it may be acceptable for cars not to be fitted with rear seat belts or inflatable impact bags or anti-roll-over bars at a certain point in time but not acceptable at some subsequent time once technical and/or public perception of the risks has changed.

In this respect, the test of a dangerous product under the GPS Regulations is similar to the test of a defective product under Part I of

[64] reg. 2, GPS Regulations.

[65] s.5(1) compare of the CPA 1987 which gives an extended meaning to "damage" that includes damage to property.

the CPA 1987, which is based on the safety persons generally are entitled to expect. Both are ultimately objective, and both set out similar criteria to be taken into account. It is debatable to what extent there is a difference between the concepts or results obtained in applying tests of an "acceptable risk" or an "expectation of safety". The former might be influenced by the expression of detailed expert opinions on extensive scientific data, formal risk analysis techniques and what amounts to "a high level of protection", whereas the latter concept is much simpler and seems to depend less on extensive expert analysis.[66]

What factors may be taken into account in determining whether the risks associated with a product are acceptable or not? The Regulations list four indications but but do not give a definitive answer to this question.

Normal and foreseeable risks

Risks that only arise in conditions of use which are not normal or not reasonably foreseeable are not to be taken into consideration for the purposes of conformity with the general safety requirement. Accordingly, this excludes risks which arise in abnormal use or abuse or misuse of the product, *provided* none of these are reasonably foreseeable. A producer will be aware of the intended use of the product but he must also take into consideration any reports which he may subsequently receive of mis-use or abnormal use. Once he is aware of this he should not avoid the information but should consider whether such use gives rise to any risks which are previously unidentified or are more serious than he previously thought, and take appropriate steps such as issuing warnings.[67]

This disregard of risks arising from abnormal or unforeseeable use should, however, be seen in context of other provisions of the Regulations which include obligations on producers to provide consumers with information to assess risks which are *not* immediately obvious without adequate warnings. This wording here is not restricted to risks which arise in normal or reasonably foreseeable conditions of use and appears to relate to all possible risks. The courts will expect a high standard from manufacturers and other suppliers, and will not readily accept that they could not have been expected to have appreciated particular risks.[68]

Duration of use

A product must be acceptable throughout its reasonably foreseeable *duration* of use. As the performance of products may decrease with age

[66] The word safe is defined for the purposes of Pt. I of the Comsumer Protection Act 1987 in s.19 as meaning "no risk or no risk apart from one reduced to the minimum . . ." so the two tests are in fact more closely related than it might at first appear.

[67] See Chap. 9 and 10 for discussions of actions involving warnings and product recall in such circumstances.

[68] See the cases cited below in connection with the due diligence defence, p.156 *et seq*.

and risk may increase or occur over time a producer would be well advised to specify in the labelling for the product such matters as the intended shelf life of the product, its intended life in use, requirements for periodic maintenance or servicing, whether it is for single use only, and so on.

Use and non-use

The definition of a safe product specifically refers to conditions of *use*.[69] This might be taken to mean that the only relevant risks are those which arise during actual use of the product, such as when it is in operation. However, it would not be safe to assume that risks which only arise during transport or storage, such as contamination or leakage when the product is not being used, should be ignored. While it is arguable that under the strict interpretation of this wording in the GPS Regulations risks arising outside the context of actual use are not relevant this does not accord with the policy of the GPS Directive,[70] and the references to maintenance and disposal later in the GPS definition do in any event imply that it is the full potential of a product to do harm throughout its lifetime that should be taken into account in determining the issue of safety.

Factors to be considered

As stated above, the Regulations specify certain *particular* points which — though not intended to be the only factors — are to be taken into account in determining whether the risks are acceptable.[71] The specified factors, which are quoted in full above, can be summarised as:

- the characteristics of the product;
- the presentation of the product;
- the effect on other products;
- the categories of consumers.

Characteristics This concerns a product's most basic qualities and performance, and would be the main consideration in situtations where there is a design defect, unsatisfactory components or ingredients, or a fault introduced in the manufacturing or assembly process, so that whatever the conditions of use the product is dangerous. Often this aspect of test of safety can be determined empirically by analysis of materials or testing in operation, with the resulting existence, or absence, of risk as the case may be being observed. In contrast with the

[69] Compare s.6 of the Health and Safety at Work Act where the safety requirements extend to maintenance cleaning and (for chemicals) transportation and disposal. See Chap. 6.
[70] In any event, these aspects are usually included in the essential requirements of New Approach Directives.
[71] This acceptability test and the factors specified are similar to those of the expectation test of defectiveness in Directive 85/374/EEC on product liability.

other three factors considered here, the issue focuses on the intrinsic qualities of the product itself.

Presentation The main considerations here are proper instructions and warnings on how to use the product safely and avoid particular hazards. These must be viewed in the light of the obligations in regulation 8, which require producers to provide consumers with the relevant information to enable them to assess the risks inherent in a product throughout the normal or reasonably foreseeable period of use, and to take precautions against them. On the other hand, warnings are not always necessary, for example where the dangerous characteristic is obvious to the user, such as the risk of cutting with kitchen knives.[72] Aside from warnings and instructions there is the broader consideration of any "indications" by the producer, which could be a positive recommendation or any indirect suggestion (such as demonstrating the use of the product in a particular context in an advertisement or by images on the package or at the point of sale). There may be situations where the applicaton of the "presentation" factor in determining safety cannot provide a satisfactory result. For example instructions for assembly or use provided may be very poorly presented but the product may have such a low level of risk that it would still be considered acceptable from the perspective of safety, albeit quite unacceptable as being unfit for its purpose, or the risk in question does not materialise, for example a fault in electrical equipment which "fails safe". The opposite of this situation is, however, much more problematical: how should products be viewed when they pose a serious risk of injury, but the producer gives an explicit warning to this effect which he would claim "cures" a danger if there is one. A common situation is an instruction for correct usage which if followed makes a product very difficult to operate and is thus likely to be ignored or forgotten by a consumer. The answer would seem to be that best practice is that the design of a product should aim to eliminate foreseeable risks as far as is possible, and warnings, or instructions will generally only be sufficient to render a product safe where they address unavoidable residual risks. This approach was put forcefully by a judge dealing with a case under the Toys (Safety) Regulations 1989[73] involving the question whether a label was sufficient to deal with a risk of suffocation, who expressed the view that labelling is relevant to cases where there are inherent risks which cannot be completely eliminated by modifying the construction and composition without altering a product's function or depriving it of its essential

[72] reg. 8 of the GPS Regulations does not require information to be provided to consumers where the risks are "immediately obvious".

[73] Now revoked and replaced by the Toys (Safety) Regulations 1995.

properties.[74] This proposition cannot, however, be taken as fully describing the duty as the statutory test to be applied is determined ultimately by what is "acceptable"; this means that there must be a degree of interplay between the presentation factors and the consideration of the material *characteristics* of the product, as well as possibly other factors too. This is the case, for example, where a range of products may be on the market with varying characteristics such as optional extra safety features. Here there may be a minimum threshold for acceptability, but the "safest" product specification does not necessarily represent the minimum acceptable risk. (The implications of "safer" products being marketed are considered more fully below.) The proposition above would also need to be qualified for situations where consumers purchase products with knowledge of real (or possibly for that matter claimed) risks they might pose.

Effect on other products Again, the focus is on what a consumer does with a product rather than any specific defect. Examples of inter-action between products which results in a new hazard would be the use of a toilet cleaner that might react with bleach, or the fitting of a certain engine component that might be suitable for some models of car but not others. Nevertheless, these products taken individually are safe and useful and their inherent risks in combination cannot in practice be reduced by a producer other than by clear labelling. In *Whirlpool (U.K.) Ltd and Magnet Ltd v. Gloucestershire County Council*,[75] the importers and retailers of an extraction hood purchased with a gas cooker were convicted of an offence against the general safety requirements because the hood was liable to overheat and burn in proximity to the cooker. This is in fact the reverse of the situation posited by the phrase in the GPS Regulations here, as it concerned an effect *from* another product rather than *on* another product, but in principle the test would work in the same way. The defendants failed to persuade the court that the hood's compliance with the relevant electrical equipment safety regulations and British Standards was sufficient to meet the legal duty; this was held to be relevant only to the issues of intrinsic qualities and safety of the hoods, and not being enough to meet the duty as regards risks of arising from interaction with the other product.

[74] Buckley J. in *R. v. Felixstowe Magistrates ex parte Top Toys Ltd*, CO/67/93 (unreported). This is a decision based entirely on the interpretation of the wording of the Toys (Safety) Regulations 1989 which describes "general principles" for safety (see Sched. 2 of the Regulations) and did not involve an interpretation of a general safety requirement. Nevertheless the general principles contained in Sched. 2 would seem to be appropriate to any product, and so the dicta in the case are of wider application than just toys. The judge went on to opine that prohibitions of certain "particular risks" referred to later in the Schedule (in this case risk of suffocation) had to be viewed as absolute in that a label or warning would not be sufficient to discharge the duty not to supply toys which carried that risk.

[75] Unreported. Divisional Court. December 13, 1993 Co/d 1359/93. The decision is summarised in *Product Liability International*, July 1994 p.107. See also the discussion below concerning the due diligence defence, p.156.

Categories of consumer A product might be unsafe where it may be used by particular categories of consumer such as children or the elderly, even where it was not even intended for them. Special precautions might be needed to render the product safe. For example, bottles nowadays incorporate child-resistant caps, and the availability of certain medicines is restricted to sale by a pharmacist or only on a doctor's prescription.[76] These are examples of the situation where the product is safe — and beneficial — when used normally, as intended, but the producer is aware of misuse and is obliged to take measures to prevent the risks. There is again overlap between the criteria here, in that warnings to parents or carers may be relevant.

A limit is placed on the acceptability of the safety of the product. The risks must not only be acceptable but they must be consistent with the overall policy requirement, set out in Article 100a(3) of the EEC Treaty of ensuring that "a high level of protection of the safety and health of persons". For example, it may be that a product includes a high level of risk which is acceptable because it is warned about but which would still not be consistent with the requirement for a high level of protection of the safety and health of persons. The courts may for instance treat certain equipment as especially hazardous and subject to high safety standards.[77]

The Regulations provide that the feasibility of obtaining higher levels of safety is not itself to be taken as a reason for considering a product to be dangerous; this contrasts with the pre-existing provisions of the CPA 1987 which included, as a factor to consider in judging safety, the existence of any means by which it would have been reasonable for goods to have been made safer.[78] It will not, therefore, necessarily be relevant that a hazard could have been eradicated or reduced in a product by a design change: the test of safety is an objective one of an assessment of the level of risks involved and their acceptability. Where a hazard exists, this does not mean that the product will automatically be dangerous for the purposes of the law. Some risks are inevitably inherent in some products (*e.g.* chain saws, explosives, motor vehicles) and the products would not be useful or desirable without the features which give rise to those risks. A legitimate aim of Community policy is to enhance consumer choice and this implies that consumers should have choice between a cheaper product which may incorporate fewer safety features and a more expensive product which may incorporate more safety features. Indeed, the goal of consumer choice is not well served by insisting that all products must incorporate every conceivable safety feature so that they become prohibitively expensive and hence generally unavailable.

[76] Directive 92/26/EEC and Medicines Act 1968, s.51.

[77] See, *e.g. R. v. Board of Trustees of the Science Museum* [1993] 3 All E.R. 853, [1993] 1 W.L.R. 1171, a case decided under s.3 of the Health and Safety at Work Act 1974 where the court inferred that air conditioning equipment is extra hazardous on account of the potential to disperse harmful legionella bacteria.

[78] s.10(2)(c), CPA 1987.

The Regulations do not deal with the converse of this point, which is that the absence of *other* safer products might be taken as evidence of acceptable risk. It may be that considerations of feasibility and prohibitive cost making such a product safer might still legitimately be considered in concluding that a product is a "safe product", but this cannot be conclusive as it would result in a situation where the level of safety of novel products or adaptors of an existing design could effectively pre-empt the test of safety by being first on the market.

Evaluation criteria for assessment of conformity with the general safety requirement

It has been said above that where specific rules of Community law contain provisions imposing safety requirements on the products which they govern, those provisions govern the safety of the product and the general safety requirement and relevant obligations under the GPS Regulations do not apply. In those situations the evaluation criteria are tailored to the products concerned by the specific Community rules.

Where there are no specific Community provisions governing the safety of a product, the assessment of conformity of a product with the general safety requirement is to be carried out in accordance with the hierarchy of criteria specified in regulation 10. Whereas conformity assessment with the essential requirements of the specific technical directives has to take place *before* a product is placed on the market and may bear the CE marking, in contrast, no product needs to be assessed for conformity to the general safety requirement as a pre-condition of being legally placed on the market, nor does it have to carry any conformity mark. (Indeed it must not bear the CE marking unless this relates specifically to an aspect covered by a New Approach Directive, such as electromagnetic compatibility.[79])

To the extent to which the general safety requirements apply to a producer, they are only likely to be checked officially when an enforcement authority decides to scrutinise a particular product. The issue of conformity with the GPS requirements will therefore only be likely to arise where the enforcement authority receives information, whether from its own market surveillance, or testing, or from an outside source, that a product already in circulation is unsafe.

Conformity with national law

The first way to demonstrate compliance with the general safety requirement under the GPS Regulations is hierarchy in terms of conformity with product safety regulations. Regulation 10(1) provides that:

> "Where in relation to any product such product conforms to the specific rules of the United Kingdom laying down the health and

[79] See the CE Marking Directive (93/68/EEC).

safety requirements which the product must satisfy in order to be marketed there should be a presumption that, until the contrary is proved, the product is a safe product".

There are some significant departures here from the source wording of the Directive, under which a product shall be *deemed* (not just presumed) safe when it conforms to the specific rules of national law of the Member State in whose territory the product is in circulation, where such rules are in conformity with the EEC Treaty, in particular Articles 30 and 36 of the Treaty of Rome on the elimination of quantitative restrictions on imports between Member States, and lay down the health and safety requirements which the product must satisfy in order to be marketed.[80]

So, under the GPS Regulations conformity of a product with national law is not necessarily by itself sufficient: a pram could, for example, comply fully with the relevant specific U.K. regulations yet fail to meet the general safety requirement, either for a particular reason not covered by the regulations such as a protruding sharp edge, or even because notwithstanding compliance there remained an "unacceptable risk 'not consistent with a high level of protection' ".[81]

Standards and codes

In the absence of Community or national rules governing safety, the conformity of a product to the general safety requirement is to be assessed having regard to the criteria set out in regulation 10(2). The stipulation of these criteria is intended not to leave the general safety requirement too open to arbitrary discretion but related to some means that allows the degree of safety to be examined in the light of official and objective criteria and of practical and available technology.[82] The criteria for assessing conformity are as follows:

"(i) voluntary national standards of the United Kingdom giving effect to a European standard; or

[80] Art. 4.1. Even if the GPS Directive's terminology were used instead there is still uncertainty about the interpretation of a product being *deemed safe*. On one approach, a court could conclude that a product is safe for the purposes of the GPS Directive where it conforms to national law *even* where it might be shown that the product would otherwise be unsafe measured against the general safety requirement when directly applied. In other words, the deemed compliance with the general safety requirement would be legally irrebuttable. But this approach is inconsistent with the safeguard clause in Art. 4.3 of the Directive which empowers a Member State to impose restrictions on a product being placed on the market or to require its withdrawal from the market where there is evidence that "despite conformity" with the general safety requirement it is dangerous, and Art. 6.1 which requires action to be taken against dangerous products. It would, of course, be unappealing for an enforcement authority to try and demonstrate that its own national law is defective or inadequate in this way.

[81] Constrast with s.10(3)(b)(i) of the CPA 1987, giving a defence of compliance with a product specific regulation. See also *Whirlpool (U.K.) Ltd and Magnet Ltd v. Gloucestershire County Council, supra.*

[82] Explanatory Note, COM (89) 162/6.

(ii) Community technical specifications; or
(iii) if there are no such voluntary national standards of the United Kingdom or Community technical specifications—
(aa) standards drawn up in the United Kingdom;
(bb) the codes of good practice in respect of health and safety in the product sector concerned; or
(cc) the state of the art and technology;

and the safety which consumers may reasonably expect."

These criteria are listed as alternatives and in an order which follows a logical hierarchy of descending importance. It is unclear from the wording of the Regulations as to what relative weight should be given to each of these assessment criteria. It is presumed that the last sentence is intended to apply in all cases under (i)–(iii) and not as a discrete test of safety in its own right[83] with the result that there is no more than a rebuttable presumption that conformity with any of the criteria means the product is safe. If a product that conforms with a UK safety regulation can still be classed legally "dangerous" then *a fortiori* so should a product meeting a standard; a consistent approach should however emerge because the criteria in Regulation 10(2) are expressed as matters "to be taken into account" in assessing conformity with the general safety requirement; conformity with a standard does not automatically deem a product safe, as the wider test under the definition of a "safe product" may still remain unsatisfied.[84]

The interplay between U.K. and European product rules and standards that arises under regulations 10 and 4 is far from straightforward. The diversity of harmonised, European and national standards can inevitably give rise to confusion and uncertainty in individual cases. For example, a national standard may set a more stringent safety requirement than the comparable European standard (such as the height of the backs of babies' highchairs and a requirement for harness attachment points). Conversely, the European standard may be more stringent or different (examples include bunk beds and step ladders). Moreover, no special significance would be attached by regulation 10 to the fact that a product conforms with statutory requirements or recognised standards of European States other than the U.K. (or any other foreign country for that matter). To be reliant as a producer on compliance with say a French recognised voluntary standard could therefore be problematical, unless such a producer is satisfied that no higher standards exists elsewhere and the standard used represents the state of the art. As more and more European standards and specifications are adopted this diversity issue should become gradually simpler, but in the meantime producers may feel compelled to err on the side of caution and take U.K.

[83] The wording of Art. 4.2 of the Directive is also unclear on this point.

[84] See, for example, *Balding v. Lew Ways Ltd, The Times,* March 9, 1995, where compliance with BS 5665 did not render a toy safe for the purposes of the Toys (Safety) Regulations 1989: "The company was not entitled to assume British Standards complied with the requirements laid down by Parliament."

recognised standards as their norms for products sold in the home market. For exports this of course detracts from the Single Market, as, without an E.C. standard, national standards could still be used barriers to trade.

"Conduct" duties — the obligations to provide information and to monitor safety in use

It has been said above that the basic obligation on producers is to place only safe products on the market. However, this obligation is not the only aspect of the GPS Regulations, which are expanded (by regulation 8) to encompass the additional aspects of providing information and monitoring use — obligations with regard to the *conduct* of the producer, in contrast with obligations as to the *quality* of products. The significance of this approach becomes apparent when the nature of offences under the GPS Regulations comes to be considered, for contravention of the requirements regulation 8 is not specified as an offence in its own right.[85]

The full wording of these obligations in regulation 8 is as follows:

"(1) Within the limits of his activity, a producer shall—

(a) provide consumers with the relevant information to enable them to assess the risks inherent in a product throughout the normal or reasonably foreseeable period of its use, where such risks are not immediately obvious without adequate warnings, and to take precautions against those risks; and

(b) adopt measures commensurate with the characteristics of the products which he supplies, to enable him to be informed of the risks which these products might present and to take appropriate action, including, if necessary, withdrawing the product in question from the market to avoid those risks.

(2) The measures referred to in sub-paragraph (b) of paragraph (1) above may include, whenever appropriate—

(i) marking of the products or product batches in such a way that they can be identified;

(ii) sample testing of marketed products;

(iii) investigating complaints; and

(iv) keeping distributors informed of such monitoring."

All these obligations are subject to the qualification that producers shall (in the wording of the Directive) observe them "within the limit of their respective activities". These words are intended to place some limit on the extent to which a given producer, in the circumstances in which he operates, can be expected to achieve compliance with the obligations. For example, the Union of Industrial and Employers' Confederations of

[85] See p.141 *et seq* below where enforcement of the GPS Regulations is considered.

Europe objected to an initial draft of the Directive which did not contain these words on the basis that manufacturers are not always involved in the maintenance or disposal of their products and should not have unqualified obligations.[86] A distinction is also to be drawn between the extent of the obligation as it applies to the different categories of persons who are included in the definition of a producer in regulation 2, namely manufacturers, representatives and suppliers. It is implicit that some account must be taken of the ability of people in these categories to fulfil the obligations. U.K. Courts may well be inclined to infer that this is a question of what is "reasonable" or "reasonably practicable" — *i.e.* they would recognise an element of fault-based or due diligence type reasoning but this may not be the correct approach as "the limits" may represent a standard akin to "best endeavours" or "practicable", requirements which English courts have treated as being of a demanding standard where such phrases are used in contracts or in legislation.[87] It may be quite unreasonable to expect representatives or suppliers, which may be small organisations or have to deal with a wide range of products, perhaps with limited resources, to be able without considerable expense to carry out extensive information, labelling or recall operations. On the other hand, it is intended that consumers should be informed of and effectively protected from serious risks. To the extent that action is taken by the manufacturer in relation to ensuring the safety of his products, obligations on representatives and suppliers in the chain presumably diminish. Thus, where the manufacturer supplies products with adequate product literature, or takes post-marketing action to inform consumers of risks or to withdraw products, representatives and suppliers would be expected to co-operate in facilitating these actions but might not be expected to take primary initiatives themselves.

Providing information on risks

The obligation to provide information is closely linked to the considerations which arise under the test of whether a product is safe or dangerous in regulation 2. The object is to provide consumers with the relevant information so as to enable them to assess the risks inherent in the product so that they may be in a position to take precautions against those risks. In other words, sufficient information and warnings must be provided so as to enable the product to be used safely. There is no requirement that the precautions for safe use will arise automatically when the product is used: it is a matter for the personal responsibility of the user how he chooses to use the product and whether he wishes to adopt any precautions at all. He is free to use the product dangerously if

[86] Business Brief No. 1631.

[87] See, *e.g. Marshall v. Gotham Co. Ltd* [1954] A.C. 360; *Adsett v. K and L Steelfounders and Engineers Ltd* [1953] 1 All E.R. 97; [1953] 1 W.L.R. 137; and *Sheffield District Railway Co. v. Great Central Railway Co.* 27 T.L.R. 451.

he wishes — subject to other legal constraints on him, such as a duty not to cause harm negligently to others. In this sense the producer is engaged in risk transference, but this has to be heavily qualified by the basic duty to supply products with the minimum acceptable risk as discussed previously.

How much information does a producer have to pass on about risks?

The obligation is to provide consumers with "the relevant information" to enable *them* to assess the risks inherent in a product. There is no elaboration of what this obligation entails either in terms of the manner of giving the information, or the substance of any necessary warnings. Clearly the information has to be legible, sufficiently prominent to be noticed, in a language understandable to the intended users, and presented in such a way that it can be understood by consumers generally. Producers will already have addressed these issues for the purposes of both the general safety requirements under the CPA 1987 and civil liability considerations, but they now face some uncertainty as to precisely how exhaustive such information has to be to meet the new *express* statutory duty.

Problems stem from the absence of a definition of "risk" in this context, and are further compounded by the language of the Directive adopted in the regulations: it would appear that this duty extends to *all* the inherent risks in a product, since this wording is not qualified as referring to only those risks which might arise in normal or reasonably foreseeable conditions of use (*i.e.* unlike the definition of "safe product"). The producer will have satisfied the general safety to place a safe product on the market provided he has adequately described, warned of risks under normal and reasonably foreseeable conditions of use at the time of placing the product on the market. A discreet obligation to provide information on risks under other conditions, whether it applies at the time of first placing the product on the market or later, is apparently illogical and impractical unless it is meant to refer only to previously unforeseen risks that have become apparent, and that would indicate the product is not in fact a "safe product" as defined.

When must the producer provide the information?

Is the duty to be interpreted as a continuing obligation to provide information after the product has been sold? There is no definite answer to this question. Obviously, the obligation to provide information must be satisfied at the time at which the product is placed on the market, having regard to the criteria for it being a safe product.[88] It presumably still exists whilst the product remains on the market, but unsold. During these times, the obligation is to provide sufficient information so as to

[88] reg. 2.

enable the consumer to be aware of the risks which are likely to arise throughout the normal or reasonably foreseeable period of use of the product, where such risks are not immediately obvious without adequate warnings. Read as a whole, however, regulation 8 seems intended to make the duties continue post-sale: there is the continuing obligation to "take appropriate action" which includes sample testing and investigating complaints after placing the product on the market. From the point of view of the policy objective of ensuring the safety of consumers, this information obligation makes little sense if it does not relate to risks which come to the attention of the producer *after* the product has reached the consumer. However, it might be argued that the legal basis of the Directive under Article 100a of the Treaty in relation to establishing the common *market* does not extend to validate any provision which relates to a product after it has left the market and indeed it has been argued by the U.K. Government that the specified duty to "withdraw" a product from the market cease to apply after a product has actually been purchased and so is no longer on the market.

In principle the duty extends to information needed for as long as the product's useful life—*i.e.* the 'normal and foreseeable period of use'. This indeterminate time period may though present problems for manufacturers, for example because it may be that a small percentage of their products (*e.g.* an enthusiasts "classic" car, or a favourite old radio set) could remain in use many years after most would be discarded or scrapped. There is no threshold in terms of numbers in circulation, or cut-off period in time to assist in dealing with such cases. The legislation unfortunately begs some hard questions as to the life-span of products in a consumerist society.

These requirements raise once again the question of whether the giving of a warning of a risk will necessarily suffice to discharge the producer's duties to inform consumers. Article 3.2 of the GPS Directive expressly states that the provision of adequate warnings by a producer does not exempt him or anyone else from compliance with the other requirements of the Directive so that, for example, provision of warnings some time after a product range has first been marketed would not excuse the fact that items already sold were dangerous and so breached the general safety requirement at the time of sale nor would necessity obviate a need to withdraw a product from the market. The GPS Regulations omit this clarifying provision, and it might therefore be inferred that the opposite to that taken in the Directive is meant to be adopted. However the obligation in regulation 8(1)(b) (which are expanded on in regulation 8(2)) can be viewed as distinct from the information obligations and it is submitted, amount to independent duties requiring producers to "take appropriate action" which may go beyond just warnings.[89] The practical issues involved in post-marketing warnings are considered again in Chapter 9.

[89] For a fuller discussion of the extent to which warning pre-empt other duties on a producer see: C.J.S. Hodges, *Product Liability, European Law and Practice* (1993), paras. 3–033 to 3–054 and *Benjamin's Sale of Goods* (1992), para. 14–036.

Testing, labelling and surveillance

The obligation on producers under regulation 8(1)(b) has two aspects. The first is to "adopt measures commensurate with the characteristics of the products which they supply, to enable them to be informed of risks which these products might present". This obligation applies both before and after the producer has placed the product on the market. The objective is two-fold. First, manufacturers, representatives and suppliers should not simply make or take steps to put products on the market without checking whether they are dangerous or without a reasonable assessment of the risks which they might involve. Secondly, they should have some responsibility in relation to post-marketing surveillance, in recognition of the fact that defects in a product or dangerousness in use might only occur or be identified after the product leaves the manufacturer. This leads on to the second aspect of the duty which is "to take appropriate action".

Examples are given in the Regulations of what might constitute appropriate measures for a producer to take. These are:

- marking the products or product batches in such a way that they can be identified. This would facilitate withdrawal of particular products or batches without the necessity of a general recall of all similar products or batches;
- sample testing of marketed products;
- investigating complaints made;
- keeping distributors informed of the results of monitoring.

Taken together, these obligations point to the conclusion that a producer should set up *systems* which enable him to be informed of the risks which appear from use of the products and to institute action to rectify the position. Indeed, these are aspects of systems which are included in the Quality Systems Standard, ISO 9000 (BS 5750). They do not though comprise an exhaustive list of measures that would satisfy the regulatory obligation; certainly a quality system would be expected to include document retention policies, arrangements for checking the quality of ingredients and components as well as the finished product, process control records, as well as systems for monitoring quality generally and auditing the system as a whole from time to time.

Taking appropriate action

Having identified a risk after a product has been placed on the market, the producer then has an obligation to "take appropriate action" to avoid these risks. Only two examples of such action are given in regulation 8, namely providing warnings or withdrawing the product from the market. However, there is a range of refinements of these options which are open to a producer faced with a potential safety problem in practice, including:

(a) taking no action because the risk is so small, or any further action would be ineffectual;
(b) including a stipulation in the product information that the product is to be used in a certain fashion or not to be used in certain circumstances;
(c) including a warning in the product information about use in particular circumstances or about the possibility of encountering specified untoward events;
(d) in the case of certain products involving unavoidable hazards, for example, medicinal products, pesticides, etc, a restriction on the availability of particular products to specialist intermediaries;
(e) a special notification of a new hazard direct to all users or outlets or specialist intermediaries;
(f) discontinuation from sale of further items of a particular batch or class, where the continued safety of the product in use cannot be guaranteed, even with appropriate warnings;
(g) withdrawal from the distribution network;
(h) recall of a product from the consumers who have previously purchased the product.

Any one (or more) of the first seven of these options is capable of falling within the scope of the producer's obligations. Selection of the option which is appropriate in the circumstances is difficult without criteria in the regulations themselves. Judgment has to be exercised by producers to decide what is necessary, in the context of the particular risks that have been identified, "to avoid those risks".[90] This should not mean total elimination of *any* risk, and it is implicit that what is intended is that the steps should render an otherwise dangerous product a "safe product" within the meaning of the Regulations, *i.e.* one that does not present any risk *or* only the minimum risks compatible with normal and reasonably foreseeable conditions of use.[91] Again the question arises of whether the cost of implementing any particular steps carries weight in determining if the producer is under a duty to act. This obligation is, like that of providing information in regulation 8(1)(a), qualified as being "within the limits of the producer's activity", so as has been suggested above the economic factor is arguably a material consideration. Nevertheless, the fact that action may be very expensive will undoubtedly carry little weight if the risk of injury posed by the product is a serious one. The civil cases in which this particular issue has been considered by indicate that the safety of consumers subjugates considerations of costs for the

[90] An official speaking at the CBI/McKenna & Co. General Product Safety Seminar, in March 1994 commented that:

> "It would not be possible for the Government to try to prescribe in detail what every producer of every product should be doing to comply with these duties. So it will be the producer's job to assess the appropriateness of these or any other measures that might be desirable, because he is the person who is best placed to know that is reasonable and practical in the light of what he knows about his products."

[91] See reg. 2.

producer of taking necessary action and potential damage to his market share and the product's reputation.

The eighth option in the list above referred to the possibility of full scale public recalls and here there is another serious interpretation difficulty with the GPS Regulations. The phrase ". . . if necessary withdrawing the product in question from the market" is taken directly from article 3 of the GPS Directive; it mirrors the basic producer's duty to place only safe products *on* the market, and so there is internal consisting in wording of the legislation. The Commission contends that this power extends to a power to recall products which have been sold to consumers or users and are in use or available for use. However, the United Kingdom has pointed out that the power is only to withdraw products "from the market": they are only "on the market" if they have not yet been sold to consumers or users. Accordingly, if this interpretation is correct, there is no duty on the producer to recall a product which has been sold by retail or supplied to its intended user, or to be precise at least no duty within the framework of the GPS Regulations.[92] There would, of course, still be a need to recall other items or batches of the same product which had not yet been sold or supplied to their consumers. It is notable that the term "recall" appears nowhere in the Directive. Apparently this is because the Commission believed that an equivalent word for "recall" does not exist in some European languages and so the word "withdrawal" has been used, although the phrase "withdrew from the market" is standard in Community internal market legislation. However, the word recall does appear in other Community documents.[93] The U.K. Government's position has been to implement the Directive exactly as worded in the original leaving the Courts to decide the correct legal meaning of the language. The matter may ultimately be resolved by the European Court giving a definitive interpretation of the words in the Directive, but even if the Commission's view is found to be correct in principle there will remain doubt whether a producer can in fact be *compelled* to undertake a public recall given the nature of the enforcement powers available to the authorities. Breach of regulation 8 is not an offence,[94] and no new enforcement powers are created by the Regulations. While further stocks of products can be forfeited, and the authorities can order the publication of

[92] See Chap. 8 on the civil liability issue of breach of a duty of care at common law.

[93] See, *e.g.*, Directive 91/356 laying down the principles and guidelines of good manufacturing practice fot medicinal products for human use, Art. 13; Directive 91/412 laying down the principles and guidelines of good manufacturing practice for veterinary medicinal products; Guide to good manufacturing practice for medicinal products; Directive 92/25 on the wholesale distribution of medicinal products for human use; Guidelines on Good Distribution Practice of Medicinal Products for Human Use, OJ No. C63/4, 1.3.94.

[94] reg. 12.

warning notices[95] and take action to block further supplies there remains no power to order a producer to recall products from consumers.[96]

Impact of these provisions

These conduct duties give a new dimension to product safety law and in effect may leave companies open to enforcement even where there is no evidence whatsoever of their products actually being unsafe or posing any risk to consumers: a "systems failure", for example in inadequate monitoring, might be a contravention of the statutory safety provision in its own right.[97] The implications of the new regime are likely to involve significant investment in the creation of safety monitoring units which constantly collect and disseminate information between manufacturers, distributors, retailers and users. There will be needs for systematic procedures for investigating and assessing complaints and for significant investment in information technology and in training managers to understand and assess technical and health risks. There will also be a requirement for technical and legal input in determining what response is appropriate in a given situation: amending instructions for use, improving warnings, packaging changes, modification, limited withdrawal or full recall (see Chapters 9 and 10). Certain lessons may be learnt from the pharmaceutical industry, which has developed and is continuing to develop extremely sophisticated product surveillance facilities and techniques — but at considerable cost.

The obligations are non-prescriptive and intended to avoid imposing requirements such as monitoring where this is inappropriate to the scale or nature of producers' activities. However, this flexibility, which industry representatives often seek in the adoption of new legislation, has possible drawbacks which can cause producers discomfort later: uncertainty in how to comply, inconsistent advice and enforcement from the authorities, and the need to seek legal advice and no guarantee that standard industry practice is necessarily sufficient to discharge the legal duties.

[95] ss.13–17, CPA 1987.

[96] Art. 8–14 of the GPS Directive which may permit the European Commission to achieve a recall order through the mechanisms in place to deal with emergency situations invoking the adopting of a formal Decision: the exercise of these procedures could throw into sharp focus the differing interpretations of the European Commission and national governments.

[97] The courts are liable to give particular weight to the "preventative" nature of safety legislation and to construe legislation unfavourably against the duty holder — see, *e.g.*, *R. v. Board of Trustees of the Science Museum* (*supra*), a decision on the Court of Appeal on the meaning of the term "expose to risks" under the Health and Safety at Work Act 1974.

THE OBLIGATIONS ON "DISTRIBUTORS"

In E.C. technical Directives the usual focus is on those who "place products on the market". This phrase is not straightforward, but it is generally understood to refer to manufacturers and importers since legislation uses specific expressions such as "supplier" (Product Liability Directive) where this is intended. The GPS Directive and GPS Regulations have more wide-ranging obligations on "distributors", which is a term with a specific meaning for these purposes defined as: "any professional in the supply chain whose activity does not affect the safety properties of a product".[98]

The meaning of "professional" here is the same as has been described above when looking at producers. This can cover not just manufacturer's representatives, agents, distributors (in the usual sense) and wholesalers, but also retailers — who would previously have had no or fairly minimal obligations under Part II of the CPA 1987. It has been noted above that a supplier in the wider sense (*i.e.* professional in the supply chain whose activity *may* affect the safety of a product) is treated as a producer and is subject to the general safety requirement and obligations of producers under regulations 7 and 8. The characteristic of a distributor that his activity *does* not affect safety is at face value more definite, but the similar questions will arise here as they do in determining the application of the producer definition: is safety affected by packaging, carriage or storage conditions; are the goods perishable; are appropriate instructions and warnings passed on properly by the person concerned? An intermediary in the supply chain such as a finance company in a lease or hire purchase arrangement is likely to be a distributor for these purposes (unless more active participation such as importation or reconditioning renders the company a producer), as is an insurance company which arranges with a supplier for replacement goods to be delivered to a consumer under a policy covering damage or theft.[99] The producer/distributor distinction therefore depends on an analysis of what they actually do in relation to the product, rather than on what their intended role is in the chain of supply.

A distributor within the definition is subject to the following distinct duties under regulation 9:

> "A distributor shall act with due care in order to help to ensure compliance with the requirement of regulation 7 above [the general safety requirement] and, in particular without limiting the generality of the foregoing —
>
> (a) a distributor shall not supply products to any person which he knows, or should have presumed, on the basis of the information in his possession and as a professional, are dangerous products; and

[98] reg. 2.

[99] *cf.* s.46(6) of the CPA 1987, which exempted from the definition of supply under the Act the supply of goods by an insured person to his insurer.

(b) within the limits of his activities, a distributor shall participate in monitoring the safety of products placed on the market, in particular by passing on information on the product risks and co-operating in the action taken to avoid those risks."

Act with due care

The extent of this obligation is indeterminate. There is no specific obligation to test or label products, such as is required in relation to producers who have to *comply* with the general safety requirement. A distributor merely has to *help* to ensure compliance but since — by definition — such a person's activities do *not* affect the product's safety properties it is hard to see that this duty can entail obligations, other than positively to monitor and pass on information as described in sub-paragraph (b). As he has to act with due care, he can only contravene this provision if he is careless or at fault in damaging the product or failing to provide the consumer with the safety information intended by the producer to accompany it. In this respect the obligation may therefore not go significantly further than the distributor's existing obligation under civil law not to cause injury through negligence. The standard of "due care" (as further qualified by reference to what a supplier should have presumed and what is within the limits of his activity) indicates that the duties may vary with the scale and sophistication of the business concerned. The DTI guidance suggests that a major retailer will be measured against higher standards than a village shop.[1] The duty goes beyond just not acting carelessly, however, as it includes the positive steps of participation, passing on information and co-operation with producers.

This requirement not to supply dangerous products is based on actual or constructive knowledge by a distributor of non-compliance with the general safety requirement. A number of cases have involved the interpretation of these elements of "knowledge" of a contravention of a requirement in similarly worded statutes[2] and it is clear that courts will impute to knowledge to a person who turns a blind eye to or acquiesces in a situation where a requirement under the legislation is not met. However, a failure to make a presumption that a product is unsafe

[1] See comment of Lord Lane C.J. in *Garrett v. Boots the Chemist Ltd* (*Monthly Review* Vol. 88, No. 12, p.238) a case concerned with the application of the due diligence defence to a contravention of requirements for pencils. See also *Hicks v. Sullam Ltd* (1983) 147 J.P. 493, D.C.

[2] See, *e.g. Ross v. Moss* [1965] 3 All E.R. 145 and *James & Son Ltd v. Smee* [1955] 1 Q.B. 78; [1954] 1 All E.R. 273, on know edge. The extension of the duty to situation were products ought to have been presumed unsafe precludes the result of the principle expressed in *Taylor's Central Garages (Exeter) Ltd v. Roper* [1951] 2 T.L.R. 284 by Devlin J. that neglecting to make reasonable enquiries is not tantamount to knowledge. One has to consider knowledge attributable in a professional capacity, *i.e.* more than that of a consumer—see the DTI guidelines Annex of definition on "professional" for these puropses, Appendix 7.

brings in new consideration, as it implies a duty on a distributor to inform himself about all the matters which are relevant to the constituents of the Regulations' definition of a "safe product".

Participate in monitoring product safety

It would seem that the obligation to participate in monitoring product safety relates only to products for which a distributor has some responsibility and not products generally, or else a distributor of a particular brand could be burdened with responsibility for other brands or suppliers.[3] The extent to which he is to participate is not spelt out but two relatively simply activities are specified. First, distributors are to pass on information on product risks. It is not stated to whom the information should be passed: consumers would be the obvious target but it might also be argued that enforcement authorities, others in the chain of supply and producers should be informed. If so, then this could be a burden, although there is the qualification that the distributor only need do what is "within the limits of his activities". Passing on information to consumers may also be involved but could be problematic: if the Directive does extend to passing on information after a product has left the market and is in the hands of a consumer, many distributors, especially retailers, will have no record of which customers may have bought which products. This obligation could not extend to keeping such records. It is presumably also meant to be a two-directional process. If a distributor becomes aware that a product is dangerous, perhaps through a consumer complaint, he should tell his supplier or the producer.

The second specific obligation is to co-operate in any action taken in relation to avoiding risks. Distributors do not have to initiate such action, merely to co-operate in it.[4] The main examples would include liaising with producers, suppliers, the enforcement authorities and testing houses and assisting with withdrawal of products from the market. Distributors will wish to have the costs of such action included in the contractual indemnities they try to obtain from suppliers and producers to protect them against the liabilities they incur to customers under the sale of goods legislation.

In view of the fact that the U.K. Government considered the nature of the obligation to participate in monitoring to be unspecific, an offence for contravention has been confined to regulation 9(a) only, resulting in the peculiar outcome that the principal duty (in the main introductory paragraph to regulation 9) is not an offence in its own right. Protection of the public from unsafe products is to be achieved by other means and this is considered further below.

[3] The reason being that the distributor in question would have to be "in the supply chain" to attract the obligations in relation to a product.

[4] This must however be seen in conjunction with the duty under reg. 9(a) not to supply a product which a distributor knows to be unsafe.

It can therefore be seen that the Regulations are partly good news for "distributors" in the traditional sense, since their duties under the Regulations are more limited than those of producers and they are less exposed to the risk of committing an offence for the supply of unsafe products than under the CPA. Retailers, however, are now exposed to additional obligations, and may also be at risk of being classed as "producers" where their retail activities may affect product safety. ("Own brand" distributors or retailers, of course, fall within the definition of producer and bear the full weight of regulations 7 and 8.)

ENFORCEMENT

The bodies responsible for seeing that product safety legislation is enforced have been described in the introduction to this chapter. The powers in this area are derived chiefly from the Consumer Protection Act 1987 which enables them to carry out investigations, serve enforcement notices on producers and other suppliers, and bring contraventions for prosecutions of the general safety requirement, safety regulations and a number of ancillary offences.

Before considering the enforcement measures that exist it is important to note that all of these measures are expressed in the legislation as being powers granted to, rather than duties imposed upon, the enforcement authorities. These authorities therefore have to exercise discretion whether or not to take formal action. In practice a large proportion of the complaints and other problems which Trading Standards Officers encounter are dealt with informally, with the suppliers concerned co-operating voluntarily in providing information about the product and sales data, and agreeing changes in product design or safety information and instructions for use provided to the customer. As can be seen from **Table 5.1** the use of written warnings and formal cautions exceeds the total number of other successful enforcement actions taken, and some of the enforcement measures available to the authorities have not been used at all.

Table 5.1 Product Safety Enforcement Statistics 01.04.88 to 31.03.93

Forfeiture Orders	299
Prohibition Notices	18*
Suspension Notices	1,702
Notices to Warn	0
Secretary of State's Notice to furnish information	0
Convictions	1,931
Written warnings and formal cautions	4,295

* This figure in fact relates to only two products, and comprises notices against four importers of one product and 14 suppliers of the other product

Source: Consumer Safety: Report by the Secretary of State for Trade and Industry for the period April 1, 1988–March 31, 1993 (HMSO)

These statistics pre-date the GPS Regulations, and cover a period before the New Approach Directives could have had a significant impact on the general level of product safety in the U.K. There are indications, however, that the effect of introducing new legislation *increases* the overall volume of enforcement action and does not (as one might presume) necessarily lead to a reduction on account of the enhanced safety of the products concerned. For instance, in the five-year period covered by the table above there were more than three times as many prosecutions for unsafe toys than there were in the preceding five-year period, despite the fact that in 1989 the Toys (Safety) Regulations gave effect to the European Toys Directive and required toys to conform to "essential requirements". On the other hand, there are examples of regulations which apparently have not had formal enforcement at all such as the Gas Appliances (Safety) Regulations 1992. (See **Table 1.12** in Chapter 1.)

Powers to obtain information and evidence

The 1987 Act contains a number of provisions designed to facilitate the exercise of the substantive enforcement powers. Enforcement officers have wide-ranging investigatory powers, and it is an offence to obstruct them intentionally or to refuse to comply with their requirements, or to fail, without reasonable cause, to any assistance or information these officers may require for the purposes of exercising their statutory functions.[5] Making false statements, either knowingly or recklessly as to the truth, is also an offence.[6] As with all offences under the Act, if a company is convicted a director or senior manager can also be prosecuted personally when the offence is attributable to his neglect or committed with his consent or connivance.[7]

Certain limits are, however, placed on the powers of the enforcement authorities, and they cannot require the production of any records that could be subject to legal professional privilege[8] in court proceedings, so permitting suppliers and others to confide freely in their legal advisers. Legal professional privilege is the only criterion for withholding records, and the fact that the holder may deem confidential other documents or, may be subject to a confidentiality agreement with a third party, that they will not be grounds for withholding them. Also no-one can be required to answer questions or give information that would incriminate that person or his or her spouse.[9] Since the word "person" is construed to include a corporation it appears that if a company is under investiga-

[5] s.32(1), Consumer Protection Act 1987. The penalty is a fine of up to £5,000.
[6] s.32(2).
[7] s.40(2).
[8] For an explanation of the circumstances in which legal professional privilege applies see *The Supreme Court Practice* (1995) Vol. 1, para. 24/5/6.
[9] s.47.

tion its board of directors could resolve not to co-operate in providing information which would be self-incriminating. However, attempts to prevent individual employees from providing information could lead to the company committing the offence of obstruction. The privilege against self-incrimination is of limited value in practice since the exercise of this right at once alerts an investigating officer to the likelihood of evidence of contravention existing, and this may be obtained by interviewing different individuals or obtaining evidence from other sources.

In obtaining statements from witnesses, enforcement officers will be mindful of the issue of admissibility of the evidence in any future proceedings. The Act does not impose any formal procedural requirements on the taking of statements but the Police and Criminal Evidence Act 1984 (PACE) together with its Codes of Practice, lay down a number of requirements which enforcement officers need to adhere to.[10] These rules require, amongst other things, that a person must be given a caution and an accurate record must be made of each interview. A person under caution is entitled to make his own statement as well as (or instead of) answering questions put to him which he should sign.[11] A producer or other supplier under investigation therefore has a number of safeguards and before agreeing to be interviewed formally under caution it will generally be prudent to seek legal advice about protecting these rights.

Test purchases

Enforcement authorities are authorised to purchase any goods and to test them themselves or obtain the services of an outside organisation to examine them.[12] There is no formal requirement to disclose the results of such tests or any report that might be written on the products concerned, but if the testing leads to a prosecution, a suspension notice or forfeiture of the product then the seller or another person with an interest in the goods[13] are entitled to have their own tests carried out.[14] Prosecutors will in practice usually disclose reports and testing data to a defendant's solicitors as part of the evidence on which the prosecution rely at trial, so that there is an opportunity to consider the results the authority has obtained and if necessary obtain a report from another expert.

Search and seizure

For most investigations into product safety dealt with by the enforcement authorities the carrying out of test purchases coupled with direct

[10] The Act provides that "persons other than police offiicers who are charged with a duty of investigating offences or charging offenders shall in the discharge of that duty have regard to any relevant provision of such a code" (s.16(7)(9), Police and Criminal Evidence Act 1984). Interviews and questioning are considered further in Chap. 6.

[11] See also s.47, Consumer Protection Act 1987. A person cannot be required to answer any question or give any information if to do so would incriminate him or his spouse.

[12] s.28(1).

[13] s.28(2).

[14] *Ibid.*

approaches to producers and suppliers for additional information is sufficient to gain all the details required to determine whether there has been a contravention of the safety provisions. Nevertheless, enforcement authorities do not have to rely on co-operation from those whose conduct is under investigation, and a duly authorised officer is entitled to enter premises to inspect any goods (without a search warrant) provided he produces evidence of his credentials if asked — normally in the form of his identity card.[15] The right to entry extends to all premises except those occupied *only* as a residence.[16] Mixed residential and business use of premises will not be within this exception.

Entry can be sought at any "reasonable hour"; the precise times of day are left undefined but would clearly include normal business hours. However, if there is an emergency situation or a suspicion that important evidence may about to be destroyed or hidden then it would seem arguable that entry would be permissible at any hour if this can be said to be reasonable in the circumstances. Provisions nevertheless exist whereby officers can seek search warrants,[17] and this would be appropriate where it is necessary to force entry since this would not be lawful without a warrant. A warrant may be granted where a Justice of the Peace is satisfied that there are reasonable grounds for believing that there is likely to be evidence on the premises of a contravention of any safety provision and that admission has been or is likely to be refused, or that seeking admission from the occupier would defeat the object of the entry, or that the premises are unoccupied.

Upon entry the powers available are to inspect any goods and examine any procedure (including arrangements for carrying out product testing) in connection with production. These powers are exercisable *for the purposes of ascertaining* whether any safety provisions have been contravened, and it is not therefore necessary for an officer to establish a prima facie case or that he holds a reasonable belief of contravention of safety provisions in order to justify a search. If however, certain criteria are met an officer can take advantage of additional powers to require the production of business records, to take copies of any records, and to seize and detain goods. The criteria for this are that the officer has to have reasonable grounds for suspecting that there has been a contravention in relation to any goods of a safety provision.[18] However, even if the officer does not have grounds for suspecting the contravention he may nevertheless exercise these additional powers if he had reasonable grounds for suspecting that the goods are manufactured or imported goods which have not yet been supplied in the U.K. since they were first manufactured or imported.[19]

As well as goods that contravene the safety provisions officers may seize and detain goods or records which may be required as evidence in

[15] s.29(1).
[16] s.29(2).
[17] s.30(2).
[18] s.29(5).
[19] s.29(4).

proceedings. The seizure powers are, however, subject to a number of provisos which include providing any test results to the person from whom they were seized.[20] The significance of this goes beyond merely giving the person an opportunity to examine the enforcement authorities findings, because the Act provides for compensation where seizure and attention of goods has occurred if there turns out to have been no contravention of any safety provision, provided the exercise of the power is not attributable to neglect or default by the person from whom the goods were seized.[21]
Under section 33 of the Act, any person having an interest in goods which have been seized can apply to the Magistrates Courts (or in Scotland, to the Sheriff) for an order for their release, but the circumstances in which such orders are made are restricted; the applicant must establish that no other proceedings have resulted in the goods being forfeited and (where no proceedings for an offence or for forfeiture have been brought) more than six months has elapsed since the seizure.

Detention of goods by customs officers

Customs officers are empowered to seize imported goods and detain them for up to two days to assist the usual enforcement authority in exercising its powers of inspection etc. The very short period of detention is merely to permit custom's officers to make preliminary enquiries and to prevent goods being sold pending further investigation by the enforcement authorities.[22]

Secretary of State's power to obtain information

In addition to these powers which are bestowed on enforcement authorities generally, the Secretary of State (who is included within the general definition of enforcement authorities)[23] has additional powers at his disposal to issue formal notices requiring a person to disclose information, produce records and permit copying of documents.[24] A notice may be served on any person who is likely to be able to furnish the information the Secretary of State requires for the purposes of making, varying or revoking safety regulations or a prohibition notice, or serving or revoking a notice to warn (see below for a description of these notices). These powers are also, however, subject to the safeguards against disclosure of privileged material described above.

Formal enforcement action

The availability of enforcement powers depends on various criteria being met: the products concerned must be categorised as "goods" or

[20] s.30(6).
[21] s.34.
[22] s.37 of the Act also authorises the Commissioners of Customs and Excise to disclose information to facilitate the exercise by an enforcement authority of its product safety powers.
[23] s.45.
[24] s.18.

"products" as defined in the legislation, and the correct grounds for exercising the power in question must exist. **Table 5.2** shows how the criteria vary. There can be important effects in practical terms as a result of these differences, for example goods may be seized on *reasonable grounds for suspicion* of contravention of safety provision but forfeiture depends on it being established that there is *actual* contravention. The Table includes the relevant unrepealed provisions of Part II of the CPA 1987 relating to the general safety requirement but as a result of the more comprehensive coverage of products under the GPS Regulations the different definitions of goods and products are now much less significant than they were under the 1987 Act; other than antiques and products sold for repair or reconditioning, for the purposes of prosecutions the only consumer products which are not caught by this range of definitions are those which are covered by Community sectoral legislation *and* which are not deemed "consumer products" by virtue of section 10(7) of the Act. Even so, all such products are subject to all the enforcement powers other than prosecution shown in **Table 5.2**.

Suspension notices

Under section 14 of the Act enforcement authorities are empowered to serve suspension notices where they have reasonable grounds for suspecting that any "safety provision" has been contravened in relation to the goods concerned. The term safety provision is defined in section 45 of the Act and comprises the general safety requirement, requirements of any Safety Regulations, (including the requirements of the GPS Regulations[25]) as well as a prohibition notice and a suspension notice. These notices prohibit the person on whom they are served from supplying the goods (or offering or agreeing to supply them or exposing them for sale) for up to six months. Notices can include a provision that the recipient keep the authority informed of the whereabouts of all the goods in question. Contravention of suspension notices is an offence.[26]

As its name indicates a suspension notice is only a temporary measure, but commercially it is disrupting and potentially very damaging to a supplier and may effectively terminate the supply of a product for good. There are nevetheless limitations because the notice only binds the persons on whom it is actually served. As the goods are already widely in circulation the use of a suspension notice against the manufacturer or importer will have little practical effect in protecting consumers, and serving hundreds of individual suspension notices on distributors and retail outlets is impractical.

[25] reg. 11(b) of the GPS Regulations provides that the requirements of the Regulations constitute safety provisions for the purposes of s.14, 16, 17 and 18 of the Act.

[26] s.14(6) as amended by reg. 11(d) of the GPS Regulations, punishment is a fine of up to £5,000 and/or up to three months' imprisonment.

Table 5.2 Enforcement powers

Consumer Protection Act Enforcement Powers	*Products subject to the powers*	*Grounds for exercise of the powers*
Search and Seizure (s.29)	any Goods[a]	*Entry into premises*: to ascertain whether there has been any contravention of any safety provision.[b] *Seisure of goods*: *either* reasonable grounds for suspicion of contravention of any safety provision[b] *or* reasonable grounds for suspicion that the goods are manufactured or imported goods which have not been supplied in the U.K. since they were manufactured or imported
Power to obtain information (s.18)	n/a	Secretary of State considers he requires information which another person is likely to be able to furnish, for the purpose of deciding whether to make/vary/revoke safety regulations/prohibition notices/notices to warn
Suspension notice (s.14)	any goods[a]	Reasonable grounds for suspicion of contravention of any safety provision[b]
Forfeiture Order (s.16 and 17)	any goods[a]	Order of the court, on grounds that there has been a contravention of a safety provision[b]
Prohibition Notice	relevant goods[c] and products[d]	Secretary of State considers the goods are unsafe
Notice to Warn (s.13(1)(b))	relevant goods[c] and products[d]	Secretary of State considers the goods are unsafe
Prosecution (s.10) (Reg. 12 of GPS Regulations)	consumer goods[e] dangerous products[f]	Contravention of CPA 1987 general safety requirement Contravention of GPS Regulations general safety requirement

[a] "'Goods' includes substances, growing crops and things comprised in land by virtue of being attached to it and any ship, aircraft or vehicle" (s.45)

[b] "'Safety provision' means the general safety requirements in section 10 . . . or any provision of safety regulations, a prohibition notice or a suspension notice" (s.43). The requirements of the GPS Regulations constitute safety provisions for the purposes of s.14 and 15 (suspension notices), 16 (forfeiture: England, Wales and Northern Ireland), 17 (forfeiture: Scotland) and 18 (power to obtain information) of the 1987 Act (reg. 11(b)).

[c] "'Relevant goods' means:
(a) in relation to a prohibition notice, any goods to which s.11 . . . applies; [see text above concerning safety regulations and note 25, page 107] and
(b) in relation to a notice to warn, any goods to which that section applies or any growing crops or things comprised in land by virtue of being attached to it" (s.13(6))

[d] "'Product' means any product intended for consumers or likely to be used by consumers, supplied whether for consideration or not in the course of a commercial activity and whether new, used or reconditioned; provided, however, a product which is used exclusively in the context of a commercial activity even if it is used for or by a consumer shall not be regarded as a product for the purposes of these Regulations provided always and for the evoidance of doubt this exemption shall not extend to the supply of such a product to a consumer" (reg. 2)

[e] "'Consumer goods' means any goods which are ordinarily intended for private use or consumption, not being:
(a) growing crops or things comprised in land by virtue of being attached to it;
(b) water, food, feeding stuff or fertiliser;
(c) gas which is, is to be or has been supplied by a person authorised to supply it by or under section 6, 7 or 8 of the Gas Act 1986 (authorisation of supply of gas through pipes);
(d) aircraft (other than hang-gliders) or motor vehicles;
(e) controlled drugs or licensed medicinal products;
(f) tobacco"
(s.10(7))

[f] "'Dangerous products' means any product other than a safe product" (reg. 2), but duties are not applicable to antiques, products for repair/reconditioning, or in so far as provisions of Community legislation are applicable.

Figure 5.1 Suspension Notice

BLANKSHIRE COUNTY COUNCIL: TRADING STANDARDS DEPARTMENT

Consumer Protection Act 1987
SUSPENSION NOTICE

To: **Dawn Tack Supplies Limited**
Of: **Tack House, Green Road, Dartford, Kent DA10 2XY**
Date of Issue: **October 3, 1994**

Pursuant to the powers contained in section 14 of the above Act, this Authority, being an enforcement authority and having reasonable cause to suspect that the goods described below contravene the relevant provisions, notify you that you are prohibited from:

(a) placing on the market, offering or agreeing to place on the market, exposing or possessing for placing on the market the article; or
(b) supplying, offering to supply, agreeing to supply or exposing for supply such goods without the consent of this Authority.

If it is your intention to move the goods to another location, this Authority must be notified immediately in writing, together with particulars of that location.

Description of goods: **Saddles for horse-riding known as "Dawn's Saddles"**

Grounds for suspecting contravention of relevant provision: **the girth straps are inadequately secured by the stitching and may break causing users to fall from the saddle and thereby suffer injury.**

ANY PERSON CONTRAVENING THIS NOTICE SHALL BE LIABLE ON SUMMARY CONVICTION TO A FINE NOT EXCEEDING £5,000 AND/OR THREE MONTHS IMPRISONMENT

Any person having an interest in the goods to which this Notice relates may apply for an order setting aside this Notice by:

(i) application to the court in which any proceedings have been commenced in relation to the goods;
(ii) if no such proceedings have been commenced, by way of complaint to a magistrates' court.

....
Signature of person receiving Notice — Signature of Authorised Officer

....

This Authority hereby consents that you may supply, offer to supply, agree to supply or expose for supply that above goods subject to the following conditions: **the girth straps are re-worked and adequately secured to the satisfaction of the Authorised Officer**

Date: ....
Signature of Authorised Officer

The person on whom a suspension notice is served must be notified by the enforcement authority of rights of appeal provided by the Act.[27] Applications by way of appeal are dealt with by magistrates' courts (or in Scotland by summary application to the Sheriff). The court can set aside the notice if it is satisfied that there has been no contravention of a safety provision. As with seizure of goods, where an enforcement authority serves a suspension notice it may be liable to pay compensation to the person served if the goods do not contravene safety provisions and the exercise of the power cannot be attributed to that person's neglect or default.[28] It is in fact unusual for an enforcement authority dealing with safety matters to be put at risk of paying financial compensation in this way; there is for instance no equivalent provision in the health and safety, food or medicines legislation. It is hard to see why, on policy grounds, manufacturers and suppliers of consumer goods should be afforded additional level of protection against enforcement action.

Forfeiture Orders (see **Figure 5.2**)

Section 16 of the Act permits enforcement authorities to apply for an order of the court for forfeiture of any goods on grounds that they contravene a safety provision. (Section 17 lays down the equivalent rules for the Scottish jurisdiction.) As with suspension notices the effect of such an order is personal to the recipient and does not have the effect of a comprehensive ban on supply of the goods concerned. The court has to be satisfied that there is a contravention but it may infer this in relation to the goods generally if it is satisfied that a representative sample are defective. When the powers were introduced it was anticipated that it would be used in conjunction with action already being taken against a supplier. The forfeiture order may be dealt with by a court at the same time as a prosecution, or an appeal against seizure or detention of goods, or it may be dealt with by a separate application. The court's powers include directions as to destruction of the goods, or their release to a designated person.

Prohibition Notices (see **Figure 5.3**)

The power to issue a prohibition notice is confined to the Secretary of State and is dealt with in section 13 of and Schedule 2 to the Act. He may serve a notice on any person prohibiting the supply, offering for supply, exposing for supply or possessing for supply of any goods which he "considers are unsafe". The notice has to state the reasons why the goods are considered unsafe and can be framed in such a way that it permits supply to continue with the consent of the Secretary of

[27] s.16.
[28] s.14(7).

Figure 5.2 Application for Forfeiture Order

BLANKTOWN MAGISTRATES' COURT

The COMPLAINT of CHARLES FARNSBARNS, ASSISTANT CHIEF INSPECTOR TRADING STANDARDS FOR BLANKSHIRE COUNTY COUNCIL ON BEHALF OF THAT COUNCIL

Of: COUNTY OFFICES, BLANKTOWN, BLANKSHIRE, BB1 1DJ

who states that: Dawn Tack Supplies Limited

of: Tack House, Green Road, Dartford, Kent DA10 2XY

on the 3rd day of October 1994

at Green Road, Dartford aforesaid did possess for supply goods, namely 24 saddles for horse-riding known as Dawn's Saddles which failed to comply with the general safety requirement contrary to regulation 13 of the General Product Safety Regulations 1994 AND the said Council applies to Blanktown Magistrates Court pursuant to section 16 of the Consumer Protection Act 1987 for an order for the forfeiture of the said goods.

....

Complaint TAKEN before me this 4th day of October 1994

Justice of the Peace for the Area aforesaid

State subject to conditions. As with the other notices, contravention of prohibition notices is an offence.[29]

Prohibition notices carry more force than suspension notices in that their effect is to determine permanently the issue of whether or not the recipient can supply the product. They are not subject to an appeal procedure through courts.[30] The notices are personal to the recipient and so they cannot be used to impose a comprehensive ban of the goods in question; to achieve this end the Secretary of State would need to implement safety regulations under section 11 of the Act. Nor can the suppliers concerned by required by these means to recall goods from the trade or consumers.[31]

Schedule 2 to the CPA 1987 lays down procedures governing the mandatory review of prohibition notices if the person affected objects.

[29] s.13(4) as amended by reg. 11(d) of the GPS Regulations, punishable by a fine of up to £5,000 or up to three months' imprisonment.

[30] The exercise of the Secretary of State could, however, be subject to judicial review. As the statute gives the Secretary of State power to issue prohibition notices in relation to goods which he "considers" unsafe he has a large measure of discretion and the courts are unlikely to interfere unless the decision is irrational and manifestly unreasonable (*Associated Provincial Picture Houses v. Wednesbury Corporation* [1948] 1 K.B. 223; [1947] 2 All E.R. 680).

[31] An amendment which would have included a provision for notices requiring recall was tabled during the passage of the Consumer Protection Bill but was withdrawn prior to enactment of the Act.

Figure 5.3 Prohibition Notice

PROHIBITION NOTICE

Consumer Protection Act 1987

Section 13

To: **The Secretary, Dawn Tack Supplies Limited**

whose Registered Office is situated at **Tack House, Green Road, Dartford, Kent DA10 2XY**

The Secretary of State considers that a saddle for horse-riding known as "**Dawn's Saddles**" being a product as defined by the General Product Safety Regulations 1994 ("the article") is unsafe. The Secretary of State considers that the article is unsafe because **the girth straps are inadequately secured by the stitching and may break causing users to fall from the saddle and thereby suffer injury.**
Accordingly the article is a dangerous product.

The Secretary of State, therefore, in exercise of his powers under Section 13 of the Consumer Protection Act 1987 hereby gives notice that you shall not (except with the consent of the Secretary of State and in accordance with the conditions, if any, on which that consent is given)

(a) place on the market, offer or agree to place on the market, expose or possess for placing on the market the article; or
(b) supply, offer or agree to supply, expose or possess for supply the article,

whether or not under the name **Dawn's Saddles.**

This notice shall come into force on **October 3, 1994.**

You may at any time make representations in writing to the Secretary of State for the purpose of establishing that the article is safe.

Dated **3rd October 1994**

Signed ....
Parliamentary Under-Secretary of State for
Consumer Affairs and Small Firms
Department of Trade and Industry

Note: Contravention of this Notice is an offence punishable on summary conviction by imprisonment for a term not exceeding three months or by a fine not exceeding £5,000 or by both (Consumer Protection Act 1987, section 13(4))

The trader concerned must be given an opportunity to make representations in writing for the purpose of establishing that his goods are safe, whereupon the Secretary of State must consider whether to revoke the notice or to appoint a person to consider the representations and investigate the matter further. In the latter case, a report is prepared for the Secretary of State taking into account any further representations (oral or written) and the Secretary of State has to decide whether to revoke, continue or vary the notice. Any variation made cannot however make the prohibition notice more restrictive than it was previously.[32]

Notices to warn

The Secretary of State is also empowered under section 13 to serve notices requiring persons who supplied (or have supplied) goods which he considers to be unsafe to publish warnings at their own expense. The Secretary of State can dictate the form and manner in which the warnings should be given, and this flexibility makes notices to warn a particularly potent threat. They can, in theory, result in a supplier having to mount a media campaign warning consumers not to use the products concerned, with all the embarrassment and expense that entails. The mere existence of this power acts as a strong incentive to suppliers who discover safety defects in their products to take voluntary measures to warn the public and in some cases to recall the goods (even though the Secretary of State cannot actually require this by a warning notice) rather than lose the initiative and have more damaging warnings (which might, for example amount to admissions for the purposes of civil proceedings) imposed upon them by Government officials. The report of the Secretary of State for Trade and Industry on consumer safety for the period April 1, 1988 to March 31, 1993 stated:

> "It has not been found necessary in the period of the Report to serve any such notice. This is because the Department has been able to secure the necessary co-operation of suppliers without the necessity of exercising this power. On other occasions the publication of a press notice has been considered to be more effect."

In the event of the power being exercised there are procedural requirements in Schedule 2 to the Act which resemble those for prohibition notices. These involve the recipient of the intended notice being advised of his rights to make representations and, if the notice is challenged in this way, provision is made for the appointment of a person to produce a report for the Secretary of State. In contrast with prohibition notices however, the intended recipient must be informed in advance of the Secretary of State's intention to issue a notice and a draft disclosed to him. He then has a period of 14 days in which to indicate that he will make representations, and a further 14 days after that in which to submit the representations themselves. The Secretary of State can only proceed to issue his notice to warn if the recipient has not responded within these time limits. As with prohibition notices, upon consideration of the report by the appointed person the Secretary of State can decide not to proceed, to serve the notice as originally drafted, or to serve it with modifications, but the modifications cannot be more onerous than the original draft notice.

[32] Sched. 2, para. 5(2).

Prosecutions

The Consumer Protection Act 1987 and the General Product Safety Regulations 1994 make provision for contravention of various of the requirements they contain to be offences, with conviction leading to penalties of fines and/or imprisonment depending on the nature of the events concerned. Decisions whether or not to bring prosecutions lie primarily with the Trading Standards Officers of the enforcement authorities as part of their overall responsibilities to police the consumer safety legislation, and even if there is a clear case of the statutory requirements being contravened they are not obliged to prosecute.[33] They may consider that the particular contravention involved can be dealt with satisfactorily by simply issuing a warning to the producer or other supplier concerned, or by obtaining an undertaking from them that the safety of their products will be improved. Alternatively, they might consider that formal action, using one of the enforcement measures outlined above, in an appropriate response to the problem. Prosecution is not, however, an alternative to these other formal enforcement measures, and it is not unusual for a prosecution to be linked to a notice. There are no hard and fast rules as to when a prosecution will be brought, and this will depend largely on the policy adopted by the Trading Standards Department concerned and whether they perceive a prosecution to be in the public interest. The factors generally taken into account are the magnitude of the danger posed to consumers by the product, whether the defect is an isolated one or indicative of a wider failure by the producer to address safety issues, the offender's attitude to the defect and the measures it takes to rectify the problem, past record in terms of safety defects and previous prosecutions, and how co-operative the person has been in disclosing details of the problem to the Trading Standards Officers. For these reasons it is difficult to predict whether or not enforcement authorities will consider that a contravention deserves prosecution, and this creates particular difficulties for suppliers who may be in two minds about whether to seek guidance of the Trading Standards Officers about safety problems, or to involve them in planning an exercise to warn customers of new discovered danger in a product or to retrieve it from the chain of supply.

A number of statutes restrict the power to bring prosecutions to specifically authorised enforcement officers or regulatory agencies[34] but there is no such restriction in the consumer safety legislation. Consequently it is open to individual consumers, consumer pressure groups or anyone else to commence private prosecutions. If a private

[33] The system in Scotland is different. If alleged offences come to the attention of a Trading Standards Officer, to initiate legal proceedings he must compile a report and send it to the local Procurator Fiscal's Office. The Procurator Fiscal will then investigate the matter and if there is sufficient evidence he will initiate a prosecution.

[34] See, *e.g.* s.38 of the Health and Safety at Work Act 1974.

prosecution is commenced, however, the Director of Public Prosecutions may have residual power to take over the conduct of the prosecution and can either continue or abandon the case.[35] In Scotland different procedural rules apply and enforcement authorities there are expressly not empowered to bring prosecutions for an offence.[36]

The duty of each enforcement authority is expressed in the Act to be specifically to enforce the legislation in its own area. This means that where products are in wide circulation any number of enforcement authorities could in principle bring a prosecution in respect of supply within their particular areas of jurisdiction. Moreover, a producer could be prosecuted in respect of each individual unsafe item placed on the market and could face Court hearings all over the United Kingdom. In practice this does not normally happen because, under the Home Authority Guidelines, an enforcement authority should liaise with the designated "Home Authority" before taking action to minimise duplication. If prosecutions follow then the prosecuting authority may group together a number of sample offences as representative of the contraventions relating to the product generally, and the Court is likely to take into account when considering sentence the fact that more than just the sample offences are involved.

Contravention of general safety requirements and the statutory defences

Offences are triable summarily (*i.e.* before a magistrates' court or Sheriff in Scotland) and are subject to a maximum fine of £5,000[37] and/or up to three months' imprisonment. Imprisonment will not apply to offences committed by companies, although as is described more fully below individuals responsible for a company's offence can be prosecuted personally and would be subject to the full range of sentencing powers.

Regulation 5 of the GPS Regulations deals specifically with the overlap of offences for breach of general safety requirements:

> "For the purposes of these Regulations the provisions of section 10 of the 1987 Act to the extent that they impose general safety requirements which must be complied with if products are to be—
> (i) placed on the market, offered or agreed to be placed on the market or exposed or possessed to be placed on the market by a producer; or
> (ii) supplied, offered or agreed to be supplied or exposed or possessed to be supplied by distributors,
>
> are hereby disapplied."

The disapplication of the Act *for the purposes of the Regulations* ensures that enforcement action cannot be taken under both the Act and the

[35] s.6, Prosecution of Offences Act 1985.
[36] s.27(4), Consumer Protection Act 1987.
[37] Reg. 17 of the GPS Regulations. s.12, CPA 1987 provides for up to six months' imprisonment for an offence against the s.10 general safety requirements. The fine is linked to 'level five' on the standard scale, an amount which can be increased by order of the Secretary of State from time to time.

Regulations in respect of the same activity. The DTI guidance treats the section 10 requirements as effectively superseded now by the GPS Regulations, with the former only having a role to play in very limited circumstances.[38]

To issue a prosecution it is necessary for the inspector to "lay an information", which is a document containing details of the alleged offence. Section 127 of the Magistrates' Court Act 1980 contains a requirement that the information must be laid within six months of the commission of the alleged offence[39] but a prosecution under the GPS Regulations can be brought up to 12 months after commission of the offence.[40] This information is checked by the magistrates court which in turn issues a summons which is then served on the defendant by the trading standards officer or his local authority's solicitor. The summons is served by sending it to the registered office of a company, or the usual place of abode of an individual defendant.[41].

It is important that the information correctly describes the specific offence with which the defendant is charged. It should for example specify that the offence consists of having "supplied" or "placed on the market" or whatever the exact allegation is in relation to the statutory offence. The Magistrates' Courts Rules require that sufficient particulars of the offence should be given as are necessary for giving reasonable information about the nature of the charge.[42] The summons will be accompanied by notes informing the defendant of the steps he has to take prior to the commencement of the hearing. In serving the summons the prosecutor may also include copies of witness statements and reports which he intends to rely on in evidence, although he is not obliged to do this because the rules governing disclosure of prosecution evidence do not impose a duty to disclose in cases for offences which are triable only summarily.[43] If the evidence is not sent, a defendant is well advised to request voluntary disclosure of copies by the prosecutor so that the whole nature of the prosecution case can be examined and a decision made by the defendant whether or not to contest the case.

If the defendant accepts his contravention of the requirements he has no defence available under the legislation (see below) then the defendant's representative attends court on the due date to enter a plea of

[38] s.10 will continue to apply to distributors (in this sense meaning persons other than the first placer on the market) of products which are subject to specific product directives where the implementing regulations only impose obligations on the person who first places the product on the market (for example regulations implementing the Personal Protective Equipment Regulations). Para. 8, DTI's Guidance, see Appendix 7.

[39] reg. 16 of the GPS Regulations. The Secretary of State has power to make Regulations increasing the time limit to 12 months for contravention of safety regulations: s.11(3)(e) and (f), Consumer Protection Act 1987.

[40] Reg. 16.

[41] There are no specific rules governing service on partnerships, and partners would be treated as individuals for the purposes of prosecution — for service requirements see r.99 of the Magistrates' Court Rules 1981.

[42] r.100(1), Magistrates' Court Rules 1981.

[43] The Magistrates' Court (Advance Information) Rules 1985 (S.I. 1985 No. 601).

guilty and to inform the court of any mitigating circumstances before penalty is imposed. If, however, the defendant intends to contest the case this would normally be notified in advance to the court and prosecution, and a date set by the court for a full trial of the issues. At the trial, it will be necessary for the prosecution to prove each element of the offence "beyond reasonable doubt" and this will entail the calling of all the witnesses unless particular facts are admitted by the defendant. A defendant might for example normally admit that he was a producer for the purposes of the alleged offence and that he supplied the goods, in which case only issue for the court to decide might be the question of whether or not the goods were unsafe. The exact nature of the defendant's case will depend on particular circumstances of the prosecution. If, for example, he is disputing the factual question as to whether a product is unsafe the defendant can put in issue those matters which go to assessing conformity with the general safety requirements.

Whilst these are technical issues which the defendants are entitled to argue that the prosecution have to prove to show that all the elements of an offence exist they are not strictly speaking matters which constitute defences. Only if all the necessary elements exist does the need arise for the defendant to establish one of the statutory defences. The burden of proving the matters concerned then lies on the defendant, but this burden is less stringent than that on the prosecution. The defendant only has to establish these matters "on the balance of probabilities" — *i.e.* that it is more likely than not that the facts are true.[44]

Regulation 14 of the GPS Regulations provides that in any proceedings where a person is prosecuted for an offence against the regulations: "It shall be a defence for that person to show that he took all reasonable steps and exercised all due diligence to avoid committing the offence.[45]

Although the standard of proof required for the defendant to prove this defence is only "on the balance of probabilities", very detailed evidence will be required to persuade the court that reasonable precautions have been implemented, and these precautions duly followed. The existence of a due diligence defence in relation to general safety requirements is not new; such a defence already existed under section 39 of the 1987 Act, In fact the wording is to all intents and purposes the same in both sets of provisions. How useful is this defence in practice? It rarely succeeds. Cases have been decided on the basis that reliance on a manufacturer's assurance or guarantee of compliance with statutory requirements is not sufficient.[46] Also, it has been held that a sampling

[44] See *R. v. Carr-Briant* [1943] K.B. 607.

[45] The relevant offences concern breach of general safety requirements (s.10, and reg. 7 of the GPS Regulations), breach of safety regulations (s.12(1), (2) or (3), CPA 1987), supply (other than as a producer) of dangerous products (reg. 9(a) of the GPS Regulations); failure to comply with prohibition notices or notices to warn (s.13(4) of the 1987 Act) and contravention of a suspension notice (s.14(6)). Also reg. 13 of the GPS Regulations (preparatory acts of offering or agreeing to supply or place dangerous products on the market, or exposing or possessing such products for supply or placing on the market). There is an equivalent reference of due diligence in s.39 of the CPA 1987.

[46] *David J.R. Taylor v. Lawrence Fraser (Bristol) Ltd* (1977) 121 S.J. 757. See also *Riley v. Webb* (1987) 151 J.P. 372.

system with only reported failures in products (as opposed to positive confirmation of compliance) was not adequate.[47] The defence does not merely mean that a person can be exonerated for exercising reasonable care; there is an obligation to take *all* reasonable precautions if there are any, and exercise *all* due diligence and one small omission will suffice to preclude the defence. There have been some recent cases under the CPA 1987 demonstrating this — and the circumstances of the cases are such that it seems that the due diligence defence will be even harder to show under the 1994 Regulations.

P&M Supplies (Essex) Ltd v. Devon County Council[48]
This case concerned a soft toy from which the eye could be detached. A director of the defendant had inspected the manufacturing methods at the Chinese production plant, and some random samples had been tested in-house in consultation with local Trading Standards Officers. The defendant failed to establish the defence, the reason being that the Court was not satisfied that a sufficient quality of toys had been tested — 378 out of 76,960 randomly sampled by the defendant, and 18 looked at by the public analyst. The prosecution brought no evidence as to what an appropriate number would have been but the court nevertheless convicted. The conviction was upheld on appeal, the reason being that the burden of proof lay with the defence to establish due diligence; the onus was on them to bring statistical evidence as to what an adequate number of tests would have been.

Coventry City Council v. Ackerman Group plc[49]
This case concerned egg boilers and exploding eggs. It was held that the absence of a warning with the product that users should not cook whole eggs in their shells the general safety requirement was breached. The defendant tried to argue that once the concerned had come to light that inexperienced microwave users might not break the eggs before cooking them they issued 80,000 labels and sent them to retailers saying:

> ". . . we would recommend that you arrange to affix the enclosed instruction labels on the lid of the individual boxes and, at the same time, we would kindly ask you to accept our sincere apologies for any inconvenience to you caused in this matter."

The two retailers involved in this case did not act on these recommendations. The defence was rejected by the court: "A mere recommendation leaves it in the discretion of the retailer to adopt the safety precaution or not. That is manifestly not enough. It is not at all surprising that the retailers involved in this case ignored the recommendation." The court held that this not only meant that the general product safety requirement was still not met by virtue of the labels. It meant also that in failing

[47] *Rotherham Metropolitan Borough Council v. Raysun* (1988) 153 J.P. 37.
[48] (1991) Crim.L.R. 832.
[49] Unreported (Divisional Court, July 13, 1994).

to inform adequately of the risks, the defendant had fallen markedly short of showing reasonable steps for the exercise of due diligence: "A retailer might quite reasonably have understood the letter, read with the label, as a mere inessential aid to better use of the egg boiler."

The moral of this case is that all warnings, but particularly post-marketing warnings, have to be clearly identified as drawing attention to an important safety issue. Diluting the strength of the warning in an attempt to minimise the commercial impact can destroy the potential due diligence defence.

Whirlpool (U.K.) Ltd and Magnet Ltd v. Gloucestershire County Council[50]
This case was discussed earlier in relation to the test of a "safe product". It involved a cooker hood which, by itself, was intrinsically safe but which apparently run the risk of fire damage when used in conjunction with certain gas hobs. The importers and retailers were unsuccessful in arguing that the general safety requirement under the 1987 Act had not been breached on account of the hood meeting all the requirements of the Low Voltage Electrical Equipment (Safety) Regulations 1989, the Low Voltage Directive, and the applicable British Standard. Where the hazard arose extraneously — *i.e.* because of its use in conjunction with another product, the court had to look at all the circumstances and adopt the general test of safety under section 10(2) of the Act. Could a defence of due diligence nevertheless succeed? The court said not. Even though evidence had been shown of the company's belief that the relevant safety certificates had been obtained and that these covered their use with these gas hobs there had, the court said, nevertheless been a failure to appreciate that there was a potential problem. Moreover, evidence had been given to the court that there was knowledge within the gas cooking appliances industry that there was a problem with hoods withstanding heat.

This case, therefore suggests that companies which do not follow closely industry developments in safety, for example through trade associations, will have problems with due diligence defences.

This case is also of interest in that Magnet argued the "retailer defence" in that they neither knew or had reasonable grounds for believing that the goods failed to comply with the general safety requiremets. It was held that their branch manager should have appreciated that there was something unsafe with the hood after the customer had first complained and before he installed his replacement. In any event, Magnet were deemed to have been remiss in not appreciating the knowledge referred to earlier that was available within the industry.

These cases would have all been decided the same way had they been brought under the GPS Regulations. In fact, the cases would have probably been even stronger had that been so; in the *Whirlpool* case had

[50] Unreported (Divisional Court, December 13, 1993 Co/d 1359/93). The decision is summarised in *Product Liability International*, July 1994, p. 107.

there been a finding of failure to participate in the monitoring of the safety of products placed on the market, the due diligence defence could not even have been pursued because of regulation 14(5) deems the defence to be unavailable where this failure has occurred. In the *Ackerman* case it would seem that the prosecution could have demonstrated a failure to comply with regulation 8 (requirements as to information) which would appear to negate a due diligence defence.

For practical purposes one of the most important applications of the due diligence defence is in relation to companies where breaches of the safety provisions are due to a failure on the part of a junior employee. *Tesco Supermarkets Ltd v. Nattrass*[51] involved a fault by a branch manager in applying correct prices to goods, and he was held by the House of Lords to be "another person" who had caused the company to contravene the requirements. The defence will only apply in such circumstances when all other appropriate precautions and controls have been in place and competent persons are appointed and supervision is properly carried out.

Where the defendant is endeavouring to establish a defence of due diligence not by reference to the precautions he took but on the basis of an allegation that the commission of the offence was due to the act or default of another person, or to reliance on information provided by another person, additional procedural requirements apply.[52] In these cases not less than seven clear days' notice before the hearing must be given to the prosecution of the fact that the defendant intends to rely on the due diligence defence, and thus notice must identify or assist in identifying the person alleged by the defendant to have caused him to commit the offence. (Failure to give the proper notice is not a complete bar to a due diligence defence but it cannot then be relied upon without the leave of the court.) If the due diligence defence is based upon reliance and information given by another the defendant must specifically demonstrate that his reliance on the information was reasonable, having regard in particular to the steps he took, and could reasonably have taken, to verify the information and whether there were any reasons for disbelieving it.[53]

Offences against the safety regulations

Section 12 of the 1987 Act specifies ways in which offences can be committed in relation to the requirement of safety regulations in force under the Act:

1. supplying goods contrary to a prohibition on supply.

[51] (1972) A.C. 153; (1971) 2 All E.R. 127. See also *R. v. British Steel* [1995] I.C.R. 586 (a Health and Safety at Work Act case) which emphasised the limits set on the scope of the *Tesco v. Nattrass* decision.
[52] s.39(2–4).
[53] s.39(4).

2. failure to carry out correctly a test or to use a procedure specified for ascertaining whether goods satisfy any requirements.
3. incorrect provision of information pursuant to safety regulations.
4. failure to supply information to another person for the purposes of that person to perform any function (or provision of false information).

The penalties on conviction are a fine of up to £5,000, or up to six months' imprisonment.

Distributor's failure to act with due care

Since under the 1987 Act there is no distinction made between a distributor (as an intermediary supplier) and a producer, a distributor (in the technical sense used by the GPS Regulations) would for these purposes face prosecution in relation to one of the offences described above. Regulation 12 of the GPS Regulations designates contravention of regulation 9(a) by a distributor as an offence — *i.e.* supplying products to any person which he knows or should have presumed are dangerous products. The procedures for prosecutions are same as those described above. The prosecution will either need to call evidence of the distributor's actual knowledge, or invite the court to infer from evidence of the information available to him at the time of the alleged offence that the dangers should have been presumed. This notion of being guilty on account of failing to presume is far from straightforward, and contrasts with the language of the 1987 Act retailer defence which is in terms of "reasonable grounds for belief". This requires the court to make an *ex post facto* judgment as to what the defendant ought to have thought, rather than determine what he *did* think about the safety of the products concerned. Given that the prosecution have the burden of proving the offence beyond reasonable doubt, any doubts the court may have about inferring what a distributor ought to have presumed will have to be resolved in the defendants favour. As noted previously, whilst the due diligence defence is available to a distributor faced with such a prosecution under the GPS Regulations, regulation 14(2) makes special provision that if the defendant has contravened regulation 9(b) (participation in monitoring the safety of products and passing on information) he is precluded from relying on the due diligence defence in relation to an alleged offence under Regulation 9(a).

Enforcement of GPS Regulations "conduct" duties

It has already been noted that the contravention of the obligations regarding the "conduct" of producers — testing, labelling, post-marketing surveillance etc. which are imposed on producers by regulation 8 and on distributors by regulation 9(b) does not give rise to any offence. It is unusual to have positive statutory duties which are not punishable in this way, but the U.K. Government took the position that the nature of these obligations referred to in the GPS Directive were not sufficiently prescriptive or clearly defined to be made subject to criminal penalties. Nevertheless, they are deemed "safety provisions" for the purposes of the 1987 Act and are thereby enforceable by suspension notices and forfeiture; as can be seen from **Table 5.2** above, neither of these enforcement measures, has as pre-requisite to being used, a requirement that the products concerned are *unsafe;* rather the power arises in relation to any contravention of a safety provision. (In contrast, the other measures of prohibition notices and notices are dependant on the products concerned being viewed as unsafe.) It is therefore impossible for an enforcement authority to enforce directly the producers' duties to test sample products, investigate complaints, mark batches or keep distributors informed of their monitoring, or to enforce against distributors the duties to co-operate in monitoring. The indirect remedy of a suspension notice or an application for a forfeiture order would be something of a blunt instrument in such circumstances. With the question of compliance here being highly judgemental, an authority might well be reluctant to risk a potentially severe financial penalty of having to pay compensation if the producer or distributor were to successfully challenge such action taken against them.

Ancillary offences

Contravention of the general safety requirements and safety regulations are the principal offences under the legislation. There are, however, numerous other offences created by the legislation which are ancillary to the principal offences and the enforcement measures:

1. Offences in relation to preparatory acts Under regulation 13 of the GPS Regulations it is an offence to offer or agree to place on the market any dangerous products, or expose or possess any such products for placing on the market, or to offer or agree to supply any dangerous products or expose or possess any such products for supply. These are all technical terms relating to different states of readiness to place products on the market, enabling prosecutions to be brought irrespective of whether or not a supply has actually occurred to a third party. The procedural steps for a prosecution will be the same as those described above in relation to an offence against the general safety requirement. The due diligence defence also applies in such cases, and on conviction penalties are the same as those described above.

2. Contravention of a prohibition notice Section 13(4): punishable by a fine of up to £5,000 and/or up to three months' imprisonment.

3. Contravention of a notice to warn Section 13(4): punishable by a fine of up to £5,000 and/or three months' imprisonment.

4. Contravention of a suspension notice Section 14(6): punishable by a fine of up to £5,000 and/or three months' imprisonment.

5. False statements to an enforcement officer Section 32(2): punishable by unlimited fine

6. Failure to comply with a notice from the Secretary of State to furnish information Section 18(3): punishable by fine of up to £5,000.

7. Furnishing false information in response to Secretary of State's notice Section 18(3): punishable by unlimited fine.

8. Obstruction of an enforcement officer or customs officer Section 32(1): punishable by a fine of up to £5,000.

9. Unauthorised persons purporting to act as an enforcement officer- Section 30(5): punishable by a fine of up to £5,000.

10. Wrongful disclosure of information obtained pursuant to statutory powers or safety regulations Section 38(1): punishable by unlimited fine and/or up to two years' imprisonment.

Additional powers to deal with persistent offenders

Fair Trading Act 1974[54]

Part III of this Act confers powers on the Director General of Fair Trading to take action against a person carrying on business who "persists" in a course of conduct which:

(a) is detrimental to the interests of consumers in the United Kingdom, whether those interests are economic or in respect of health, safety or other matters; and
(b) is to be regarded as "unfair to consumers".[55]

Unfair conduct for these purposes consists of contraventions of any enactments which impose duties, prohibitions or restrictions enforceable by criminal proceedings, or conduct which amount to a breach of contract or breach of some other obligation which would justify civil remedies.[56] It is not a prerequisite for the exercise of the Director's

[54] Pt. II of this Act provided for a Consumer Protection Advisory Comittee to which adverse consumer trade practices could be referred. The system was not considered workable and the Committee fell into desuetude in 1982.
[55] Fair Trading Act 1973, s.34(1).
[56] subs.34(2) and (3).

powers that the person concerned shall have been convicted, or even any proceedings commenced.

The Director is under a duty to act on complaints he receives from consumers or others (such as a consumer pressure group or even a competitor of the subject of the complaint) as well as any other information collected by or furnished to him. The action consists of requesting written assurances that the unfair conduct (and any similar conduct) will cease. If the person concerned refuses to give the assurance sought, or gives an assurance but later fails to observe it, the Director can resort to bringing proceedings before the Restrictive Practices Court for an order to be made against him.[57] Failure to comply with such an order would amount to contempt of court, and would render the person liable to fines, sequestration of assets or imprisonment.

Special provision is made for "interconnected bodies corporate" — *i.e.* groups of companies: the court can direct that an order made against one company shall bind the whole group, and if a company against which an order has been made joins a group (or its existing group expands) the Director can apply to have the scope of the order extended to cover the newly related companies.[58]

These powers supplement the primary enforcement regime of the Consumer Protection Act 1987 and may give consumers a useful additional means of complaining about products which might fall short of breaching specific regulatory safety requirements; a product might, for example, be safe according to all the statutory definitions, but the sales practices might lead to danger because it is unfit for the buyer's particular purposes' contrary to the Sale of Goods legislation. The OFT obtained 70 assurances between 1991 and 1994, mostly relating to Trade Descriptions offences, breach of implied contractual terms with consumers or failures to carry out repair work properly. In 1992 assurances were given by two directors of a company that they would refrain from contravening various safety regulations applying to electrical goods. A number of assurances were also obtained in relation to the supply of defective motor vehicles.[59]

Injunctions restraining the Commission of crimes

Local authorities are exceptions to the general rule that only the Attorney General may bring an action in the civil courts for an injunction to restrain the commission of crimes. Section 222 of the Local Government Act 1972 permits local authorities to bring the necessary civil proceedings if they "consider it expedient for the promotion or protection of the interests of the inhabitants of their area", and since

[57] The court may accept a formal undertaking from the person concerned in lieu of an order — s.37(1).

[58] s.40. See *Re: British Concrete Pipe Association* [1983] I.C.R. 215; [1983] 1 All E.R. 549.

[59] See Annual Reports of the Director General of Fair Trading.

local authorities (in their capacity as weights and measures authorities) have the duty to enforce safety legislation within their areas the remedy of an injunction may be granted to them if the court is satisfied that the circumstances are sufficiently serious. It is not necessary however for the local authority to demonstrate that all other statutory remedies, such as notices or obtaining the conviction, have been exhausted. Infringement of the criminal law by itself is not sufficient to justify the remedy. It was suggested in one House of Lords decision that it must be shown that the defendant in the civil proceedings must be shown to be "deliberately and flagrantly flouting the law".[60] This test was an attempt to encapsulate a wide range of circumstances in which the civil courts would grant relief when the criminal courts had not yet had an opportunity to deal with a prosecution and so determine whether or not an offence was actually being committed. However, deliberate contravention will not be treated as the *only* test by the court asked to grant the injunction. In *City of London Corporation v. Bovis Construction Ltd*,[61] a case concerning contravention of a noise control notice, Bingham LJ said:

> "The essential foundation for the exercise of the court's discretion to grant an injunction is not that the offender is deliberately and flagrantly flouting the law but the need to draw the inference that the defendant's unlawful operations will continue unless and until effectively restrained by the law and that nothing short of an injunction will be effective to restrain them".

Here the court granted a temporary injunction at a time when criminal proceedings for breach of the notices were still pending.

Although this approach does not appear to have been adopted yet there would be no bar in principle against local authorities (or the Attorney General[62] seeking injunctions to prevent the sale of unsafe products, or to compel with compliance with, for example, a suspension notice or prohibition notice which (if not complied with) might otherwise not have their intended effect at once and would only render the offender liable to criminal penalties at a later date.

Liability of persons other than principal offenders

In addition to what is termed the 'principal offender' it is possible for other persons also to be liable in respect of an offence. Where a company is convicted and the offence is shown to have been committed "with the consent or connivance of, or to be attributable to any neglect" on the part of any director, manager or similar officer such a person may be prosecuted personally.[63] The same principle applies to companies

[60] See *per* Lord Bridge in *Stafford Borough Council v. Elkenford Ltd* [1077] 1 W.L.R. 324, 330.
[61] [1992] 3 All E.R. 697.
[62] The Attorney General's powers may be more limited than those of local authorities under s.222, see *Gouriet v. Union of Post Office Workers* [1978] A.C. 135.
[63] s.40(2), Consumer Protection Act 1987.

managed by their members, and individual shareholders or a parent company managing the affairs of its subsidiary can also be accountable for the principal offenders offence.[64]

There is also provision for liability on the part of anyone else who *causes* an offence to be committed. Section 40(1) provides that:

> "Where the commission by any person of an offence . . . is due to an act or default committed by some other person in the course of any business of his, the other person shall be guilty of the offence and may be proceeded against and punished by virtue of this paragraph whether or not proceedings were taken against the first-mentioned person".

Although it is not necessary for the principal offender to be convicted in order for the secondary offender to be liable it nevertheless has to be proved that the principal offender would have been liable if prosecuted. The provision can apply in a variety of circumstances, for example where a component supplier has introduced a defect into an otherwise safe product, or where goods have become damaged or tainted by being stored or transported by another party. Unlike some applications of the due diligence defence it does not, however, extend to situations where an individual employee is personally responsible for causing a safety defect because in such a situation the proviso that the secondary offender must be acting in the course of a business of *his* is not met.[65]

Public Order Act 1986

This Act is concerned with various forms of harassment, threats and offensive behaviour. It makes provision for specific criminal offences relating to deliberate tampering with or contamination of products, hoaxes and blackmail attempts. The offences, which are subject to stiff penalties are set out as follows in section 38:

(1) It is an offence for a person, with the intention—

(a) of causing public alarm or anxiety, or

(b) of causing injury to members of the public consuming or using the goods, or

(c) of causing economic loss to any person by reason of the goods being shunned by members of the public, or

(d) of causing economic loss to any person by reason of steps taken to avoid any such alarm or anxiety, injury or loss,

to contamination or interfere with goods, or make it appear that goods have been contaminated or interfered with, or to place goods which have been contaminated or interfered with, or which appear to have been contami-

[64] s.40(3).

[65] See *Warwickshire County Council v. Johnson* [1993] 1 All E.R. 299 concerning s.20(2)(a) of the CPA 1987 (misleading price claims) where a shop manager was held not personally liable under another provision for the same reason.

nated or interfered with, in a place where goods of that description are consumed, used, sold or otherwise supplied.

(2) *It is also an offence for a person, with any such intention as is mentioned in paragraph (a), (c) or (d) of subsection (1), to threaten that he or another will do, or to claim that he or another has done, any of the acts mentioned in that subsection.*

(3) *It is an offence for a person to be in possession of any of the following articles with a view to the commission of an offence under subsection (1)—*

  (a) *materials to be used for contaminating or interfering with goods or making it appear that goods have been contaminated or interfered with, or*

  (b) *goods which have been contaminated or interfered with, or which appear to have been contaminated or interfered with.*

(4) *A person guilty of an offence under this section is liable—*

  (a) *on conviction on indictment to imprisonment for a term not exceeding 10 years or a fine or both, or*

  (b) *on summary conviction to imprisonment for a term not exceeding six months or a fine not exceeding the statutory maximum [£5,000] or both.*

(5) *In this section "goods" includes substances whether natural or manufactured and whether or not incorporated in or mixed with other goods.*

(6) *The reference in subsection (2) to a person claiming that certain acts have been committed does not include a person who in good faith reports or warns that such acts have been, or appear to have been, committed.*

6 Products for use at work

Products used for business purposes are subject to general safety requirements contained in the Health and Safety at Work, etc., Act 1974. The principles are distinct from those in consumer safety legislation, and the law is enforced separately by Health and Safety Executive inspectors.

Products for use at work are categorised for these purposes as either articles or substances. Designers, manufacturers, importers and suppliers have various obligations in relation to product design, intrinsic safety, warnings and instructions. The general safety requirements are supplemented by more detailed regulations which are specific to different types of product.

INTRODUCTION

The legislation described in the previous chapter is concerned primarily with consumer protection and products for private use or consumption. As has been seen, the definitions of products in this legislation are meant to exclude capital goods and products used solely in the context of a trade or business.

In the U.K., product safety in the workplace has been regulated within the overall context of health and safety at work legislation, and treated as a strand of the statutory protection afforded to workers. This approach recognises that safety in the use of such products, which may be highly technical and require skilled operation, is closely related to an employer's arrangements for safe systems at work and proper supervision and training of workers. An employer in any case has direct responsibilities for the provision of safe plant and equipment for his workforce and for ensuring that care is taken in relation to the use of chemicals.[1] The regulation of workplace products in this way enables health and safety inspectors to take enforcement action, rather than having to enlist the involvement and support of local authority trading standards officers.

[1] s.2(2), Health and Safety at Work Act 1974, the Provision and Use of Work Equipment Regulations 1992, Employers Liability (Defective Equipment) Act 1969, and the Control of Substances Hazardous to Health Regulations 1994.

In a number of instances a clear distinction between consumer and workplace products cannot be made; for example telephones, computer hardware or tins of paint, may readily be used for business purposes or at home. Producers of such goods are subject to both the consumer protection and workplace product safety regimes and, for that matter, may be subject to the scrutiny and powers of the two distinct sets of enforcement authorities as well. While manufacturers and suppliers will need to be aware of the requirements of both systems it is fair to say that a fundamental division of product safety legislation in this way does not fit comfortably with the commercial realities of placing products on the market. Increasingly, largely as a result of European influence, product safety regulations for consumer and workplace products are converging with measures such as the Supply of Machinery (Safety) Regulations 1992 that apply to both areas. Nevertheless, the continuing existence of the dual statutory arrangements is recognised in such regulations which preserve the separate enforcement powers of the regulatory bodies according to the context in which the product is being used.

Regulatory control

In 1972 the Robens Committee published a landmark report on the need to overhaul legislation dealing with health and safety.[2] The report stated the proposition that: "the first step in the promotion of safety and health at work is to ensure, so far as may be practicable, that plant machinery, equipment and materials are so designed and constructed as to be intrinsically safe in use". The Committee made two particular recommendations in this respect: firstly, that there should be a general statutory obligation on those making and marketing plant, machinery and equipment for industrial and commercial use, to ensure it is designed and constructed to comply with the safety requirements. Secondly, that there should be comprehensive powers of control over toxic substances allied to a general statutory obligation on manufacturers to ensure adequate safety testing of new substances before they are marketed for industrial use.

It was in response to this report that Parliament enacted the Health and Safety at Work, etc., Act 1974 (HSWA) which is the foundation for what has become a highly developed system of hazard-specific regulations, general statutory obligations and enforcement powers governing all aspects of workplace safety.[3] The Act established as a statutory body the Health and Safety Commission (HSC) which has overall responsibility for promoting health and safety measures and more specifically a duty to develop and present regulation for the Secretary of State to then adopt. A separate body, the Health and Safety Executive (HSE) has

[2] Report of the Robens Committee on Safety and Health at Work (1972 Cmnd. 5034).
[3] Northern Ireland is subject to broadly equivalent legislation in the form of the Health and Safety at Work (Northern Ireland) Order 1978.

responsibility for enforcement and other advisory and support functions to assist the HSC. Unlike under consumer protection legislation ministers do not hold enforcement powers under the 1974 Act.

The basic provisions relating to product safety are found in section 6 of the Act which apply to all *articles* or *substances* for use at work. These duties are imposed on anyone who manufacturers, imports, supplies or (in the case of articles) designs products for use at work, and they expressly require such products to be safe for use, properly tested, and supplied with adequate information and instructions. Breach of these duties is a criminal offence.

The general duties are supplemented by health and safety regulations made pursuant to powers under the Act. As regards hazardous substances, there are now detailed regulations covering testing and notification to the authorities by manufacturers, the supply of safety data, and use of containers and packaging. The supply of a number of products is banned altogether. As regards plant and machinery, there is a range of regulations, most notably the Supply of Machinery (Safety) Regulations 1992, which lay down specific safety criteria.

The HSWA contains provisions relating to enforcement of the general duties and regulations. The sole enforcement authority in relation to section 6 of the Act is the HSE,[4] whose inspectors are based in offices around the country. The measures available to these officers are service of formal notices requiring improvements. In safety arrangements or prohibition of activities contravening safety requirements. In addition to a range of supplementary powers to carry out investigations, interviews and collect documents, health and safety inspectors may commence prosecutions.

SUPPLY OF PLANT, MACHINERY AND MATERIALS ETC

The key provisions are contained in section 6(1) of HSWA and are as follows:

> "It shall be the duty of any person who designs, manufactures, imports or supplies any article for use at work . . .
>
> (a) to ensure, so far as is reasonably practicable, that the article is so designed and constructed that it will be safe and without risks to health at all times when it is being set, used, cleaned or maintained by a person at work;
>
> (b) to carry out or arrange for the carrying out of such testing and examination as may be necessary for the performance of the duty imposed on him by the preceding paragraph;

[4] reg. 4(5)(a) of the Health and Safety (Enforcing Authority) Regulations 1989.

(c) to take such steps as are necessary to secure that persons supplied by that person with the article are provided with adequate information about the use for which the article is designed or has been tested and about any conditions necessary to ensure that it will be safe and without risks to health at all such times as are mentioned in paragraph (a) above and when it is being dismantled or disposed of; and

(d) to take such steps as are necessary to secure, so far as is reasonably practicable, that persons so supplied are provided with all such revisions of information provided to them by virtue of the preceding paragraph as are necessary by reason of its becoming known that anything gives rise to a serious risk to health or safety."

The duty holders

It will be seen that the duty is the same in principle in relation to the designer, manufacturer, importer or other supplier of products covered by this section, but the nature of the duty will be qualified in two ways. First, it is confined to matters within the control of that particular person.[5] Second, it is a duty framed in terms of what it is *reasonably practicable* for the person in question to do in relation to the product. Section 6(2) of the Act contains a supplementary provision whereby the designer or manufacturer is under an additional duty: "to carry out or arrange for the carrying out of any necessary research with a view to the discovery and, so far as is reasonably practicable, the elimination or minimisation of any risks to health or safety to which the design of an article may give rise".

Manufacturers and designers are not defined in terms, but they include persons to whom design or manufacture is sub-contracted, and include manufacturers and designers of components as well as finished products. It can therefore be important to clarify with sub-manufacturers/designers precisely who is undertaking responsibility for testing, examination or research into safety aspects of the product in its completed form. It is not a requirement for importers or other suppliers to repeat any testing, examination or research which has been carried out by the designers or the manufacturers, in so far as it is reasonable for them to rely on the results.[6]

Importers for these purposes are persons who import products into the United Kingdom. (This legislation is not derived from E.C. directives and hence the term "importer" has a much narrower sense than in relation to the European consumer safety legislation.) The duties have no application to products not supplied in the U.K. and that are

[5] s.6(7).
[6] s.6(6).

produced only for export.[7] The duties of importers are more onerous than on the other duty holders because the Act makes them responsible for defects or other breaches of section 6(1) directly due to the fault of a foreign designer or manufacturer; this is irrespective of the fact that aspects of development or production are beyond an importer's direct control.[8]

Supply in this context means supplying by way of sale, lease, hire or hire purchase, whether as principal or agent.[9] Thus, distributors and commercial agents are suppliers within the scope of the legislation, as are retailers for trade customers. Special provisions exist in relation to leasing and other finance arrangements. Section 6(9) of the Act distinguishes "ostensible suppliers" (the finance organisation acquiring an interest solely for the purpose of financing the transaction for the customer) from "effective suppliers" (*i.e.* the person actually supplying the goods under the financing arrangement). Where this takes place by way of hire purchase, conditional sale, credit sale or lease it is the effective supplier who is deemed to have the duty to comply with section 6 and the ostensible supplier is immune.[10]

There are separate duties on persons who erect or install articles in premises for use by persons at work. The duty is expressed as one to ensure, so far as is reasonably practicable, that nothing about the way in which the article is erected or installed makes it unsafe or a risk to health when it is being set, used, cleaned or maintained.[11]

There can be no contracting out as such from obligations imposed by statute which are personal to the duty holders. This is not to say that a manufacturer or other supplier can never rely upon tests or precautions devised by others. There may be many circumstances in which it is not just permissible but even necessary to seek specialist external advice in order to discharge the statutory duty. The Act makes special provision for the responsibilities to be transferred where an article (but not a substance) is designed, manufactured, imported or supplied on behalf of or to another person. In such circumstances provided there is a *written undertaking* that the other person will take specified steps sufficient to ensure safety the designer, manufacturer, importer or supplier (as the case may be) is given immunity.[12] This provision is useful in a range of circumstances where, for example, suppliers of components and materials may have little knowledge or control over the design and production of the finished goods, or they do not have the testing capability to deal with safety checks and the manufacturer is taking a co-ordinating

[7] Various regulations, including ones implementing New Approach Directives are of wider scope and extend to exports to Europe. See for example the definitions of "supply" in reg. 3(2) of the Electromagnetic Compatibility Regulations 1992 and "placing on the market" in the Notification of New Substances Regulations 1993.

[8] s.6(8A).

[9] s.53(1).

[10] See also the Health and Safety (Leasing) Regulations 1992 (S.I. 1992 No. 1524).

[11] s.6(3).

[12] s.6(8).

role for this purpose, or where a product is supplied for incorporation into larger systems. The main purpose of this section is to facilitate customers ordering custom-built articles which the manufacturer might not be able to verify as being safe for the conditions of use. It is commonly the case that suppliers', printed terms and conditions include clauses deemed to be written undertakings from the purchaser for these purposes. Such clauses may be effective in certain circumstances, although better protection against liability is afforded by there being a discrete written agreement drawn up specifically for the purpose of the supply in question. Even then this will not necessarily confer complete immunity for two reasons. Firstly, the person is relieved of the duty only to the extent that it is reasonable having regard to the terms of the undertaking (thus requiring undertakings to be comprehensive), and secondly because the provision only works to relieve liability in respect of paragraph (a) of sub-section 6(1), leaving undiminished the other duties relating to testing and provision of information contained in paragraphs (b) to (d).

The meaning of 'article for use at work'

Work is defined for the purposes of the HSWA as meaning work as an employee or as a self-employed person, and an employee is at work throughout the time when he is in the course of his employment (but not otherwise); a self-employed person is at work throughout such time as he devotes to work as a self-employed person.[13] It is not clear, however, if the "use" and "user" for the purposes of these requirements is to be treated as being used by the purchaser (*i.e.* the organisation acquiring the product) or if instead it relates to use of the individual workers, a distinction which might be material in some circumstances, for instance the degree of detail provided in safety information and instructions[14] and it may be that the answer to this question varies depending on the circumstances in which products are to be employed; for example, some equipment might be deemed as not sufficiently safe if it is not provided with an easy-to-follow operator's manual, as opposed to a complex set of technical instructions to the purchasing company.

An "article for use at work" means:

(a) any plant (including machinery, equipment or appliances) designed for use or operation (whether exclusively or not) by persons at work, and

(b) any article designed for use as a component in any such plant.[15]

This definition is not without its difficulties. While it clearly applies to things such as tools and machinery used for the performance of work

[13] s.52.

[14] See HS(G) 27, para. 6.

[15] s.53(1). Note, there are separate provisions in relation to fairground equipment, see s.6(1)A.

related tasks the terms "equipment" encompasses very much more. In *Coltman v. Bibby Tanks Ltd*,[16] a case under the Employer's Liability (Defective Equipment) Act 1969, it was held that a large ship which sank due to defects in its hull was "equipment". In *Knowles v. Liverpool City Council* dealing with interpretation of the same Act,[17] it was held that a flagstone being handled by a worker in the course of his employment was also "equipment". In decisions in cases dealing with the interpretation of the terms "article" used in section 175(1) of the Factories Act 1961[18] a similarly broad interpretation has been given to the term, for example to include water being treated in a filter house. For the purposes of the HSWA the definition is probably to be viewed in the same way as it is in these related statutes, except that it is more confined on account of the separate provision in relation to "substances", the definition of which is discussed below.

It would appear, therefore that all products and raw materials, regardless of whether they are used as means of production or are themselves in production, are covered by this section dealing with articles, unless covered elsewhere as substances. However, there was a case which drew the line at purely experimental products. In *McKay v. Unwin Pyrotechnics Ltd*[19] the Divisional Court dealt with a case where a dummy mine had exploded injuring a person carrying out the first trials and demonstrations. In this case the person injured was a self-employed explosives expert engaged as consultant in the design, testing and manufacture of the mine. It was held that the particular product was not designed or manufactured *for use at work*, but rather *to determine whether it could be used at work*.

The legislation is not restricted to articles supplied new and for the first time. Second-hand products, goods supplied for refurbishment and re-supply, recyclable materials and even waste can attract the responsibilities laid down by section 6. In such circumstances the user, in passing on products in a transaction for financial consideration for them to be used by persons at work elsewhere becomes a supplier in his own right and becomes subject to obligations in the same way the original suppliers were. This may have a number of ramifications, as discussed further below. If, however, there is not a supply in the meaning of the Act, for example if products are merely sent away for servicing, repair or refurbishment section 6 would not apply to that arrangement.[20]

[16] [1988] A.C. 276.

[17] *Knowles v. Liverpool City Council* [1993] 4 All E.R. 321; [1993] 1 W.L.R. 1428.

[18] *Longhurst v. Guildford, Godalming and District Water Board* [1963] A.C. 625; *Cox v. S. Cutler & Sons Ltd* [1948] 2 All E.R. 665.

[19] [1991] Crim L.R. 547.

[20] Note, however, that if the product owner thereby exposes the employees of the repair or service organisation to risks he may contravene s.3 of the HSWA, *i.e.* there is a duty on an employer to ensure that persons not in his employment but who may be affected by his undertaking are not thereby exposed to risks to their health or safety. The fact that the repair or service operations are not under the control of the product owner will not necessarily exonerate the latter from liability. (See also *R v. Associated Octel Ltd* [1995] I.C.R. 281).

Duty to make articles safe

There are no definitions of the term "safe" or "risk" even though they are used throughout the HSWA. It is clear however that one must consider safety in the broadest sense as risk to anyone (not just the immediate user) must be taken into account. The Act provides that risks for these purposes: "shall be treated as including risks attributable to the manner of conducting and undertaking, the plant or substances used for the purposes of an undertaking and the condition of premises so used or any part of them".[21] The legislation is concerned not only with risks *to* persons at work but also protecting persons other than persons at work against risks to health or safety arising out of or in connection with the actual persons at work.[22]

These descriptions serve to clarify the subjects to which risks apply for the purposes of the Act, but not what a risk actually is. The Royal Society Study Group report on Risk: Analysis, Perception and Management described risk as: "the probability that a particular adverse event occurs during a stated period of time, or results from a particular challenge". British Standards treat risk as: "a combination of the probability, or frequency, of occurrence of a defined hazard and the magnitude of the consequences of the occurrence".[23] In BS4778 safety is defined as: "the freedom from unacceptable risks of personal harm". It is notable that this definition of safety is not based on absence of risk *per se*. The standard notes that: "it is implied that for the consequences of an event to be defined as a hazard, *i.e.* a potential for causing harm, there is some risk to the human population and therefore safety could not be guaranteed, even if the risk is accepted when judged against some criterion of acceptability."

In the Approved Code of Practice to the Management of Health and Safety at Work Regulations 1992 the following description of risk appears:

"(a) A hazard is something with the potential to cause harm (this can include substances or machines, methods of work and other aspects of work organisation;

(b) risk expresses the likelihood that the harm from a particular hazard is realised;

(c) the extent of the risk covers the population which might be affected by a risk; *i.e.* the number of people who might be exposed and the consequences for them.

Risk therefore reflects both the likelihood that harm will occur and its severity."

On the few occasions that the courts have been called upon to examine the meaning of risk within the context of the HSWA they have been

[21] s.1(3).
[22] s.1(1)(b).
[23] BS 4778: Quality Vocabulary: Part 3: Section 3.2 Glossary of International Terms (1991).

remarkably reticent. In one case the Court of Appeal even went so far as to say there is no need to define or analyse the meaning of risks of safety.[24] The meaning of risk was nevertheless considered by the Court of Appeal in *R. v. Board of Trustees of the Science Museum*,[25] a case concerning section 3 of the HSWA and the duties of employers to ensure that persons outside their employment are not exposed to risks. It was held that a risk is to be taken as conveying the idea of a possibility of danger not an actual danger, and that a risk therefore exists whether or not people are exposed to the danger in any given situation. In this case the risk in question was Legionnaires' Disease that might be contracted from air conditioning cooling towers, and the risk was held to exist irrespective of there being no proof of inhalation by persons nearby or even the presence of legionella pneumophilia bacteria in the equipment. It was argued by the defendant that this reasoning would render anyone with such equipment liable to prosecution. It was the court's view that: "subject only to the defence of reasonable practicability, section 3(1) is intended to be an absolute prohibition. Bearing in mind the imperative of protecting public health and safety so far as it is reasonably practicable to do so, the result could be faced with equanimity".[26]

What is more, the Court of Appeal has held that the analysis of both risk and the defence of reasonable practicability is limited to purely objective considerations, which means that a manufacturer or other supplier cannot argue that his particular resources or the technical knowledge of his staff for instance were such that he could not have been expected to know about a particular risk.[27]

Although it has to be acknowledged that there has been no case in which section 6 itself has been considered judicially for these purposes the practice of the courts has been to interpret the various sections as being consistent with one another. On the existing authorities it must be taken that designers, manufactures, importers and suppliers are subject to an absolute duty based on a duty to *ensure* the absence of risk. Exposure to any risk will suffice, and the remoteness of the incidence of that risk is merely a factor which bears upon the defence of reasonable practicability of being able to take steps to avoid the danger. This approach is at odds with that taken by the Royal Society Study Group and others who view risk in terms of the potential attaching to a given hazard, and who import notions "acceptability" of inevitable danger and "likelihood" of harm in the overall assessment of a product's risks. It also appears that the strict legal interpretation of the 1974 Act highlights a significant conceptual divergence between health and safety legislation on the one hand and consumer protection legislation on the other. The essential difference is that in health and safety legislation the

[24] *R. v. Kenchington Little plc*, Court of Appeal Criminal Division February 17, 1993 (unreported).
[25] [1993] 3 All E.R. 853; [1993] 1 W.L.R. 1171.
[26] *Ibid.*, at 859 and 1178 respectively.
[27] *R. v. Kenchington Little plc, op. cit.*

primary duty is apparently one to provide absolutely safe products, whereas in consumer legislation it is recognised that this primary safety question must be judged against criteria involving criteria of acceptable levels of minimum risk.[28] Under the law for work products the onus is on the person supplying the products to show it was not reasonably practicable to do more to ensure safety; under consumer safety law the onus is to show due diligence.

It is clear though that in considering whether a product is safe and without risks a criterion that must be taken into account is that of the reasonable foreseeability of the occurrence in question.[29] This mitigates the strictness of the duty somewhat so that it may not be truly "absolute" as the courts have suggested, although paradoxically it also highlights another element of risk which must be considered, which is foreseeable misuse for example by an operator or by a person disposing of the product. If for example an item of electrical equipment used in a confined space is likely to be towed around by users by its power cable regardless of the provision of a suitable handle, the designers and manufacturers should realise this and make the electrical couplings themselves strong enough to withstand the strain. This is clear from the changes made to the wording of section 6 in 1988, which had previously confined the duty to supply safe products to situations where they were *properly used*, and which exonerated the suppliers if their instructions for use were not followed.[30] However, the effect of this revised section is to require manufactures and so on to anticipate situations where misuse by individual users is to be expected and, where practicable, design out risks and provide suitable precautions to prevent harm in those circumstances.

So far as is reasonably practicable

As has been seen above, the duty to ensure safety is qualified by use of the phrase *so far as is reasonably practicable*, a qualification that appears throughout health and safety legislation and which has become a term of art. Section 40 provides that the onus on proving that it is not reasonably practicable to do more than has in fact been done to satisfy the duty on the designer, manufacturer, supplier or importer as the case may be. For practical purposes therefore this operates as a defence to the otherwise strict duties to ensure safety. (See above in the discussion of risk.)

The classic exposition of the phrase was given by Asquith L.J. in *Edwards v. National Coal Board*[31]:

[28] See the definition of safe product in reg. 2(1) of the General Product Safety Regulations 1994.

[29] s.6(10). See *Larner v. British Steel plc* [1993] 4 All E.R. 102 for a review of the authorities relating to reasonable foreseeability of risks as an element of duties to ensure safety.

[30] See the amending provisions of the Consumer Protection Act 1987, s.36 and Sched. 3.

[31] [1949] 1 K.B. 704. See also *West Bromwich Building Society v. Townsend* [1983] I.C.R. 257.

> "Reasonably practicable is a narrower term than physically possible, and implies that a computation must be made in which the quantum of risk is placed in one scale, and the sacrifice, whether in money, time or trouble, involved in the measures necessary to avert the risk, is placed in the other; and that, if it be shown that there is a gross disproportion between them, the risk being insignificant in relation to the sacrifice, the person upon whom the duty is laid discharges the burden of proving that compliance was not reasonably practicable. This computation falls to be made at a point of time anterior to the happening of the incident complained of."

An HSE guidance note states that this test is to be applied on an objective basis, emphasising that in considering the cost no allowance must be made for the size, nature or profitability of the business concerned.[32] This guidance goes on to say that where the difficulty and cost are high, and the risk is comparatively unimportant, there is no need to take action. The fundamental difficulty with this way of interpreting the duty is that it views manufacturers' obligations entirely in the abstract, and there are no points of reference as to exactly what — as a practical matter — should be done to meet the statutory requirement. The courts are equally reluctant to lay down principles of law of general application where they feel that it is essentially a factual question which has to be determined on a case-by-case basis. In many instances it may be possible to find such a point of reference in health and safety regulations dealing with the specific product in question or analogous requirements for products which have similarities. (For example, the legislation on machinery may contain useful lists of safety features in the applicable "Essential Requirements" which can be taken as analogous to or indicative of what is reasonably practicable even where the regulations themselves do not apply to the product.) It cannot be concluded, however, that the absence of a specific provision in health and safety regulations precludes any further question of what is reasonably practicable, as regulations may not reflect the current state of the art or what is widely accepted as good manufacturing practice in the particular industry in question.[33] Moreover, demonstrating that what has been done is the universal practice in an industry is not of itself proof that a duty has been discharged so far as is reasonably practicable, and will only be one factor to be weighed in the evidence.[34] The courts will

[32] HS(G)27(rev) Substances for Use at Work: The Provision of Information.

[33] There may be some doubt as to whether safety regulations, or European Directives, that are not yet in force in the U.K. can be taken as a criterion of what is reasonably practicable. In *R. v. Birmingham City Council, ex parte Ferrero Ltd* [1990] 154 J.P. 661, *The Times*, March 3, 1990, it was held that regulations not yet in force should not be taken into account for purposes of determining compliance with the general safety requirements in the Consumer Protection Act 1987. "The object of a delay between publication and coming into force of regulations was to enable manufacturers to take steps to comply with them, rather than find themselves immediately in breach", *per* Hutchinson J.

[34] *Martin v. Boulton and Paul (Steel Construction) Ltd* [1982] I.C.R. 366.

not necessarily condone an industry-wide practice if it fails to meet an objective test of what is reasonably practicable.

An HSE Guidance note on section 6 adopts the dictum of Asquith L.J. and restates that in relation to product safety in the following way:

> "The requirement to ensure 'so far as is reasonably practicable' means that in the design, manufacture, supply, erection and installation of articles account should be taken not only of the likelihood of risks to safety and health but also their severity, the physical and practical problems of reducing or removing them and whether the money and time involved in such step would be disproportionate to the result that can be obtained. If the risks are substantial, then it would be reasonably practicable to go to considerable trouble and expense to find ways of reducing or removing them . . .
>
> Consideration should be given to ensuring so far as is reasonably practicable, that the best known health and safety practices, techniques and knowledge have been incorporated in the design and manufacture, etc., and that there are adequate margins of safety. This would include such factors as design strength, guarding of dangerous parts, construction of enclosures, provision of safety devices, construction of electrical apparatus for use in potential explosive atmospheres, double insulation techniques, extraction of dust and fume, etc".[35]

When considering reasonable practicability the courts are obliged to take into account Approved Codes of Practice, *i.e.* codes which have been formally adopted by the HSC pursuant to section 16 of the Act. Other formal HSE guidelines, or other recommendations issued by third parties will be influential as well. The HSE has published a list of standards that may be relevant — see *Standards Significant to Health and Safety at Work* to which reference is made by its advisory and enforcement officers.[36] This contains British Standards, and also international and European standards. The 1989 edition was still current at the start of 1995, and so it is necessary to make further enquiries as to the up to date position.

Testing, examination, research

Duties in relation to *testing* and *examination* are imposed on all designers, manufacturers, importers and suppliers, but as was noted above there is a separate duty specifically relating to "necessary research". The two types of obligation therefore need to be considered separately.

Testing and examination

The Act lays down no more than the barest requirement that testing and examination should be carried out as is necessary to ensure compliance

[35] *Articles and substances for use at work; Guidance for designers, manufacturers, importers, suppliers, erectors and installers* (Guidance Note GS8).

[36] *Standards Significant to Health and Safety at Work,* April 1989.

with the statutory duties regarding supply of safe products, including the duty to provide adequate safety information. This leaves the duty holders to determine what they consider necessary for their particular products and their intended markets. Very much more specific testing obligations are laid down by some of the health and safety regulations, in particular those governing machinery and chemicals. (See below.) Where regulations provide a comprehensive set of requirements the general duty to test and examine under section 6 may be effectively otiose.

An HSE guidance note[37] makes the following general points:

- The major part of testing and examination takes place at the production stage. This need not necessarily be duplicated by others in the supply chain where it is reasonable to rely on the results.
- Responsibility for deciding what testing to carry out lies with the individual designer, manufacturer, importer or supplier as the case may be but ultimately only the courts can give a definitive judgment, based on objective expert evidence, as to what testing and examination is necessary in the particular circumstances.
- Testing should be sufficient to check whether the product performs its function properly, and the components are liable to failure or fatigue under normal conditions and predictable extremes of use; whether moving parts are adequately guarded; whether any in-built safety devices function as designed; whether noise which may be hazardous is produced unnecessarily.

Simple component parts may require only basic testing to ensure that they meet specification and do not pose hazards in transportation. More sophisticated products, for example complex equipment used for building services, may require testing and examination throughout its period of manufacture, assembly and even commissioning. Testing on the part of the designers and manufactures of products will often need to be sufficiently comprehensive to cover all the potential risks. This may therefore include testing of individual components and raw materials, testing during the manufacturing process, for example for sound welding or correct assembly of goods, as well as testing of the finished product.

Section 6(6) provides that:

> "Nothing in the preceding provisions of this section shall be taken to require a person to repeat any testing, examination or research which has been carried out otherwise than by him or at his instance, in so far as it is reasonable for him to rely on the results thereof for the purposes of those provisions".

The testing may be carried out in-house where the facilities exist. Where the testing required involves specialist skill or equipment, or where the

[37] *Articles and substances for use at work: Guidance for designers, manufacturers, importers, suppliers, erectors and installers* (Guidance Note GS8).

tests are very extensive, there is no bar to a manufacturer or other supplier commissioning tests from the third party which is a testing house or laboratory, or carrying out design testing with other manufacturers.

Research

Designers and manufacturers of articles have additional duties in relation to carrying out "any necessary research", which entails a more fundamental examination of safety than just testing and examination. The HSE guidance describes the aim of the research as being: (a) to discover any risks associated with the product itself; and (b) to eliminate or minimise known or discovered hazards so far as is reasonably practicable. The guidance goes on to indicate that this will entail a thorough scrutiny of the appropriate published literature to determine whether adequate research has already been undertaken which can be relied upon. It also entails such things as an examination of the properties of the product itself, whether alternative designs or production techniques can reduce the scope for misuse, the need for instructions and warnings to be given, whether the product can operate safely in conjunction with other products and materials in which it might be incorporated or used alongside and an appraisal of the full extent of the risk to users. Such research should also be sufficient to identify appropriate testing and examination that may be needed later at the production and supply stage.

Provision of adequate information

The responsibility for providing adequate information lies with all designers, manufacturers, importers and suppliers, and this forms an important link in the chain of responsibilities, thus enabling the ultimate user to discharge his own obligations under the HSWA to ensure the safety of his own employees. A number of regulations require users to carry out thorough assessments of the properties of the products they use in the workplace and the provision of product safety information will often be a critical element of this risk assessment task. Compliance with this obligation pre-supposes that there has been sufficient research and testing, and that the proper conditions of use have been identified by the manufacturer. The duty to secure that information is provided is not qualified by the phrase "so far as is reasonably practicable", and as such is an absolute duty which must be observed or all in the supply chain may be at risk of prosecution.

Section 6 does not prescribe the manner of giving safety warnings, nor does it require that the information accompanies the product every time there is a delivery. There is no actual requirement to send safety information in writing. Prudent manufacturers and suppliers will, however, ensure that safety information is documented, and that a file is maintained evidencing that this has been done and recording any changes in the safety data that take place at the time. Manufacturers and other suppliers are therefore at liberty to devise their own formats, using for example, operating manuals, information sheets, labels, decals, videotapes or possibly just a letter setting out the relevant details. It must be borne in mind, however, that certain product specific regulations may contain more explicit labelling requirements, for example those relating to maximum working pressures for pressure vessels,[38] as well as specific requirements for written safety instructions to accompany products as under the Supply of Machinery (Safety) Regulations 1992.[39] It will also be necessary to take into account any applicable CE marking requirements (see Chapter 3). Where safety symbols are used these should be consistent with those laid down in existing regulations to avoid confusion, in particular the Safety Signs at Work Regulations 1980.[40] The HSE guidance also stresses that care should be taken to present the information clearly and precisely, avoiding excessive detail which may obscure the essential facts.

No criteria are given as to what amounts to "adequate" information in the Act. Where there are specific labelling requirements these are not necessarily equivalent to complying with the duty, as they may be regarded as merely the basic minimum legal requirements which could have to be supplemented to meet the requirements of section 6.

HSE guidance on the provision of information for substances lists the following factors as affecting the adequacy of the information supplied:

(a) the properties of the substance;
(b) the hazards of the substance;
(c) the reasonably foreseeable uses;
(d) the quantity being supplied;
(e) the anticipated knowledge and competence of the user.

The factors will be broadly similar in relation to articles. Adequacy will have to be considered mainly in relation to the research and testing that has been carried out at the design and manufacturing stage. The list demonstrates that it is not just the nature of the product itself but also the circumstances in which it is going to be used that need to be taken into account when considering the information.

Each person in the supply chain is, to the extent that it is reasonable, able to rely on the information generated and provided to him by others. The initial responsibility lies with the designer or manufacturer, but the duty to communicate this further lies with each person in the supply chain. The responsibility lies with intermediate suppliers to supplement this information with any further information relevant to any processing assembly or re-packaging of products they may have carried out.

[38] Sched. 2, Simple Pressure Vessels Regulations 1991.
[39] Sched. 3, para. 1.7.4.
[40] See also BS 5360 and 5378.

Continuing duty to provide information

The 1988 changes to section 6 have imposed a continuing obligation on designers, manufacturers, importers and suppliers positively to provide revised safety information to their customers if they become aware of a serious risk to health or safety. This might for example be the discovery of an inherent defect or a concern about previously unforeseen misuse. In contrast to the information duties in relation to new products, however, this obligation is qualified in so far as it is reasonably practicable to secure that the information is provided. Another limitation is that the duty to inform applies in relation to the person supplied, and not necessarily the ultimate user.

The full extent of this duty is not entirely clear. It may be implicit that there is a requirement to monitor and assess the level of risks associated with any reports of product failures or accidents to determine whether or not there is a need to publish further information.[41] It is certainly implicit that a manufacturer or other supplier should develop some criteria by which to judge the *seriousness* of the risk to health and safety in the absence of any definition of this phrase in the legislation. The reasonably practicable qualification means that the cost of issuing warnings can be balanced against the degree of risk.

The lack of definition here means that making decisions as to whether to publish information is fraught with difficulty, and there are close parallels with the problems in determining whether or not to undertake a product recall. Risks of trivial injury need not be taken into account, but it is less clear whether it is possible to discount the potential for serious injury when the chance of this occurring may be extremely small. A cautious approach should be taken given that the legal interpretation of risk for these purposes is not, or has been seen, one of minimum or acceptable risk but absolute risk.

The qualification of reasonably practicable also imposes some limitation on the lengths a manufacturer or other supplier must go to to reach users. It will generally be acceptable to disregard previous customers whose products can no longer be expected to be in use, but it may be nevertheless necessary to take into account second-hand users and dealers to the trade for the purposes of guarding against common law claims, even though they are not persons supplied for the purposes of the legislation. Where records of past customers exist it will be difficult to argue that it is not reasonably practicable to contact them, however long ago the product was supplied. HSE guidance indicates that manufacturers and suppliers may be required to go further than this and contact customers via trade journals and advertisements. At this point, however, the costs/benefit equation imported by the reasonably practicable test may need to be considered and a judgment made as to

[41] Contrast reg. 8 of the General Product Safety Regulations 1994 and the duty to monitor consumer products.

whether the expense incurred in use of the media is proportionate to the risk involved.

Product specific regulations

Without diminishing the importance of the product safety obligations under section 6 of the HSWA, increasing attention is focusing on measures intended to define with much greater particularity the design and construction criteria that should be met for specific products or classes of products. As has been seen in Chapter 3 the directives promoting the implementation of the European Single Market have added considerable impetus to this process by including the safety considerations among the Essential Requirements that products must meet in order to be lawfully supplied throughout the Community and to be accompanied by the relevant CE mark. These New Approach directives cover work products such as simple pressure vessels, construction products, machinery, personal protective equipment, active implantable medical devices, gas appliances, telecommunications terminal equipment and hot water boilers.[42] The U.K. legislation implementing these requirements is enacted by use of powers in the European Communities Act, rather than the HSWA powers so these are not true health and safety regulations. (Nevertheless, as will be seen later in this chapter, they are enforced by the HSE as if they were in many respects the same as regulations made under the HSWA.) These provisions generally revoke existing U.K. regulations that would otherwise impose inconsistent requirements but there has not been wholesale revocation of these pre-existing regulations, and even those that are revoked may continue to exist for a limited life span to 1996 or beyond.

A list of regulations relevant to workplace products is contained in Appendix 4. The regulations of the widest general application are the Supply of Machinery (Safety) Regulations 1992 (as amended) which implement the Machinery Directive.[43] They provide a useful example of the U.K. approach to the "New Approach" Directives. These regulations impose a series of requirements governing design and the construction of machinery. They have also been extended from the beginning of 1995 to cover safety components — components separately supplied to fulfil a safety function[44] — such as additional add-on guarding, and certain lifting equipment.[45] "Machinery" is widely defined and includes an assembly of linked parts or components, at least one of which moves, with appropriate actuators control and power circuits and which are joined together for a specific application, such as for the processing,

[42] See Appendix 4.
[43] S.I. 1992 No. 3073.
[44] The full definition of "safety component" is at reg.2(2) added by the Supply of Machinery (Safety) (Amendment) Regulations 1994.
[45] reg. 7A.

treatment, moving or packaging of a material.[46] The definition also covers so-called "inter-changeable equipment" modifying the function of a machine and an assembly of machines arranged so that they function as one. Certain equipment is specifically excluded from the scope of the regulations including steam boilers, tanks and pressure vessels, storage tanks and pipelines for petrol, fuel and dangerous substances, means of transport (but not vehicles used in the mineral extraction industry) and manually powered machinery (except certain lifting equipment).[47] The regulations are also inapplicable to most electrical equipment[48] (provided the risks are mainly of electrical origin), machinery for export to a country outside the European Economic Area which does not carry CE marking[49] and to the extent that the risks associated with the machinery are covered by other E.C. Directives.[50]

The requirements apply to machinery first supplied or put into service in the E.C. before January 1, 1993.[51] Further duties in relation to safety components and lifting equipment only apply from January 1, 1995.[52] However both set of requirements are subject to transitional arrangements. The regulations do not apply to machinery first supplied or put into service on or before December 31, 1994 which complies with U.K. health and safety legislation as at December 31, 1992.[53] In the case of safety components and lifting equipment the transitional arrangements provide that existing equipment may be supplied until December 31, 1996 provided it meets the health and safety legislation in force in the U.K. on June 14, 1993.[54]

The regulations require that machinery and safety components must meet detailed "essential health and safety requirements"[55] governing all aspects of design and construction including the characteristics of guards and protection devices; control equipment, for example starting and stopping devices; protection against mechanical hazards; protection against other hazards such as fire, explosion, temperature and electricity; maintenance requirements and the provision and form of instructions, markings, warnings or other indicators accompanying or placed on machinery. In particular these require that all machinery and safety components supplied must be accompanied by detailed instructions on safe installation and use.[56] The regulations also specify detailed requirements for certain categories of machinery such as woodworking machinery and for underground work, certain lifting operations and machinery and mobile machinery.

[46] reg. 4.
[47] reg. 5 and Sched. 5.
[48] reg. 10(1)(b).
[49] reg. 6.
[50] reg. 10(1)(a).
[51] reg. 7.
[52] reg. 7A.
[53] reg. 8.
[54] reg. 8A.
[55] reg. 12(1)(a) and Sched. 3.
[56] Sched. 3, para. 1.7.4.

The manufacturer, his authorised representative in the E.C. or in the case of non-E.C. manufacturers, the importer of the goods,[57] is responsible for ensuring that these essential health and safety requirements are met and for ensuring that the machinery is safe.[58] He must also ensure that the machine can be safely assembled and put into service.[59] He is responsible for compiling a file of technical information relating to the machinery including drawings and specifications[60] ("the technical file") and ensuring that the equipment satisfies the essential health and safety requirements — this is known as the conformity assessment. In most cases the manufacturer can itself issue the so-called "declaration of conformity" (or in certain limited circumstances a "declaration of incorporation"[61]). However, special attestation procedures apply to certain higher risk machinery involving submission of the technical file to an approved body.[62]

Except for equipment intended for assembly with or incorporation into other machinery (which must be accompanied by a "declaration of incorporation"), all machinery covered by the regulations must bear a CE mark properly affixed by the manufacturer or other responsible person.[63] The CE marking requirements do not apply to safety components but these must be accompanied by a special declaration of conformity with the essential health and safety requirements laid down in the regulations. It is an offence for the manufacturer to place the CE marking on machinery unless it satisfies the essential health and safety requirements, or to attach any markings to machinery which reduces the visibility or legibility of CE marking or is likely to create confusion with CE markings.[64] However, the regulations provide that where the CE mark has not been properly affixed to machinery the enforcing authority must give the manufacturer notice of the problem before taking formal enforcement action, except where the machinery is unsafe when the main enforcement provisions apply.[65]

Although the principal requirements of the regulations rest with the manufacturer or importer of the goods, intermediate suppliers and distributors also owe a general duty to ensure that the machinery or safety components they supply are safe.[66] Suppliers of used or second-hand machinery fall outside the scope of the regulations as these do not apply where the goods have been previously used or put into service in the Community or, after January 1, 1994 the European Economic Area.[67]

[57] The "responsible person" as defined in reg. 2(2).
[58] regs. 11 and 12.
[59] reg. 12(2).
[60] regs. 13–15.
[61] regs. 22 and 23.
[62] regs. 14–18, 20, 21 and Sched. 4.
[63] reg. 12(1)(d).
[64] reg. 25.
[65] reg. 28. See Sched. 6 for the main enforcement provisions, and the enforcement section of this chapter.
[66] reg. 11(2).
[67] reg. 11(4).

CHEMICALS

In the same way that general duties are laid down in relation to articles there are similar (but not identical) provisions in relation to the supply of substances. The term "substances" in the HSWA means "any natural or artificial substance including micro-organisms whether in solid or liquid form or in the form of a gas or vapour".[68] HSE guidance[69] advises that the term substances includes things commonly termed materials, chemicals, mixtures and preparations and gives as examples paints, adhesives, solvents, oils and cleaning fluids. It also cites less obvious examples that may be deemed substances such as clay, sand or wood and even toxins produced by plants or animals. This definition is meant to supplement that given to *articles* so that together the provisions of Section 6 cover all products supplied for use at work.

Duty to supply safe products

The general duties in relation to substances are found in section 6(4) and are as follows:

> "It shall be the duty of any person who manufactures, imports or supplies any substance:
> (a) to ensure, so far as is reasonably practicable, that the substance will be safe and without risks to health at all times when it is being used, handled, processed, stored or transported by a person at work or in premises to which section 4 above applies [non-domestic premises];
> (b) to carry out or arrange for the carrying out of such testing and examination as may be necessary for the performance of the duty imposed on him by the preceding paragraph;
> (c) to take such steps as are necessary to secure that persons supplied by that person with the substance are provided with adequate information about any risks to health or safety to which the inherent properties of the substance may give rise, about the results of any relevant tests which have been carried out on or in connection with the substance and about any conditions necessary to ensure that the substance will be safe and without risks to health at all such times as are mentioned in paragraph (a) above and when the substance is being disposed of; and
> (d) to take such steps as are necessary to secure, so far as is reasonably practicable, that persons so supplied are provided with all such revisions of information provided to them by

[68] s.53(1), HSWA. "Micro-organism" includes any microscopic biological entity which is capable of replication.

[69] HS(G)27 Substances for Use at Work: The Provision of Information.

virtue of the preceding paragraph as are necessary by reason of its becoming known that anything gives rise to serious risk to health or safety."

In comparing these requirements with those in section 6(1)(a) for articles it can be seen that the structure is largely the same, so the discussion on the interpretation of those aspects which are the same will not be repeated here. The main differences in relation to these provisions on substances are that there is no reference to a designer and consequently there are correspondingly greater duties on manufacturers, suppliers and importers to carry out testing and to make available results of available results about relevant tests and other information. Nevertheless any duty imposed on a person is qualified as being a duty to do things only which are within his control.[70] The duty to ensure safety is expressed in terms of how the product is to be *used, handled, processed, stored or transported* by a person at work, or in non-domestic premises which are made available to persons as a place of work or as a place where they may use plant or substances provided for their use there.[71] This recognises that substances may not be capable of being made entirely safe because of their inherently hazardous characteristics and serves to place emphasis on duties in relation to the way in which substances are kept and their safety in carriage. The existence of inherent hazards does not however lessen the fundamental duty to ensure safety, and it may be that there are means available that can reduce the level of risk — for example, by the inclusion of an additional compound to reduce volatility, or the provision of a type of container which minimises the possibility of accidental spillage.

The supplementary provisions of section 6 discussed previously also apply here (*i.e.* additional responsibilities on importers for substances manufactured abroad, the liability of "ostensible suppliers", and the supplementary duty on manufacturers of substances to carry out or arrange any necessary research with a view to discovery and elimination on minimisation of risk to health and safety to which the substance may give rise[72]).

However, there is no provision for written undertakings by purchasers to deal with safety measures for substances as there is in relation to articles. There is also no specific safety duty on persons who are intermediaries who perform operations with substances (for example processing under contract) akin to that on erectors and installers of articles,[73] although such persons would be covered by other general duties under the HSWA in terms of ensuring the safety of their own employees and persons who may be affected by their operations.[74]

Even more so than in relation to the legal provisions relating to articles, when considering substances reference needs to be made to

[70] s.6(7), HSWA.
[71] s.4(1), HSWA.
[72] s.6(5).
[73] s.6(3), HSWA.
[74] ss. 2 and 3, HSWA.

health and safety regulations which amplify the general duties in the HSWA for research and testing, labelling, packaging, transportation and the giving of information to users about safe use and disposal. These are summarised in the sections below.

Testing, examination and research

Manufacturers, suppliers and importers of substances are heavily reliant on published research and data to discharge their duties, at least as far as established chemical substances are concerned. Suppliers of novel substances, or substances intended for use in new applications, will often need to undertake primary research, a matter now covered by more specific regulations summarised below. HSE guidelines indicate sources of relevant information which include the Approved Guide to the Classification and Labelling of Substances and Preparations Dangerous for Supply (second edition)[75]; guidance material published by the HSE or other authoritative bodies on substances and processes such as Guidance Note EH40 (*Occupational Exposure Limits*) and various HSE Toxicity Reviews; experience obtained and information gathered as a result of previous activities; technical reference sources (text books, journals, scientific papers, etc); professional institutions, trade associations, trade unions and specialist consultancies.[76]

A duty to undertake research (as opposed to testing and examination) lies solely with the manufacturer[77] for the purposes of discovering and eliminating or minimising any risk to health and safety to which the substance may give rise, subject to the necessary research having been reliably carried out by others.[78] HSE guidelines indicate that matters for a manufacturer's consideration might include any chemical similarity to known carcinogens and mutagens; searching for safer substitutes or investigation of safer methods of work with the substance; a full evaluation of the properties of the substance given the extent of its use and quantity involved, and possibly the identification of hygiene and exposure standards and recommendations for appropriate exposure monitoring and health surveillance.[79]

As with all product safety issues it is not sufficient to look at just these generally applicable requirements, and any product-specify legislation must be considered. The safety evaluation process for pesticides or medicines, for example, will generally be part of the overall regulatory approval process. Even where there are no product-specific requirements there may still be obligations stemming from European legislation to carry out research or to collate material health and safety data.

[75] Document approved by the HSC on 18.10.94 for the purposes of the Chemicals (Hazard Information and Packaging for Supply) Regulations 1994.

[76] See *Substances for use at work: The provision of information* (Guidance Note HS(G)27 (Rev)).

[77] s.6(5).

[78] s.6(6).

[79] See *Articles and substances for use at work: Guidance for designers, manufacturers, importers, suppliers, erecters and installers.* (Guidance Note GS8).

Notification of New Substances Regulation 1993

These requirements, giving effect to Directive 67/548/EEC, are intended to promote the Community's goal of ensuring that the toxicology of new chemicals is fully assessed before they are made available. The HSE is appointed as the Competent Authority for the U.K. for notification purposes. Its functions are broadly to evaluate the effect the new chemicals might have on man and the environment and to liaise with the competent authorities of other Member States and the European Commission. An incidental effect of the notification requirements is that the HSE and their Community counterparts become aware of commercial activities that are of interest sooner than they would otherwise be in relation to new product development.

The regulations work by stipulating that new substances cannot be placed on the market (which includes for these purposes importation) unless they are either exempted from the regulations or have been subject either to the full or the reduced notification requirements. Substance is defined for these purposes with more particularity than in the HSWA and means "a chemical element or compound in the natural state or obtained by any production process, including any additive necessary to preserve the stability of the product and any impurity deriving from the process used, but excluding any solvent which may be separated without effecting the stability of the substance or changing its composition".[80] Mixtures or solutions of two or more substances (deemed "preparations" for these purposes) are also subject to the regulations.

A *new* substance for these purposes is one that is not listed in the European Inventory of Existing Commercial Chemical Substances (EINECS),[81] which is a list of some 110,000 substances which had been supplied in the community between 1971 and 1981.

A wide range of substances are in fact excluded from the scope of the regulations, because they are subject to other product-specific regimes, including active ingredients in medicinal products, cosmetics and substances exclusively for use in food.[82] Also, these notification requirements do not apply where substances have already been notified to the Competent Authority of another Member State.[83]

Full notification "Full notification" is required prior to placing one tonne or more per year of a new substance on the market. Supplying the chemical or making it available to another person in the Community or importation are all treated as placing on the market for the purposes of these regulations.[84] A full notification to the Competent Authority comprises:

[80] reg. 2.
[81] *Ibid.*
[82] See reg. 3(2) for a full list of excluded substances.
[83] reg. 3(3).
[84] reg. 2(1).

(a) a technical dossier with information evaluating the foreseeable risks which the new substance may create for human health and the environment, containing all relevant data and the results of tests stipulated in the regulations;
(b) a certificate in writing from the body carrying out the test for the purposes of the technical dossier confirming adherence to the principles of good laboratory practice;
(c) a declaration concerning the unfavourable effects of the substance in terms of its various foreseeable uses;
(d) if a substance is classified as a "dangerous substance"[85] proposals for how it should be dealt with under the relevant regulations (see below);
(e) in the case of a substance manufactured outside the Community, where appropriate a statement by the manufacturer that the notifying person had been appointed as his sole representative for the purposes of submitting a notification;
(f) if so desired, a statement that the notifier requests (on reasonable grounds) that the notification be exempted from certain testing requirements involving animals.[86]

The information to be obtained in the technical dossier for a full notification will include the composition of the substance and its physiochemical properties; precise details of the production process and the levels of exposure at that time; the proposed uses of the substance and details of any resulting waste products; recommended precautions for packaging, storage, handling, transportation and emergency measures; toxicological and ecotoxicological studies; and means of disposal or recycling.[87] At various threshold limits of quantities involved (ranging from 10 to 5,000 tonnes) additional notification requirements are triggered whereupon the Competent Authority may require certain additional tests of studies to be carried out.[88]

Duties are imposed on the Competent Authority receiving notification to carry out an assessment of the real and potential risks created by the substance to human health and the environment, which has to include recommendations on appropriate testing methods and safety precautions.[89] Substances which have been through the full notification procedure may, in the absence of any objection by the Competent Authority, be placed on the market 60 days after the notification has been received.[90] The Competent Authority can, however, at any time after notification require further information, verification or confirmation tests where further evaluation of the risks is required.[91]

[85] *i.e.* a dangerous substance for the purposes of Chemicals (Hazard Information and Packaging) Regulations 1994.
[86] reg. 4.
[87] reg. 4(a) and Sched. 2, Pt. A.
[88] reg. 5.
[89] reg. 16.
[90] reg. 8(1) and (2).
[91] reg. 9.

Reduced notification The "reduced notification" requirements apply where a person is responsible for placing a new substance on the market in a total quantity of less than one tonne per year. The requirement here is for a technical dossier and the other information as described above in relation to full notifications, but the technical dossier can be less extensive.[92] For quantities of substances below 100 kg per year the information requirements for technical dossier are even less.[93] Where the substances with a reduced notification are subsequently supplied in greater quantities then, as under the full notification procedure, additional notification and testing duties may arise.[94] Where the reduced notification requirements apply, substances can be placed on the market 30 days after notification subject to any objection by the Competent Authority.[95]

There are also requirements for follow-up information from the notifier of a substance, which include:

(a) changes in the quantity of the substance placed on the Community market by him;
(b) new knowledge which he may have concerning the effects of the substance;
(c) new uses of which he may be aware for the substance;
(d) any change in composition of the substance as given in the technical dossier;
(e) any change in his status as manufacturer, importer or representative.[96]

Provision is made for another manufacturer, importer or representative of the same substance to make use of the particulars and data previously notified by someone else with that previous notifier's consent.[97] This will enable the subsequent notifier to refer to the results of tests or studies included in the technical dossier which has already been submitted. The fact that a substance had been notified may be evident to a prospective notifier from its publication in the European List of Notified Chemical Substances ("ELINCS")[98] but the regulations require that he obtains confirmation of prior notification somewhere in the Community from the Competent Authority and at the same time demonstrates a genuine intention to market the substance concerned.

[92] See reg. 6(1)(a) and Sched. 2, Pt. B.
[93] s.6(2) and Sched. 2, Pt. C. See also reg. 6(4) which deems a number of substances as having already been notified, in particular substances placed on the market in quantities of less than 10 kg per year per manufacturer, and substances of less than 100 kg per year per manufacturer intended solely for the purposes of scientific research. In such circumstances there may be a requirement to mark the substance (in addition to any other warnings) with the words *"Caution — substance not yet fully tested"* (reg. 6(7)).
[94] reg. 6(8) and (9).
[95] reg. 8(3) and (4).
[96] reg. 10.
[97] reg. 13.
[98] See OJ No. C 361, 17.12.1994, p. 1. The presence of a substance in the ELINCS does not dispense any new importer and/or manufacturer placing it on the market from having to notify it in accordance with the regulations.

There are additional rules under which a notifier may exercise rights to require a Competent Authority to keep confidential the information contained in the notification which, if disclosed, might harm its competitive position. There are limits to these rights and confidentiality cannot be claimed in relation to certain basic information about the substance or, for example, in relation to the summary tests of toxicological and ecotoxicological tests.[99]

Council Regulation (EEC) Number 793/93 on the Evaluation and Control of the Risks of Existing Substances

This European regulation complements the Notification of New Substances Regulations 1993 in that it requires the evaluation of *existing* substances. These are defined as substances listed in the European Inventory of Existing Commercial Substances (EINECS).[1]

Part 1 of the Council regulation deals with systematic data reporting. Any manufacturer who has produced or any importer who has imported an existing substance in quantities exceeding 1,000 tonnes per year at least once in the three years prior to March 1993 is required to submit to the European Commission information specified in an Annex to the Council regulation. The data requirements are similar to those in relation to that contained for the technical dossier for a full notification in relation to a new substance.

For substances produced or imported in quantities above 10 tonnes per year but below 1,000 tonnes per year over the same three-year period data must be supplied. Here the notification requirements are not as extensive as that required for a reduced notification in relation to a new substance, and concern only basic information about identification, quantities made/imported, labelling and pattern of use.[2]

The European Commission is to identify for priority treatment substances requiring immediate attention because of their potential effects on man or the environment. Additional obligations arise here for relevant manufacturers and importers. Under Part 2 of the regulation, "priority list substances" are allocated to individual Member States whose competent authorities are given responsibility for their evaluation and producing a report for the European Commission with recommendations for future action.

As a European Council regulation these requirements took direct effect in the Member States on June 4, 1993. The British Government has supplemented the requirement by means of the Notification of Existing Substances (Enforcement) Regulations 1994 which provide the HSE and

[99] See reg. 18 for the confidentiality provisions and a full list of items in relation to which confidentiality cannot be claimed. Reg. 19 also imposes duties of confidentiality on the Competent Authority in relation to the information disclosed to it.

[1] OJ No. C 146 A, 15.6.1990, p. 1. This is intended to be a comprehensive list of substances supplied in the Community between 1971 and 1981.

[2] Annex IV.

Her Majesty's Inspectorate of Pollution[3] with a range of enforcement powers, including notices which are used to ensure that the Council regulation is carried into effect. The 1994 regulations also make provisions for offences for failure to comply with the Council regulation.

Provision of information

The obligations in relation to provision of information for substances are slightly different to those which apply for articles. The basic duty to ensure the substances are safe and without risks to health at all times when being used, etc., cannot be regarded in isolation where substances are inherently dangerous and their safety is dependent on the user appreciating the exact nature of the dangers and being aware of any special arrangements for handling, processing, storage and transportation.

It is not just the inherent dangers of some substances that causes greater emphasis to be put upon the provision of information. Generally substances will not have been developed for specific applications. Manufacturer or importer cannot so easily predict the use to issues products might be put after being supplied in bulk or unfinished form as raw materials; safety may depend on the volumes the purchaser handles, the way in which the chemicals are stored, the properties of other chemicals with which they are mixed and their use in a wide variety of processes. Ensuring that a substance can be disposed of safely will often involve reliance on the information which the manufacturer provides. Even where substances are supplied in their finished form, for example paints or cleaning fluids, there is still considerable scope for misuse, spillage, or contact with other materials that might have unexpected consequences. Whereas the dangers in relation to an article used at work will commonly be obvious or within well-known parameters (such as operating unguarded machinery) more detailed consideration often needs to be given to the long term effects of substances arising out of prolonged exposure and potential inhalation, ingestion or absorption on contact.

The significance of these differences is reflected in the contrasting wording of the information obligations for substances and articles. Section 6(4)(c) includes (in relation to the information manufacturers, importers or suppliers should provide) references to the "results of any relevant tests" and "the inherent properties of the substances" instead of (as in relation to the equivalent provision for articles) the "use for which it is designed". It is worth noting that the information obligations of a manufacturer, importer or supplier have to be considered in the light of the proviso in the HSWA that any absence of safety or risk to health in a product are to be disregarded in so far as the case in which it

[3] In Scotland, Her Majesty's Industrial Pollution Inspectorate.

would arise could not reasonably be foreseen.[4] However, as with the obligations in relation to articles, there is a continuing duty to provide persons previously supplied with the substance with new information that comes to light about anything giving rise to a serious risk to health or safety, and so knowledge of a problem that a particular customer might encounter would require action to be taken to add to an existing information package.[5]

The provisions of the HSWA are unspecific as to the methods of communicating adequate safety information. Obviously warnings and information cannot always accompany a chemical in the same way they can with an article. This places the onus on the manufacturer, importer or supplier to determine what is suitable in any particular circumstances, as well as how often information needs to be provided or repeated. Under the terms of section 6 information may be given informally, and need not even be in writing although it will always be prudent for important information of this nature to be recorded in some way. Where the user has specific requirements and direct contact with the manufacturer is feasible, it may be that there will be an ongoing dialogue, where the manufacturer can possibly provide an information service and training for the users' staff.

In most instances the manner of communication will be achieved in a combination of two main ways: through labelling of the container or packaging of the product itself, and through more detailed formal data sheets. Both of these approaches are now subject to legislation as far as dangerous substances are concerned.

The Chemicals (Hazard Information and Packaging for Supply) Regulations 1994 ("CHIP")

These regulations contain information requirements for all dangerous substances except those excluded from their scope because they are covered by other legislation. Whether or not a substance is dangerous for these purposes has to be determined by reference to the "Approved Supply List" approved by the Health and Safety Commission.[6] Regulation 3 contains the full list of exclusions, which include medicinal products (as defined by the Medicines Act 1968) foods (as defined by the Food Safety Act 1990) pesticides (approved under the Food and Environment Protection Act 1985) and certain waste materials.

These regulations use a slightly different terminology to the HSWA, distinguishing between substances and preparations (meaning mixtures or solutions of two or more substances).[7] The definition extends to

[4] s.6(10).
[5] s.6(4)(d).
[6] See Information Approved for the Classification and Labelling of Substances and Preparations Dangerous for Supply (2nd. Ed.) (18.10.94) (ISBN 0 7176 0858 1) (also available on diskette).
[7] reg. 2.

chemicals which may be used by consumers as well as work-place products and consequently the enforcement provisions permit enforcement not only by the HSE but also the local authorities where a supply takes place from a shop or other retail outlet or by direct sales to the public, for example by mail order.[8]

A substance or preparation is deemed *dangerous for supply* if it appears in Part I of the Approved Supply List, or if it is a substance which falls within a category of danger listed in CHIP as explosive, oxidising, extremely flammable, highly flammable, flammable, very toxic, toxic, harmful, corrosive, irritant, sensitising, carcinogenic, mutagenic, toxic for reproduction or dangerous for the environment.[9]

CHIP contains a general prohibition on the supply of a substance or preparation dangerous for supply unless it has been first *classified* in accordance with the regulations.[10] The classification is carried out in accordance with the criteria set out in the Approved Supply List, or by reference to the categories of danger described above (in which case an investigation will need to be carried out to assess the properties of the substance concerned against the criteria contained in the regulations). This classification process identifies the information requirements for the next stages which are mandatory labelling and a provision of data sheets.

Labelling of dangerous chemicals A supplier (or importer) is not permitted to supply a substance or preparation dangerous for supply unless designated particulars are clearly shown on its receptacle, and on the outermost layer of packaging if the information on the receptacle would not otherwise be visible.[11]

The labelling requirements only apply in relation to substances or preparations dangerous for supply which are supplied in *packages*. The specific meaning given to the word "package" is a "package in which substance or preparation is supplied which is liable to be individually handled during the course of supply". It includes the receptacle containing the chemical, any other packaging associated with it, and any pallet or other device enabling receptacles to be handled as a unit, vehicles and freight containers (other than tank containers) are not packages for these purposes.[12] Larger quantities of chemicals not in packages are dealt with under separate rules (see below).

The labelling requirements also do not apply where the quantity involved is so small that there is no reason to fear danger to persons handling them (except when they are explosive, very toxic or toxic or sensitising).[13] There are also derogations from some of the labelling

[8] reg. 16(2)(b).

[9] See Sched. 1, Pt. I of CHIP.

[10] Where a substance has been notified under the Notification of New Substances Regulations 1993 (see above) the substance is classified in conformity with that notification (reg. 5(3) of CHIP).

[11] reg. 9(1).

[12] reg. 2(1) (see below for requirements relating to transportation equipment).

[13] reg. 9(7).

requirements in relation to quantities of less than 125 millilitres.[14] The rules are also less extensive for certain transfers between work places where the substances or preparations involved are not going to be used or processed or opened.[15]

The information required in such labels is:

(a) the name, address and telephone number of a person in a European Member State who is responsible for supplying the substance or preparation (whether it is manufacturer, importer or distributor);
(b) the name of the substance, which here means its official name in the Approved Supply List or otherwise an internationally recognised name if it is unlisted. (For preparations the information is the trade name or other designation);
(c) the following additional particulars[16]:
    (i) the indication or indications of danger and the corresponding symbol or symbols (if any);
    (ii) the risk phrases (set out in full);
    (iii) the safety phrases (set out in full);
    (iv) the EEC number (if any)[17];
(d) where a preparation is intended for sale to the general public, the nominal quantity (nominal volume or nominal mass) must appear as well, and the labelling must also identify the *constituents* of the preparation which result in the preparation being classified as dangerous for supply. The requirements in relation to the EEC number do not apply to preparations.

To complicate matters further, certain preparations are subject to special rules done in their labelling, for example paints and varnishes containing lead, products containing isocyanates, or epoxy constituents.[18]

The various indications of danger and corresponding symbols required can be seen in **Figure 6.1.**

The designated risk phrases (of which there are 62, although some have to be combined where more than one category of risk fits the classification) are contained in Part III of the Approval Supply List. These phrases do no more than state a risk in simple terms; examples are "Irritating to Eyes" and "Causes Burns".

The required safety phrases are found in Part IV of the Approved Supply List. The safety phrase is a standard phrase giving advice on safety precautions which are appropriate for the substance or preparation concerned.[19] There are 52 possible safety phrases which can apply,

[14] reg. 9(8).
[15] reg. 9(6).
[16] These are to be ascertained in accordance with Pt. I of Sched. 6 (reg. 9(2)(c)).
[17] The EEC number means either the number assigned in the Approved Supply List, or in the case of substances not in that List, the number specified in EINECS or in ELINCS as the case may be (reg. 2(1)) and the words "EEC label" where the substance appears in Pt. I of the Approved Supply List.
[18] See Sched. 6, Pt. II.
[19] The full texts of safety phrases are found in Parts III and IV of the Approved Supply List.

Figure 6.1

SCHEDULE 2

Regulation 2(1)

INDICATIONS OF DANGER AND SYMBOLS FOR SUBSTANCES AND PREPARATIONS DANGEROUS FOR SUPPLY

Column 1 *Indication of danger*	Column 2 *Symbol-letter*	Column 3 *Symbol*
Explosive	E	
Oxidizing	O	
Extremely flammable	F+	
Highly flammable	F	
Very toxic	T+	
Toxic	T	
Harmful	Xn	
Corrosive	C	
Irritant	Xi	
Dangerous for the environment	N	

Source: **CHIP Regulations 1994.**

Figure 6.2

METHANOL

Highly flammable **Toxic**

200-659-6
EEC label

Toxic by inhalation and if swallowed
Keep out of reach of children
Keep container tightly closed
Keep away from sources of ignition
No smoking
Avoid contact with skin

Supplied by
Sykes, Warner and Foster Ltd
Rue de Hart, Derrickville
Brussels Belgium
Tel 000 1111 2222

Example of a supply label for a substance

AUNTIE MARY'S PATENT CLEANSER
Contains trichloretheylene

Harmful
1 litre

Possible risk of irreversible effects
Do not breathe vapour
Wear suitable protective clothing and gloves

Mixed by:
Sykes, Warner and Foster Formulations Ltd
Rond Point Mosselmans, Derrickville
Brussels, Belgium
Tel 000 1111 2222

Example of a supply label for a preparation

Source: HSE's booklet "The Complete Idiot's Guide to CHIP".

and these include such as "Keep out of the Reach of Children", "Keep Container Tightly Closed", "Avoid Contact with Skin". All dangerous preparations to be supplied to the general public must bear certain relevant safety phrases. Also (where they are classified as very toxic or corrosive) and where it is physically impossible to give the information on the package itself, packages must be accompanied by precise and easily understandable instructions for use, including, where appropriate, instructions for the destruction of the empty package.

Examples of labels for a dangerous substance or dangerous preparation are shown in **Figure 6.2.**

CHIP also prescribes the methods of marking or labelling packages, including requirements for the label to be clearly and indelibly marked on a part of the package reserved for that purpose, and securely fixed with its entire surface in contact with the packaging.[20] The colour and nature of the marking must make it stand out from the background and the writing of such a size and spacing as to be easily read horizontally when the package is set down normally. There are further specific requirements for the dimensions of labels (depending on the capacity of the package).[21] If the package is an awkward shape, also small which is unsuitable to attach a label to comply with the normal requirements the label must be attached in some other appropriate manner.[22] The language used must normally be English, except where the chemical is intended for supply in another Member State where it can be an official language of that state.[23]

Indications such as "non-toxic" or "non-harmful" or any other statement indicating that the product is not dangerous are not permitted on the packaging.[24]

Safety data sheets The CHIP regulations contain important requirements which, for the first time, have imposed a positive obligation to provide a data sheet for dangerous chemicals. The requirement falls upon any supplier.[25] However the duty to supply data sheets is not restricted to situations where dangerous chemicals are supplied in packages, and extends to other means of supplying them.

The information that must be contained in the data sheet as set out in Schedule 5 to the regulations which comprises a list of headings which are as follows:

1. Identification of the substance/preparation and company/undertaking;
2. Composition/information on ingredients;
3. Hazards identification;

[20] reg. 11.
[21] reg. 11(5).
[22] reg. 11(7).
[23] reg. 11(8).
[24] reg. 9(5).
[25] reg. 2(1) and reg. 6(2).

4. First-aid measures;
5. Fire-fighting measures;
6. Accidental release measures;
7. Handling and storage;
8. Exposure controls/personal protection;
9. Physical and chemical properties;
10. Stability and reactivity;
11. Toxicological information;
12. Ecological information;
13. Disposal considerations;
14. Transport information;
15. Regulatory information;
16. Other information.

The information to be provided has to be such as to enable the recipient of the substance or preparation to take the necessary measures relating to protection of health and safety at work (and the protection of the environment). Guidance has been published by the Health and Safety Commission in the form of an Approved Code of Practice, relating to the contents of the Safety Data sheet.[26] The particulars given in the safety data sheet must be in English, except that where a substance or preparation is supplied to a recipient in another Member State the safety data sheet may be in an official language of that state.[27] The data sheet must clearly show its date of first publication or latest revision.[28] In provisions which mirror the section 6 obligations regarding information, the regulations require safety data sheets to be revised (and clearly marked "revision") if any significant new information comes to light about safety or protection of the environment. In contrast with section 6 however the requirement to supply the revised data sheet is limited to notifying only recipients who received the chemical in the previous 12 months.[29] The data sheets have to be provided free of charge no later than the date on which the chemical is first supplied to the recipient.[30] It is not necessary to keep supplying the same safety data sheets each time there are repeat orders of the same products to the same person.

Responsibility to provide a data sheet arises at each stage in the supply chain of a dangerous chemical. Initially data will come from manufacturers, and processors or distributors repackaging the product will also be under an obligation to adapt the information as necessary for their own customers. In some situations it may be appropriate

[26] Safety Data sheets for substances and preparations dangerous for supply (2nd. Ed.) — Guidance on reg. 6 of the Chemicals (Hazard Information and Packaging for Supply Regulations 1994) (*Approved Code of Practice*). For further guidance on see The Popular Guide — CHIP 2 for Everyone (HS(G) 126), the Approved Guide to the Classification and Labelling of Substances and Preparations Dangerous for Supply (L63) and The Complete Idiot's Guide to CHIP (INDG — 151L).

[27] reg. 6(6).

[28] reg. 6(1).

[29] reg. 6(4).

[30] reg. 6(4).

simply to pass on information received in a data sheet that has already been prepared, although it will be necessary to check that the data is still valid and applicable to the circumstances for which the chemical is being supplied. The only exception to this principle of continuous provision of data sheets throughout the supply chain is in relation to chemicals sold through a shop or other retail outlet to the general public. A safety data sheet need not be provided here if sufficient information is furnished to enable users to take necessary precautions, but one must still be provided by the retailer (free of charge) if a person who intends to use the chemical at work requests it.[31]

There is not an obligation on the recipient of the chemical to pass the data sheet onto an employee or contractor, although this situation is covered by the general duties under the HSWA to take all reasonably practical steps to secure the safety of such persons and their relevant information from the data sheet should still be given to the actual users.[32]

For a certain high risk chemicals there is a requirement on the supplier to notify a "Poisons Advisory Centre" of the information required to be in the safety data sheet, and this information would have to be kept up-to-date.[33] At the end of 1994 no official body had yet been appointed to fulfil the function of this Centre, although various poisons information units already operate in the public health services around the U.K. and provide points of reference for information of this nature.

Packaging and transportation

Various regulations deal with safe packaging and carriage of dangerous chemicals. For packaging, CHIP contains a general requirement for packages to be suitable for their purpose and designed, constructed maintained and closed so as to prevent spillages when subject to the stresses and strains on normal handling. Packaging must be capable of withstanding contact with the substance or preparation in question. Receptacles with replaceable closures must be capable of being re-closed without the contents escaping.[34]

There are additional provisions in CHIP dealing with child-resistant fastenings (by reference to designated British and ISO Standards) and a prohibition on packaging dangerous chemicals in a way likely to attract or arouse the curiosity of children. Tactile warnings are also required for chemicals with indications of danger that are very toxic, corrosive, harmful, extremely flammable or highly flammable.[35] Further more

[31] reg. 6(5).
[32] Section 2(2) HSWA. See also the Control of Substances Hazardous to Health Regulations 1994 which impose duties to assess risks and ensure protection against chemical hazards.
[33] reg. 14.
[34] reg. 8.
[35] reg. 12.

complex packaging requirements and other precautions for safety during transportation are contained in a variety of regulations dealing with specific types of transport including road and rail and storage in harbours.[36] Some of these regulations also contain separate classification and labelling requirements.

Prohibited products

It has generally not been the approach in the U.K. to impose total bans on hazardous substances. The need for regulatory approval produce and supply high risk products such as medicines and pesticides prevents many particularly dangerous compounds from being made widely available, but the legislative approach has been directed more generally towards imposing onerous duties on those using chemicals to assess and control their risks.[37] Notable exceptions are some forms of asbestos which have been banned since the mid 1980s.[38] However, while the supply of some particular kinds of asbestos is banned altogether many of the restrictions are framed in terms of prohibiting particular applications of individual types of asbestos, rather than as blanket prohibitions.

As for specific prohibitions, polychlorinated biphenyls (PCBs) and polychlorinated terphenyls (PCT's) can no longer be supplied under pollution legislation.[39] After the adoption of the Montreal Protocol on the ozone layer European Community states restricted the use of chlorofluorocarbons (CFC's) by a Community regulation.[40] Restrictions have been placed on the use of cadmium in pigments, certain plastics and a number of other products[41] and on pentachlorophenol.[42] The Control of Substances Hazardous Health Regulations 1994 list 11 catego-

[36] The Carriage of Dangerous Goods by Road and Rail (Classification, Packaging and Labelling) Regulations 1994; the Carriage of Dangerous Goods by Rail Regulations 1994; the Road Traffic (Carriage of Dangerous Substances in Road Tankers and Tank Containers) Regulations 1992; the Road Traffic (Carriage of Dangerous Substances in Packages etc) Regulations 1992; the Road Traffic (Carriage of Explosives) Regulations 1989; the Radioactive Substances (Carriage by Road) (Great Britain) Regulations 1974; the Road Traffic (Training of Drivers of Vehicles Carrying Dangerous Goods) Regulations 1992; Dangerous Substances in Harbour Areas Regulations 1987; Freight Containers (Safety Convention) Regulations 1984; Ionising Radiations Regulations 1985; Classification and Labelling of Explosives Regulations 1983; Packaging of Explosives for Carriage Regulations 1991; Placing on the Market and Supervision of Transfers of Explosives Regulations 1993; the Pressure Systems and Transportable Gas Containers Regulations 1989.

[37] See the Control of Hazardous to Health Regulations 1994; the Control of Asbestos at Work Regulations 1987; and the Control of Lead at Work Regulations 1980.

[38] See the Asbestos (Prohibitions) Regulations 1992, replacing earlier regulations of the same name made in 1985, and the Asbestos Products (Safety) Regulations 1985 (as amended).

[39] The Control of Pollution (Supply and Use of Injurious Substances) Regulations 1986.

[40] Regulation 3322/88, OJ L 297, 31.10.1988 (as subsequently amended).

[41] Environmental Protection (Controls on Injurious Substances) (No. 2) Regulations 1993.

[42] Environmental Protection (Controls on Injurious Substances) Regulations 1993.

ries of substances which are prohibited for a number of specified purposes.[43] Various other applications of individual chemicals are restricted by other regulations.[44]

There is no comprehensive list published of products banned or restricted in the U.K. but reference can be made to the United Nations consolidated list of restricted products which identifies both U.K. and European Community-wide restrictions.[45]

ENFORCEMENT

The Health and Safety at Work Act confers enforcement powers on inspectors (who may operate under a variety of titles) who are formally appointed by the relevant enforcing authority. The only enforcing authority in relation to section 6 is the Health and Safety Executive, but when considering specific regulations reference may need to be made either to the Health and Safety (Enforcing Authority) Regulations 1989 or to the individual regulations themselves to determine whether the production or supply of the products in question takes place in premises subject to the jurisdiction of the Health and Safety Executive or, as may be the case, some other body. Usually it is the local authority which is designated the enforcing authority for the purposes of health and safety legislation for premises such as offices, catering services, or premises used for storage, retail or wholesale distribution.

Powers to obtain information and evidence

Inspectors have very extensive powers under section 20 of the HSWA enabling them to enter premises to carry out inspections and to compel witnesses to answer questions which go further than those which are available to the police for the enforcement of the general criminal law. Rules for admissibility of evidence in relation to court proceedings, and in particular the Police and Criminal Evidence Act 1984 also have to be taken into account in so far as they affect the way in which the inspectors actually take their evidence.

Powers of entry

An inspector can enter any premises at any reasonable time (or at any time at all if he believes there is a dangerous situation[46]). The only

[43] reg. 4 and Sched. 2.

[44] See the Environmental Protection (Controls on Injurious Substances) Regulations 1992 on lead in paint, mercury in textiles and DDB.

[45] Consolidated List of Products whose Consumption and/or Sale have been Banned, Withdrawn, Severely Restricted or not Approved by Governments (fifth issue, 1995) United Nations publication, available from HMSO.

[46] ss.20(1) and (2)(a), (b) and (c).

criterion for exercising this power is that the inspector has reason to believe that it is necessary for him to enter "for the purpose of carrying into effect any of the relevant statutory provisions within the field of responsibility of the enforcing authority which appointed him". This amounts to a very broad authority to investigate compliance with the relevant legislation as well as investigating complaints or accidents. Supplementing these general powers of entry are additional powers to make such examinations and investigations as may be necessary in the circumstances,[47] to direct that premises, or anything in the premises, be left undisturbed pending investigation,[48] and to take measurements and photographs and make other records.[49]

Examination and detention of items of evidence

Inspectors can undertake various steps in relation to the investigation of physical evidence which include:

- taking samples of any articles or substances, or atmospheric samples[50];
- dismantling or testing to any article or substance appearing to be a cause or likely cause of danger,[51] or taking possession of it and detaining it for as long as is necessary for it to be examined, or to preventing it being tampered with, or ensuring it is available for use as evidence in proceedings.[52]

In the event that an inspector orders dismantling or other testing it is open to the manufacturer (or other person under investigation) to be present at the time.[53] If an inspector detains items he is required to leave a notice giving particulars identifying what he has taken and, if it is practicable to do so, to leave a sample for future identification.[54] Where an inspector fails to leave such a sample it may result in evidence based on subsequent testing being rendered inadmissible, as it has been held (in a Scottish case[55]) that where an inspector goes beyond merely taking a sample and detains the whole of the evidence entirely the rule requiring the inspector to leave a sample behind must be followed strictly.[56]

Disclosure of documents

An inspector can require the production of any books or documents which have to be kept pursuant to statutory requirements, or any other

[47] s.20(2)(d).
[48] s.20(2)(e).
[49] s.20(2)(f).
[50] s.20(2)(g).
[51] s.20(2)(h).
[52] s.20(2)(i).
[53] s.20(4).
[54] s.20(6).
[55] *Skinner v. John G. McGregor (Contractors) Ltd*, 1977 S.L.T. (Sh. Ct.) 83.
[56] s.20(3). No rules have been made concerning the conduct for inspectors in relation to taking samples, although regulations permit ministers to make regulations for this purpose.

documents which he deems necessary to see for the purposes of his investigations. This gives access to virtually all written evidence,[57] the only exception being documents which are subject to legal privilege.[58] This power may be used to obtain reports, correspondence, internal memoranda and any other documents, whether or not marked confidential and however incriminating about a product or the conduct of someone supplying it. In the event of proceedings being brought, such documents can, subject to the usual rules of admissibility of evidence, be considered by a court. There is a question, as yet unresolved, as to whether an inspector who has carried out and completed his investigation, may subsequently require the production of more documents during the actual course of a prosecution. It is arguable that an inspector's entitlement to such documents is limited to the purposes of making an "examination" and "investigation" and cannot be used as a means of extracting documents from the defendant already facing proceedings to bolster the prosecution case.[59]

The questioning of witnesses

An inspector can require any person whom he has reasonable cause to believe to be able to give any information relevant to his examination or investigation to answer such questions as he thinks fit, and has signed a declaration of the truth of his answers.[60] It is an offence not to answer such questions, or to attempt to prevent another person from answering.[61] A person being questioned is entitled to nominate a person to be present. This does not necessarily have to be a lawyer. No rules are laid down as to the role of such a person and how actively they can participate in the interview; in practice inspectors exercise a discretion to allow such a person to advise the interviewee.

This provision would appear to give inspectors free rein to carry out interviews and to obtain evidence, but there are restrictions on the use to which this evidence can be put in proceedings. Answers given by a person pursuant to these powers is inadmissible in evidence against that person (or their spouse) in court, although this does not prevent an inspector who has acquired knowledge of that evidence subsequently seeking admissible evidence from another witness (such as an employee or colleague) to corroborate the facts.

In practice, a more important constraint on the taking of evidence for use in proceedings is the inter-relationship of these powers with the requirements of the Police and Criminal Evidence Act 1984 (PACE).

[57] s.20(2)(k).

[58] s.20(8).

[59] The point arises because of the language used in s.20(2)(k)(ii) restricting the power to obtain documents to those necessary for an inspector to see for the purposes of examination or investigation pursuant to s.20(2)(d), which appears to be separate from the purpose of obtaining further evidence to bolster a prosecution case.

[60] s.20(2)(j).

[61] s.33(1)(e) and (f).

These rules were specifically drawn up to codify police powers for the collection of evidence. However, the Act applies equally to persons other than police officers who have a duty to investigate breaches of the criminal law[62] and it is therefore relevant to the exercise of investigative powers by inspectors such as HSE inspectors and local environmental health officers where they are investigating criminal offences. It is a question of fact in each case as to whether inspectors collecting evidence and inspecting premises are "investigating offences" and therefore whether PACE applies. Just questioning a person simply to obtain information or his explanation of the facts would not normally constitute an interview for the purposes of PACE and there is no need to caution the person questioned. An interview is defined more narrowly as the questioning of a person regarding his involvement or suspected involvement in a criminal offence or offences.[63]

Of particular importance are the powers of detention, treatment and questioning which are governed by Code of Practice C issued under PACE. Under Code C if an inspector has grounds to suspect that a person who he intends to question has committed a criminal offence then he must caution that person before questioning him. If the proper caution is not administered, his answers will not be admissible in evidence if proceedings are subsequently brought. The Criminal Justice and Public Order Act 1994 has made modifications to the "right to silence" of a person being interviewed. Failure to mention material information or to explain incriminating circumstances under questioning may lead to the court drawing adverse inferences — in effect the court might reject a defence on grounds which were not disclosed at the investigation stage.[64] The Code also contains specific guidelines regarding the interview — an accurate record must be made.

PACE interviews usually only take place after a preliminary investigation has been completed and where it is felt that criminal charges may be brought. If it is possible that the person under investigation will be prosecuted as a result of the investigation, inspectors will almost always issue a formal caution and conduct the interview under PACE, to ensure that any evidence obtained is admissible. The key difference here is that the interviewee is not under an obligation to give answers.

Supplementary powers of Inspectors

The specific powers described above are supplemented by provisions which state that an inspector can require any person "to afford him such facilities and assistance . . . as are necessary to enable the inspector to exercise any of the powers conferred on him . . .", and also to exercise

[62] s.67(9), PACE.

[63] Code of Practice C, PACE.

[64] ss.34–39. . The recommended standard caution wording is now: *"You do not have to say anything. But it may harm your defence if you do not mention when questioned something you later rely on in Court. Anything you do say may be given in evidence."*

"any other power which is necessary . . ." for the purposes of carrying any relevant statutory provisions into effect. These apparently unlimited powers have the potential to be very important but they have not been defined by any judicial decisions and they may serve little practical purpose other than to authorise formally incidental activities of inspectors such as commissioning reports, paying fees and making general enquiries. It can be inferred from the Scottish decision referred to earlier[65] that the detailed requirements attaching to the exercise of specific powers contained elsewhere in section 20 are definitive in the areas they cover (such as seizure of products), and so inspectors cannot rely on these supplementary powers to do anything which a specific power would not permit.

Formal enquiries

Separate from the powers exercisable by individual inspectors are provisions contained in section 14 and section 27 of the HSWA. These enable the HSC to direct that a special report is drawn up or a formal inquiry be held into any accident, occurrence or other situation that may have safety implications.[66] The HSC can serve a notice requiring anyone to furnish it with information that it requires.[67]

Restrictions on disclosure of information

The information obtained by the HSC, the HSE or other inspectors actually under their statutory powers is subject to restrictions on its publication or disclosure or anyone else except with the consent of the person who gave the information. Unauthorised disclosure or use is a criminal offence.[68] The main exceptions to this rule are for disclosure to another enforcing authority, or where the disclosure is authorised by the specific statutory provision, or the disclosure is made for the purposes of any legal proceedings.[69]

Formal enforcement action

Where infringements are discovered or complaints about a product are considered justified inspectors will commonly issue written warnings and seek undertakings from the manufacturer or supplier in question; these are steps which have no direct legal consequences and which fall short of formal enforcement action. An inspector may, however, proceed

[65] *Skinner v. John G. McGregor (Contractors) Ltd*, 1977 S.L.T. (Sh.Ct.) 83.

[66] s.14. See also the Health and Safety Inquiries (Procedure) Regulations 1975 for the manner in which inquiries are conducted.

[67] s.27.

[68] s.33(1)(j).

[69] s.28, HSWA.

by way of statutory notices requiring action to be taken or preventing further supply of a product. In situations of serious danger, products may be seized.

The approach that has been taken to regulating the safety of workplace products in the context of health and safety at work legislation has not resulted in the creation of special enforcement mechanisms comparable to those contained in consumer protection legislation aimed at manufacturers and suppliers. There are no equivalents in the HSWA of suspension notices, forfeiture orders, or notices issued by the Secretary of State. There are no provisions giving the authorities power to order recall or repair and no express obligation to withdraw products from the market. Unless specific regulations make special provision for their own enforcement one has to consider the powers generally available to inspectors when dealing with risks to health and safety in the workplace, consisting of the ability to serve mandatory notices, and the power to seize products in certain circumstances.

Improvement notices

If an inspector is of the opinion that a person: (a) is contravening statutory requirements or; (b) has contravened statutory requirements in circumstances that make it likely that the contravention will continue or be repeated then he may serve an improvement notice ordering the person concerned to remedy the contravention.[70] This would entail an inspector demonstrating either non-compliance with one of the features of section 6 of the HSWA, or contravention of regulations to which the Act's powers apply. Such a notice must comply with a number of formalities and must:

- specify the provision or provisions which the inspector believes are not being complied with;
- give particulars of the reasons why he is of that opinion;
- specify the period of time within which the person is required to remedy the contravention, being a period of not less than 21 days.

In addition, a notice may have a schedule attached setting out the steps which the inspector would regard as sufficient to remedy the contravention.[71] These notices are not commonly issued in relation to products (although they are much used in relation to places of work) and could be used for example to require modifications to the design of a product, or the carrying out of research on safety in use, specify the message to be conveyed by an appropriate warning. This may give wide scope for enforcement in relation to products as yet unsold, but the scope is narrower in relation to products which have already been placed on the market. Here, an improvement notice might only be effective in as much

[70] s.21, HSWA.
[71] s.23(2).

as it could compel compliance with the duties to provide additional safety information to persons already supplied with products.[72] Even so the power to order additional safety information to comply with section 6 would seem to be restricted to requiring the recipient of a notice to inform the person *to whom he supplied the products*, and not to publish warnings more widely to dealers and end users. As the effect of any such notice is limited to the individual recipient, where products are in a chain of supply it will be necessary for notices to be served on each supplier concerned, and possibly also on the end user.[73]

A more difficult question arises in relation to products already sold to end users which need retrofitting or repairing to render them safe. It would appear to be the case that once a supply of unsafe products has taken place an offence may have been committed under section 6 or specific regulations, but this would be a "once and for all" contravention which cannot be remedied retrospectively. A manufacturer or supplier's legal obligations here would appear to be restricted to whatever contractual warranties he has given or are implied by law in relation to the buyer's rights to reject or to have defects rectified and an inspector may not require the recall of products or work to be carried out when there is no express requirement to this effect in the legislation. However, it might, in some cases be implicit in the duty to warn customers of danger that they should be advised to return goods to the manufacturer for necessary remedial work, or to purchase additional safety equipment or to have a retrofit carried out, and a carefully worded improvement notice might approximate to a way of an inspector ordering a form of mandatory recall.

Prohibition notices

Prohibition notices differ from improvement notices in that they take immediate effect, and there is no requirement for an inspector to demonstrate that statutory requirements have actually been contravened. The criterion here is that the inspector should be of an opinion that the activity in question involves a risk of serious personal injury. Such a notice may also be served in anticipation that activities carried out by the person concerned will involve a risk of serious personal injury.[74] At the same time, a prohibition notice can be used in any circumstances where an improvement notice could have been served. A specimen prohibition notice is shown in **Figure 6.3.**

[72] ss.6(1)(d) and 4(d) of the HSWA.

[73] See sub-ss.6(1)(d) and 6(4)(d). It may be however that where a specific regulation requires mandatory labelling or other information to accompany a product (*e.g.* the CHIP Regulations) an improvement notice might compel a supplier to remedy the breach by giving the requisite information to the actual user. It is uncertain how a notice would work in such circumstances.

[74] s.22, HSWA.

Figure 6.3 Specimen Prohibition Notice

Serial No. *P/10/RCM*

Health and Safety at Work, etc Act 1974, sections 22, 23 and 24

PROHIBITION NOTICE

To: *ABC Limited*
The Industrial Estate
Blanktown
Berks BB1 1SQ

trading as ***Daniels Office Equipment***

I ***Ruth Catherine Matthew*** one of Her Majesty's Inspectors of Health and Safety being an Inspector appointed by an instrument in writing made pursuant to section 19 of the said Act and entitled to issue this notice of ***HSE House, London Road, Blanktown, Berks BB1 1HM. Telephone 01256 123456***

hereby give you notice that I am of the opinion that the following activities, namely:-

The manufacture and supply of typists' chairs described in your sales catalogue as "Easy-Sit office chair"

which are being carried out by you/~~about to carried out by you/~~under your control at your address above ~~involve~~, or will involve ~~(a) a risk~~/an imminent risk, of serious personal injury.

I am further of the opinion that the said matters involve contraventions of the following statutory provisions:-

Section 6(1)(a) of the Health and Safety at Work, etc. Act 1974

because ***the chairs are unstable and liable to collapse, and persons using them at work and thereby at risk of injury***

and I hereby direct that the said activities shall not be carried on by you or under your control immediately~~/after unless~~ the said contraventions and matters ~~included in the schedule, which forms of this notice~~, have been remedied.

I further direct that the measures specified in the schedule which forms part of this notice shall be taken to remedy the said contravention(s) or matters.

Signature: ***R.C. Matthews*** Date: ***1.1.1995***

SCHEDULE

The chairs should be modified to confirm with the requirements of British Standard BS5459 Part 2 for strength, stability and structural safety of office seating

The formalities attaching to such a notice are that it must:

- state the inspector's opinion that there is a risk of serious personal injury;
- specify the matters which give rise to the risk;
- identify any statutory requirements which he believes have been broken, giving particulars as to why he holds the belief;
- direct that the activities in question shall not be carried out by or under the control of the person on whom the notice is served unless the matters specified have been remedied.

The prohibition can take effect immediately, or within a period of time specified in the notice.[75]

As with an improvement notice, a prohibition notice may (but need not) include directions in a schedule as to the measures to be taken to remedy any contravention or any other matter to which it relates. Such directions can be framed by reference to any Approved Code of Practice, or in such a way as to offer the person on whom the notice is served a choice between different ways of remedying the situation.[76]

As a means of enforcing product safety a prohibition notice is a blunt instrument, carrying as it does the threat of total cessation of trading in relation to the product concerned on the part of the recipient. However, like improvement notices, it would be necessary to have a series of notices across the supply chain wholly to prevent further sales, as well as action to prevent end users being exposed to danger. In practice, prohibition notices are rare (on average only five or six per annum in recent years for contraventions of section 6) and the threat of a notice may well be sufficient to prompt manufacturers or other suppliers to take steps which they could not positively be required to take pursuant to an improvement notice. Such a threat will, however, only be effective if the producer or other supplier concerned maintains an interest in the particular product or market concerned. If supply of the products in question has ceased, or the suppliers have gone out of business or cannot be traced, then there would be no continuing activities upon which a prohibition notice could bite and an inspector would be limited to taking steps to seize the goods as described below.

Seizure in cases of imminent danger

An option available to an inspector is to seize and render harmless articles or substances for use at work where he has reasonable cause to believe, in the circumstances in which he finds such a product, that it is a cause of imminent danger of serious personal injury.[77] This power is distinct from the investigative powers contained in section 20 of the HSWA to take samples or to detain products for their preservation. In

[75] s.22(4), HSWA.
[76] s.23(2), HSWA.
[77] s.25, HSWA.

appropriate cases rendering harmless the product may include its destruction. There are, however, rules relating to providing a person from whose premises the product has been taken with a sample for his own purposes, and the provision of a signed report of the circumstances in which the product was seized.[78]

Powers to detain articles and substances are also given to customs officers in relation to goods imported into the U.K. It is not necessary for a customs officer to believe that there is any imminent danger of serious personal injury, and he may seize imported products for the purposes of facilitating the functions of any enforcing authority or an inspector. Products seized in this way can be detained for only up to two working days,[79] but by then an inspector should be in a position to exercise the other enforcement powers available.

Appeals against enforcement action

There are no means of lodging appeals against the seizure of products in cases of imminent danger, or against the exercise by inspectors of their powers in relation to inspection, detention of products and documents all requiring persons to give information. If a manufacturer or supplier is minded to challenge the exercise of such powers his remedies would be restricted to requesting the court to exercise his powers of judicial review, for example on the grounds that the action taken by the inspector has exceeded his jurisdiction or authorisation, or that the inspector's decision has been so unreasonable that it is not one which an inspector acting properly could have made or there has been some procedural error or failure to comply with conditions attaching to the exercise of the power.[80] Alternatively a civil action may lie for delivery up of goods unlawfully detained.

For improvement and prohibition notices, the Act lays down appeals procedures which involve the recipient making an application to industrial tribunal.[81] An application has to be sent to the tribunal within 21 days from the date the notice is served (although the tribunal is empowered to extend the time period). An appeal has the effect of suspending the operation of an improvement notice until the proceedings are disposed of or withdrawn. Appealing may also suspend the effect of a prohibition notice, but only if the tribunal gives an interim direction that this will be so.[82] On hearing the application, the tribunal can either cancel or affirm a notice; in affirming it it may do so either in its original form or with modifications.[83] A tribunal can rephrase a notice

[78] s.25(2) and (3).

[79] s.25(A), HSWA.

[80] For the general principles and procedural rules applicable to judicial review see *The Supreme Court Practice* (1995), Order 53.

[81] s.24, HSWA. See also the Industrial Tribunals (Improvement and Prohibition Notices Appeals) Regulations 1974.

[82] s.24(3)(b).

[83] s.24(2).

to make its terms more precise.[84] In a case involving allegedly unsafe child seats in shopping trolleys it was decided that a retailer who had challenged a prohibition notice precluding their use did not have to prove they were safe. The onus lay on the inspector to show that the criterion for a prohibition notice of a serious risk of personal injury[85] existed. (The standard of proof here is that of the balance of probabilities and not the criminal standard of proof beyond reasonable doubt.)

Prosecutions

The HSWA contains provisions relating to a considerable number of offences in relation to breach of general duties under the Act, contravention of health and safety regulations or non-compliance with the requirements of inspectors. The courts which will have jurisdiction in relation to proceedings of such offences and the maximum penalties vary depending on the nature of the contravention concerned. In England and Wales proceedings for an offence can only be instituted by an inspector or with the express permission of the Director of Public Prosecutions.[86] In Scotland prosecutions are conducted under the auspices of the procurator fiscal.

Table 6.1 illustrates the number of prosecutions brought under section 6 of the Act in recent years. In comparison with the number of prosecutions brought in respect of the general safety requirement on consumer protection legislation prosecutions are relatively infrequent and the fines are relatively low. (Data is not available in relation to convictions in respect of contravention of health and safety regulations.)

Table 6.1 Prosecutions under Section 6 of the Health and Safety at Work etc Act 1974

	1988–89	1989–90	1990–91	1991–92	1992–93
Number of informations laid	31	31	38	47	27
Number of convictions	25	25	34	39	19
Average fine	£781	£550	£844	£1,299	£1,676

Source: Data provided by the HSE's Statistical Information Department.

A prosecution may be brought irrespective of whether or not other enforcement action has been taken in the form of statutory notices or seizures of products. The outcome of appeal proceedings before an industrial tribunal in relation to a notice does not, of itself, determine

[84] *Chrysler (U.K.) Ltd v. McCarthy* [1978] I.C.R. 939.
[85] *Readmans Ltd v. Leeds City Council* [1992] C.O.D. 419.
[86] s.38, HSWA.

whether or not an offence has been committed, which is a question which has to be resolved in separate criminal proceedings.

Most prosecutions in relation to unsafe products are "triable either way" which is to say that proceedings in England and Wales can be dealt with "summarily" in the magistrates' court or on "indictment" in the Crown Court.[87] Under the rules governing the time in which proceedings have to be brought[88] there are no time limits within which an inspector has to commence a prosecution for these "either way" offences.[89] Certain of the ancillary offences (see below) are only triable summarily and for these offences the normal rule for time limits is prosecutions must be commenced within six months from the date when the offence was allegedly committed. However, these rules are modified by the HSWA so that proceedings may be commenced in relation to offences by designers, manufacturers, importers or other suppliers within six months from the date on which evidence comes to the knowledge of the enforcing authority which is sufficient to justify a prosecution,[90] or within three months of a formal HSC enquiry or a coroner's inquest indicating a contravention of relevant statutory requirements.[91]

The maximum fine available to magistrates is £20,000[92] in relation to section 6 offences and £5,000 in respect of offences under health and safety regulations. In the event of a prosecution being referred to the Crown Court there is no maximum on the amount of the fine that may be imposed upon conviction, either in relation to section 6 offences or contravention of health and safety regulations.[93]

Prosecutions in respect of unsafe products may be brought either in relation to a failure to discharge the general duty under section 6, or in respect of a contravention of a health and safety regulation which is applicable to the product. Where specific regulations are breached it is more likely that an inspector will proceed in the latter way, although this may result in a lower penalty being imposed.

In any prosecution the burden of proof lies with the inspector who must establish the commission of the offence to a criminal law standard of proof, *i.e.* beyond reasonable doubt.[94] In relation to section 6 this will require establishing all the requisite evidence of the offence, including the status of the defendant as a designer, manufacturer, supplier or importer as the case may be and, more importantly, the existence of a risk within the legal meaning of that term. One element of the offence that an inspector does not have to prove, however, is the issue of whether it was reasonably practicable for the defendant to do more than

[87] For the position in Scotland and Northern Ireland see the notes accompanying **Table 6.2**
[88] s.127, Magistrates' Court Act 1980.
[89] See *Kemp v. Liebherr-GB Ltd* [1987] 1 All E.R. 885; [1987] 1 W.L.R. 607.
[90] s.34(3), (4) and (5).
[91] s.34(1).
[92] s.33(1A), HSWA.
[93] s.33(1A) and (3).
[94] *Woolmington v. D.P.P.* [1935] A.C. 462.

he in fact did to deal with the risk. Once the prosecution have shown a prima facie breach of duty section 40 of the HSWA expressly provides that the onus of proving the limits of what is reasonably practicable is placed on the defendant. However, the burden of proof on the defendant here is less onerous than on the prosecution, so that it only has to be established on the balance of probabilities.[95] This is of considerable important in practice as there are no specific legal defences to circumstances of section 6; although it is not a formally designated as such, proof of reasonable practicability by a defendant operates as if it were a defence.

One way in which allegations of contravening product safety requirements can be defended is to demonstrate compliance with an Approved Code of Practice. Again this is not a defence as such but would serve to undermine the prosecution case because such codes are admissible as evidence in their own right.[96] Of particular importance will be situations in which a British Standard or some other recognised guide applies, either because it is itself recognised as an Approved Code of Practice under section 16 of the HSWA[97] or because such a standard is designated as being applicable for the purposes of showing compliance with the requirement.[98] It remains possible, however, that if an inspector regards a product as unsafe in spite of it meeting the technical requirements of relevant standards there might be a prosecution under section 6 alleging that the product is nevertheless not sufficiently safe or, for example, lacks appropriate instructions for use. This must be the case in relation to regulations implementing "New Approach" Directives which contain so-called "safeguard clauses" establishing action to be taken against dangerous products.[99] Certain regulations do however specifically provide that compliance with their requirements will be a full defence in relation to proceedings brought under the Act.[1]

Health and safety regulations made pursuant to the HSWA commonly provide that it will be a defence in criminal proceedings for the accused

[95] *R. v. Carr-Briant* [1943] K.B. 607; [1943] 2 All E.R. 156.

[96] Conversely, failure to adhere to an Approved Code of Practice is prima facie evidence of guilt unless the defendant can demonstrate compliance in some alternative way to observance of the Code. See s.17 HSWA and *West Cumberland By Products Ltd v. D.P.P.* [1988] R.T.R. 391.

[97] The following British Standards were until 1995 approved as Approved Codes of Practice under Section 16 of the Health and Safety at Work Act 1974: BS 697: 1977 rubber gloves for electrical purposes; BS 1870 Part I: 1979 safety footwear other than all rubber and all plastic moulded types; BS 1870 Part II: 1976 specification for lined rubber safety boots; BS 1870 Part III: 1981 specification for poly-vinyl chloride moulded footwear; BS 5169: 1975 fusion welded steel air receivers; BS 5426: 1976 workwear. As of 1995 these approvals have ceased to apply.

[98] See, *e.g.* various harmonised standards relevant for the purposes of the Personal Protective Equipment (E.C. Directive) Regulations 1992 and listed in Commission Communication in the framework of the implementation of Council Directive 89/686/EEC (94/C 359/06), OJ No. C 359 16.12.1994 p.7.

[99] See Chap. 4.

[1] Such a provision can also extend to a requirement for the cancellation of an improvement or prohibition notice where Regulations are complied with, see for example reg. 33(2) of the Construction Products Regulations 1991 and reg. 5(2) of the Electro-Medical Equipment (EEC) Requirements Regulations 1988.

to prove that he took all reasonable precautions and exercised all due diligence to avoid the commission of the offence.[2] Due diligence defences also appear in a number of regulations giving effect to New Approach Directives, for example the Simple Pressure Vessels (Safety) Regulations 1991. (See below in relation to the enforcement of such regulations.) Here again the onus of proof on the defendant in establishing the defence is on balance of probabilities, and not proof of the point beyond reasonable doubt.

Where a person is convicted of an offence the HSWA gives the courts power, in addition to (or instead of) imposing a penalty in the normal way, to order the defendant to remedy matters which are in breach of the statutory requirements. If such an order is made it has the effect that the person concerned cannot be further liable in respect of those matters under the relevant statutory requirements during the time specified in the order for remedying the breach.[3]

The HSWA also creates a series of additional offences as sanctions for failing to comply with the various enforcement powers given to inspectors and others. These ancillary offences and the penalties that may be imposed are set out in more detail in **Table 6.2.**

Liability of persons other than principal offenders

In common with many regulatory statutes the HSWA contains two provisions whereby there can be secondary as well as a principal offenders. The first arises where the commission of an offence is "due to the act or default of some other person".[4] It is not a pre-requisite of conviction as a secondary offender that proceedings are actually taken against the principal offender.[5] This provision could be used in relation to a third party whose activities affect the safety of a product, for example where the manufacturer has engaged an outside designer or a consultant, and this person has caused there to be the commission of an offence in relation to the manufacturer's product, or where an employee has acted in a way that has caused there to be a defect.[6] It is possible that this provision might also be used to convict a person who has maliciously tampered with a product, although such a case would normally be dealt with under the general criminal law.[7]

[2] See Chap. 5 for a discussion of due diligence.

[3] s.42.

[4] s.36, HSWA. Note that it is not necessary for this other person to be acting in the course of a business, as is required by the equivalent provision under s.40(1), Consumer Protection Act 1987.

[5] It is nevertheless a requirement for the prosecution to demonstrate that the principal offender would have been convicted if prosecuted.

[6] In this respect see also s.7, HSWA, general duties of employees at work. See also *Tesco Supermarkets Ltd v. Nattrass* [1972] 1 A.C. 53; [1971] 2 All E.R. 127, concerning the question of whether an employee is to be treated as a separate person for the purposes of an offence.

[7] Public Order Act 1986, section 38—see Chapter 5, p.165.

Table 6.2 Main and Ancillary offences and penalties under HSWA

Main Offences	Mode of Trial*	Maximum Penalty**
Failure to discharge duty under s.6 (general duty of safety of products) (s.33(1)(a))	Magistrates' Court or Crown Court	£20,000 fine Unlimited fine
Contravening any health and safety regulations (s.33(1)(c))	Magistrates' Court or Crown Court	£5,000 fine Unlimited fine
Ancillary Offences		
Contravention of the requirement of an imposed notice or prohibition notice. (s.33(1)(g))	Magistrates' Court or Crown Court	£20,000 fine Unlimited fine and/or up to two years imprisonment
Intentionally obstructing an inspector or custom's officer in the exercise or performance of his powers and duties. (s.33(1)(b))	Magistrates' Court	£5,000 fine
Preventing or attempting to prevent another person from appearing before an inspector or from answering questions. (s.33(1)(f))	Magistrates' Court	£5,000 fine
Contravention of any requirement imposed by an inspector under s.20 (general powers of inspectors). (s.33(1)(e))	Magistrates' Court	£5,000 fine
Contravention of any requirement imposed by an inspector under s.25 (seizure of products where an imminent danger). (s.33(1)(e))	Magistrates' Court or Crown Court	£5,000 fine Unlimited fine
Contravention of a requirement under s.27 (notice to provide information to the HSC). (s.33(1)(i))	Magistrates' Court or Crown Court	£5,000 fine Unlimited fine
Knowingly or recklessly making a false statement in response to a request to furnish information pursuant to relevant statutory provisions. (s.33(1)(k))	Magistrates' Court	£5,000 fine
Intentionally making a false entry in a record or document required under a statutory provision. (s.33(1)(l))	Magistrates' Court	£5,000 fine
Failure to comply with a Court order made under s.42 (order made on conviction to remedy a contravention). (s.33(1)(o))	Magistrates' Court or Crown Court	£20,000 fine Unlimited fine and/or up to two years imprisonment

* The Courts listed here are those for England and Wales. In Scotland for magistrates' court read Sheriff Court (or District Court) and for Crown Court read High Court. In Northern Ireland, for Crown Court read High Court.
** As at December 31, 1994.

The other provisions concerning secondary offenders apply specifically in relation to corporate bodies, in relation to which section 37 of the HSWA provides as follows:

"(1) where an offence under any of the relevant statutory provisions committed by a body corporate is proved to have been committed with the consent or connivance of, or to have been attributable to any neglect on the part of, any director, manager, secretary or other similar officer of the body corporate or a person who was purporting to act in any such capacity, he as well as the body corporate shall be guilty of that offence and shall be liable to be proceeded against and punished accordingly;

(2) where the affairs of a body corporate are managed by its members, the preceding sub-section shall apply in relation to the acts and defaults of a member in connection with his functions of management as if he were a director of the body corporate."

Whether a person is sufficiently senior in an organisation to be saddled with responsibility as a manager within sub-section (1) of these provisions will depend on all the circumstances of the case. In a recent case brought under the Fire Precautions Act 1971[8] it was held that this type of offence is aimed at "only those who were in a real position of authority, the decision-makers within the company, who had both the power and responsibility to decide corporate policy and strategy". An employee in charge of a shop during the general manager's holiday was not a "manager" for these purposes.[9]

The meaning of section 37 is otherwise fairly clear. Its effect is to impose personal liability contingent upon there being liability on the part of a company. It is not necessary for the company's offence to be *wholly* attributable to the conduct of the individual concerned; it may be sufficient that attribution can be apportioned to him among the rest of the management.[10] However, a director or other senior person should not be found guilty simply because the company for whose management he is responsible is guilty of an offence; it is necessary for the prosecution to show conduct specifically amounting to consent, connivance or neglect on his part.[11] The burden of proof of establishing these elements of the offence will lie on the prosecution in addition to the separate burden of proof in relation to there having been an offence by the company, upon which the individual's liabilities are contingent. There are no statutory defences available to individuals in relation to this provision, for example in terms that they may have relied upon someone else.[12] The liability is though contingent on the liability of their company as principal offender.

[8] *R. v. Boal* [1992] Q.B. 591; [1992] 3 All E.R. 177.

[9] In cases of doubt over the seniority of the individual prosecutions may instead be brought in respect of contravention of s.7, HSWA.

[10] *Wotherspoon v. H.M. Advocate* (1978) J.C. 74.

[11] See *Lewin v. Bland* [1985] R.T.R. 171, *Huckerby v. Elliott* [1970] 1 All E.R. 189 and *Re: City Equitable Fire Insurance Co.* [1925] Ch. 407.

[12] Compare with ss.23 and 25 of the Fair Trading Act 1973.

Cases brought under these provisions generally require a very detailed examination of where responsibility lies within the corporation and the way in which management supervision is exercised. In relation to the development or sale of products a director or other senior officer is as a matter of general principle not required to supervise his co-directors or to acquaint himself with all the details of the product or the running of the company. Where a responsibility is properly delegated this will usually discharge an individual's responsibilities.[13] This will always be a question of fact which can only be determined ultimately by the courts in individual cases. In a prosecution brought under trade descriptions legislation,[14] the managing director of a company which imported brake lights which the manufacturer had wrongly marked as being an approved type was convicted on grounds that the company's offence was attributable to his neglect, the neglect here consisting of failing to check whether his co-director had consulted an authoritative source on the legality of the goods. The court was influenced in particular by the fact in this case that this was the first time this particular product had been obtained and the director should have made more active enquiries with his colleague as to the checks that had been carried out.

The formal designation of responsibility for safety in relation to a particular matter, especially if in writing, will often be determinative of the issue of whether or not a duty was personal to the individual concerned for the purposes of the offence. In a Scottish case dealing with a workplace accident the Director of Roads of a local council was convicted on the basis that he had not taken a series of steps which were allocated to him by the company's safety policy which gave rise to a personal duty which the court held he had not discharged.[15] *A fortiori*, where it is written into a person's contract of employment that he has certain personal responsibilities for matters which materially affect a product's safety he can be found guilty under this section where it can be shown that his role is not properly carried out and there is a causal link with the company to committing the offence.

Enforcement arrangements for other product safety regulations

As has been noted previously a number of recent sets of regulations implementing New Approach Directives relating to specific types of products are not formally adopted as regulations pursuant to the HSWA. They stand alone as regulations made by ministers under powers contained in section 2(2) of the European Communities Act 1972. Regulations made in this way can repeal or amend Acts of Parliament or other regulations.[16] Consequently it is necessary for these regulations

[13] *Huckerby v. Elliott* and *Lewin v. Bland*, cited above.
[14] *Hirschler v. Birch* [1986] 151 J.P. 396.
[15] *Armour v. Skeen* [1977] S.L.T. 71.
[16] Section 2(4).

either to contain or to adopt by reference measures enabling them to be enforced by the relevant authorities. The way in which this has been done has varied in relation to different regulations.

The U.K. legislation implementing New Approach Directives now generally contain provisions for enforcement authorities to issue compliance notices where a product does not fully comply with the Directive or CE marking has been wrongly affixed. This procedure will not, however, be applicable when the non-compliance renders the product unsafe. Here the manufacturer can be obliged to withdraw the product from the market. A variety of approaches have been taken for these purposes. Some regulations are to be treated as *safety regulations* within the meaning of the Consumer Protection Act 1987 (see for example the Electrical Equipment (Safety) Regulations 1994) with certain modifications; others may incorporate provisions which are virtually identical to those in the 1987 Act.[17] Some regulations, for example the Supply of Machinery (Safety) Regulations 1992 and the Simple Pressure Vessels (Safety) Regulations 1991 cross-refer to and incorporate by reference some or all of the enforcement provisions of the HSWA (in relation to such products for use at work) as well as the Consumer Protection Act 1987 (where the products concerned are for consumer use). In contrast, some regulations, for example the Personal Protective Equipment (E.C. Directive) Regulations 1992 and the Electrical Equipment, etc., (Certification) Regulations 1990 merely incorporate some elements of either the 1974 or the 1987 Act enforcement provisions. Certain regulations also provide that compliance with their requirements in relation to the product will act as a defence in relation to offences brought under the HSWA or in relation to enforcement notices brought by health and safety inspectors.[18]

The absence of consistent approach to the drafting of enforcement measures therefore requires careful consideration of individual regulations where the consequences of contravening the requirements have to be examined.

CIVIL LIABILITY FOR DEFECTIVE WORKPLACE PRODUCTS

There are two forms of strict liability under statute relating to workplace products that cause personal injury. A producer may be liable by virtue of Part I of the Consumer Protection Act 1987 for defective products, this statute applying to persons injured in the workplace as well as consumers. An employer may also be strictly liable under the Employer's

[17] See, *e.g.* the Construction Products Regulations 1991.

[18] See n.1, p.215, *supra.* — further example is reg.2(3) of the Electrical Equipment (Safety) Regulations 1994.

Liability (Defective Equipment) Act 1969. This Act makes the employer liable where a defect in the equipment has caused an injury to an employee and the defect is attributable wholly or partly to the fault of the third party (who need not necessarily be identified). The supplier of the product to the employer may then be obliged to indemnify him under contractual warranties arising under the contract of sale. Civil liability under these provisions is discussed more fully in Chapter 8 below.

A manufacturer's or supplier's contravention of section 6 does not of itself create a cause of action on which a civil claim can be based. Section 47 of the HSWA expressly precludes an injured person having a claim directly based on non-compliance with Section 6, but this non-compliance will often be strong evidence that there has been negligence or some other breach of duty on the part of the manufacturer or supplier.[19]

In contrast, a breach of a duty imposed by health and safety regulations is, so far as it causes damage, actionable except in so far as the regulation itself provides otherwise.[20] Thus, a person who can demonstrate, for example, that a failure to provide adequate information about a chemical substance contrary to the Chemicals (Hazard Information and Packaging) Regulations 1994 caused him injury would be entitled to claim damages for this breach of statutory duty, subject only to the defence of reasonable precautions and due diligence contained in the regulations being made out by the defendant.

[19] See s.11 Civil Evidence Act 1968. Generally, the conviction will be admissible as evidence and has the effect of shifting the relevant burden of proof to the defendant.

[20] s.47(2).

7 The impact of the GPS Regulations on business

The GPS Directive is clearly a measure which has far-reaching implications for consumers and industry. However, it should be seen in the context of the EU as a whole, by bringing product safety standards and enforcement in some Member States up to the level which pertains in the U.K., Germany, France and the Netherlands. It may be the case that the Directive will have little effect in practice in Member States which have a well-established existing regime of product safety regulation and experienced enforcement officers. In other States, however, the practical effect remains entirely unclear. Nevertheless, indications are that responsible competent authorities in all Member States are seriously considering their enforcement responsibilities — they cannot ignore the Directive because it is there.

Reassessment of operations

Companies would be well advised to consider their products, systems contracts, insurance and affairs in the light of the General Product Safety Regulations. A general Action List intended to provoke ideas, rather than to indicate legal requirements in all cases, is at **Table 7.1.**

Table 7.1 Action List

- Are my products safe?
  - Have I identified all the regulations, standards and codes of practice that apply to them?
  - Do they have acceptably minimum risks, given their use?
  - Do they have appropriate characteristics, packaging, assembly instructions, labelling, instructions for use, advertising and promotional material, maintenance?
  - Are they properly designed, tested, manufactured, packaged, distributed, stored?
- Do I have appropriate systems for:
  - ensuring that my products are safe when they leave my control?

  - ensuring that my products are safe to use?
  - being informed of problems in use?
  - monitoring developments in scientific and technical knowledge?
  - assessing and testing information and returned products?
  - communicating with retailers and others in the supply chain?
  - taking appropriate action to inform customers and users of risk assessment information, whether pre-existing or new?
- instituting an effective recall?
- Is my contractual documentation with my suppliers and customers satisfactory? (see **Table 7.2**)
- Have I taken all reasonable steps and exercised all due diligence to avoid committing an offence? How will I prove this if challenged?
- How well do I know my local TSO?
- Is my product liability insurance cover adequate? Does it extend to recall costs?

Safety systems

An increased emphasis in product safety regulation should lead commercial operators to consider their systems for safety control. Safety control is not necessarily the same as quality assurance. Manufacturers, distributors and retailers should reassess their product safety obligations and how they can demonstrate that they comply. Manufacturers should consider whether they have adequate systems for promoting safety at each stage: design, research, development, manufacture, packaging, distribution, use and, ultimately, disposal. Distributors and retailers should reassess the impact which their activities might have on product safety. Particular importance should be given to the safety aspects in product information (warnings, instructions for use, etc) which need the application of experience and careful judgment. Then there is the need to have systems for dealing with problems (information on suppliers, customers, batches and prudent crisis management plans and procedures). The ability to institute an effective recall will be important and this involves having established and practised procedures which could be implemented quickly, including having the facilities to identify and contact customers and users of their products and to liaise with appropriate expert advisers, whether technical, scientific, PR or legal.

The new obligations on producers to monitor safety in use and to take appropriate action will involve the need to check labelling systems, perhaps manufacturing processes, and certainly storage and stock control. A product or batch should be identifiable and traceable before and, ideally, after supply. The GPS Regulations specifically state that appropriate measures might include marking of products or product batches in such a way that they can be identified, sample testing of marketed products, investigating complaints made and keeping distributors informed of such monitoring.

Producers of consumer goods will be required to provide relevant safety information to enable customers "to assess the risks inherent in a product *throughout the normal or reasonably foreseeable period of its use*". For some products it may be possible to provide this information once and for all when the product is supplied. However, the new duty is continuous. Thus, there is a duty to continue to provide information on new risks which come to light after a product has been sold. This is in contrast to the position under the Product Liability Directive, under which information acquired after the product has been put into circulation is expressly irrelevant to the question of whether the product is defective, the test of defectiveness being decided at the time at which the product is put into circulation.

Will it be enough to say "this product deteriorates with age and/or continued use"? Seemingly not: sufficient information must be given to enable customers not only to identify and understand particular risks but also to assess them. This implies producers having to establish extensive post-marketing surveillance departments which will need effective methods for the reporting and communication of information relating to the safety of the product in use (including complaints), collecting and disseminating information between users, retailers, distributors and manufacturers, scrutinising the on-going public and scientific literature in relation to identical and similar products, storing and continuously analysing all such information, and taking appropriate action when required.

There may be demand for significant investment in information technology and in training managers to understand and assess scientific and medical risks. There will certainly be need for scientific, technical and legal input in determining what response is appropriate in a given situation: amending instructions for use, improving warnings, packaging changes, modification, limited recall or full recall.

Certain lessons may be learnt from the pharmaceutical industry, which has developed and is continuing to develop extremely sophisticated product surveillance facilities and techniques — but at considerable cost. Multi-million pound companies are able to afford such luxuries, but smaller concerns might not.

Product surveillance also generates a considerable amount of data. Not only does the existence of extensive quantities of documentation or computerised information lead to storage problems, there are implications concerning potential discovery in civil litigation (with a considerable increase in cost) and criminal prosecution. The Directive does not impose a specific obligation to retain records, whether for a specified period or at all, but this may be implicit from producer's general obligations. Document retention policies will have to be carefully considered in the light of this new regulatory regime and in the light of the Product Liability Directive. Whilst a rule of thumb under the latter has been 10 years plus a year or two for certain categories of documents to take account of periods of limitation, under the GPS Directive different considerations will come into play. Records of product development, for example, may have to be kept indefinitely to assist in meeting the obligations for monitoring safety throughout a product's life span. In the regulatory context, one may wonder to what extent will Trading Standards Officers expect or require to see monitoring records? Will failure to have up-to-date, well organised and accessible data itself be a cause for enforcement action?[1]

Contract documents

Contractual documentation should be re-assessed as suggested in **Table 7.2.**

Table 7.2 Assessment of contract documentation

- does it provide appropriate indemnities or exclusions of liability?
- does it provide for appropriate standards of safety in products supplied?
- does it set out who is to have what obligations for sampling, testing, storage, distribution or providing information on products — and who is not to have these obligations?
- does it include obligations to maintain information on customers and use to which products are put in practice, including complaints and returns, and to pass on full information in the chain of distribution, whether back towards producers or forwards to users?
- does it cover the obligations of appropriate parties in relation to co-operation in issuing warning notices or recall?
- whose obligation is it to hold insurance?
- is the contract governed by English law and does it provide for any disputes to be subject to the English courts? If not, do you understand your liability under the laws of other relevant countries?

The answers to these questions will, of course, vary depending on the circumstances of the product and of the commercial bargaining strength of the parties involved. The invalidity of certain exclusions of liability in relation to consumers should be noted: see **Chapter 8**.

Enforcement and insurance

It benefits all operators to establish a close and continuous dialogue with local enforcement officers and to be capable of talking to national

[1] See Chaps. 5 and 6 on enforcement

officials and the Commission where products are sold in other Member States. Particular notice should be taken of the fact that although breaches of the obligations in regulations 8 and 9(b) of the GPS Regulations are not criminal offences in the United Kingdom, the same may not be true in other States. Their general laws on workplace products are not harmonised and so their requirements cannot be assumed to be equivalent to the U.K.'s. The main consequences might therefore be experienced in trading in Member States where the consumer safety regime is new (*e.g.* Portugal, Spain, Italy and Greece) and where problems emerge simultaneously in more than one State which trigger the international notification provisions. This is yet another example of the extension of European regulatory control over the marketing and manufacture of products which combines with New Approach Directives and developing environmental and health and safety legislation.

Those companies which can demonstrate a good track record in relation to product safety and high quality systems producing high quality products, particularly through certification with BS EN 1S0 9000, may be able to negotiate a reduction in liability insurance premiums.

Increased costs under the new regime

It is difficult to accept the view of the Commission that "there are no special financial consequences in [the Directive] for business, although the measures will encourage such businesses to keep proper records and data, where these are not already required by other Community national measures . . ." and that the Directive might result only in "a small extra cost".[2] The Commission has also stated that the minimal extra direct costs on manufacturers should be compensated by the economic benefits of the harmonised and efficient safety net provided by the Directive through, amongst other things, reduction in unfair competition, accidents product liability claims and barriers to trade.[3]

This Directive constitutes a significant increase in the regulation of producers. It exposes them to onerous obligations throughout the foreseeable lives of their products, backed by criminal sanctions, and entails material cost implications. A great deal will depend on the manner of implementation in each country's laws, and the vigour with which powers are exercised by the national authorities.

[2] Impact statement with COM (89) 162/6.
[3] Written Question No. 932/89, OJ No. C 283/4. 12.11.90.

8 Product liability

Most of the legislation considered in this book is regulatory law governing product safety, backed by criminal sanctions. Community product liability law has the principal aim of providing financial compensation for damage, but is also aimed at encouraging the design, manufacture and marketing of safe products. This chapter considers the three theories of product liability law: breach of contract, negligence and strict liability for defective products under Part II of the Consumer Protection Act 1987.

PRODUCT LIABILITY AND PRODUCT SAFETY

This book is concerned with the safety of products. Most of the legal provisions which are discussed are regulatory in character, *i.e.* they relate to duties on those who market products to ensure that they are safe, backed up by enforcement powers of regulatory authorities under the criminal law. There is, however, a separate system of law which arises under civil law and is concerned with the payment of compensation for injuries caused by negligence or by a defective product. This area of civil law is known as product liability. One of the principal policy aims in the imposition of liability for damage caused by a defective product is concerned with achieving product safety by means of encouraging producers of products to design, manufacture and market products which are safe.[1]

A study of product safety would therefore be incomplete without mention of the law of product liability. This chapter therefore outlines the law of product liability in England and Wales.[2] This analysis is not intended to be an exhaustive legal discussion but to highlight those

[1] The first recital to Council Directive 85/374/EEC of July 25, 1985 on the approximation of the laws, regulations and administrative provisions of the Member States concerning liability for defective products mentions not only the harmonisation of Community rules on trade as part of the creation of the internal market but also the protection of the consumer's health and property.

[2] The law of negligence in Northern Ireland and, with some differences, in Scotland is the same as in England and Wales. Strict liability under the Consumer Protection Act 1987 is also the same, since that Act applies to Scotland and the Consumer Protection (Northern Ireland) Order 1987 has the same provisions as the Act.

aspects of product liability law which are important from the point of view of product safety. In particular, it draws attention to practical aspects which should be borne in mind from the point of view of designing, manufacturing and marketing products.[3]

A person who suffers injury caused by a product may be able to bring a claim on one or more of three bases (causes of action):

- a claim for breach of a term of a contract of sale if he has bought the product[4];
- a claim in negligence, *i.e.* that the product has not been designed or manufactured or marketed with due care;
- a claim in strict liability under Part I of the Consumer Protection Act 1987 for damage caused by a defective product.

These three approaches will now be examined in turn.

CONTRACT LIABILITY

A claim for breach of contract depends upon the existence of a contract which contains a term which has been breached. The most usual types of contract are those for sale and purchase, hire purchase or other credit purchase, or bailment (transfer of possession without ownership). Under English law, it is not necessary that a contract should be in writing for it to be legally enforceable unless the sale of land is involved. In order to be legally enforceable, however, the following conditions must be fulfilled:

- sufficient agreement between the parties (an offer and final and unqualified acceptance on that offer)[5];
- certainty as to the terms which have been agreed[6];
- consideration (something of value given by both parties unless it is a promise under seal)[7]; and
- an intention to create binding legal relations.[8]

It is in general unusual for contracts to contain a clause which specifies that a product which is the subject of the contract will not be dangerous or defective or cause injury and that the seller or manufacturer of the product will be liable in the event that the buyer or a third party is injured. However, commercial contracts frequently contain conditions relating to the quality of the product and it can usually be argued that considerations of safety are implicit in aspects of quality.

[3] For a more detailed examination see C.J.S. Hodges *Product Liability: European Laws and Practice* (1993).
[4] Or possibly for misrepresentation or breach of a collateral warranty.
[5] *Peter Lind & Co. Ltd v. Mersey Docks & Harbour Board* [1972] 2 Lloyd's Rep. 234.
[6] *G. Scammell & Nephew Ltd v. Ouston* [1941] A.C. 251.
[7] *Currie v. Misa* (1875) L.R. 10 Ex 153 at p. 162.
[8] *Zakhem International Construction Ltd v. Nippon Kokkan KK* [1987] 2 Lloyd's Rep. 596.

Furthermore, terms are implied into contracts for the sale of goods and services sold in the course of a business as to the "satisfactory quality" and "fitness for purpose" of the goods or services. By Section 14 of the Sale of Goods Act 1979[8a], goods are of satisfactory quality if they:

> "meet the standard that a reasonable person would regard as satisfactory, taking account of any description of the goods, the price (if relevant) and all the other relevant circumstances."

There is no implied condition as to satisfactory quality as regards defects specifically drawn to the buyer's attention before the contract is made or, if the buyer examines the goods before the contract is made, as regards defects which that examination ought to reveal. Where the buyer, expressly or by implication, makes known to the seller (or to a credit-broker involved in the transaction) any particular purpose for which the goods are being bought, there is an implied condition that the goods supplied under the contract are reasonably fit for that purpose, whether or not that is a purpose for which such goods are commonly supplied, except where the circumstances show that the borrower does not rely, or that it is unreasonable for him to rely, on the skill or judgment of the seller or credit-broker.[9]

These statutory implied terms may (subject to the Unfair Contract Terms Act 1977, see below) be negated or varied by express agreement, or by the course of dealing between the parties, or by such usage as binds both parties to the contracts. An express condition does not negate an implied statutory condition unless inconsistent with it.[10]

Where goods supplied under a contract for the sale of goods are not of satisfactory quality or are unfit for their purpose, it is no defence that the seller has exercised all reasonable care in the supply of goods.[11] Inadequate labelling or instructions for use do give rise to liability.[12] In principle, contributory negligence by the buyer is not a defence to a contractual claim, although it may lead to a reduction in the damages.[13]

Nevertheless, under the Unfair Contract Terms Act 1977, a contracting party may not exclude or restrict his liability in respect of the above implied terms (as to conformity of goods with description or sample, or as to their quality or fitness for a particular purpose) as against a person dealing as a consumer, and may only rely on such implied terms as against a person dealing otherwise than as a consumer insofar as the term satisfies the requirement of reasonableness.[14]

The Unfair Contract Terms Act 1977 also provides that a person may not exclude or restrict his liability for death or personal injury resulting

[8a] As amended by the Sale and Supply of Goods Act.

[9] s.14(3), Sale of Goods Act 1979.

[10] Sale of Goods Act 1979, s.55.

[11] *Frost v. Aylesbury Dairy Co. Ltd* [1905] 1 K.B. 608, CA.

[12] *Wormell v. RHM Agriculture (East) Ltd* [1986] 1 All E.R. 769; [1986] 1 W.L.R. 336.

[13] *Basildon District Council v. J.E. Lesser (Properties) Ltd* [1985] Q.B. 839; [1985] 1 All E.R. 20.

[14] Unfair Contract Terms Act 1977, s.6(2) and (3).

from negligence by reference to any purported contractual term or "notice given to persons generally or to particular persons". Such a notice would generally manifest itself in a manufacturer's "guarantee" supplied with products.[15] A person may not exclude or restrict his liability for negligence in respect of other loss or damage in so far as the term or notice satisfies the requirement of reasonableness.

Similarly, under the Unfair Terms in Consumer Contracts Regulations 1994[16] any term in a contract between a seller or supplier and a consumer which has not been individually negotiated, including where it has been drafted in advance and the consumer has not been able to influence the substance of the term, will be unfair and not binding on the consumer where, contrary to the requirement of good faith, it causes a significant imbalance in the parties' rights and obligations under the contract to the detriment of the consumer. Terms which have the object or effect of excluding or limiting a legal liability of a seller or supplier in the event of death of a consumer or his personal injury resulting from an act or omission of that seller or supplier, or of excluding or hindering the consumer's right to take legal action, are included in the indicative list of terms which may be regarded as unfair.

Liability for loss or damage arising from use of defective consumer goods supplied for private use or consumption resulting from negligence in manufacture or distribution cannot be excluded or restricted by reference to any contract term or notice contained in or operating by reference to a guarantee of the goods.[17] This ban does not apply as between parties to a contract where possession or ownership of the goods passed: its principal effect is to negate exclusion clauses for negligence in "consumer guarantees" provided by manufacturers.

The courts are required to take into account a number of factors in determining whether an exclusion clause is reasonable and in particular they must have regard *inter alia* to the strengths of the bargaining positions of the parties; whether the customer received an inducement to agree to the term; whether the customer knew or reasonably would have known of the existence and extent of the term; and whether the goods were manufactured or adapted to the special order of the customer.[18]

FAULT LIABILITY: NEGLIGENCE

Negligence[19] is one of the civil wrongs actionable under the common law of tort. Common law is not codified by statute but is understood to

[15] s.2, Unfair Contract Terms Act 1977.
[16] The Unfair Terms in Consumer Contracts Regulations 1994, S.I. 1994 No. 3159.
[17] s.5, Unfair Contract Terms Act 1977.
[18] Unfair Contract Terms Act 1977, Sched. 2.
[19] See generally R.A. Percy, *Charlesworth & Percy on Negligence*, (1990) and R.W.M. Dias, *Clerk & Lindsell on Torts*, (1989).

be part of the generally existing law of England and Wales and is declared by judges in concordance with the precedents of previously decided cases.

A cause of action lies in negligence where a person has breached a duty which is imposed upon him to take care and the breach has resulted in damage to the complainant. The elements of negligence are therefore:

(a) a relationship between the parties in which the law imposes a duty of care;
(b) breach of the duty of care, *i.e.* conduct by the defendant which falls below a particular standard of care;
(c) which causes damage which is not too remote.

The classic statement of the law was given in 1932, by Lord Atkin:

> "The rule that you are to love your neighbour becomes in law, you must not injure your neighbour; and the lawyer's question, "Who is my neighbour?" receives a restricted reply. You must take reasonable care to avoid acts or omissions which you can reasonably foresee would be likely to injure your neighbour. Who, then in law is my neighbour? The answer seems to be — persons who are so closely and directly affected by my act that I ought reasonably to have them in contemplation as being so affected when I am directing my mind to the acts or omissions which are called in question."[20]

This establishes the general concept of reasonable foresight as the criterion of negligence. The test for the existence of a duty of care is "what the defendant ought to have contemplated as a reasonable man".[21] A person will be liable for the natural and probable consequences of his act, but not the possible consequences.[22] He is entitled to assume that the consequences will be normal unless he has actual notice to the contrary. Lord Atkin continued:

> ". . . a manufacturer of products, which he sells in such a form as to show that he intends them to reach the ultimate consumer in the form in which they left him, and with the knowledge that the absence of reasonable care in the preparation or putting up of the products will result in injury to the consumer's life or property, owes a duty to the consumer to take that reasonable care."[23]

There is little doubt that every person in the chain of design, manufacture and supply of a product owes a duty to take reasonable care to avoid causing injury to a consumer or user by his careless act or failure to act. A general duty of care has also been held to be owed to an unborn child (born with injuries caused by pre-natal neglect).[24] Under

[20] *Donoghue v. Stevenson* [1932] A.C. 562 per Lord Atkin at p. 580.
[21] *Bourhill v. Young* [1943] A.C. 92, per Lord Wright, at p. 107.
[22] *Searle v. Wallbank* [1947] A.C. 341.
[23] *Ibid*, p. 599.
[24] *B v. Islington Health Authority* [1991] 1 Q.B. 638.

the Congenital Disabilities (Civil Liability) Act 1976 a person will be liable in damages to a child where he would have been liable to the parent for an occurrence affecting the parent which causes the child to be born disabled. It is now established that a duty of care exists where "nervous shock" (here treated as a recognised form of psychiatric damage) is caused, as opposed to more tangible physical injury. However, the class of persons to whom the duty not to cause nervous shock is owed is limited to parent, child, husband and wife[25] and rescuer.[26] Claimants must have close proximity to the accident in space and time (including people who experience the aftermath of the accident) and have seen or witnessed the accident or damage personally rather than been told about it.[27]

It is irrelevant that there may be a possibility of intermediate examination, unless that was contemplated. The issue is whether the product was intended to reach the consumer or user, subject to the same defect as it had when it left the manufacturer.[28] Where an intermediate examination is made, a producer is not liable for defects which that examination did or should have revealed. The chain of causation is broken.

Whilst there is therefore minimal difficulty in establishing the existence of a duty of care by the manufacturer in the case of product defects, the same is not always true of proving breach of duty and causation. The standard of care applicable in any given case is, as a matter of law, that of "reasonable care", *i.e.* the level of foresight of a prudent and reasonable man.[29] The standard is obviously flexible and not absolute, depending on the circumstances. Matters which would be taken into account[30] include:

(i) The magnitude of the risk The greater the risk the more care should be taken.[31] For more dangerous products, such as explosives, "the law exacts a degree of diligence so stringent as to amount practically to a guarantee of safety."[32] At the other extreme, the degree of risk may be so small that no special care need be taken, but this is subject to considerations of cost and practicability.

(ii) The likelihood of injury "People must guard against reasonable probabilities but they are not bound to guard against fantastic possibilities".[33] Both a greater risk of injury and a risk of greater injury are relevant.[34]

25 *McLoughlin v. O'Brian* [1983] 1 A.C. 410, *Alcock v. Chief Constable of South Yorkshire Police* [1991] 3 W.L.R. 1057, H.L.
26 *Chadwick v. British Railways Board* [1967] W.L.R. 912.
27 *Hanbrook v. Stokes Brothers* [1925] 1 K.B. 141.
28 *Grant v. Australian Knitting Mills* [1936] A.C. 85.
29 *Blyth v. Birmingham Waterworks* (1856) 11 Ex. 781.
30 *Morris v. West Hartlepool Steam Navigation Co. Ltd [1956] A.C. 552, per* Lord Reid at 574.
31 *Read v. J. Lyons & Co. Ltd* [1947] A.C. 156, at 173.
32 *Donoghue v. Stevenson, supra* 612 *per* Lord Macmillan.
33 *Fardon v. Harcourt-Rivington* (1932) 146 L.T. 391, *per* Lord Dunedin at 392.
34 *Paris v. Stepney B.C.* [1951] A.C. 367, H.L.

(iii) The gravity of the consequences The more serious the consequences for the intended or reasonably forseeable user, the greater the care which must be taken.

(iv) The cost and practicability of overcoming the risks Commercial factors may be considered here and also, it is suggested, the importance of the product. For example ". . . if all the trains in this country were restricted to a speed of five miles an hour, there would be fewer accidents but our national life would be intolerably slowed down. The purpose to be served, if sufficiently important, justifies the assumption of abnormal risk".[35] Thus, a high risk of death, serious injury or side effects may be acceptable in a pharmaceutical product which offers significant therapeutic benefit.

A defendant will not have been negligent if he has acted consistently with the "state of the art". This standard is based on an objective assessment of a reasonable standard to be expected of that defendant. Conduct by the defendant in accordance with common and approved practice by others in similar situations is evidence of what constitutes the reasonable standard of care in a given situation,[36] but is not necessarily conclusive. Similarly, compliance with statutory requirements[37] or industry standards is evidence of attainment of the standard of care but is not conclusive, since these may only set minimum standards. For example, it will be negligent to fail to depart from a common practice in the face of knowledge of a known danger.[38] Where an activity requires some special skill or competence then the test:

> "is not the test of the man on the top of a Clapham omnibus . . . but the standard of the ordinary skilled man exercising and professing to have that special skill. A man need not possess the highest expert skill . . . it is sufficient if he exercises the ordinary skill of an ordinary competent man exercising that particular art".[39]

Thus, in the context of medical negligence, the standard is to act in accordance with a responsible body of expert opinion skilled in the specialisation, even if another similar body holds a contrary view.

Whether the standard of care has been attained in any given case is a question of fact for the judge. Issues arise as to whether the damage caused was too remote from the defendant's negligence to be compensated by the law. This is an extensive and complex topic and is partially considered in the context of damages, below. The test of remoteness of damage is reasonable foreseeability. Damages for personal injury are not recoverable in negligence for pure economic loss.[40]

[35] *Daborn v. Bath Tramways Ltd.* [1946] 2 All E.R. 333, *per* Asquith L.J. at 336.
[36] *Vancouver General Hospital v. McDaniel* (1934) 152 L.T. 56, *per* Lord Alness at 57.
[37] *Franklin v. The Gramophone Co. Ltd* [1948] 1 K.B. 542.
[38] *Brown v. John Mills & Co. (Llanidloes) Ltd* (1970) 8 K.I.R. 702, C.A.
[39] *Bolam v. Friern Hospital Management Committee* [1957] 1 W.L.R. 582 at 586.
[40] *Department of the Environment v. Thomas Bates & Son Ltd* [1991] 1 A.C. 499. Damages for economic loss may be recoverable for negligent advice in special circumstances.

Liability for death or personal injury resulting from negligence cannot be excluded or restricted by contract or by a notice given to persons generally.[41] However, in the case of other loss or damage a person can limit his liability in respect of negligence provided that the contract term or notice is reasonable.[42]

Principal defences

Contributory negligence

Where the plaintiff's damage is caused partly by the fault of the defendant and partly by the fault of the plaintiff himself, the court will reduce the damages recoverable to a just and equitable extent in the light of the plaintiff's share of responsibility.[43] The burden of proving the plaintiff's contributory fault and its causation is on the defendant and the standard of care is the same as in negligence.[44] Contributory negligence is not strictly a defence but an apportionment of liability.

Voluntary agreement to assume the risk: volenti non fit injuria

It is an absolute defence for the defendant to show, on the balance of probabilities, that notwithstanding a breach of reasonable care by the defendant, the plaintiff: (a) agreed to that breach; and (b) consented to waive his right of action against the defendant in respect of that breach. The plaintiff's agreement may be express or implied but it must be freely given and made with full knowledge of the nature and extent of the risk being run.[45] The circumstances must show that the plaintiff accepted that the risk would fall solely on him. In essence, the defence involves formal transference of risk to the plaintiff and his responsibility for causation. It is not sufficient that the plaintiff saw the danger and decided to run the risk: if his decision was unreasonable he will be contributorily negligent, but in order for the defence of *volenti non fit injuria* to exempt the defendant from his negligence, the plaintiff must have agreed, expressly or by implication, to exempt the defendant from liability.

In the context of products, which may involve risks which are more or less apparent, the existence and extent of written warnings to purchasers and/or consumers can be of crucial importance. The outcome of cases may turn on the precise words used in product information and their prominence and the date on which they were issued or changed.

Subject to certain exemptions designed to protect particular classes of persons, a person may contractually exclude liability for his negligence.

[41] Unfair Contract Terms Act 1977, s.2(1).
[42] Unfair Contract Terms Act 1977, s.2(2).
[43] Law Reform (Contributory Negligence) Act 1945.
[43] Law Reform (Contributory Negligence) Act 1945.
[45] *Woolridge v. Sumner* [1963] 2 Q.B. 43.

A written exemption clause will be construed strictly against a defendant who seeks to rely on it. However, liability for death or personal injury caused by negligence in the course of business cannot be excluded or restricted. Liability for other negligence loss or damage in the course of business may only be excluded to the extent that it is reasonable.[46] Reasonableness is measured according to defined criteria including the relative strength of the parties' bargaining positions; whether the customer received an inducement to agree to the term; the availability of contracts with others without a similar term; whether the customer knew or ought reasonably to have known of the existence and extent of the term.[47]

Burden of proof

In negligence, as in every type of civil law action unless specifically otherwise provided for by statute or common law, the burden of proof falls on the plaintiff to establish each element necessary for liability. The standard of proof required is "the balance of probabilities".[48] In a recent medical negligence case, the House of Lords firmly upheld the strict burden on the plaintiff of showing that but for the defendant's conduct the injury would not have occurred. Thus, where there are several possible causes, the plaintiff must establish that the defendant's conduct was a cause: doubt will destroy the claim.[49] A legal inference of negligence can be drawn from the evidence, if this is so on the balance of probabilities, even though the matter is not completely clear. Thus, where the precise mechanism of causation is not understood, the plaintiff can still succeed in showing that the defendant's conduct "materially contributed to the risk" of injury.[50] Where the plaintiff proves that an event occurred but cannot establish anything more about causation, it is reasonable to infer negligence where the event would not have happened in the ordinary course of things without negligence by somebody, and the circumstances point to negligence by the defendant, rather than any other person.[51]

Employer's Liability (Defective Equipment) Act 1969

Where an employee suffers personal injury in the course of his employment in consequence of a defect in equipment provided by his employer

[46] Unfair Contract Terms Act 1977, s.2. See also the Unfair Terms in Consumer Contracts Regulations 1994, discussed above.

[47] *Ibid*, Sched. 2.

[48] *Donoghue v. Stevenson, supra*, at 622 *per* Lord Macmillan.

[49] *Wilsher v. Essex Area Health Authority* [1988] A.C. 1074.

[50] *McGhee v. National Coal Board* [1973] 1 W.L.R. 1.

[51] This is described by the maxim *res ipsa loquitur*: see *Grant v. Australian Knitting Mills* [1936] A.C. 85 in which a manufacturer of woollen underwear found to contain a chemical irritant was liable for a wearer's dermatitis.

for the purposes of the employer's business and the defect is attributable wholly or partly to the fault of a third party (whether identified or not), this Act deems that the injury shall also be attributable to negligence on the part of the employer, whether or not he is liable in respect of the injury in some other way. The Act does not confer a new cause of action, but amends the unsatisfactory position under the common law after *Davie v. New Merton Board Mills Ltd*[52] under which an employer would not be liable to his employee who suffered injury caused by a defective tool negligently manufactured by a third party provided that the employer had obtained the tool from a reputable supplier or manufacturer and had made such inspection as was reasonable in the circumstances. It is still necessary to prove that the equipment was defective, that this was attributable to fault on the part of a third party, and that this caused the injury. The term "equipment" has been given a wide meaning to include a ship[53] rather than just equipment on it, and a flagstone which was being handled by a council employee engaged in paving.[54]

BREACH OF STATUTORY DUTY

As an alternative to suing in negligence, it is sometimes possible to found a civil claim on the breach of a statutory duty. However, the circumstances in which this is possible are limited and probably of little practical importance in relation to product liability. In order to establish this type of civil liability, a plaintiff must show that:

(a) the injury he has suffered is within the ambit of the statute;
(b) the statutory duty imposes a liability to civil action;
(c) the statutory duty was not fulfilled; and
(d) the breach of duty has caused his injury.[55]

In relation to the first two criteria, the general rule is that:

> ". . . where an Act creates an obligation, and enforces the performance in a specified manner . . . that performance cannot be enforced in any other manner . . . Where the only manner of enforcing performance for which the Act provides is prosecution for the criminal offence of failure to perform the statutory prohibition for which the Act provides, there are two classes of exception to this general rule."[56]

The exceptions where a civil claim may be founded are:

[52] [1959] A.C. 604, H.L.
[53] *Coltman v. Bibby Tankers; Derbyshire, The* [1988] A.C. 276, H.L.
[54] *Knowles v. Liverpool City Council* [1993] I.C.R. 6, C.A.
[55] See generally on this topic *Clerk & Lindsell on Tort*, Chap. 14.
[56] *Lonrho Ltd v. Shell Petroleum Co. Ltd (No. 2)* [1982] A.C. 173 at 185.

- ". . . where on the true construction of the Act it is apparent that the obligation or prohibition was imposed for the benefit or protection of a particular class of individuals as in the case of the Factories Acts and similar legislation."
- ". . . where the statute creates a public right (*i.e.* a right to be enjoyed by all those of Her Majesty's subjects who wish to avail themselves of it) and a particular member of the public suffers . . . 'particular direct and substantial' damage 'other and different from that which was common to all the rest of the public.'"[57]

Breach of statutory duty and civil liability

The question arises, has the implementation of the General Product Safety Directive in the 1994 Regulations affected this position? On the face of it it might do, and there is certainly not the same degree of clarity that there is in relation to Part II of the 1987 Act.

It is in everyone's interests that the existence or not of a civil remedy in relation to breach of a statutory duty is clear. This is the case for example in relation to the Health and Safety at Work Act (section 47 excludes civil liability for the general duties), but is not made clear in the Regulations. More importantly, section 41 of the Consumer Protection Act 1987 makes it crystal clear that civil liability can arise in relation not just to Part I, but also to safety regulations made pursuant *to the Act.* The section provides expressly that the general safety requirement under Part II of the Act is not actionable. The same result could have been achieved at the stroke of a pen in drafting the 1994 Regulations. This was raised on more than one occasion during the consultation stage, but the risk the U.K. Government could have faced in so doing was that individual claimants might have tried to establish that they had direct claims against the Government for barring rights given by the GPS Directive, relying upon the *Francovich* decision of the European Court.[58]

Whether the GPS Regulations are meant to confer individual rights to claim damages for contravention of their requirements is therefore an open question and it is left to interpret the effect of the Regulations on the basis of general principles. Does the fact that the 1987 Act has an exclusion of civil liability in relation to its general safety requirement, and the 1994 Regulations do not, imply that civil liability *does* arise? Should the 1994 Regulations, although not "safety regulations" for the purposes of the 1987 Act, be treated as equivalent to such and therefore actionable like the other Regulations? There can be no clear answer to

[57] *Ibid.* at 186.

[58] *Francovich v. Italian Republic* [1992] I.R.L.R. 84. Damages are an appropriate remedy against a Government where it has failed to implement a directive properly, thus depriving individuals of a remedy. See also *Kirklees Metropolitan Borough Council v. Wickes Building Suppliers Ltd* [1993] A.C. 227

these questions until such time as a precedent has been determined by the courts, and if the absence of any authority some six years after the enactment of strict liability of the 1987 Act is anything to go by, it could be a considerable period of time before such an authority exists. Nevertheless, it is submitted that the 1994 Regulations are not in fact actionable as a claim for breach of statutory duty; firstly, for the following reasons based on case law in which the same question has arisen in relation to other statutes in the past and, secondly, by reference to the existence of the Product Liability Directive.

- "Where an Act creates an obligation, and enforces its performance in a specified manner . . . that performance cannot be enforced in any other manner" (Lord Tenterden C.J. in *Doe d. Murray v. Bridges*).[59]
- Where the only manner of enforcing performance for which the Act provides is prosecution for the criminal offence of failure to perform the statutory obligation or for contravening the statutory prohibition which the Act creates, there are two classes of exception to this general rule (Lord Diplock in *Lonrho Ltd v. Shell Petroleum (No. 2)*).[60]
- The first exception is where the obligations or prohibitions are imposed for the benefit or protection of *a particular class of individuals*. The other exception is where the statute creates a right for the general enjoyment of the public, and the plaintiff can show that he had suffered "particular, direct and substantial" damage which is other and different from that which was common to all the rest of the public.

Neither of the exceptions to the general rule applies in relation to the 1994 Regulations. Even though they are for the *benefit* and *protection* of consumers, consumers here consist of the general public and not a particular class thereof. Neither do the Regulations confer any public rights of enjoyment as such.

The European dimension to the question stems from particular wording in the General Product Safety Directive recitals, which says that it "does not affect victims' rights within the meaning of Council Directive 85/374/EEC on 25 July 1985" (the Product Liability Directive) and in Article 13 which states "this Directive shall be without prejudice to Directive 85/374/EEC".

The wording of the Directive is of direct relevance to the interpretation of the 1994 Regulations since, under Community Law, implementing legislation must be construed "purposively" in a way that results in the intended effect of the Directive.[61] The effect of the 1994 Regulations giving rise to civil liability would be to cut across the Product Liability Directive in a way which cannot have been intended in the adoption of

[59] (1831) 1 B&Ad. 847 at 859. Approved in *Lonrho Ltd v. Shell Petroleum (No. 2)* [1982] A.C. 173.
[60] [1982] A.C. 173.
[61] *Van Colson v. Land Nordrhein-Westfalen* [1984] E.C.R. 1891 at 1909 and 1910–11.

the General Product Safety Regulations; this would, for instance, ignore the rights of Member States to adopt a development risk defence and to exclude primary agricultural products and put financial caps on damages, as well as the inclusion of a component manufacturer defence and a 10-year long stop on claims.

STRICT LIABILITY FOR A DEFECTIVE PRODUCT UNDER THE CONSUMER PROTECTION ACT 1987

Overview of strict liability

Strict liability was introduced into the law of United Kingdom jurisdictions on March 1, 1988 through Part I of the Consumer Protection Act 1987 ("CPA").[62] Part I of the CPA was enacted to implement the European Directive on strict liability.[63] Part II governs aspects of regulatory law concerning product safety and is discussed elsewhere in this work. The Directive was introduced to achieve an approximation between the laws of Member States in relation to liability for damage caused by defective products. The laws of some Member States on fault liability (negligence) had been developed by reversing the burden of proof in this situation so that strict liability already applied. This was true in, for example, France, Germany, Italy and the Netherlands.[64] However, the introduction of strict liability was a novel concept in other Member States such as the United Kingdom and Ireland.

Under strict liability, the producer of a defective product is liable for damage caused by it. The term "producer" is defined widely to include a manufacturer of a finished product, the manufacturer of a component and a person who puts his own name or trademark on a product so as to appear to be the producer. Where the producer cannot be identified, a supplier of the product will be liable. Damage is only claimable for death, personal injury and damage to what may generally be described as personal property. The protection of the CPA is therefore aimed at consumers and individuals rather than commercial concerns. There are seven specific defences, the most important of which is the "development risks" defence, and important limitation provisions. In general, claimants who are able to take advantage of the CPA provisions are able to establish liability more simply and cheaply than if they have to prove negligence. Proof of strict liability does not require proof of fault, which

[62] In Northern Ireland through the identical Consumer Protection Act (Northern Ireland) Order 1987.

[63] Council Directive 85/374/EEC of July 25, 1985 on the approximation of the laws, regulations and administrative provisions of the Member States concerning liability for defective products.

[64] For a complete analysis of European Product Liability Law see C.J.S. Hodges, *Product Liability: European Laws and Practice* (1993).

is why it is called "strict". These provisions will now be examined in more detail.

Products covered

Liability under Part I of the CPA applies to damage caused by a product. A product is defined to mean any goods or electricity or a product which is comprised in another product, such as a component part or raw material.[65] In considering the definition of a product under the CPA, the restriction on the applicability of the CPA in the commercial and industrial context should be remembered in view of the limitation on the damage which is claimable, as discussed below. The term "goods" includes substances, growing crops and things comprised in land by virtue of being attached to it and any ship, aircraft or vehicle.[66] Building materials, whether before or after they have been incorporated into buildings, are "goods" but the buildings or permanently immovable structures themselves would not be. The Government has said that liability is not intended to extend to pure information, such as defective printed matter.[67] Information provided by defective computer software might therefore not give rise to liability, although that would not be true of defective operation of the machinery in which the software is incorporated.

The CPA does not cover game or agricultural produce which has not undergone an industrial process.[68] Agricultural produce is defined as any produce of the soil, of stock-farming or of fisheries.[69] There is some uncertainty as to the interpretation of the phrase "industrial process" in the CPA and the linked phrase "initial processing" in Article 2 of the Directive.

Defectiveness and safety

Consideration of product safety is at the heart of product liability. The test of whether there is a defect in a product is:

> "if the safety of the product is not such as persons generally are entitled to expect; and for those purposes 'safety' in relation to a product, shall include safety with respect to products comprised in that product and safety in the context of risks of damaged property, as well as in the context of risks of death or personal injury."[70]

[65] s.1(2), CPA.
[66] s.45(1), CPA.
[67] "Guide to the Consumer Protection Act 1987", Department of Trade and Industry, HMSO.
[68] s.2(4), CPA.
[69] s.1(2), CPA.
[70] s.3(1), CPA.

This establishes the "expectation" test of defectiveness. It is sometimes referred to as the "consumer expectation test", which is not entirely accurate since the test should be objective and ultimately independent of the interests of both consumers and producers. In determining the safety which persons generally are entitled to expect from a product, all the circumstances are to be taken into account. Certain specific considerations are mentioned specifically in the CPA:

"(a) the manner in which, and purposes for which, the product has been marketed, its get-up, the use of any mark in relation to the product and any instructions for, or warnings with respect to, doing or refraining from doing anything with or in relation to the product;

(b) what might reasonably be expected to be done with or in relation to the product; and

(c) the time when the product was supplied by its producer to another;

and nothing in this section shall require a defect to be inferred from the fact alone that the safety of a product which is supplied after that time is greater than the safety of the product in question."[71]

The above list is not exclusive and may include other considerations, such as price. There are, as yet, no decided cases which would illustrate how these considerations are to be applied in practice. However, it should be well understood that safety is a variable and relative concept and that absolute safety is unobtainable. Some useful products are intrinsically dangerous but should not be defective. Examples would include kitchen cutting equipment, DIY tools, fireworks, rodent poison and fuel. On the other hand, a product which conforms to its design criteria may be defective under the CPA.

The references quoted above to the manner of marketing, instructions for use and warnings associated with a product show that the expectation of safety may be qualified or even increased by the use of labelling and other product information, including advertising. In certain cases, the degree of prominence (*e.g.* its location and size on product information) may be relevant. Care should be taken to ensure that statements made in all product information, whether labelling, instructions or advertising, is consistent.

The test for defectiveness of a product is to be applied at the time when the product was supplied. If a product was not defective at that time, liability under the CPA cannot arise for failure to issue warnings about a product which was already in circulation, although this is subject to negligence liability. However, the CPA makes clear that the design of and information supplied with other products of the same type must be reassessed once information comes to the attention of the producer as to problems with the use of the product. This follows from

[71] s.3(2), CPA.

the reference in the CPA to consideration of "the use to which it could reasonably be expected that the product will be put".

A product should not be defective at the time of supply if it becomes dangerous only after extensive use, or after its reasonable or stated life. In some circumstances, a product which is liable to become less safe over time may be defective at the time at which it is put into circulation unless it is supplied with an adequate warning. However, the producer should not be liable if the consumer uses a product after the marked expiry date.

Who is liable?

The policy of the legislation is that there should be a commercial entity within the European Community which is identifiable by an injured consumer and who can be liable to him. Accordingly, liability may attach to a manufacturer, processor, "own-brander", importer into the Community or, where one of the above is not identifiable, by someone in the supply chain.

The principal concept is that of a "producer" which is defined as meaning:

"(a) the person who manufactured it;

(b) in the case of a substance which has not been manufactured but has been won or abstracted, the person who won or abstracted it;

(c) in the case of a product which has not been manufactured, won or abstracted but essential characteristics of which are attributable to an industrial or other process having been carried out (for example, in relation to agricultural produce), the person who carried out that process."[72]

Liability is also extended to any person who, by putting his name on the product or using a trademark, or other distinguishing mark in relation to it, has held himself out to be the producer of the product.[73] This would generally apply to a chain-store retailer or mail order operator who has not been involved in the manufacture of the product but sells it under his own name, thereby presenting himself as the sole producer. This person is generally referred to as an "own-brander".

Any person who supplied a product which has caused damage may also be liable if certain conditions are fulfilled. The conditions are that:

(a) the person who suffered the damage requests the supplier to identify one or more of the persons who are primarily liable, as discussed above (*e.g.* the producer, importer or person who has held himself out to be the producer);

[72] s.1(1), CPA.
[73] s.2(2)(b), CPA.

(b) the request is made within a reasonable period after the damage occurs and at a time when it is not reasonably practicable for the person making the request to identify all those persons; and
(c) the supplier fails, within a reasonable period after receiving the request, either to comply with the request or to identify the person who supplied the product to him.[74]

The extent to which certain aspects of this secondary liability of suppliers and the request mechanism conform to the Directive are unclear.

No exclusion of liability

Liability under the CPA may not be limited or excluded by any contract term, notice or any other provision.[75]

Claimable damage

Damage is claimable under the CPA for death, personal injury or any loss of or damage to any property, including land.[76] There is no liability for loss of or any damage to the product itself, or for the loss of or any damage to the whole or any part of any product which has been supplied with the product in question comprised in it.[77] This provision is obviously relevant to packaging and components.

Damage to property is only claimable if, at the time it is lost or damaged, the property is not:

(a) of a description or property ordinarily intended for private use, occupation or consumption;
(b) intended by the person suffering the loss or damage mainly for his own private use, occupation or consumption.[78]

In respect of damage to property, although not in the case of death or personal injury, section 5(4) of the CPA provides that:

> "No damages shall be awarded . . . in respect of any loss of or damage to any property if the amount which would fall to be so awarded . . . apart from this sub-section and any liability for interest, does not exceed £275".

This provides a jurisdictional threshold under which no claims for damage to private property will succeed if damages of less than £275 are awarded at trial. This provision is inconsistent with Article 9 of the

[74] s.3, CPA.
[75] s.7, CPA.
[76] s.5(1), CPA.
[77] s.5(2), CPA.
[78] s.5(3), CPA.

Directive, in which the financial threshold of 500 ECU acts as a deduction which is to be made from all awards of damages in respect of property claims.

The burden of proof

The plaintiff has to prove the damage, the defect and the causal relationship between damage and defect.[79] This is a basic principle of English law and is the same, for example, in relation to negligence. Proof of causation of injury can sometimes present problems, particularly in relation to products which act inside the human body or where there are possible alternative causes.[80]

Defences

Six specific defences are available to defendants under section 4 of the CPA:

1. The defect is attributable to compliance with any requirement imposed by or under any enactment or with any Community obligation The effect of this defence is more limited than might at first be thought. The defect must have been caused by compliance with a mandatory provision. The situation should arise only rarely. Compliance with a harmonised or national standard would not qualify.

2. The defendant did not at any time supply the product to another This is intended to excuse people while they are making products or who keep them after they have made them.

3. Non-commercial supply This is intended to excuse gifts, private non-business sales and sales in aid of charity. The precise wording of section 4(1)(c) of the CPA is somewhat complex.

4. The defect did not exist in the product at the relevant time This is an important defence. "The relevant time" generally means the time at which the producer supplied the product to another.[81] A person who supplies a product which is not defective when he supplies it is entitled to rely on the defence. However, the burden is on him to show that the product was not defective when he supplied it, perhaps because it was correctly manufactured and went with appropriate instructions. He will have to show that the product became defective later and this may be difficult. Was the product supplied with any or correct or substituted

[79] Directive, Art. 4.
[80] *Wilsher v. Essex Area Health Authority* [1987] A.C. 750.
[81] s.4(2), CPA.

instructions? Was the defect due to faulty installation, mishandling or mis-use, lack of maintenance or other interference? The need is apparent for producers and suppliers to have full and accurate records in order to be able to establish some of these matters.

5. The state of scientific and technical knowledge at the relevant time was not such that a producer of products of the same description as the product in question might be expected to have discovered the defect if it had existed in his products while they were under his control This defence is known as the "development risks" defence. It is not quite the same as the "state of the art" concept which arises in negligence. It is likely to be a very important defence to the manufacturers of innovative products, particularly pharmaceuticals, chemicals and those involved in aerospace. Whilst the general purpose of the legislation is to place responsibility for the design, manufacture and marketing of safe products squarely on producers and suppliers, this defence recognises that certain innovative products may contain hazards which are unknown and unknowable and about which accurate or any warnings cannot be given. The risk of using these products is therefore transferable to the consumer on the basis that the products are intrinsically useful and that innovation should be encouraged.

The essence of this defence is that the state of knowledge was such that the defect was not discoverable when the product was supplied.[82] The wording of this defence in section 4(1)(e) of the CPA is complex and is not the same as the wording in Article 7(e) of the Directive. The European Commission has concluded that the CPA wording is inconsistent with the Directive and should be rectified.

The state of knowledge of the producer or supplier is irrelevant to this defence. What must be shown is the objective state of scientific and technical knowledge at the time. This means that prudent manufacturers should identify and be familiar with the relevant scientific, technical and medical literature and have monitored the use of their products and similar products. Since scientific and technical knowledge is constantly developing, periodic reassessment of the safety of products is called for.

The defect must have been one which could not have been discovered at the time. This implies that a prudent manufacturer should carry out proper testing on his products and, once again, monitor their use and the use of similar products. The extent to which a manufacturer is expected to go in terms of the detail, cost and duration of tests prior to marketing is an issue which has not been made clear.

6. The defect constituted a defect in a product in which the product in question had been comprised and was wholly attributable to the design of the subsequent product or to compliance by the producer of

[82] The definition of "the relevant time" is given in s.4(2), CPA and is the same as that mentioned in relation to the previous defence.

the product in question with instructions given by the producer of the subsequent product This rather complex wording is intended to apply where a finished product is defective because of a defective component.

Contributory negligence

Where the damage is caused partly by defect in a product and partly by the fault of a person suffering the damage, the liability of the defendant may be reduced or extinguished, in accordance with normal principles.[83]

Limitation and expiry

The rules for limitation of actions, whether for personal injuries or damage to property, are the same under the CPA as for personal injuries under the Limitation Act 1980. Claims are barred after the expiry of three years from whichever is the later of:

"(a) the date on which the cause of action accrued; and
(b) the date of knowledge of the injured person or, in the case of loss of or damage to property, the date of knowledge of the plaintiff or (if earlier) of any person in whom this cause of action was previously vested"

The date of knowledge in section 11A of the Limitation Act 1980 is defined in relation to personal injury claims as the time at which the plaintiff became aware, or should reasonably have become aware, of the damage, the defect and the identity of the producer.[84] Identical provisions in relation to damage to property are included in section 5(5) to (7) of the CPA in relation to England, but these do not extend to Scotland.

However, claims under the CPA are subject to the overriding cut-off that they may not be brought after the expiry of 10 years from "the relevant time". The meaning of the relevant time in section 4(2) of the CPA has been referred to above but generally means the time at which the product was first supplied.

PRACTICAL CONCLUSIONS

Certain practical conclusions for designers, manufacturers and suppliers of products should be clear from the above product liability provisions. Prudent organisations will take care that they are aware of the state of

[83] Law Reform (Contributory Negligence) Act 1954 and s.6(4), CPA.
[84] CPA, Sched. 1, Part I, amending the Limitation Act 1980 by inserting a new s.11A.

scientific and technical knowledge and that their products and processes conform to state of the art standards. Appropriate testing and assessment will be carried out, both on the products themselves and on the information supplied with them. Proper information will be supplied so as to lead to the appropriate and safe use of products. Monitoring of one's own and similar products in use is advisable and appropriate action should be taken in response to information acquired.

9 Practical advice: product information and warnings

What instructions and warnings should be given by a producer about his product? When should a product be recalled? This chapter summarises the position which is reached in practice when one combines the different duties which arise under the various provisions of criminal and civil law which are discussed in more detail elsewhere in this book.[1]

Regrettably, the legal position in relation to warning and recall is both confusingly diverse and ill-defined. The approaches under regulatory law on general product safety and under product liability law are at the stage of establishing general principles but have not as yet been developed into rules which are more specific in helping people to know what the law requires them to do in particular circumstances.

PRODUCT INFORMATION: INSTRUCTIONS AND WARNINGS

The purpose of a warning

Satisfactory product information can render an otherwise unsafe product safe. Conversely, the absence of satisfactory product information can render a product unsafe which might have been safe with such information. A manufacturer or supplier must give adequate information so as to enable the product to be used as intended and so that the user is adequately warned of risks which he may encounter in using the product. In policy terms, the risk of the residual hazard is transferred from the producer to the user: The essence of a warning is that it allows the user to confront and avoid the hazard which it describes in an otherwise unreasonably dangerous product. If the warning is ignored then the causal link between the manufacturer's action in putting the product on the market and an injury to the user is broken.

[1] For a more detailed analysis of product liability theory, see C.J.S. Hodges *Product Liability: European Laws and Practice* (1993) Chap. 3.

The function of a warning, therefore, is:[2]

(a) to warn users of the hazards associated with the product;
(b) to instruct users on the safe uses, operation and maintenance of the product;
(c) to inform users of the consequences of failure to heed the warnings and instructions.

The same legal approach underlies instructions for safe use and warnings of hazards. The term "warning" will therefore be used to refer to both. The questions which need to be considered under both are:

- when is a warning required?
- how much information need be given?
- to whom need the information be given?

These questions give rise to further particular issues of who bears the risk of:

- an unknown hazard?
- misuse of the product by the user?
- a hazard which is only identified after the product is sold?

When is a warning required?

In general a warning is required when a product is unreasonably dangerous without it. A warning is required of dangers associated with the product which are not obvious and arise from its intended use or foreseeable misuse. In general terms, a warning is not required of hazards of which the user is aware and voluntary assumed and, possibly also, of hazards which are reasonably forseeable by the user. The precise position needs to be considered under the General Product Safety Regulations, CPA Part II and the civil law of fault liability (negligence[3] and strict liability for defective products in CPA Part I).

It has been held in a regulatory case under the Toys (Safety) Regulations 1989, which require a label and/or packaging and instructions for use "to draw the attention of users or their supervisors fully and effectively to the risks involved in using them and to the ways of avoiding such risks", that labelling is relevant both to cases of inherent risk as well as to cases where a label will avoid such risks.[4] In this case, Mr Justice Buckley drew a distinction between, on the one hand, clear risks, perhaps those included specifically as "Particular Risks" in the Regulations which toys must not be present, which it would not therefore be possible to obviate by a label, and, on the other hand,

[2] C.J. Wright, *Product Liability: The law and its implications for risk management,* (1989), p.123.
[3] *Grant v. Australian Knitting Mills Ltd* [1936] A.C. 85 at 105; *Farr v. Butler Bros & Co* [1932] 2 K.B. 606.
[4] *R. v. Felixstowe Magistrates' Court, ex parte Top Toys Ltd* (1993) unreported.

inherent risks which, provided they are commensurate with the ability of the users, may and should be met by suitable labelling. These comments were obiter and may only apply in the specific context of these Regulations. It is difficult to draw a general conclusion in the product liability context in the absence of further judicial guidance.

The test of safety in the GPS Regulations includes considerations of the information which accompanies a product:

> "The presentation of the product, the labelling, any instructions for its use and disposal and any other indication or information provided by the producer."[5]

This formulation of safety is very similar to the test of a defective product under strict civil liability:

> "The manner in which . . . the product has been marketed, its get-up . . . and any instructions for, or warnings with respect to, doing or refraining from doing anything with or in relation to the product;"[6]

Under fault liability a person has a duty to warn of dangers which are reasonably foreseeable, in other words dangers which he knew or ought to have known about which involve sufficiently serious risk. He is therefore liable for damage caused by a hazard of which he had actual or constructive knowledge and could reasonably have warned about. Such knowledge will generally have come from an understanding of the product, its intended use and the uses to which it could reasonably be expected to be put, or knowledge of risks or uses that all acquired subsequent to supplying it, particularly through complaints or reports of adverse events. This understanding will be governed by information from the manufacturer's design and testing of the product, scientific and technical information from external sources and post-marketing information as to the uses to which it is actually put and the possible situations of hazard which may be encountered. A producer can have no liability in negligence for failure to warn of dangers which are undiscoverable despite the exercise of reasonable care. What is reasonable will depend upon general (and not necessarily consumer) expectation, the manner of marketing, instructions and warnings and the general state of scientific and technical knowledge.

The duty to warn does not cease at the time of marketing the product. It continues in relation to dangers which are identified post-marketing in relation to products still in circulation or use, as discussed in Chapter 8. This is in contrast to strict liability, where there is no on-going liability in relation to a product after it has been placed into circulation.[7]

Many safety aspects of products are governed by specific regulations or standards. Compliance with such provisions is not, as a matter of law, a defence to a product liability claim.[8]

[5] Directive 92/59/EEC, Art. 2(b); The General Product Safety Regulations 1994, reg. 2(1).

[6] Consumer Protection Act 1987, s.3(2).

[7] CPA 1987, ss.3(2)(c) and 4(1)(e).

[8] Unless, in a claim for damage caused by a defective product, the defect is attributable to compliance with any requirement imposed by or under any enactment or with any Community obligation, CPA s.4(1)(a).

Compliance will be evidence that the requisite duty of care has been met or that the product is not defective. Although there is little authority on the compliance of products with Regulations made under New Approach Directives,[9] the historical approach of the courts has tended to be that statutory requirements merely set a minimum standard and may not supersede more general duties in relation to safety nor pre-empt the courts' jurisdiction to determine standards of care. In the Canadian case of *Buchan v. Ortho Pharmaceutical (Canada) Ltd*[10] the judge said, of warnings given in connection with complications that could arise from taking the defendants' contraceptive pill:

> "Although the recommended wording of the package insert was presumably followed by Ortho (Canada) I do not think this ends the matter. The Food and Drug Directorate can require that certain warnings be given but these surely are minimal warnings. If a manufacturer knows of risks that are material there is, in my opinion, a duty upon the manufacturer, in a case of this type where there can be a package insert, to warn of such risks and to warn the consuming public whether or not any such warning is required by the Food and Drug Directorate".

It may be arguable, however, that whilst a general rule of pre-emption of product liability will not apply in relation to compliance with statutory regulatory requirements, the standard of care in individual circumstances should not exceed the regulatory standard. The considerable increase in product regulation, particularly since the mid-1980s, and its wide and onerous scope, may affect the courts' approach and eventually lead, if not to the establishment of a general pre-emption defence of compliance with regulatory requirements, at least to the equation in practice of such compliance with satisfaction of the standard of care required at civil law. Much is likely to depend on the extent to which the regulatory requirements are comprehensive or precise in covering the relevant safety aspects — similar to the test of the applicability of GPS requirements in relation to product-specific requirements.[11]

Regrettably the principles regarding duty to warn about products that are put on the market, and in particular to warn about subsequently discovered dangers in products previously viewed as safe without specific warnings, are not well defined. The explanation for this was put succinctly by an Australian Appeal Court judge:

> "It is a question of fact in each case whether the duty owed has been breached. It is not a question of law. The manufacturer and retailer

[9] In *Whirlpool (UK) Ltd v. Gloucestershire County Council* (1993) unreported, the Divisional Court held that suppliers were required to do more than merely comply with a harmonised safety standard in order to comply with the general safety requirement in s.10, CPA in the context of the Low Voltage (Safety) Regulations 1989.

[10] (1984) 46 OR (2d) 113.

[11] See Chapter 4.

must act reasonably in placing its product on the market. The almost infinite variety of circumstances forbid any categorical exegesis of the manner of performance of the relevant duty of reasonable care."[12]

Some of the cases approach the issue in terms of instructions for correct usage — the classic situation of avoidance of a marketing defect. In other cases the concern is with the issue of enabling the consumer to confront and avoid a possible danger, or at least to weigh up the pros and cons and make an informed choice. Some cases have approached the issue as being one of whether the manufacturer ought to have responded to the seriousness of risk by taking steps to recall the product from consumers.[13]

The law concerning a duty to warn of unusual but serious consequences has developed furthest in the field of medical malpractice, where patients who have suffered side effects claim that they would not have consented to treatment had they known more than the doctor disclosed. Such cases have important differences in the context of the warnings which make extrapolation to directly purchased consumer products difficult, on account of the supply being through a "learned intermediary" and need to take into consideration a risk/benefit equation which arises from the fact that patients are in need of treatment in some way and, unlike most products which are purchased, have little freedom to choose between various options. Nevertheless, the courts have grappled in this context with two difficult problems:

1. What should be the correct response of a manufacturer during the period between emergence of the suspicion that the product might represent a health and safety risk and the later establishment that the suspicion was justified?
2. What weight should be given, when deciding on the correct response in terms of warning, to the *likelihood* of a person being harmed on the one hand, and the *gravity* of harm should it arise on the other hand.

In English medical negligence law, the courts consider adequacy of warnings against the background of the practice accepted as proper by "a responsible body of medical men skilled in that particular art,"[14] but it is also established that where a substantial risk of grave adverse consequences exists the court might expect a warning even if this has not been the general practice in the profession.[15] An example of such a level of risk has been given as the risk of stroke from a surgical operation estimated at 10 per cent.

It would be enormously helpful to manufacturers if the genesis of a duty to warn could be correlated to specific statistical evidence of risk

[12] *Thompson v. Johnson & Johnson* (1992) 3 Med. L.R. 148.

[13] *Walton v. British Leyland U.K. Ltd* (1978) unreported, *Wright v. Dunlop Rubber Co. Ltd* (1972) 13 K.I.R. 255.

[14] *Bolam v. Friern Hospital Management Committee* [1957] 2 All E.R. 118.

[15] *Sidaway v. Board of Governors of the Bethlem Royal Hospital* [1985] 1 A.C. 871.

and straightforward percentages representing vulnerable consumers, but it is simply not possible to lay down firm rules of this nature because each situation is different. In some cases the courts have touched upon this type of analysis: The 10 per cent figure was in a Canadian case and is obviously a material level of risk for a serious injury.[16] In an Australian medical negligence case[17] a doctor was found negligent for not disclosing a 1 in 14,000 risk of blindness from an eye operation because he should have appreciated the patient's desire to know of the risk. In the *Ortho (Canada)* case the judge, in finding the company negligent, relied heavily on epidemiological evidence (which the company was deemed to know about) showing an association between usage of the pill and the risk of stroke at 19 per 100,000 (as opposed to 1 per 100,000 for non-users).

In the *Ortho* case the court looked specifically at the question of the rarity of the side effect. The court was prepared to adopt the proposition that even if a certain risk is a mere possibility which ordinarily need not be disclosed, yet if its occurrence carries serious consequences, as for example, paralysis or even death, it should be regarded as a material risk requiring disclosure. In this context the Court was prepared to say the risk of stroke, was without question a material risk.

In the Australian case of *Thompson v. Johnson & Johnson* the trial judge gave the following statement which is a convenient summary of how the Courts can generally be expected to view rare but serious events:

> "As a general proposition it appears to me to be obvious that where the possible consequences of the contraction of a condition include death, even though the risk of any contraction may be very small, a potential purchaser is, at least, entitled to know of the existence of that risk and to be able to choose whether or not it will be accepted. This does not mean that it is necessary to provide warnings with respect to every conceivable possibility which might arise from the use of every conceivable product. Many risks are well understood through ordinary human experience, others are clearly not so and in relation to them a proper compliance with the duty of care resting upon the manufacturer or distributor may well require that reasonable steps are taken to provide appropriate information.
>
> Another dimension might be . . . where . . . a new problem could be seen to have arisen in relation to what has been long regarded as a generally safe product. Such a history might well be relied upon by consumers as indicating to them that no possible danger could arise from its use. Accordingly they could be, in some situations, misled into assuming a higher degree of safety than that which is either recognised as existing by the manufacturers and distributors of the product more than that which ought to have been reasonably recognised existing by those persons."

[16] *Reibl v. Hughes* [1980] 25 C.R. 880.

[17] *Rogers v. Whitaker* (1993) 4 Med. L.R.

The *Thompson* case, which was decided ultimately by the Appeal Division of the Supreme Court of Victoria, provides a useful illustration of a claim in respect of a rare but serious reaction, in this instance the involving of the contraction of toxic shock syndrome (TSS) by a woman using tampons manufactured and distributed by two Johnson & Johnson companies in New Zealand and Australia. The findings of the court were that there was a relationship between the use of tampons and TSS in a very small percentage of women, and that this claimant had indeed suffered TSS. Liability turned, on what the companies knew and ought to have known about this small risk at particular times and what, as a consequence, they should have done about it. Between April and September 1980 various studies in America began to show this association, although the authorities suspected that it was related to the method of manufacture because one particular brand (not that of Johnson & Johnson) seemed to be prevalent in use arising the affected women. At the end of September Johnson & Johnson in America were asked to provide warnings on their products and the Australasian companies knew about this soon afterwards. They discussed the position with the regulatory authorities in Australia and New Zealand.

At the start of October 1980 there were press reports of a TSS case in New Zealand which prompted the New Zealand authorities to warn women to avoid using tampons for the time being, although they subsequently took a different view and a few weeks later the New Zealand authorities agreed the wording of a warning to go in packets and asked that they be in place by April 1981. In Australia the authorities issued a news release discussing the "very small risk" of TSS associated with tampons and stressing that most reports of the syndrome had originated in America, and there was also press coverage in both countries. The authorities in neither country supported a suggestion that Johnson & Johnson might write to medical practitioners advising of the risks.

The claimant became unwell with TSS towards the end of January last. The evidence was that she had purchased the products in November/December. Strict liability laws did not apply here. The critical question before the Court was, therefore, had the companies acted negligently in not providing warning labels, advertisements and other media publicity between realising the potential for the risk and the risk materialising for the plaintiff? The plaintiff lost her case, the reasoning of the Court being as follows:

- It was reiterated that where the picture was unclear and the nature of the condition was as serious as it was known to be (*i.e.* risk of death — see the cases above) the defendants came under a duty to take reasonable steps to draw the attention of the risk (albeit very small) of contracting TSS to the very large number of users.
- The situation confronting the defendants was not such as to necessitate them carrying out a recall.

- An immediate duty to draw the attention of users to the risk through warnings in packets was not warranted, taking into account the uncertainty of the position with only one known case in Australasia, and the attitude and reaction of the public authorities there. In any event, it would not have been feasible to put warnings into packets for several months, and this was in fact done by February 1981. The evidence was that in October and November 1980 there was much publicity about the matter of TSS anyway, which was relevant to the question of whether failure to place press advertisements constituted negligence.
- Similarly, an allegation that the medical profession should have been directly informed by the defendants was rejected, again because the defendants conduct was consistent with the recommendations of the authorities.

It was of critical importance to ascertain the exact state of play at the time the injury occurred. The outcome in the *Thompson* case could easily have been different if the woman's purchase and use of the product had been rather later, and there had by that time still been no warnings issued extensively by the companies.

The principles discussed above evolved primarily in relation to a duty to exercise care — *i.e.* in the context of the law of negligence. As has been explained earlier, the legal issues in a strict liability claim are conceptionally different — liability turns upon the existence of defect, and this in turn requires an examination of the general expectations of consumers. In the absence of authority, how does one apply this expectation test to an alleged defect? Given the fact that very few products can never be said to be totally safe in all their applications, and some products which are genuinely useful nevertheless have inherent dangers (*e.g.* razor blades, petrol) some element of "reasonableness" must be imported into any analysis of consumers expectations.[18] If this is so, it is probable that a court would say that the general expectations of consumers is that an unusual but very serious risk that cannot be eliminated from a product through other means is at least made known to them.

The extent to which a hazard should be warned against will rest on the magnitude of the risk of it occurring, both in terms of the statistical chance that the hazard will occur and the seriousness of the injury which can be expected to result if it does. Thus the wording, prominence and class of warning, contra-indication or instruction will be dictated by similar considerations.

In strict liability, a producer will not *prima facie* be liable for dangers in his product which are obvious or common knowledge, since the product should not fail the test of defectiveness on this account. No warning need therefore be given of such hazards. Conversely, there are certain

[18] For a full discussion on the expectation test see C.J.S. Hodges, *Product Liability: European Laws and Practice* (1993), pp. 104–107.

situations in which any warning would be inadequate since it would not render an otherwise defective product safe. Examples would be products which may be used by people who would not comprehend a warning (children, people with linguistic or mental handicap) or where a hazard may arise so quickly that the danger could not be avoided.

The issue of whether a product is defective is decided on the basis of the expectation of safety given by the product. This expectation is not based on the expectation of the producer alone, although since the scientific factual enquiry into the characteristics of a product will inevitably be focused on the scientific data and knowledge of the producer, his understanding of the use to which the product could reasonably be expected to be put and the hazards which might arise will inevitably influence the court in many cases. It is not reasonable for a producer to ignore information about hazards merely because he finds it unconvincing.[19] Equally, it is suggested that it is incorrect to base the test on the consumer's expectation and that the correct approach is for the test to be objective, *i.e.* what people generally expect.

Many alleged failure to warn cases involve detailed analysis of complex scientific, technical and medical evidence as to the precise state of knowledge at a particular time. In court, the detailed wording of any warning which was given is examined minutely. This is a largely artificial analysis since it often takes place against a continuously changing background of information and knowledge such that it is difficult to define a precise moment at which a certain wording was appropriate or should have been altered. Further, the efficacy of minor alterations in wording which might occupy an obscure position in lengthy product information can be questioned.

How much information?

Applying the same principles discussed above, the question is whether the warning has allowed the user adequately to identify, assess and, if so wished, avoid or minimise the hazard. In short, has the warning made the product safe?

In the regulatory context, importers of microwave egg boilers imported from the Far East were convicted of failure to comply with the general safety requirement under section 10 of the Consumer Protection Act 1987 in responding to knowledge that the products were not safe to cook eggs, unless yolks and whites were pierced or tipped into a container prior to cooking, by having 80,000 labels printed and distributed to retailers with the recommendation that the labels be affixed to the lids of the products' boxes. The Divisional Court held that a mere recommendation to retailers left it to the latter's discretion to adopt the

[19] *Buchan v. Ortho Pharmaceutical (Canada) Ltd* (1984) 46 O.R. (2d)113 a Canadian case applying English law principles.

safety precautions or not. In this case, that was manifestly not enough and the products remained unsafe since retailers ignored the recommendation, which entirely failed to inform retailers of the risks.[20]

Similar issues about the adequacy of information arise under the Health and Safety at Work Act 1974: see Chapter 6. HSE guidance issued on the requirement for "adequate information" in section 6 of the HWSA states:

> "In deciding how much information should be available designers, manufacturers, importers and suppliers should aim to strike a balance between the provision of excessive and of inadequate information. Some hazards are common to all articles and need not be spelt out, *e.g.* any article may be hazardous if dropped from sufficient height. On the other hand, it is not sufficient merely to draw the attention of a user to the dangerous nature of the article. Reference should also be made to the specific nature of the hazards, including any noise hazards, and the best means of reducing or removing them. Information should also be available in order that the user may use the supplied article safely. If the information is not sufficient, the health or safety of those using the article may be endangered. Manufacturers, etc. should attempt to present the information clearly and precisely and avoid the provision of excessive information which may lead to the essential facts becoming obscured."[21]

In relation to liability in negligence, it has been held (in the context of recall, discussed further in Chapter 10) that a duty of care can extend to making "a clean breast of the problem" where the manufacturer alone is aware of the risk. The duty is higher where the manufacturer can palliate the worst effects of a failure which could never decisively be guarded against.[22]

In general, it is suggested that relevant considerations in assessing how much information to give to whom might include:

(a) the degree of danger involved;
(b) whether the wording used is a sufficient warning of the degree of danger[23];
(c) whether the warning is sufficiently prominent having regard to the magnitude of the risk: *i.e.* the size and colour of the print; its inclusion in the product literature or also on the packaging or product itself; the use of alternative means of communication such

[20] *Coventry City Council v. Ackerman Group plc* (1994) unreported.

[21] Articles and substances for use at work: Guidelines for designers, manufacturers, importers, suppliers, erectors and installers (HSE Guidance Note GS8).

[22] *Walton and Another v. British Leyland (U.K.) Limited and Others*, 1978; Judgment of Willis J. reproduced in *Product Liability Casebook* (Lloyd's of London Press Limited, 1984), p. 131.

[23] *Vacwell Engineering Co. Ltd v. B.D.H. Chemicals Ltd* [1971] 1 Q.B. 88, in which a label with the warning "harmful vapour" was insufficiently forceful for a chemical which exploded on contact with water, where the manufacturer should have known this but did not.

as letters to distributors, learned intermediaries or users or use of media announcements;

(d) whether an attempt has been made to render the warning intelligible to the relevant user: it is advisable to be as explicit and full as possible and where the warning is addressed to lay persons to use simple language. Particular problems of comprehension arise with children and people who do not understand the language in which the warning is given. The additional use of recognised symbols can go some way to overcoming this problem.

Factors (a) to (d) above are interdependent. The purpose of a warning is to seek to influence the behaviour of product users. However, a person will only be influenced by a warning if he or she reads it and appreciates it. Levels of both reading and comprehension vary within the population and are exacerbated by factors such as age, language and ability to see. If a producer aims his written warnings at an average comprehension age of, say, nine years, he may over-simplify, whereas if he puts in too much detail the emphasis of the warning may be lost. Warnings therefore involve compromise and careful judgment.

In some of the United States jurisdictions, requirement (b) has been expanded from the giving of general information into requiring an adequate explanation of:[24]

- the precise nature of the hazard (*e.g.* poisonous, flammable, eye irritant);
- how to avoid the hazard (use only in a well-ventilated area, no naked flames; wear protective goggles, keep out of reach of children);
- the possible consequences (may cause streaming of the eyes; highly flammable);
- any remedial action (bathe eyes in clean water; use only carbon dioxide fire extinguishers).

The ISO/IEC Guide 51 on Guidelines for the inclusion of safety aspects and standards[25] states that warning notices shall:

- be conspicuous, legible and durable;
- be worded in the official language(s) of the country were the product is intended to be used — unless one of the languages associated with a particular technical field is more appropriate:
- be concise and unambiguous;
- state the hazards involved and/or give ways in which risks may be reduced.

Although these Guidelines relate to information provided when products are first marketed, the same principle should apply to post-marketing information. The Guidelines continue:

[24] See C.J. Wright, *Product liability: the law and its implications for risk management* (1989), p. 128.
[25] Adopted as CEN/CENELEC Memorandum No. 9, 1994/06.

When instructing the persons concerned as to	*The recommended wording should include*
What to avoid	"no", "do not" or "prohibited"
What to do	"shall be"
The nature of the hazard	"caution", "warning" or "danger" as appropriate (see below for the meaning of these signal words)
The nature of the safe conditions	The noun appropriate to the safety device

The "signal words" referred to above should be used in relation to warning statements in standards and the following hierarchy respected:

- **"DANGER"** to call attention to a high risk;
- **"WARNING"** to call attention to a medium risk;
- **"CAUTION"** to call attention to a low risk.

Inconsistent marketing

Under both fault and strict liability principles, the focus is not only likely to be on consistency between the instructions for use and warnings supplied with the product but also the wider informational activities of the producer in advertising and generally promoting his product: the general "manner of marketing". Expectations of safety may inadvertently be created by advertising or the statements of sales representatives, which information provided with, or in connection with, the product will be unable to qualify satisfactorily. "Over selling" a product may undo the careful accuracy of printed product information.

Symbols and pictograms

Directives may provide that symbols and pictograms may — or even should — be used in relation to the labelling of products and in information and instructions for use supplied with products.

For example, Directive 89/392/EEC on machinery[26] specifies that a manufacturer must provide warnings of residual risks, preferably using readily understandable pictograms. Directive 93/42/EEC on medical devices specifies that symbols shall be used wherever appropriate in order to comply with essential requirements specified in the Directive in relation to the labelling of medical devices. In other words, symbols are to be preferred to words.

[26] See the Supply of Machinery (Safety) Regulations 1992 (S.I. 1992 No. 3073) as amended.

The following are examples of standards which provide useful symbols:

- ISO 7000 Symbols for use on equipment — Index and synopsis (a compilation of 1140 symbols) Second edition 1989.11.01
- EN 20780:1993 (ISO 780: 1985) Packaging, Pictorial marking for handling of goods.
- EN 980 Terminology, Symbols and Information provided with Medical Devices: Graphical Symbols for use in the labelling of medical devices.

Whilst the Community and industry enthusiastically pursue use of symbols in product labelling, there remains a gap in the public's understanding of safety information on labels, which will have to be bridged. A questionnaire survey in 1995 by the Confederation of Family Organisations in the European Community (COFACE) in eight EU states, involving mostly women, 40% of whom had children living with them, asked for identification of seven hazard symbols. Only a small minority could recognise them all, with about 40% identifying three or less. Only 13% correctly stated the meaning of all the symbols. The majority of participants believed that people do not read safety recommendations, do not understand or remember them, consider that they already know how to use products and underestimate the risks of use.

Misuse

To what extent must the manufacturer anticipate the unintended use, re-use, misuse or abuse of his product? If he can anticipate that the product may be used in a dangerous fashion, what must he do?

The conformity assessment of products subject to regulation under New Approach Directives is generally based on their operation when properly installed, maintained and used in accordance with the manufacturer's intended purpose. However, the essential requirements may qualify the circumstances of use for the intended purpose(s) by referring not only to the normal use of the product but also uses which could reasonably be expected. This is stated, for example, in Annex I of Directive 89/342/EEC on machinery which continues:

> "The machinery must be designed to prevent abnormal use if such use would engender a risk. In other cases the instructions must draw the user's attention to ways — which experience has shown might occur — in which the machinery should not be used."

The essential requirements under this Directive continue to describe numerous specific hazards which must be taken into account and, where residual risks remain, the manufacturer must provide warnings. Instructions must also accompany machinery for safe use, handling, assembly, dismantling, adjustment, maintenance and training, and should draw attention to ways in which the machinery should not be used.

In relation to product liability, section 3(2) of the CPA specifies that one of the factors to be taken into account in concluding whether there is a defect in a product is its expected use: what might reasonably be expected to be done with or in relation to the product. The expectation test adopted here is likely to approximate to the foreseeability test under fault liability: both are based on reasonableness.[27] On this basis, damage caused by any unsafe use of a product which can reasonably be foreseen, on an objective basis, will give rise to liability unless it is warned against or designed out of the product. However, one may foresee that a product may be used wrongly or abused (the approach under fault liability) without reasonably expecting it (under strict liability). The qualification of *reasonable* expectation ought to remove abuse from the equation. Contributory negligence by a user will reduce liability.[28] Thus careless misuse will reduce the damages.

In a rare decision in this area, the Federal Appellate Court in Frankfurt[29] held in January 1989 that the manufacturer of Orciprenaline aerosol for asthma had provided insufficient warnings against excessive use. The package information instructed three inhalations to be taken, each five minutes apart with the next inhalation no less than two hours later. The patient was in the habit of taking multiple inhalations, against which there was no specific warning, and ultimately he died. The Court held that:

> "Risks which can arise in the case of improper use and overdosage of drugs must always be warned about by the pharmaceutical enterprise unless, and to the extent under which it can be anticipated that these risks are known to every patient. This obligation is not limited in any case to the hazards that arise from accidental misuse or overdosage resulting from carelessness. Instead it extends to every type of misuse that the pharmaceutical enterprise can anticipate . . . It is basically not necessary to warn against the hazards occurring as a result of excessive use of drugs, or against abuse that must be considered unreasonable. However, in the case of drugs that are intended — like a metered dose aerosol in asthma attacks — to be used by the patient himself in dramatic situations, warnings against the dangers occurring in the case of excessive use are also necessary."

Who should be warned?

In fault liability the duty is to warn users who it is reasonably foreseeable may be injured, but this might also be extended to non-users

[27] Foreseeability of misuse is the basis of liability in the U.S. under both strict liability (comment h to s.402A of the Restatement (Second) of Torts 1965) and fault liability (comment j to s.395 of the Restatement).

[28] Art. 8(2).

[29] BGH, [1989] NJW, 1542 FF.

who may reasonably be affected by the defect.[30] The foreseeability test can result in an extension of the class who should be warned to include a second-hand purchaser in a case where the danger is particularly serious, and a reduction in the class to employers (rather than all individual employee users). If a product is dangerous, a warning must be issued if it is intended to be used or will foreseeably be used by unskilled users, but not if it is supplied for skilled users.[31]

Foreseeability is subject to the exception that a warning need only reach an intermediary where the product reaches the ultimate users through such a person. This person — in the medical field often called the "learned intermediary" — is someone who assumes responsibility in place of the ultimate user for selecting the product for use by that user.[32] This principle has been applied to doctors, teachers and hairdressers.

The CPA Part I is silent on who should be warned. It would follow from sections 3(2)(c) and 4(1)(d) of the CPA that the primary consideration is whether the warning was present with the product at the time it was put into circulation. The other possibility of holding that a warning must reach any person who conceivably may be exposed to injury is manifestly impracticable. It remains to be seen whether considerations of reasonableness will be applied to reach a compromise between these extremes and expand or restrict the class in a similar manner as fault liability.

[30] Thus a person who continued to expose themself to radioactivity after being warned of the danger would not be able to claim for subsequent damage.

[31] See U.S. decisions on use of electricity by a householder *Troszynski v. Commonwealth Edison Co.* (1976) 356 N.E. 2d 926 (warning required) and a skilled electrician *Peterson v. B/W Controls Inc.* (1977) 366 N.E. 2d 144 (no warning required).

[32] *Holmes v. Ashford* [1950] 2 All E.R. 76, C.A.: and *Kuback v. Hollands* [1937] 3 All E.R. 907. However, the "learned intermediary" rule has been held inapplicable to oral contraceptives in some U.S. jurisdictions, where the warning must reach the user: *MacDonald v. Ortho Pharmaceutical Corp.* (1985) 475 N.E. 2d 65 (Mass.); *Odgers v. Ortho Pharmaceutical Corp.* (1985) 602 F. Supp. 867 (D.C. Mich.); *Stephens v. G.D. Searle & Co* (1985) 602 F. Supp. 379 (Mich); *Lukaszewicz v. Ortho Pharmaceutical Corp.*. (1981) 510 F. Supp. 961 (Wis).

10 Practical advice: II. post-marketing obligations and recall

The GPS measures extend responsibility for product safety post-marketing. In product liability, although exposure under the Consumer Protection Act Part I is to be measured only at the time of supply of a product, liability for negligence continues and there is an on-going duty to act reasonably in relation to products which are marketed or sold.

Some products, notably pharmaceuticals, have specific regulatory requirements in relation to recall. When facing new adverse safety information about a product, it is important to evaluate all options and assess the risk of perceived hazards and then act reasonably.

One of the most difficult problems to face producers and suppliers is what to do when evidence emerges that a currently marketed product is, or may be, dangerous. What options are available? Should the product be recalled? Who should be told and how much?

Decisions on safety issues involve identification of all relevant hazards, assessment of the degree of risk associated with each hazard and with the foreseeable use of the product, assessment of the risk-benefit ratio involved in foreseeable use of the product and whether the product can be used safely, taking into account the instructions for use and warnings for the product.

The proper carrying out of each step in this sequence is subject to regulatory scrutiny under the GPS Regulations and civil scrutiny under fault liability: a decision which is clearly wrong can lead to criminal and/or civil liability.[1] Although the details differ under these two systems of liability, the basic approach is the same: a producer and, to a lesser extent, a supplier has a duty to take appropriate measures to ensure that users and others will not be harmed by his product. There is no established law on what might be an appropriate measure in any given circumstances. The standard of exercising reasonable care in negligence is deliberately generalised in order to be applicable in any circumstances which may arise. A decision by the courts on what was reasonable in particular circumstances will only be given on a case-by-case basis. The GPS Regulations likewise mention only "appropriate

[1] See the discussion in Chapter 5.

measures" but do make clear that "where appropriate" this includes recall from the market. As discussed elsewhere,[2] recall from the market does not necessarily extend to recall of products sold to consumers.

In a recent negligence case, the court said:

> "A manufacturer's duty of care does not end when the goods are sold. A manufacturer who realises that omitting to warn past customers about something which might result in injury to them must take reasonable steps to attempt to warn them, however lacking in negligence he may have been at the time the goods were sold."[3]

In contrast to the continuing exposure under fault liability, no liability arises under the strict product liability provisions of Part I of the CPA to issue further product information or to recall after a product has been placed into circulation.[4]

Post-marketing obligations in New Approach Directives

Although New Approach Directives are essentially concerned with the conditions for placing products on the market, their detailed provisions can include aspects under which conformity with essential requirements effectively requires on-going obligations. The continuous approved operation of a quality system will also require on-going obligations in relation to the effective recording and assessment of notifications of adverse incidents and complaints. Product type approval and approval of a quality system by a notified body may also effectively imply on-going market surveillance by a manufacturer.

An example of the extension of conformity assessment to include risks which may occur throughout a product's life can be taken from the Machinery Directive, although similar provisions appear in many other New Approach Directives. The essential requirements under the Machinery Directive, which specify the general principles of the health and safety requirements for marketing, include:

> "(a) . . . to eliminate any risk of accident throughout the foreseeable lifetime of the machinery. . .
>
> (b) eliminate or reduce risks as far as possible (inherently safe machinery design and construction); take the necessary protection measures in relation to risks that cannot be eliminated; inform users of the residual risks due to any shortcomings of the protection measures adopted . . ."[5]

The safeguard clause in New Approach Directives

All New Approach regulatory Directives include a standard "safeguard clause" under which the competent authorities of a Member State shall

[2] Chapter 5.
[3] *E. Hobbs (Farms) Ltd v. The Baxenden Chemical Co Ltd* [1992] 1 Lloyd's L.R. 54.
[4] CPA 1987, ss.3(2)(c) and 4(1)(e).
[5] Directive 89/392/EEC on machinery, Annex I, Requirement 1.1.2(b).

take all appropriate measures to withdraw or prohibit the placing on the market of a product or to restrict its free movement, even if it is accompanied by one of the means of attestation, where it finds that the product might compromise the safety of individuals, domestic animals or property. Where such a measure is taken in relation to a product which is accompanied by one of the means of attestation, the Member State must inform the Commission within a given period of time, indicating the reasons for its decision and in particular whether the non-conformity results from:

(a) non-compliance with the general clause in the Directive or the essential safety requirements;
(b) incorrect application of the harmonised standards; or
(c) a shortcoming in the harmonised standards themselves.

The Commission must then consult the Member State and refer the matter to the Standing Committee which is concerned with the implementation of the Directive. Where, after consultation with the Committee, the Commission finds that the Member State's action is justified, it will inform all Member States that, all else being equal, they are also obliged to prevent the product in question from being placed on the market. Where failure of the product to comply results from a shortcoming in the harmonised or national standards, the standards shall be examined by the Standing Committee. This examination may also take place where a Member State or the Commission considers that the harmonised standards do not fully satisfy the general clause or the essential safety requirements. In the light of the opinion of the Committee, the Commission notifies the Member States whether or not the standard in question should continue to enjoy the presumption of conformity. If it is inadequate, it will be withdrawn from the authorised list of published references.[6]

General product safety requirements

Obligations on producers and distributors under the General Product Safety Regulations 1994 in relation to post-marketing and recall are discussed in detail in Chapter 5. The major provisions are that a producer shall, within the limits of his activity:-

(a) provide consumers with the relevant information to enable them to assess the risks inherent in a product *throughout the normal or reasonably foreseeable period of its use*, where such risks are not immediately obvious without adequate warnings, and to take precautions against those risks;
(b) adopt measures commensurate with the characteristics of the products which they supply, to enable them to be informed of risks which these products might present (including sample testing of

[6] Council Resolution of 7.5.85 on a new approach to technical harmonisation and standards, O.J. 1985 No. C 136/1, 4.6.85.

> marketed products, investigating complaints and keeping distributors informed of such monitoring) and *to take appropriate action including, if necessary, withdrawing the product in question from the market* to avoid these risks[7] (emphasis added).

Similarly, a "distributor" as defined in regulation 2(1) has an obligation under regulation 9(3), within the limits of his activities, to participate in monitoring the safety of products placed on the market, in particular by passing on information on the product risks and co-operating in the action taken to avoid those risks.

However, breach of none of these obligations is a criminal offence under regulation 12. Nevertheless, if a third party suffers damage, failure to comply with one of these obligations may give the third party a civil remedy in damages on the basis of the producer's breach of statutory duty.

Product specific requirements on recall: pharmaceuticals

Certain product types are subject to particular regulatory requirements in relation to recall. This is illustrated by reference to pharmaceuticals. Safeguarding public health by means of the safety and quality of medicines is given a high priority in European Community legislation dealing with the internal market for such products. Directives dealing with manufacture and wholesale dealing include requirements for withdrawal or recall of medicinal products from the market. Since these measures are authorised under Article 100A of the EEC Treaty on the basis of control of the *market*, as with Directive 92/59/EEC on general product safety, there may be uncertainty as to the extent to which the provisions in relation to recall from the market extend to products which have been sold to consumers and may therefore be considered to be no longer on the market.

Certain obligations have existed under English law in relation to facilitating recall for over 20 years. The holders of a marketing authorisation or product licence, a manufacturer's licence or a wholesale dealer's licence must "keep such documents as will facilitate the withdrawal or recall from sale, supply or exportation of any medicinal product to which the licence relates."[8] The holder of a product licence is also subject to an obligation to notify the licensing authority forthwith of any such decision to withdraw a product and to state the reason for that decision.[9]

Manufacturing

Commission Directive 91/356/EEC of June 13, 1991 lays down the principles and guidelines of good manufacturing practice for medicinal

[7] Directive 92/59/EEC, Art. 3.2; General Product Safety Regulations 1994, Reg. 8.

[8] Medicines for Human Use (Marketing Authorisations etc.) Regulations 1994, (S.I. 1994 No. 3144), Reg. 7(3) and The Medicines (Standard Provisions for Licences and Certificates) Regulations 1971 (S.I. 1971 No. 972), Sched. I, para. 6, Sched. II, para. 9 and Sched. III, para. 4.

[9] Ibid., Sched. I, para. 8.

products for human use.[10] This requires a manufacturer to establish and implement an effective pharmaceutical quality assurance system. Article 13 of this Directive[11] provides:

> "The manufacturer shall implement a system for recording and reviewing complaints together with an effective system for recalling promptly and at any time the medicinal products in the distribution network. Any complaint concerning a defect shall be recorded and investigated by the manufacturer. The competent authority shall be informed by the manufacturer for the defect that could result in a recall or abnormal restriction on the supply. Insofar as possible, the countries of destination shall also be indicated. . . ."

The *Guide to Good Manufacturing Practice for Medicinal Products* issued by the European Commission[12] expands on the above provisions in relation to complaints and product recall:

> "Principle
>
> All complaints and other information concerning potentially defective products must be reviewed carefully according to written procedures. In order to provide for all contingencies, and in accordance with Article 28 of Directive 75/319/EEC, a system should be designed to recall, if necessary, promptly and effectively products known or suspected to be defective from the market.
>
> Complaints
>
> 8.1 A person should be designated responsible for handling the complaints and deciding the measures to be taken together with sufficient supporting staff to assist him. If this person is not the Qualified Person, the latter should be made aware of any complaint, investigation or recall.
>
> 8.2 There should be written procedures describing the action to be taken, including the need to consider a recall, in the case of a complaint concerning a possible product defect.
>
> 8.3 Any complaint concerning a product defect should be recorded with all the original details and thoroughly investigated. The person responsible for Quality Control should normally be involved in the study of such problems.
>
> 8.4 If a product defect is discovered or suspected in a batch, consideration should be given to checking other batches in order to determine whether they are also affected. In particular, other batches which may contain reworks of the defective batch should be investigated.

[10] Commission Directive 91/412/EEC includes similar provisions for veterinary medicinal products, OJ No. L 228/70 17.8.91.

[11] These provisions were implemented in the United Kingdom through the Medicines (Standard Provisions for Licences and Certificates) Regulations 1971, (S.I. 1971 No. 972) as amended *inter alia* by the Medicines (Standard Provisions for Licences and Certificates) Amendment Regulations 1992, (S.I. 1992 No. 2846).

[12] See *The Rules Governing Medicinal Products in the European Community: Volume IV* Commission of the European Communities, 1992.

8.5 All the decisions and measures taken as a result of a complaint should be recorded and referenced to the corresponding batch records.

8.6 Complaints records should be reviewed regularly for any indication of specific or recurring problems requiring attention and possibly the recall of marketed products.

8.7 The Competent Authorities should be informed if a manufacturer is considering action following possibly faulty manufacture, product deterioration, or any other serious quality problems with a product.

Recalls

8.8 A person should be designated as responsible for execution and coordination of recalls and should be supported by sufficient staff to handle all the aspects of the recalls with the appropriate degree of urgency. This responsible person should normally be independent of the sales and marketing organisation. If this person is not the Qualified Person, the latter should be made aware of any recall operation.

8.9 There should be established written procedures, regularly checked and updated when necessary, in order to organise any recall activity.

8.10 Recall operations should be capable of being initiated promptly and at any time.

8.11 All Competent Authorities of all countries to which products may have been distributed should be informed promptly if products are intended to be recalled because they are, or are suspected of being defective.

8.12 The distribution records should be readily available to the person(s) responsible for recalls, and should contain sufficient information on wholesalers and directly supplied customers (with addresses, phone and/or fax numbers inside and outside working hours, batches and amounts delivered), including those for exported products and medical samples.

8.13 Recalled products should be identified and stored separately in a secure area while awaiting a decision on their fate.

8.14 The progress of the recall process should be recorded and a final report issued, including a reconciliation between the delivered and recovered quantities of the products.

8.15 The effectiveness of the arrangements for recalls should be evaluated from time to time."

Wholesale dealing

Similar requirements in relation to having a recall system, but not a system to handle complaints, are included in the Directive on the wholesale distribution of medicinal products for human use.[13] This

[13] Council Directive 92/25/EEC of March 31, 1992, OJ No. L 113/1, 30.4.92. Implemented in the United Kingdom by The Medicines (Standard Provisions for Licences and Certificates) Amendment Regulations 1993, (S.I. 1993 No. 883).

imposes the requirement for a person engaged in wholesale distribution of medicinal products to possess an authorisation[14] granted by a Member State, for which holders must fulfil certain minimum requirements including having an emergency plan which ensures effective implementation of any recall from the market ordered by the competent authorities or carried out in cooperation with the manufacturer or holder of the marketing authorisation for the product concerned. Such a person is also subject to the European Commission's *Guidelines on Good Distribution Practice of Medicinal Products for Human Use*[15] which include the following points under the heading "Emergency plan and recalls":

"25. An emergency plan for urgent recalls and a non-urgent recall procedure should be described in writing. A person should be designated as responsible for execution and co-ordination of recalls.

26. Any recall operation should be recorded at the time it is carried out and records should be made available to the competent authorities of the Member States on whose territory the products were distributed.

27. In order to ensure the efficacy of the emergency plan, the system of recording all deliveries should enable all destinees of a medicinal product to be immediately identified and contacted. In case of recall, wholesalers may decide to inform all their customers of the recall or only those having received the batch to be recalled.

28. The same system should apply without any difference to deliveries in the Member States having granted the authorisation for wholesaling and in other Member States.

29. In case of batch recall, all customers (other wholesalers, retail or hospital pharmacists and persons entitled to sell medicinal products to the public) to whom the batch was distributed should be informed with the appropriate degree of urgency. This includes customers in other Member States than the Member State having granted the wholesaling authorisation.

30. The recall message approved by the holder of the marketing authorisation, and, when appropriate, by the competent authorities, should indicate whether the recall should be carried out also at retail level. The message should request that the recalled products be removed immediately from the saleable stock and stored separately in a secure area until they are sent back according to the instructions of the holder of the marketing authorisation."

Withdrawal of a marketing authorisation

The above provisions are, of course, concerned with the regulatory requirements for manufacturers and wholesale dealers to have *procedures*

[14] In the U.K. referred to as a wholesale dealer's licence under s. 8(3) of the Medicines Act 1968.
[15] OJ No. C 63/4 1.3.94.

and systems for product recall but they do not deal with when such procedures and systems should be operated. Under Community law, the threshold for the withdrawal of a marketing authorisation for a medicinal product (as distinct from a manufacturing authorisation or wholesale dealing authorisation) is, *inter alia*, where "it proves that the medicinal product is harmful in the normal conditions of use . . ."[15a]

In order to justify a competent authority taking regulatory action by withdrawal of a marketing authorisation, the test is, therefore, essentially that the product must be *harmful* or *unsafe* when used normally as intended.

It is unclear whether these regulatory powers should be regarded as defining the standard upon which a recall decision should be taken or as a "long stop" which sets the outer parameters within which a product recall is justified. It would certainly be prudent for manufacturers to adopt the latter construction.

Recalls of Consumer Products in U.S. Distribution[16]

Considerable assistance in considering the practicalities of operating recalls in a regulated environment can be obtained from comparison with pre-existing United States Federal legislation. The importance of a hazard assessment and the categorisation of hazards into priority classes should be particularily noted.

In the U.S., approximately 15,000 types of consumer products,[17] are regulated by the Consumer Product Safety Commission (CPSC) pursuant to several federal statutes, including the Consumer Product Safety Act (CPSA),[18] the Federal Hazardous Substances Act (FHSA),[19] the Flammable Fabrics Act,[20] and the Poison Prevention Packaging Act.[21]

[15a] Council Directive 65/65/EEC of January 26, 1965 on the approximation of provisions laid down by law, regulation or admistrative action relating to medicinal products, as amended, Act. 5, OJ No. 1965 369/65, 9.2.65. This is implemented in the U.K. under the Medicines For Human Use (Marketing Authorisations Etc.) Regulations 1994 (S.I. 1994 No. 3144), Reg. 6(1).

[16] This section has kindly been contributed by Kathleen M. Sanzo who is of Counsel with the international law firm Morgan, Lewis & Bockius.

[17] Consumer product is defined under the CPSA as "any article or component part thereof, produced or distributed (i) for sale to a consumer for use in or around a permanent or temporary household or residence, a school, in recreation, or otherwise, or (ii) for the personal use, consumption or enjoyment of a consumer in or around a permanent or temporary household or residence, a school, in recreation, or otherwise; . . ." 15 U.S.C. § 2052(a)(i). Products used by consumers but which are not regulated by CPSC as consumer products include foods, drugs, medical devices and cosmetics, motor vehicles, boats, pesticides, airplanes, and firearms.

[18] 15 U.S.C. § 2051 *et seq.*

[19] 15 U.S.C. § 1261 *et seq.* This Act regulates toys and other articles intended for use by children, fireworks, juvenile products such as cribs, rattles, pacifiers, bicycles, and any substance or mixture of substances which is toxic, corrosive, an irritant, a strong sensitizer, flammable or combustible.

[20] 15 U.S.C. § 1191 *et seq.* This Act regulates clothing, textiles, vinyl plastic film, children's sleepwear, carpets and rugs, mattresses and mattress pads.

[21] 15 U.S.C. § 1471 *et seq.* This Act regulates packaging for substances which present toxicity concerns to young children (*e.g.* prescription drugs, household chemicals such as lye).

Every manufacturer, including importers, distributor, and retailer of a consumer product distributed in U.S. commerce who obtains information which reasonably supports the conclusion that the product fails to comply with an applicable consumer product safety rule established by the CPSC, contains a defect which could create a subsantial product hazard,[22] or presents an unreasonable risk of serious injury or death, must immediately inform the CPSC of such information, unless the reporter has actual knowledge that the CPSC has already been adequately informed.[23] Failure to file a section 15(b) report on a timely basis can result in substantial fines of up to $1.25 million.[24]

Once a section 15(b) report has been filed, CPSC will initiate a process by which to determine whether to order the product manufacturer, distributor, or retailer to undertake corrective action to remedy the product defect or to remove the product from commerce. CPSC's authority for requiring corrective actions, including recalls, relating to consumer products derives from section 15(c) and (d) of the CPSA, 15 U.S.C. § 2064(c) and (d),[25] and section 15(b) and (c) of the FHSA, 15 U.S.C. § 1274(b) and (c). These provisions authorise CPSC to require a manufacturer, distributor, retailer, or importer to notify the public of a defective product, or to repair, replace or refund the purchase price of the product (minus a reasonable allowance for use, if the consumer has had the product for more than one year), if CPSC determines that the product poses a substantial product hazard under the CPSA, if the product constitutes a banned hazardous substance[26] under the FHSA, or if it is a toy or other children's article which contains a defect which creates a substantial risk of injury to children under the FHSA. The CPSA prohibits manufacturers or others from charging consumers to participate in a recall.[27]

Prior to mandating any form of corrective action, CPSC must give interested parties, including consumers and consumer organizations, a formal hearing before an administrative law judge assigned to the CPSC.[28] Pursuant to the laws governing such hearings, an aggrieved

[22] A substantial product hazard is defined under section 15 of the Consumer Product Safety Act, 15 U.S.C. § 2064(a), as either "a failure to comply with an applicable consumer product safety rule which creates a substantial risk of injury to the public, or a product defect which (because of the pattern of the defect, the number of defective products distributed in commerce, the severity of the risk, or otherwise), creates a substantial risk of injury to the public." *Id.*

[23] 15 U.S.C. § 2064(b). CPSC asserts that pursuant to section 30(d) of the CPSA, manufacturers of products regulated under the FHSA, FFA, and PPPA must also submit section 15(b) reports to the Commission. 43 *Fed. Reg.* 34989 (August 7, 1978).

[24] 15 U.S.C. § 2069(a).

[25] Under section 12 of the CPSA, a federal district court also may declare a product to pose an imminent hazard and issue a mandatory order requiring public notice, recall, repair, replacement of or refund for the hazardous product, 15 U.S.C. § 2061(b).

[26] Toy or children's articles are also considered banned hazardous substances if they do not meet certain CPSC product standards, for example, with respect to size or sharp edges: 15 U.S.C. § 1261(f)(1)(D) and § 1261(q)(1).

[27] 15 U.S.C. § 2064(e)(1).

[28] Such hearings are conducted in accordance with section 554 of the Administrative Procedure Act, 5 U.S.C. § 554.

person can appeal the decision of the administrative law judge to a federal court, and ultimately, to the U.S. Supreme Court.

In addition to mandating corrective actions, the Commission also has the authority to apply to a U.S. district court for a preliminary injunction against the sale or distribution of products in interstate commerce, pending completion of the hearing relating to the mandatory corrective action.[29] Thus, CPSC can prevent the distribution of a company's product while the legality of the proposed corrective action is being litigated in the administrative hearing. Consequently, CPSC has authority to significantly interrupt product distribution and thus motivate manufacturers to voluntarily undertake recalls, foregoing their statutory right to an administrative hearing.

Consequently, despite the extensive procedures outlined in the CPSA and FHSA statutes for mandatory recalls or other corrective action and for administrative due process associated with such mandatory corrective actions, the process is used infrequently. Since the passage of the CPSA and the creation of the Commission in 1972, there have been less than ten instances in which the Agency has initiated an administrative hearing, and only one or two instances in which a full administrative hearing was completed. Instead, most recalls of consumer products are undertaken pursuant to the Commission's regulations for voluntary corrective actions.

Recalls and other corrective actions, whether voluntary or mandatory, are directed and managed by the Office of Compliance and Enforcement, Division of Corrective Actions (CECA). Once the CECA staff becomes aware of a defective product, through a report pursuant to section 15(b) of the CPSA, a consumer complaint, a news account or other source of information on a product defect and/or injury,[30] the CECA staff investigates the alleged incident of injury or product defect. If the product incident involves a death or serious injury, CECA will usually send an investigator to the site and prepare an epidemiological investigative report (EIR). CECA staff then will make a preliminary hazard assessment which it will provide to the product manufacturer or other responsible party.[31]

In the hazard assessment, CECA staff will determine whether the product presents a substantial product hazard, according to a hazard priority system. The hazard priority system classifies hazards into three levels of severity: Class A, B, or C hazards.

- Class A hazard exists when a risk of death or grievous injury or illness is likely or very likely, or serious injury or illness is very likely.

[29] 15 U.S.C. § 1264(g)(1).

[30] CPSC and its field officers routinely monitor newspapers for accounts of deaths or serious injuries involving consumer products, review death certificates issued by coroner's offices, and track product-related injuries through hospital emergency room statistics computer system, the National Electronic Injury Surveillance System ("NEISS").

[31] For imported products, CPSC will ordinarily contact the importer first because it has no jurisdiction over foreign companies.

- Class B hazard exists when a risk of death or grievous injury or illness is not likely to occur, but is possible, or when serious injury or illness is likely, or moderate injury or illness is very likely.
- Class C hazard exists when a risk of serious injury or illness is not likely, but is possible, or when moderate injury or illness is or is not likely, but is possible.

Class A hazards require the most comprehensive recall plan, while Class C hazards ordinarily involve a much less detailed plan. Once the CECA staff makes its internal determination as to the appropriate hazard classification, it will notify the manufacturer or other responsible party by letter of its preliminary hazard determination and request submission of a voluntary corrective action program ("CAP"), usually within ten days. Depending on the seriousness of the hazard, a company can often obtain an extension of time to respond to the CPSC.

Voluntary corrective action plans are specifically authorised by CPSC regulation.[32] A voluntary CAP is signed by the affected company, but is not legally binding on either the Company or the CPSC. Thus, CPSC can seek, and has often sought, broader or more extensive remedial actions if the originally proposed corrective action is ultimately found not to be sufficient to protect the public.[33]

By regulation, a voluntary CAP is required to include the following types of information:

- a statement of the nature of the alleged hazard and alleged defect or non-compliance and potential injury presented;
- a description of the methods of notifying affected consumers and others such as distributors (*e.g.*, press releases, letters etc.) and draft copies of any proposed notices and proposed releases;
- a description of the product;
- a description of the corrective action to be taken (*i.e.* repair, replacement, discard, or some combination etc.);
- other information relating to correction of the product in the distribution chain;

Pursuant to regulation, the voluntary CAP should be signed by the manufacturer and submitted to the Commission. However, once such a remedial plan is accepted by the Commission in writing, any information submitted by the manufacturer to the Commission with the section 15(b) report which likely initiated the recall or the recall itself, may be released to the public. Consequently, it is general practice for the Commission not formally to accept such plans in writing in order for the

[32] See 16 C.F.R. § 1115.20.

[33] It is not unusual for the Commission to request a second recall notice or campaign to be administered if it concludes the first recall was not sufficiently effective. For example, Hedstrom, a U.S. playground equipment manufacturer, was required to do a second recall notice for an allegedly defective children's swing. General Electric was required to undertake a similar second recall notice for an electric coffee maker which allegedly posed a fire hazard.

information which the manufacturer submits to remain non-disclosable.[34]

The scope of a recall notice and the precise corrective action can be negotiated with CECA staff. If CPSC is consulted prior to the initiation of a consumer product recall, CPSC often will insist on a joint press release of the product recall. In addition, depending on the severity of the hazard, CPSC will often request that the recall be publicized in relevant magazines (*e.g.*, notice of toy recall published in parenting magazines), posters or notices in retail stores, radio and newspaper wire services and, at times, a video news release for satellite distribution. Generally, the more likely it is that the company can identify specifically the purchasers of its product, the more likely it will be that CPSC will allow a more targeted recall notice. Similarly, if a company can demonstrate through production or other records that the recall should be limited to specific lots of product or manufacturing time frames, CPSC likely will agree. CPSC increasingly has requested companies to provide to consumers some form of incentive, for example, cash payment, coupon or price discount for a new product, in addition to product repair or replacement, to motivate consumers to respond to the recall notice.[35]

Finally, after the principal components of the recall have been undertaken, CPSC will conduct site visits of retailers to determine compliance with the terms of the recall and will require the company to submit weekly, monthly, or quarterly status reports, for some defined number of months or years, indicating the number of responses the company has received.

Consequently, although there are comprehensive laws which address the conditions under which a recall or other corrective action for a consumer product can be mandated, such laws are only rarely used in the U.S. Instead, most U.S. manufacturers find it less costly and more expeditious to undertake corrective actions voluntarily through negotiation with the CPSC.

The current English law

There is little legal authority on the issue of what steps satisfy the criminal or civil standards of care such that a manufacturer or seller knows what is expected in reacting to post-marketing information and, in particular, when he will be found negligent if a recall is not instituted. Receipt of information which may require urgent investigation, such as

[34] Section 6 of the Consumer Product Safety Act governs the release of information by CPSC. Under section 6(b), there are specific provisions which protect certain classes of information submitted to CPSC by manufacturers from being released to the public by CPSC. Manufacturers should study these provisions carefully prior to submitting product-related information to the CPSC in connection with a hazard analysis or recall.

[35] The average U.S. consumer response rate to recalls is less than 15%, even when the product is a critical safety device, such as smoke detectors or infant car seats.

a report of the product causing death, may even so not legally be considered to be a situation of any great urgency in which other action is necessarily urgent.[36] At least in all but the most urgent cases, the law would seem to expect thorough and careful investigation and consideration of the seriousness of the situation and the options and not necessarily a precipitate and unilateral response, such as which is often demanded by the media.

In the Australian case *Thompson v. Johnson and Johnson Pty Ltd and Anor*[37] discussed in Chapter 9, the Court of Appeal of Victoria said that a manufacturer must "act with whatever promptness fairly reflects the nature of the information and the seriousness of the possible consequence" and must balance all the relevant factors including "the magnitude of the risk and the degree of probability of its occurrence, along with the expense, difficulty and inconvenience of taking alleviating action and any other conflicting responsibilities which the defendant may have".

The court in the *Thompson* case was clearly influenced by the attitude of the regulatory authorities. Future cases in England and Wales will be influenced — particularly in establishing the standard of care to be applied in considering whether the manufacturer was or was not negligent — by industry codes of conduct in relation to recall and whether a company has and follows a crisis/recall plan. Important industry codes include The Society of Motor Manufacturers and Traders' *Code of Practice on Vehicle Safety Defects* (1992) and The British Retail Consortium's *Guidelines and Checklist for Product Recall* (1994), copies of which are reprinted in Appendices 5 and 6.

A rare English decision in the regulatory context established some very pertinent points. First, the nature and speed of a manufacturer's response to information that his product may be unsafe depends upon an assessment of the nature and level of risk involved. Even a risk of a serious hazard such as death needs to be considered against its incidence. Even the enforcement authorities have a duty to consult the manufacturers before taking precipitate action. In quashing a suspension notice issued under section 14 of the Consumer Protection Act 1987 following the death of a three year old child who choked on the feet of a new Pink Panther plastic toy contained in a Kinder Surprise chocolate egg and assembled by her father, on the ground of taking into account an irrelevant consideration, failure to take into account relevant matters, procedural impropriety and irrationality, Mr Justice Hutchison said:

> *"This was not, in truth, a situation of any great urgency. Of course, where a little girl has died, it cannot be doubted that the case requires urgent investigation—but that is another matter. Given the huge number of Kinder*

[36] *R. v. Birmingham City Council, ex parte Ferrero Ltd, The Times*, March 3, 1990: a case in which the death of a child caused by a toy led to national publicity and service of a suspension notice by a local authority, which was set aside on technical grounds, but here the Judge criticised the authority's reliance on irrelevant factors.

[37] *Thompson v. Johnson and Johnson Pty Ltd and Anor* [1991] 2 V.R. 449 and 475.

Surpise eggs that had been sold over the years, and the fact that . . . it is to be inferred that many of the other toys sold during those years had contained small parts as easily detachable and as dangerous to small children as the foot of the Pink Panther, Jennifer's death did not call for precipitate or unilateral action. [The Trading Standards' Officer] perception of the problems would, I am satisfied, have been entirely different had he done what I find he ought to have done, which was to make urgent arrangements for consultation with company representatives, in order fully to inform himself of all the matters which [were relevant]."[38]

We describe below a series of responses open to a manufacturer or supplier. It is suggested that the degree of knowledge or suspicion of hazard which a manufacturer must have in order to trigger one of the responses must rise incrementally. If the producer has a relevant degree of knowledge or suspicion of a risk but does not respond by taking the step(s) appropriate to that degree of knowledge or suspicion and the seriousness of the hazard, then he will be at fault, although it will still be necessary to prove that the "correct" response would have avoided the injury in the case in question. This could be described as the "graded response" principle. No doubt the standards to be expected will be significantly influenced by the requirements of any applicable regulatory law, as discussed earlier in relation to general product safety or product specific directives.

The leading English decision in relation to negligence establishes that once a manufacturer becomes aware of a sufficiently serious defect he owes a duty of care to the public to recall all batches.[39] In this case, British Leyland were held to have been faced over a period of about a year until October 1974 with "mounting and horrifying evidence" of wheels coming adrift from Allegro cars. This followed the introduction of tapered roller bearings in the rear hub assembly which had to be adjusted in a different way, so as to give end float. Earlier models had been fitted with roller bearings. The company's expert consensus attributed the bearing failure, the judge indicated wrongly, to carelessness or unfamiliarity with the new technique of end float adjustment on the part of mechanics, producing overtightening. The company introduced a new washer as a modification "to provide an additional bearing retention safety feature". Nine months later, the chief engineer wrote:

"the design was introduced to satisfy performance demands at lower cost, and it is true to state that provided design requirements are adhered to no problem would be experienced. Unfortunately the design is not idiot proof and will therefore continuously involve risk. The risk becomes greater as vehicles become older and ever more carelessly maintained. Had we incorporated the large washer from the commencement the risk would have been tolerable . . . Engineer-

[38] *R. v. Biringham City Council, ex parte Ferrero Ltd* (1990) 154 JP 661, 9 Tr Law 148.

[39] *Walton and Another v. British Leyland (U.K.) Limited and Others* 1978; Judgment of Willis J. reproduced in *Product Liability Casebook*, (Lloyd's of London Press Limited, 1984), p. 131.

ing have considered the possibility of a recall action but do not favour it owing to the fact that it would damage the product, and historically the response is too low to guarantee fixing the problem and thereby remove our liability".

It was decided that a recall campaign at a cost of £300,000 was not justified and that instead an intensive education campaign to franchised outlets should be mounted. A letter to distributors said "We recommend that you should fit this [larger] washer to each hub when attention is being given to the rear hub or rear brake servicing". The judge criticised this wording as at best ambiguous and at worst misleading and as giving no idea of the urgency of the problem. He considered these steps to give instructions to dealers as "totally inadequate" and left those outside this limited safety net in ignorance of the risk to which the company knew they were subject. When a problem became apparent with a car which the plaintiff subsequently purchased, the franchisee was held not to be liable for only fitting a new washer to the rear offside wheel. The garage which serviced the car was not liable since it knew nothing of the larger washer modification or its importance. The manufacturer was, however, liable for the plaintiff's damage when the rear nearside wheel came off the car after bearing collapse.

The judge formulated the duty of care as follows:

> "The duty of care owed by Leyland to the public was to make a clean breast of the problem and recall all cars which they could, in order that the safety washers could be fitted. I accept, of course, that manufacturers have to steer a course between alarming the public unnecessarily and so damaging the reputation of their products, and observing their duty of care towards those whom they are in a position to protect from dangers of which they and they alone are aware. The duty seems to me to be the higher when they can palliate the worst effects of a failure which, if Leyland's view is right, they could never decisively guard against. They knew the full facts; they saw to it that no one else did. They seriously considered recall and made an estimate of the cost at a figure which seems to me to have been in no way out of proportion to the risks involved. It was decided not to follow this course for commercial reasons. I think this involved a failure to observe their duty of care for the safety of the many who were bound to remain at risk, irrespective of the recommendations made to Leyland dealers and to them alone . . .
>
> It was, in my view, their duty to ensure that all cars still in stock and unsold by the time the washer palliative was proven were fitted with this safety feature before sale.".

The practical requirement in order to be able to operate a recall successfully[40] is that all distributed items of the product should be traceable. In order to limit the extent of the recall, it is advisable to be

[40] See H. Abbott, *Managing Product Recall* (1991).

able to trace at least to the level of production batches. This will avoid an unnecessarily wide recall, a waste of time and cost and ultimately an unsuccessful recall. A recall cannot be planned retrospectively. The use of crisis management techniques (planning, training, simulation, standard operating procedures) is spreading in industry.

In practice, arguments often revolve around whether appropriate and adequate wording was used at the relevant time in an instruction for use or a warning which was in fact given, rather than whether the producer should have recalled the product instead of revising the wording of a pre-existing warning so as to make it more explicit. It bears repetition that criticism of acting inappropriately or too late must therefore be raised as a matter of negligence not strict liability, except in a contaminated product case.

What steps are appropriate?

The appropriate level of response to a hazard depends on the degree of risk which that hazard presents. Risk assessment depends on the availability of reliable information and the proper assessment and evaluation of that information. In other words, the requirements are for facts and judgment. In practice, however, it is often the case that decisions need to be taken on the basis of information which is inadequate and/or unverified and/or incomplete and/or subsequently proved to be wrong. There is also often considerable pressure to reach and implement decisions and lack of time. The quality of the decisions taken may therefore be heavily based on the judgment of those taking them. The process of reaching these decisions can be assisted by applying a logical sequence of steps.

The following questions may be of assistance here in providing a useful matrix of steps for management to take. The list should not be considered to be definitive or exclusive, still less based on any legal authority. It is a list assembled from the authors' experience and based on common sense.

Background facts

1. What is the product: what are its intended and known uses?
2. How many items of the product are in circulation?
3. What information do users have (from any source) about how to use the product safely?
4. Is the product used by the general public or by professionals?
5. What similar products are available to users?

Assessing the risk of the hazard

1. What is the hazard?
2. What causes the hazard?
3. Does the hazard only occur in certain situations which may be defined?

4. What are its effects?
5. What is its incidence? Note that in order to answer this question it is necessary to know: (a) the number of occurrences of the hazard (numerator); and (b) the number of times the product is used, (denominator) which may or may not be the number in circulation.
6. Are special groups affected, *e.g.* children, the infirm, people in a particular geographical location?
7. Are only special groups affected?
8. How serious are the consequences, *e.g.* death, personal injury?
9. Are the effects reversible?
10. How predictable is the hazard?
11. Is the hazard avoidable? What steps are possible or feasible to avoid it occurring?

In cases of difficulty, it may be helpful to consider the following questions in addition to those listed above:

12. What, if anything, is the general and approved practice in this situation?
13. What is the attitude of the regulatory authorities?
14. Do competitor products have the same hazard or how do they avoid it?
15. Would particular measures unnecessarily alarm users or the general public and present a greater risk to public safety (*e.g.* patients being afraid to take medicines of which the overall therapeutic benefits exceeds the risk of the hazard)?

It will be particularly relevant for a court to know what view is taken by those who are expert and experienced in risk assessment in the given field.

Consideration of the above questions should lead to an informed and objective assessment of the risk first that the hazard may occur and secondly of the consequences if it does occur.

What steps can be taken?

Consideration may now be given to defining what step(s), if any, could be taken which would enable the hazard to be avoided and the product used safely.

(a) Do nothing: no change is justified in existing product information.
(b) Inform distributors, *e.g.* to check for problems on next service.
(c) Inform appropriate regulatory authorities.
(d) Amend product information issued with new products, *e.g.* a stipulation that the product is not to be used under certain circumstances.
(e) Amend product information issued with new products to include a warning in the product information about use in particular circumstances or about the possibility of encountering specified untoward events.

(f) In the case of certain products carrying unavoidable hazards (*e.g.* medicinal products, pesticides etc.), a restriction on the availability of the particular products to specialist intermediaries.
(g) A special notification of a new hazard direct to all users or outlets or direct specialist intermediaries.
(h) General advertisements in the media and/or press releases.
(i) Discontinuation from sale of further items of a particular batch or class, where the confirmed safety of the product in use cannot be guaranteed, even with appropriate warnings.
(j) Informing distributors and users to carry out modifications to the product (retrofit).
(k) Recall of items already sold of a particular batch or product.

If a range of options are open, it would be reasonable for the producer to adopt the option which is cheapest, provided this is consistent with achieving swift communication to users of appropriate information on how to avoid the hazard. Considerations of the magnitude of the risk may also be relevant. For example, a hazard which produces a very low level of risk (*e.g.* malfunction in a rear windscreen defrost circuit identified in spring), even if it occurs regularly, hardly calls for an immediate recall or retrofit of all affected vehicles from the safety point of view (although commercial considerations may lead to different decisions being adopted). On the other hand, even the rare occurrence, or potential occurrence, of serious personal injury or death would justify urgent and extreme measures, such as recall and/or discontinuance.

Different considerations may apply to different types of product. The question of safety has been approached in a particular manner in relation to medicines. For medicinal products the fundamental question is whether the benefits of use of the product exceed the risks of its use. It is accepted in relation to medicines that some risks are always associated with their use. In some situations, the risks may be high, but these are accepted because of the potential benefit which the product may bring in alleviating the risk of disease which is already present. In contrast, most consumer products are not designed to overcome pre-existing risk but simply to confer a benefit (usually involving achieving greater facility with less physical effort in a shorter time and perhaps with increased comfort). For the majority of consumer products, the risk-benefit equation will be less important than with healthcare products, since the general expectation will be that the former products involve a high level of health and safety and no risks, or risks reduced to a minimum.

Warnings

Important considerations in relation to the relevance, formulation and timing of warnings are discussed in Chapter 9. Many of the principles considered there can apply to the general post-marketing and recall situation and the reader should cross-refer to that chapter.

The need for a logical assessment

Inexperienced manufacturers and distributors are often panicked into making bad decisions in relation to insuring the continued safety of products post-marketing. The question is often asked by such people "Should we recall the product?". This approach fails to analyse the risks involved and the available options, as set out above, and jumps to a conclusion which may be quite unjustified and inappropriate. Even though the available information and time may be against one, the best decisions both in terms of safety and in terms of defending a negligence action are those which are taken by applying appropriate analysis and assessment of the risks of the situation and of the available options.

Standard ISO 8402 (EN 28402, BS 4778), which defines a quality vocabulary, does not include a definition of recall. A definition is included in standard EN 46001, which applies EN 29001 to medical devices, which are products in which safety and recall issues can be particularly relevant. Significantly, the definition of recall in EN 46001 is expanded to include not only the return of a product to the supplier but also its modification at the site of installation, or its exchange or destruction, in accordance with the instructions contained in an advisory notice. Such action is defined to be taken in accordance with the standard only where there is a risk of death or serious deterioration to the state of health.

11 Advertising and safety

Previous chapters have highlighted the close relationship between the safety of products and the way in which they are marketed to their intended users. This chapter looks at the legal and other regulatory controls on the way products are advertised.

A DELUGE OF DIRECTIVES

Recent assertions by Sir Leon Brittain, Vice President of the European Commission, that the flow of new legislation from Brussels has slowed down "considerably" is not supported by the statistics. European Union rules and regulations are in fact emerging at an ever increasing rate. Figures published by the Commission show that the total of new directives and regulations rose from 1,602 in 1993 to 1,800 in 1994. A great number of these require the member states to harmonise their laws to ensure that products are uniformly safe throughout the community. In many instances the U.K. already has a body of law, regulations and voluntary codes which cover the area so wholesale change to U.K. law is not required. This is particularly so in the context of marketing and safety and this chapter looks at the general overall scheme for controlling advertisements with particular emphasis on product safety.

In 1978 the European Commission initially attempted to introduce a uniform regime across Europe whereby all complaints of both misleading and unfair advertising would be resolved by the local courts. This was particularly abhorrent to the U.K. with its well developed system of control resting in part on the criminal law principally through the Trade Description Act 1968 and in part on self regulation principally the codes of the Advertising Standards Authority ("the ASA") in existence since 1961.[1]

Largely as a result of U.K. opposition the E.C. Directive was amended to drop the provisions relating to unfairness and Council Directive

[1] The Broadcasting Act 1955 required the broadcasters to draw up a code and this lead the rest of the industry to realise that they also needed a code. The Advertising Association developed the first edition of the British Code of Advertising Practice based on an international code (the International Code of Advertising Standards) prepared by the International Chamber of Commerce. The ASA was created in 1961 to adjudicate upon complaints that the Code had been broken.

84/450 on Misleading Advertisements was adopted instead. Four years later the Directive was incorporated into U.K. law by the Control of Misleading Advertisements Regulations 1988.

Table 11.1

E.C. Directive	**U.K. Law or Code**
Draft directive on Misleading and Unfair Advertising 1978	• Trade Descriptions Act 1968 • Fair Trading Act 1973 • Consumer Credit Act 1974 • Consumer Protection Act 1987 • Numerous General Safety Regulations • Medicine Act 1968 • British Code of Advertising and Sales Promotion (BCASP) • The Association of British Pharmaceutical Industries Code of Practice for the Pharmaceutical Industry ("the ABPI Code") • The Proprietary Association of Great Britain's Code of Standards of Advertising Practice ("the PAGB Code")
84/450 Misleading Advertisements	• Control of Misleading Advertisements Regulations 1988
Draft amendment to 84/450 to permit comparative advertising	• Trade Marks Act 1994
89/552 TV Broadcasting	• Broadcasting Act 1990 • ITC Code of Advertising Standards and Practice ("The ITC Advertising Code") • The Radio Authority Code of Advertising Standards ("The Radio Code")

89/622 Labelling of Tobacco Products	• Tobacco Products Labelling (Safety) Regulations 1991
92/41 Amending 89/622	• Tobacco Products Labelling (Safety) Amended Regulations 1993 • Tobacco for Oral Use (Safety) Regulations 1992

Table 11.1 demonstrates the extent of the U.K.'s laws and codes for regulating advertisements and demonstrates how the U.K. has complied with the E.C. directives and/or draft directives.

This table demonstrates at a glance that there are many laws and codes governing advertising. This chapter briefly reviews these to the extent that they impact upon safety issues.

Trade Descriptions Act 1968

The Act makes it a criminal offence for a person in the course of a trade or business either:

(a) to apply a description which is false to a material degree to any goods; or
(b) to supply, or offer to supply, any goods to which a false trade description is applied.

For the offence to be committed the trade description must be false. This includes descriptions which, though not false, are misleading, that is to say, are likely to be taken as an indication of any of the matters specified in the Act. A trade description is defined broadly and includes "fitness for purpose, strength, performance, behaviour or accuracy".[2] It is important to bear in mind that it is the impact upon the consumer's mind which is important. Advertising frequently focuses upon the safety of a product and any unsupported claims of safety could result in prosecution and, if successful, a substantial fine and/or imprisonment.

Fair Trading Act 1973

Advertisers must be mindful of the provisions of U.K. competition law which regulate their business relations with consumers and competitors generally. This includes how they conduct their advertising. Advertisers must ensure that their advertising is not detrimental to consumers. In

[2] s.2, Trade Description Act 1968.

particular, they must have regard for section 34 of the Fair Trading Act 1973 which provides that:

> "where it appears to the director[3] that the person carrying on a business has in the course of that business persisted in a course of conduct which —
> (a) is detrimental to the interests of consumers in the United Kingdom, whether those interests are economic interests or interests in respect of health, safety or other matters, and
> (b) in accordance with the following provisions of this section is to be regarded as unfair to consumers,
> the director shall use his best endeavours, by communication with that person or otherwise, to obtain from him a satisfactory written assurance that he will refrain from continuing that course of conduct and from carrying on any similar course of conduct in the course of that business".

Section 34(3) of the Fair Trading Act 1973 provides that conduct may be regarded as unfair if:

> ". . . it consists of things done, or omitted to be done, . . . in breach of a duty . . . owed to any person by virtue of any enactment or rule of law and enforceable by civil proceedings . . ."

Provided that it could be shown that the advertising in some way breached a regulation, such as the Control of Misleading Advertisements Regulations 1988, it would appear that the Director-General could approach errant advertisers directly to prevent advertising without having to wait for a complaint to be made to the ASA first (see below). The conduct to which the section relates must be "detrimental to the interests of consumers". Advertising which misleads on issues of safety is bound to be detrimental to the interests of consumers and an advertiser who misleads in this way could be asked to stop by the ASA and/or be asked by the Director-General of Fair Trading for a written assurance that adverts will stop.

Consumer Credit Act 1974

Financial "safety" as well as physical safety is increasingly being required of advertisements. Particularly stringent rules apply to advertising of financial products and services. Financial advertising must not mislead, whether by exaggeration, omission or otherwise. Section 46 of the Consumer Credit Act 1974 makes advertising that is misleading a criminal offence. The ITC Code[4] expressly stresses the need for advertisements to comply with the Consumer Credit (Advertisements) Regu-

[3] The Director General of Fair Trading.
[4] See below.

lations 1989. The advertising of credit products poses a number of difficult problems. For example, under the Consumer Credit (Advertising) Regulations 1989, when advertising credit products, certain items must be included in the advertisement, for example, the APR. The Consumer Credit (Total Charge for Credit) Regulations 1980 provide a number of formulae for calculating the APR. When the major credit card issuers introduced annual fees, in order to render comparisons between different forms of credit effective, the Association of Payment Clearing Services (APACS) with the agreement of card issuers introduced a new formula to take account of the annual fees and also the impact of different credit limits on the APR. The position, unclear to those in the industry, has become virtually impenetrable to the layman. In order to make things more intelligible the Office of Fair Trading has highlighted two European Council Directives — the Consumer Credit Directive (1987) and the APR Directive (1990), which the U.K. has so far not implemented. The OFT has reported that legislation must be introduced requiring that only the APR formula in the APR Directive is used. The formula does not refer to an annual fee, or to a credit limit. In the meantime the same credit limit figure should be used in comparisons of APR while the current rules are still in place.

Consumer Protection Act 1987

Courts can also look at the way products are marketed in determining whether they are safe and those which do not comply with consumer safety provisions may be seized, forfeited and destroyed. A number of parties involved with the sale of a product must now be mindful of how it is marketed, since the liability incurred under the Consumer Protection Act 1987[5] for defective or dangerous goods can fall on the manufacturer, supplier, distributor, and even the importer of the product into a Member State of the European Union or someone who holds himself out to be a producer of goods, *i.e.* an own-brander. Section 2(2) of the Consumer Protection Act 1987, provides that any person who puts his name on the product or uses a trade mark, or other distinguishing mark in relation to the product, has held himself out as the producer of the product. However, in order for the person applying the trade mark or putting his name on the product to be caught, he must be actually holding himself out as a producer. Those who produce promotional material must be very careful because their statements may create expectations of safety. Indeed dealers and trade associations may also incur liability under the Consumer Protection Act 1987 if they come into the supply chain, either as principal or agent.[6]

In the United States, liability was found to rest with a publisher who had endorsed defective shoes simply by placing its seal of approval on

[5] Enacting the European Product Liability Directive 1985.
[6] See s.46 and the definition of supply.

the advertisement.[7] However, it should be emphasised that the liability was not strict, and the bulk of U.S. decisions are based on the involvement of the advertiser in the marketing of the product. The position of licensors and franchisers is similarly difficult. Mere permission to use a trade-mark may fix the licensor with liability under the Consumer Protection Act 1987.

General Safety Regulations

The Secretary of State has power[8] to regulate and control the packaging and labelling of dangerous products. There are a raft of safety regulations which the Secretary of State has made under the Consumer Protection Act 1987.[9] Previously such powers were granted under the Consumer Protection Act 1961. For example:

(i) Baby products — (in addition to general furniture safety regulations) These regulations cover prams, carrycots, furniture, packaging and medicine. Generally the regulations provide that certain safety requirements must be met, with regard to the stability of prams and carrycots, and locking and parking devices. Regulations also prohibit the sale or supply of children's medicines except in child-resistant containers.

(ii) Clothes These regulations cover children's clothing, nightwear, and dressing-gowns. These regulations are intended to prevent the use of inflammable material in children's clothing.

(iii) Heating, lighting, electrical and cooking appliances There are regulations covering gas cooking appliances, oil heaters and lights and a range of other heating and lighting equipment. Regulations cover plugs, and a number of other household electrical appliances. The regulations generally control emissions, and safe construction of appliances.

(iv) Chemicals (Hazard Information and Packaging for Supply) Regulations 1994 These regulations contain a requirement that any person who supplies any "substance dangerous for supply", as provided for in a long list, must not advertise them for sale unless mention is made in the advertisement of the hazard or hazards presented by the substance.

(v) Miscellaneous In addition to these, there are safety regulations which cover cosmetic products, dangerous and intoxicating substances, motor vehicles, bicycles, toys and food.

Anyone marketing a product must be very conscious of these safety regulations, as their breach is a criminal offence which may render the

[7] *Hanberry & Hearst Corp.* [276 Cal. App 2d 680].
[8] s.2(2), European Communities Act 1972 and s.11, Consumer Protection Act 1987.
[9] s.11.

company and its directors liable to criminal prosecution. The manner in which consumers are encouraged to use the goods in any advertisement may be used as evidence that the product is unsafe. Offering to supply products which are unsafe is an offence in its own right, even if they are not actually supplied.[10]

Medicines Act 1968

Great care is also required for the advertising of medicines and related products. The codes relating to the advertising of such products state that there must be compliance with the Medicines Act 1968 and the Food Labelling Regulations 1984. In addition breach of provisions of the Act or the Regulations may constitute criminal offences.

The Medicines Act 1968[11] provides that it is an offence to issue false or misleading advertisements and representations. An advertisement will be false or misleading if:

"(a) it falsely describes the description of the medicinal products to which it relates, or

(b) it is likely to mislead as to the nature or quality of medicinal products of that description or as to their uses or effects,"

An advertisement or representation will be taken to be likely to mislead as to the uses or effects of a medicinal product of a particular description if it is likely to mislead as to any of the following:

"(a) any purposes for which medicinal products of that description can with reasonable safety be used;

(b) any purposes for which such products cannot be used; and

(c) any effects which such products when used, or when used in any particular way referred to in the document, advertisement or representation, produce or are intended to produce."

Consumers must not be misled as to the quality of a product. Quality covers a property or an attribute or a distinguishing characteristic. An example of a misleading statement as to quality therefore includes where one manufacturer claims bio-equivalence with another medicinal product when this is not in fact the case.

The ABPI Code

The Association of British Pharmaceutical Industry Code covers the promotion of medicinal products to the medical and allied professions. It applies to companies which are members of the Association of the British Pharmaceutical Industry and any other companies which agree to abide by its terms. The Code attempts to stamp out exaggerated or

[10] Reg. 13 of the GPS Regulations.
[11] s.93.

all-embracing claims, prevents the use of superlatives, and ensures that all comparisons are factual, fair and capable of substantiation. Complaints may be submitted to the ABPI Committee by individuals or other companies and the alleged breaches are then notified to the company concerned. However, all that the Committee can do is to seek an undertaking from the company not to continue with a practice which is in breach of the Code. The company which remains in breach of the Code may eventually be expelled from the Association.

The PAGB Code

The Proprietary Association of Great Britain Code covers "over-the-counter" medicinal products and does not apply to advertisements which are directed to health professionals or organisations connected with the wholesale or retail distribution of medicines. It is concerned only with advertisements directed to the general public. The Code's emphasis is to ensure that misleading advertisements are not published, that all descriptions, claims and comparisons are capable of substantiation, and are balanced and fair. The PAGB deals informally with all complaints, and any promotional material is vetted prior to its use by the PAGB.

There are a number of common factors which can be extracted from the codes. In general, advertising must be legal, decent, honest and truthful. There must be due consideration for protection of privacy and the prevention of exploitation of the individual. Advertisements must not contain descriptions, claims or illustrations which directly or by implication mislead the public about the product or service advertised or about its suitability for the purpose recommended. Scientific terms and statistics when quoted must be properly used. When making claims about price, visual and verbal representations of actual and comparative prices and cost must be accurate and incapable of misleading by undue emphasis or distortion. There must be no likelihood of consumers being misled as a result of comparative advertisements. The basis of comparison in comparative advertising must be equivalent between products compared.

Broadcasting

Historically the U.K. advertising industry has regulated itself. The courts are reluctant to intervene and the overall trend in Europe has been to promote self-regulation. Self-regulation is only effective if the self-regulatory bodies are given sufficient powers and are seen to exercise these powers. If a regulator is unable to take positive action, then it will be subject to the whims of those with commercial strength. A number of codes dictate advertising practice.

ITC Advertising Code

The control of advertisements transmitted over television, satellite and cable services is provided for in the Broadcasting Act 1990.[12] This states that the Independent Television Commission ("ITC") must draw up a code governing advertising standards and practice (the ITC "Code"), and do all it can to ensure the ITC Code is adhered to. The Code was adopted with special regard to the need to give effect to television advertising as required by E.C. Directive 89/552 on Television Broadcasting and the 1989 Council of Europe Convention on Transfrontier Television.

The Code has special provisions on standards of advertising. The rules impinging on safety issues are:

16. Appeals to fear
17. Superstition
18. Unacceptable products or services
19. Health and safety
20. Motor cars and driving
21. Protection of the environment
23. Misleadingness
25. Comparisons
40. Alcoholic drink
41. Advertising and children
42. Financial advertising
43. Health claims, medicines and treatments

These all impact on safety issues and, in particular, rule 19 provides that no advertisement may encourage behaviour prejudicial to health and safety. This does not preclude responsible advertisements of products and services which, used to excess or abuse, could endanger health or safety. For example no advertisement may encourage or condone dangerous, inconsiderate or competitive driving practices or breach of the Highway Code. References to top speed or acceleration in advertisements for motorcars or other motor products must not imply that speed limits may be exceeded and there is to be no accompanying suggestion of excitement or aggression.

The Radio Code

The responsibility for radio advertising rests with the Radio Authority. The Radio Authority is obliged[13] to draw up a code of standards and practice and ensure that these are adhered to. However, both the ITC and the Radio Authority are empowered by the Act to impose requirements which go beyond their respective codes of practice.

[12] s.9.
[13] s.93, Broadcasting Act 1990.

The ASA

By contrast, the code governing the print media, cinema and video advertising is not imposed by Statute. The Committee of Advertising Practice publishes the British codes of Advertising and Sales Promotion.[14] The ASA monitors the enforcement of this Code and receives and deals with complaints.

The basic principle is that all advertisements should be "legal, decent, honest and truthful". They should be prepared with a sense of responsibility to consumers and to society. Particularly under the heading Safety the Code provides that advertisements should not show or encourage unsafe practices except in the context of promoting safety. Particular care should be taken with advertisements addressed to or depicting children and young people.

The latest edition of the Code was launched on January 16, 1995 and came into effect on February 1. It has been criticised as being unnecessary censorship. The critics point to two recent complaints. One is an advert which showed a child sipping a drink of sweetened carbonated water and its head shooting off, another showed a mother bending to nibble her baby daughter's bottom. The ITC disapproved and decided the first was frightening to children and the second sexually provocative. The Code now has specific sections detailing rules for:

46. Alcoholic drinks
47. Children
48. Motoring
49. Environmental claims
50. Health and beauty products and therapies, sub-divided into
    (a) general
    (b) medicines
    (c) vitamins, minerals and food supplements
    (d) cosmetics
    (e) hair and scalp
51. Slimming
55. Financial services and products
66. Cigarettes

The Control of Misleading Advertising Regulations 1988

A greater sanction now exists under the Control of Misleading Advertising Regulations 1988 which implements the E.C. Misleading Advertising Directive 1984. In the case of misleading advertising, the Director General of Fair Trading has the power to seek an injunction to prevent the advertiser from publishing the offending advertisement in the

[14] Currently in its 9th ed. (January 1995).
[15] [1989] 2 All E.R. 266.

future. In the case of *Tobyward*[15] the ASA successfully persuaded the Director-General to act to take out an injunction to prevent the release of the advertising. In *Tobyward*, the advertiser was the manufacturer of a slimming aid. A number of claims were made as to its effectiveness. The advertisers, despite being advised not to do so by the ASA, persisted in publishing a copy of the advertisement which contravened the Code. The ASA referred the whole matter to the Director-General who applied under the Misleading Advertising Regulations for an injunction to prevent further publication. An injunction was granted to prevent publication of the advertisement, and any similar advertisement. The court paid particular regard, in deciding whether to award the injunction, to the following factors:

(a) There was a strong, prima facie case that the advertisements were likely to affect the behaviour of the person to whom they were addressed by making false claims for advertiser's products.
(b) The nature of the court order must not be so general that the advertiser can get away with minor changes, nor so vague that the advertiser does not know what to do.
(c) An injunction is not subject to the condition that the Director-General give a cross-undertaking for damages. A cross-undertaking is not needed where there is a strong prima facie case.

Overview

In addition to the Director-General of Fair Trading, the Advertising Standards Authority plays a key role supervising the advertising industry. Prior to the Control of Misleading Advertisements Regulations 1988, the ASA could take no steps against an advertiser who failed to comply with one of its rulings. The principal disincentive to breaching the Code lay in the adverse publicity which would follow, or expulsion from a trade organisation to which the advertiser belongs.

An advertiser who now breaches the Code and then does not respond to the recommendations and criticisms of the ASA may, if the advertising is deemed to be misleading, risk being restrained from further advertising by the Director-General of Fair Trading obtaining an injunction. Since the Regulations allow for an application for an interlocutory injunction, there is a way of preventing the damage which such an advertisement might do. Where a potential audience would be deceived if the advertisement were allowed to be published, the court is likely to grant an interlocutory injunction. An advertiser who continues to advertise in breach of an injunction risks a hefty fine for contempt of court. Broadcasters are also susceptible to actions for breach of statutory duty if they fail in their duty to ensure compliance with their respective Codes (the individual bringing the case must have suffered special

[15] [1989] 2 All E.R. 266.

damage, or the case must be brought by the Attorney-General). In addition, self-regulatory bodies are statutory bodies which are susceptible to judicial review if they fail to behave reasonably.

The restraint which advertisers in the U.K. do demonstrate is proof of the way the combination of self-regulation and statutory controls successfully govern advertising.

CIVIL SANCTIONS

In serious cases, where a company publishes advertisements containing statements which are likely to make people think less of a competitor or his goods, that competitor may be able to sue the advertiser in defamation. The competitor is most likely to secure an interlocutory injunction to stop the advertisement. In cases where justification or fair comment is going to be pleaded as a defence the U.K. courts will be extremely reluctant to grant an interlocutory injunction.

Defamation

There are two actions in respect of the publication of material which is defamatory. An action for libel, where the material is written down or published in some other permanent form or is broadcast,[16] or an action for slander where the words were used in ordinary speech or some other transient form.

In order for an action in defamation to be made out, there must be a publication (*i.e.* communication from one person to another person of material concerning a third person). The matter must be defamatory in nature. The question of what is defamatory in nature has been construed by the courts to generally mean anything which is likely to make right thinking people think less of the person being allegedly defamed. An allegation that a competitor's product was unsafe will give the company producing the product a cause of action in libel if the producer can satisfy the court that the lack of safety is such that the audience will think less of the company producing the product rather than just thinking less of the product. If the latter is the case the producer will only have an action for slander of goods (see below).

Advertisers must be wary of defaming competitors according to the natural and ordinary meaning of the words which they use, but also by attaching innuendo meanings to words, and inferences which the public may be expected to draw from the use of ordinary words. The courts have repeatedly said that one must consider, not only the words which are actually used but also what conclusions might reasonably be drawn

[16] s.1, Defamation Act 1952.

from their use. In addition advertisers must bear in mind that the meaning which they intended is not relevant if an ordinary person could reasonably have drawn a negative meaning from the particular words used.

The law of defamation, in addition to allowing inferences to be drawn from ordinary words also recognises that some words have technical slang meanings or indeed meanings that depend on a specialist knowledge possessed by a limited number of people.[17] In this case ordinary words may bear special meanings other than their natural and ordinary meaning because of extrinsic facts or circumstances. These "legal innuendos" pose a potential trap to an advertiser using words which are understood to have special meanings to persons to whom it is published.

Slander of goods

In an action for slander of goods (also known as malicious falsehood or trade libel) the plaintiff must show:

(a) the words complained of were untrue;
(b) that they were published maliciously; and
(c) that the plaintiff has thereby been caused special damage or is exempted from proving special damage by reason of the provisions of section 3 of the Defamation Act 1952.

This last exemption provides that in an action for slander of goods it is not necessary to allege or prove special damage if the words used were calculated to cause pecuniary damage in respect of an office, profession, calling, trade or business held by the person at the time of the publication. Contrary to actions in defamation, it is not necessary to show that right thinking members of the public would be inclined to think less of the plaintiff in order to succeed.

Qualified privilege

There is a defence to defamation, where a statement is made in pursuance of a legal, social or moral duty to a person who has a corresponding duty or interest to receive it. Alternatively qualified privilege may be relied on for statements made for the protection or furtherance of an interest to a person who has a common or a corresponding duty or interest to receive such a statement. This defence can be defeated if the plaintiff can show that the defendant was actuated by malice. Advertisers may seek to argue that the statements that they

[17] *Winyard and another v. Tatler Publishing Co Ltd and Others*, Independent Law Reports August 16, 1991.

make were for the protection or furtherance of consumers' interests. Courts have constantly drawn attention to the difference between what is in the public interest and what the public are interested in, and it would prove extremely difficult for an advertiser to satisfy a court that defamatory statements were made in the consumers' interest.

Misrepresentation

An advertisement, if it goes beyond a mere "puffing" of the advertisers' product, may amount to a representation, and if false, a misrepresentation. A misrepresentation occurs when:

> "one person makes a false representation (who may be called 'the representor') to another (who may be called 'the representee') which has the object and result of inducing the representee to enter into a contract or binding transaction with him, the representee may, in general and subject to certain circumstances which may preclude him from so doing, elect to regard the contract as rescinded."[18]

A misrepresentation may be fraudulent, innocent or negligent. To be fraudulent, the misrepresentation must have been made in the knowledge that what was stated was false or the representor must have been reckless, not caring whether it was true or not. If damage is suffered as a result of the fraudulent misrepresentation, then, under common law, in addition to the right to rescind the contract, the representee may recover damages.

In relation to negligent misstatement, under common law both the remedies of rescision and damages are available to a successful plaintiff. Under the Misrepresentation Act 1967 (the "1967 Act"), however, unlike the common law, a plaintiff need not demonstrate a duty of care between the parties and the burden of proof is reversed and it is for the representor to prove his reasonable belief rather than the representee having to prove that the representor failed to take reasonable care. Under common law the remedy for innocent misrepresentation lies in the right of rescission and does not extend to damages.

The 1967 Act provides that:

> "Where a person has entered into a contract after a misrepresentation has been made to him, and—
> (a) the misrepresentation has become a term of the contract; or
> (b) the contract has been performed;
> or both, then, if otherwise he would be entitled to rescind the contract without alleging fraud, he shall be entitled, subject to the provisions of this Act, notwithstanding the matters mentioned in paragraph (a) and (b) of this section."

The Act also provides that damages may be recoverable even though the misrepresentation was not made fraudulently. If the person making the

[18] Halsbury's Laws of England, 4th edition.

representation would be liable to damages in respect of it had the misrepresentation been made fraudulently, that person may be so liable notwithstanding that the misrepresentation was not made fraudulently, unless he proves that he had reasonable grounds to believe and did believe up to the time the contract was made that the facts represented were true. The Act also provides that a court may award damages in lieu of rescission.

Misrepresentation is very different from mere puff. If a person praises his own goods, in an unspecific manner, this will not usually amount to a representation at all. Where, however, that person incorporates facts into the statement then the statement as a whole may be deemed to constitute a representation. If that statement contains an actionable misrepresentation, then it is no defence to allege that the facts were hidden in generalities.

Intellectual property rights

On the other hand, a competitor may seek to rely on an intellectual property right to prevent what it considers unfair advertising. The advantage to the competitor of seeking to do this rather than relying on a defamation action is that an interlocutory injunction is more commonly granted. An action in defamation is an action to protect reputation, whereas an action based on intellectual property rights is an action to protect a property right. English law has always afforded greater protection to property than reputation. In addition, an advertisement may give rise to an action for passing-off; for example, the advertiser may be attempting to pass off his product as that of a competitor.

Trade marks and advertising

There are certain civil remedies available to competitors of advertisers who feel that their own products have been unduly disparaged in the advertising. This will apply most particularly in the area of comparative advertising.

A comparison with another's product may seek to take undue advantage of the other's well known trade mark. For example where a manufacturer of smell-alike perfumes made comparisons with perfume manufactured under the mark "CHANEL". Use of a competitor's trade mark in comparative advertising was deemed a trade mark infringement in the U.K. where the trade mark was registered in Part A of the Trade Marks Register (which will be the case for most distinctive trade marks) (section 4(1)b of the Trade Marks Act 1938). However, the Trade Marks Act 1994 anticipating a draft E.C. directive on comparative advertising has removed the prohibition on comparative advertising in the U.K. where reference is made to another's trade or service mark.

Under section 10(6) of the Trade Marks Act 1994, comparative advertising by reference to another's trade or service mark is no longer a trade mark infringement. The Trade Marks Act 1994 is the U.K.'s implementation of the Trade Mark Harmonisation Directive, and the relevant section of the Act provides that:

> "Nothing in the preceding provisions of the section shall be construed as preventing the use of a registered trade mark by any person for the purpose of identifying goods or services with those of the proprietor or a licensee.
>
> But any such use otherwise than in accordance with honest practices in industrial or commercial matters shall be treated as infringing the registered trade mark if the use without due course takes unfair advantage of, or is detrimental to, the distinctive character or repute of the trade mark".

In addition there are a number of directives at European Council level on comparative and misleading advertising. The most recent comparative advertising directive is still in draft form, and its final wording is not yet agreed. The U.K. is running the risk of having to introduce two forms of legislation in order to implement the Trade Mark Harmonisation Directive and the Comparative Advertising Directive once it is in a final form. Trade mark users attempted to lobby Parliament, while the Trade Mark Bill was being debated, to introduce a provision so that anyone intending to use a trade mark in comparative advertising would have to notify the trade mark owner first, but this was unsuccessful.

In order to ascertain how the new legislation may be interpreted in the future in the context of comparisons on safety issues it is instructive to look at some of the cases which have been decided under section 4(1)b of the Trade Marks Act 1938. In *Duracell v. Ever-Ready*,[19] the plaintiffs complained that the defendants had by means of "knocking advertising" infringed two of their trade marks, being the name "DURACELL" and the get-up of the batteries. The advertisement compared the lifetimes of the batteries sold by Duracell Batteries Ltd, and those sold by the Ever-Ready Corporation, Inc. Even though the defendants referred to the corporate name, it was held that the corporate name did include the trade mark (despite the statements in the earlier case of *Pompadour v. Frazer*[20] to the contrary). The advertisements consisted of two pictures of the batteries (in black and white), with the indications "long" and "longer", next to a picture of a body-builder and King Kong with the indications "strong" and "stronger", and alternatively a racehorse and a picture of the cartoon character "Road Runner". It is likely that this case would, under the new legislation, turn on whether the activity of the advertiser was considered to be an "honest practice in industrial or commercial matters," and whether the

[19] [1989] F.S.R. 71.
[20] [1966] R.P.C. 7.

advertiser's use of its competitors' trade mark was detrimental to the repute of the competitors' trade mark.

In *Compaq v. Dell*,[21] the defendant computer company placed two advertisements containing photographs of both the plaintiff and defendant's computer systems, each accompanied by a price and an identification of the system. The plaintiffs alleged that the advertisements represented that both systems were basically and essentially the same. However it was found that the plaintiff's and defendant's computers were materially different. Hence the claims might amount to an injurious falsehood. In addition the price representations were not capable of being justified. Such misrepresentations would almost certainly mean that the activity remains a trade mark infringement even under the new Act. Similarly misrepresentations on safety issues incorporated in an advertisement using a competitor's trade mark would be an infringement.

Although comparative advertising will now be able to refer to a competitor's trade mark without being a trade mark infringement, it must be in accordance with "honest practices in industrial or commercial matters". It is not at all clear what this actually means, and whether this introduces a *mens rea* element into the trade mark infringement action or whether it is the practice which must be honest, so that the yardstick by which honesty is measured differs depending on the industry. It would seem that a number of the decided cases would remain trade mark infringements under the new law, where they were misleading or in some way dishonest. However, it would also appear that an honest comparison would be allowed when the Act's provisions become effective.

Passing-off

The tort of passing-off was introduced to prevent one company representing its goods as the goods of another. In order to show passing-off it is necessary to show:

(a) a misrepresentation;
(b) made by a trader in the course of a trade;
(c) to prospective customers or ultimate consumers of his goods or services;
(d) which is calculated to injure the business or goodwill of another trader (in the sense that this is a reasonably foreseeable consequence); and
(e) which causes actual damage to the business or goodwill of the trade by whom the action is brought.

A passing-off action is an action to protect goodwill. However, for this tort to have any application to advertising there must be some misrepre-

[21] [1992] F.S.R. 93.

sentation. If there is no confusion between the trade marks or the get-up of the actual products, then there will be no passing-off. A previous attempt to allege unfair trading because the defendant's advertising had adopted the tenor of the plaintiff's successful advertising, did not succeed.[22]

In the *Pub Squash* case, the defendant's advertising had adopted the style of the plaintiff's campaign. The plaintiff had been able to successfully illustrate that its lemon squash could conjure up simultaneous images of masculinity and nostalgia. However, since there was no confusion between the parties' trade marks or get-up of the actual products, there was no passing-off.

By contrast, in *Elida Gibbs v. Colgate Palmolive*,[23] the defendants used a marketing campaign based on a theme whereby a comparison was made between a tree and its roots and a human tooth and its roots. The plaintiff alleged that it had used the same theme for an advertising campaign some 30 years previously. The campaigns were not identical but were based on the same theme using a tree. The plaintiff therefore sought interlocutory relief to prevent the defendants from passing-off their product as that of the plaintiffs.

An injunction was awarded because:

- prior to the commencement of the plaintiff's campaign, there was no relevant reputation attached to the tree theme in England;
- the defendants were aware of the plaintiff's position;
- if both products were launched at the same time there would be confusion in the minds of the public, and here, the plaintiffs entered the market first.

This was a *quia timet* action, initiated to prevent commencement of the defendant's advertising campaign. In this case a similar advertising campaign was successfully challenged on the basis that to allow it to proceed would cause confusion in the minds of the public.

In the U.K., there is no law on unfair competition and so it is difficult for a competitor to challenge an advertiser's campaign on the basis that it is very similar to his own. The Paris Convention on the Protection of Industrial Property Rights 1883 (the "Paris Convention") provides that signatory states are bound to assure nationals protection against unfair competition. Unfair competition is defined as being any act which creates confusion by any means whatever with the establishment, the goods, or the industrial or commercial activities of a competitor. The U.K. has not implemented this into its legislation, but other countries in the European Union have.

In summary, in order to be able to attack a competitor's advertising campaign one has to show that:

(a) it was misleading; or

[22] *Cadbury-Schweppes v. Pub Squash* [1981] R.P.C. 429.
[23] [1988] F.S.R. 93.

(b) there has been a passing-off; or
(c) it contains comparisons which refer to the competitor's trade mark, and from November 1994 the use of the competitor's trade mark is not in accordance with honest practices in industrial or commercial matters, or otherwise takes advantage of, or is detrimental to the distinctive character and repute of the competitor's trade mark.

Under (a), assistance can be gained by reference to the various codes of practice mentioned previously. Under (b), there are, it would appear two forms of confusion which may give rise to an action in passing-off. The first is that the public may be confused as to who manufactured the products; the second is that the public may be confused into thinking that the goods of the alleged infringer are manufactured under a licensing agreement with the real manufacturer. Such an implication is rare, but not unknown.

Copyright

If an advertiser copies some or all of a competitor's advertising, this may give rise to a copyright infringement. As in passing-off this type of action is in practice rare, but not unknown. The first problem to overcome is that the work must actually attract copyright, by virtue of the nature of the material or the intellectual or entrepreneurial activity that produced it. Advertising material will generally be an artistic work within the meaning of the Copyright, Designs and Patents Act 1988; or possibly (depending on content) a literary work. Artistic works must be original, and there must be the requisite skill, judgment and labour which goes into their production.

The next hurdle to overcome is to prove that there has been an infringement. Copyright protection does not confer a monopoly protection, and it is necessary to show that the defendant's infringement is causally connected with the production of the allegedly copied work. Such a connection may be intended if the plaintiff's work was first, and there are striking similarities between the two works (*Harman Pictures v. Osborne*).[24] There is some support for the proposition that a work may be subconsciously copied (*Rees v. Melville*),[25] and such copying may be of relevance in the world of advertising. Probably the biggest problem for advertisers who attempt to protect their work by seeking to enforce their copyright is the so-called expression/ideas dichotomy which pervades copyright law. What copyright protects is the expression of ideas, not the ideas themselves. Judges differ in their view of how far "expression" actually extends.

Wrongful interference with trade or business

The so-called "economic" torts may give rise to possible causes of action for advertisers' competitors. This tort is made out when one person uses

[24] [1967] 2 All E.R. 324.
[25] [1911–16] MacG. Cop. Cas. 96.

unlawful means with the object and effect of causing damage to another.[26] The essence of the tort is that the plaintiff must have suffered loss as a result of the defendant interfering with its business. There must be some unlawful means going beyond mere spiteful interference.[27] "Unlawful means" include procuring another to break a contract with the competitor or a breach of confidence. The competitor must also show that the advertiser set out with the object of harming it (even though this does not have to be the predominant purpose of the advertisers' action).[28] In summary, this tort is unlikely to be a useful weapon in the armoury when seeking to attack a competitor's advertisement. It will only be applicable in a case where advertising forms part of a vendetta between advertiser and competitor. If the advertising is misleading, this may be the "unlawful means" platform from which to launch an action.

CONCLUSION

It is a commonly-held view that the advertising industry in the U.K. is self-regulated, and because of the limited powers of the regulators, this essentially means it is not regulated at all. However, not only can the Director-General of Fair Trading act to stop misleading advertising, but it is also clear that there are a raft of regulations to which advertisers must pay heed or else incur criminal liability or render themselves civilly liable to their competitors. As the number of regulations both at national and E.C. level increases, advertisers will need to take more and more care about the way they market, sell and advertise their products being ever mindful of the civil actions competitors may pursue against them.

[26] *Merkur Island Shipping Corporation v. Loughton* [1983] 2 A.C. 570.
[27] *Allen v. Flood* [1985-89] All E.R. 52.
[28] *Lonrho v. Fayed* [1992] 1 A.C. 448.

12 Product Safety under Public Scrutiny

The safety of a company's products can become a public issue. This presents management with a series of serious challenges. How do managers protect consumer trust in the company, manage information, manage the dimensions of the crisis, select a proper tone of response?

The ultimate option is "product recall". How does management consider and balance the cost of lost reputation, and define the risk and scope of a recall problem?

Communicating in a crisis is a challenge. How does management decide how much to say, when and to whom? Who should speak on the company's behalf?

Companies should be prepared for how to manage a crisis. What is a suitable preparedness programme and how should it be implemented?

PRODUCT SAFETY ON THE PUBLIC AGENDA

Under normal circumstances, managers are expected to plan for and handle day-to-day problems within the confines of their business. Managers are selected, remunerated and promoted, at least in part, for their ability to pick up and solve problems before they reach threatening proportions.

Any experienced operational manager will recognise that normal product and quality regimes are constantly in need of supervision and updating. There is no machine, no process that cannot be improved, especially when human beings are involved in operating, servicing or repairing it.

Well-organised companies detect and solve faults within tight company check systems and controls. But the themes and discussions within this book recognise that failures in product safety do occur — sometimes jeopardising consumers and the general public, with all the liability implications that follow.

This chapter addresses the problems that arise when product faults emerge from under the control of management or check systems and burst into the public domain.

Managing under the glare of public attention

Immediately product problems are escalated outside a company, the rules change. Every action, every decision is put under the glare of public and media attention. Suddenly management faces a series of new and unknown challenges, which combine to hinder the efforts to solve the operational problems faced by the company. Normal management becomes crisis management.

THE CHALLENGES FOR MANAGEMENT

While every product problem will differ, once the situation emerges into the public arena, the following characteristics apply:

- The circumstances will be unexpected with the timing compounding the problem. Many situations reach crisis proportions at weekends, during national holidays or at other times when key executives are unavailable.
- Management will have insufficient information upon which to base the pressing decisions needed to reduce or solve the problem. Additionally those facts that are available will be distorted by rumour or speculation.
- Situations will escalate at an accelerating pace, leaving management with a sense of loss of control. Events will appear to be dictated by individuals and groups acting from outside; suddenly the future is apparently being shaped by regulators, governments, consumer groups and the media.

In many cases, corporate management react to these unfamiliar circumstances by adopting a siege mentality, attempting to shut out the world. Quickly, long-term strategic plans are sacrificed in a scramble for short-term solutions.

Protecting consumer trust in the company

When a serious product safety fault or contamination occurs, the situation will threaten the bonds of trust and confidence that lie at the heart of the relationship between successful manufacturers and their customers and consumers.

Perrier faced a world-wide crisis when the Food & Drink Administration in the USA found benzene in samples of mineral water at a higher level than normal. While the health or safety risks may have been minimal, the drop in sales figures, from the moment the possible contamination problem was revealed, indicated how brand values and consumer confidence can be quickly undermined.

When corporate reputations and public trust are at risk, then management must address fundamental decisions in deciding the future of the product at fault.

Since the company is being forced to act within full public view, a short-term sacrifice may be necessary to save the brand or product line. Suddenly handling a product fault is escalated and takes on long-term, strategic dimensions. At this point market share and even company survival may be at stake.

Managing information

Under normal conditions businesses are organised to gather and analyse facts and data before taking decisions. Information technology has increased management dependence on accurate information. A public crisis however surrounds a company with media discussion and speculation, which is fuelled by rumour — whether benign or malicious. Wide experience of working alongside corporate management in crisis has demonstrated that any product safety issue involves constant conflict between facts and perceptions. Thus the company is faced with the problem of separating fact from fiction — all at a time when the outside world is demanding answers, reasons, decisions and reassurance.

Now in the maelstrom of a crisis, management is forced to address twin tasks if the situation is to be wrested back under control:

- First, technical and management expertise must be brought to bear on the product problem.
- Secondly, and of equal importance, communications need to be tightly managed, so that rumour and speculation can be countered and controlled.

These twin management tasks must be brought into play quickly in order to provide key decision-makers with the best available facts upon which to base strategic objectives and plans. Since accurate data is unlikely to be available, a collection point needs to be established into which all information must be fed for analysis, collation and assessment.

Cadbury-Schweppes received a series of consumer complaints that glass had been found in Nerds, a coloured sugar candy. The unusual product name excited media interest and the number of consumer complaints climbed. Technical and production data were not available until production analysis and quality checks had been completed in the USA. To ensure key decisions could be made, an information network was set up, linking the crisis management and recall planning teams to the hotline bureau, media monitoring cells, the police investigation centre and an independent forensic laboratory. Using dedicated fax and modem links, all data was gathered, analysed and collated at one point within the company. Thereafter the corporate crisis management team were able to assess the depth and scope of the product contamination, basing decisions on the best available information.

Managing the dimensions of the crisis

The first sign that a company is facing a serious problem frequently comes when the switchboard lights up like a Christmas tree. Often before corporate management has had a chance to appreciate the gravity of the situation, consumer complaints flood in while the media will bombard the company with questions. Suddenly a product safety issue becomes public property with all the inherent risks for company reputation and the future of the business.

Anchor Butter detected a fault on the production line when a screw tumbler went out of alignment, causing metal to be shaved off into butter due for packing. An order was issued that the affected product was to be quarantined pending destruction; but somehow the affected batch was put out into the distribution chain in error. Management only realised what had happened when the media reported the fault and ran the story. Late on a Friday evening the plant at Swindon was inundated with press calls, followed the next day by a wave of consumer complaints, many of which turned out to be mischievous.

The speed of build up and volume of calls can quickly swamp telephone and fax handling capacities. At the same time the range of queries and demands for information can distract key managers from vital decision-making tasks. At such times external audiences gain attention at the expense of employees, who are equally keen to know what is happening — after all, their company is under the spotlight and their jobs could appear to be at risk.

The tone of the management response

In the middle of a product crisis, corporate management become so deeply involved in solving product and business problems that human considerations are often forgotten. But the tone of response to public and consumer concerns will be remembered long after product problems have been solved. Again managers face dual challenges in, on the one hand, making hard commercial decisions while at the same time being seen to display concern and understanding of the reaction of customers and consumers.

The various communications channels and techniques available to a company are discussed later in this chapter. But the tone of communications must be a factor for consideration in evolving strategic plans.

Product recall — the ultimate option

As soon as safety problems are catapulted onto the public agenda, corporate management must start considering the ultimate solution of product recall. Eventually, if customer and consumer trust appears to be severely undermined, then recall may be the only option left open to the company.

Johnson & Johnson quickly recognised the threat to Extra Strength Tylenol, when the analgesic drug was spiked with cyanide before being put back on retail shelves, causing death and injuries. The Chief Executive publicly took personal control of the situation, thus demonstrating J&J's commitment to the defence of product integrity and consumer safety. Tylenol returned on relaunch, eventually regaining, and even increasing, market share in the tough USA marketplace.

A fault in filters on a product line caused bone slivers to drop into a bone marrow baby feed. As soon as consumer complaints were received, Heinz, the manufacturers, made a wide, strategic assessment of the potential impacts on this popular product. In light of likely concerns, the company ordered an immediate and complete withdrawal in order to protect their bond of trust with mothers. Corporate management had recognised the urgent need to protect the overall portfolio of baby foods at the expense of losing one product within the range.

Balancing the cost of reputation

When corporate management accepts the need to recall a product, the CFO will be watching costs mount for withdrawing the product, compensating consumers and customers plus the replacement of stock. At the same time the hidden costs can never be accurately calculated for such items as management time and operational disruption. For a public company, any undermining of corporate reputation is quickly reflected in downward stock movements. At the time of the Tylenol recall it was estimated that $3 billion worth of shares were traded in Johnson & Johnson stock. However that share price recovered and market share was regained as shareholders and the general public recognised the corporate responsibility which had driven the decision to withdraw the analgesic in such an open and honest manner.

Defining the risks and scope of the recall problem

The logistical and operational challenges of any product recall will be daunting. Limited product freezes or distribution "holds" or national product lifts will involve complex tracing and recovery problems. Recalls at multinational levels can present extreme difficulties within international distribution networks, where the assessment of the risk to consumers may be difficult to define in detail.

Product handling by several different shippers and hauliers complicates and obscures vital facts needed for tracing the depth and likely spread of affected product. Finally batch coding might not have been used in handling documentation, especially in less sophisticated markets such as in Central Europe or the Pacific Rim.

When planning for a multinational recall of Export Bier, Heineken found that the sheer volume of the problem made it difficult to determine whether potentially affected products had reached retail outlets, thus putting consumers at risk, although rigorous product tracking systems were in place. The quantity of potentially affected stock, 17 million bottles in 152 markets, slowed trace analysis and risk assessment.

Communications within a recall plan

But when a well-known brand or product is declared unsafe — whether true or not — logistical problems must be considered alongside the communications demands of the situation. Again management must be ready to respond to queries and explain the situation in a coherent, consistent manner.

When the Food & Drink Administration in the USA detected traces of benzene in Perrier, each operating subsidiary was permitted to manage communications with a minimum of direction or constraint from Source Perrier in France. The resultant confusion caused by conflicting messages undermined the confidence of the public. It took several weeks of tightly focused communications, backed by a world-wide advertising campaign, to arrest escalation and bring the situation under control.

Only when consumer concerns begin to be allayed can realistic assessments be made of future options beyond recall, when relaunch can become a possibility.

Assessing attitudes behind the headlines

One of the major problems for companies in crisis is gauging the true attitudes of consumers in the market-place. Since the media are the most vocal group, it is tempting to react to the adverse publicity, which surrounds any serious product safety or liability case.

But as soon as a crisis hits, management instead must seek to research behind the headlines to assess true opinions. This is the time to set up market research to track customer, consumer and general public attitudes to the threatened product while also assessing the way the company is seen to be handling the situation.

Mattesson Walls recalled Pepperami sticks when a fault in pasteurisation processes caused salmonella incidents in the U.K. From the day that the recall was announced, research was conducted on a daily basis amongst key audience groups. Early results detected sympathy for the company and a desire for the return of the product. This trend continued positively and permitted Mattesson Walls to successfully predict the timing and tone of the relaunch of Pepperami, which took place only six months after the national recall.

Hotlines as research tools

The wide use of carelines and hotlines offers another market research tool, giving a company direct access to consumer attitudes. Thus when a product safety crisis hits, hotline staff need briefing and training to undertake simple research and recording tasks in addition to handling queries and complaints. However staff should be made aware that journalists use this route to gather further information under the disguise of being a consumer. Special arrangements should be put in place for picking up and passing press queries to the appropriate media handling group within the crisis management team.

THE CHALLENGE TO COMMUNICATE

As has been seen earlier in this chapter, when a product safety or liability problem reaches crisis proportions under the glare of public and media scrutiny, management faces the dual tasks of solving the problem and controlling communications. The latter task is often unfamiliar and daunting for decision-makers used to managing within the safe confines of their company.

Deciding whether to speak out

Because the siege mentality appears a safe option when a crisis takes hold, management may be tempted to ignore or delay answering queries and questions. This is a dangerous tactic when health or safety of consumers is at risk, since unanswered concerns become magnified and fears grow, especially if press speculation is fanning public concerns. Thus management must seek to adopt a proactive, responsive communications stance.

Today the spread and speed of communications propel business into a rapidly changing global market-place. Regrettably when product problems arise, the same communications efficiency drives situations out of the control of management. When regulators, the media and interest groups become involved, the problem escalates.

In the middle of a crisis, when the headlines are accusing the company of unsafe practices or lax procedures, there may seem to be clear grounds for not communicating. Some of the reasons that are offered could be:

- "We do not know all the facts."

- "We do not know how to solve the problem yet."
- "We risk admitting liability."
- "We do not have anyone qualified to speak."

All these are sound reasons for staying silent. Regrettably "no comment" and "The Company were not willing to take part in this programme", have become media shorthand for guilt. As readers, viewers and listeners, we have been led to interpret such responses as coming from companies who have something to hide. Under such circumstances, silence is not golden, rather it can indict the organisation in the eyes of the public.

Managing interested parties

Once any business or company is under the glare of public scrutiny, corporate management can become overwhelmed by the number and groups that take an interest in the product problem. Familiar business partners will rapidly seek reassurances. Customers and consumers will start calling in increasing numbers, followed by the media who will doggedly follow up every lead in pursuit of a story. Once health and safety aspects surface, regulators, governments and even ministries start pressing for information. Citizen and pressure groups may recognise an opportunity to use the situation to their own ends. Calls from local politicians or elected representatives may follow.

At the same time internal pressures will build as employees attempt to express their concerns and seek reassurance on the future of their jobs. Trade unions and works councils will ask to meet with management in order to gain a better picture of the circumstances.

All these and other external groups will have cause to seek answers, reasons, reassurance and confirmation of the facts. In the dynamic situation of a crisis, rumours will be circulating fast, adding to the confusion. At such a moment, management needs to identify all those groups and individuals who will be watching and judging the company.

Answering individual queries and needs

Once audiences have been identified, it will be necessary to decide the particular concerns of each one. Only then can communications be planned that will be capable of answering the diverse needs of internal and external groups.

Audiences must be segmented and their needs must be tended individually. As examples of varied requirements, communications must be extended to reach the following such groups at the time of a crisis:

The company

- Employees and their families because they fear for their jobs.

- Trade unions who need to be seen to be protecting interests of their members.
- The local community who will be concerned about the possible impact on employment and supporting services in the area.

The business community

- Consumers because they are worried for their health or safety.
- Customers because they will be concerned about their own businesses.
- Suppliers who wonder if their contracts are at risk.

Influencers

- Regulators who need to know if rules have been breached.
- Health and safety officers who need to know what went wrong.
- Ministers who expect to be asked questions, especially if they have responsibility for the industry or business sector.
- Politicians who will be asked for an opinion — particularly local ones.
- The media who need a story — now.

Since many of these groups talk to each other, it is preferable to communicate simultaneously to them all. This integrated approach requires detailed planning, which has to be conducted against tight timelines.

Preparing communications and messages

When Quaker Oats had to recall the Honey Monster and Sugar Puffs breakfast cereal, communications had to be developed quickly. Advertisements, letters, telephone briefing scripts, press releases plus management briefings to employees and salesforces, all had to be prepared within 12 hours for use in 16 markets.

In getting ready to speak out, clear objectives must be set which steer all communications towards maintenance of confidence while building back trust and reputation. It has been proved in many crisis situations that consistency, clarity, accuracy and timeliness are essential elements. If any of these principles are breached, information will be sought elsewhere, thus undermining the authority of corporate management teams.

Keeping these principles in mind, a team dedicated to communications needs to draw up a list of key messages, which can be delivered to all audiences. Since those messages will be seen as an expression of corporate policy and direction, it is important that the detail is cleared by the key decision-makers who have strategic responsibility for managing the situation. Subsequently, as circumstances alter, the messages will need amendment and clearance before being disseminated.

Selecting communications channels

While messages are being developed, it will be necessary to decide the best way of reaching each individual or group. It is to be hoped that in most cases channels will exist already; otherwise speedy, efficient communications conduits must be selected. Internally, cascade briefing procedures or electronic links may be in place and should be used.

The value of well briefed staff is often ignored, especially when many other priorities are pressing. However employees know most about their company and have a stake in communicating good news on behalf of management. If they have been told the facts, employees will act as ambassadors, especially in the local community, where interest levels will be high. In this context, sales staff become important since they represent the most immediate link to many customers; however problems can arise when it becomes necessary to brief them quickly when they are on the road, visiting customers.

The portfolio of spokespeople

When faced by the media in a crisis, a company should deploy fully briefed spokespeople who have been trained to handle adverse interviews. Since consistency and accuracy are so important, it is better to limit the number of spokespeople to those who can be kept fully up to date as the situation develops. Townsend Thorensen never recovered after the Chief Executive had stated that the "Herald of Free Enterprise" could not have left Zeebrugge harbour with the bow doors open, when the media knew he was wrong. This fatal mistake occurred because the Chief Executive had not been briefed on the accident before he spoke out. Many product safety and liability incidents will turn upon technical or scientific information, which should be communicated by experts. It is rarely feasible for a CEO or a corporate spokesperson to be able to handle such specialist subjects. Thus additional specialist spokespeople should be trained and made available when required.

Hotlines as communications tools

Hotlines were discussed earlier in this chapter in the context of market research. After careful briefings, trained operators can communicate essential messages as part of their response conversations. Thus hotlines should be viewed as a suitable conduit to consumers and the general public, especially since skilled operators can quickly build trust with callers.

Understanding the press

The course of product safety or liability incidents cannot be forecast accurately, except in anticipating media behaviour once the problem reaches the public agenda. Journalists will besiege the company with calls in the initial blitz. Suddenly management faces a wave of highly vocal, critical, cynical and judgmental people, who will be demanding information on the incident, background on the company, financial data plus pictures — of the product, the plant, the CEO, of anything and everything. All these demands will be made against very tight timelines.

The press are likely to be present at any serious incident, particularly if health or safety is at stake. Thus management needs to understand the needs of the media, so that communications plans can respond accordingly. For a news editor, your bad news represents a good story. Journalists will be tasked to find out the facts, preferably taking back a story or angle which is exclusive to the newspaper, radio or TV station.

While all journalists will present their queries in different ways, each will be seeking to answer four basic questions:

- What happened?
- Who/what is to blame?
- How dangerous is it?
- What is being done about it?

Since most managers do not deal with the press on a regular basis — especially under crisis conditions — it is forgotten that newspapers and the electronic media are all businesses. Journalists are in competition with each other with limited time being a further driving element. Twenty-four hour news services have essentially destroyed the concept of deadlines — news is needed *now*.

Finally, it should be remembered that only limited space is ever available to explain the company's complex product safety and liability situation. Journalists will be seeking facts and figures that can be delivered in a manner which is easily understood often by audiences and readers who have little or no knowledge of the business or industry in trouble.

Communicating through the media

If management can appreciate these facts about the media and their needs, then the press can be recognised as a potential asset to a company in a crisis. Because of the speed and reach of media communications, news programmes and newspapers can be used to talk directly to large audiences at short notice.

Pepsi-Cola used nationwide TV to tell U.S. consumers that it was not possible to insert items into tins of cola. Footage of sophisticated high speed cleansing lines and bottling operations were shown across the USA when claims were made that syringes had been found in Pepsi cans. This communication device reassured customers and began to cast doubt upon what, subsequently, proved to be a series of hoax claims.

PREPARING AHEAD OF THE PROBLEM

Until this point we have considered how serious product safety and liability situations can be handled. The remainder of this chapter will consider some of the preparation measures that can be taken to anticipate and handle these high intensity, high pressure, high profile situations.

The need for a preparedness programme

As has been seen throughout this book, the incidence levels for product failure remain constant, with safety and liability problems arising in all industries. Thus the first step in getting ready is for management to think the unthinkable — "it could happen to us". This important mindset leads to acceptance of the need to have sound plans in place which are constantly kept up to date. Thereafter, once plans have been devised and codified, it is necessary to embark on a progamme of training at all management levels.

Since crisis situations place exceptional demands upon management, plans need to be robust and well prepared. This specialist task may require the assistance of experienced crisis counsellors and communications experts, who are likely to recommend a preparedness programme to cover:

- An updated assessment of threats and risks for the business.
- Review of current operational and communications plans.
- Development of crisis management guidelines and manuals.
- Preparation of special crisis plans, procedures and systems.
- Programme of training for crisis managers, spokespeople plus technical and management support staff.

Preparing the front line

One aspect of preparedness often forgotten concerns the "front line" in any company — the consumer complaints department, secretaries to key executives, switchboard operators, receptionists and security staff. Day by day this relatively junior group of employees operates at interfaces with the world outside. In these key positions they will pick up important early warning signals, for example an increase in levels of complaints for one particular product, a journalist asking tricky questions, a suspicious call which could precede a threat message.

When the crisis hits, many of the front line troops will be involved in handling a tidal wave of calls. Mattesson Walls handled over 1,300 calls in the first 24 hours after recalling Pepperami. Hoover were receiving 2,000–3,000 calls each day and up to 4,000 letters a week at the height of the crisis associated with free flight promotions. Companies should consider how to handle such volumes — is a standby hotline facility needed?

The first step in preparing the front line is briefing and training the troops. Simple seminars can be run which explain and practice roles and responsibilities. Interactive follow-up sessions will generate ideas for special procedures for handling calls under crisis conditions.

Testing and validating plans

Wide experience of handling product safety or liability cases in the public domain shows that procedures and preparedness measures need to be flexible and robust. Once detailed planning has been completed it is necessary to test and validate teams, procedures and systems to ensure that all will stand up to the rigours of high pressure crisis situations. Since objective assessment is needed at this important final stage, it may be necessary to call upon the assistance of external crisis trainers. Depending on the levels of training and experience of the participants, testing and validation can call upon one of the following generic formats:

- *Desktop decision simulations:* management teams are presented with various situations within an unfolding crisis scenario. Decisions and actions are taken, calling upon in-place plans, procedures and management systems. Scenarios escalate, as problems become more complex against reducing timelines. Key decisions and events are analysed as the session proceeds with lessons being recorded for subsequent consideration.
- *Live play simulation sessions:* scenarios are depicted via telephone calls, faxes, memos, briefings, newscasts and reports plus role playing. Crisis managers have to respond with operational and communications actions. After an intense period of play, exercise activities are analysed to highlight lessons and requirements for additional training.
- *Test exercises:* sophisticated simulation techniques are used to augment routine operational tests with the objective of analysing how crisis management actions would dovetail into operational actions during a serious incident. In the case of scenarios based upon safety failure or liability cases, simulation could augment routine recall exercises. Post exercise analysis and follow up is recommended as the next preparedness step.

CONCLUSION

Once details of a product safety incident or liability case get into the public domain, the rules change as key decision-makers attempt to manage escalating situations under the glare of public and media scrutiny.

The challenges in managing the resultant crisis demand sophisticated and far reaching operational procedures which act in concert with integrated communications to the array of internal and external audiences, who will be demanding answers, decisions and reassurance.

The pressures of these high profile situations are such that corporate management must get itself prepared through a comprehensive programme of preparedness planning and training. Only then will companies be ready to anticipate and handle product safety and liability incidents that escalate to crisis proportions.

13 Managing the producer's risk

INTRODUCTION

The legislative pressures for safe products continue to increase: strict liability, the New Approach Directives and now the General Product Safety Directive. But it is commonplace for some producers to assert that they already make safe products. The key question is: How do they know? An objective measurement is necessary to be able to answer the question accurately.

Measurements of quality are not always measurements of safety. A product can be satisfactory according to the first without being so against the second. For example, a lift stuck on the ground floor is safe, but it does not meet the quality standard for lifts because it will not go up and down when asked.

Insurance claims are sometimes quoted as evidence of safety, with a low claims record pointing to good product safety. While this may be true, the number of intermediaries between a victim of a defective product and the insurer can include an insurance broker, a loss adjuster, a forensic accountant and a solicitor. All are in the business of reaching a financial settlement and charge a fee for their advice. However, they are dealing with the past and examining a retrospective picture. As we have seen in the first part of this book, the future demands for product safety will be different.

The management of product safety will have to acquire a higher profile. We must ask: how safe should our products be? The supplementary question is: how will we know that we have reached the target? For many companies these commonly acknowledged goals will be subsumed into their traditional thinking. The status quo has to be preserved. Change spells danger.

The increasing demands made on producers suggests that fresh management thinking is advisable. A serious reappraisal of product safety management is required. Experience shows that for companies with liability-sensitive products a change of culture may be needed. The pages that follow seek to promote this approach. It is more a question of strategy than tactics. Some of the methodologies and techniques have appeared elsewhere.[1] Here we are concerned with general management principles.

[1] H. Abbott *Product Risk Management* (1992).

THE MORAL DILEMMAS

> The position of codes of ethics, mission statements and policies as a background to product safety are reviewed. The importance of training in difficult moral situations for top managers is recommended and the value of a human life in cost-benefit exercises is examined. The moves towards corporate responsibility can give rise to a moral dilemma when things go wrong.

Product safety is achieved by management. Management is performed by people. They make the decisions. Often these are straightforward for those with experience and knowledge. The difficulties arise when the situation is not clear cut. Then, whatever the experience and knowledge, another factor can appear in the frame. The ethics of the organisation will influence the course of events, for good or ill.

Corporate integrity is a luxury reserved for strong organisations. Consider some examples: Bearing in mind the weak bottom line, just how safe should we make this new product? Is it worth the damage to the company's image and market share, to recall a product in a borderline case? At a critical time in a national advertising campaign, should an extortionist be paid to go away? Is every widely used product claim capable of full substantiation? Do we admit liability for damage caused by a defective product, or deny it because of the risk of a flood of similar claims?

The management will take their lead from the top. In many companies, the most senior executives will have no direct part to play in product safety. Day to day responsibility will be delegated to a level or two down from them, until something goes wrong. Then top corporate morality can be exposed to the media spotlight. Carefully crafted statements will be made, attitudes will be adopted, blame swiftly sidestepped, reassuring press releases will appear and shoulders glanced over.

But what are these managers like? In the 1980s the picture that emerged from the U.S. was not attractive. A survey of 671 managers found that a quarter of them believed that ethics could impede a successful career. More than a half would bend the rules to get ahead.[2] Another survey revealed that 55 per cent of the American public considered that most corporate executives were dishonest. Nearly 60 per cent thought that white collar crime occurred very often.[3] During a ten-year period about two-thirds of America's top 500 companies were involved in some form of illegal behaviour.[4]

[2] "Ethics are nice, but they can be a handicap some executives declare," *Wall Street Journal*, September 8, 1982.

[3] *Hong Kong Business Today* reporting a *New York Times*/CBS poll, September 1985.

[4] S.W. Gellerman, "Why good managers make bad ethical choices," *Harvard Business Review*, July/August 1985.

In recent years the activities of some companies in the U.K. have done little to improve confidence in our industrial leaders. Examples are: the British Airways dirty tricks campaign against Virgin, the closure of the Bank of Credit and Commerce International, Polly Peck, County NatWest and so on. Groucho Marx said that honesty and fair dealing were the secret of success. He added, "If you can fake that you've got it made."

Codes of ethics

All this concerns corporate ethics. Moral philosophy is the discipline of what is morally good and bad, right and wrong. It essentially comprises issues fundamental to practical decision making, which is linked to many other fields. Ethics is occupied with moral values and not so much with factual knowledge. It is human conduct as it ought to be, rather than what it actually is.

Normative ethics is primarily concerned with establishing standards of conduct. It is associated with general theories of how we ought to live. A central question is whether human activities should be judged right or wrong solely according to their consequences. Applied ethics deals with practical moral problems, such as human rights, justice and the value of a human life. The latter is a question that can arise in the management of product safety, as we shall see.

Business ethics is important to product safety. The first course in the subject was offered by Harvard Business School in 1915. Yet, according to a speaker at a U.S. conference of the Risk and Insurance Management Society, 91 per cent of the world tells lies regularly at work and at home. But everyone believes that they belong to the other 9 per cent.[5]

Unfortunately unethical organisational practices are commonplace. A review of the Wall Street Journal[6] during one week provided over 60 articles, illustrating how moral issues are inherent in almost every business situation. The reports included conflicts of interest, hiding information, taking unfair advantage, rule violations and being an accessory to unethical acts.

How then should this issue be tackled? There is no lack of published advice, much of it to be found in the U.S. In the 1970s and the 1980s many U.S. corporations established their own code of ethics. This followed the realisation that it was no longer acceptable to retreat behind the refuge that an action was within the law. It had to be morally acceptable as well. There was the dual test of legal and moral acceptability. Society expected companies to be accountable for their actions. Profit was no longer the only goal.

A U.K. survey, by the Institute of Business Ethics, found that only 28 per cent of the 500 participants had published codes against 60 per cent

[5] "Ethics painted in shadows of gray" *Business Insurance*, May 13, 1991.

[6] T. O. Charrington, D. J. Charrington "A menu of moral issues. One week in the life of the *Wall Street Journal*", *Journal of Business Ethics*, 11 1992.

of U.S. companies. Among the U.K. companies that have brought in a code are British Telecom, Cadbury Schweppes, Lloyds Bank, Barclays Bank, the House of Fraser and British Airways with its Code of Business Conduct.[7]

The U.K. Institute of Management believes that "Ethics should be a top priority for every manager." even though it "can be far from an easy task in today's cut-throat world of business." A document[8] explaining its Code of Conduct and Guides to Professional Management Practice says: "Relying upon collective and corporate responsibility applied in policies is insufficient in itself." The manager still has a responsibility to ask questions and act on information within any direct sphere of authority. Paragraph 3 of the Code is:

> "The discharge of one's duties as a professional manager also involves the acceptance and habitual exercise of ethical values, among which a high place should be accorded to integrity, honesty, loyalty and fairness."

Personal values to which the manager adheres outside the organisation will be called into use or question, as well as values within it. In difficult cases the manager is advised to challenge assumptions regarding the organisation's expectations of him. The manager should be fully aware of the organisation's mission and purposes set out in a short, succinct statement from top management. Relationships with government and statutory bodies should not only be within the law but also be governed by exemplary standards of ethics.

There must be a regard for the short and long-term effects and possible consequences within society of present and proposed actions.

This is expanded to include:

> "A keen awareness of issues of strict liability should be developed. This may extend to the recall of an unexpectedly substandard product. Any consequences of actions that could reasonably be agreed to be bad should lead to discussions with a view to self-regulation of organisational practices. As a principle, the manager should have due regard to the expectation that the organisation has a short and long-term duty of care for individuals, communities and the physical environment."

The following part of the Guides says an organisation must "Communicate to the public truthfully and without intent to mislead by slanting or suppressing information."

One U.S. survey[9] found that in large companies with a code of ethics only 55 per cent had been distributed to their employees. Further, only 12 per cent provided ethics training. Some codes were found to demand a higher standard of conduct than individuals followed in their private

[7] *The Times*, September 25, 1993.
[8] S.M. Evers, "The Manager as a Professional", *The Institute of Management Corby* 1993
[9] T. Thompson, "Rhetoric and reality", *CA Magazine*, August 1992.

lives. The survey concluded that many companies took the easy way out with the visible trappings, but ignored the tough issues that got to the core of the business. Too often senior executives lacked the capability to make ethical choices, beyond the simplistic and obvious. Although they believed that they were people of the highest moral integrity, they did not have a developed sense of moral reasoning. There was a gap between the words and the actions. An example was the situation when a major product was found to be unsafe, in a way that was not evident when it was first marketed. Did the company insist that all was well, say nothing or go public with the truth?

There is one code that has been known since the sixteenth century. That much misunderstood man, Nicolo Machiavelli, in *The Prince*, set out a code of conduct. It was one that many subscribed to in practice but found repellent in theory. Successful governments were always ready to act ruthlessly to obtain their ends. He taught that, in the final resort, the rights and wrongs of an action could only be decided on what it was meant to achieve, and whether it successfully achieved it. Companies adopt similar principles, perhaps without appreciating that they do so.

Corporations are not rational beings. They are organisations established by human beings with the specific object of making a profit. As law and morality are not always synonymous, one authority has suggested that a company should establish a Moral Audit Committee.[10] It would be concerned with identifying and appraising aspects of the company's operations which may cause harm. The guiding principles would be found in the code of ethics. On the disclosure of information "the goal of communication is to tell the truth under all circumstances." This no doubt admirable precept makes several assumptions, one of which is that the truth is actually known so that it can be told.

The practical problem is how to ensure compliance with the code. One source[11] says that there are three areas that a corporation's leaders should address personally:

1. Commit to the goal of ethical conduct and serve as a role model.
2. Strive toward openness.
3. Establish and implement rules, policies and procedures to achieve the goal.

But such altruistic aims present a dilemma in practice. One expert says:

> "Decent instincts are not always strong enough to hold up under the adverse and complex conditions managers inevitably encounter . . . management concerns about ethics have seemed to centre on two great fears: the fear that living up to ethical obligations will impose an immediate cost on the bottom line, and that employees who adopt unethical standards will pose a financial liability down the road . . . at

[10] S.A. Ostapski, C.H. Isaacs, "Corporate Moral Responsibility and the Moral Audit", *Journal of Business Ethics*, 11 1992.

[11] M.M. Dolecheck, C.C. Dolecheck, "Ethics: take it from the top" *Business*, 12 January/March 1989.

the same time the fear of ethics costing too much prevents the formulation of an effective response."[12]

Mission statements and policies

An increasing number of U.K. companies are adopting a mission statement. This may not be as ambitious as a code of ethics. It can set out in simple terms what the company is aiming to achieve. Some are called policy statements, which may be supported by guidelines. Often they are commendably short.

The idea behind a mission statement is to provide the foundation on which other actions can be built. For example, strategic planning for subsidiary operations or determining a company's focus when dealing with complex situations. Small firms seldom have a mission statement or, at least, only develop one when a crisis strikes.

The importance of a quality function may be included in a mission statement. The quality manual for BS EN ISO 9000 should have its own commitment by the chief executive. The Health and Safety at Work, etc., Act 1974, section 2(3) requires a written policy for every firm with five or more employees: ". . . each firm must write its own policy according to its own need." A product safety policy is being adopted by companies as legislation gets more onerous and products become more sophisticated.

So far we have considered codes of ethics, mission statements and policies. This is the received wisdom from the literature and the gurus. The way in which the experts say it should be done. The public face of corporate concern as fashioned for dissemination. But what of these altruistic aims in practice? In the management of product safety?

The crux of the whole problem can be stated very simply. When the consequences are serious the theory and the practice do not always agree. Usually, when a big product liability incident looms pragmatism takes over. No-one suggests that the code of ethics should be sent for to indicate the actions that should be taken. Indeed, it is unlikely that the company's leaders will give it a second's thought before taking action. Subsequently the gloss of hindsight may be able to make sure that the horse was to be found in its rightful position before the cart, from the very beginning. Because the code will have been launched with a flourish. Grave leaders will have nodded solemnly over its portentous words. They will have made imposing speeches to the assembled multitude below. Acclaim will have been heard.

The present writer has never known a reference to a code of ethics in a product liability incident. Even when, on one occasion, it was fixed to the wall in reception to meet all who arrived to manage the incident. In some cases the leaders acted in a very ethical manner. Agonising deeply

[12] L.L. Nash, "Good Intentions Aside" Harvard Business School Press, 1993.

over the best action to take. These impressive occasions were more a reflection of the ethics of the individuals making the decision, than any code or mission statement. Corporate morality and codes of ethics were not part of the scenario.

However, the future presents a different aspect from the past. Legislation imposes greater demands on producers and consumers are far more aware of their rights today. The rules of the game are changing so that the way in which the game is played will have to change too. It is time for some soul-searching by the leaders of companies. Responsibility for product safety cannot be delegated and paying lip service to it is no longer enough. The public are much more cynical now about what they are told or led to believe. They have been conned too often to be otherwise: the Irish bishop with a 17–year-old illegitimate son; the judge who smuggled drink; the government minister whose private life was less than some thought it should have been; the policeman who burgled on his beat. Then there was the Governor of the Bank of England telling everyone that they had to observe pay restraint, but took a 17 per cent pay rise himself.

We must confine ourselves to the problems of product safety. It is certainly advisable for a company to establish a product safety policy and make sure that it is widely publicised. The words should be the result of considerable consultation within the company, with contributions sought from a range of employees.The need to broadcast serious management commitment almost goes without saying.

The policy will have to be supported by a strategy and tactics, which are discussed in this book. A policy by itself is useless. Each company has to develop its own scheme of things. Ready-made solutions contain ready-made weaknesses. When all this has been done it must be tested. Unless, that is, circumstances arrive which present the real thing.

Training exercises

Importantly, top managers should run exercises to measure their response to difficult moral scenarios. This is not something that can be learned from a book or a lecture. The best training has to be that which is as close to real life as possible.

One well tried method uses a scenario written around a company's actual products, people, organisation and market. It is fiction but can be based on a current product safety difficulty, if that is appropriate. The story will have incomplete and second-hand information, red herrings and the occasional lie — just like real life. One morning a dozen or so senior managers assemble and are divided into two separate, equally balanced syndicates. The scenario is unfolded before them in a paper-fed exercise. At specific points decisions have to be made, action taken and the risk scored. Later the two syndicates come back together and each presents to the other the results of its deliberations. Frequently, this is a most revealing time as diverging decisions and action will have been taken about the same situation. The risk scores may well illustrate it in a clear manner. The advantage is that the exercise is heuristic. There is no expert or consultant to say what *should* have happened. The managers learn from themselves. This is of great importance as it is their company after all.

A number of simulation exercises will ensure that the senior managers appreciate the moral problems — and their personal reaction to them. It is not so much that they will teach themselves the right things to do, but rather to avoid the wrong things. There can be no universal guide to the awkward product safety incident. Each one is different.

Cost–benefit exercises

One ethical problem which it is appropriate to include here is: what is the value of a human life? Every product can be made safer at a price. How much will a company pay to improve the safety of its product? Or, to put it more directly, by how much will it be prepared to reduce its profit to increase the safety of its product? At this stage we are concerned with the moral dilemma.

The landmark case is the much quoted *Ford Pinto* car. Very briefly, the incident happened in May 1972 in California, when Richard Grimshaw was offered a lift by a family friend in her new Pinto car. There was an accident on Interstate Route 15. The petrol tank was located 7 inches from the rear bumper. It ruptured in the crash and the car burst into flames. The family friend died and her passenger only just survived. In 1978, in the first of a series of court actions, he was awarded $127.8 million, of which $125 million was punitive damages. What is frequently overlooked is that these figures were reduced on appeal, to $6 million for compensatory damages and $3.5 million for punitive damages.

During the case one of Ford's retired senior design engineers gave evidence. He spoke of the cost–benefit exercise which had been carried out during the design of the Pinto. Later a U.S. magazine, *Mother Jones*, published some of the documents. A life was valued at $200,000, an injury at $67,000 and a vehicle at $700, to give a "benefit" of $49.5 million. The cost of moving the petrol tank to a safer position was $131 million, at $11 a vehicle, see **Table 13.1**. It was not cost-effective. Typical of the headlines of the day was "Ford goes on trial for homicide after car crash deaths."

But the cost–benefit exercise is a familiar technique widely used by engineers. Each one has to be evaluated in context and care is needed in

Table 13.1 The Ford Pinto cost-benefit exercise

Benefits

Savings — 180 burn deaths, 180 serious burn injuries, 2,100 burned vehicles
Unit cost — $200,000 per death, $67,000 per injury, $700 per vehicle
Total benefit — 180 × ($200,000) + 180 × ($67,000) + 2,100 × ($700) = $49.5 million

Costs

Sales — 11 million cars, 1.5 million light trucks
Unit cost — $11 per car, $11 per truck
Total cost — 11,000,000 × ($11) + 1,500,000 × ($11) = $137 million

selecting the parameters applied. We have to beware of safety mania. The essential principle must be that the money available for safety is spent in proportion to the risk. It assumes that a finite sum is available for safety and that the size of the risk is known.

For some organisations the information is available. British Rail has considerable experience of this type of cost-benefit exercise. They say that if it costs more than £2 million to avoid a death they will rarely go ahead. In road schemes the figure is much less, at £683,000. In public transport each progressive advance in safety saves fewer lives at greater cost. In the U.S., according to *Fortune*,[13] the value of a life varies with the organisation making the assessment. It ranges from $2 million to $5 million, from $1 million to $7.5 million and to a low figure of $650,000.

These figures relate to a statistical life and not an identified one. The traditional approach to valuing life equated one to the value of a person's future stream of economic output, plus a notional sum for the pain, grief and suffering felt by those affected by a given person's death. This approach is being revised. Named family lives are priceless, as are those that appear in the media. The five-year-old, blond haired, blue eyed girl, called Mary, who needs a large sum for a life saving operation, will attract the money once the media run the story. Another, in a similar condition but unknown, may well die in obscurity and become merely a fatality statistic.

For the producer, however, the cost–benefit exercise will contain one major element that has to be taken into account: market share. Quite apart from societal responsibilities, the company will be concerned about the impact on sales of a serious product safety incident. The pragmatic approach is to conform to the state of the art, the law and keep the risks as low as reasonably practicable. Always remembering that no product can be immune from risk. Some of the residual risks have to be accepted, because business is founded on risk. The skill lies in choosing which risks to retain and which to reduce or transfer to third parties.

[13] D. Seligman "How much money is your life worth?" *Fortune*, March 3, 1986.

Corporate responsibility

One attempt to bring home corporate responsibility following a major disaster failed. As the *Herald of Free Enterprise* ro-ro ferry was leaving Zeebrugge on March 6, 1987 the sea entered the car deck through the bow doors, which had been left open. The vessel capsized and 192 people died. Subsequently a charge of corporate manslaughter was brought against P & O European Ferries. After 27 days in the Central Criminal Court the judge directed the jury to acquit the defendants on all charges. In his eyes the prosecution case was unsustainable.

The question of corporate governance has been addressed by the Cadbury Report, issued on December 1, 1992. The Stock Exchange expects compliance with the Code of Best Practice by member firms or an explanation of failure to comply. It sets out a framework of checks and balances that should govern the way in which a company is run. It emphasises that the company should be run by the board, that roles should be clearly defined, and that independent non-executive directors should have a powerful voice in monitoring its affairs. No one individual should have "unfettered power of decision."

A different suggestion for identifying responsibility was in a proposal published in 1991. The London law firm of Davies Arnold Cooper proposed a Corporate Accountability Bill. It provided that corporations themselves should be liable for the acts of their managers. Companies would have to carry out annual audits of their safety systems and publish independent auditor's reports.

The Centre for Business and Public Sector Ethics at Cambridge was established in 1988, and is endorsed by Adrian Cadbury. It has two aims:

1. The study of ethical dilemmas and conflicts within business and public sector organisations.
2. Encouraging and pinpointing priorities for the expression of corporate social responsibility.

The London Business School has a Department of Business Ethics and Social Responsibility. In the U.S. there are 500 courses on business ethics and virtually all the country's business schools teach the subject.

But it seems that these initiatives have little influence, because they may be out of touch with the reality of business. The problem with the advice often given is that it points to moral absolutism. In other words, the executive always has to do the right thing, even if it wrecks the company.

The moral dilemma can arise when the balance goes wrong. It is then that training in ethical decision making will come into play. Then that the code or mission statement or policy will be put to the test. And so will the moral integrity of the executives who established it. A time for standing up for counting to take place.

"The great Austrian wine scandal" Case History on page 430 shows what can happen when ethics are ignored.

A not-so-hot line on ethics

The long salami of *la polizia* has collared various advertising executives in Italy, including one from Young & Rubicam, who was detained for allegedly paying a kickback to obtain part of a government advertising campaign. This would not be funny except that Y & R operates a special "ethics hotline".

A spokesman in New York said: "There is a telephone number for staff about ethical limits; they can check appropriateness of action and check policy."

So what about the guy in Italy? "Ah, yes," said the spokesman. Apparently he is expected to be released soon — which might give him a chance to call the hotline before it's too late.

Sunday Times
July 4, 1993

THE RISK MANAGEMENT STORY

Risk management is seen as being dominated by insurance considerations, with little active contribution to risk control. In relation to product safety, total quality management and BS EN ISO 9000 have their limitations while an appreciation of the human factor is in its infancy. An in-house champion of product safety can make a major difference to producing safer products.

Products are made safer by reducing their risks. The overall means by which this can be achieved is called risk management — product risk management. One of the many definitions of risk management is: the discipline for living with the possibility that future events may cause harm.[14] Another is that risk is the compound estimate of the probable frequency, probable severity and public perception of harm. The theory is concerned with the key elements of risk assessment, risk control and risk financing. But the theory and the practice rarely coincide.

The problem for risk management in industry is that it is usually a euphemism for insurance management. Many a risk manager in industry achieved his title by substituting "Risk" for "Insurance" on his office door. Then, instead of developing the classic principles he just went on dealing with the company's insurance brokers. Of course, there are exceptions, but there are not too many of them.

The idea of risk management can be traced back to the U.S. in the 1950s. In the following decade came the concept of the cost of risk and ten years later the Europeans started to talk about risk management. A holistic approach was recommended and a range of disciplines was developed.

Practitioners formed themselves into representative organisations which have become world-wide. The biggest is the U.S. Risk & Insurance Management Society with over 3500 members; in the U.K. there is the Association of Insurance & Risk Managers in Industry and Commerce; there is the South African Risk & Insurance Management Association and the Australian Institute of Risk Management; and the French have the Association pour le Management des Risques et des Assurances de l'Enterprise.

A new concept of "risk partnership" has been proposed[15] as being a more correct representation of the relationship between insured and insurer, than the more generally used term "risk transfer". This is in line with the future concept of risk management. Its role may not be limited

[14] H.F. Kloman, "Rethinking Risk Management", *The Geneva Papers on Risk & Insurance*, 17 No. 64 July 1992.

[15] J.W. Reid, "The Cost of Risk and the Concept of Risk Partnership", Management of Risks in Engineering Conference, Basel, The Geneva Association, November 1993.

to the integrated management of pure risks but extended to an organisation's global management of risk, arising from both external and internal sources. This strategic dimension of risk management points to top management's responsibility for it.

A discussion of future trends in risk management[16] identified a number of issues. It should be a concurrent engineering function, not a separate specialist's task. Because risk managers are often also insurance buyers without peer control they may have blurred vision. There is a lack of qualitative data as insurance companies do not publish or share loss statistics. The gap between insured risks and insurable risks is increasing while risk management is a long term issue, as is company survival.

The problems with risk management

An academic view of risk management is provided by a Royal Society report on risk.[17] It steps back from industrial risk management and draws attention to the lines of thinking that may be influential in the formation of public policy. It says that, as there are basic differences in terminology, the term risk management has no single meaning. At a general level it has three essential elements:

- setting goals;
- interpreting information;
- taking action to influence human behaviour or physical structures or both.

Some have argued that risk assessment and risk management are overlapping but separate tasks. In public policy, risk management refers to quantifying estimated risks and evaluating them against likely benefits. A provocative argument in the report is that disasters and systems failures often look "predictable" only with hindsight: "The implication is that at the margin risk management regimes should be designed to promote resilience against unsuspected catastrophes, rather than rely on seeing them coming." The "Titanic effect" postulates that attempting to place emphasis on anticipating risks may itself contribute to the crisis it seeks to avoid.

Quantitative risk assessment is criticised by some who are sceptical of claims to be able to quantify risks with high degrees of accuracy, particularly where changing human behaviour can make a crucial difference. See page 336. There are sharp limitations in the current state of knowledge about how risk is handled in human organisations. There are considerable variations in corporate safety policies in transnational organisations, for even apparently contradictory approaches seem to yield similar outcomes.

[16] "Future Trends in Risk Management Discussion", Management of Risks in Engineering Conference, Basel, The Geneva Association, November 1993.
[17] "Risk: Analysis, Perception and Management", The Royal Society, London 1992.

In dealing with product safety in industry the weaknesses of risk management are those that face the activity as a whole. Managers now have to deal with a whole mix of exposures including social, economic, regulatory and competitive factors. The increasing amount of legislation from the E.C., as we have seen in the first part of this book, adds to the load. To cope with this situation one authority[18] has proposed five steps for the development of risk management:

1. Risk communication The over-riding objective should be the aim of communicating risks intelligently to other managers. It will be important to avoid the tendency to over-emphasise risks with low probabilities and under-estimate those with high ones. Few companies make a serious attempt to measure their product risks in a logical and structured manner, let alone disseminate the information.

2. Consolidation of disciplines The fragmentation of risk management has to be prevented. The various aspects tend to focus on their own specialisation, which excludes the possibility of cross-fertilisation. For example, for product liability pre-loss activities do not always link up with potential post-loss actions.

3. Long-term thinking The business climate today encourages short-termism. We should be concerned with the long-term costs of today's actions. The E.C. Directive on Liability for Defective Products has a 10-year cut-off for the possibility of a product liability action.

4. Catastrophe management The risk of catastrophe seems to be increasing. Yet there is an unwillingness to consider worst case situations. Perrier's multi-national recall cost over £125 million and a serious loss of market share, even though the product was no danger to health.

5. Role of the insurance industry Despite assertions to the contrary, the industry has put little real emphasis on risk control and risk research. Underwriters have generally failed to develop strong risk assessment skills. Few underwriters have an understanding of the formal techniques of product hazard analysis and risk assessment. These shackles have to be thrown off if risk management is to develop fully.

These views were reflected by one expert[19] who said:

> The growing disillusionment of British risk managers, with the way the country's insurance industry is run and regulated, [has] channelled itself into a determined search for new risk management paradigms, reflecting a greater emphasis on front-end risk prevention and as little reliance on traditional insurance as possible.

[18] H.F. Kloman, "Rethinking Risk Management", *The Geneva Papers on Risk & Insurance*, 17 No. 64 July 1992.

[19] C. Best, "U.K. Risk Managers Seek New Horizons", *Risk Insurance*, June 1993.

Cost of risk

The total cost of a risk management function in an organisation is the cost of risk. It has been defined as the sum of:

- Net insurance premiums;
- Unreimbursed losses;
- Risk control and risk prevention; and
- Administrative costs.

This cost of risk concept has been studied in the U.S. a number of times since 1979. Buried in a report[20] on 847 organisations is some surprising information about risk management departments in the U.S. The average had only 4.67 people for an average of 11,000 employees and an average revenue of $1.7 billion. Missing from the list of activities, for which they were responsible, are the essential functions of risk control and risk prevention. The introduction to the study says:

> "Since in the past we received few responses to questions regarding risk control costs, risk control expenditures were not requested in the survey and are therefore excluded from the data presented in this report."

One can but wonder whether the poor response was due to the fact that there was no risk control responsibility and that the respondents were in fact insurance departments — regardless of their title.

The difficulty with the cost of risk control is knowing where to stop. It can include all or part of: a quality function, research and development, purchasing, production, distribution, legal activities, training, insurance, human resources — indeed virtually every function in a company can make a contribution to a greater or lesser extent. Another aspect is an examination of direct and indirect costs, which again produces insurmountable difficulties in reaching a firm conclusion.

Here, then, is the problem with risk management in industry. It is also the problem with product risk management. No-one knows what it really costs. The result is that product safety is often left to the quality function, almost by default. Because nobody else claimed responsibility, the quality manager took it over, along with all the other odds and ends. When this happens product safety becomes a quality problem, whereas many other factors have a part to play. The wider remit of product risk management is ignored, its elements scattered among other parts of the company. Consequently there is no consolidation, no synergy, no input from public relations, company secretarial, marketing, sales, and so on.

Total Quality Management and BS EN ISO 9000

Companies that claim to have TQM often believe that they are very unlikely to have a product safety problem. But "quick fix expectations

[20] Tillinghast, *Cost of Risk Survey* 1991.

are misplaced. TQM is, after all, a radical new approach to business management. The true benefits will be longer term."[21] The fact is that TQM cannot confer immunity from product liability exposures, however well it is implemented. Human beings are involved and they are fallible, see below.

Total Quality Management requires a dramatic culture change from top to bottom in a company, if it is to be worthwhile. Unlike BS EN ISO 9000, it focuses on the customer. Surveys by major international consultancies have thrown doubt on the effectiveness of TQM. A cross-section of 100 British companies in industry and commerce, with employees ranging from 50 to 10,000, contributed to one survey of Total Quality.[22] The report says "The concept of Total Quality as the way to improve business performance belies the fact that, reportedly, 80 per cent of their programmes fail". The report concluded that the emphasis of many approaches was too much on quality and not enough on total. For those companies where TQM is successful safer products will result, if only because that is what the customers will demand.

The new British Quality Foundation has embraced TQM with fervour. The organisation has prestigious leaders, the backing of the Department of Trade and promotes the U.K. Quality Award for best practice in Total Quality Management. It remains to be seen how successful this latest initiative will be and whether it will have any impact on product safety. The Japanese Kaizen philosophy, like TQM, aims at total consumer satisfaction by continuous improvement through quality in gradual stages, without any significant incremental costs.

No standard has received as much publicity as BS EN ISO 9000. It must be pointed out that it cannot *of itself* guarantee safety. Indeed, a company fully conforming to the standard can successfully produce a defective product. This is because it is the manufacturer who decides on the specification to which his product must conform. Of course, specifications have been wrong before now and certification bodies cannot expect to be expert in the detail of every product. A number of major companies, who make safety-critical products, have not sought conformance to the standard. They and others still audit their suppliers whether they have BS EN ISO 9000 or not. The standard has value in ensuring management disciplines and generating data which can make a significant contribution to product safety.

The human factor

All the words about risk management and its techniques have one fundamental weakness. They tell us precious little about the contribution people, rather than machines, make to product safety. In any

[21] B. Witcher, J. Whyte, "The Adoption of Total Quality Management in Northern England", Durham University Business School, 1992.

[22] A.T. Kearney, "Total Quality: Time to Take Off the Rose Tinted Spectacles", London, 1992.

industrial system human beings have to be involved, sooner or later. Even the 100 per cent mechanical or electronic checks need people in their design, manufacture, maintenance and calibration. A mistake on the part of human beings has to be a factor in product failure. It is often called operator error. The provision of fail-to-safe design or redundancy to accommodate primary failure has the same weakness, albeit to a lesser extent.

In attempting to predict human reliability, psychologists recognise that people doggedly persist in making the facts of a situation fit their existing frameworks. It is called a mind-set and is adopted in preference to devising new frameworks to fit the facts. There can be a pattern of faulty diagnosis, followed by the impeccable implementation of inappropriate decisions, stubbornly resistant to contra-indications. In everyday life an example is when we go to search for the car keys and discover we are unlocking the garden shed.

Data on operator error suggest that a reliable operator is 99.99 per cent perfect in a routine job, but much less reliable in emergencies. Techniques are being developed to assign numbers to the probability of human error. They are usually called Human Reliability Assessment (HRA).[23] For example, sequences of letters or digits are entered on keyboards in many companies by human beings thousands of times a day. Some of these will have product safety implications, such as Statistical Process Control. It has been found by HRA that the probability of error is about three times as great with digits as it is with letters. A safety-related keyboard on a production line should use letters whenever possible in preference to numbers, to help reduce the possibility of operator error.

Two of the factors in HRA are important to product safety. The first relates to the requirement to assess systems during the design stage, which will allow potentially hazardous operations to be avoided at an early point. The alternative is to design the system regardless of the human factor and only realise the unacceptability of a hazard when a safety incident occurs. The second is that in some circumstances human functions are of special importance for safety. This will occur when the overall rate of failure is dominated by the value assessed for human error. When this happens extra non-human precautions must be taken, or the human element reduced, or both.

Because people are always around, they may not be taken into account when safety-critical operations are established. Conversely, when something does go wrong, it is often easiest to blame the softest target, the human being. The fact of the matter is no-one really knows for certain the contribution people, rather than machines, make to product safety.

[23] "Study Group of Human Factors second report: Human Reliability Assessment — a Critical Overview." Advisory Committee on Safety of Nuclear Installations. Health and Safety Commission (HMSO London 1991).

An in-house champion

Establishing a product safety programme can be difficult. To some it will be a new idea and as such must be viewed with great circumspection. Rather like the apprehensive manner in which one creeps towards a stalled firework. The establishment will see it as a threat to well-preserved empires. Naturally, there will be no overt opposition to the proposals for a new way of reducing the product risks. Indeed, they will be openly welcomed, if not actually accepted and acted upon. People rely on the tried and tested methods and are reluctant to change them. This is particularly true of large corporations, which in some ways resemble a very large ship. Once committed on a set course it takes a long time to alter it. Which is understandable if past performance indicates that the adopted methods have been successful — so far.

But, as we have already seen in the first part of this book, the future is going to be different from what has gone before. The past may no longer be a satisfactory guide to the future. A serious review of how product safety is managed becomes necessary. It looks as though the usual risk management ways will be of little help. Total Quality Management and BS EN ISO 9000 have a contribution to make but cannot in themselves be the answer.

To establish and maintain a product safety programme needs a champion. He will gather together the principles from others and assemble them to fit the unique exposure of his company. There is no point in reinventing the wheel when so much information is already available. He may come from a variety of disciplines: quality, marketing, technical, financial or even (in one case) human resources. His function is less important than his determination. Three examples illustrate the point.

An effective product safety programme in one company is led by its champion who works alongside the quality man. Together they have had a major impact on both product safety and quality. They operate in such a way that each complements the other, while at the same time each stands clear in his own right. Their reporting lines are separate and only meet in the office of the chief executive. The products are to be found in highly demanding environments which do not tolerate failure. It is not surprising that such success has led to an increasing market share. An instance of the fact that consistent and demonstrable product safety can be profitable.

A very different approach is to be found in a company which has all the technical functions, apart from production, under one man. Product safety is paramount and the various departments have it at the top of their priorities, a fact which the champion keeps in high profile. This is not to say that other responsibilities are ignored, rather that they have to be fulfilled almost as a matter of course. Unlike the previous example the production process is simple and the product low tech.

The champion in a third company is the managing director who has reporting to him a conventional management structure. He sees his main function as making sure that the products are as safe as possible. To achieve this aim he relentlessly probes, questions and checks the activities of those who report to him. He personally follows up any deviations that could affect safety. He expresses his commitment by saying "If I am not seen to give product safety top priority I cannot expect anyone else to do the same."

The three companies seek the same objective but reach it by different management structures. The principles they use are very similar, although the products could not be more different. Nothing about product safety can be set in concrete: suppliers change, specifications get revised, plant and equipment are replaced and improved, markets shift, customers' requirements alter and legislation becomes tougher. Therefore, a product safety programme must be active and dynamic if it is to succeed. To make this happen a champion is needed to keep up the pressure. The essential characteristic is unremitting persistence. Product safety is a journey not a destination.

THE PRESSURES ON PRODUCERS

> Producers are caught between the opposing pressures of new legislation to make products safer and strict liability for the damage caused by defective products. Regulatory bodies have increased powers to protect purchasers. Codes of practice, benchmarking and standards are looked at in connection with product safety.

Figure 13.1 The pressure on producers

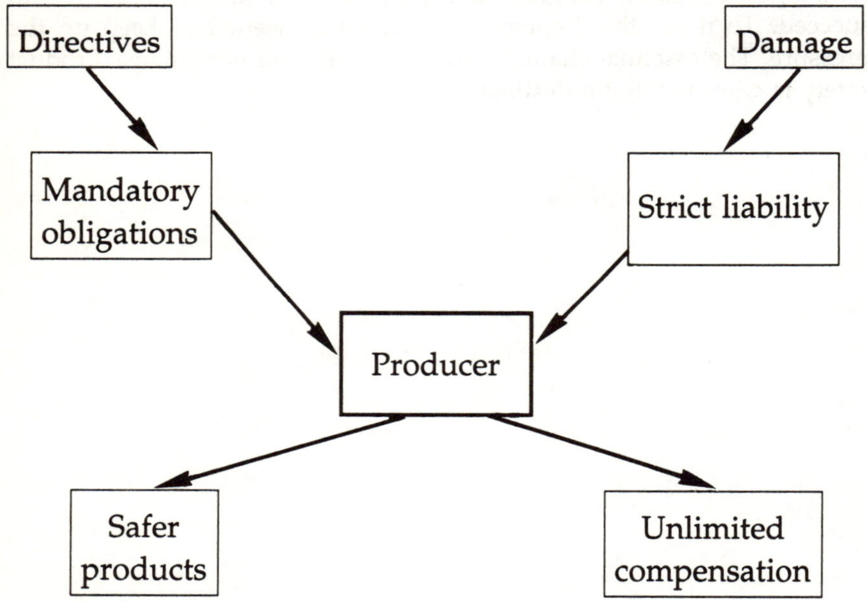

A company concerned with products faces pressures from two opposite directions, — see **Figure 13.1.** On the one hand there are the ordinances aimed at making products safer. On the other hand there is strict liability and the threat of unlimited damages, for the harm caused by a defective product, and the possibility of a product recall. The producer is caught in a pincer movement between the two. The one seeks to protect the user, while the other provides a route for him to obtain compensation if harm does occur. Either way it can cost the producer money. In addition, shareholders have to be satisfied, market share protected and good relations maintained with the media. The overall effect is to improve product safety as producers look to reduce their exposures caused by product defects. Some of the pressures are examined below.

Directives

In the first part of this book both general and product-specific directives were reviewed. Their implementation across the Member States is by no means uniform, which complicates matters for exporters. In addition, judicial systems vary as does the legal culture in different countries. The E.U. has eleven official languages. Directives for individual products can be considerable documents. For example, a vehicle has to conform to some 50 directives; the 1976 Cosmetic Directive was amended 24 times up to 1992. All this involves producers in costs, from keeping up with the paperwork to implementing its requirements. Following the progress of just one directive from first proposal to final adoption can need stamina and determination. The E.C. Directive on Liability for Defective Products had a gestation period of eleven years and the General Product Safety Directive one of four years. The confusing CE mark is part of the provisions of the New Approach Directives. It has no explicit implication for product safety and is not a safety mark, despite a popular view to the contrary.

Standards

Conforming to a standard does not necessarily confer immunity from a product liability action and take the pressure off a producer. Some standards have little or nothing to do with safety. The complexity of the position is illustrated by the way in which the safety provisions of the General Product Safety Directive interrelate with those of other directives, which deal with safety. The heavily promoted BS EN ISO 9000 is not concerned with product safety. It provides for a management system capable of assuring production in accordance with a specification. It does not determine the quality or fitness for purpose of a product.

Generally speaking, a standard can be seen as a rebuttable presumption of non-defectiveness. This means that conformance to the provisions of a standard may be an advantage. But the standard itself may be wrong, inadequate or not address safety at all. An example of a standard being called into question was the recall by Boots of a Caterpulla toy in November 1993. The company said that there was a problem with a small plastic bobble that could become detached during play and "although the toy meets all current British and European toy safety standards (specifically BS 5665 1989, part 1/EN71, part 1) we have decided to withdraw the current stock."

Under Part II of the Consumer Protection Act 1987, the Secretary of State used to have the power to approve standards as benchmarks for safety, in respect of the general safety requirement. Compliance with an approved standard ensured that the reference goods automatically satisfied the general safety requirement. Seventy-seven standards or parts of standards were so approved in the five years from 1988. The

Regulations implementing the E.C. Directive on General Product Safety revoked these provisions and cancelled the approval of the standards.

Regulation 10 implements the criteria which may be used in assessing the conformity of a product with the general safety requirement. They do not permit the introduction or continuation of the *absolute* defence which compliance with an approved standard provided. Instead compliance with the appropriate standard, code of practice, state of the art and technology, etc will carry a rebuttable *presumption* that the product is safe. If a product complies with a harmonised standard of safety, that is mandated under an E.C. directive, the supplier has the *assurance* that the product meets the relevant safety requirements set out in that directive. In these circumstances the general safety requirement of the General Product Safety Directive will not be applicable.

An independent study, commissioned by the Consumer Safety Unit of the Department of Trade and Industry, showed that consumer groups had mixed reactions to the value of the standard approvals system for consumers. Neither was there any clear evidence that the approvals system was considered indispensable by manufacturers and suppliers in general.

Some organisations operate a system of certification marks for product compliance. Examples are the Kitemark of the British Standards Institution, the Association of Short-Circuit Testing Authorities' diamond certification symbol and the British Electrotechnical Approvals Board with its "BEAB Approved" mark.

Regulatory bodies

Today regulatory bodies have increased powers to take action to protect consumers and others. The local Trading Standards Officers and Environmental Health Officers are examples of the regulators who can apply pressure on producers. There are 126 local Trading Standards Departments. Under Part II of the Consumer Protection Act 1987, as described in Chapter 5, producers who offend against the safety regulations can be served with a prohibition notice or a notice to warn. In another field, as described in Chapter 6, the Health and Safety Executive enforces the provisions of the Health and Safety at Work, etc., Act 1974.

An example illustrates what can happen. A local Consumer Services Department had a product tested against the relevant British Standard, following a complaint from a user. It was found to contravene the Low Voltage Electrical Equipment (Safety) Regulations 1989. A Trading Standards Officer visited the producer for a series of interviews, under the Police and Criminal Evidence Act 1984. The producer was prosecuted in a magistrates' court and fined nearly £1,000 and costs. The consequence was that the product had to be recalled. The recall advertisement, in 13 newspapers, cost £40,000. The total cost was several times that amount, when lost sales were taken into account.

The co-ordination of enforcing legislation at local level in the U.K. is carried out through LACOTS,[24] the Local Authorities Coordinating Body on Food and Trading Standards. The organisation was created in 1978 and, strictly speaking, has no power to force local authorities to act in a particular way. The management committee consists of elected members of the local authorities of England, Wales and Scotland. The Home Authority Principle was introduced by LACOTS. The concept makes enforcement authorities responsible for the goods and services provided by companies in their area. The Principle includes a form of arbitration aimed at resolving disputes between local authorities. The lion's share of funding for Trading Standards Departments comes from the Department of Trade and Industry.

A European approach has closely followed LACOTS. The Product Safety Enforcement Forum of Europe (PROSAFE)[25] comprises representatives of European enforcement officers, with the European Commission and the EFTA secretariat having observer status. The aim of PROSAFE is the coordination of the provision, collection and exchange of information, uniform enforcement action and the solution of problems connected with harmonised enforcement.

There is one potential pressure which it is impossible to quantify at present. Under the General Product Safety Directive the E.C. can set up a Committee on Product Safety Emergencies (Article 10). This would seem to be a supra-national body with draconian powers: "Member States shall take all necessary measures to implement the decisions adopted [by the Committee] under this procedure within less than 10 days" (Article 11.3).[26] It remains to be seen just how this body will be used and how it will exercise its powers.

Codes of practice, guidelines, good manufacturing practice

Many industries have codes of practice under a variety of names. They are recommendations, usually drawn up by an authoritative body, describing what is accepted as good practice in particular circumstances. They may or may not be mandatory. Some are internationally acceptable. An example is that for the design, selection of materials, manufacturing and operating procedures for the production of chemical plant items for onerous conditions. The Codex Alimentarius sets world-wide standards for food production and processing. It was established in 1963 by the Food and Agricultural Organisation of the UN and the World Food Organisation.

There are codes of practice for product recall by the Society of Motor Manufacturers and Traders, the Association of the British Pharmaceutical Industry, the Bicycle Association of Great Britain, the British Retail Consortium and the Association of Manufacturers of Domestic Electrical

[24] See page 100.
[25] See page 79.
[26] See page 91.

Equipment. There is no complete list of U.K. codes for food, although the Institute of Food Science and Technology has identified some 400, whose subjects vary from protective clothing to mechanically separated meat. Contributions came from 131 different organisations. There are over a dozen statutory codes relating to food issued by the Ministry of Agriculture, Fisheries and Food and the Department of Health.

The effect of a code will obviously depend on individual circumstances. A guide is provided by the Food and Drink Good Manufacturing Practice of the Institute of Food Science and Technology. The Food Safety Act 1990 provides a defence of due diligence and the taking of all reasonable precautions. In a product safety case, the ability to prove that all reasonable steps had been taken would be assisted by showing that the provisions of the Good Manufacturing Practice had been followed.

As with standards, a relevant code of practice should be treated as the minimum that should be achieved.

Benchmarking

One of the main pressures on producers is the competition. The "best-in-class" can set the target by which the other players are judged. Benchmarking is the means by which a company measures its performance against the best and then seeks to emulate or exceed it. The best industry practices are used to establish operating targets. A comparatively recent phenomenon, it has generated articles, books, conferences and, of course, consultants.

Short Brothers of Belfast is the world's oldest aircraft manufacturer, and part of Canada's Bombardier Corporation since 1989. In 1991 Shorts introduced benchmarking as part of its quality management strategy. Of two benchmarking studies, the more ambitious compared seven of Shorts manufacturing procedures with 28 worldwide competitors. Overall the survey found that Shorts were as competitive as any in the world in five of the seven procedures. The other two demanded the re-engineering of operating systems and practices.

Motorola tackled defect rates by the application of benchmarking. The U.S. manufacturer of communication equipment, computer systems and semi-conductors employs some 100,000 people world-wide. In 1981 the chairman, Bob Galvin, launched his campaign to "Meet the Japanese Challenge." The motivation came from a lack of success compared with Japanese television sets, car radios and memory chips. The target was a ten-fold improvement in quality in five years. This was achieved, but by then the Japanese had moved on. It led Motorola to their Total Customer Satisfaction campaign and the aim of Six Sigma Quality by 1992. The latter was a reduction of the defect rate to 3.4 per million units.

The company took big advertisements in the press to announce that this was the aim, in order to meet the Japanese competition. When the campaign started the defect rate was 6,000 per million. Motorola freely admits that it missed its target, but it got the defect rate down to 40 per million, although some operations did achieve the target. The reduction resulted in a saving of $700 million in manufacturing costs. The next target was to cut manufacturing defects by 90 per cent every two years throughout the 1990s and to get the defect rate down to one per million by the year 2001.

There is a concept similar to benchmarking which has a place in strict liability. This is the state of the art defence in Part I of the Consumer Protection Act 1987. Section 4(1)(e) says that it is a defence to prove:

> "that the state of scientific and technical knowledge at the relevant time was not such that a producer of products of the same description as the product in question might be expected to have discovered the defect if it had existed in his products while they were under his control."

It is also referred to as the development risks defence. From this it will be seen that it could be incumbent on a producer to make sure that he is fully up to date with the safety attributes of competitive products. Benchmarking could be a means of achieving this.

Strict liability

The other type of pressure on producers comes from the introduction of strict liability, discussed in Chapter 8. The millions of words spoken and written on the subject, since it first publicly emerged in the 1970s, have had a serious impact on certain producers. Now, it is on the statute book of many countries. Generally speaking, there are two elements of strict liability in tort that put pressure on producers.

First, is the removal of the need to prove negligence. If a person suffers harm because of a defective product, he can recover compensation by showing that the producer put the product into circulation and that the defect was the cause of the damage. The need to show in addition that the producer was negligent no longer arises. This has increased the exposure of producers, as sooner or later every producer will make a defective product.

Secondly, in the U.K., is the threat of large, unlimited damages that can be awarded in compensation. Awards running into seven figures have already been made in personal injury cases. However, it must be said that there have been few reports to date of a strict liability action being brought under Part I of the Consumer Protection Act 1987.

The effect of these provisions has been to cause perceptive companies to review their management of product safety. In particular this has applied to those making liability-sensitive products such as food, cosmetics, toiletries, toys, DIY products, leisure and sports goods, domestic electrical products, cars and automotive products, baby products, and health care products. Producers of other, perhaps less obvious, products have also been concerned; they include filter aids, railway equipment, ink, gloves, dyes, doors, building resins and lifts.

A major result of strict liability, in the U.K., has been the significant increase in the number of product recalls, see page 364. Another factor is that consumers are far more aware of their rights today. Indeed, they are virtually encouraged to complain when a product is not satisfactory for any reason. Consumer expectations have never been higher.

DESIGN FOR SAFETY

Because a design defect can be serious a design review programme is important. It must start with the concept by asking "should we be doing this anyway?" Throughout the whole programme product safety has to be the leading item on the agenda. Software has a special position, as an evaluation of its failure rate cannot be made before the system is deployed. The design team should consist of members from a variety of disciplines.

It can be a long road from the concept of a new product right through to a fully operational production line. The time-scale may be measured in years for cars and aircraft. But for other products it may only be a matter of weeks before a concept finds its way into the marketplace, a flavour change in a food for instance. Whatever the time-scale, the period prior to first production will be critical in determining the safety of the product. Design defects are serious because they affect all production. A manufacturing error will be limited to a batch or a run.

If the design process is to be managed successfully a formalised system is essential. Not all that many companies have a design management system, which sets out the checks and balances to be followed. Even among those that do have such a system, there will be some in which it is honor'd more in the breach than the observance.

The design review programme There can be no one ideal system. Each company has to determine what is best for its operations. Whatever is adopted, it must have structure and logic with built-in fixed stages, when defined approvals have to be obtained before moving on to the next phase. There is a British Standard called Guide to Managing Product Design, BS 7000. In its 20 pages the word safety appears only twice, although by inference it can be read into every page, because it is so general. For example, the quality of design is said to have four key elements: avoid unnecessary complexity, variety and costs, and minimise or eliminate features known to cause quality problems. It is difficult to imagine anything more unremarkable.

Case histories[27] of the practical effect of design review systems provide a valuable insight into the reality. A large manufacturer had an elaborate design review process which applied to new products and major product redesigns. An in-depth critique found the documentation highly inadequate. There was no means of tracking product performance in the field and linking it to the original design effort. Accident investigations were delegated to insurance claims adjusters, which resulted in the loss of valuable safety-related information.

[27] G. Eads, P. Reuter, *Designing Safer Products* (The Institute for Civil Justice, Rand Corporation, Santa Monica 1983).

Another company had formal procedures, used checklists and failure modes effects analysis. But the other aspects of the safety review process were basically informal. There was little attention to the review of advertising and instruction manuals. The former was delegated to the legal department. It was left to intuition to decide how to communicate with consumers. A big retailer marketed a complete range of goods manufactured by third parties. There was an elaborate tracking network to investigate failures in the field. The safety review of new products, however, relied principally on product engineers in the company's laboratory. There was no formal design review process. There was a remarkable difference between the apparatus devoted to failures in the field and the in-house management of design.

There is a salutary lesson to be learnt from the experience of the U.S. National Aeronautics and Space Administration. A 1982 in-depth critique concluded: "the NASA's Safety Program is a superior model of how to manage complex engineering projects where the potential for catastrophic consequences to human health and safety make even a single accident intolerable." The Program was a paradigm of formalism with complete documentation and explicit exploration of safety consequences. It inculcated concern for safety into its own and its contractors' engineers.

In 1986 The Challenger space shuttle exploded on blast off due to a design defect, killing the seven crew. The House of Representatives Committee on Science and Technology reported that "the safety, reliability and quality assurance programs within NASA were grossly inadequate". It recommended that the risk management activities needed review in order to define a complete risk management programme. The Committee said that it realised that the lessons to be learned were universally applicable. One lesson is not to take a system at face value and judge on appearances. See also page 350.

The first question When the concept for a new product is proposed the key safety question that should be asked is: "Should we be doing this anyway ?" It is worth remembering that some large organisations have got a fundamental idea spectacularly wrong but pressed on regardless. Just a word can still bring a wry smile to the lips: Brabazon, Edsel, ground nuts in Africa, Sinclair's three-wheeler and Hoover's free flights.

Certain products present greater demands than others where safety is concerned, despite apparent marketing attractions. For example, it was proposed, in a cosmetics company, that a popular product should be changed to incorporate therapeutic properties. The strong marketing argument was that it would provide a classic opportunity of fragmenting a market to increase brand share. Investigations soon revealed that the new product would have to meet the requirements of the Medicines Act 1968. The company had no experience of the Act's safety requirements and felt that an attempt to conform would take them out of their competence. The idea was dropped.

Another company manufactured a safety-critical car component. They were forced into a recall after it had caused fires in some vehicles. A product redesign programme was initiated to overcome the design weakness, that had caused the fires. An estimate of the cost and likely effectiveness of the redesign made the company pause and reconsider. They decided to drop the product entirely. Their experience made them realise that it was not a market they wanted to be in, because the penalties were too great.

There are no independent data on which products are most likely to cause harm. As discussed in Chapter 1 the nearest approach is the Home Accident Surveillance System (HASS) of the Department of Trade and Industry, which is concerned with products which are *involved* in accidents. There are around 1,000 different product categories. In a recent year 140,000 accidents were investigated at 18 hospitals. The Consumer Safety Unit of the DTI also carries out research on accidents in which certain products are involved and publishes detailed reports on its work. Alongside the HASS, there is a similar survey by the Leisure Accident Surveillance System. The E.C. has a similar system called the European Home and Leisure Accident Surveillance System (see page 82), which was originally based on the HASS. In the U.S. there is the National Electronic Injury Surveillance System of the Consumer Product Safety Commission. For companies with home or leisure products these data sources may provide valuable background information when new products are being considered.

How Safe? In an ideal world someone ought to tell the designer how safe the new product should be. But this can be a very awkward piece of information to provide. The reasoning is that, as no product can be totally safe, it is quite unrealistic to instruct the designer to make the product safe. It is also unrealistic to leave the question open by default or let the designer work it out for himself. It has to be a management responsibility.

Where there are relevant safety standards or codes of practice they will give the yardstick. Otherwise state of the art or custom and practice may point the way. Ideally a measure is required against which the new product must perform, such as a maximum number of defined failures per million units or operations.

The General Product Safety Directive lays down that a product must, under normal and reasonably foreseeable conditions of use, including duration, not present any risk, or only the minimum risks considered as acceptable and consistent with a high level of protection for the safety and health of persons see page 45.

An example of the levels of risk that individuals will accept is in a document on the tolerability of risk.[28] The general risk of death in a

[28] "The Tolerability of Risk from Nuclear Power Stations", Health & Safety Executive, HMSO 1992.

traffic accident is 1 in 10,000, the general risk of death in a fire or gas explosion at home is 1 in 1 million and the risk of being killed by lightning is 1 in 10 million. None of these factors stops us using the roads, having gas central-heating or walking the dog in the park.

The Health and Safety Executive lays down that an employer must ensure that any risk is reduced as far as reasonably practicable or to a level which is as low as reasonably practicable (ALARP). The higher or more unacceptable a risk is the more, proportionately, the expenditure necessary to reduce it.

Unfortunately we do not live in an ideal world. It has yet to become commonplace to attempt to measure the safety of many products in a meaningful way, during the product development process. As regulatory product liability exposures increase, many producers will have to adopt a more professional approach to this vital question.

It is important to have safety as a leading item on the agenda during the whole development phase. At particular points a hazard analysis and risk assessment exercise should be carried out to provide a formal measure of risk. There is a range of techniques available for applying logic and structure, from those which are sophisticated and computer based to simple methods, which have been reviewed elsewhere.[29] Individual circumstances will determine which are most appropriate. The assessments should be formal, recorded and approved as acceptable by the design team.

Software The position of software in product safety design is such that it demands special mention. As the sophistication and complexity of products increase so does the importance of software. "It is a dominant component in many safety-critical systems and this development poses special problems for risk management."[30] An example is the much-quoted failure-rate requirement for standard flying control systems in modern aircraft of 10^{-9}, or one in one billion.

One expert[31] emphasised the dangers from computer operators and engineers using sophisticated software without being able to judge the reliability of the software or without having access to the source code. An example was an accident to a Lufthansa Airbus in Warsaw, which resulted in one killed and the total loss of the aircraft. The cause was a safety code hidden in the source code, which prevented braking by the flaps as long as both wheels were not firmly on the runway. The Lufthansa pilots were unaware of this fact. The U.S. National Research Council reported "many of the same kinds of mistakes that played a role in the Challenger accident, (see page 348) are now being repeated with shuttle flight software, especially with respect to the belief that

[29] H. Abbott, *Product Risk Management* (1992).

[30] "Risk: Analysis, Perception and Management", The Royal Society, London 1992.

[31] A. Puri, "Validation of Computational Analysis Procedures with respect to Product Liability and Consequential Loss", Management of Risk in Engineering Conference, Basel, The Geneva Association 1993.

safety precautions for established programs like the shuttle do not need to be as stringent as those for new programs." Among the problems were an overreliance on contractors and faults in the verification and validation process for software.

In software development it is not possible to evaluate the failure rate before the system is deployed. Which means that its reliability cannot be measured in advance. This is a major philosophical question in relation to the validity of statistical measures applied in design. The fundamental problem is that software behaves in a discontinuous way, which may not be encountered in other engineering disciplines. The Ministry of Defence, however, specifies that the appropriate route is to quantify design integrity through formal mathematical methods. These ideas are incorporated in the Interim Defence Standard 00/55. There are those who question this approach. The human-computer interface is at the heart of the debate about safety-critical systems, which are intolerant of errors made by humans in times of stress.

The design team and the price of safety The team should have a cross-section of disciplines in its membership. The engineers or scientists should be leavened, for example, by representatives from purchasing, manufacturing, sales, marketing and legal. Availability of raw materials or components can influence safety; some designs are easier to replicate than others so manufacturability can be important for product safety; a clear description of just who will use the product can affect how hazards are designed out and safety is designed in; the words that go with a product, the instructions, warnings, claims and directions, should be built in at the earliest stage; legal requirements may have a great part to play in the design of some products.

The work of the team should be logged. Its meetings should be for action and not merely for the exchange of information. One of the difficult areas that can arise is how much to spend on improving the safety of the product. Product safety has a price, see also page 328. It may have to be a trade-off between what funds are available and additional safety features. There are few products that could not be made safer at a price. The management skill lies in choosing the optimum checks and balances.

Prior to the GPS Regulations one legal requirement for deciding if consumer goods comply with the general safety requirement was to be found in the Consumer Protection Act 1987. It was:

> "the existence of any means by which it would have been reasonable (taking into account the cost, likelihood and extent of any improvement) for the goods to have been made safer. (section 10(2)(c))."

"Safe" is defined as there being "no risk, or no risk apart from one reduced to a minimum" that death or personal injury will be caused, (section 19(1)).

A Rand survey[32] put this problem, the price of safety, into perspective:

[32] G. Eads, P. Reuter, *Designing Safer Products* (The Institute for Civil Justice, Rand Corporation, Santa Monica 1983).

> "The cost of eliminating *all* design-related hazard associated with consumer product use is likely to be prohibitive. The marginal cost of reducing low probability injury will probably exceed any reasonable estimate of the benefit."

The design process involves elements of organisation and decision-making that are poorly understood. The increasing rate of change in safety legislation complicates the issue. Hence the need for a design team drawn from a number of disciplines. There is, however, a significant difference in the safety of products used by consumers and those used by industry. The legal settings are different and the skill and organisation of the users are also different. Purchasers of industrial goods will have experience in their performance while consumers will be virtually an unknown quantity. The views and opinions of relevant industrialists and consumers can have an important voice in the deliberations of the design team. It is dangerous to assume what such views and opinions would be, without actually finding out.

It will be the job of the design team to navigate its way through this labyrinth and ensure that the best decisions are taken.

An unusual example of a possible design failure on a massive scale is the "Frame 65 and the loss of the *Derbyshire*" Case History on page 413.

SOME SENSITIVE AREAS

> An explanation is given of a method of avoiding manufacturing errors by the adoption of Hazard Analysis Critical Control Point. Product traceability is an important asset in product safety management, with record keeping a key element in its success. The use of pictographs in providing product information — warnings, directions and instructions — has advantages in multi-ethnic societies. As the new legislation requires producers to monitor the safety of products already on the market, there is now a requirement for customer contact departments to be proactive rather than reactive.

Preventing manufacturing errors

Having developed an agreed design it has to be faithfully reproduced, time and time again. It is the need for exact repetition that can give rise to problems and cause defects. Broadly speaking, a manufacturing error will be limited to a batch and have a smaller impact than a design defect, which will run through every unit made. However, some manufacturing errors have been very serious.

In 1978 a tiny hole in one $7^{1}/_{2}$oz can of salmon resulted in two deaths, a national recall and a dramatic fall in demand for canned fish. Over Christmas in 1985 a baby food had to be recalled because of a 1cm by 3cm hole in the lining of a spray drier; the total cost of that opening was between £30 and £40 million. Perhaps the most famous of all manufacturing errors would have been the snail-in-the-ginger-bottle case, if it had gone to proof (*Donaghue v. Stevenson*, see Case Histories "Lord Atkin and the snail in the ginger beer bottle" page 426).

One of the aims of product safety management is to reduce the risk of a manufacturing error and provide a positive response should one occur. There is a plethora of information on manufacturing management methods: codes of practice, good manufacturing practice, total quality management, statistical process control, computer integrated manufacturing and so on. There is even a choice of quality gurus: Juran, Deming, Crosby, not one of whom agrees exactly with the others.

None of these methods is exclusively intended to ensure product safety. Some may well have an influence on it but do not have it as a prime aim. The management procedure specifically designed for product safety is Hazard Analysis Critical Control Point (HACCP). It was brought into prominence by the Food Safety Act 1990, although it is by no means a new concept. It dates back to the 1960s in the U.S. where it was developed by Pillsbury and the U.S. Army Natick Laboratories for the National Aeronautics and Space Administration. Its principles can be applied to any industry where product safety is paramount.

The concept has the objective of ensuring that a product is safe by identifying the hazards in the manufacturing process and either eliminating or controlling them. It is primarily concerned with product safety, although there is a product quality dividend. The idea is to get it right the first time and build safety into the product. To fix the disease before the symptoms appear. Fundamentally it is the formalised application of common sense, in a logical and structured manner. There is no magic.

No official HACCP procedure has so far been agreed. The nearest is a 1993 draft document from the UN Codex Alimentarius Commission. The first report of the Richmond Committee on the Microbiological Safety of Food (1990), recommended that HACCP should be widely applied throughout the U.K. food industry. It is probably only a matter of time before it becomes official in one way or another.

The traditional inspection and testing methods for product safety only tell what has already happened. They provide retrospective knowledge of the effectiveness or otherwise of past processes. If the results are unsatisfactory the product has to be rectified or discarded. Far better to get ahead of the game and prevent the defects arising in the first place. Different attitudes are demanded from management and the workforce if a HACCP is to succeed. The methods of control move from the laboratory to the production line. For those familiar with process Failure Modes Effects Analysis HACCP can be seen as a plain man's version. Indeed, one expert[33] said that "HACCP is FMEA in a food safety role."

The Food Safety Act 1990 introduced a new defence for anyone charged with an offence under the Act. This is "for the person charged to prove that he took all reasonable precautions and exercised all due diligence" (section 21(1)). Evidence of a thorough HACCP procedure would do much to demonstrate this requirement. It is one of the chief reasons why HACCP has received such publicity in the technical and professional press.

The Codex Alimentarius document sets out seven principles for HACCP (see **Figure 13.2**):

1. Identify the hazards and assess their risks. An accurate up-to-date flow diagram of the process is essential. The preventative measures to control the hazards must be specified.
2. Identify the Critical Control Points (CCP) where the optimum control of a hazard can be obtained. These can be a location, practice, procedure or process at which a control is implemented to prevent a hazard arising or reduce it to an acceptable level. The term control means what it says and is *not* a synonym for testing or checking.
3. Identify the critical limits which provide the minimum level for safety. An example is a milk pasteuriser which has to operate at 72°C for 15 seconds or better.

[33] M. Easter, Reading Scientific Services Limited.

Figure 13.2 Constructing a HACCP plan

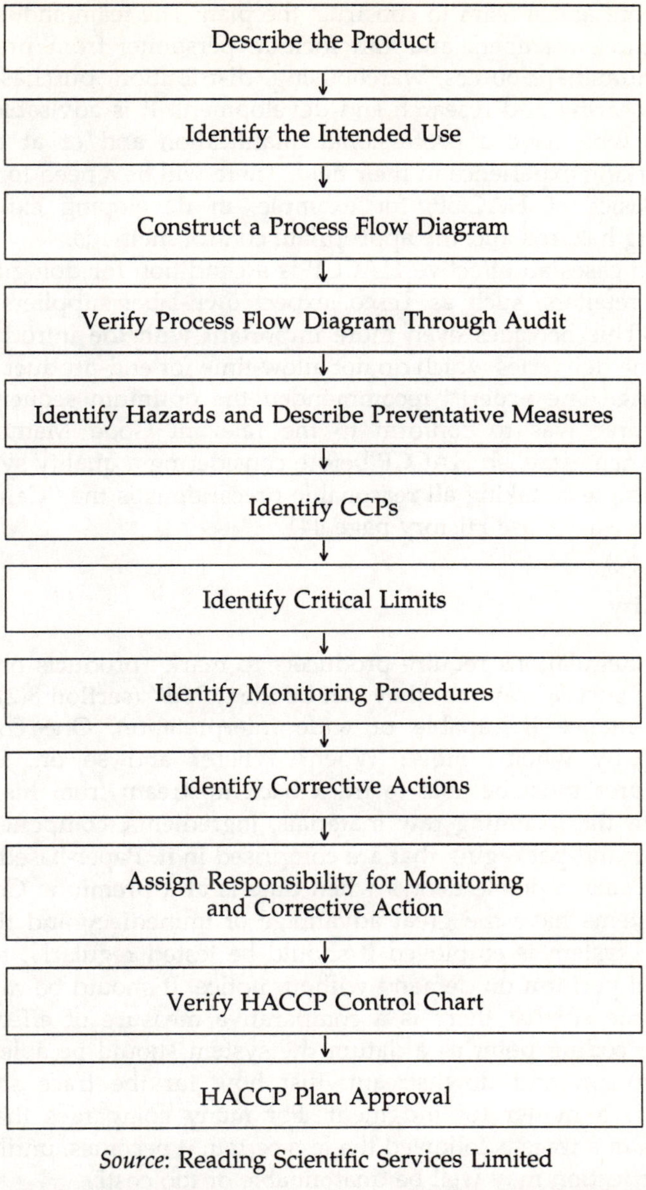

Source: Reading Scientific Services Limited

4. Identify the monitoring procedures which demonstrate that the controls are effective. An example would be a thermometer chart which indicates the temperature and duration of pasteurisation.
5. Identify the corrective actions that must be undertaken if the target CCP is not achieved.
6. A verification system must be in place which audits the CCPs to ensure that the preventative measures have been fully implemented.
7. Keep records. If called upon these could be crucial in showing due diligence and that all reasonable precautions were taken.

To implement a HACCP requires demonstrable senior management commitment and a team to construct the plan. The team should have a core of three members and can include personnel from production, quality, human resources, warehousing, distribution, purchasing, process engineering and research and development. It is advisable to seek members who have a professional qualification and/or at least five years working experience in their field. There will be a need for training in the basics of HACCP; for example, in developing expertise in identifying hazards and the appropriate control methods.

In some cases an effective HACCP is a condition for doing business. Multiple retailers, such as Tesco, expect own-label suppliers to have HACCP. This becomes even more important with the introduction of just-in-time deliveries which do not allow time for end-product checking and testing. One expert[34] recommended the optimum sequence for a manufacturer was to conform to the relevant Good Manufacturing Practice, then establish HACCP before considering a quality system.

An example of taking all reasonable precautions is the "Cancer scare that never was" Case History page 441.

Traceability

The GPS Regulations require producers to mark "products or product batches in such a way that they can be identified" (section 8(2)(i)). This simple sentence is capable of wide interpretation. One could ask: Identified by whom? How? When? Where? and so on. Ideally a manufacturer must be able to track back upstream from his finished product to the incoming raw materials, ingredients, components, subassemblies and packaging that are comprised in it. Paper-based systems can cause unacceptable delays when time is at a premium. Computer-based systems have the great advantage of immediacy and flexibility. Whatever system is employed it should be tested regularly, to ensure that it will perform on demand without notice. It should be carried out against time so that there is a comparative measure of effectiveness. Using the coding point as a datum the system should be able to track both upstream and downstream. Just how far the trace should be pursued is a matter for judgment. For many companies the further downstream a trace is followed the less certain it becomes, until all track is lost. Perfection may well be unattainable or too costly.

There are always companies which assume that if necessary they could run rapid trace, without ever actually having done so. A product liability incident may reveal weaknesses, rather late in the day. The obvious needs to be stated: traceability cannot be put in place retrospectively.

The type and position of batch and serial numbers on the finished product have to be chosen with care. Some recall advertisements have to

[34] S.B. Petitt, "HACCP — Theory and Practice", Leatherhead Food RA Programme for Food Industry Managers, 1993.

resort to complicated diagrams and explanations to tell the public what to look for. One for a television set listed 36 different numbers each up to 12 digits long. The recall of a dimmer switch applied to 36 two-letter combinations in a badly laid out confusing list, see **Figure 13.3**. A trailing socket needed a screwdriver to get at the vital information to identify the affected units, see **Figure 13.4**, page 358. In some instances the key figures are swamped by surrounding information, which makes location difficult even for those with good eyesight. A lavatory pan had a complete set of codes on the inside of the base, where they were totally inaccessible once the product was plumbed in place. It would seem that in some cases the numbering system and its location is determined more for the convenience of the manufacturer than the public.

Computer-controlled ink-jet coding has great flexibility and provides excellent traceability. Using such a system, a jam manufacturer produces 40 million units a year, each one of which has a unique number on the bottom of the jar. The development of bar codes has important applications in this field. Portable checking devices and fixed-position scanners can confirm that encoded product information is correct, as well as checking along the distribution chain to the point of sale. Bar codes can be read on individual units, outer cases, pallets, printed circuit boards and the spare aircraft wings of the Royal Air Force. Other developments

Figure 13.3 Newspaper recall advertisement

IMPORTANT ANNOUNCEMENT

CONCERNING

A possible fault on 400 watt Push Action Brass Dimmer Switches and other Push 400 watt Metal Dimmer Switches purchased under the following brands:

ROYALE, J.D. BEARDMORE, GOLD MEDALLION, GUILDFORD BRASS, HERITAGE BRASS, HOME AUTOMATION, HOMEBASE, INTERBRASS, JEDO, KNOBS & KNOCKERS, MASTERBRASS, MICROMARK, MODRIC, PIK-A-PAK, SILVER MEDALLION, SUSSEX BRASSWARE, WALSALL GALLERY.

PLEASE CHECK ANY OF THE ABOVE PUSH ON/OFF 400 WATT DIMMER SWITCHES PURCHASED SINCE 1ST JANUARY 1988 to see if the Electronic Module attached to the rear appears as follows:

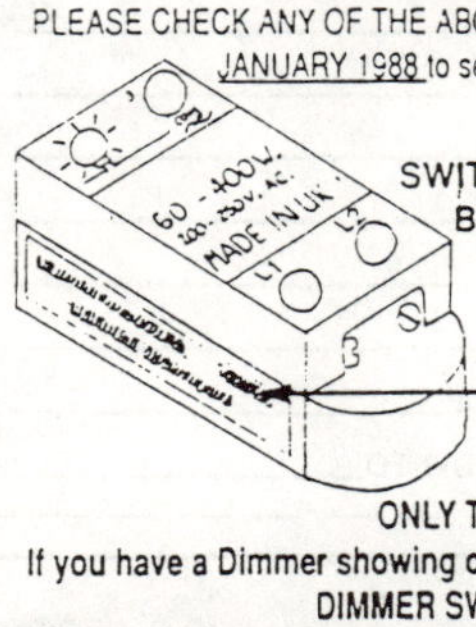

SWITCH OFF AT MAINS BEFORE CHECKING!

Black in colour and showing any of the following codes. An 'X' followed by any of AL, BL, CL, DL, EL, FL, GL, HL, IL, JL, KL, LL, AM, BM, CM, DM, EM, FM, GM, HM, IM, JM, KM, LM, AN, BN, CN, DN, EN, FN, GN, HN, IN, JN, KN, LN

The wattage will be shown on the Electronic Module as 60–400W

ONLY THE CODES LISTED ABOVE ARE CONCERNED.

If you have a Dimmer showing one of the above codes, PLEASE TELEPHONE THE HOME AUTOMATION DIMMER SWITCH HELPLINE ON 0249 443511 IMMEDIATELY.

IT IS ESSENTIAL THAT THE SWITCHES ARE CONNECTED TO THE EARTHING SYSTEM OF THE HOUSE.

Source: Daily Telegraph, August 31, 1990. it also appeared in the *Daily Mail, Daily Express, Daily Mirror* and the *Sun*. A mass of information jammed into too small a space. There are 36 codes to search through. No indication of the hazard. Helpline should be a Freephone

Figure 13.4 Newspaper recall advertisement

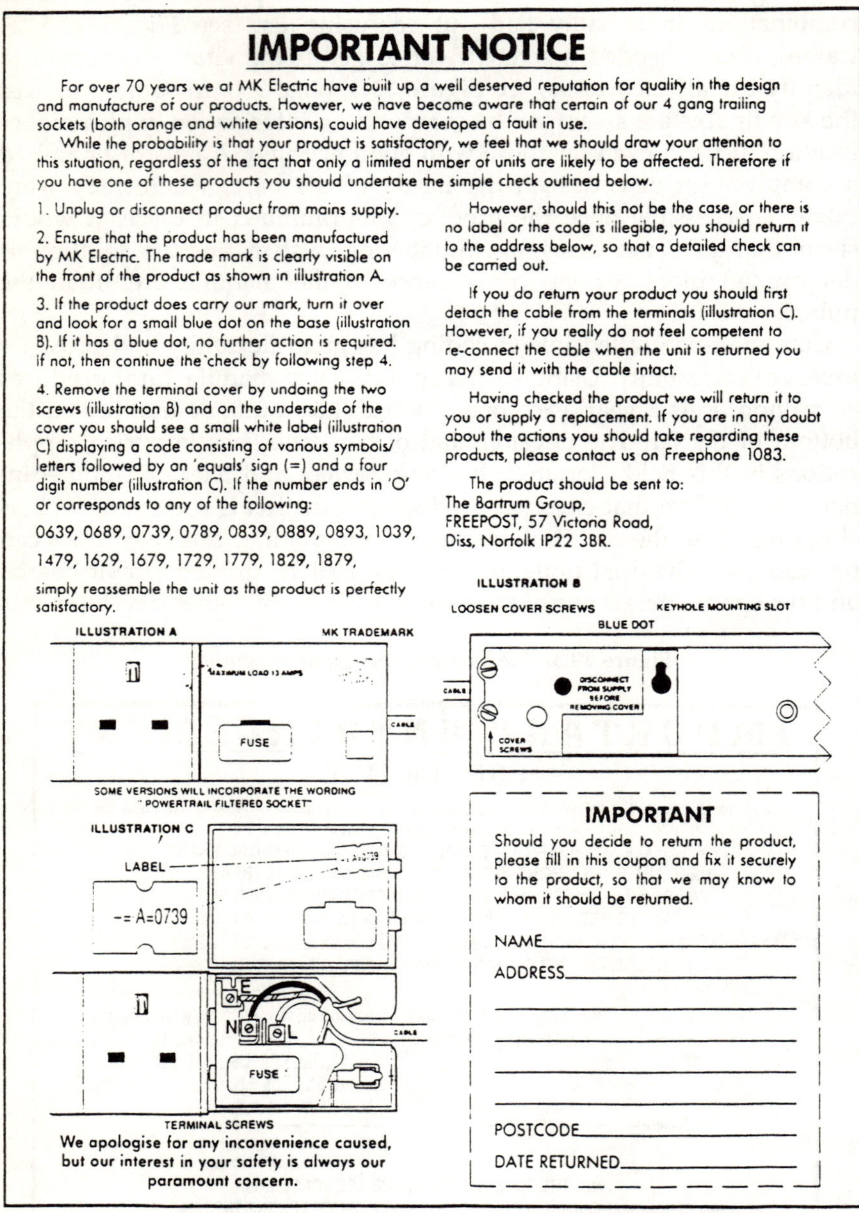

IMPORTANT NOTICE

For over 70 years we at MK Electric have built up a well deserved reputation for quality in the design and manufacture of our products. However, we have become aware that certain of our 4 gang trailing sockets (both orange and white versions) could have developed a fault in use.

While the probability is that your product is satisfactory, we feel that we should draw your attention to this situation, regardless of the fact that only a limited number of units are likely to be affected. Therefore if you have one of these products you should undertake the simple check outlined below.

1. Unplug or disconnect product from mains supply.

2. Ensure that the product has been manufactured by MK Electric. The trade mark is clearly visible on the front of the product as shown in illustration A.

3. If the product does carry our mark, turn it over and look for a small blue dot on the base (illustration B). If it has a blue dot, no further action is required. If not, then continue the check by following step 4.

4. Remove the terminal cover by undoing the two screws (illustration B) and on the underside of the cover you should see a small white label (illustration C) displaying a code consisting of various symbols/letters followed by an 'equals' sign (=) and a four digit number (illustration C). If the number ends in 'O' or corresponds to any of the following:

0639, 0689, 0739, 0789, 0839, 0889, 0893, 1039, 1479, 1629, 1679, 1729, 1779, 1829, 1879,

simply reassemble the unit as the product is perfectly satisfactory.

However, should this not be the case, or there is no label or the code is illegible, you should return it to the address below, so that a detailed check can be carried out.

If you do return your product you should first detach the cable from the terminals (illustration C). However, if you really do not feel competent to re-connect the cable when the unit is returned you may send it with the cable intact.

Having checked the product we will return it to you or supply a replacement. If you are in any doubt about the actions you should take regarding these products, please contact us on Freephone 1083.

The product should be sent to:
The Bartrum Group,
FREEPOST, 57 Victoria Road,
Diss, Norfolk IP22 3BR.

We apologise for any inconvenience caused, but our interest in your safety is always our paramount concern.

IMPORTANT

Should you decide to return the product, please fill in this coupon and fix it securely to the product, so that we may know to whom it should be returned.

NAME__________

ADDRESS__________

POSTCODE__________

DATE RETURNED__________

Source: Daily Telegraph, July 21, 1990. The wording is verbose and the identity of the product is not immediately apparent. A screwdriver is needed to discover if the code is *not* affected. No indication of the hazard. The formidable layout requires determiniation to understand

in automatic identification include radio frequency identification, optical character recognition and voice recognition.

Problems can arise in obtaining a trace for low-value high-volume components, such as fasteners and small plastic items, used in the assembly of a finished product. Batch numbering of the products themselves is often impractical and yet they can have a critical role in the overall safety of a product. One company produces 1.75 million eyelets a year, which can end up in a pair of shoes or in electrical equipment. A solution to this potential exposure is to arrange for single sourcing or block sourcing. The latter is the method whereby only one supplier is used for a fixed period. This can be tied into the product traceability system on a time basis, which will restrict the trace to one source. The alternative is to take the code on the packaging that contains the items and carry it through to the ready-use bins on the production line.

Record retention is a key element in traceability. A company should have a policy on who keeps what, where and for how long. There is surprisingly little official guidance on what form the retention of records should take or the period for which they should be retained. The E.C. Directive on Liability for Defective Products provides that an action, regarding a defective product, cannot be brought more than ten years after it was supplied. The limitation period in tort is six years. Time begins to run from when the cause of action accrues. Bearing in mind the cost of document retention, one authority[35] makes the following recommendations for retention:

- If, for reasons of bulk, it is difficult to retain all documentation a digest could be considered.
- All parts of a company should be made aware of a document retention policy and the method of retention.
- Retention periods should be related to when a particular product was last produced. Ten years from cessation of production might be appropriate for key data, with two or three years for other data.
- Records of supplier relationships should not be ignored.

Product information

The information that is supplied with a product is part of the product, as far as liability is concerned. A particular difficulty today arises because of our multi-ethnic society. Some end-users may not understand instructions and warnings because of their lack of familiarity with the language in which they appear. Nevertheless, it is the responsibility of the producer to convey his message to the user. A member of a ship's crew suffered injury because he did not follow the warnings on certain

[35] S. Pearson, "To keep or not to keep?", *Product Liability International*, London, November 1993.

cleaning agents. The words were in Dutch and German which he could not read. He was awarded £4,000 in an action he brought against the shipping line (*French v. Olau Line (UK) Ltd* 1983). In another case a farmer misunderstood the instructions on a container of herbicide. The court held that the instructions and warnings were clear and the fault lay with the farmer in not following them (*Wormell v. RHM Agriculture (East) Ltd* 1987).

A plaintiff emigrated to the U.S. from Portugal in 1971. In 1978 there was an explosion of a truck tyre rim when a tyre was being mounted. The warnings provided were in English but were not followed. The plaintiff, who was injured in the explosion, won an appeal in the New Jersey Supreme Court on account of the injuries he suffered (*Campos v. Firestone Tire & Rubber Company* 1984) The judgement said:

> "In view of the unskilled or semi-skilled nature of the work and the existence of many in the work force who do not speak English, warnings in the form of symbols might have been appropriate, since the employee's 'ability to take care of himself' was limited."

It is preferable to use illustrations rather than words whenever possible. A series of pictographs can overcome problems of communication in a multi-ethnic society. In safety-critical applications it will be an advantage to test their effectiveness. There is a U.S. standard (ANSI Z535.3 1991) for such an exercise. It requires 85 per cent correct answers and a maximum of 5 per cent critical confusions from a panel of 50 people. For severe hazards, which could result in death or serious injury, a warning is rejected if the figures are less than 90 per cent and more than 1 per cent respectively.

Although the E.C. Product Liability Directive does not refer to specific language requirements, many technical directives do. The Machinery Directive says:

> "Such warnings [of residual risks] should preferably use readily understandable pictographs and/or be drawn up in one of the languages of the country in which the machinery is to be used, accompanied, on request, by the languages understood by the operators, Annex B 1.7.2."

Product safety information can be divided into the following:

- a warning of danger;
- a direction for use;
- an instruction for effectiveness;
- claims for attributes.

It is essential to keep the parts separate and convey all that a reasonable user would expect to have available for the safe use of the product. There is a duty to warn if the danger is not obvious or not readily discoverable. Claims must be capable of documented substantiation. A producer must take into account foreseeable misuse. People use products in ways that the designer did not intend. The use of a product can be limited by giving an exclusive list of applications or by listing specifically those applications which are unacceptable.

Misuse is different from abuse. Indeed, it may depend on the user whether misuse or abuse has occurred. A young well-educated executive could be expected to have greater powers of discrimination than an ailing pensioner who left school at 14. The market into which the product is sold will influence the information that accompanies it. The GPS Regulations mention children as a category of consumer to whom particular attention has to be paid. A product sold to a company with a highly skilled workforce does not have the same requirements as a product available to anyone in the High Street.

According to the GPS Regulations, the areas taken into account when deciding if a product is defective, include the characteristics of the product, its effect on other products, instructions, presentation, labelling and "the categories of consumer at serious risk when using the product, in particular children" (section 2(d)). From this it will be seen that it is not only the information that accompanies the product itself that is taken into account, but also the marketing through the media, points of sale, representatives, customer service departments, etc. Training of personnel with responsibilities in these areas, in the potential exposure they could create, is advisable. A ill-considered, casual or off-hand remark could have serious consequences for the user of a safety-critical product.

An example of the importance of telephone support for consumers is provided by the computer company Dell. They have 100 staff running a free, 24–hour, seven-days-a-week hot-line. The staff undergo a two-week induction course followed by a three- to five-week customer support course. Microsoft's technical support operation increased from 32 people to 220 in three years, to deal with 3,000 calls a day.

Feedback from the market

Many companies have departments that deal with customers. They handle complaints, enquiries and give advice on a reactive basis. They supply information in response to specific requests. In some companies the work is included in a function such as marketing, sales or public relations. The requirements of the GPS Regulations suggest that these activities may need to be reviewed and upgraded. The emphasis will have to be more pro-active than reactive. There will be a need to find out what is happening, rather than just allow the information to come in and respond to it.

There is a positive duty on producers to keep themselves informed of the risks their products might present and to investigate complaints. Producers and distributors have to monitor the safety of products placed on the market and pass on information about product risks. The implication is that producers should establish which products are on the market and where they are. This is far easier said than done and in certain cases will be impossible with any degree of accuracy. In-house records will be the prime source, but when agents, merchants and factors are involved in the distribution chain, complications will arise. One tobacco company *thought* it had some 220,000 outlets, but had no way of being certain.

Contact with a market can be by letter, fax, phone and personal visit. Further, several different departments in a company may have contact with one point of sale: sales, marketing, distribution, technical and accounts. To meet the requirements of the GPS Regulations, a producer will have to have an efficient system of ensuring that positive monitoring of the products is recorded, and that there is positive feed-back to consumers when it is necessary. The degree to which this is done will obviously depend on individual circumstances. For large companies it can probably be incorporated into existing activities, but smaller companies may well find it an additional expense.

To meet the requirement for the regular monitoring of the market the database will have to be interrogated. The GPS Regulations do not specify that information must be obtained from consumers, only from the market. Nevertheless, any producer will want to be informed of the views of those who actually use his products. Mounting concern of consumers about the safety of a product can provide an indication that action will be necessary. Presumably sample testing could be contracted out to an approved laboratory or test house, who would apply an agreed definition of a safe product.

The GPS Regulations require that complaints are investigated. This is normal practice but the analysis of complaints may need revision. These are often a list of who complained about what and how it was dealt with, or a categorised tabulation. Such presentations can conceal trends and not provide the pointers to movements of particular types of complaint. The best analyses are comparative, using graphs or indexes to show movement and red flag potential exposures. Swift corrective action can then be taken.

The GPS Regulations say that producers must provide consumers with information about any risks in a product throughout its "normal or reasonably foreseeable period of its use" (section 8(1)(a)). They have a duty to keep distributors informed of the results of the monitoring activities. It follows that a scheme of communication will have to be devised to ensure that this is done on a positive basis. To close the loop this information needs to be fed back in-house to those departments with relevant responsibilities — quality, manufacturing, research and development, technical, etc.

A fairly recent development in consumer contact is called Careline. This is the printing of a special free telephone number, on the packaging of consumer products, to be called for advice, help, complaints and the like. They have been in use in the U.S. since the 1970s. The first in the

U.K. was for Van den Bergs' Flora margarine in December 1990. The packaging says: "Phone Flora Food Company 0800 446464 (U.K. only). Questions comments or suggestions about Flora ? Call us FREE Monday to Friday 8 am to 8 pm." Since then other companies, such as Kraft and Kellog, have adopted the idea. A survey[36] found that 83 per cent of branded products in a U.S. supermarket had a Careline number; the figure for France was 30 per cent, for Germany 15 per cent and only 8 per cent for the U.K. Household products were the greatest users but there were none on the OTC or own-label products surveyed in Europe. Comments from the U.S. on Careline numbers included:

> The Careline offers consumer feedback. It's a quality control device that gives us the ability to right wrongs quickly. [*Household products manufacturer*]
>
> If you catch a complaint early you can avoid a lawyer. It's worth a chat and $5 off coupon. [*Pharmaceutical company*]

The development of the concept could provide valuable support to producers' responsibilities under the GPS Regulations, so they know what is happening to their products once they have left the factory gate. For example, in 1993 Nutricia, Europe's second biggest baby food supplier, recalled two million jars of Olvaritt across the Continent, because of possible contamination. Although Nutricia stressed that normal consumption would not harm babies, more than 8,000 called a special free telephone helpline.

[36] "The Careline Report", L & R Group Limited London 1993.

MANAGEMENT CONSIDERATIONS FOR A DEFECTIVE PRODUCT

> Once a potentially dangerous product leaves the factory gate it must be recalled. The number of recalls has increased in recent years as tougher legislation has been introduced, consumers have become more aware and management techniques have improved. The proportion of defects in a batch is but a guide to decision making. Risk perception can play a vital role, but it is a little understood subject.

Introduction

The most obvious way to deal with a defective product is to know that it has been made and correct it before despatch. But at times information about defects will only become available after a product has left the factory gate. This may be revealed through use, as when a drug's side-effects are manifested only after it has taken for a period. With some short shelf-life products the defect may need time to be discovered. For example, micro-organisms have to grow to be disclosed and nature will not be hurried too much, although modern conductance methods of determination have speeded up analysis. Extended use can result in unforeseen problems, as these advertisements show:

> "It has been found that under particular conditions — especially very high usage over a long period of time — metal fatigue can occur in certain soldered joints causing malfunction." [*Sunday Times*, February 28, 1993]
>
> "During the course of our continuous quality assurance programme we have discovered that, in extreme circumstances, the plastic casing of the plug of a detachable mains lead supplied as an accessory . . . could fracture. This lead meets all relevant British Safety Standards and will operate perfectly normally but it has been found that when subjected to unusually rough treatment a fracture could leave pins exposed." [*Sunday Times*, July 11, 1993]

This chapter is concerned with products that are found to be defective after they have left the factory gate. It should be read in conjunction with Chapter 10. Depending on the circumstances, there are four actions that can be taken. The producer can:

- *Recall*. Remove a product from a point along the distribution chain between the producer and the consumer. The term is used to include retrofit, when the producer arranges to visit a consumer to rectify a defect, on a washing machine for instance.
- *Publish a direction*. For example, a message to doctors to modify the circumstances in which a drug is used or a restriction on the incorporation of a component or ingredient in an end-product

- *Stop distributing*. This prevents products reaching the point of sale eventually, but lacks urgency.
- *Ignore it*. If the risks are thought to be low, companies have been known to look the other way and take a chance on the outcome.

All options are adopted at some time or other and the reason for the choice made will depend on the company. A recall is initiated usually, but not always, when there is the possibility of damage. There are times when there is no danger but the distribution of a product may be stopped because the price is wrong, the colour does not match the label, there are unimportant errors in the instructions, etc. Unlike some countries, the U.K. has no mandatory provision in law for the recall of defective products, apart from pharmaceuticals. However, regulatory bodies and Government departments can achieve the same result by other means, such as prohibition notices, banning supply and press releases.

There is a product recall flow chart on page 386 and a comprehensive summary of the principles. The more important considerations are dealt with in the following pages.

Recalls are increasing

During the 1980s and into the 1990s recalls increased in frequency to become virtually commonplace. Scarcely a week passes without a recall advertisement appearing in the press; *The Times* carried three different ones in a single issue. However, it is not entirely a modern phenomenon. Beer contaminated with arsenic was recalled in the year 1900 in the north west of England, when over 70 people died and 6,000 became ill. The more recent increase is due to:

1. Legislation becoming tougher, as we saw in the first part of this book. The introduction of strict liability in 1987 brought with it the potential of large, unlimited damages, for the harm caused by a defective product. This accelerated recalls as producers sought to protect themselves from possibly serious costs. Whereas, once upon a time, there was a tendency to turn a blind eye to a defective product, the new situation concentrated the minds of executives.

   The "essential requirements" of the New Approach Directives include product safety. As the standards which spell out these requirements are a Community obligation, products which fail to conform to them are an exposure for the producer. When this happens a recall may be the prudent action.

   The General Product Safety Directive brings additional pressure to bear on producers. There is an obligation to place only safe consumer products on the market. Yet in the E.C. there are 45 million accidents a year which involve consumer products. If a product on the market is found not to be safe the provisions of the law are contravened and a recall may be the only sensible action.

Under the Consumer Protection Act 1987, Part II, the Secretary of State has powers to enforce certain actions, which are summarised in the Consumer Safety Report.[37] Under Voluntary Withdrawals, the majority of which concerned toys followed by electrical products, it says:

> "It should be noted that, where possible, enforcement authorities prefer to negotiate voluntary withdrawal of suspect goods, rather than use suspension notices or apply forfeiture orders, because this approach enables the goods to be removed from the market immediately. In the period of the Report [1988–1993] local authorities reported 1,237 voluntary withdrawals."

In the same period 1,702 suspension notices were served, mainly for furniture and furnishings, with toys and nightwear some way behind. A suspension notice prohibits the person upon whom it is served from supplying specified goods for up to six months. It may also require that person to keep the enforcement authority informed as to the whereabouts of the goods in question.

The Report says that 299 forfeiture orders were made, during the five years, on the grounds that the goods contravened a safety provision; toys and electrical products again led the list. In the same period there were over 2,000 cases brought for offences under the Act, with convictions in 1,931 cases.

2. Consumers are much more aware and perceptive today. They are encouraged to complain, with help available from leaflets, books and the Consumer Advice Bureaux. The media run stories about the attitude of recalcitrant manufacturers who fail to meet the demands of complainants. Each month 700,000 members of *Which?* are given a list of unsafe products and those on recall. Features recount the actions of producers, often after the threat of legal action. Today major consumer product companies have sophisticated departments which handle consumer complaints. They find that it is a way of stopping molehills becoming mountains and reflects the increased muscle of consumers.
3. Recalls are more acceptable now and can turn a necessity into a virtue. When recalls were unusual the announcement of one would be the subject for gossip and comment. The advertisements were somewhat strained and almost shamefaced, as if the company did not entirely relish having to admit it had made a bad one. With the passing of time and the increasing frequency of recalls the approach has changed. By careful presentation the company can be seen to be on the side of the consumers, protecting them from harm. Reassurance underlies advertisements explaining that the company is ever on the look out for anything which might cause difficulty. For instance:

[37] "Consumer Safety", Report by the Secretary of State for Trade and Industry for the period April 1, 1988 – March 31, 1993, HMSO London 1993.

> "The modification is designed to improve the safety of the window lock in exceptional circumstances, where considerable force is applied to the window." [*Sunday Times*, November 1993]
>
> "We have become aware through these additional safety checks that in some circumstances the [toy] dog's eyes work loose under pressure. Our concern is in public safety and the confidence of our customers and we are as a precaution alerting the public to the situation and withdrawing the toy dogs . . . from circulation." [*The Times*, May 29, 1993]

This change of attitude enables companies to reduce the potential downside of a recall and get over the message of being a thoughtful and caring organisation. It has minimised the reluctance to recall that existed some years ago.

Number of recalls

There are no independent, objective data on the number of recalls, apart from those for vehicles. Subjective opinion is that they have increased significantly. Food, drink and domestic electrical products are frequently called back and also products associated with children, sport and leisure, as well as cosmetics, toiletries, household and DIY products. The surprising variety of products that have been recalled is shown by the following examples: a horse feed supplement, slippers, nightwear, petrol, a necklace, tyres, a glue gun, a lock, a mixing bowl set, book, moss killer, anorak, swing, car ramp, dinghy, firework, car jack, aquarium, bunk bed, tadpoles, handcuffs and aircraft.

Recalls of vehicles and their components conform to the voluntary codes of practice agreed by the Department of Transport and the representative bodies of the motor industry. The first code was introduced in 1979 and applies to all motor vehicles sold in the U.K. In 1982 a further five codes were introduced. All code of practice recalls are monitored by the Department of Transport, which publishes a regular summary of them. Between 1980 and 1992, each year the number of campaigns, as the recalls are called, ranged from 55 to 96 and the number of vehicles affected from 219,528 to 1,333,673. In 1992 the U.S. National Highway Traffic Safety Administration was involved in 187 recalls of 10 million vehicles.

There is no means of discovering the number of silent recalls, those of which the public are not aware. For example, a supermarket chain may recall a product from within its own distribution system or a producer may be able to contact certain customers direct, without the need for any publicity. During 1990 the U.S. Food & Drug Administration recorded 2,352 recalls of food, cosmetics, drugs and medical instruments, with only about five appearing on the nightly TV news. The U.S. Consumer Product Safety Commission is involved with the recall of about 250 products a year.

Risk classification

A method of categorising risk is essential, if the means of managing a recall is to have any logic and structure. Each company should develop its own method to fit its own unique exposure. It is important to appreciate that this is a *risk* classification: the probability and severity of harm. Examples should be given of the hazards that could cause the risk in each category. The following is a guide:

- Class 1 Serious ill health or the possibility of death. Botulism, electrocution, ineffective critical drug.
- Class 2 Probable reversible ill health, fatal risk low. Food poisoning bacteria, mechanical pinch trap, improperly calibrated thermometer.
- Class 3 Remote chance of ill health. Labelling violation, aesthetic defects, out-of-life.
- Class 4 No health consequences. Legal contravention, non-performance, poor packaging.

Where appropriate the classification should be associated with damage to property, commercial damage to a brand name or company image.

Another method is to categorise how far from the end of the production line the defective batch should be pursued. This is usually called the recall depth or level. The more serious the risk the closer to the end-user the recall will reach. The following is an example:

- Level 1 End-user or consumer. Often will require going public because the individuals who hold the product will be unknown.
- Level 2 Points-of-sale. Not always readily identifiable, especially with fast moving consumer products.
- Level 3 Third party distributors, factors, merchants. Usually identifiable but not under direct control.
- Level 4 Company-owned, remote depots, distribution centres and warehouses. Under direct control.
- Level 5 In-house warehouse.

The greatest cost and smallest response rate will be at Level 1. Costs will diminish and response rates increase the nearer Level 5 is approached.

Proportion of defects

The most frequent reason for having to remove a product from the market is that it may cause death, injury, damage to property or commercial damage. If the defect is due to a failure of design then all products made to that design will be implicated. If the failure is due to a manufacturing error, the number of units will be limited to a batch or production run. When a proportion of units is involved it may be possible to measure the size of the probability. Some examples follow:

- A batch of refill packs for an asthma medicine was recalled when it was found that the proportion of defects was 14 in 182,000, or **0.0077 per cent**.

- A bottled beer was recalled because it was estimated that **1 per cent** of 17 million bottles in seven countries could contain glass splinters.
- An adult tonic was recalled because of a manufacturing error being discovered in two bottles of a batch of 15,600, or **0.013 per cent**.
- A recall was initiated in Europe for a toy after the manufacturers received eight complaints (including two of injuries) out of 120,000 units sold, or **0.0067 per cent**.
- A car manufacturer recalled 51,000 top-of-the-range models after it had found three faulty seat belt anchorages, or **0.006 per cent**.
- A recall of 12 million bottles of a health drink was initiated because it was estimated that 1 in 1,000, or **0.1 per cent**, could break at the neck when opened.
- Tiny pieces of plastic in cans of beer resulted in the recall of 900,000 of them. A company expert said "I'd guess only about 10 cans are affected", or **0.001 per cent**.

As will have been seen from this range, proportions of defects alone cannot provide the answer: the selection above varies from 0.001 per cent to 1 per cent. They may help reach a decision in individual circumstances, depending on the seriousness of the risk. In very serious incidents just one defective unit can cause a major national recall, see page 382.

In many situations the proportion of defects will not be known at all. Indeed, one of the difficulties is that the producer may not know, with any degree of accuracy, how many units are on the market, let alone in the hands of consumers. He may not have a perfect picture of the number of points of sale either. With short shelf-life products an informed estimate may be the only guide.

Not all recalls are initiated because the product is defective or potentially dangerous. For example, the world-wide recall of 160 million bottles of Perrier mineral water in 1990 was to protect the brand name, as the product itself did not pose a threat to health. Kodak Instant Cameras were recalled because they infringed Polaroid's instant photography patents. In 1990 a U.S. judge in Boston awarded Polaroid $909.4 million in compensation for the infringement. In 1991 Wall's canned meat products had to be recalled because there was a chance that horse meat could have been substituted for beef. The company said that there was a possibility that it had been the victim of malpractice in the meat trade. In 1987 Spring Bathrooms sought 3,500 baths labelled as being made with Perspex acrylic sheet, which was incorrect. The High Court gave ICI, manufacturers of Perspex, a judgement prohibiting Spring from selling any more wrongly labelled baths.

Risk perception

Statistical data on defect ratios have limitations. These assessments do not take into account the perceived risk. Statistical information, such as we have seen above, contains an element of subjective judgment. Similarly the hazard analysis and risk assessment techniques, Failure Mode Effects Analysis and Fault Tree Analysis for instance, assume that the analyst has taken into account every possible route to failure. But the human factor, (see page 336) has to be part of the equation, and humans are biased and fallible. So are experts.

It follows that a figure for defect proportions cannot be the only criterion for deciding whether to recall or not. In addition, the perception of the risk must be taken into account. The social scientists find that it involves people's beliefs, attitudes, judgments and feelings, as well as social and cultural values. The perceptive risk is multi-dimensional and means different things to different people. It is not surprising, therefore, that the social scientists do not have a common view, despite an increase in the amount of investigative work carried out.

There have been many conferences, scientific meetings and articles on the subject; two journals have been launched. Further, the provision of risk information to the public has gained prominence. The General Product Safety Directive requires producers to affix to their products suitable warnings regarding their risks. They must monitor the safety of the products they have already placed on the market and inform consumers of any risks they find. The legislation does not have a comprehensive definition of risk but shuffles off the responsibility on to others, see below. The main lines of thinking on risk perception have been set out in a report[38] by the Royal Society, supported by a bibliography of 183 references. For the purpose of recall, the review that follows can only give an idea of the breadth of the subject and point to factors that should be considered.

It is wrong to think that an acceptable level of risk can be established for all hazards. Three approaches can be used to determine what is acceptable:

- Professional judgments, standards, codes of practice.
- Formal hazard analysis and risk assessment.
- Extrapolation from data on behaviour towards existing hazards.

According to the report: "There can be no single all-purpose number that expresses the acceptable risk for a society. The best one can hope to find is the most acceptable alternative in a specific problem." The concept of acceptable risk is being replaced by tolerable risk. This is defined by the Health and Safety Executive as: "The willingness to live with a risk to secure certain benefits and in the confidence that it is being properly controlled." From this developed the principle that risks should be As Low as Reasonably Practicable (ALARP). It requires a trade-off between risk and benefit. The HSE states that "the judgment on what is tolerable is not a scientific but a political matter".

[38] "Risk: Analysis, Perception and Management", Report of a Royal Society Study Group, London 1992.

The question of what consumers will accept or tolerate, in a product liability exposure, can be fraught with difficulty. Especially as the producing company will have to make assumptions on behalf of its consumers, who initially will be unaware of the risks to which they are exposed. If the product benefits are comparatively meagre on the human scale, then the risk which people will be prepared to live with to secure the benefits conferred will be negligible. In a developed society the benefits conferred by many consumer goods would be discarded if there were any serious perceived risks. The producer will have to step into the shoes of the HSE's politicians to decide what is tolerable. In a potential recall this decision will have a heightened importance.

There is a conflict between objective or statistical risk on the one hand and subjective or perceived risk on the other. The Royal Society report addresses the question as to whether objective risk assessment can ever be free from the fundamentals of judgment. One expert argued that there were "large of elements of intuition" on the part of administrators in construing, from frequency statistics, what risks are acceptable to the public. As we have already seen, the importance of the human contribution to failure is well-recognised but not very susceptible to measurement. When making a recall decision, a producer would perhaps be wise to view with circumspection the data presented by his in-house experts on the proportion of defects. Yet in practice such data is rarely questioned in professional detail. Reliance is usually placed on the opinion of a familiar individual manager, without appreciating that he may have been biased and judgmental in reaching his conclusions. The pressure of events and the consequences of a major recall can tend to exclude a critical appraisal of the basic data.

Individuals have an enormous capacity for storing past perceptions and calling on them when evaluating a new situation. Tornadoes are more feared than diabetes, in spite of the fact that the former causes fewer deaths than the latter. Too, it is important to distinguish between the voluntary and the involuntary assumption of risk, especially for product recall. If a product on the market has a concealed dangerous defect the people who use it involuntarily assume the risk it presents to them. By initiating a recall of the product and publishing information about it, the assumption of risk becomes voluntary for those who become aware of the notification but ignore it. An example would be a car owner who took no action after receiving a recall notification by recorded delivery, which the vehicle manufacturer could prove.

Work on the effect of low mortality hazards with high disability outcomes is quoted in the Royal Society report. These qualitative characteristics are an important factor in perceived risk: examples are permanent brain damage, protracted terminal cancer and paralysis from the neck down, which were assessed as being worse than death. There is also a distinction between individual and societal risk: a snakebite and nuclear radiation. These two dimensions of perceived risk are independent and the HSE distinguishes between them in its approach to risk assessment. When respondents are asked to judge a range of hazards the most notable is the dread risk, found in nerve gas, crime and nuclear weapons for example. The higher the perceived risk the more people want its current risks reduced and strict regulation introduced. If dread risks exist in a consumer good the decision to recall is straightforward: for instance, botulism in food, the danger of electrocution in a domestic appliance or a choking hazard for children. The confirmed dread risk makes the recall decision itself.

Attitudes to risk and danger are influenced by the cultural bias that is shared by a group. People select certain risks for attention to defend their preferred lifestyle and to be able to blame others. Most of our knowledge about hazards and danger comes second-hand from the media, politicians, scientists and government agencies. This emphasises that risk perception is multi-disciplinary and that the real world does not necessarily match that presumed by experts.

One worker observed that certain events led to ripples of secondary consequences, which could go far beyond the initial impact of an event. It is called social amplification and can include loss of sales, regulatory constraints, litigation, community opposition and investor flight. The social framing of risk experts' assessments always involves a judgment, which may be different from that adopted by the public. An example concerned the presence of a contaminant called dioxin in a herbicide; it is the same toxin as that released at Seveso in 1976 which affected many local residents. In the U.K. the debate over the safety of a herbicide was only resolved when it was realised that the initial scientific evaluation depended on an assumption, that the product would always be made and used under strictly controlled conditions. Experts had assumed that manufacturing conditions never varied to allow contaminants, such as dioxin, to be produced and that drums of herbicide were always delivered with full, intelligible instructions. Agricultural workers were only too well aware that their environment rarely approximated to the idealised laboratory conditions, assumed by the scientists. The latter imagined that farmers would always comply with the stated instructions, such as correct solvents, spray nozzles and pressure valves under the prescribed weather conditions while wearing protective clothing.

Producers are responsible for the consequences of the foreseeable misuse of their products, although not the abuse of them. They must be well informed of the circumstances in which they will be used. On occasion users discover weaknesses in products which can pose a threat to safety. This can lead to a recall and a review of the product development procedures that allowed the weakness to get through undetected.

There have been few definitive studies of risk communication, yet it is a vital part of a producer's responsibility to ensure the safety of the users of his products. Recall advertisements are an example but they vary greatly in their quality, from those which are simple and uncomplicated to those which verge on the incomprehensible. Now the E.C. has a system for the rapid exchange of information (Rapex, see page 85), provided for in Article 8 of the General Product Safety Directive. The Annex to the Directive sets out the detailed procedures to be followed and continues that "It is impossible to lay down specific criteria as to what, precisely, constitutes an immediate and serious risk; in this regard, the national authorities will therefore judge each individual case on its merits." This failure to provide any guidance on the definition of risk means that in practice each national authority will establish its own definition. There has to be a possibility that there will be a variety of definitions, from a selection of the 15 national authorities.

The Royal Society report raises several significant dilemmas and paradoxes about the conflicting goals of risk communications. It lists four conceptual approaches which have been identified in the literature:

1. *The top-down or one-way transmission.* This could be a message about a hazard or risk from an expert to a non-expert audience. A recall advertisement or notification is in this category, as well as press releases from government agencies and regulatory bodies. The report says: "The one-way model of risk communication has been the target for much criticism, in particular on the grounds that by assuming an altruistic communicator it implicitly devalues the perspectives and knowledge of the risk bearers."
2. *The two-way exchange or dialogue.* The U.S. National Research Council sees risk communication as an interactive process of exchange of information and opinion among individuals, groups and institutions. It highlights the critical role of feedback and interaction.
3. *Actions, messages, signs and symbols.* Depending on the context, action and inaction on the part of the risk managers can speak louder than words, by sending important messages which may conflict with official communications. A classic case is that of Tylenol in the U.S. in 1982, see page 382.
4. *Participation and empowerment of risk-bearing groups in the decision-making process.* This focuses on the important question of the public groups' right to know about the risks they face. It implies such a role in the tolerable risk concept discussed above.

Much of the advice on risk communication lacks direct empirical validation, either in terms of its effectiveness or its capacity to avoid unintended consequences. One worker showed that the credibility of the communicator was critically dependent on the trust placed in him: "If we do not trust the source then we will not trust the message."

This whole field of risk perception has been virtually ignored, not only in the circumstances of product recall but also in the management of product liability generally. Now, with the added responsibility placed on producers to warn them about risks, it should not be neglected.

An example of risk perception is the "Camelford water contamination incident" Case History on page 420.

The dread risk of botulism is illustrated in "The fatal pot of yoghurt" Case History on page 437.

PRODUCT RECALL PLAN

A key factor in a successful recall is the appointment of the recall co-ordinator. The manager who can make the decision to initiate a recall must be named in the plan. Care is needed to ensure that the recall notification fulfils its objectives. A 100 per cent response rate will not be achieved in a national recall. Plans for relaunching the product should be put in hand at the earliest opportunity; examples are given of how this was done in a number of companies. The key elements of a product recall plan are examined alongside a flow chart.

Recall Co-ordinator

The appointment of the Recall Co-ordinator is a key factor in product recall. He should be in place before the event so that he can familiarise himself with the possible actions and their consequences. The latter are more important than they may appear to be at first sight, especially in the techniques and nuances of presentation. Mistakes in communications can have expensive results. The most significant and far reaching actions may well have to be made within a few hours of the confirmation of the existence of a defective product on the market. These can affect the whole course of the recall and ultimately its cost.

It is an advantage for the Recall Co-ordinator to be responsible for having the plan written, not necessarily writing it himself. Indeed, if each specialist makes his own contribution this will encourage his commitment to the outcome, if the plan is put into effect. There is a flow chart on page 386 followed by a summary of the principles. The extent and detail will very much be influenced by a company's unique product liability exposures. It may be a considerable manual for a safety-critical product in wide distribution or a brief procedure for a non-critical component supplier who manufactures to customers' specification. The plan must be widely accepted and thoroughly tested if it is to enable a recall to be managed successfully. Regular review and updating is essential.

One survey[39] found that, apart from vehicles, recalls did not deal adequately with unsafe products. The particular problems were

- lack of definition of what constitutes a recall;
- poor use of advertising of recall notices and safety warnings;
- inadequate, incomplete and inaccurate information;
- no specific target response to the recall to be aimed at;
- no consistency in the decision process;

[39] "Improving recalls of unsafe products" 'Consumers' Association, London 1993.

- no requirement for the speed of action necessary;
- unidentifiable warnings;
- recalls sometimes not free of charge;

The recall decision (see below) will confirm the risk classification and the level to which the product is to be pursued. Then it becomes the responsibility of the Recall Co-ordinator to manage the recall. In this he can be supported by a *small* committee of two or three, with additional specialists co-opted as necessary.

The recall decision

Whether to recall or not can be a difficult decision to make. In extreme cases it is straightforward. If the product is known to have caused death or injury then the decision makes itself. A knowledgeable company, with a strong bottom line and experienced management, will usually be able to rely on previous incidents to reach a solution. The difficulties arise when there is not enough evidence one way or the other, there is insufficient time to gather any more and experience is lacking. Examples illustrate what can happen.

A domestic electrical product had been on sale for several years, enjoying a modest but unspectacular success. Each Christmas the promotional activities were stepped up as it was a popular present, especially for elderly people. One December the manufacturer's local Trading Standards Officer reported that a lady in Leamington Spa had suffered an electric shock while using the product. Her identity and further details were not available. The company immediately put the incident at top priority. A search of company records revealed nothing untoward, but could not conclusively prove that a rogue had not been produced. Strong requests for more information met with little response, except to confirm that the lady received the shock in normal use of the product. The approvals organisation, whose symbol the product carried, were adamant that there should be an immediate recall. The manufacturer's holding company directors joined a meeting of the incident management team.

These corporate executives found it hard to believe that a decision had to be based on so little hard information. The meeting wallowed around because there were no markers to indicate which direction to take. Eventually the threat of a press release from the approvals organisation forced a reluctant recall decision. By some adroit public relations the recall was carried out successfully. No-one ever did discover what happened at Leamington Spa. No other incident was reported and no defective units were found.

The second example demonstrates the advantage of experience and planning ahead. A food company announced it was to make some employees redundant in a cost cutting exercise. A note was received that the product had been contaminated by an anonymous employee in a grudge attack to protest against the redundancies. The local newspaper splashed the story in a banner headline on the front page. The company had a well-tested crisis management plan which was immediately activated. The only information about the contamination was vague. As a matter of urgency a specialist laboratory checked all ingredients, packaging and final product in an extensive operation. In the meantime consultants advised that the circumstances strongly indicated that the attack was a hoax. No recall was initiated. No contamination was found. The company put out a press release saying that all checks had proved negative but that experts were keeping a very close eye on the situation. Nothing further was heard of the tamperer.

Sometimes, however, even the best laid plans do not help. An engineering company made a safety-critical component, whose users reported a small handful of possible failures. The manufacturer had a thorough product safety management system with comprehensive hazard analysis and risk assessment records. At a meeting of the senior executives these were reviewed in great detail. A probability tree was constructed on the whiteboard. There was no agreement on whether or not to go for an expensive recall. In the end the managing director called for a vote on a recall. It was a tie, at three for and three against. The managing director thereupon decided against a recall. There were no unusual consequences following that decision.

It should be established who has the authority to take a recall decision. As a rule of thumb, the greater the risk the more senior should be the manager. The multiple retailers who stock many fast moving consumer products (Boots have 50,000 products, Sainsbury's 17,500 and Argos 7,500) have well-tried systems which accommodate this situation as a matter of course. For them recalls are virtually part of everyday life. Mostly they will be for defects which pose little or no threat to consumers, such as an incorrect price.

For other companies, without this wealth of experience, the need to make a recall decision can catch them unawares. They will find that the one commodity lacking is time. Assessing the aspects reviewed here — risk classification, the significance of the proportion of defects, risk perception, let alone the ethical considerations — needs experience and training. Without these essential factors there can be a danger that corporate martyrdom will lead to a very expensive exercise. This means a misguided belief in doing the apparent right thing, whatever the cost. An appreciation of the choices available and the techniques that can be adopted can avoid the penalties of moral absolutism.

Recall notification

The communication, to those who hold the product, of the actions to be taken to initiate a recall is called the notification. There will be a number of versions depending upon the recipient and the means of transmission. The public notification will be by an advertisement in the national press, specialist publications or posters at the points of sale. There are a number of essential features which an advertisement should carry, which can include:

- A means of attracting attention to the purport of the message. "Important Announcement" and "Important Notice" lack the impact of "Safety Notice", "Urgent Recall" and "Product Recall." The advertisement should declare its difference from offers, sales and promotions. A cluttered layout will frustrate the object of the exercise, see **Figure 13.3** page 357 and **Figure 13.4** page 358.
- The name and address of the producer.
- A description of the product. An illustration will capture attention more effectively than words alone, especially for domestic electrical products, see **Figure 13.5** page 378.
- A means of identifying the defective batch. This may be by a serial number, sell-by date or period of purchase. On occasion the purchaser may be asked to examine the product to establish whether the defect exists.
- The hazard should be given in simple terms, so that those who hold the product know the risk they run in using it.
- Limitations of use. These may range from an instruction to stop use immediately to a restriction on specific applications.
- Instructions on what to do with the product. Some will have to be returned to the point of sale, some may require a coupon to be returned to the producer with the purchaser's name and address and others may ask that a specialist agency is contacted to arrange for a repair.
- Free telephone number for enquiries. The operators must be trained and log all calls. It is often advisable to retain an outside agency to carry out this work, to prevent the calls getting in the way of the producer's regular business. For example, The BT Customer Communication Centre at Bristol has a computer integrated telephony system which can recognise nominated numbers. The service is script driven. When a designated number is dialled the operator calls up a prompt screen which gives the script, previously agreed with the customer. All calls are logged and analysed to the depth required by the customer. Reports can be provided by the day, week or month. The cost is 65p per operator minute.

The success of a recall advertisement may not be as great as imagined, although placing it may give the manufacturer a feeling of having done the right thing. For example, the single insertion of a recall advertisement in 13 national newspapers cost £40,000; in addition there were insertions in specialist publications. Out of the 9,675 units that had been sold just 115 were returned, including some competitors' products. Business notifications will have additional information regarding payment, reporting of stocks held and returned, a contact point, and storage and shipment of returned product.

Figure 13.5 Recall notification example

BLACK & DECKER®

SAFETY NOTICE

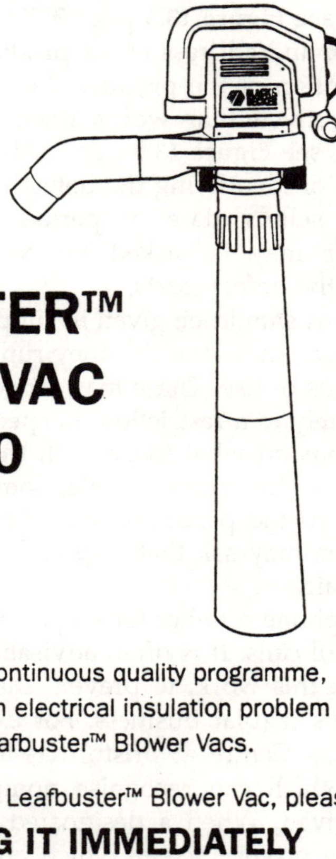

LEAFBUSTER™
BLOWER VAC
GW150

In the course of our continuous quality programme,
we have discovered an electrical insulation problem
on all of our Leafbuster™ Blower Vacs.

If you possess a GW150 Leafbuster™ Blower Vac, please

CEASE USING IT IMMEDIATELY

and contact us at your earliest convenience.

We have set up a helpline on:
Freephone 0800 252661
to take your calls each day between 9.00am and 5.00pm
(including Sat/Sun until 21st November 1993).
Or simply call your local Black & Decker Service Centre
(see Yellow Pages for details).
Your co-operation in this matter is appreciated.

Source: The Times, November 12, 1993. Clear, simple direct. Product instantly identifiable, Hazard given and alternative contact instructions

An analysis[40] of 97 recall advertisements between 1990 and 1992 showed:

- 29 per cent had no heading which indicated that it was a safety issue or recall;
- 70 per cent did not make clear what the hazard was;
- 12 per cent failed to say there was either a hazard or a safety defect;
- 47 per cent said there was safety problem but did not say what it was;
- 33 per cent gave no telephone contact number;
- 25 per cent only offered a freephone number.

The National Readership Survey, funded by the press and agencies, is based on questionnaires completed by 35,000 people twice a year. From this the DTI can recommend those newspapers which would give the optimum chance for purchasers, of a product under recall, to see an advertisement. In theory it would be possible to reach 92 per cent of the population, but not every reader will see every page or even notice a recall advertisement if they did.

Apart from advertising, the notification can be transmitted by fax, letter, telex, telephone, personal visit and press release. Under section 42 of the Consumer Protection Act 1987 the Secretary of State has the power to compel suppliers to publish at their own expense Notices to Warn about unsafe goods. The Secretary of State may specify the form and manner of the notice as well as the occasions on which it should be published. In the five years to 1993 this power was not used but the Department of Trade and Industry has published its own press notices.

Response rates

The proportion of units returned out of those sold is one measure of the effectiveness of a recall. For consumer goods in particular, a major difficulty will be that there may be no accurate figure for the number available for recall. For example, food, drink, cosmetics, toiletries, hair preparations and the like may have been used by the time a recall is announced. Short shelf-life products add to the difficulty. Too, people who do see the notification will ignore it, throw away the offending product or postpone action. Others will not be reached by the information.

A survey[41] of 2,000 randomly selected adults found that guarantee cards were widely noticed, with 84 per cent remembering having received one in the previous year. About six in ten of those who received cards returned them, with domestic appliances having the biggest rate. Only 4 per cent of respondents said that guarantee cards were a means of enabling manufacturers to contact them in the event of

[40] *Ibid.*
[41] *Ibid.*

a recall. Of those who failed to return guarantee cards a third said that there was no point in doing so.

There are no independent data on response rates, with the exception of vehicles. The Vehicle Inspectorate of the Department of Transport monitors recalls, which have the advantage of the Driver and Vehicle Licensing Agency's computers' data on Vehicle Identification Numbers and the registered keepers' names and addresses. The expectation on recall performance is a response rate of 50 per cent after six months, 70 per cent after 12 months and 100 per cent after 18 months. A recall is terminated by agreement between the manufacturer and the Inspectorate, when 100 per cent of the vehicles have been corrected or the response rate has remained static for some time. The average response rates on closed recalls for two fiscal years were:

	1991/92	1992/93
Cars	84.8%	80.35%
HGVs	72.8%	73.47%
Buses	85.3%	93.1%
Motorcycles	86.5%	86.12%

In the U.S. the National Highway Traffic Safety Administration found that over a 20-year period up to 1985 the average response rate was 54 per cent. Even with the great benefit of the DVLA, it will be seen that the possibility of achieving a total recall is unlikely. There is precious little published information on other response rates, compared with the initial publicity announcing the recalls. An exception was the well-reported case of the Nova Fritex deep-fat fryer in 1976, when 18,703 units were sought in Belgium and the U.K. A series of three recall advertisements and an intense company effort by ITT Europe, who owned Nova, recovered 90 per cent. The company called this "an exceptional achievement: in the USA a return rate of 25 to 50 per cent for a recall is considered very satisfactory."[42]

A remarkable result was claimed by Perrier in their world-wide recall, which they announced in full-page advertisements in the U.K. on February 15, 1990. The *Financial Times* of February 27, 1990 reported "Perrier has recalled more than 90 per cent of its world stock of 160m bottles by yesterday. All production had been returned in Britain, North America, Asia and the Far East, Perrier said."

A major story in 1992 involved a Candy washer/drier, following the death of an elderly woman because of a fire in her machine. Initially the product had been recalled in March 1991. A year later less than 16 per cent had been modified to make them safe. The Consumers' Association had taken an interest in the case and presented evidence at the inquest. It showed that the appliance had a foreseeable fault condition. The CA also said that they had evidence of several other serious fires which had

[42] J.M. Groocock *et al*, "The Recall of the Nova Fritex" *Quality Assurance*, London June, 1978.

involved the product. A video of a Candy washer/drier in flames in a laboratory received intense media coverage. A headline in *The Times* was "Minister's plea after drier death". Further recall advertisements were published in the national press on four separate occasions and the company wrote to 15,000 known purchasers. The campaign started in the August and by the end of the November 72 per cent of the 42,000 appliances had been checked.

Topvogue recalled a lightbulb sensor socket in December 1990, which had been sold by mail order. Despite this data source, a month later only 16 per cent had been returned. The Director of the British Electrotechnical Approvals Board is quoted[43] as saying that a company is doing very well if it achieves an 18 to 22 per cent return. Zanussi claimed a 90 per cent response for 18,000 Slimline dishwashers in 1988. They attributed this very high rate to the co-operation of retailers who made their sales records available and the fact that the product had only been on sale for a few months.

Relaunch

The activity surrounding the recall of a major product can divert attention from an important factor that is often overlooked. If the product is likely to suffer damage to its brand image a way of retrieving the situation will be required. A brand image can be one of a company's greatest assets, even though it may not appear in the balance sheet. It is advisable to set up, as soon as possible, a small team with the task of relaunching the product. It should be separate from the management of the recall, although it must be familiar with its circumstances.

Market research may be essential to reveal the impact of the recall on the consumers' appreciation of the brand. It is dangerous to make assumptions from the security of an ivory tower. There is no substitute for first hand information from those on the Clapham omnibus. This will help in answering fundamental questions. How many people know about the recall? Are those that do know concerned enough to stop buying? How can they be reassured? Would it be advisable to repackage? Should the name be changed or modified? How important will it be to distinguish the relaunched product from the previous version? Or would it be better not change anything? What would be the best way of communicating with the public? How much will a relaunch cost? Have we got the money?

Some people will reject indefinitely a product that has been recalled, whatever the circumstances and whoever was at fault. For example, a very long memory was responsible for an elderly couple not buying corned beef. In 1993 they said that they would "never have it in the house" after that "awful business in Scotland". This turned out to be a

[43] See n. 36, *supra*.

reference to the Aberdeen typhoid outbreak of 1964, when one tin of Argentine corned beef put 400 in hospital. A similar case was that of the lady who stopped buying canned salmon when Mr and Mrs Farmer died after eating some from one can, for Sunday tea in August 1978. Despite reassurances in the 1990s, the lady adamantly refused to have anything to do with any canned fish, let alone salmon, because she said, "You never know".

The John West canned salmon recall[44] received significant national coverage in the media, as it was the biggest recall in the U.K. up to that time. The cause was botulism and the cost was put at £2 million. To recover the situation an £80,000 advertising campaign was launched in November 1978. It was backed by the British Association of Canned and Preserved Foods Importers and Distributors in co-operation with the canned salmon industry in the U.S. and Canada and the can making industry of North America and the U.K. It had been agreed by the U.K. Department of Health and Social Security. The headline used was CANNED SALMON IS CLEARED! and the copy included "You can now buy canned salmon with confidence."

In June 1979 sales were reported to be back to 75 per cent of what they had been before the Farmers' tragedy, when they were £50 million a year. The Canned Salmon Consumer Bureau had been established to provide recipes and information. Then, in 1982, the story started all over again. There were two cases of botulism in Belgium, one fatal, caused by eating the same brand of canned salmon. A Manchester family became ill after eating salmon. The Minister of Health told the House of Commons that 10 million cans were retained in warehouses, after his department had put out a public health warning. By September all had been examined at three checking stations but sales had dropped like a stone.

The most spectacular relaunch was in the U.S.[45] Seven people were murdered in September 1982 by Extra-Strength Tylenol capsules, of lot number MC 2880, that had been laced with cyanide. Sales of Tylenol were $400 million and represented a third of the over-the-counter analgesic market; the capsule version had sales of $175 million. About $40 million was spent on advertising. The product was sold by McNeil Laboratories a subsidiary of Johnson & Johnson. In one of the many company discussions James Burke, the Chief Executive Officer of J & J, said: "The most positive reassurance you can give [the consumer] is a tamper-resistant package and we're going to give it to her." He believed that it was no good trying to sell the product without first providing reassurance. Burke went to every media network to explain that the murders were an act of terrorism against the entire health care delivery system, and by extension the food delivery system. It was not an attack on J & J.

[44] H. Abbott, "The first mouse died at three o'clock", *Product Liability International*, London, December 1983.

[45] H. Abbott, "The story behind the Tylenol story", *Product Liability International*, London, January 1991.

Telephone research was carried out to discover what the public really felt about the disaster. It was repeated daily to provide the best possible knowledge base. In the corporate incident room Burke said: "Gentlemen, the idea here is not just to save the franchise or some part of the franchise but to restore the franchise to full blooming health, the thirty-five [per cent] share and build it." In a TV interview he said: "Have no doubt. None of us have any doubts, that we are going to have a business in Tylenol. The question is how big it is going to be and how long it will take."

Two million pieces of literature were sent to doctors, nurses, dentists and hospital managers. An advertising programme, told people who had thrown Tylenol capsules away, that they could get free replacements. Tens of thousands of feet of film were shot of interviews with users and non-users. The company medical adviser, Dr Thomas Gates, talked about the situation on TV. Using satellite communication a 30 city tele-conference was held for the media. Burke showed the new "tamper-proof triple-sealed" packaging to Phil Donahue, the anchor man on his prime time TV programme Sixty Minutes.

The relaunch started on November 11 with 60–second TV commercials followed by national advertising in the New Year. Then, four years after recovering market share the story started all over again, just like the canned salmon story. In February 1986 a woman in New York died after taking cyanide-laced Tylenol capsules. Immediately J & J recalled all the product and replaced the capsules with a new caplet form. Up to $150 million was spent in promoting the new appearance, full-page advertisements were placed in 400 newspapers offering free exchange of customers' capsules. Mailgrams were sent to 100,000 doctors, hospitals and pharmacies in a major information sampling programme. Subsequent consumer research showed that the public felt that J & J had made an adequate response to the crisis.

The Farley National Sales Conference was being held at an hotel in Bath on Friday December 20, 1985. The Marketing Director had just presented the incentive awards and told the delegates that the company had done well, when he was called to the telephone. He returned to the conference to report that a recall of Farley baby food was to be initiated.[46] The sales team retained some of the hotel rooms to devise a policy, prepare press statements and responses. Over Christmas a separate relaunch group was established to prepare for the resumption of sales. In 1985 Farley, owned by Glaxo, were number three in the baby food market with a 24 per cent share. The media led with the story, eventually the product was taken off the market and the company was sold by Glaxo to Boots. In 1994 Boots sold Farley to H.J. Heinz.

In the New Year of 1986 market research was carried out twice a week for four weeks to discover the state of goodwill towards the company. The large majority of respondents thought that the company had acted

[46] H. Abbott, "Salmonella at Farley's", *Product Liability International*, London, August 1988.

speedily, responsibly and correctly. A full page advertisement on January 19, 1986 thanked customers for their support and listed the eight Farley products that were not affected. The advertisement did not achieve its aim and seemed to resurrect memories of the crisis. The planned repeat was abandoned.

With the Farley product off the market for nine months the competition moved in. Wyeth claimed its total market share had increased 11 per centage points to 51 per cent, and Milupa had 10 per cent of the market compared to 4 per cent before the recall. Boots planned a campaign to relaunch the baby food range to health care professionals in the autumn. This reveals the great difficulty that faced the relaunch. Under the voluntary code of advertising, based on the World Health Organisation's International Code of Marketing Breast-milk Substitutes 1981, baby-milk products cannot be advertised directly to the consumer — in this case the mothers who buy the product. So one of the foundations of a marketing exercise could not be employed. A video was made for showing to the health professionals. New packaging was tamper-evident and emphasised the Farley Seal of Quality Assurance. The packs carried "We're Back for Good" and "Discover how you can rest assured with Farley's". A market share of 15 per cent was regained.

The Perrier relaunch in 1990, after the world-wide recall,[47] was badly fumbled. The company's image was damaged by an inept press conference on February 14, followed by contradictory statements about how the contamination with benzene came about in the first place. Full-page advertisements appeared on February 15 in the U.K. national newspapers saying that there were "very slight traces of impurity in some bottles of Perrier though at levels which represent no hazard to health." A helpline telephone number was given. Some 1,700 calls were received from consumers and the trade, all of which were logged. Over the whole period the following enquiries were received: 5,000 from the media, 7,000 from the trade, 15,000 from consumers and 100 from scientists, engineers, chemists and universities. Within 10 days of the recall 93 per cent of the U.K. population knew of the contamination.

On February 27 more full-page advertisements appeared in the newspapers saying the problem had been solved. New quality control procedures were in place and the new bottles of Perrier would be easy to identify. Again a helpline telephone number was given. At the end of March a £4 million relaunch campaign started to recapture the 60 per cent market share. About the same time it was reported that the gas, which gave the water its bubbles, came from an underground source separate from the water itself. The gas was added to the water at ground level. This fact was to rebound on the relaunch campaign. More full-page advertisements appeared on March 26 announcing a new 750 ml bottle size and a label carrying "New Production."

The next day this was called a rip-off in the press because it concealed a 10p-a-litre price rise compared to the previous 1 litre bottles. Perrier

[47] H. Abbott, *Managing Product Recall* (1991).

said that the 750 ml size was standard throughout Europe and made restocking faster. In April the words "naturally sparkling" were to be dropped from the Perrier label in the U.S., as the Food and Drink Administration considered them to be inaccurate. In the U.S. there was a series of giveaways, television advertisements, talk-show appearances and radio advertisements. In the U.K. Sainsbury's told Perrier that it would not stock the product until the label had been changed from "naturally carbonated" to "carbonated natural" mineral water. In June 1990 group sales were at 60 per cent of the previous level but there were difficulties in regaining share in the U.S. In August U.K. sales were claimed to be at 75 per cent of the level before the recall. The monitoring company MEAL estimated that Perrier had spent £2.6 million on press and television advertising since the relaunch.

At the end of August the Ministry of Agriculture, Fisheries and Food announced that Perrier was to be relabelled. The decision had been agreed by the European Commission and the French Government. It would be called "Natural Mineral Water Fortified with Gas from the Spring." The *Wall Street Journal* said that the announcement was another blow to the company's reputation. *The Economist* said: "Just as it was forgetting its troubles with benzene, Source Perrier has been caught out again." By the end of the year Perrier's share of the U.K. sparkling mineral water was 24 per cent compared to 49.6 per cent in July 1989.

Summary of the key elements of a product recall plan

See **Figure 13.6, page 386,** the Society of Motor Manufacturers and Traders' Code of Practice on Vehicle Safety Defects (Appendix 5) and the British Retail Consortium Guidelines and Checklist for Product Recall (Appendix 6).

Product defect A producer can learn about a defective product from a number of sources. The most common is from in-house departments, such as quality assurance and field personnel. Properly managed consumer complaints can give a warning of trouble ahead, by looking for variations from the normal. Regulatory bodies may receive a complaint directly from a consumer, which is then taken up with the producer. A criminal attack may immediately suggest a recall, but a more considered response may rest on the ability to recall should it become necessary.

Recall Co-ordinator (see page 374) This key appointment needs a seasoned and experienced professional with plenty of management muscle. He can come from a variety of functions. It will probably be an advantage to support the Co-ordinator with a *small* product recall committee. At the beginning of a major recall the committee will be in continuous session. Alternates should be named in the plan so that the normal business of the company can continue.

Figure 13.6 Product recall flow chart

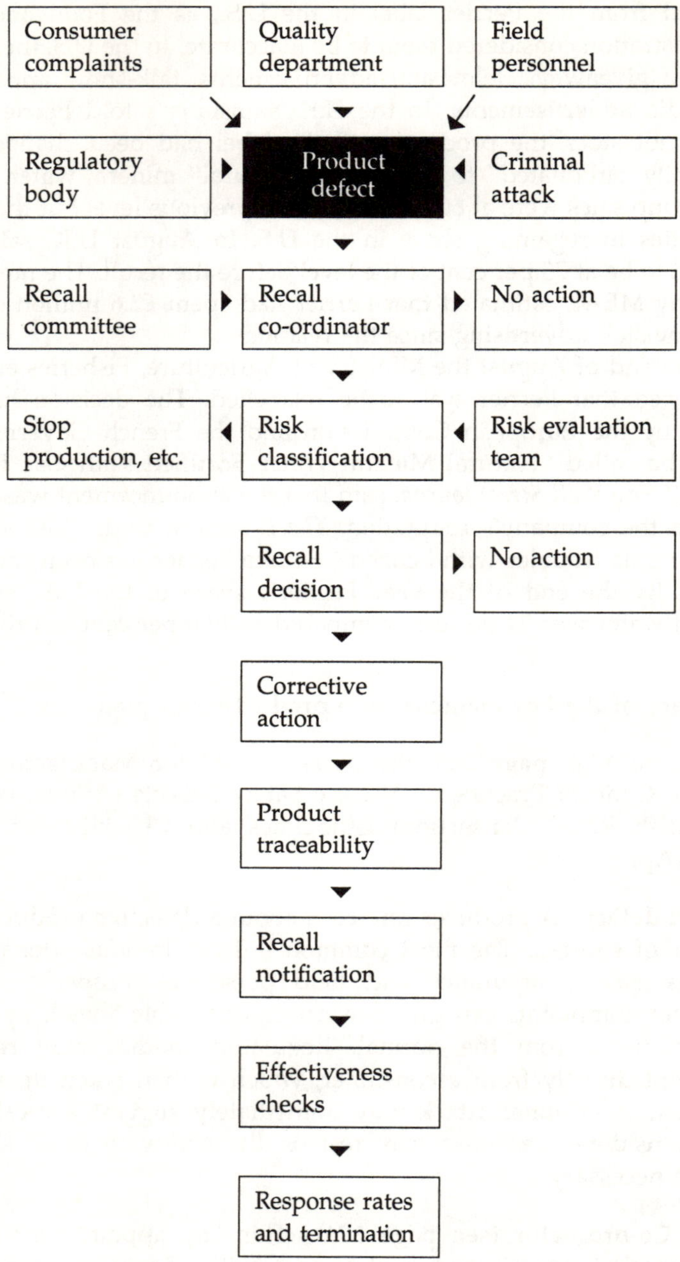

Make sure you manage the recall and do not allow the recall to manage you.

Scource: H. Abbott, *Managing Product Recall*, (1992)

Risk classification (see page 368) The first step, and at times the most difficult one, is to confirm that a hazard actually does exist. Then, by examining its probability and severity, the risk can be classified. A *small* evaluation team of experts, internal and possibly external, is required to allocate an individual classification to the risk. The plan must contain a classification table by which it can be achieved. From this action a number of major decisions will flow, one of which may be to stop production until the problem has been fully investigated.

Recall decision (see page 375) The recommendation to initiate a recall will come from the Co-ordinator but the decision will be made by a separate and senior manager. The classification given to the risk will determine who it is. In many companies the chief executive will make the decision. In a criminal attack the tough decision may be not to recall until the situation has clarified.

Corrective action To do this the administrative mechanism by which it can be achieved has to be in place, before the notification is published. The usual practice for fast moving consumer products is a refund or replacement. Other products may require an *in situ* repair or modification

Product traceability (see page 356) A successful recall will use a scalpel not a cold chisel. It must be able to delineate the defective product batch and uplift that, and that alone. The more kindred products that have to be uplifted, to ensure that the defective batch itself is recovered, the greater the cost. Product traceability is the foundation of success. It must enable the company rapidly to discover which ingredients and packaging have been comprised into which end products, to whom they have been sent and when.

Recall depth (see page 368) An early decision has to be made on how far along the distribution chain the product is to be pursued. The further from the factory gate, the more difficult it becomes, the higher the total cost, the smaller the chances of success and the greater the publicity. The risk classification will indicate the recall depth.

Recall notification (see page 376) The essential parts of any communication to users should be listed in the Plan. They include: a description of the product, batch number, a description of the hazard, instructions on what action to take and a helpline phone number. Model approved advertisements are an advantage when time is limited.

Effectiveness checks Two figures are required to monitor the progress of a recall. The number of units out in the field should be known, although it may not always be possible to discover it with any precision. The number of units returned should be reported regularly to build up a picture of progress. If the latter figure is taken as a percentage of the former the effectiveness of the recall is determined. To carry out effectiveness checks needs good administration and record keeping. The plan should have the details of the system to be used.

Response rate and termination (see page 379) This is one measure of the success of a recall. The chance of getting back all the defective units in a national recall is nil. It follows that at some time a decision will have to be taken to dismantle the special arrangements for managing the recall, and let the regular routines handle the tail. The decision to terminate should be taken by the manager who initiated the recall.

Contact lists A surprising number of people may have to be contacted in a recall. The means of doing so must be listed in the plan. A regular update is essential but unfortunately is often overlooked. Apart from company employees the list can include the company lawyer, doctor, insurance broker, public relations agency, major customers and suppliers, Trading Standards Officer, union representatives, trade association and Government bodies.

Outside agencies A company may need help and advice in a major recall. The agencies that can provide it should be selected and their contact details incorporated in the plan. Examples are field marketing companies, experienced public relations agencies, specialist laboratories and management consultants.

Spokesperson The nominated spokesperson, and alternate, must be specifically trained in media relations, especially in adversarial situations. The media may well expect to hear from the chief executive or senior director rather than a public relations representative. It is essential to capture the information flow and, for radio and TV, insist on live and not recorded interviews.

Incident room and facilities In a major recall a separate room should be available for the Recall Co-ordinator and his team. It will require certain facilities which have to be immediately to hand. They can include dedicated phone lines both incoming and outgoing, fax, copier, flip charts, stationery, refreshment, controlled access, log book, word processor, secretarial assistance, etc.

Legal position It must be very clearly stated in the plan. The responsibility can be influenced by when the contamination occurred. If it was in-house then the company itself will have a liability under the Consumer Protection Act 1987, Part I. For this reason alone the time of contamination should be established as soon as possible. A requirement that is not always as simple as it may appear.

Insurance Cover is available for product recall. It is expensive and requires an established plan. A statement of the company's position regarding cover should be in the plan, together with insurance broker contact details.

Costs The plan should include the means by which relevant costs can be captured, as far as possible.

Test the plan A plan cannot be said to be established unless it has been realistically tested. A simulation exercise is effective, with a scenario written to include the people, products and market of the company.

14 The producer's control systems

The problem with quality control systems is that they are subject to human frailty: such as 100 per cent inspection which can never be 100 per cent effective. Quality assurance led to documented systems and ISO 9000. This standard lists the key factors in an organisation and requires a written description of how they are managed. Assessment of management systems for ISO 9000 can be carried out internally, by the customer or by an independent certification body. Total quality management is based on never ending quality improvement to identify weaknesses and reorganise management to take account of customer needs.

MANAGEMENT SYSTEMS

In order to achieve end results, every organisation whether a one man business or a multi-national corporation, must have aims and direction. There must be a plan of how the end result is to be reached. The plan may be predetermined, or develop as work proceeds.

But whether written down, or kept in the head of the person running the business, the plan must exist. Such a plan is a management system. All businesses must have management systems, even though they may not realise they exist.

For a very small organisation it is possible for the person running the business to pass verbal instructions to staff as they need them. In larger organisations communications problems increase with the length of the chain of command. In addition to lack of clarity and hence misunderstanding of verbal instructions, they tend to go in one direction only, top downwards. The end results are not always clear to everyone performing part of the task. Hence input or communication back to the top, is limited.

Management systems must define communications routes, both for instructions and for describing aims to be achieved. Such systems can exist in many different forms, and except in the very simplest of organisations, written data is essential.

PROCESS CONTROL

Everything which needs to be done to produce a product can be called a process. Processes include:

- deciding customer needs;
- designing specific products;
- manufacturing operations;
- inspection or checking operations;
- producing operating instructions to the customer.

Processes are a combination of physical tasks and administrative tasks which together are required to achieve the end result which a customer will buy.

Since the time man was able to write, written instructions have been used to control processes. As the world has become more sophisticated, so the instructions have become more complex. They include drawings, photographs and computer software.

The essential data needed to undertake a process is:

- description of starting materials;
- process parameters to be controlled;
- process measurements;
- output characteristics and acceptance criteria.

Without this data, the process operator cannot work. Some of the data can be provided by verbal instructions (*e.g.* descriptions of starting materials). But much will be too complex to rely on verbal communication. Imagine trying to explain how to measure a complex shape without some form of drawing. Errors would be certain if dimensions are not written down.

Disputes would be certain if no record of the controls are generated. Records are needed both within the organisation, and to give confidence to the customer.

Quality control systems

In most cases of manufacturing, a supplier agrees end results, or a product description with the customer. The supplier may define a product description and the customer chooses the supplier based on the declared performance claims (*e.g.* a domestic washing machine). The customers' measure of the "quality" of the product is how closely the supplier meets that product description.

The product description can be for general performance characteristics, or for specific dimensions. The customer may want a pump which will move liquid at a given rate, not being worried about the type of pump or how it is constructed. Alternatively, a piece of material may be supplied to be painted with a specific coating to a specific thickness, or machined to specific toleranced dimensions.

The manufacturer is expected, by the customer, to control and measure the processes needed in order to achieve the required results.

Since the 1940s quality control systems in the form of documented inspection systems, have been in place in order to give assurance that measurement control will take place. Such systems created "Inspectors" whose job is to ensure acceptance criteria are achieved at each stage of the process.

A quality control system comprises:

- process method statements;
- equipment operating instructions;
- inspection data — drawings, specifications etc;
- inspection criteria and tolerances;
- production and inspection records requirements.

Today, almost every manufacturer has some form of quality control system, and often advertises product on the basis of careful inspection before release for sale.

Whilst a quality control system ensures a mechanism is in place which will permit comparison of every product with the criteria agreed between the manufacturer and its customer, there are problems.

Problems of quality control systems

Systems which rely on people, are subject to human frailty. 100 per cent inspection, never leads to 100 per cent rejection of defective items. The inspector "misses" some rejects, which are then provided to the customer.

This of course is known to the customer, and may be acceptable for high volume, low cost products. For example the customer may accept a box of 1,000 wood screws in which three screws have no slot in the head. These are discarded.

Acceptable rejects

The principle led to the operation of tables of "Acceptable quality levels" which were defined in the British Standard series BS6000. A level of acceptance of "undiscovered rejects" can be agreed between manufacturer and customer.

However this weakness can be exploited by the better manufacturer, competing on whatever low a level of rejects which will be guaranteed. The situation became very difficult for the west in the 1970s when the Japanese were able to provide products with very low levels of defectives.

Japanese manufacturers aimed at a concept of zero rejection, perhaps not absolutely attainable, but making the agreements between western manufacturers and their customers seem very poor.

Process capability

The Japanese recognised that the way to prevent reject product being provided to the customer was not simply by inspecting, but by considering the process itself. In many cases, the process methods could be improved to reduce the chances that rejects would be produced.

This initiated the development of a number of methods of reviewing the actual processes by which work was undertaken. It recognised the factors which affect those processes, not simply the process methods and inspection criteria, but the people and their effect.

The five key factors are:

- people;
- equipment;
- materials;
- methods;
- environment.

All have an effect on the process, all can contribute to the success of the process. Measuring the total capability of the process involves rather more than simply inspecting the final product.

Work was undertaken to change process methods to increase the chances of the process yielding consistent results. Training operators not only in how to perform their own actions, but to understand the significance of their process to other related processes, took place. Everyone must understand the goals the company aims to achieve, and all must work continually to achieve those goals.

All of the key factors must be considered for all processes.

Probably the most important factor to evolve from process capability studies is that the quality of the product is determined by actions at all stages of product life. From concept, through design and production, to use, all actions are significant and must be controlled.

A further important factor is that consideration must be given not only to product which fails to meet specification, but also results of normal production, such data can help to predict potential future problems and enable them to be avoided.

Measurement and continual review and improvement of the capability of a process to reduce rejections has lead to many management systems based on statistical control of the process.

SPC (statistical process control) is a powerful tool in the quest for zero rejections. However, to a large extent it has been applied to manufacturing processes, not the supporting administrative processes. It is a tool used by the design department in determining manufacturing methods, not in controlling the design process itself.

Whilst quality control systems can be developed to improve the chances of a customer receiving the expected quality of product, alone they are unlikely to give an absolute guarantee of conformance.

In the U.K. an enormous amount of work has been undertaken on SPC by the automotive industry, from whom information is readily available.

Standardisation

Part of the requirements of each customer will be some form of product specification, an agreement between supplier and customer of what is expected. A problem for the supplier is to be sure he understands precisely what the customer wants. This problem can be exacerbated when the customer does not know, or perhaps has not yet decided.

A further problem exists when customer needs vary slightly from one customer to another. Variations in product specification which change the process parameters is not only expensive, but likely to lead to the product failing to meet customer needs and thus being rejected.

Standardisation of process is desirable as it increases efficiency and saves costs. It makes the production processes simpler and thus reduces the risk of failure. The aim of a management system must be to employ as many standard processes as possible.

In businesses which specialise in custom built products, the range of work undertaken is such that standard processes can be built up to produce totally individual end products, but each process is in itself standard.

The possible variations which can be built into a farm tractor are almost infinite, over a million in the Ford range. Yet the manufacturer does not have a million production lines, most processes are standard. The individuality comes from the way in which the standard process routes are put together.

Standardisation in design and marketing

Standard process routes must be taken into account at the earliest opportunity. In defining the products which will be sold, or in designing the manufacturing methods and materials to be used, standard methods must be considered.

The use of product standards assists this process. The customer who is unsure of the needs of the product will be attracted to the claim of compliance with a national product standard. Such standards are evolved over a relatively long period of time and incorporate product or performance characteristics which are the basis for inspection measurements.

The use of standards can have dangers when the customer does not understand the extent of the requirements of the standard. In particular, since some standards cover safety aspects of the product, not all standards ensure the product is safe.

Customers must beware of agreeing to claims that a product meets a national standard, unless they are clear of the requirements of the standard. Kite marks on the product, only mean the requirements of the applicable standard have been met, not necessarily that the product is safe, or performs in a particular manner.

Product standards can reduce the customer's desire to incorporate individual needs, and hence increase the manufacturer's ability to standardise process routes.

Product standards ensure measurement characteristics are clearly agreed, and indeed measurement methods are practical and possible. A current problem being debated on European Community water quality, is that of whether the desired specification of impurities can actually be measured by currently known techniques.

Product standards can be seen as a restriction to trade, especially where such standards vary between countries. The harmonisation of product standards in the European Community has been much slower than was envisaged in the mid 1980's. But without such standards many more variations will be required in process routes, and the advantages in relation to product conformity of standardisation will be less.

As E.C. Product Directives are issued we will become familiar with the CE mark on the goods. The CE mark indicates the product meets the requirements of the relevant directive. Whilst these requirements are based on safe operation, each directive defines specific requirements to be met. Again the customer needs to understand the standards the product is claimed to meet, and not assume safe operation on the basis of the CE mark.

Quality assurance

As discussed, the rapid concept changes associated with Japanese products in the 1960s and 1970s, was primarily a result of the development of quality control systems.

In the U.K. there was also concern that the concept of inspectors filtering out rejects was not the answer. It was costly, in that a significant amount of product was wasted, and since employees were being paid to produce product which was not sold. Indeed, in the "piece work" payment systems used at that time the incentive was simply to produce. It was the inspector's job to find the rejects, a separate process to the production process.

Driven largely by the Ministry of Defence and the Defence Procurement Programme for NATO, the U.K. considered how it could improve product conformity, and management systems.

Just as the Japanese realised processes were affected by a number of factors including the people and the equipment, the U.K. came to the same conclusion. Perhaps because of a difference in culture, however, the conclusion reached in the U.K. was that the problem lay with management.

It was considered that much of the problem was a direct result of poor communication between the process operator and his manager. The resultant action was a proposal made in 1968 by MoD, whereby key elements of management of an operation should be controlled.

A significant difference in the U.K. approach was that the management system must consider not only the management of production processes, but also key administrative processes. The most significant administrative processes were:

- purchasing;
- design processes;
- documentation control;
- traceability and records.

Documented system

The unique concept of the U.K. proposal was that the method of control must be written down. The aims of the organisation must be clearly stated in a policy which everyone understands. (Perhaps in Japanese culture this existed without the need for it to be written.)

The policy must be supported by further written procedural documents defining the standard methods to be employed to achieve the results. The whole system is then supported using clear data and instructions which are needed to perform the operations.

Once written, it is possible for managers to establish the methods are followed by observing work being performed and reviewing the records. This technique was defined as "internal auditing".

In 1979 a British Standard BS5750 was introduced which defined the key business process which should be included in a management system. The world's first National Standard set of criteria

The issue of BS5750 expanded the need for control to further non-manufacturing areas, review of customer orders, and identifying staff training needs.

As interest in the U.K. approach grew, many other countries adopted a similar approach. The Canadian approach was perhaps the most comprehensive, but national standards equivalent to BS5750 grew in most European countries, South Africa and Australasia.

The International Standards Organisation, ISO, recognised the need and value in combining individual approaches. In 1987 EN 9000 series, based on BS5750 was issued. BS5750 was amended to come into line with this document and the European equivalent EN29000 was issued. In 1994 the standard became BS EN ISO 9000.

BS EN ISO 9000

The set of standards in the BS EN ISO 9000 series is probably the most widely accepted and used ISO document. Management systems the world over are now being constructed using the models of BS EN ISO 9001, 9002 and 9003.

Since 1991, even the Japanese have adopted the principle of documented systems, albeit incorporating their proven developed quality control systems.

Whilst the some organisations continue to produce their own criteria as a basis for comprehensive management systems, there are few today which do not base their requirements on BS EN ISO 9000. The motor industry has recently brought its requirements into line with this world standard, albeit adding additional criteria to those of BS EN ISO 9000, to meet its specific needs.

- **BS EN ISO 9000** is a set of documents.
- **BS EN ISO 9000** defines the basic concept and method of operation of management systems.
- **BS EN ISO 9001** defines the content of management systems for organisations both designing and manufacturing products.
- **BS EN ISO 9002** defines the content of management systems for organisations manufacturing to customer defined designs.
- **BS EN ISO 9003** defines the content of management systems where simple quality control will control product conformity.
- **BS EN ISO 9004** is a series of guidance documents to aid the use of the standard in specific areas of business and for specific situations.

The documents are revised every five years.

The standard does not define levels of quality to be achieved, it does not reference specific product standards and it does not define how a company is to be operated.

It lists the key factors which affect the management of any organisation and requires the organisation to describe in writing how these factors are managed. BS EN ISO 9000 management systems are unique to each organisation, they explain to staff how the organisation is operated and define everyone's responsibility and level of authority. The system contains all the information needed to run the business in respect of ensuring product quality conforms with customer agreed requirements.

Active system

The system is active, it recognises errors will occur and makes provision for investigation and correction.

Internal audits and reviews make sure the processes are correctly described, and are followed as standard operations.

Provisions for corrective action ensure weaknesses and errors in the system are detected and gradually eliminated.

Just as no quality control system can guarantee zero defectives reaching the customer by 100 per cent inspection so no management system built around BS EN ISO 9000 will be perfect. But operating the system and using the evidence it provides is a sound basis for constant improvement.

Problems with quality assurance systems

The greatest problem with quality assurance systems is that the concept is not easy to understand. The idea that by defining how an organisation is managed, will ensure the customer gets a quality product is not obvious.

Quality management systems compliant with a BS EN ISO 9000 model (BS EN ISO 9001, BS EN ISO 9002 or BS EN ISO 9003) are often evaluated or assessed by customers as a measure of capability to meet the needs of contracts which may be placed. In recent years, third party (independent) evaluation of management systems has been used to save the customer undertaking his own assessment, although some companies continue to assess their suppliers themselves.

Third party certification establishes only that the system addresses the requirements in an appropriate manner in relation to the scope of work agreed between the company and the certification body. There may be no system for activities undertaken which are not included in the scope. Neither can the third party body demand extra requirements beyond those in the agreed assessment standard.

For example a company may make two types of product and gain third party certification for only one.

The scope of approval, or extent of the certified system must be established by the customer.

The customer must also establish that the methods of control defined by the supplier will meet his needs. There may be specific controls needed by the customer which are not included in the supplier's system. These controls would have to be requested as an agreed contractual condition. Examples may include specific levels of qualification for operators (*e.g.* welder qualifications).

The concept is workable when used between a customer and supplier who both have BS EN ISO 9000 systems, as each understand the potential problems. But are more difficult when the customer does not have such systems.

There is a great weakness when the customer is the general public. Despite the growth of adoption of BS EN ISO 9000 in service organisations which serve the public, there is still a low level of understanding of the concept by the "man-in-the-street".

After "approval"

BS EN ISO 9000 management systems must be operated to ensure they work effectively. They depend on analysis of problems to ensure they become fully effective.

Current pressure from the marketplace to gain approval in order to be able to compete, leads companies to simply install a set of procedures which address the requirements of the standard. Provided these procedures are followed at assessment, approval results. But the system will not be fully effective. It will contain errors which will only come to light as it is operated.

The system must change as both customer needs (the marketplace), and the company changes. Yet many companies fail to realise this part of the concept. Changes are often reluctantly included in systems as a result of demands of the customer or certification authority under threat of loss of orders or certification.

The system will detect the need for changes, but it is up to the company to act on these "signs". The system is capable of predicting failure, BS EN ISO 9000 makes provision to avoid such problems, but it is up to the company to take the actions.

Guarantee of product conformity

For every contract placed with another organisation there is a risk of being dissatisfied with the result and contract requirements not being understood. The more the customer knows about its supplier the lower the risk. Equally the less well the product can be specified to the supplier, the higher the risk. Thus where the supplier is required to design a product which is not understood by the customer, the risk of failure is extremely high. This is often the case for example with computer software, where product conformity (even from internal suppliers) is very low.

The risk is minimised by effective communication between customer and supplier. Clear specifications must be agreed and understood. The customer should know how the supplier intends to process the work and ensure those processes will meet his needs. The customer needs to agree the manner in which the supplier will carry out checks to ensure the product meets the specification, and any limitations on those checks and weakness in standards which may form part of the specification.

Most important, the customer must establish the work is within the capability of the supplier, and the supplier must recognise the limits of his own capability. Probably the greatest reason for product failure is the company taking on work beyond its capability, but it happens regularly, especially in difficult economic times.

Depending on the nature of the contract, quality control systems may be appropriate to control the end result. Alternatively a quality assurance system may be considered more appropriate, incorporating an acceptable quality control system and inspection techniques. There is a model in BS EN ISO 9003 which requires a documented management system for a quality control process, although very few companies have yet been approved to BS EN ISO 9003, preferring BS EN ISO 9001 or BS EN ISO 9002.

If the BS EN ISO 9000 approach is to be used, then the customer must ensure the extent of the system, and the type of products covered, is appropriate to needs. The controls of the system, often described generally as a Quality Manual, must be established and the system determined appropriate in terms of the contract being placed.

Where design is involved, the customer has a right to be involved in the design process, particularly at final review, and should include this in the contract requirements if not an automatic part of the supplier's system.

Whatever the approach to be demanded, or to be taken by the supplier, customers must be aware of the risk and make an effort to reduce this by their own actions.

Regardless of management systems, errors can always occur. The application of simple safeguards such as determining the supplier's previous experience with similar work, or consulting other customers are obvious but often forgotten.

Management systems help to reduce the chance of error and improve assurance. But no management system is totally effective and should never be regarded as such.

Management systems in design

Design is the most difficult task or process associated with the production of a product. Poor designs will not only fail to meet customer expectations, but will create problems in production and after sales costs.

Just as for production processes, management systems can be defined to control the design process. Frequently design organisations are reluctant to attempt to define their design processes using the excuse that it restricts natural flair of their designers. Yet if management systems are concerned with effective communications, it is frequently the case that communications between the designer and the outside world is the poorest in the company.

BS EN ISO 9001 defines the elements of a management system for design. The requirements are apparently very simple considering the complexity of the normal design process. But as BS EN ISO 9000 does not define how to run the business, only aspects to be controlled, so the same is true for design. Controls are needed in respect of inputs, outputs, design development and review of outputs against requirements and constraints.

However, the standard sets the company the task of defining how these controls are managed. It is this task which is left up to the company. In order to complete the task, the company must understand exactly how the design process operates.

Defining design systems

In order to define effective management systems to control the design process BS EN ISO 9001 is not much use on its own.

An expansion on the terminology is provided in BS EN ISO 9004. However this document does not give advice on how to construct a design system.

The problem is that BS EN ISO 9000 documents attempt to cover all types of design for all sizes of organisation and products. Design control is unique to the specific organisation and its methods may not be common to other organisations.

BS5750 : Part 4 : 1990 looks at the specific requirements of the standard, but as with BS EN ISO 9004 only expands on the words of BS EN ISO 9001 and provides little real guidance.

A British Standard BS7000 : 1989 has the title: "Guide to managing produce design", and in a mere 21 pages attempts to give guidance on the subject. Whilst covering the subject; except for initial ideas, most companies would find the document lacking in any detail. Perhaps the most useful section is the Bibliography which directs the reader to more useful references.

In considering the references and their advice it is clear that the simplistic points required to be included by BS EN ISO 9001 : Clause 4 are the essentials. But they will be different for every company. Returning to the basic concept of quality assurance — that of process standardisation; how much standardisation can be built into the design processes.

The BS EN ISO 9001 requirements

Without restating the guidance referred to above, and with no attempt to produce a definitive guide to the writing of design systems, it is worth considering the reasoning behind the sub-clause of BS EN ISO 9001 Clause 4.

4.4.1 Is the general clause which requires the design system to be proceduralised. Earlier considerations in this section have considered the value of documented systems and the controls and improvements which can be achieved.

4.4.2 Design Planning A formal design planning system must exist in order that the various design processes needed to meet a specific design task are identified and co-ordinated. It follows that responsibility for the various processes must be clear and inter-relation of the design functions must be established. Multi-functional designers must be working towards the same goal with the same general information.

4.4.3 Design input Although types of input are not specified they will be extensive. The primary input is to specify what the customer expects to obtain. This expectation may go far beyond that which is defined in the contract. It will cover regulations and legislation applicable to the product which may not even be known to the customer. Such considerations must ensure the product is safe to use.

It may also be necessary to consider the end use of a component by the customer which may not be known at the initial stage of design. Similarly other designs may be taking place for compatible components in the final product. Hence the customer may be required to co-ordinate the design activities of many suppliers. Consider the design of a house and its fittings to meet the customer's final "specification".

Other design inputs will include producibility, serviceability and reliability; availability of raw materials, service conditions to be encountered and possible disposal after use, close co-operation between the customer and designer increases the chances of the customer being satisfied with the end result.

Design output The company must decide how its design data is to be presented. Design data must be communicated to others who must understand what is intended. Consideration must of course be given to the design input requirements and ensure they have been satisfied by the design proposals including product safety which is specifically mentioned. Manufacturing capability must also be considered and the quality control system of the producer must be taken into account in measurement requirements.

Design verification The design must be practical, it must not only meet design inputs, but it must be capable of being manufactured. The design output requirements need to be reviewed and thought about. This is the stage the customer should be involved, even when the direct customer is the manufacturing unit of the company. This is the real danger point. Design may be beyond the capability of manufacturing, in this case the design is not acceptable. There must be feedback of previous problems. There must also be a system to feedback data related to similar designs both from current production and previous designs now in service.

Design changes As mentioned earlier, all design data may not be available before the process commences. As changes are needed, the system must accommodate them and ensure everyone is informed. Failure to do this wastes important time and effort.

Design validation The revision to BS EN ISO 9001 in 1994 includes a new clause with this title. Design validation means ensuring the designed product will meet the required performance characteristics. This is the point that the customer must be involved. At this stage, the end use must be known. It is possible that design validation cannot be undertaken until after a product has been made, but that does not prevent it being planned and undertaken. Design process cannot be considered complete until the customer is satisfied that the result meets the intended need. If the product fails then this must be fed back to the designer and taken account of in future decisions. The system has failed and the weaknesses must be identified and prevented from recurring.

An effective design system is an effective communication system. Decisions are recorded and the reason for reaching conclusions are documented. The designers must be able to learn from previous mistakes. The system must be constantly revised to prevent the recurrence of error and constantly improve.

A management system in design which controls the design process, can ensure consistency in the process. It need not restrict the creative flair of the designer, but will ensure key stages are not overlooked. It also ensures the design is clearly understood by those who are required to make the product.

Unless design is formalised in a management system consistency will not be achieved. BS EN ISO 9001 defines the basic requirements for a design management system. It concisely defines the basic requirements.

ASSESSING BS EN ISO 9000 SYSTEMS

First party audit

If a management system has been defined in accordance with BS EN ISO 9001, 9002 or 9003, the company must carry out an assessment to make sure all requirements have been adequately addressed. The company must be sure the system is a true reflection of the manner in which it really operates.

In order to define a system, management must understand the processes which are involved. Systems must reflect reality, not be descriptions of what they would like to happen, or what the customer may expect.

Internal audit must be undertaken by employees independent of the process being audited. The aim of internal audit is to verify the content of the documented system. The auditor is not interested in excuses or practical problems. If the systems does not define what really happens it is non-compliant.

Second party audit

When satisfied the system reflects what actually happens, the customer may be allowed to review the controls in order to gain confidence that his work will be processed correctly. Such an audit is called a second party audit.

The problems with second party audits are:

- They cost the customer money in providing auditor time and expense.

- Companies with many customers are subject to frequent audit, each time having to devote time and effort to the customer's auditors.
- It would be impractical to expect the general public to undertake an audit, if they are the customer.

Third party auditing

In the last ten years, Independent Certification Bodies have been set up. Third party bodies undertake assessment of management systems to the requirements of BS EN ISO 9000 standards. When found compliant, the third party body issues the company with an approval certificate.

The approval relates to a specific scope of work. The scope may be the whole, or just part of the activities the company undertakes. The scope is defined on the certificate issued to the company.

Third party bodies are authorised to work in specific areas by Accreditation Councils, in turn authorised by National Government to evaluate the Certification bodies. Certification Bodies indicate their authorisation by permitting their approved companies to use the Accreditation Council mark. In the U.K., the Accreditation Council is the NACCB (National Accreditation Council for Certification Bodies). The "Tick and Crown" logo is now widely recognised.

Certification bodies are not legally obliged to obtain accreditation, and some certification bodies undertake work outside their accredited scope. Only companies assessed by certification bodies operating within their scope of accreditation are permitted to use the accreditation mark. Thus the Crown and Tick logo in the U.K. shows the third party assessment was undertaken correctly.

Whilst there is no requirement for a certification body to gain accreditation, there is equally no reason for a professional certification body not to demonstrate its competence to the accreditation authority. Certification without accreditation must be viewed with suspicion.

Most industrial countries have set up accreditation councils similar to NACCB. Whilst the marks are not the same, the accreditation process is. An ISO Guide has been defined for assessment of certification bodies and a European Standard (EN45012) is used by all European Accreditation Councils.

Differences between audits

The company's own audit is probably the one which goes deepest into the system. The auditors are aware of the company's real problems and will know the people best. The problem with a compliance statement from the company itself is that it may not be believed by its customers.

The second party audit will concentrate on issues related to specific requirements of the customer. If certain processes are unlikely to be needed, the auditor may not waste time auditing the controls. Hence the audit of one customer may not be acceptable to another. In practice it has been found that even two project teams from the same organisation do not trust each other's audit.

The third party audit is the most remote. The auditors do not know the people in the organisation nor possibly have data related to past performance before the audit. At the same time, the fresh independent review of the system often reveals problems which the company and its customers have been too close to, to fully analyse. The third party body is probably more aware of the range of customer expectations than the company or any one of its customers.

The third party body is supportive of standardisation of process controls. It reviews systems against all potential orders and is less likely to demand systems supportive of specific customer variations.

Third Party Certification costs the company money. The cost is based on the complexity and size of the system, generally related to the size of the company being assessed. Costs vary from around £2,000 for a small company, to perhaps £20,000 for a company employing over a thousand people.

Some small companies feel the cost of certification, when demanded by their customer, is an unfair financial penalty. Some feel BS EN ISO 9000 is not applicable to small organisations.

The standard can be used by any size of organisation, but has limited value in a company of less than five employees, where communication is simple. However there is a value in clearly defining the company's objectives and the manner in which they are achieved. The key is to define a system appropriate to the size and complexity of the operation.

Savings have been proved in very small operations which exceed the costs of certification, equally, with an inappropriate system, BS EN ISO 9000 simply adds to costs. Guidance is being produced by certification bodies in association with the U.K. Federation of Small Businesses which will help to avoid the pitfalls.

Guarantees of third party certification

The guarantee given by third party certification is simply that a system exists which meets the requirements of the assessment standard for the defined scope of work.

It does not guarantee that product produced will meet customer requirements. It only gives assurance that systems are in place which, provided they are operated correctly, will identify customer needs and translate those needs into appropriate end results.

Third party approval does not remove the need for detailed purchase contracts or the accurate specification of contractual conditions. It does not ensure the systems in place will meet specific needs of a particular customer. But it does mean the supplier is aware of regulatory or legislative requirements related to the product and has a capability of producing the product to meet these requirements.

Third party approval means the systems of the supplier are real and reflect what actually happens. It is up to the customer to decide whether this type of control is appropriate to the order being placed. Every customer has a right to see the Quality Policy of its suppliers. The Automobile Association (AA) has produced a very readable document for its members.

When purchasing from a third party approved supplier, the customer should determine the assessment standard used and the scope of approval granted. The customer should also establish the approval is current — approvals can be and are withdrawn.

BS EN ISO 9000 systems in product conformity

European Community Product Directives may invoke modules which demand BS EN ISO 9000 management systems. Depending on the directive and the module used, the applicable standard may be BS EN ISO 9001, BS EN ISO 9002 or BS EN ISO 9003.

The management system may be only a part of the controls applied in order to affix a "CE Mark" to the product. It is possible that type testing and/or production testing by the Notified Body may also be required. However the BS EN ISO 9000 assessment by the third party, or Notified Body is affected by the fact it is related to product conformity.

The same considerations would apply to the assessment of management systems using BS EN ISO 9000 for other product conformity schemes.

The main difference is assessment methodology is related to the fact that an agreed set of requirements exist which the product must meet. Systems must be in place which ensure these requirements are complied with, regardless of specific customer needs.

The quality control arrangements must be appropriate to demonstrate compliance with the requirements of the conformity scheme. In particular levels of sampling may be specified. The assessment must include the specific needs of the specified product conformity scheme.

In practice this means more emphasis will be placed on inspection techniques and inspection records. The audit will include not only looking at the system to deal with defectives, but the action taken as a result of defectives being produced. There will be a greater emphasis on product recall.

In addition, the Certification Body will evaluate the capability of the processes in producing acceptable product.

BS EN ISO 9003

In product conformity schemes, where the product design is provided, conformity may be demonstrated by inspection systems alone. Such systems are defined in BS EN ISO 9003.

BS EN ISO 9003 systems are management systems which define quality control systems.

The problem with ISO 9003 was that some key elements of a full management system had been left out. In particular Contract Review and Audit had been excluded. This has resulted in the standard rarely being used by third party bodies and its value being debased.

The 1994 revisions to BS EN ISO 9003 strengthen the requirements considerably. The standard has now become a complete system for the purpose of defining the essential controls of a quality control system.

It is likely that as the changes are recognised, greater use will be made of BS EN ISO 9003. The standard has already been incorporated into the EC Product Directive for Personal Protective Equipment and will increase in use for product conformity schemes.

As a basis for product conformity of simple operations with a single manufacturing process, BS EN ISO 9003 can be helpful to small organisations. Its requirements are more appropriate to organisations with short communications chains and thus simple management systems. But there is still a need to raise the standing of BS EN ISO 9003 in the eyes of customers.

Future developments

Quality controls continue to develop and improvements in techniques are built both on existing tools (*e.g.* SPC) and by totally new methods.

Quality assurance is also developing with the BS EN ISO 9000 standards constantly under review. The issue of the 1994 versions of BS EN ISO 9001, 9002 and 9003 is only the first stage in a planned development cycle towards a total restatement expected by the year 2000. (Vision 2000 as stated in BS EN ISO 9000 itself.)

The emphasis given to improvement of quality, and quality as a key factor in business success, has made many companies look beyond existing systems. In recent years the concept of total quality management, (TQM), has been developed. TQM is based on never ending quality improvement. Since it is a continual process, a goal can never be achieved. Hence approval of a company's system which ensures total quality is difficult.

Measurement of progress is achieved through award schemes. Such schemes started in Japan, but the U.S. Baldridge award is perhaps best known. In the last few years an equivalent European Scheme EFQM and a U.K. scheme (BQF) have been put in place.

The schemes are based on measurement of achievement of excellence against specific criteria, each criterion carrying a score. The criteria relate to the manner in which the company manages its affairs and works to determine and meet its customer's expectations.

The award is made annually to the best company, yet even the best is unlikely to score more than 70 per cent of the available marks. Many companies see such schemes as a way of identifying weaknesses and reorganising their management to take more account of their customer needs.

Total Quality Management is not the same as Quality Assurance, but a BS EN ISO 9000 system is the foundation on which to build a management system which will embody TQM principles.

BS EN ISO 9000 will gradually cover all processes in an organisation and demand documented management systems. Controlling product safety is a process which must be managed. It thus needs a management system to measure its success. Whether that happens through BS EN ISO 9000, TQM or some other means, remains to be seen. Management systems give a possible route to the future of improved product safety management.

15 Case histories

INTRODUCTION

The great value of case histories lies in the explanation of what went wrong. In some cases the start of a major incident can be so trivial as to be quite unremarkable at the time: the Camelford story began because one key fitted two locks; the removal of sugar from hazelnut puree, intended for yoghurt, led to the death of Annie Newton and put 26 people in hospital.

Crime was the cause of the addition of an unauthorised chemical to Austrian wine, which devastated the country's export market and necessitated emergency cabinet meetings and a change in the law — but no-one was harmed. The threat that a popular product can give one cancer will grab the headlines, especially if it is beer. However, this product safety case history demonstrates how an industry acted swiftly to prevent the threat becoming a reality.

The most famous product liability case history is that of the snail-in-the-ginger beer bottle and Lord Atkin's judgment, which influenced the relevant law throughout the world. The story of how he reached this judgment, with the help of his family over Sunday lunch at his holiday home in Wales, gives fascinating background.

One story is very much open-ended. The largest British ship to be lost at sea was the *Derbyshire*, in 1980 near Japan. It now lies nearly three miles beneath the sea and all on board were lost. The cause of the disaster is in dispute. There have been official investigations, professional papers, a book, a BBC TV programme and strong pressure from the families of the crew. The question in contention is: Was it a design defect ?

CASE HISTORIES

The common feature of these case histories is, as might be expected, the human factor. This was discussed above at page 336 where it was said that we know precious little about the contribution people, rather than machines, make to product safety. Whether the product is a ship or a pot of yoghurt the failure of human beings can have fatal consequences.

Acknowledgment is made to *Product Liability International*, Lloyd's of London Press, where some of this material originally appeared.

FRAME 65 AND THE LOSS OF THE *DERBYSHIRE*

When a product is nearly 300 metres long and displaces 200,000 tonnes its disappearance becomes a matter of great concern. Especially with serious loss of life, little trace of the disaster and no possibility of finding out what went wrong. It is a potential product liability case on a massive scale, with the question of a design defect which involved many experts and sorrowing families for ten years.

The largest British ship to be lost at sea was the *MV Derbyshire*. She was the length of three football pitches, as wide as a motorway and one of the Bridge class of six oil/bulk/ore (O/B/O) carriers, built between 1971 and 1976 by Swan Hunter. She sank in Typhoon Orchid in the western Pacific south of Japan in 1980.

About 20 bulk carriers are lost each year from a variety of causes such as war, collision, grounding, fire, explosion, capsizing and structural failure. One of these losses will be unexplained, out of the total of 5,000 bulk carriers world-wide. A BBC TV Panorama current affairs programme in February 1993, called "Scandal at Sea", dealt with the unsafe condition of some bulk carriers. It said that in the previous three years 44 had sunk with the loss of 300 lives. One of the problems was the difficulty in finding corrosion and cracks in holds the size of cathedrals, in the limited time that surveyors had available — "Bigger has not meant safer for the giants of the seas." About 80 per cent of the world's shipping insurance was placed at Lloyd's of London; in 1992 it paid out claims totalling £5 billion.

The OBOs appeared in the mid 1960s and provided great flexibility as they could carry ore, grain in bulk and oil. To be able to do this required a very complex design, with the holds clear of bulkheads or cross girders. The strength of the vessels had to rely on the integrity of the whole and accurate construction.

The Bridge class were built on Teesside at a yard which closed in 1980. The ships were fabricated in sections welded together on the slip, which required precision because of the forces to which such long structures would be subjected. Each section weighed about 70 tonnes, with some being assembled upside down. The precise alignment of all parts made a major contribution to the overall strength of the vessel; they were checked by a Lloyd's surveyor. A senior representative of the Bibby Line, which owned the *Derbyshire,* supervised the construction of four of the ships, although not the *Derbyshire* itself, which was the last of the six.

One part of the vessels subsequently received a great deal of attention: an investigation by the Department of Transport, a paper at the Royal Institution of Naval Architects (RINA), a book, *A Ship Too Far,* and much pressure from the Derbyshire Families Association and the seafaring unions. It was Frame 65, situated at a point just forward of the superstructure, about a third of the way from the stern. Here there was a change in the structural configuration at the end of a line of holds. The transverse bulkhead of Frame 65 had two main strength members which abutted it at right angles on one side. On the opposite side there was a matching pair, which had to be correctly aligned to preserve the integrity of the structure. The forward pair had a major part to play in the flexural strength of the ships.

The RINA paper asked the question:

> "Should they be continued through the bulkhead or should they be terminated on one side of the bulkhead? If the latter course is adopted, particular care must be taken to weld the structural components accurately so as to preserve continuity and so maintain the structural strength of the hull . . . it is necessary that there be proper alignment between the members on each side of the transverse bulkhead and that the welding is of high quality."

In *A Ship Too Far* the authors say that the key factor was:

> "The relationship between the forward two-thirds of the ship and the last one-third (where the accommodation and superstructure are placed). We know that four of these ships had one port and one starboard longitudinal girder extending [back] from the bow to Frame 65 to give it longitudinal strength. At Frame 65 this was stopped at the forward side of the bulkhead. Crudely then, you have two structures welded at this point. That was not the way the ships were designed."

The RINA paper continues: "Perhaps on account of the modular approach to the fabrication of the hull, significant misalignment of the two longitudinal members was found . . . [which] would be associated with high local stresses. The amount of misalignment varied from ship to ship in the class, and estimates of its magnitude vary from source to source." The importance of any misalignment was central to the disquiet over the loss of the *Derbyshire.*

To complicate matters five of the ships changed their names, with the first being successively called the *Furness Bridge, Lake Arrowhead, Marcona Pathfinder, World Pathfinder* and *Ocean Sovereign*. All six were repaired at various times and places, with Frame 65 featuring in every case. The first of the class, for example, *Furness Bridge,* had extensive cracks (one of 450mm) repaired in the vicinity of Frame 65 in February 1982.

The third ship of the class was the *Kowloon Bridge*. In 1986 she was carrying 160,000 tonnes of iron ore from Canada to the Hunterston terminal on the Clyde. After a bad Atlantic crossing she anchored in Bantry Bay on the coast of southern Ireland in an unseaworthy condition. The weather worsened and the anchor cable parted, forcing the master to put to sea and send out a Mayday call as the ship was taking in water. The RAF airlifted the 28 crew to safety in Cork. Early the following morning the *Kowloon Bridge* hit the Stag Rock, eventually breaking in three. The ship had had a series of problems at Frame 65 with a number of repairs being carried out between April 1982 and November 1986 when, as the RINA paper says, "Ship breaks at Frame 65 as she sinks, having struck a rock at no. 3 hold."

The *Derbyshire* was loaded with iron ore for Japan when she encountered the typhoon off the island of Okinawa and sank, with all crew and two wives. It was not until six days after her last radio contact that a search was mounted. One of the search aircraft reported an oil slick 20 miles from the *Derbyshire's* last known position, and a search vessel reported oil rising to the surface at that point. Six weeks later one of the ship's seriously damaged lifeboats was found drifting 250 miles away. In due course £11 million was paid as an insurance claim for the loss of the ship. The relatives received an average of £5,000 each.

Investigations into major disasters seem to take time to get started and then there may be several which do not always reach the same conclusion. So it was with the *Derbyshire.* Of special interest, now that today we have strict liability in many countries, is the concern as to whether a ship is "equipment" under the strict liability provisions of the Employers Liability (Defective Equipment) Act 1969. In 1986 the *Financial Times* Commercial Law Reports had the headline "Shipowners face negligence claims for providing defective vessel", over a case in the Queens Bench Division (Admiralty Court) brought by the estate of the late Third Engineer of the *Derbyshire* against Bibby Tankers. The plaintiff contended that the design and construction of the ship were defective in that her longitudinals were not continuous through the transverse bulkhead at Frame 65, in accordance with Lloyd's Rules then in force. It was submitted that because of such defects the ship was unseaworthy, that she broke in two at about Frame 65, which was immediately forward of the bridge and accommodation, with the result that the after superstructure and bridge sank rapidly.

Section 1 of the short Act applies strict liability in tort to an employer if an employee is injured by defective equipment, which the employer has supplied for the purpose of his business. The word "equipment" includes plant and machinery, vehicles, aircraft and clothing. The injury an employee suffers, because of defective equipment supplied by his employer is attributable to the negligence of the employer, even if the defect can be laid at the door of a third party, against whom the employer may have a cause of action. The liability imposed by the Act cannot be limited or excluded. The judge said that it would be manifestly absurd not regard a ship as equipment, otherwise a workman would be deprived of the remedy intended by Parliament and ships then would escape the legislative net. The effect of this decision was that the case against the shipowner could go ahead, without affecting the rights that Bibby may have against Swan Hunter.

But the Court of Appeal did not agree. The following year they overturned the judgment and decided that a ship was *not* equipment for the purposes of the Act. This meant that the shipowners were not liable for any defects in the vessel, which were attributable to the manufacturer's fault and which resulted in loss of life. An *FT* headline cancelled out the previous one with "Defective ship does not constitute equipment".

Then it was the turn of the House of Lords to overturn that judgment. Their Lordships held that:

> "There was no more essential equipment for the setting up of and carrying out the business of a shipowner than the ship or ships with which the business is carried on . . . they were the tools of his business and there was no ground for treating the word 'equipment' as excluding this particular type of chattel of whatever size or construction employed by a trader in carrying out his trade."

The E.C. Directive on Liability for Defective Products defines a product as a movable, even though incorporated into an immovable (and somewhat strangely to a layman includes electricity in the definition as well). In the U.K. Part 1 of the Consumer Protection Act 1987, which gives effect to the Directive, does not use the word movable but defines products as "any goods". It then defines goods as including "substances, growing crops and things comprised in land by virtue of being attached to it and any ship, aircraft or vehicle".

The loss of the *Kowloon Bridge* prompted another enquiry to be ordered by the Secretary for Transport. It lasted 46 days and produced a volume of transcript for each day. The Wreck Commissioner asked ". . . why did none of the other ships get lost by having the after part falling off . . . None of the others was lost in this way, yet there is evidence that as far as these cracks in way of Frame 65 are material at all the other ships had rather more cracks than the *Derbyshire* ever had". The final report included "The combination of circumstances necessary to postulate separation of the hull at Frame No. 65 is very unlikely, though some element of doubt must remain". On day 40 a scrap metal merchant unloaded in the yard outside Church House, Westminster, where the enquiry was being held, a large section of the Frame 65 cut out of the wreck of the *Kowloon Bridge* by divers.

In June 1990 there was a further twist in the story of Frame 65. An illegal underwater film of the *Kowloon Bridge*, broadcast on Tyne Tees television, showed "massive structural damage" between the bridge and the cargo section. Then came the paper at the RINA, based on an earlier report which the Wreck Commissioner had refused to consider. The paper is highly technical and focuses on hull stressing and fatigue in large bulk vessels. It seeks to lend support to the theory that the *Derbyshire* suffered a structural failure in the aft end of the cargo section. Pages are devoted to calculations and diagrams concerning Frame 65.

An idea of the passions generated by this case can be gained from the manner in which the President opened the discussion on the paper:

> "I want it to be very clear that we as the RINA, are in a professional engineering institution where interests are in technology, not in politics, and certainly not in the apportionment of blame for any

accident. We agreed that the paper be discussed on its technical merits only."

The following speakers were not exactly reticent in voicing their opinions on the paper they had just heard.

The first said: ". . . there can hardly have been a paper read before any technical institution which so utterly failed to meet its objectives as this one has." The second said: "It is therefore disappointing for me to see a theory used prematurely to imply the tragic loss of the *Derbyshire* can be explained so simply." The third said: "It is disappointing that a paper should be published which . . . so totally fails to substantiate its claims."

But not all were so vehement in their disagreement. Another contributor to the discussion said: "I have thoroughly enjoyed reading and digesting this intriguing paper which is a credit to [the authors]." Other comments were:". . . an interesting and generally helpful paper", and "a fascinating and convincing paper." A surveyor who was concerned with the class, but not the *Derbyshire,* said: "Basically misalignment was almost chapter and verse throughout the whole construction. The so-called checks and building maintenance of form checks were virtually non-existent." In total 22 people contributed to the discussion.

The Chief Inspector of Marine Accidents reviewed the paper and other published material on the loss of the *Derbyshire*. His report, in 1991, said that there was nothing new in the RINA paper or in the other material: "Every ship, indeed every structure, must have its weakest point. For the structural arrangements in way of Frame 65 of *DERBYSHIRE* to have caused the ship's loss requires a good deal of supposition beyond the evidence of a comparatively weak point." Later he wrote:

> "On the alleged misalignment of longitudinal at Frame 65, which is fundamental to any question of fault in construction, the extent of misalignment in *DERBYSHIRE* (if any) has not been established. There is nothing in the paper that would be likely to make a re-hearing attach causative fault to the builder or any other party."

In March 1991 the Secretary of State for Transport, in answer to a Parliamentary question, said he had concluded that the formal investigation into the loss of the *Derbyshire* should not be re-opened.

Less than two weeks later *The Times* published a letter from the Shadow Transport Minister deploring the Minister's statement. She wrote:

> "I am shocked by the Secretary of State's announcement on March 25 without any regard to the petition signed by over 75,000 people, the early day motion signed by a significant number of MPs and representations made by the National Union of Rail, Maritime and Transport Workers. The conclusions of the department's original investigation have been fundamentally challenged by new scientific evidence and television pictures. The enquiry must be re-opened."

At the end of 1993 the International Transport Workers Federation put up £320,000 to conduct a side-scan sonar search for the wreck. Representatives of the Derbyshire Families Association claimed that computer analysis by oceanographic experts had indicated that the ship was lying in two halves 21.5 nautical miles apart. The aim of the underwater search was to show exactly where the ship had split in two and whether Frame 65 had been the critical stress point. The Department of Transport said if "100 per cent photographic evidence" was produced the chief inspector of marine accidents could re-open the enquiry.

In June 1994 the survey ship *Shin Kai Maru* located at least seven large pieces of wreckage about 2.8 miles down 800 miles south of Japan. The sonar scan was studied at the University of Wales in Cardiff. In its report The International Transport Workers' Federation concluded:

> "The hypothesis that the *Derbyshire* sank due to massive structural failure in the way of frame 65 is certainly strengthened by the evidence recovered on the ITF's expedition. It is also supported by analysis undertaken by the University of Wales of the video evidence of the bow section. . . What we believe happened, on the basis of the evidence recovered, is that the inhabited section of the vessel, abaft frame 65, separated from the rest of the ship and sank almost immediately. The sonar evidence supports this, the research confirms frame 65 as a weak point, the sisterships all suffered cracking in this area and the fact that no messages were ever sent by the crew gives this hypothesis added weight. . . Many questions about how the *Derbyshire* came to be so completely destroyed remain to be answered. It is clear that the conclusions drawn by the authorities can not now be justified. Further research, including a new expedition to gather more evidence from the wreckage field, must be undertaken without delay. The U.K. Government has an ideal opportunity to set an example to others, and the ITF hopes they are ready to grasp the nettle."

At the end of November 1994 there were fresh allegations about the standards of construction at the Swan Hunter shipyard, which had built the *Derbyshire* and her sister ships. A BBC TV documentary centred on key bolts which secured the rudder. Faults with rudder assembly bolts could have contributed to the loss of the ship by leaving her exposed broadside on to the typhoon in which she sank.

Sources

1. "MV DERBYSHIRE" Report of Court No. 8075 Department of Transport 1989 HMSO ISBN 0 11 550896 1.
2. R. E. D. Bishop, W. G. Price, P. Termarel. *A Theory on the loss of the MV Derbyshire* 1991.
3. "Derbyshire: Review of New Material", Marine Accident Investigation Branch Department of Transport, March 14, 1991.

4. D. Ramwell, T. Madge, *A Ship Too Far* 1992.
5. *Lloyd's List* July 13 and October 10, 1993; July 25 and November 24, 1994
6. "Report of the ITF *Derbyshire* mission", International Transport Workers" Federation, London, July 1994.

THE CAMELFORD WATER CONTAMINATION INCIDENT

Some products we have at home are available on demand. They come without packaging and cannot be returned if they are defective. Examples are gas, electricity and water, together with the telephone service and broadcasts. The calorific value of gas could be wrong, the voltage of the electrical supply could be inadequate or the water could be contaminated. Misrouted telephone calls could lead to problems, while an inaccurate news bulletin can cause much trouble. But in every case a product recall is impossible. It has to be right first time.

Correcting a mistake in these products can be very difficult. If people perceive there to be a risk, there is a risk, whether one exists scientifically or not. The public perception is the key. Once the public has made its collective mind up, it is a struggle to change it. Especially when the situation develops into an "us" and "them" fight. We know that the initial response to an incident can set the tone. Get that wrong and there will be years of argument, meetings, investigations and public enquiries. Which is just what happened at Camelford in Cornwall. This product liability case depended on whether it could be proved that contaminated water caused certain illnesses, or whether they would have occurred anyway. It also developed into public mistrust not only of the product quality but also the producer's ability to manage an incident properly and to tell the truth.

It all started because one key fitted two locks, which led to two public enquiries and the Court of Appeal.

John Stevens was a relief driver working for ISC Chemicals of Avonmouth. He drove a road tanker of aluminium sulphate to the North Cornwall Lowermoor treatment works of the South West Water Authority (SWWA). He arrived at 4.30 pm on Wednesday July 6, 1988. It was his first visit and there was no-one about, for the SWWA employee who worked at the plant was not present. The gate was locked.

He had a key given to him by a colleague. Later, the water unions would say that it must have been one of several keys, provided for contractors, to break a strike five years earlier. The unions said that they had raised the question of surplus keys several times with the SWWA. Despite assurances to the contrary, nothing had been done.

Unlocking the gate, John Stevens drove in to find several unmarked tanks. He had been told to deliver his load into the tank on the left. But there were two. However, he found that his key would unlock a hatch set in the ground. He assumed that this had to be the destination for the aluminium sulphate. By 5.45pm he had discharged 20 tonnes of the chemical by mistake into the chlorine contact tank. The concentrated aluminium sulphate passed straight into a treated water reservoir, which fed the Lowermoor distribution network. Camelford's 9,000 people and St. Miniver's 2,500 were among those who used this water.

An automatic alarm sounded in the Authority's control room at Exeter. The stand-by duty officer could not be contacted until 11 pm. He was at a dog training class.

That night a programme was started of flushing mains water into rivers. This had the effect of drawing more concentrated water into the complex distribution system. There was no detailed or systematic monitoring of the actions taken.[1]

At Exeter Crown Court John Stevens would say that he had subsequently returned to the Lowermoor site. He had pointed out to the SWWA supervisor the tank into which he had discharged the chemical. He claimed that the supervisor told him not to let the incident go any further. The Authority would sort it out. The Authority blamed ISC for the mistake. The load should have been delivered on July 4 or 5 and before 4 pm. The driver did not contact the SWWA before making the delivery as he was supposed to do, so that the plant could be attended.

The effects of the contamination were widespread. In total there were potentially 12,000 residents and 8,000 holidaymakers at risk. There was "much anger and mistrust as a result of the contradictory, confusing and sometimes inappropriate advice given to consumers by Water Authority staff."[2] What happened next has become part of the local folk lore.

The *Sunday Times* published a major feature on residents' reactions. Tea formed into a repellent brown lump that rapidly coalesced around a globule of curdled milk. Coffee reacted in a similar way. Solar heating panels on the roof of a house corroded. The water in the river at Camelford bridge turned bright blue, with many fish dead. A local doctor said that patients complained of dry and burning mouths, abdominal pains, diarrhoea, itching rashes and mouth ulcers. Holidaymakers at Helston, who complained to the SWWA, were told that the water was safe to drink despite containing a translucent milky sludge. Attempts to make ice cream failed because of a tainted and metallic taste. Chickens, ducks and lambs unaccountably died. Customers at a hairdressing salon had hair that turned green. A flautist "developed huge blisters all over the gums under my upper lip" after drinking tea.

On July 14, 1988 the SWWA wrote to its customers saying that it had instituted an enquiry into the incident. It apologised for "the wrong and inconvenience" caused and acknowledged that some "may have suffered particular damage as a result of this incident." Claims for compensation would be considered. The statement ended with "The Authority confirms that the water from Lowermoor Treatment Works now has the right alkalinity and is safe to use and drink." As we will see, this sentence was used in a High Court case for exemplary damages, brought against the water company four years later.

The Cornwall and Isles of Scilly Health Authority, on August 25, 1988, wrote to all householders concerned. It had received a report from the

[1] "Water pollution at Lowermoor North Cornwall", July 1989, HMSO.
[2] "Water pollution at Lowermoor North Cornwall", November 1991, HMSO.

Senior Medical Officer in the Division of Toxicology and Environmental Health, a report prepared for the SWWA and an analysis by the Camelford Scientific Advisory Panel of over 200 questionnaires. The householders were told "there is no reason to expect long term or delayed harm . . . some people will have experienced unpleasant effects, but these should be relatively short lived." The Health Authority was to survey 1,000 residents and said it was undesirable to use water from the hot tap for drinking or cooking.

Some £38,000 had been paid in compensation by the SWWA, according to *The Times* in December 1988. Sums ranged from £1,800 for bottles of mineral water to £11,000 for poisoned exotic fish and a total of £20,000 for sickness. It reported that the concentration of aluminium in the water supply had risen to 3,000 times the E.C. limit.

A mains and reservoir cleaning exercise was mounted by the SWWA in October 1988. The object was to remove as far as possible any deposited aluminium compounds. It was hoped to complete the work by Christmas but it was not finished until March the following year.

The North Cornwall Residents' Association was set up at the beginning of 1989. It requested the Parliamentary Ombudsman to investigate the absence of health care in the aftermath of the incident. Almost immediately the Government appointed the Lowermoor Incident Health Advisory Group, under Professor Dame Barbara Clayton, to report on the matter. The subsequent acceptance by the Government of the Clayton report meant that the Ombudsman was powerless to take any action.

A year after the mistake at Lowermoor, a public meeting was held by the North Cornwall Residents' Association. Those attending included an expert toxicologist, a local MP and a Cornwall County Councillor. A full public enquiry was called for and a meeting with the Secretary of State.

The day before the meeting the Clayton report was published. It said that "the main cause of ill-health among residents of North Cornwall is psychosomatic." No significant absorption of aluminium would have occurred. There would be no toxic effects and no long term ill-health. The report made a number of recommendations. These included a survey of pregnancy outcomes and the provision of a special clinic for people who continued to be unwell; the latter was afterwards attended by 120 people.

The Residents' Association promptly rejected the report. They found it "highly unscientific and based on minimal direct evidence". Only 14 residents had been interviewed, each for less than 10 minutes. There were "numerous contradictions and blatant untruths".

The Parliamentary Under Secretary of State for Health responded to the call for an enquiry. He said that the Clayton report had dealt with the incident comprehensively and authoritatively. It had been accepted by the Health Authority. The Minister said "There is no longer any purpose in such meeting nor any form of further enquiry." This was followed by a letter from the Administrative Secretary of the Clayton group who said "There is nothing to be gained by a public meeting such as you called for."

The Southwest Environmental Protection Association was an "independent advisory group which monitors and advises on environmental matters." It published a critique of the Clayton report, rejecting in detail much of its evidence and the conclusions drawn. It too called for a public enquiry.

The effect of the aluminium sulphate was to make the water more acidic. The Clayton report said that pH readings of 3.9 to 5.0 had been recorded; this is the logarithmic index that measures the acidity of a solution. A pH below 7 indicates acidity and one above alkalinity. Contact by the highly acidic water with constructional materials, used in domestic plumbing, gave rise to high metal concentrations in hot and cold tap water in some cases. Very few examples of a high lead concentration were recorded, because lead pipes are not widely used for the soft Lowermoor water. In the initial stages very high copper levels were encountered but these fell to normal values. Zinc concentrations behaved in a similar manner.

The World Health Organisation's and the E.C.'s guideline value for aluminium in drinking water is 200 millionths of a gram per litre. It is also a requirement of the U.K. Water Supply (Water Quality) Regulations 1989. The level of aluminium in the water supply in the Camelford area fell below 1,000 millionths of a gram per litre a few days after the incident, according to the Clayton report. But it did not drop to the guideline value until after the whole system had been cleaned and flushed out. A monitoring programme, which examined levels of aluminium, iron, manganese and pH values, showed that in 1989 96.0 per cent of more than 2,000 samples complied with the limits. In 1990 the proportion was 99.6 per cent.

The trial of the SWWA on criminal charges started at Exeter Crown Court on December 4, 1990. The prosecution opened with "From top to bottom the story is one of bungling and incompetence, a failure of staff to follow their own procedures. . . ." Later the Chairman denied that there had been an attempt to cover up the incident but accepted criticisms of the operation and supervision at Lowermoor. After a 17-day trial the Authority were fined £10,000, with £25,000 prosecution costs, for causing a public nuisance. The taxpayers had to find the money. The South West Water Authority was succeeded by South West Water plc, which did not take over any criminal liability from the former body.

After the trial the Southwest Environmental Protection Association said the verdict would help the 1,000 civil cases being prepared. Next day the shadow minister for environmental protection repeated the demands for a full enquiry. One family said that they were spending £100 a month on bottled water. The head of corporate affairs for the SWWA said "the thing has been going on for two and a half years and I cannot believe there is anything more to say that has not been uncovered before 12 good men and true".

Two months before the trial the Lowermoor Incident Advisory Group was reconvened, again under Professor Dame Barbara Clayton. The Group had five members, supported by a secretariat from the Department of Health. Medical, scientific and technical advice was received from 80 people. The terms of reference were "to assess reports which have become available since July 1989 of persistent symptoms and clinicopathological findings amongst people who were resident in the Camelford area at the time of the Lowermoor incident . . ." and to advise on the findings.

The second Clayton report was published in November 1991. It runs to 51 pages as opposed to 22 for the first report, and deals with the problems in much greater depth. About 400 people continued to attribute health complaints to the incident. The Group accused some sections of the media of inaccuracy in referring to the findings of its previous report, in particular the *Guardian*. It said "In fact we never doubted that symptoms being reported were other than real and that the incident caused a great deal of mental and physical suffering to the community".

The report said:

> The research reported to us does not provide convincing evidence that harmful accumulation of aluminium has occurred, nor that there is a greater prevalence of ill-health due to toxic effects of the water in the exposed population. After examination of all the available information on serum aluminium concentrations in the exposed population, including sampling procedures, we consider that sample contamination is the most likely explanation for the report of raised values in a small series of specimens collected several months after the incident. Although some measures of impaired performance were reported in a series of psychological tests conducted on small groups from the Lowermoor population this is not at all surprising since the groups were self-selected people who presented because of complaints of memory impairment.
>
> We do not believe, nor have we ever said, that people in the Lowermoor area are imagining the symptoms, or that their illness is caused by "hysteria." [This is a reference to reports in the *Guardian*.] We still have no doubt that the incident itself and subsequent events have led to real suffering in the community. The physical problems associated with all the worry and concern and the psychological harm could last a long time for some people. Such a situation is well recognised following major accidents.
>
> The reported symptoms such as muscle pains, fatigue and memory loss are common in all populations and the evidence suggests that rates of these symptoms are not excessive in the Lowermoor population. In our judgement it is likely that these symptoms would have occurred in the normal course of events. We believe that they have been attributed to the incident as a result of the heightened awareness provoked by the incident and subsequent events. The incident was

unique, and the precise doses of aluminium and other contaminants received by the residents are unknown; therefore, although we have no reason to predict any late consequences, we cannot exclude them categorically.

The Department of Health put out a press release about the report headed "'No lasting physical harm expected' say experts". The Parliamentary Under Secretary of State for Health (a different one from 1989) took the unusual step of writing to the householders in the Lowermoor area. He sent a summary of the report so that they could see what it 'actually says'. The headline in the *Sunday Times* was "Poison inquiry report branded a whitewash".

The chairman of the North Cornwall Residents' Association said "it was a fudge before and they have fudged again". Research at the Royal London Hospital had been commissioned by lawyers representing victims. It was said to have evidence that more than 50 people, who drank the contaminated water, had intellectual impairment. A study at a Bodmin hospital found that 90 per cent of those who drank the water had serious memory defects.

In March 1992 a group action, by 180 people who allegedly suffered harm from the contaminated water, was heard in the Queen's Bench Division. The master statement of claim sought damages from South West Water Services Ltd for failure to take reasonable care to supply wholesome water.

It was claimed, *inter alia*, that the water supplied was a defective product for which the water company was liable under the Consumer Protection Act 1987, section 2(1). [This is from Part 1 of the Act which provides for strict liability in tort following the E.C. Directive on Liability for Defective Products.] The defendants admitted liability but not the plaintiff's claim for exemplary damages. The plaintiffs said that they had been wilfully and deliberately misled as to the true state of affairs by the letter of July 14, 1988, mentioned above. There were allegations of withholding information and inadequate action to minimise the effects of the incident. Finally, when they did find out the truth of the matter, their feeling of indignation was justifiably aroused by the high-handed manner with which the water company had dealt with the incident. Mr Justice Wright ruled that they were entitled to pursue a claim for exemplary damages for the tort of public nuisance.

In November the Court of Appeal overturned that judgment, because exemplary damages could not be claimed for a public nuisance. In the course of delivering judgment Lord Justice Stuart-Smith said ". . . anger and indignation was not a proper subject for compensation, it was neither pain nor suffering".

In May 1994 an appeal settlement was reached in Truro by 158 out of 160 of the people who allegedly suffered harm because of the incident.

LORD ATKIN AND THE SNAIL IN THE GINGER BEER BOTTLE

The most famous case history of them all concerns the possibility that there could have been a snail in a bottle of ginger beer. The judgment is well-known but the story behind the case is less familiar.

The world at the beginning of the 1930s was a very different place and provides the background to the story. The collapse of the United States stock markets started the world economic crisis. The *Graf Zeppelin* flew around the world and Richard Byrd flew over the North Pole. Gandhi began his civil disobedience campaign and the Allied occupation of the Rheinland came to an end. In Germany, the National Socialists gained over 100 seats from the moderates in the elections; Pierre Laval became the Premier of France; in the U.K., Oswald Mosley started his New Party and Ramsey McDonald formed a National Government to balance the Budget. The British Broadcasting Corporation was five years old in 1931, the year in which Chaliapin sang at the London Lyceum, when Noel Coward's *Cavalcade* could be seen at the Adelphi and the musical *White Horse Inn* at the Coliseum was having a huge success.

Early in the summer of 1932, the Atkin family as usual spent some time at their holiday home, called Craig-y-don, at Aberdovey in Wales. After attending church every Sunday morning there was a large family lunch, complete with the traditional roast joint. Grandfather Atkin took much pride in carving and used the occasion to conduct a discussion. On several Sundays the lunchtime talk concerned a case that had recently been heard by the House of Lords, but for which judgment had yet to be given. There was conversation around the table about a snail in a ginger beer bottle and a question about who is my neighbour.

Grandfather was Lord Atkin, a famous Lord of Appeal, who was one of the greatest common lawyers of the twentieth century. The case is known to everyone who has studied English law and it created one of the most profound shifts in legal thinking. Its name is a byword to students of common law and product liability through the world. *Donoghue v. Stevenson* has been called the greatest civil case between the wars. A book by Geoffrey Lewis tells of the part played by Lord Atkin.

What was alleged to have happened was this. Just before 9 pm one evening towards the end of August 1928, Mrs May Donoghue and a friend went into the Wellmeadow Cafe in Paisley, Scotland. The friend ordered, from Francis Minchella who owned the cafe, an ice cream and a ginger beer for Mrs Donoghue and a pear and an ice for herself. The ginger beer was in a dark opaque glass bottle and Mr. Minchella poured part of the contents into a tumbler containing the ice cream. Mrs Donoghue drank some. Then, as her friend poured the remainder of the ginger beer into the tumbler, a snail "floated out of the said bottle. In consequence of the nauseating sight of the snail in said circumstances, and of the noxious condition of the said snail-tainted beer consumed by her, the pursuer (Mrs Donoghue) sustained the shock and illness hereinafter condescended on".

Mrs Donoghue took her case to Walter Leechman, a renowned campaigning Glasgow solicitor, because she had been off work for a few days and had spent a short time in Glasgow Royal Infirmary. She sued David Stevenson, the ginger beer manufacturer, for damages of £330. Eventually the case found its way to the House of Lords on the preliminary question of whether such a claim could ever be well-founded, assuming the facts to be proved.

However, Stevenson died soon after the House of Lords decision and the case never went to trial as to the facts. Stevenson's executors settled with Mrs Donoghue for £100. So no one ever knew whether the snail did exist or not. Ten years later Lord Justice MacKinnon said, "to be quite candid I detest that snail".

The appeal in the House of Lords on December 11, 1931 was heard by a Board of five: Lords Thankerton and Macmillan, two Chancery lawyers — Lords Buckmaster and Tomlin — and Lord Atkin. Judgment was reserved until May 26, 1932, when a three to two split favoured Mrs Donoghue. Atkin was strongly supported by Thankerton and Macmillan on the one side, while Buckmaster's dissent received only a slight contribution from Tomlin.

A fascinating insight into the relationship between Law Lords is provided by a letter sent, a fortnight before the judgment was given, to Atkin by Lord Wright, another Lord of Appeal.

"Dear Atkin

I have been reading with admiration your magnificent and convincing judgment in the snail case — also Macmillan's which is very good. I am glad this fundamental rule of law will now be finally established.

It seems as if (alas!) I were fated to differ from old Scrutton in the first two cases from this Court I have to deal with! I hope you will have a pleasant vacation.

Yrs

Wright

I find Buckmaster on snails very disappointing. I have not seen Tomlin's efforts on the same subject".

(Scrutton was a famous judge who sat in the Court of Appeal; Wright and Atkin had been his pupils 40 years previously).

Lord Buckmaster's judgment showed that his thinking was rooted in English contract law, by which a stranger to a contract had no rights under it. A manufacturer's contract with someone, to use care and skill about the manufacture of an article, could not give anyone else any rights under the contract. To this rule he felt there were only two exceptions: if the article was dangerous in itself or if the article had some defect known to the manufacturer. Neither of these exceptions applied to the bottle of ginger beer.

To Lord Buckmaster it followed that Mrs Donoghue had to seek the wider principle: that every manufacturer owed a duty to anyone using the article to see that it was carefully made. He thought that was "simply to misapply to tort doctrines applicable to sale and purchase". The consequences of this would be serious for trade and commerce and a potential for mischief almost limitless.

Lord Atkin, like Lord Buckmaster, knew that the result of the appeal would have a great effect on the law of civil liability for carelessness. Having thought about the situation very deeply — and discussed some of its principles over Sunday lunch with his family — he stated his general conception of a manufacturer's liability in words that have been quoted ever since:

> "A manufacturer of products, which he sells in such a form as to show that he intends them to reach the ultimate consumer in the form in which they left him, with no reasonable possibility of intermediate examination, and with the knowledge that the absence of reasonable care in the preparation or putting up of the products will result in an injury to the consumer's life or property, owes a duty to the consumer to take that reasonable care."

According to Geoffrey Lewis in his biography of Lord Atkin, the decision in *Donoghue v. Stevenson* "received only a modest welcome in the professional journals of the day". A short article in the *Law Quarterly Review* praised the Scots Lords for overriding the scruples of their English colleagues — Thankerton and Macmillan were Scots — but Atkin was born in Queensland and came to Wales when he was four years old. The *Solicitor's Journal* said that the decision would "govern millions of small transactions every day in the whole of the United Kingdom". There were appreciative articles from Canada and Australia.

Lord Atkin was prominent in another judgment when his radical dissenting speech made him a public figure. This was in the dark days of 1941 in the case of *Liversidge v. Anderson* when he alone among 10 judges found a different view, which the years have finally vindicated in a House of Lords ruling. Liversidge was detained under the Emergency Regulations 18B which gave the Home Secretary (Sir John Anderson) power to detain without trial or charge. The plaintiff wanted to know the grounds for his detention and Lord Atkin upheld that right.

Little is known about Atkin's private life. He had eight children, an addiction to drama and he liked the low humour of the music hall. When he died in Aberdovey at the age of 77 in 1944 he had been a judge for over 30 years. Atkin was a strong judge who would come to a clear conclusion and stick to it. He had a compelling sense of right and wrong with much kindness, courtesy and patience. In reaching his decision in *Donoghue v. Stevenson*, Atkin and his colleagues had, in Geoffrey Lewis' words:

> ". . . found a tangled mass of old decisions but no decision of the House directly in point. The step which they took to bring order to

> the chaos was one which was impelled by the ordinary needs of British society and the assumptions which it made about right and wrong. In retrospect the decision now seems so clearly right and just that it makes one marvel at the state of the law before 1932".

Mr Minchella was still in business in 1933. Mrs Donoghue died in her sons's house in Glasgow in 1958. David Stevenson's firm continued to produce ginger beer until the late 1950s and fell to the redevelopers in the 1960s. The Wellmeadow Cafe also gave way to redevelopment in Paisley and became part of the car park of the Co-op funeral parlour.

In 1982, the Australian Broadcasting Corporation marked the 60th anniversary of the case by broadcasting a special feature. In the same year, the University of British Columbia held a seminar and dinner. More recently, in 1989, guests of the Law Society of Scotland sat down to a commemorative lunch in Edinburgh's Signet Library. Those invited included direct descendants of participants in the case. The menu was significant:

Memorial cake and ginger beer
Escargots Donoghue
Carrot and ginger soup
Veal Scollopino Minchella
Mousse *Mullen v. Barr*

Mullen v. Barr was a similar action in 1929.

Press reports indicate no illness among the guests.

Sources

1. G. Lewis, *Lord Atkin* (1983).
2. J. S. Ashworth (Ed.) *Product Liability Casebook* (1984).
3. *The Scotsman*, March 31, 1989.
4. *The Daily Telegraph*, April 5, 1989.
5. D. Cassidy "Snail's place", *Post Magazine*, June 1, 1989
6. *The Times*, August 29, 1990.
7. H. Abbott, *Product Risk Management* (1992).

THE GREAT AUSTRIAN WINE SCANDAL

This is a product liability story with a difference. There were no deaths, no injuries, no damage to property but there was very serious commercial damage which extended to ten countries. It ended with calls for ministerial resignations, emergency cabinet meetings, a new law, prison sentences and the devastation of Austria's export wine trade of £20 million a year.

Not many substances can be legally added to wine. Usually just residual amounts of sulphur dioxide and sorbic acid to prevent oxidation and stop fermentation. The most common illegal substance is sugar, which is only officially allowed for certain wines made from grapes grown in cold climates. A chemical called diethylene glycol was the cause of the scandal that hit the Austrian wine business in the mid 1980s, when it was found in their wines.

The adulteration was carried out to turn cheap wines into expensive ones. The press had a field day — "Chemical Ordinaire" in the *Economist* — but would insist in calling the chemical anti-freeze, which is monoethylene glycol. Diethylene glycol has applications in making parchment softer, keeping tobacco moist, in the printing of textiles and the manufacture of cosmetics. Despite many reports to the contrary, it is not poisonous in its own right, although drinking 10 bottles of adulterated wine quickly could have a serious effect, quite apart from the impact of the alcohol.

April 25, 1985 The Austrian Ministry of Agriculture in Vienna notify the West German authorities that wine had been contaminated. Two-thirds of Austria's wine exports go to West Germany, mainly by bulk tanker.

May 13, 1985 The Health Ministry in Bonn requests the Lander (Provincial) governments to carry out checks on Austrian wines. The Lander are constitutionally responsible for health and environmental problems.

May 1985 In Rhine-Palatinate 1.5 million bottles of suspect wine are withdrawn. It contains up to 10 gms per litre of diethylene glycol. The lethal dose is said to be 110 gms per litre.

July 10, 1985 West German supermarket chains withdraw Austrian wine from sale and cancel contracts for between four and five million bottles. The West German Health Ministry has issued a warning that Austrian wines had been doctored with "car anti-freeze", to sweeten them and pass them off as superior varieties.

July 11, 1985 A dispute is developing between Austria and West Germany over the delay in alerting the West German public to the danger of the contaminated wine. In Cologne 490,000 litres of wine with 5.2 gms per litre of diethylene glycol were seized; Hesse confiscated 70,000 bottles and Saarland more than 2,000. West German experts said that anything over 0.1 gms per litre could lead to a kidney infection.

July 16, 1985 West Berlin impounded all Austrian wine while Switzerland withdrew bottles from sale.

July 18, 1985 *The Times* reported that sales of Austrian wine in Germany has collapsed. Austria claimed that most of the contaminated bottles were discovered by its own inspectors before they left the country. The Minister of Agriculture, Gunter Haiden, said that the problem had been discovered "10 weeks ago" and that it was well under control.

July 19, 1985 Austrian and West German health authorities are to blacklist 135 Austrian wines. The British Ministry of Agriculture advised wine merchants to remove all Austrian wines from their shelves and told the public not to drink any. Samples contaminated with "anti-freeze" had been found in South Yorkshire, but an Austrian trade spokesman said that Britain was unlikely to be affected.

July 20, 1985 The *Economist* reported that 90 per cent of Austrian wine exporters may have been involved. Some wine growers "are suspected of having had a hand in the fiddle by helping middlemen obtain certificates of origin for fake 'superior' wine". The scandal was starting to escalate rapidly. In Washington the U.S. Government ordered importers and wholesalers to stop selling Austrian wines until they had been tested. Three Austrian wines sold in the U.S. had been found to be contaminated. In West Germany the wine trade said that there had been a drop in overall business and one million bottles of Austrian wines had been confiscated. In Austria 20 growers had been charged with illegally adding diethylene glycol to their products to enhance the taste.

July 23, 1985 Food safety officials throughout the E.C. were alerted by the Commission about the exact destination of imported Austrian wine. The *Financial Times* said that there was considerable anger in Brussels that Vienna "had taken more than two months to tip-off the Commission". The Commission said that 1.5 million litres of adulterated wine had been sold in the Community. Health officials warned of the possibility of permanent kidney damage or death through consumption of the adulterated wine. Already confusion was beginning over the amount of diethylene glycol that had been discovered and the effect it could have. In Austria itself people were warned for the first time to stop drinking domestic wine.

July 24, 1985 The media were now calling it "The great anti-freeze wine scandal". The Austrian wine growers attacked the wine merchants and joined the farmers' union in demanding the resignation of the Minister of Agriculture. The adulterated wine came mainly from the Burgenland province and had been found in Switzerland, the Netherlands, Britain, France, Greece, Hong Kong, Poland and North America. Legal proceeding were under way in Austria against 39 wine merchants. Reuter quoted the chairman of the farmers' union as saying that a wine mafia operated in Austria, doctoring vintages to improve quality and profits, with the backing of "high-ranking" politicians. In Vienna the Minister of Health called for Europe's toughest wine purity law to be enacted. In West Germany authorities in Lower Saxony had found wine from Burgenland with 16 gms per litre of diethylene glycol. In a fresh twist two varieties of German wine from Rhine-Hessen had been found with 0.2 gms per litre of the chemical.

July 25, 1985 The Austrian authorities were trying to find out how to dispose of 4.5 million litres of contaminated wine. A new wine industry law was promised in the autumn. The Austrian Minister of Agriculture refused to resign but acknowledged that the scandal was more widespread than at first thought. Four West German wines containing diethylene glycol had been withdrawn.

July 26, 1985 The *Financial Times* was now referring to "Austria's devastating wine scandal" which had assumed world-wide proportions. The U.S. Treasury Department's Bureau of Alcohol, Tobacco and Firearms said that consumers should not drink Austrian wine until it had found out which brands were safe. Austrian television reported a wine with 48 gms per litre of diethylene glycol. The Austrian Chancellor was to chair a crisis meeting of all those concerned with the scandal. Vienna had an emergency telephone number for people who were worried about having drunk contaminated wine. In Britain the Ministry of Agriculture advised retailers to remove all Austrian wine from their shelves or risk prosecution if it was found to be contaminated.

July 27, 1985 The Austrian media were dominated by the story. There were 200 suspect brands traded by 40 firms and seven people had been arrested. The previous year Austria had exported nearly 48 million litres of wine, which had come from the country's 53,000 growers, 52 co-operatives and 1,582 shippers. It was claimed that diethylene glycol could impart "a rounded smooth sweetness" to otherwise unremarkable vintages. The chemical was cheap, easily obtainable and virtually undetectable. It could transform an ordinary vintage into a high grade wine. One calculation estimated that 1,000 grams costing £5 would treat 1,000 litres of wine. It was ironic that Austria was the first country to perfect a method of detecting diethylene glycol down to 5 mg per litre.

July 28, 1985 The headline in the *Sunday Times* was "More toxic wine found on sale in British shops". A chemist called Otto Nadraski was credited with the discovery in 1976 that diethylene glycol considerably increased the sweetness of wine. Unlike sugar it was difficult to detect and could change an ordinary Spatlese into an expensive Trockenbeerenauslese. Nadraski is alleged to have sold his secret to Josef Grill, one of Austria's biggest wine exporters, who then produced Trockenbeerenauslese containing 16 gms per litre of diethylene glycol. Both men are in jail. Nadraski is also thought to have sold his recipe to several others before he was arrested. In 1986 he was to get a five year prison term. There were now 192 contaminated Austrian wines, 11 producers were pending trial and 40 companies were under investigation.

The Austrian deputy trade commissioner in London believed that an Austrian exporter was responsible for the adulteration coming to light. The exporter had asked for a tax refund on the chemicals he had used in processing his wine "out of sheer greed and stupidity". Puzzled customs officers raised the alarm. Another source thought that a disgruntled vineyard worker had tipped off the authorities. Yet another believed that a sharp increase in the production of top quality labels had aroused suspicion. Austria's £20 million wine export market was in ruins with 10 countries now banning all its wines.

July 30, 1985 An emergency session of the Austrian cabinet promised the new law next month. There would be: a general ban on adding extra sugar to sweeten higher quality wines, cuts in the maximum permissible yields per acre, more detailed labels of origin, and a curb on the bulk export of wine. The system would be analogous to the Appellation Controlee legislation in France. It was still not clear how long the adulteration had been going on. Vienna claimed that they were first notified in late 1984 but West German investigators had evidence pointing to the use of the chemical in 1981 and 1982.

July 31, 1985 There were now 20 people in detention. A quarter of the total quantity of contaminated wine, 1.4 million litres, had been seized at Karl Siegfried Peer's supermarket. Japan was shunning Australian wine because of unclear pronunciation and spelling which had confused it with Austrian. In Britain contaminated wine bottled in Germany had been found in Hertfordshire, Avon and Merseyside.

July 31, 1985 The head of the Food Science Laboratory of the Ministry of Agriculture said: "There is no accepted technology for analysing this particular contaminant and now a large number of labs are suddenly being asked to produce data quickly". He was testing eight bottles a hour 14 hours a day. A liaison team was to co-ordinate the work of all laboratories. The most accurate method was first to screen the sample by gas chromatography, which would indicate whether or not a component having the characteristics of diethylene glycol was present. If this test was positive the sample was then put through a mass spectrometer, which could identify the specific molecules comprising diethylene glycol. Many laboratories could carry out the first step, but the equipment for the second determination cost 10 times that for the first.

August 3, 1985 The chemical had been found in nine brands of West German wine.

August 6, 1985 More than 10 million litres of wine have been impounded in Austria and 362 brands blacklisted. Five more wine merchants had been arrested bringing the total number of people in detention to 31. They are being held pending investigations and no formal charges have been laid.

August 12, 1985 The new 25 point law to be presented to the Austrian Parliament at the end of the month is "unworkable and over-bureaucratic", according to the opposition Peoples Party. Further calls were made for the resignation of the Minister of Agriculture.

August 14, 1985 In West Germany three top civil servants resigned in the Rhine Palatinate. This followed the discovery of diethylene glycol in a West German sekt. Bonn released a blacklist of 800 Austrian and 31 West German wines, half of them from West Germany's biggest wine merchant Ferdinand Pieroth. In Austria a wine merchant was declared bankrupt, the first financial victim of the scandal. This was Bruder Grill run by Josef and Richard Grill who would both receive 10-year prison sentences next year.

August 17, 1985 What *The Times* called "the greatest consumer scandal in Austria's history" turned out to be six separate scandals

- the sale of *qualitat* certificates for wines that do not meet the statutory requirements;
- the addition of diethylene glycol;
- the discovery of artificial wine consisting of water, chemicals and the refuse of grapes;
- the discovery that three companies making fruit juices had been adding diethylene glycol to their grape juice;
- table wine had been watered down by up to 30 per cent; and
- half Austria's red wine was white wine coloured red by Italian wine.

August 16, 1985 The *Financial Times* listed eight Italian wines that contained diethyelene glycol, with some of the vintages going back to 1984. Two of the wines had been best buys in the *Sunday Telegraph Good Wine Guide*. Sainsbury's had stopped selling Austrian wine.

August 21, 1985 A leading Austrian wine merchant was arrested for irregularities in labelling. The total arrested was now 45.

August 28, 1985 There was a noisy demonstration against the proposed new wine law by 4,000 farmers and vintners outside the Austrian Chancellery.

August 30, 1985 The Austrian Parliament approved the new law despite opposition.

August 31, 1985 In Japan diethylene glycol was found in two brands of Japanese wine. Imported wine from Austria had been part of a blend produced by Manns, a subsidiary of Kikkoman the soy sauce and food giant. Manns' wines were marketed as Japanese products, as any wine with more than 5 per cent domestic grape could be sold as a Japanese product.

September 16, 1985 The president of Kikkoman is due to resign soon over the growing scandal in its Manns subsidiary, seven of whose directors have already resigned. A coincidental revelation was that the high-cost Manns Estate wines were 95 per cent extremely inexpensive bulk wine from Austria.

October 18, 1985 A wine dealer who pleaded guilty to adding diethylene glycol to wine was given a 15-month suspended sentence. There were now 60 people awaiting trial.

February 7, 1986 Austrian wine exports fell by almost half last year and 13 per cent fewer Austrians were drinking wine. Confidence in the industry had been 'shattered".

May 31, 1986 The two Grill brothers were each jailed for 10 years for their part in the scandal. The chemist Otto Nadraski, who first proposed using diethylene glycol, got five years. Their cellar overseer received a two-year suspended sentence. They had adulterated six million litres of wine with the chemical.

September 12, 1986 A wine dealer was sent to prison for eight years for selling 14 million litres of wine adulterated with diethylene glycol.

September 22, 1986 The difficulty of disposing of the adulterated wine could be solved by mixing it with salt to melt the ice on the winter roads. The mixture was much less harmful than salt by itself and would melt ice at much lower temperatures.

January 27, 1991 Until 1985 Britons drank about 1.25 million bottles a year of Austrian wine. By the end of the decade this had dropped to 90,000 bottles. However, the wine was starting to make a modest comeback with most large supermarkets stocking at least one brand. Both Sainsbury's and Harrods had top estate wines on their shelves.

1992 The overall export figure was significantly lower than it had been before the diethylene glycol scandal. However, Austrian wine exports were a quarter up on the previous year, with those to Germany up by a third and those to Britain by more than a half. The German market took over three-quarters of the total, followed by Sweden and France. Compared to 1991 the exports to Japan dropped by 70 per cent and those to the U.S. by 39 per cent

Throughout the story there had been no reports of illness or death.

THE FATAL POT OF YOGHURT

The beginning of a product safety incident can sometimes only be identified with hindsight, to which the producer was not privy when it happened. Further, an apparently purely local case can escalate very rapidly into national concern over general food safety. The admission of a 15-year-old girl to the Victoria Hospital in Blackpool, on Tuesday May 30, 1989, was the first indication that something serious was amiss. She had creeping paralysis which made it difficult for her to chew, swallow or move her eyes. Unknown to anyone at the time, the origin of her illness lay on the other side of the country, miles away in Kent.

Two weeks later the Secretary of State for Health was making a statement in Parliament defending his Department's actions, that followed this and other hospital cases. He was attacked by the Opposition for his failure to ensure the safety of the nations's food supply. There was a leader in *The Times* and a six-column headline.

By Sunday June 4, a 27–year-old man, with the same symptoms as the girl, was also in the Victoria Hospital. That morning, the *Sunday Times* reported, 21–year-old Adam Cooper a Liverpool Polytechnic student woke up with what he thought was a bit of a hangover. Two hours later he was on a ventilator in the Royal Preston Hospital. At first all three patients were diagnosed as suffering from Guillain Barre syndrome, a rare nervous disease of the nervous system, or bulbar polio a type of polio which affects the head. Tests ruled out bulbar polio.

Then two children seriously ill with the same symptoms were transferred to Manchester. The mother of one of the first victims soon followed. In Manchester a paediatric neurologist at Booth Hall Children's Hospital thought he was dealing with a sudden influx of three Guillain Barre cases. The brother of one of the first three patients was admitted with the same symptoms on June 9. The neurologist realised that the odds against two members of the one family having Guillain Barre were huge and immediately thought that it must be botulism. He had never seen a case but telephoned the Communicable Diseases Centre in London, which sent a team of specialists to Blackpool. The next day, a Saturday, 20 doctors and officials met at the Victoria Hospital and set up an incident room to co-ordinate action. They agreed that the most likely cause of the illnesses was a foodborne infection, probably *Clostridium botulinum.*

To confirm their diagnosis serum from the victims was injected into mice, half of whom had previously been treated with anti-toxin. Public health officials interviewed the patients. By the Sunday afternoon of June 11, the common feature of their food was identified as hazelnut yoghurt, made by Acorn Foods of Preston. The first public statement was put out by the Department of Health on June 12. Sainsbury's, Tesco, Boots and Safeway had cleared their shelves before the shops opened. The next day *The Times* had front page headlines: "Nationwide alert over poison yoghurt" and "Ten seriously ill in botulism outbreak" with a large photograph of Robin Marsden, the owner of Acorn Foods.

There were now 17 reported cases of botulism. Three-year-old Emma Ford was poorly but stable at Booth Hall Children's Hospital, her 14-month-old brother Mark was said to be "improving" according to *The Times*; their parents were at their bedsides. A 74–year-old grandmother, Annie Newton, became a victim four days after eating a pot of yoghurt. Other suspected victims included a boy of six and a policeman from Rochdale.

Many of the patients were treated with horse serum. The animals are inoculated with the toxin, which produces anti-bodies against the botulism in their blood. The serum is extracted and the anti-bodies used to treat the patients; it is effective only when given early while the toxin is circulating in the patient's blood. The toxin usually arises in food which has been inadequately sterilised and the most common source is contaminated tinned food. The onset of an attack can be very sudden when it is the toxin itself that is ingested, rather than the bacteria which produce the toxin in the gastrointestinal tract.

By June 13, the source of the toxin had been traced to hazelnut puree made by Youngs Fruits of Folkestone in Kent. The factory continued to produce citrus and soft fruit purees to flavour yoghurt but had stopped making the hazelnut variety. The hazelnuts came from Spain and samples were undergoing tests. The Managing Director of Youngs, Dr Christopher Young, was quoted as saying:

> "I am jolly proud of our standards and record. The company has been established for many years and has a high reputation in the food industry. We would stress that the diagnosis has not been confirmed but the matter is under investigation by the health authority and ourselves. Until the outcome of these investigations, it would be premature to comment further."

Eight dairies obtained supplies of hazelnut puree from Youngs but no cases of botulism had been linked to them. Acorn Foods had bought 36 cans of hazelnut puree from Youngs and had produced 7,000 pots of yoghurt from them before production was stopped.

On June 13, the incident became a political matter with a clash in Parliament between the Secretary of State for Health, Kenneth Clark, and the chief Opposition spokesman on health, Robin Cook. The Minister made a statement on the outbreak. He said that the Department of Health had first been informed of the diagnosis of botulism on the evening of June 9. He congratulated the neurologist at Manchester on his prompt action in alerting the Communicable Disease Centre. He said that between 1922 and 1985 there had been only nine outbreaks of botulism in Britain, compared with 216 in the U.S. between 1971 and 1985, and 115 in France between 1978 and 1984. The last British case which had resulted in death had been in 1978. He rejected suggestions that his Department had failed to act quickly in informing the public of the dangers.

Robin Cook criticised the Government's action on research in the food supply. He said that the Bristol Food Research Laboratory had not been able to carry out any research in food processing the previous year, because of the cut in the Government grant for work on salmonella poisoning:

> "When is the House of Commons going to see the regulations on food hygiene which has been with the Secretary of State in draft form for two years? When will the Government start to reverse its irresponsible cuts in research into food safety? Will he confirm that there are currently 430 unfilled vacancies for environmental health officers?"

The Minister said that Mr Cook knew very well that the hygiene regulations had nothing to do with cases of botulism. After consultations, the regulations would be produced as soon as possible. The Bristol research station had not been engaged in food safety research relating to botulism. Resources for environmental health were a matter for local government.

Also on June 13 *Clostridium botulinum* toxin Type B was detected in a can of hazelnut puree made by Youngs. The next day the toxin was found in a pot of hazelnut puree. On the Thursday the mice which had not been treated with anti-toxin started to die. The total number of people affected by the outbreak was 26. Annie Newton died in the Victoria Hospital. She had been on a life-support machine for eight days. The original press release from the Department of Health warned the public not to eat *any* hazelnut yoghurt. The major supermarkets withdrew the product, including own-label, and destroyed thousands of pots.

At the Environmental Health Congress in 1989, Dr Richard Gilbert the director of the Public Health Services food hygiene laboratory made a speech. He warned manufacturers not to alter the formula of their foods without regard to the process, because it may no longer apply when the amount of sugar and salt was reduced. It was the removal of sugar from the hazelnut puree, intended for yoghurt, that was responsible for the outbreak. The sugar had maintained the correct acid/alkali balance which inhibited the growth of bacteria.

On September 2, 1991 Youngs Foods pleaded guilty at Preston Crown Court to selling hazelnut puree unfit for human consumption. For the defence it was said that the hazelnuts came from a reputable supplier and that any bacteria would have been killed in the roasting process. Environmental health officers had found mould growing around the entrance to the processing room, chutes leading to the vessels were left uncovered and there was dirty equipment, walls and ceilings. The company, which once had a turnover of £1.5 million, was fined £3,000 and went into receivership with debts of £222,000.

In 1990 Parliament approved the Food Safety Act, which introduced all due diligence and the requirement to take all reasonable precautions, and the Food Hygiene (Amendment) Regulations came into force, which lay down the maximum temperature for certain products in the food chain.

Sources

Economist, Financial Times, Independent, Mail on Sunday, Sunday Times, The Times, Western Morning News.

THE CANCER SCARE THAT NEVER WAS

Bad news sells newspapers, for we all read the latest scare stories. The tabloids thrive on them as millions are attracted by the splash headlines. The broadsheets, too, make sure that there is a good crop of nasties to catch the attention, albeit on an inside page. Certain words are guaranteed to draw the reader, a collection like: cancer, beer and whisky for instance. However, they provide a product safety story which demonstrates that the public can be protected from an apparent danger before it can develop. This case history is told in two parts. First, a sketch of what the press said, followed by what the experts were actually doing about it.

In 1978 the *Sunday Times* headline was "US test on food chemicals raise new cancer fear". The story said that nitrates and nitrites had been suspected for more than a decade of causing stomach cancer. There was evidence that they could cause other cancers as well. The Massachusetts Institute of Technology had found that rats given large quantities of nitrite developed cancer of the lymph glands. There was a possibility that the two chemicals could cause Hodgkin's disease, leukaemia and breast cancer in humans. About 20 per cent of all meat products contained nitrates and/or nitrites. The chief scientific adviser to Ministry of Agriculture Fisheries and Food (MAFF) said "we can't get rid of the nitrites altogether or we would run straight into the botulinum problem". This was because the nitrites prevented botulism by preserving the meat.

The same year there was a report in a West German magazine that nitrosamines had been found in 111 beers, out of 158 that had been checked by Professor Preussmann at Heidelberg's Cancer Research Centre. The centre had examined 3,000 food and drink products of 170 types over two years for traces of the carcinogen nitrosamine.

On January 11, 1979 a link between cancer and beer was made for the public in a *Daily Telegraph* headline: "Beer tests for cancer substance." This was a reference to the German work. The Brewers Society said that there was no indication of what the danger level would be and that it would take 250,000 years for the average beer drinker to consume a teaspoonful of nitrosamine.

In April 1979 *Business Insurance* picked up the story with "Insurers monitor probe of carcinogens in beer". It reported that the work in Heidelberg would take another six months to evaluate. The Brewers Society put out another press release which included: "We're satisfied by all the available evidence that our beers are just as safe and wholesome as they were when brewing started 3,000 years ago and there's no reason why beer drinkers should not continue to enjoy their favourite brands." A statement which conveniently overlooked the case in Manchester in 1900 when arsenic in beer killed 70 and put 6,000 in hospital.

Across the Atlantic in the U.S. the New England Institute of Sciences had investigated nitrosamines in whisky. The *Wall Street Journal* in August 1979 reported this under "Cancer Agent Found in Several Brands of Scotch Whisky." It said that "cancer-causing nitrosamines" had been detected in Chivas Regal, Black & White, J & B, Ballantines's Sandy Scot and Cutty Sark. The amounts ranged up to two parts per billion (ppb) and levels of 10 ppb had caused cancer in laboratory animals. The amount that would be carcinogenic for humans was not known. Small amounts of the chemical had been found in beer, bacon and cosmetics.

In the U.K. the *Guardian* also ran this story about "cancer on the rocks." The beers affected were named as Guinness, Newcastle Dark Ale, Skol, Heineken from Holland, Fosters from Australia, Kirn from Japan and St Pauli Girl from West Germany. The concentrations detected ranged up to seven ppb. The *Daily Telegraph* joined in with "'Cancer Risk' for Scotch Drinkers" over a report on the findings. The *Financial Times* in similar vein had "Cancer risk found in Scotch whisky brands."

The following month the *Wall Street Journal* had the headline "Tests by the FDA find 28 beers with agent that causes cancer". The highest nitrosamine reading was in Schlitz beer at seven ppb while Coors had a no detectable level. These results had been released by the FDA, which said that they were confident that nitrosamine could be eliminated, through changes in the kilning of the barley malt used in the brewing process.

The good news came twelve months later when the *Wall Street Journal* headline was "FDA finds reduced nitrosamine levels in a survey of beers". Brewers were said to have "significantly reduced" the level of the chemical in their beers in a survey of more than 100 brands. Domestic and imported beers were down to an average of one ppb of nitrosamine. The addition of sulphur during kilning had prevented the formation of nitrosamines. The FDA considered five ppb the level at which it would take action against a brewer. Three beers were affected by this decision: Cerveceria India had recalled its India beer, San Miguel's dark beer from Manila had been detained as had Samuel Smith's Pale Ale from Tadcaster, England. The Schlitz beer was down to the two ppb level.

So much for the popular press. Behind the scenes the powerful beer industry had moved into action to protect the public and its interests. The report in the *Wall Street Journal*, that nitrosamine levels had been significantly reduced, was the result of international co-operation and some intensive scientific investigations. The headlines in the press concealed a story more interesting than the copy beneath them revealed.

We must take a step back for a moment to explain the source of nitrosamines. Nitrates have a wide variety of applications, in explosives, fertilisers, chemical intermediaries and in curing meat. The Romans found that nitrates would preserve meat and give it an attractive pink colour. But it was not until 1899 that it was discovered that the active agent was not the nitrate, but nitrite. The nitrate is broken down to nitrite which preserves meat such as ham and bacon by killing the bacteria, especially the deadly *Clostridium botulinum* — hence the remark by MAFF.

Under some conditions nitrites can combine with amines, which are found in food and the human body, to form nitrosamines. In the 1950s these were found to be powerful carcinogens and teratogens, which create gross abnormalities in living cells. In 1968 the respected weekly medical journal, the *Lancet*, warned that as nitrites could form nitrosamines in food it was "a matter of gravest concern". The situation in malting and brewing is slightly different. Here the reaction is between the oxides of nitrogen in malt kiln gases and naturally occuring amines in the germinating barley.

In 1970 the recently formed Medical Advisory Group, which advised the U.S. Brewers Association, held its second meeting. Among the issues discussed was the possible contamination of malt beverages with substances such as nitrosamines and aflotoxins. Two years later a committee of MAFF recommended limits on all nitrates and nitrites in food. In 1976 the Laboratory of the Government Chemist determined the level of nitrosamines in 500 foods, to ensure that the concentrations were below the level considered to be a risk to humans.

The German work in Heidelberg had been carried out with a Thermal Energy Analyser, which could detect very small quantities of specific substances. At that time it was the only instrument of its type. In March 1979 the Brewers Society in the U.K. decided to fund an instrument at a cost of £22,000 for the brewing industry research association, now BRF International near Redhill in Surrey. Inevitably it became known as the Tea Machine. The Norwich laboratory of MAFF had previously obtained a Tea Machine to examine a range of products, including beer and Scotch.

By 1979 several organisations were cooperating to tackle the nitrosamine problem. In the U.K. there was the Brewers Society as well as similar organisations in the U.S., Canada and Australia. Together they gathered under the umbrella of the International Medical Advisory Conferences, which met annually in each country in turn. At the Melbourne meeting in 1979[3] there was a report on the Heidelberg investigations. Extensive research had discovered that malt was a major source of nitrosamines. It was recommended that they should be reduced to the lowest level because they could be possible carcinogens. Malt is the major raw material in the production of both beer and whisky. A grant was funded in the U.S. to study the indirect firing of malt kilns, in an effort to reduce the formation of the nitrosamines.

In the U.K. working parties, driven by close cooperation between the Brewers Society, the Maltsters Association of Great Britain and MAFF,

[3] T. B. Turner, V. L. Bennett, "Forward Together", Alcoholic Beverage Medical Research Foundation, Baltimore, Maryland, 1993.

looked at two aspects: kilns and nitrosamines. The former was important because of the introduction of North Sea gas in place of anthracite or oil. Indirect fired kilns would help in reducing nitrosamine formation but were less efficient than direct fired kilns. In the malting process the grain, usually barley, is steeped in water to start germination and then allowed to grow for a few days before being kilned to stop growth and impart flavour. It was found that amines were formed in the rootlets during the growing phase. The application of bromate effectively reduced rootlet growth and consequently the availability of amines. Adding sulphur to the kiln also hampered the nitrosating action which led to the formation of nitrosamines.

Thus, by the end of 1979, the scientific solution to the problem was available. The U.K. maltsters then introduced a voluntary limit of five ppb of nitrosamine in malt which would produce, as a rule of thumb, 0.5 ppb in beer, well below the accepted threshold in the U.S. To check conformance to this level samples of malt, domestic beers, and "green" beers for export to the U.S., used to arrive by taxi at Redhill for analysis by the Tea Machine. Up to 2,000 samples of beer and malt were analysed each year at this time and a replacement Tea Machine, bought in 1990, now cost £37,000.

In 1989 the International Medical Advisory Conference met in Eastbourne. One of the subjects discussed was the risk from nitrosamines. It was reported that a safe limit of one ppb had been set for beer and that in the previous decade beers had been reduced to, or below, this level.

Apart from nitrosamine, the nitrites had come under suspicion because they could interact with the haemoglobin of the blood and reduce its capacity to carry oxygen, from the lungs to the tissues. This is a different reaction from that between the oxides of nitrogen in malt kiln gases and the amines in germinating barley. The Preservatives in Food Regulations 1989 permit the use of nitrate and nitrite, at specified levels, as curing agents for meat products and as preservatives in certain cheeses. The addition of nitrate and nitrite to food for babies and young children is forbidden. The Water Supply (Water Quality) Regulations 1989, which incorporate the provisions of an E.C. Directive (80/778/EEC), set limits of 50 mg/l for nitrates and 0.1 mg/l for nitrite (mg/l is milligrams per litre or parts per million).

A report in 1992 by the U.K. Steering Group on Chemical Aspects of Food Surveillance[4] found that three-quarters of the average human intake of nitrate came from vegetables. Vegetarians have a considerably higher estimated average nitrate intake but still well below the acceptable level. The benefit derived from eating vegatables is not affected

The Steering Group's report said: "The main public health issue remains that of exposure to [nitrosamines] and the potential carcinogenicity of such compounds. There is no epidemiological evidence

[4] "Nitrate, Nitrite and *N*-Nitroso Compounds in Food: Second Report", Food Surveillance Paper No. 32, 1992, HMSO, London.

available to associate causally current dietary intakes of nitrate with cancer." Neither are there any "unequivocal epidemiological studies available to link dietary exposure to nitrite with cancer". But the majority of nitrosamine compounds "which have been tested can induce cancer in laboratory animals."

The report concluded that there was no cause for concern for current dietary intakes of nitrate or nitrite. However, levels should be kept as low as possible. It also concluded that: "In view of current uncertainties regarding exposure to [nitrosamine] compounds in food we recommend that it would be prudent to continue to reduce levels . . . in food wherever possible."

In 1992 the Steering Group reported on a survey of 172 samples from 65 brewery companies. In 94 per cent of the cases the nitrate concentrations were below the E.C. limit for drinking water. A possible explanation for the result was "that at least some of these brewers have taken steps to reduce the nitrate content of their ingredients as part of their strategy for eliminating [nitrosamines]." It had also been reported[5] that internationally there had been a major investment to install special burners in malt kilns, or modify them to indirect heating, which had resulted in much less production of nitrosamines during malting.

In 1994 BRF International was analysing 800 samples a year for nirtosamines, bringing the total since the commencement to 14,000. They find that all beers are less than 0.5 ppb, and that most are below 0.2 ppb compared to the U.S. limit of five ppb.

It is worth remembering that there is no evidence that nitrosamines produce cancer in humans. The considerable international work was undertaken to eliminate any possibility that this could be the case.

[5] T. Wainright "The Chemistry of Nitrosamine Formation: Relevance to Malting and Brewing", *Journal of the Institute of Brewing* January–February 1986.

APPENDICES

Appendix 1: Council Directive 92/59/EEC of June 29, 1992, on general product safety

THE COUNCIL OF THE EUROPEAN COMMUNITIES,

Having regard to the Treaty establishing the European Economic Community, and in particular Aricle 100a thereof,

Having regard to the proposal from the Commission,

In co-operation with the European Parliament,

Having regard to the opinion of the Economic and Social Committee,

Whereas it is important to adopt measures with the aim of progressively establishing the internal market over a period expiring on December 31, 1992; whereas the internal market is to comprise an area without internal frontiers in which the free movement of goods, persons, services and capital is ensured;

Whereas some Member States have adopted horizontal legislation on product safety, imposing, in particular, a general obligation on economic operators to market only safe products, whereas those legislations differ in the level of protection afforded to persons; whereas such disparities and the absence of horizontal legislation in other Member States are liable to create barriers to trade and distortions of competition within the internal market;

Whereas it is very difficult to adopt Community legislation for every product which exists or may be developed; whereas there is a need for a broadly-based, legislative framework of a horizontal nature to deal with those products, and also to cover lacunae in existing or forthcoming specific legislation, in particular with a view to ensuring a high level of protection of safety and health of persons, as required by Article 100a(3) of the Treaty;

Whereas it is therefore necessary to establish on a Community level a general safety requirement for any product placed on the market that is intended for consumers or likely to be used by consumers; whereas certain second-hand goods should nevertheless be excluded by their nature;

Whereas production equipment, capital goods and other products used exclusively in the context of a trade or business are not covered by this Directive;

Whereas, in the absence of more specific safety provisions, within the framework of Community regulations, covering the products concerned, the provisions of this Directive are to apply;

Whereas when there are specific rules of Community law, of the total harmonisation type, and in particular rules adopted on the basis of the new approach, which lay down obligations regarding product safety, further obligations should not be imposed on economic operators as regards the placing on the market of products covered by such rules;

Whereas, when the provisions of specific Community regulations cover only certain aspects of safety or categories of risks in respect of the product concerned, the obligations of economic operators in respect of such aspects are determined solely by those provisions;

Whereas it is appropriate to supplement the duty to observe the general safety requirement by an obligation on economic operators to supply consumers with relevant information and adopt measures commensurates with the characteristics of the products, enabling them to be informed of the risks that these products might present;

Whereas in the absence of specific regulations, criteria should be defined whereby product safety can be assessed;

Whereas Member States must establish authorities responsible for monitoring product safety and with powers to take the appropriate measures;

Whereas it is necessary in particular for the appropriate measures to include the power for Member States to organise, immediately and efficiently, the withdrawal of dangerous products already placed on the market;

Whereas it is necessary for the preservation of the unity of the market to inform the Commission of any measure restricting the placing on the market of a product or requiring its withdrawal from the market except for those relating an event which is local in effect and in any case limited to the territory of the Member State concerned; whereas such measures can be taken only in compliance with the provisions of the Treaty, and in particular Articles 30 to 36;

Whereas this Directive applies without prejudice to the notification procedures in Council Directive 83/189/EEC of March 28, 1983, laying down a procedure for the provision of information in the field of technical standards and regulations and in Commission Decision 88/383/EEC of February 24, 1988 providing for the improvement of information on safety, hygiene and health at work;

Whereas effective supervision of product safety requires the setting-up at national and Community levels of a system of rapid exchange of information in emergency situations in respect of the safety of a product and whereas the procedure laid down by Council Decision 89/45/EEC of December 21, 1988 on a Community system for the rapid exchange of information on dangers arising from the use of consumer products should therefore be incorporated into this Directive and the above Decision should be repealed; where it is also advisable for this Directive to take over the detailed procedures adopted under the above Decision and to give the Commission, assisted by a committee, power to adapt them;

Whereas, moreover, equivalent notification procedures already exist for pharmaceuticals, which come under Directives 75/319/EEC and 81/851/EEC, concerning animal diseases referred to in Directive 82/894/EEC, for products of animal origin covered by Directive 89/662/EEC, and in the form of the system for the rapid exchange of information in radiological emergencies under Decision 87/600/Euratom;

Whereas it is primarily for Member States, in compliance with the Treaty and in particular with Articles 30 to 36 thereof, to take appropriate measures with regard to dangerous products located within their territory;

Whereas in such a situation the decision taken on a particular product could differ from one Member State to another; whereas such a difference may entail unacceptable disparities in consumer protection and constitute a barrier to intra-Community trade;

Whereas it may be necessary to cope with serious product-safety problems which affect or could affect, in the immediate future, all or a large part of the

Community and which, in view of the nature of the safety problem posed by the product cannot be dealt with effectively in a manner commensurate with the urgency of the problem under the procedures laid down in the specific rules of Community law applicable to the products or category of products in question;

Whereas it is therefore necessary to provide for an adequate mechanism allowing, in the last resort, for the adoption of measures applicable throughout the Community, in the form of a decision addressed to the Member States, in order to cope with emergency situations as mentioned above; whereas such a decision is not of direct application to economic operators and must be incorporated into a national instrument; whereas measures adopted under such a procedure can be no more than interim measures that have to be taken by the Commission assisted by a committee of representatives of the Member States; whereas, for reasons of co-operation with the Member States, it is appropriate to provide for a regulatory committee according to procedure III(b) of Decision 87/373/EEC;

Whereas this Directive does not affect victims' rights within the meaning of Council Directive 85/374/EEC of July 25, 1985 on the approximation of the laws, regulations and administrative provisions of the Member States concerning liability for defective products;

Whereas it is necessary that Member States provide for appropriate means of redress before the competent courts in respect of measures taken by the competent authorities which restrict the placing on the market of a product or require its withdrawal;

Whereas it is appropriate to consider, in the light of experience, possible adaptation of this Directive, particularly as regards extension of its scope and provisions on emergency situations and intervention at Community level;

Whereas, in addition, the adoption of measures concerning imported products with a view to preventing risks to the safety and health of persons must comply with the Community's international obligations.

HAS ADOPTED THIS DIRECTIVE:

TITLE 1: Objective—Scope—Definitions

Article 1

1. The purpose of the provisions of this Directive is to ensure that products placed on the market are safe.

2. The provisions of this Directive shall apply in so far as there are no specific provisions in rules of Community law governing the safety of the products concerned.

In particular, where specific rules of Community law contain provisions imposing safety requirements on the products which they govern, the provisions of Articles 2 to 4 of this Directive shall not, in any event, apply to those products.

Where specific rules of Community law contain provisions governing only certain aspects of product safety or categories of risks for the products concerned, those are the provisions which shall apply to the products concerned with regard to the relevant safety aspects of risks.

Article 2

For the purposes of this Directive:

(a) *product* shall mean any product intended for consumers or likely to be used by consumers, supplied whether for consideration or not in the course of a commercial activity and whether new, used or reconditioned.

However, this Directive shall not apply to second-hand products supplied as antiques or as products to be repaired or reconditioned prior to being used, provided that the supplier clearly informs the person to whom he supplies the product to that effect;

(b) *safe product* shall mean any product which, under normal or reasonably foreseeable conditions of use, including duration, does not present any risk or only the minimum risks compatible with the product's use, considered as acceptable and consistent with a high level of protection for the safety and health of persons, taking into account the following points in particular;

- the characteristics of the product, including its composition, packaging, instructions for assembly and maintenance,
- the effect on other products, where it is reasonably foreseeable that it will be used with other products,
- the presentation of the product, the labelling, any instructions for its use and disposal and any other indication or information provided by the producer,
- the categories of consumer at serious risk when using the product, in particular children.

The feasibility of obtaining higher levels of safety or the availability of other products presenting a lesser degree of risk shall not constitute grounds for considering a product to be "unsafe" or "dangerous";

(c) *dangerous product* shall mean any product which does not meet the definition of "safe product" according to point (b) hereof;

(d) *producer* shall mean:

- the manufacturer of the product, when he is established in the Community, and any other person presenting himself as the manufacturer by affixing to the product his name, trade mark or other distinctive mark, or the person who reconditions the product,
- the manufacturer's representative, when the manufacturer is not established in the Community or, if there is no representative established in the Community, the importer of the product,
- other professionals in the supply chain, insofar as their activities may affect the safety properties of a product placed on the market.

(e) *distributor* shall mean any professional in the supply chain whose activity does not affect the safety properties of a product.

TITLE II: General safety requirement

Article 3

1. Producers shall be obliged to place only safe products on the market.
2. Within the limits of their respective activities, producers shall:

- provide consumers with the relevant information to enable them to assess the risks inherent in a product throughout the normal or reasonably foreseeable period of its use, where such risks are not immediately obvious without adequate warnings, and to take precautions against those risks.

  Provision of such warnings does not, however, exempt any person from compliance with the other requirements laid down in this Directive.

— adopt measures commensurate with the characteristics of the products which they supply, to enable them to be informed of risks which these products might present and to take appropriate action including, if necessary, withdrawing the product in question from the market to avoid these risks.

The above measures shall for example include, whenever appropriate, marking of the products or product batches in such a way that they can be identified, sample testing of marketed products, investigating complaints made and keeping distributors informed of such monitoring.

3. Distributors shall be required to act with due care in order to help to ensure compliance with the general safety requirement, in particular by not supplying products which they know or should have presumed, on the basis of the information their possession and as professionals, do not comply with this requirement. In particular, within the limits of their respective activities, they shall participate in monitoring the safety of products placed on the market, especially by passing on information on product risks and co-operating in the action taken to avoid these risks.

Article 4

1. Where there are no specific Community provisions governing the safety of the products in question, a product shall be deemed safe when it conforms to the specific rules of national law of the Member State in whose territory the product is in circulation, such rules being drawn up in conformity with the Treaty, and in particular Articles 30 and 36 thereof, and laying down the health and safety requirements which the product must satisfy in order to be marketed.

2. In the absence of specific rules as referred to in paragraph 1, the conformity of a product to the general safety requirement shall be assessed having regard to voluntary national standards giving effect to a European standard or, where they exist, to Community technical specifications or, failing these, to standards drawn up in the Member State in which the product is in circulation, or to the codes of good practice in respect of health and safety in the sector concerned or to the state of the art and technology and to the safety which consumers may reasonably expect.

3. Conformity of a product with the provisions mentioned in paragraphs 1 or 2 shall not bar the competent authorities of the Member States from taking appropriate measures to impose restrictions on its being placed on the market or to require its withdrawal from the market where there is evidence that, despite such conformity, it is dangerous to the health and safety of consumers.

TITLE III: Obligations and powers of the Member States

Article 5

Member States shall adopt the necessary laws, regulations and administrative provisions to make producers and distributors comply with their obligations under this Directive in such a way that products placed on the market are safe.

In particular, Member States shall establish or nominate authorities to monitor the compliance of products with the obligation to place only safe products on the market and arrange for such authorities to have the necessary powers to take the appropriate measures incumbent upon them under this Directive, including the possibility of imposing suitable penalties in the event of failure to comply with the obligations deriving from this Directive. They shall notify the Commission of the said authorities; the Commission shall pass on the information to the other Member States.

Article 6

1. For the purposes of Article 5, Member States shall have the necessary powers, acting in accordance with the degree or risk and in conformity with the Treaty, and in particular Articles 30 to 36 thereof, to adopt appropriate measures with a view, *inter alia*, to:

(a) organising appropriate checks on the safety properties of products, even after their being placed on the market as being safe, on an adequate scale, up to the final stage of use or consumption;
(b) requiring all necessary information from the parties concerned;
(c) taking samples of a product or a product line and subjecting them to safety checks;
(d) subjecting product marketing to prior conditions designed to ensure product safety and requiring that suitable warnings be affixed regarding the risks which the product may present;
(e) making arrangements to ensure that persons who might be exposed to a risk from a product are informed in good time and in a suitable manner of the said risk by, *inter alia*, the publication of special warnings;
(f) temporarily prohibiting, for the period required to carry out the various checks, anyone from supplying, offering to supply or exhibiting a product or product batch, whenever there are precise and consistent indications that they are dangerous;
(g) prohibiting the placing on the market of a product or product batch which has proved dangerous and establishing the accompanying measures needed to ensure that the ban is complied with;
(h) organising the effective and immediate withdrawal of a dangerous product or product batch already on the market and, if necessary, its destruction under appropriate conditions.

2. The measures to be taken by the competent authorities of the Member States under this Article shall be addressed, as appropriate, to:

(a) the producer;
(b) within the limits of their respective activities, distributors and in particular the party responsible for the first stage of distribution on the national market;
(c) any other person, where necessary, with regard to co-operation in action taken to avoid risks arising from a product.

TITLE IV: Notification and Exchanges of Information

Article 7

1. Where a Member State takes measures which restrict the placing of a product or a product batch on the market or require its withdrawal from the market, such as provided for in Article 6(1)(d) to (h), the Member State shall, to the extent that such notification is not required under any specific Community legislation, inform the Commission of the said measures, specifying its reasons

for adopting them. This obligation shall not apply where the measures relate to an event which is local in effect and in any case limited to the territory of the Member State concerned.

2. The Commission shall enter into consultations with the parties concerned as quickly as possible. Where the Commission concludes, after such consultations, that the measure is justified, it shall immediately inform the Member State which initiated the action and the other Member States. Where the Commission concludes, after such consultations, that the measures is not justified, it shall immediately inform the Member State which initiated the action.

TITLE V: Emergency situations and action at Community level

Article 8

1. Where a Member State adopts or decides to adopt emergency measures to prevent, restrict or impose specific conditions on the possible marketing or use, within its own territory, of a product or product batch by reason of a serious and immediate risk presented by the said product or product batch to the health and safety of consumers, it shall forthwith inform the Commission thereof, unless provision is made for this obligation in procedures of a similar nature in the context of other Community instruments.

This obligation shall not apply if the effects of the risk do not, or cannot, go beyond the territory of the Member State concerned.

Without prejudice to the provisions of the first subparagraph, Member States may pass on to the Commission any information in their possession regarding the existence of a serious and immediate risk before deciding to adopt the measures in question.

2. On receiving this information, the Commission shall check to see whether it complies with the provisions of this Directive and shall forward it to the other Member States, which, in turn, shall immediately inform the Commission of any measures adopted.

3. Detailed procedures for the Community information system described in this Article are set out in the Annex. They shall be adapted by the Commission in accordance with the procedure laid down in Article 11.

Article 9

If the Commission becomes aware, through notification given by the Member States or through information provided by them, in particular under Article 7 or Article 8, of the existence of a serious and immediate risk from a product to the health and safety of consumers in various Member States and if:

(a) one or more Member States have adopted measures entailing restrictions on the marketing of the product or requiring its withdrawal from the market, such as those provided for in Article 6(1)(d) to (h);

(b) Member States differ on the adoption of measures to deal with the risk in question;

(c) the risk cannot be dealt with, in view of the nature of the safety issue posed by the product and in a manner compatible with the urgency of the case, under the other procedures laid down by the specific Community legislation applicable to the product or category of products concerned; and

(d) the risk can be eliminated effectively only by adopting appropriate measures applicable at Community level, in order to ensure the protection of the health and safety of consumers and the proper functioning of the common market, the Commission, after consulting the Member States and at the request of at least one of them, may adopt a decision, in accordance with the procedure laid down in Article 11, requiring Member States to take temporary measures from among those listed in Article 6(1)(d) to (h).

Article 10

1. The Commission shall be assisted by a Committee on Product Safety Emergencies, hereinafter referred to as 'the Committee', composed of the representatives of the Member States and chaired by a representative of the Commission.

2. Without prejudice to Article 9(c), there shall be close co-operation between the Committee referred to in paragraph 1 and the other Committees established by specific rules of Community law to assist the Commission as regards the health and safety aspects of the product concerned.

Article 11

1. The Commission representative shall submit to the Committee a draft of the measures to be taken. The Committee, having verified that the conditions listed in Article 9 are fulfilled, shall deliver its opinion on the draft within a time limit which the Chairman may lay down according to the urgency of the matter but which may not exceed one month. The opinion shall be delivered by the majority laid down in Article 148(2) of the Treaty for adoption of decisions by the Council on a proposal from the Commission. The votes of the representatives of the Member States within the Committee shall be weighted in the manner set out in that Article. The Chairman shall not vote.

The Commission shall adopt the measures in question, if they are in accordance with the opinion of the Committee. If the measures proposed are not in accordance with the Committee's opinion, or in the absence of an opinion, the Commission shall forthwith submit to the Council a proposal regarding the measures to be taken. The Council shall act by a qualified majority.

If the Council has not acted within 15 days of the date on which the proposal was submitted to it, the measures proposed shall be adopted by the Commission unless the Council has decided against them by a simple majority.

2. Any measure adopted under this procedure shall be valid for no longer than three months. That period may be prolonged under the same procedure.

3. Member States shall take all necessary measures to implement the decisions adopted under this procedure within less than 10 days.

4. The competent authorities of the Member States responsible for carrying out measures adopted under this procedure shall, within one month, give the parties concerned an opportunity to submit their views and shall inform the Commission accordingly.

Article 12

The Member States and the Commission shall take the steps necessary to ensure that their officials and agents are required not to disclose information obtained for the purposes of this Directive which, by its nature, is covered by professional secrecy, except for information relating to the safety properties of a given product which must be made public if circumstances so require, in order to protect the health and safety of persons.

APPENDIX 1

TITLE VI: Miscellaneous and final provisions

Article 13

This Directive shall be without prejudice to Directive 85/374/EEC.

Article 14

1. Any decision adopted under this Directive and involving restrictions on the placing of a product on the market, or requiring its withdrawal from the market, must state the appropriate reasons on which it is based. It shall be notified as soon as possible to the party concerned and shall indicate the remedies available under the provisions in force in the Member State in question and the time limits applying to such remedies.

The parties concerned shall, whenever feasible, be given an opportunity to submit their views before the adoption of the measure. If this has not been done in advance because of the urgency of the measures to be taken, such opportunity shall be given in due course after the measure has been implemented.

Measures requiring the withdrawal of a product from the market shall take into consideration the need to encourage distributors, users and consumers to contribute to the implementation of such measures.

2. Member States shall ensure that any measure taken by the competent authorities involving restrictions on the placing of a product on the market or requiring its withdrawal from the market can be challenged before the competent courts.

3. Any decision taken by virtue of this Directive and involving restrictions on the placing of a product on the market or requiring its withdrawal from the market shall be entirely without prejudice to assessment of the liability of the party concerned, in the light of the national criminal law applying in the case in question.

Article 15

Every two years following the date of adoption, the Commission shall submit a report on the implementation of this Directive to the European Parliament and the Council.

Article 16

Four years from the date referred to in Article 17(1), on the basis of a Commission report on the experience acquired, together with appropriate proposals, the Council shall decide whether to adjust this Directive, in particular with a view to extending its scope as laid down in Article 1(1) and Article 2(a), and whether the provisions of Title V should be amended.

Article 17

1. Member States shall adopt the laws, regulations and administrative provisions necessary to comply with this Directive by June 29, 1994 at the latest.

They shall forthwith inform the Commission thereof. The provisions adopted shall apply with effect from June 29, 1994.

2. When these measures are adopted by the Member States, they shall contain a reference to this Directive or be accompanied by such a reference on the occasion of their official publication. The methods of making such a reference shall be laid down by the Member States.

3. Member States shall communicate to the Commission the text of the provisions of national law which they adopt in the area covered by this Directive.

Article 18

Decision 89/45/EEC is hereby repealed on the date referred to in Article 17(1).

Article 19

This Directive is addressed to the Member States.

ANNEX: DETAILED PROCEDURES FOR THE APPLICATION OF THE COMMUNITY SYSTEM FOR THE RAPID EXCHANGE OF INFORMATION PROVIDED FOR IN ARTICLE 8

Done at Luxembourg, 29 June, 1992

For the Council
The President
Carlos Borrego

1. The system covers products placed on the market as defined in Article 2(a) of this Directive.

Pharmaceuticals, which come under Directive 75/319/EEC and 81/851/EEC, and animals, to which Directive 82/894/EEC applies and products of animal origin, as far as they are are covered by Directive 89/662/EEC, and the system for radiological emergencies which covers widespread contamination of products (Decision 87/600/Euratom), are excluded, since they are covered by equivalent notification procedures.

2. The system is essentially aimed at a rapid exchange of information in the event of a serious and immediate risk to the health and safety of consumers. It is impossible to lay down specific criteria as to what, precisely, constitutes an immediate and serious risk; in this regard, the national authorities will therefore judge each individual case on it merits. It should be noted that, as Article 8 of this Directive relates to immediate threats posed by a product to consumers, products involving possible long-term risks, which call for a study of possible technical changes by means of directives or standards are not concerned.

3. As soon as a serious and immediate risk is detected, the national authority shall consult, insofar as possible and appropriate, the producer or distributor of the product concerned. Their point of view and the details which they supply may be useful both to the administrations of the Member States and to the Commission in determining what action should be taken to ensure that the consumer is protected with a minimum of commercial disruption. To these ends the Member States should endeavour to obtain the maximum of information on the products and the nature of the danger, without compromising the need for rapidity.

4. As soon as a Member State has detected a serious and immediate risk, the effects of which extend or could extend beyond its territory, and measures have been taken or decided on, it shall immediately inform the Commission. The Member State shall indicate that it is notifying the Commission under Article 8 of this Directive. All available details shall be given, in particular on:

(a) information to identify the product;
(b) the danger involved, including the results of any tests/analyses which are relevant to assessing the level of risk;
(c) the nature of the measures taken or decided on;
(d) information on supply chains where such information is possible.

Such information must be transmitted in writing, preferably by telex or fax, but may be preceded by a telephone call to the Commission. It should be remembered that the speed with which the information is communicated is crucial.

5. Without prejudice to point 4, Member States may, where appropriate, pass information to the Commission at the stage preceding the decision on the measures to be taken. Immediate contact, as soon as a risk is discovered or suspected, can in fact facilitate preventive action.

6. If the Member State considers certain information to be confidential, it should specify this and justify its request for confidentiality, bearing in mind that the need to take effective measures to protect consumers normally outweighs considerations of confidentiality. It should also be remembered that precautions are taken in all cases, both by the Commission and by the members of the network responsible in the various Member States, to avoid any unnecessary disclosure of information likely to harm the reputation of a product or series of products.

7. The Commission shall verify the conformity of the information received with Article 8 of this Directive, contact the notifying country, if necessary, and forward the information immediately by telex or fax to the relevant authorities in the other Member States with a copy to each permanent representation; those authorities may, at the same time as the transmission of the telex, be contacted by telephone. The Commission may also contact the Member State presumed to be the country or origin of the product to carry out the necessary verifications.

8. At the same time the Commission, when it considers it to be necessary, and in order to supplement the information received, can in exceptional circumstances institute an investigation of its own motion and/or convene the Committee on Emergencies provided for in Article 10(1) of this Directive.

In the case of such an investigation Member States shall supply the Commission with the requested information to the best of their ability.

9. The other Member States are requested, wherever possible, to inform the Commission without delay of the following:

(a) whether the product has been marketed in its territory;
(b) supplementary information it has obtained on the danger involved, including the results of any tests/analyses carried out to assets the level of risk,

and in any case they must inform the Commission as soon as possible of the following:

(c) the measures taken or decided on, of the type mentioned in Article 8(1) of this Directive;
(d) when the product mentioned in this information has been found within their territory but no measures have been taken or decided on and the reasons why no measures are to be taken.

10. The Commission may, in the light of the evolution of a case and the information received from Member States under point 9 above, convene the above Committee on Emergencies in order to exchange views on the results

obtained and to evaluate the measures taken. The Committee on Emergencies may also be convened at the request of a representative of a Member State.

11. The Commission shall, by means of its internal co-ordination procedures, endeavour to:

(a) avoid unnecessary duplication in dealing with notifications;
(b) make full use of the expertise available within the Commission;
(c) keep the other services concerned fully informed;
(d) ensure that discussions in the various relevant committees are held in accordance with Article 10 of this Directive.

12. When a Member State intends, apart from any specific measures taken because of serious and immediate risks, to modify its legislation by adopting technical specifications, the latter must be notified to the Commission at the draft stage, in accordance with Directive 83/189/EEC, if necessary, quoting the urgent reasons set out in Article 9(3) of that Directive.

13. To allow it to have an overview of the situation, the Committee on Emergencies shall be periodically informed of all the notifications received and of the follow-up. With regard to points 8 and 10 above, and in those cases which fall within the scope of procedures and/or committees provided for by Community legislation governing specific products or product sectors, those committees shall be involved. In cases where the Committee on Emergencies is not involved and no provisions are made under 11(d), the contact points shall be informed of any exchange of views within other committees.

14. At present there are two networks of contact points: the food products network and the non-food products network. The list of contact points and officials responsible for the networks with telephone, telex and fax numbers and addresses is confidential and distributed to the members of the network only. This list enables contact to be established with the Commission and between Member States in order to facilitate clarification of points of detail. When such contacts between Member States give rise to new information of general interest, the Member States which initiated the bilateral contact shall inform the Commission. Only information received or confirmed through contact points in Member States may be considered as received through the rapid exchange of information procedure.

Every year the Commission shall carry out a review of the effectiveness of the network, of any necessary improvements and of the progress made in the communications technology between the authorities responsible for its operation.

Appendix 2: General Product Safety Regulations 1994 (S.I. 1994 No. 2328)

Dated October 3, 1994 and made by the Secretary of State as a Minister designated for the purposes of section 2(2) of the European Communities Act 1972 in relation to measures relating to consumer protection as regards general product safety;

Now, the Secretary of State, in exercise of the powers conferred on him by section 2(2) of that Act and of all other powers enabling him in that behalf hereby makes the following Regulations:

Citation and commencement

1.—(1) These Regulations may be cited as the General Product Safety Regulations 1994 and shall come into force on 3rd October 1994.

(2) Nothing in these regulations applies to a medicinal product for human use to which the Medicines for Human Use (Marketing Authorisation Etc.) Regulations 1994 apply.[1]

Interpretation

2.—(1) In these Regulations—

"the 1968 Act" means the Medicines Act 1968;

"the 1987 Act" means the Consumer Protection Act 1987;

"the 1990 Act" means the Food Safety Act 1990;

"commercial activitiy" includes a business and a trade;

"consumer" means a consumer acting otherwise than in the course of a commercial activitiy;

"dangerous product" means any product other than a safe product;

"distributor" means any professional in the supply chain whose activity does not affect the safety properites of a product;

"enforcement authority" means the Secretary of State, any other Minister of the Crown in charge of a Government Department, any such department and any authority, council and other person on whom functions under these Regulations are imposed by or under regulation 11;

"general safety requirement" means the requirement in regulation 7;

"the GPS Directive" means Council Directive 92/59/EEC on general product safety;

"the 1991 Order" means the Food Safety (Northern Ireland) Order 1991;

"producer" means

[1] Amended by Medicines for Human Use (Marketing Authorisation Etc.) Regulations 1994 (S.I. 1994 No. 3144).

(a) the manufacturer of the product, when he is established in the Community, and includes any person presenting himself as the manufacturer by affixing to the product his name, trade mark or other distinctive mark, or the person who reconditions the product;

(b) when the manufacturer is not established in the Community—

(i) if the manufacturer does not have a representative established in the Community, the importer of the product;

(ii) in all other cases, the manufacturer's representative; and

(c) other professionals in the supply chain, insofar as their activities may affect the safety properties of a produced placed on the market;

"product" means any product intended for consumers or likely to be used by consumers, supplied whether for consideration or not in the course of a commercial activity and whether new, used or reconditioned; provided, however, a product which is used exclusively in the context of a commercial activity even if it is used for or by a consumer shall not be regarded as a product for the purposes of these Regulations provided always and for the avoidance of doubt this exception shall not extend to the supply of such a product to a consumer;

"safe product" means any product which, under normal or reasonably foreseeable conditions of use, including duration, does not present any risk or only the minimum risks compatible with the product's use, considered as acceptable and consistent with a high level of protection for the safety and health of persons, taking into account in particular—

(a) the characteristics of the product, including its composition, packaging, instructions for assembly and maintenance;

(b) the effect on other products, where it is reasonably foreseeable that it will be used with other products;

(c) the presentation of the product, the labelling, any instructions for its use and disposal and any other indication or information provided by the producer; and

(d) the categories of consumers at serious risk when using the product, in particular children,

and the fact that higher levels of safety may be obtained or other products presenting a lesser degree of risk may be available shall not of itself cause the product to be considered other than a safe product.

(2) Reference in these Regulations to the "Community" are references to the European Economic Area established under the Agreement signed at Oporto on 2nd May 1992 as adjusted by the Protocol signed at Brussels on 17th March 1993.

Application and revocation

3. These Regulations do not apply to—

(a) second-hand products which are antiques;

(b) products supplied for repair or reconditioning before use, provided the supplier clearly informs the person to whom he supplies the product to that effect; or

(c) any product where there are specific provisions in rules of Community law governing all aspects of the safety of the product.

4. The requirements of these Regulations apply to a product where the product is the subject of provisions of Community law other than the GPS Directive insofar as those provisions do not make specific provision governing an aspect of the safety of the product.

5. For the purposes of these Regulations the provisions of section 10 of the 1987 Act to the extent that they impose general safety requirements which must be compiled with if products are to be—

(i) placed on the market, offered or agreed to be placed on the market or exposed or possessed to be placed on the market by producers; or
(ii) supplied, offered or agreed to be supplied or exposed or possessed to be supplied by distributors,

are hereby disapplied.

6.—(1) Sub-paragraph (ii) of paragraph (b) of sub-section (3) of section 10 of the 1987 Act is hereby repealed.

(2) The Approval of Safety Standards Regulations 1987 are hereby revoked.

General safety requirement

7. No producer shall place a product on the market unless the product is a safe product.

Requirement as to information

8.—(1) Within the limits of his activity, a producer shall—

(a) provide consumers with the relevant information to enable them to assess the risks inherent in a product throughout the normal or reasonably foreseeable period of its use, where such risks are not immediately obvious without adequate warnings, and to take precautions against those risks; and
(b) adopt measures commensurate with the characteristics of the products which he supplies, to enable him to be informed of the risks which these products might present and to take appropriate action, including, if necessary, withdrawing the product in question from the market to avoid those risks.

(2) The measures referred to in sub-paragraph (b) of paragraph (1) above may include, whenever appropriate—

(i) marking of the products or product batches in such a way that they can be identified;
(ii) sample testing of marketed products;
(iii) investigating complaints; and
(iv) keeping distributors informed of such monitoring.

Requirements of distributors

9. A distributor shall act with due care in order to help ensure compliance with the requirements of regulation 7 above and, in particular, without limiting the generality of the foregoing—

(a) a distributor shall not supply products to any person which he knows, or should have presumed, on the basis of the information in his possession and as a professional, are dangerous products; and
(b) within the limits of his activities, a distributor shall participate in monitoring the safety of products placed on the market, in particular by passing on information on the product risks and co-operating in the action taken to avoid those risks.

Presumption of conformity and product assessment

10.—(1) Where in relation to any product such product conforms to the specific rules of the law of the United Kingdom laying down the health and safety requirements which the product must satisfy in order to be marketed there shall be a presumption that, until the contrary is proved, the product is a safe product.

(2) Where no specific rules as are mentioned or referred to in paragraph (1) exist, the conformity of a product of the general safety requirement shall be assessed taking into account—

(i) voluntary national standards of the United Kingdom giving effect to a European standard; or
(ii) Community technical specifications; or
(iii) if there are no such voluntary national standards of the United Kingdom or Community technical specifications—
   (aa) standards drawn up in the United Kingdom; or
   (bb) the codes of good practice in respect of health and safety in the product sector concerned; or
   (cc) the state of the art and technology

and the safety which consumers may reasonably expect.

Enforcement

11. For the purposes of providing for the enforcement of these Regulations—

(a) section 13 of the 1987 Act (prohibition notices and notices to warn) shall (to the extent that it does not already do so) apply to products as it applies to relevant goods under that section;
(b) the requirements of these Regulations shall constitute safety provisions for the purposes of sections 14 (suspension notices), 15 (appeals against suspension notices), 16 (forfeiture: England, Wales and Northern Ireland), 17 (forfeiture: Scotland) and 18 (power to obtain information) of the 1987 Act;
(c) (i) subject to paragraph (ii) below a weights and measures authority in Great Britain and a district council in Northern Ireland shall have the same duty to enforce these Regulations as they have in relation to Part II of the 1987 Act, and Part IV, sections 37 and 38 and subsections (3) and (4) of section 42 of that Act shall apply accordingly;
   (ii) without prejudice to the provisions of paragraphs (a) and (b) above and subparagraph (i) above, insofar as these Regulations apply:
      (aa) to products licensed in accordance with the provisions of the 1968 Act, [or which are the subject of a marketing authorisation within the meaning of the Medicines for Human Use (Marketing Authorisations Etc.) Regulations 1994][2] [or authorised in accordance with the provisions of The Marketing Authorisations for Veterinary Medicinal Products Regulations 1994][3] it shall be the duty of the enforcement authority as defined in section 132(1) of the 1968 Act to enforce or to secure the enforcement of these Regulations and sections 108 to 115 and section 119 of and Schedule 3 to that Act shall apply accordingly as if these Regulations were regulations made under the said Act;

[2] Amended by Medicines for Human Use (Marketing Authorisation Etc.) Regulations 1994 (S.I. 1994 No. 3144).

[3] Amended by The Marketing Authorisations for Veterinary Medicinal Products Regulations 1994 (S.I. 1994 No. 3142).

(bb) in relation to food within the meaning of section 1 of the 1990 Act, it shall be the duty of each food authority as defined in section 5 of the 1990 Act to enforce or to secure the enforcement of these Regulations, within its area, in Great Britain and sections 9, 29, 30 and 32 of that Act shall apply accordingly as if these Regulations were food safety requirements made under the said Act and section 10 of that Act shall apply as if these Regulations were regulations made under Part II of that Act; and

(cc) in relation to food within the meaning of article 2 of the 1991 Order, it shall be the duty of the relevant enforcement authority as provided for in article 26 of that Order to enforce or to secure enforcement of these Regulations in Northern Ireland and articles 8, 29, 30, 31 and 33 of that Order shall apply accordingly as if these Regulations were food safety requirements made under that Order and article 9 of that Order shall apply as if these Regulations were regulations made under Part II of that Order;

(d) in sections 13(4) and 14(6) of the 1987 Act for the words "six months" there shall be substituted "three months"; and

(e) nothing in this regulation shall authorise any enforcement authority to bring proceedings in Scotland for an offence.

Offences and preparatory acts

12. Any person who contravenes regulation 7 or 9(a) shall be guilty of an offence.

13. No producer or distributor shall—

(a) offer or agree to place on the market any dangerous product or expose or possess any such product for placing on the market; or

(b) offer or agree to supply any dangerous product or expose or possess any such product for supply,

and any person who contravenes the requirements of this regulation shall be guilty of an offence.

Defence of due diligence

14.—(1) Subject to the following paragraphs of this regulation, in proceedings against any person for an offence under these Regulations it shall be a defence for that person to show that he took all reasonable steps and exercised all due diligence to avoid committing the offence.

(2) Where in any proceedings against any person for such an offence the defence provided by paragraph (1) above involves an allegation that the commission of the offence was due

(a) to the act or default of another, or

(b) to reliance on information given by another,

that person shall not, without leave of the court, be entitled to rely on the defence unless, not less than seven days before, in England, Wales and Northern Ireland, the hearing of the proceedings or, in Scotland, the trial diet, he has served a notice under paragraph (3) below on the person bringing the proceedings.

(3) A notice under this paragraph shall give such information identifying or assisting in the identification of the person who committed the act or default or gave the information as is in the possession of the person serving the notice at the time he serves it.

(4) It is hereby declared that a person shall not be entitled to rely on the defence provided in paragraph (1) above by reason of his reliance on information supplied by another, unless he shows that it was reasonable in all the circumstances for him to have relied on the information, having regard in particular—

(a) to the steps which he took, and those which might reasonably have been taken, for the purpose of verifying the information; and
(b) to whether he had any reason to disbelieve the information.

(5) It is hereby declared that a person shall not be entitled to rely on the defence provided by paragraph (1) above or by section 39(1) of the 1987 Act (defence of due diligence) if he has contravened regulation 9(b).

Liability of persons other than principal offender

15.—(1) Where the commission by any person of an offence to which regulation 14 above applies is due to the act or default committed by some other person in the course of a commercial activity of his, the other person shall be guilty of an offence and may be proceeded against and punished by virtue of this paragraph whether or not proceedings are taken against the first-mentioned person.

(2) Where a body corporate is guilty of an offence under these Regulations (including where it is so guilty by virtue of paragraph (1) above) in respect of any act or default which is shown to have been committed with the consent or connivance of, or to be attributable to any neglect on the part of any director, manager, secretary of other similar officer of the body corporate or any person who was purporting to act in any such capacity he, as well as the body corporate, shall be guilty of that offence and shall be liable to be proceeded against and punished accordingly.

(3) Where the affairs of a body corporate are managed by its members, paragraph (2) above shall apply in relation to the acts and defaults of a member in connection with his functions of management as if he were a director of the body corporate.

(4) Where a Scottish partnership is guilty of an offence under regulation 14 above (including where it is so guilty by virtue of paragraph (1) above) in respect of any act or default which is shown to have been committed with the consent or connivance of, or to be attributable to any neglect on the part of, a partner in the partnership, he, as well as the partnership, shall be guilty of that offence and shall be liable to be proceeded against and punished accordingly.

Extension of the time for bringing summary proceedings

16.—(1) Notwithstanding section 127 of the Magistrates' Courts Act 1980 and article 19 of the Magistrates' Courts (Northern Ireland) Order 1981, in England, Wales and Northern Ireland a magistrates' court may try an information (in the case of England and Wales) or a complaint (in the case of Northern Ireland) in respect of proceedings for an offence under regulation 12 or 13 above if (in the case of England and Wales) the information is laid or (in the case of Northern Ireland) the complaint is made within twelve months from the date of the offence.

(2) Notwithstanding section 331 of the Criminal Procedure (Scotland) Act 1975, in Scotland summary proceedings for an offence under regulation 12 or 13 above may be commenced at any time within twelve months from the date of the offence.

(3) For the purposes of paragraph (2) above, section 331(3) of the Criminal Procedure (Scotland) Act 1975 shall apply as it applies for the purposes of that section.

Penalties

17. A person guilty of an offence under regulation 12 or 13 above shall be liable on summary conviction.

(a) imprisonment for a term not exceeding three months; or
(b) a fine not exceeding level 5 on the standard scale;

or to both.

Duties of enforcement authorities

18.—(1) Every enforcement authority shall give immediate notice to the Secretary of State of any action taken by it to prohibit or restrict the supply of any product or forfeit or do any other thing in respect of any product for the purposes of these Regulations.

(2) The requirements of paragraph (1) above shall not apply in the case of any action taken in respect of any second-hand product.

8th September 1994

Ferrers
Minister of State
Department of Trade and Industry

Appendix 3: Consumer Protection Act 1987 (c.43)

An Act to make provision with respect to the liability of persons for damage caused by defective products; to consolidate with amendments the Consumer Safety Act 1978 and the Consumer Safety (Amendment) Act 1986; to make provision with respect to the giving of price indications; to amend Part I of the Health and Safety at Work etc. Act 1974 and sections 31 and 80 of the Explosives Act 1875; to repeal the Trade Descriptions Act 1972 and the Fabrics (Misdescription) Act 1913; and for connected purposes. *[15th May 1987]*

Be it enacted by the Queen's most Excellent Majesty, by and with the advice and consent of the Lords Spiritual and Temporal, and Commons, in this present Parliament assembled, and by the authority of the same, as follows:

Part I

Product Liability

1.—(1) This Part shall have effect for the purpose of making such provision as is necessary in order to comply with the product liability Directive and shall be construed accordingly.

(2) In this Part, except in so far as the context otherwise requires—

"agricultural produce" means any produce of the soil, of stock-farming or of fisheries;

"dependant" and "relative" have the same meaning as they have in, respectively, the Fatal Accidents Act 1976 and the Damages (Scotland) Act 1976;

"producer", in relation to a product, means—

(a) the person who manufactured it;

(b) in the case of a substance which has not been manufactured but has been won or abstracted, the person who won or abstracted it;

(c) in the case of a product which has not been manufactured, won or abstracted but essential characteristics of which are attributable to an industrial or other process having been carried out (for example, in relation to agricultural produce), the person who carried out that process;

"product" means any goods or electricity and (subject to subsection (3) below) includes a product which is comprised in another product, whether by virtue of being a component part or raw material or otherwise; and

"the product liability Directive" means the Directive of the Council of the European Communities, dated 25th July 1985 (No. 85/374/EEC) on the approximation of the laws, regulations and administrative provisions of the member States concerning liability for defective products.

(3) For the purposes of this Part a person who supplies any product in which products are comprised, whether by virtue of being component parts or raw materials or otherwise, shall not be treated by reason only of his supply of that product as supplying any of the products so comprised.

2.—(1) Subject to the following provisions of this Part, where any damage is caused wholly or partly by a defect in a product, every person to whom subsection (2) below applies shall be liable for the damage.

(2) This subsection applies to—

(a) the producer of the product;
(b) any person who, by putting his name on the product or using a trade mark or other distinguishing mark in relation to the product, has held himself out to be the producer of the product;
(c) any person who has imported the product into a member State from a place outside the member States in order, in the course of any business of his, to supply it to another.

(3) Subject as aforesaid, where any damage is caused wholly or partly by a defect in a product, any person who supplied the product (whether to the person who suffered the damage, to the producer of any product in which the product in question is comprised or to any other person) shall be liable for the damage if—

(a) the person who suffered the damage requests the supplier to identify one or more of the persons (whether still in existence or not) to whom subsection (2) above applies in relation to the product;
(b) that request is made within a reasonable period after the damage occurs and at a time when it is not reasonably practicable for the person making the request to identify all those persons; and
(c) the supplier fails, within a reasonable period after receiving the request, either to comply with the request or to identify the person who supplied the product to him.

(4) Neither subsection (2) nor subsection (3) above shall apply to a person in respect of any defect in any game or agricultural produce if the only supply of the game or produce by that person to another was at a time when it had not undergone an industrial process.

(5) Where two or more persons are liable by virtue of this Part for the same damage, their liability shall be joint and several.

(6) This section shall be without prejudice to any liability arising otherwise than by virtue of this Part.

3.—(1) Subject to the following provisions of this section, there is a defect in a product for the purposes of this Part if the safety of the product is not such as persons generally are entitled to expect; and for those purposes "safety", in relation to a product, shall include safety with respect to products comprised in that product and safety in the context of risks of damage to property, as well as in the context of risks of death or personal injury.

(2) In determining for the purposes of subsection (1) above what persons generally are entitled to expect in relation to a product all the circumstances shall be taken into account, including—

(a) the manner in which, and purposes for which, the product has been marketed, its get-up, the use of any mark in relation to the product and any instructions for, or warnings with respect to, doing or refraining from doing anything with or in relation to the product;
(b) what might reasonably be expected to be done with or in relation to the product; and
(c) the time when the product was supplied by its producer to another;

and nothing in this section shall require a defect to be inferred from the fact alone that the safety of a product which is supplied after the time is greater than the safety of the product in question.

4.—(1) In any civil proceedings by virtue of this Part against any person ("the person proceeded against") in respect of a defect in a product it shall be a defence for him to show—

(a) that the defect is attributable to compliance with any requirement imposed by or under any enactment or with any Community obligation; or

(b) that the person proceeded against did not at any time supply the product to another; or

(c) that the following conditions are satisfied, that is to say—

(i) that the only supply of the product to another by the person proceeded against was otherwise than in the course of a business of that person's; and

(ii) that section 2(2) above does not apply to that person or applies to him by virtue only of things done otherwise than with a view to profit; or

(d) that the defect did not exist in the product at the relevant time; or

(e) that the state of scientific and technical knowledge at the relevant time was not such that a producer of products of the same description as the product in question might be expected to have discovered the defect if it had existed in his products while they were under his control; or

(f) that the defect—

(i) constituted a defect in a product ("the subsequent product") in which the product in question had been comprised; and

(ii) was wholly attributable to the design of the subsequent product or to compliance by the producer of the product in question with instructions given by the producer of the subsequent product.

(2) In this section "the relevant time", in relation to electricity, means the time at which it was generated, being a time before it was transmitted or distributed, and in relation to any other product, means—

(a) if the person proceeded against is a person to whom subsection (2) of section 2 above applies in relation to the product, the time when he supplied the product to another;

(b) if that subsection does not apply to that person in relation to the product, the time when the product was last supplied by a person to whom that subsection does apply in relation to the product.

5.—(1) Subject to the following provisions of this section, in this Part "damage" means death or personal injury or any loss of or damage to any property (including land).

(2) A person shall not be liable under section 2 above in respect of any defect in a product for the loss of or any damage to the product itself or for the loss of or any damage to the whole or any part of any product which has been supplied with the product in question comprised in it.

(3) A person shall not be liable under section 2 above for any loss of or damage to any property which, at the time it is lost or damaged, is not—

(a) of a description of property ordinarily intended for private use, occupation or consumption; and

(b) intended by the person suffering the loss or damage mainly for his own private use, occupation or consumption.

(4) No damages shall be awarded to any person by virtue of this Part in respect of any loss of or damage to any property if the amount which would fall to be so awarded to that person, apart from this subsection and any liability for interest, does not exceed £275.

(5) In determining for the purposes of this Part who has suffered any loss of or damage to property and when any such loss or damage occurred, the loss or damage shall be regarded as having occurred at the earliest time at which a person with an interest in the property had knowledge of the material facts about the loss or damage.

(6) For the purposes of subsection (5) above the material facts about any loss of or damage to any property are such facts about the loss or damage as would lead a reasonable person with an interest in the property to consider the loss or damage sufficiently serious to justify his instituting proceedings for damages against a defendant who did not dispute liability and was able to satisfy a judgment.

(7) For the purposes of subsection (5) above a person's knowledge includes knowledge which he might reasonably have been expected to acquire—

(a) from facts observable or ascertainable by him; or
(b) from facts ascertainable by him with the help of appropriate expert advice which it is reasonable for him to seek;

but a person shall not be taken by virtue of this subsection to have knowledge of a fact ascertainable by him only with the help of expert advice unless he has failed to take all reasonable steps to obtain (and, where appropriate, to act on) that advice.

(8) Subsections (5) to (7) above shall not extend to Scotland.

6.—(1) Any damage for which a person is liable under section 2 above shall be deemed to have been caused—

(a) for the purposes of the Fatal Accidents Act 1976, by that person's wrongful act, neglect or default;
(b) for the purposes of section 3 of the Law Reform (Miscellaneous Provisions) (Scotland) Act 1940 (contribution among joint wrongdoers), by that person's wrongful act or negligent act or omission;
(c) for the purposes of section 1 of the Damages (Scotland) Act 1976 (rights of relatives of a deceased), by that person's act or omission; and
(d) for the purposes of Part II of the Administration of Justice Act 1982 (damages for personal injuries, etc.—Scotland), by an act or omission giving rise to liability in that person to pay damages.

(2) Where—

(a) a person's death is caused wholly or partly by a defect in a product, or a person dies after suffering damage which has been so caused:
(b) a request such as mentioned in paragraph (a) of subsection (3) of section 2 above is made to a supplier of the product by that person's personal representatives or, in the case of a person whose death is caused wholly or partly by the defect, by any dependant or relative of that person; and
(c) the conditions specified in paragraphs (b) and (c) of that subsection are satisfied in relation to that request.

this Part shall have effect for the purposes of the Law Reform (Miscellaneous Provisions) Act 1934, the Fatal Accidents Act 1976 and the Damages (Scotland) Act 1976 as if liability of the supplier to that person under that subsection did not depend on that person having requested the supplier to identify certain persons or on the said conditions having been satisfied in relation to a request made by that person.

(3) Section 1 of the Congenital Disabilities (Civil Liability) Act 1976 shall have effect for the purposes of this Part as if—

(a) a person were anwerable to a child in respect of an occurrence caused wholly or partly by a defect in a product if he is or has been liable under section 2 above in respect of any effect of the occurrence on a parent of the child, or would be so liable if the occurrence caused a parent of the child to suffer damage;
(b) the provisions of this Part relating to liability under section 2 above applies in relation to liability by virtue of paragraph (a) above under the said section 1; and
(c) subsection (6) of the said section 1 (exclusion of liability) were omitted.

(4) Where any damage is caused partly by a defect in a product and partly by the fault of the person suffering the damage, the Law Reform (Contributory Negligence) Act 1945 and section 5 of the Fatal Accidents Act 1976 (contributory negligence) shall have effect as if the defect were the fault of every person liable by virtue of this Part for the damage caused by the defect.

(5) In subsection (4) above "fault" has the same meaning as in the said Act of 1945.

(6) Schedule 1 to this Act shall have effect for the purpose of amending the Limitation Act 1980 and the Prescription and Limitation (Scotland) Act 1973 in their application in relation to the bringing of actions by virtue of this Part.

(7) It is hereby declared that liability by virtue of this Part is to be treated as liability in tort for the purposes of any enactment conferring jurisdiction of any court with respect to any matter.

(8) Nothing in this Part shall prejudice the operation of section 12 of the Nuclear Installations Act 1965 (rights to compensation for certain breaches of duties confined to rights under the Act).

7. The liability of a person by virtue of this Part to a person who has suffered damage caused wholly or partly by a defect in a product, or to a dependant or relative of such a person, shall not be limited or excluded by any contract term, by any notice or by any other provision.

8.—(1) Her Majesty may by Order in Council make such modifications of this Part and of any other enactment (including an enactment contained in the following Parts of this Act, or in an Act passed after this Act) as appear to Her Majesty in Council to be necessary or expedient in consequence of any modification of the product liability Directive which is made at any time after the psssing of this Act.

(2) An Order in Council under subsection (1) above shall not be submitted to Her Majesty in Council unless a draft of the Order has been laid before, and approved by a resolultion of, each House of Parliament.

9.—(1) Subject to subsection (2) below, this Part shall bind the Crown.

(2) The Crown shall not, as regards the Crown's liability by virtue of this Part, be bound by this Part further than the Crown is made liable in tort or in reparation under the Crown Proceedings Act 1947, as that Act has effect from time to time.

Part II

Consumer Safety

10.—(1) A person shall be guilty of an offence if he—

(a) supplies any consumer goods which fail to comply with the general safety requirement;
(b) offers or agrees to supply any such goods; or
(c) exposes or possesses any such goods for supply.

(2) For the purposes of this section consumer goods fail to comply with the general safety requirement if they are not reasonably safe having regard to all the circumstances, including—

(a) the manner in which, and purposes for which, the goods are being or would be marketed, the get-up of the goods, the use of any mark in relation to the goods and any instructions or warnings which are given or would be given with respect to the keeping, use or consumption of the goods;
(b) any standards of safety published by any person either for goods of a description which applies to the goods in question or for matters relating to goods of that description; and

(c) the existence of any means by which it would have been reasonable (taking into account the cost, likelihood and extent of any improvement) for the goods to have been made safer.

(3) For the purposes of this section consumer goods shall not be regarded as failing to comply with the general safety requirement in respect of—

(a) anything which is shown to be attributable to compliance with any requirement imposed by or under any enactment or with any Community obligation;

(b) any failure to do more in relation to any matter than is required by—

(i) any safety regulations imposing requirements with respect to that matter;

(ii)[1] any standards of safety approved for the purposes of this subsection by or under any such regulations and imposing requirements with respect to that matter;

(iii) any provision of any enactment or subordinate legislation imposing such requirements with respect to that matter as are designated for the purposes of this subsection by any such regulations.

(4) In any proceedings against any person for an offence under this section in respect of any goods it shall be a defence for that person to show—

(a) that he reasonably believed that the goods would not be used or consumed in the United Kingdom; or

(b) that the following conditions are satisfied, that is to say—

(i) that he supplied the goods, offered or agreed to supply them or, as the case may be, exposed or possessed them for supply in the course of carrying on a retail business; and

(ii) that, at the time he supplied the goods or offered or agreed to supply them or exposed or possessed them for supply, he neither knew nor had reasonable grounds for believing that the goods failed to comply with the general safety requirement; or

(c) that the terms on which he supplied the goods or agreed or offered to supply them or, in the case of goods which he exposed or possessed for supply, the terms on which he intended to supply them—

(i) indicated that the goods were not supplied or to be supplied as new goods; and

(ii) provided for, or contemplated, the acquisition of an interest in the goods by the persons supplied or to be supplied.

(5) For the purposes of subsection (4)(b) above goods are supplied in the course of carrying on a retail business if—

(a) whether or not they are themselves acquired for a person's private use or consumption, they are supplied in the course of carrying on a business of making a supply of consumer goods available to persons who generally acquire them for private use or consumption; and

(b) the descriptions of goods the supply of which is made available in the course of that business do not, to a significant extent, include manufactured or imported goods which have not previously been supplied in the United Kingdom.

(6) A person guilty of an offence under this section shall be liable on summary conviction to imprisonment for a term not exceeding six months or to a fine not exceeding level 5 on the standard scale or to both.

(7) In this section "consumer goods" means any goods which are ordinarily intended for private use or consumption, not being—

[1] Repealed by regulation 6(1) of the General Product Safety Regulations 1994.

(a) growing crops or things comprised in land by virtue of being attached to it;
(b) water, food, feeding stuff or fertiliser;
(c) gas which is, is to be or has been supplied by a person authorised to supply it by or under section 6, 7 or 8 of the Gas Act 1986 (authorisation of supply of gas through pipes);
(d) aircraft (other than hang-gliders) or motor vehicles;
(e) controlled drugs or licensed medicinal products;
(f) tobacco.

11.—(1) The Secretary of State may by regulations under this section ("safety regulations") make such provision as he considers appropriate for the purposes of section 10(3) above and for the purpose of securing—

(a) that goods to which this section applies are safe;
(b) that goods to which this section applies which are unsafe, or would be unsafe in the hands of persons of a particular description, are not made available to persons generally or, as the case may be, to persons of that description; and
(c) that appropriate information is, and inappropriate information is not, provided in relation to goods to which this section applies.

(2) Without prejudice to the generality of subsection (1) above, safety regulations may contain provision—

(a) with respect to the composition or contents, design, construction, finish or packing of goods to which this section applies, with respect to standards for such goods and with respect to other matters relating to such goods;
(b) with respect to the giving, refusal, alteration or cancellation of approvals of such goods, of descriptions of such goods or of standards for such goods;
(c) with respect to the conditions that may be attached to any approval given under the regulations;
(d) for requiring such fees as may be determined by or under the regulations to be paid on the giving or alteration of any approval under the regulations and on the making of an application for such an approval or alteration;
(e) with respect to appeals against refusals, alterations and cancellations of approvals given under the regulations and against the conditions contained in such approvals;
(f) for requiring goods to which this section applies to be approved under the regulations or to conform to the requirements of the regulations or to descriptions or standards specified in or approved by or under the regulations;
(g) with respect to the testing or inspection of goods to which this section applies (including provision for determining the standards to be applied in carrying out any test or inspection);
(h) with respect to the ways of dealing with goods of which some or all do not satisfy a test required by or under the regulations or a standard connected with a procedure so required;
(i) for requiring a mark, warning or instruction or any other information relating to goods to be put on or to accompany the goods or to be used or provided in some other manner in relation to the goods, and for securing that inappropriate information is not given in relation to goods either by means of misleading marks or otherwise;
(j) for prohibiting persons from supplying, or from offering to supply, agreeing to supply, exposing for supply or possessing for supply, goods to which this section applies and component parts and raw materials for such goods;
(k) for requiring information to be given to any such person as may be determined by or under the regulations for the purpose of enabling that person to exercise any function conferred on him by the regulations.

(3) Without prejudice as aforesaid, safety regulations may contain provision—

(a) for requiring persons on whom functions are conferred by or under section 27 below to have regard, in exercising their functions so far as relating to any provision of safety regulations, to matters specified in a direction issued by the Secretary of State with respect to that provision;
(b) for securing that a person shall not be guilty of an offence under section 12 below unless it is shown that the goods in question do not conform to a particular standard;
(c) for securing that proceedings for such an offence are not brought in England and Wales except by or with the consent of the Secretary of State or the Director of Public Prosecutions;
(d) for securing that proceedings for such an offence are not brought in Northern Ireland except by or with the consent of the Secretary of State or the Director of Public Prosecutions for Northern Ireland;
(e) for enabling a magistrates' court in England and Wales or Northern Ireland to try an information or, in Northern Ireland, a complaint in respect of such an offence if the information was laid or the complaint made within twelve months from the time when the offence was committed;
(f) for enabling summary proceedings for such an offence to be brought in Scotland at any time within twelve months from the time when the offence was committed; and
(g) for determining the persons by whom, and the manner in which, anything required to be done by or under the regulations is to be done.

(4) Safety regulations shall not provide for any contravention of the regulations to be an offence.

(5) Where the Secretary of State proposes to make safety regulations it shall be his duty before he makes them—

(a) to consult such organisations as appear to him to be representative of interests substantially affected by the proposal;
(b) to consult such other persons as he considers appropriate; and
(c) in the case of proposed regulations relating to goods suitable for use at work, to consult the Health and Safety Commission in relation to the application of the proposed regulations to Great Britain;

but the preceding provisions of this subsection shall not apply in the case of regulations which provide for the regulations to cease to have effect at the end of a period of not more than twelve months beginning with the day on which they come into force and which contain a statement that it appears to the Secretary of State that the need to protect the public requires that the regulations should be made without delay.

(6) The power to make safety regulations shall be exercisable by statutory instrument subject to annulment in pursuance of a resolution of either House of Parliament and shall include power—

(a) to make different provision for different cases; and
(b) to make such supplemental, consequential and transitional provision as the Secretary of State considers appropriate.

(7) This section applies to any goods other than—

(a) growing crops and things comprised in land by virtue of being attached to it;
(b) water, food, feeding stuff and fertiliser;
(c) gas which is, is to be or has been supplied by a person authorised to supply it by or under section 6, 7 or 8 of the Gas Act 1986 (authorisation of supply of gas through pipes);
(d) controlled drugs and licensed medicinal products.

12.—(1) Where safety regulations prohibit a person from supplying or offering or agreeing to supply any goods or from exposing or possessing any goods for supply, that person shall be guilty of an offence if he contravenes the prohibition.

(2) Where safety regulations require a person who makes or processes any goods in the course of carrying on a business—

(a) to carry out a particular test or use a particular procedure in connection with the making or processing of the goods with a view to ascertaining whether the goods satisfy any requirements of such regulations; or

(b) to deal or not to deal in a particular way with a quantity of the goods of which the whole or part does not satisfy such a test or does not satisfy standards connected with such a procedure.

that person shall be guilty of an offence if he does not comply with the requirement.

(3) If a person contravenes a provision of safety regulations which prohibits or requires the provision, by means of a mark or otherwise, of information of a particular kind in relation to goods, he shall be guilty of an offence.

(4) Where safety regulations require any person to give information to another for the purpose of enabling that other to exercise any function, that person shall be guilty of an offence if—

(a) he fails without reasonable cause to comply with the requirement; or

(b) in giving the information which is required of him—

(i) he makes any statement which he knows is false in a material particular; or

(ii) he recklessly makes any statement which is false in a material particular.

(5) A person guilty of an offence under this secton shall be liable on summary conviction to imprisonment for a term not exceeding six months or to a fine not exceeding level 5 on the standard scale or to both.

13.—(1) The Secretary of State may—

(a) serve on any person a notice ("a prohibition notice") prohibiting that person, except with the consent of the Secretary of State, from supplying, or from offering to supply, agreeing to supply, exposing for supply or possessing for supply, any relevant goods which the Secretary of State considers are unsafe and which are described in the notice.

(b) serve on any person a notice ("a notice to warn") requiring that person at his own expense to publish, in a form and manner and on occasions specified in the notice, a warning about any relevant goods which the Secretary of State considers are unsafe, which that person supplies or has supplied and which are described in the notice.

(2) Schedule 2 to this Act shall have effect with respect to prohibition notices and notices to warn; and the Secretary of State may by regulations make provision specifying the manner in which information is to be given to any person under that Schedule.

(3) A consent given by the Secretary of State for the purposes of a prohibition notice may impose such conditions on the doing of anything for which the consent is required as the Secretary of State considers appropriate.

(4) A person who contravenes a prohibition notice or a notice to warn shall be guilty of an offence and liable on summary conviction to imprisonment for a term not exceeding six[2] months or to a fine not exceeding level 5 on the standard scale or to both.

[2] For the purposes of enforcing the General Product Safety Regulations 1994 regulation 11(d) of those Regulations provides that the period is three months.

(5) The power to make regulations under subsection (2) above shall be exercisable by statutory instrument subject to annulment in pursuance of a resolution of either House of Parliament and shall include power—

(a) to make different provision for different cases; and
(b) to make such supplemental, consequential and transitional provision as the Secretary of State considers appropriate.

(6) In this section "relevant goods" mean—

(a) in relation to a prohibition notice, any goods to which section 11 above applies; and
(b) in relation to a notice to warn, any goods to which that section applies or any growing crops of things comprised in land by virtue of being attached to it.

14.—(1) Where an enforcement authority has reasonable grounds for suspecting that any safety provision has been contravened in relation to any goods, the authority may serve a notice ("a suspension notice") prohibiting the person on whom it is served, for such period ending not more than six months after the date of the notice as is specified therein, from doing any of the following things without the consent of the authority, that is to say, supplying the goods, offering to supply them, agreeing to supply them or exposing them for supply.

(2) A suspension notice served by an enforcement authority in respect of any goods shall—

(a) describe the goods in a manner sufficient to identify them;
(b) set out the grounds on which the authority suspects that a safety provision has been contravened in relation to the goods; and
(c) state that, and the manner in which, the person on whom the notice is served may appeal against the notice under section 15 below.

(3) A suspension notice served by an enforcement authority for the purpose of prohibiting a person for any period from doing the things mentioned in subsection (1) above in relation to any goods may also require that person to keep the authority informed of the whereabouts throughout that period of any of those goods in which he has an interest.

(4) Where a suspension notice has been served on any person in respect of any goods, no further such notice shall be served on that person in respect of the same goods unless—

(a) proceedings against that person for an offence in respect of a contravention relation to the goods of a safety provision (not being an offence under this section); or
(b) proceedings for the forfeiture of the goods under section 16 or 17 below.

are pending at the end of the period specified in the first-mentioned notice.

(5) A consent given by an enforcement authority for the purposes of subsection (1) above may impose such conditions on the doing of anything for which the consent is required as the authority considers appropriate.

(6) Any person who contravenes a suspension notice shall be guilty of an offence and liable on summary conviction to imprisonment for a term not exceeding six[3] months or to a fine not exceeding level 5 on the standard scale or to both.

(7) Where an enforcement authority serves a suspension notice in respect of any goods, the authority shall be liable to pay compensation to any person having an interest in the goods in respect of any loss or damage caused by reason of the service of the notice if—

[3] See n.2 above.

(a) there has been no contravention in relation to the goods of any safety provision; and
(b) the exercise of the power is not attributable to any neglect or default by that person.

(8) Any disputed question as to the right to or the amount of any compensation payable under this section shall be determined by arbitration or, in Scotland, by a single arbiter appointed, failing agreement between the parties, by the sheriff.

15.—(1) Any person having an interest in any goods in respect of which a suspension notice is for the time being in force may apply for an order setting aside the notice.

(2) An application under this section may be made—

(a) to any magistrates' court in which proceedings have been brought in England and Wales or Northern Ireland—
   (i) for an offence in respect of a contravention in relation to the goods of any safety provision; or
   (ii) for the forfeiture of the goods under section 16 below;
(b) where no such proceedings have been so brought, by way of complaint to a magistrates' court; or
(c) in Scotland, by summary application to the sheriff.

(3) On an application under this section to a magistrates' court in England and Wales or Northern Ireland the court shall make an order setting aside the suspension notice only if the court is satisfied that there has been no contravention in relation to the goods of any safety provision.

(4) On an application under this section to the sheriff he shall make an order setting aside the suspension notice only if he is satisfied that at the date of making the order—

(a) proceedings for an offence in respect of a contravention in relation to the goods of any safety provision; or
(b) proceedings for the forfeiture of the goods under section 17 below,

have not been brought or, having been brought, have been concluded.

(5) Any person aggrieved by an order made under this section by a magistrates' court in England and Wales or Northern Ireland, or by a decision of such a court not to make such an order, may appeal against that order or decision—

(a) in England and Wales, to the Crown Court;
(b) in Northern Ireland, to the county court;

and an order so made may contain such provision as appears to the court to be appropriate for delaying the coming into force of the order pending the making and determination of any appeal (including any application under section 111 of the Magistrates' Courts Act 1980 or Article 146 of the Magistrates' Courts (Northern Ireland) Order 1981 (statement of case)).

16.—(1) An enforcement authority in England and Wales or Northern Ireland may apply under this section for an order for the forfeiture of any goods on the grounds that there has been a contravention in relation to the goods of a safety provision.

(2) An application under this section may be made—

(a) where proceedings have been brought in a magistrates' court for an offence in respect of a contravention in relation to some or all of the goods of any safety provision, to that court;
(b) where an application with respect to some or all of the goods has been made to a magistrates' court under section 15 above or section 33 below, to that court; and

(c) where no application for the forfeiture of the goods has been made under paragraph (a) or (b) above, by way of complaint to a magistrates' court.

(3) On an application under this section the court shall make an order for the forfeiture of any goods only if it is satisfied that there has been a contravention in relation to the goods of a safety provision.

(4) For the avoidance of doubt it is declared that a court may infer for the purposes of this section that there has been a contravention in relation to any goods of a safety provision if it is satisfied that any such provision has been contravened in relation to goods which are representative of those goods (whether by reason of being of the same design or part of the same consignment or batch or otherwise).

(5) Any person aggrieved by an order made under this section by a magistrates' court, or by a decision of such a court not to make such an order, may appeal against that order or decision—

(a) in England and Wales, to the Crown Court;
(b) in Northern Ireland, to the county court;

and an order so made may contain such provision as appears to the court to be appropriate for delaying the coming into force of the order pending the making and determination of any appeal (including any application under section 111 of the Magistrates' Courts Act 1980 or Article 146 of the Magistrates' Courts (Northern Ireland) Order 1981 (statement of case)).

(6) Subject to subsection (7) below, where any goods are forfeited under this section they shall be destroyed in accordance with such directions as the court may give.

(7) On making an order under this section a magistrates' court may, if it considers it appropriate to do so, direct that the goods to which the order relates shall (instead of being destroyed) be released, to such person as the court may specify, on condition that that person—

(a) does not supply those goods to any person otherwise than as mentioned in section 46(7)(a) or (b) below; and
(b) complies with any order to pay costs or expenses (including any order under section 35 below) which has been made against that person in the proceedings for the order for forfeiture.

17.—(1) In Scotland a sheriff may make an order for forfeiture of any goods in relation to which there has been a contravention of a safety provision—

(a) on an application by the procurator-fiscal made in the manner specified in section 310 of the Criminal Procedure (Scotland) Act 1975; or
(b) where a person is convicted of any offence in respect of any such contravention, in addition to any other penalty which the sheriff may impose.

(2) The procurator-fiscal making an application under subsection (1)(a) above shall serve on any person appearing to him to be the owner of, or otherwise to have an interest in, the goods to which the application relates a copy of the application, together with a notice giving him the opportunity to appear at the hearing of the application to show cause why the goods should not be forfeited.

(3) Service under subsection (2) above shall be carried out, and such service may be proved, in the manner specified for citation of an accused in summary proceedings under the Criminal Procedure (Scotland) Act 1975.

(4) Any person upon whom notice is served under subsection (2) above and any other person claiming to be the owner of, or otherwise to have an interest in, goods to which an application under this section relates shall be entitled to appear at the hearing of the application to show cause why the goods should not be forfeited.

(5) The sheriff shall not make an order following an application under subsection (1)(a) above—

(a) if any person on whom notice is served under subsection (2) above does not appear, unless service of the notice on that person is proved; or
(b) if no notice under subsection (2) above has been served, unless the court is satisfied that in the circumstances it was reasonable not to serve notice on any person.

(6) The sheriff shall make an order under this section only if he is satisfied that there has been a contravention in relation to those goods of a safety provision.

(7) For the avoidance of doubt it is declared that the sheriff may infer for the purposes of this section that there has been a contravention in relation to any goods of a safety provision if he is satisfied that any such provision has been contravened in relation to any goods which are representative of those goods (whether by reason of being of the same design or part of the same consignment or batch or otherwise).

(8) Where an order for the forfeiture of any goods is made following an application by the procurator-fiscal under subsection (1)(a) above, any person who appeared, or was entitled to appear, to show cause why goods should not be forfeited may, within twenty-one days of the making of the order, appeal to the High Court by Bill of Suspension on the ground of an alleged miscarriage of justice; and section 452(4)(a) to (e) of the Criminal Procedure (Scotland) Act 1975 shall apply to an appeal under this subsection as it applies to a stated case under Part II of that Act.

(9) An order following an application under subsection (1)(a) above shall not take effect—

(a) until the end of the period of twenty-one days beginning with the day after the day on which the order is made; or
(b) if an appeal is made under subsection (8) above within that period, until the appeal is determined or abandoned.

(10) An order under subsection (1)(b) above shall not take effect—

(a) until the end of the period within which an appeal against the order could be brought under the Criminal Procedure (Scotland) Act 1975; or
(b) if an appeal is made within that period, until the appeal is determined or abandoned.

(11) Subject to subsection (12) below, goods forfeited under this section shall be destroyed in accordance with such directions as the sheriff may give.

(12) If he thinks fit, the sheriff may direct that the goods be released, to such person as he may specify, on condition that that person does not supply those goods to any other person otherwise than as mentioned in section 46(7)(a) or (b) below.

18.—(1) If the Secretary of State considers that, for the purpose of deciding whether—

(a) to make, vary or revoke any safety regulations; or
(b) to serve, vary or revoke a prohibition notice; or
(c) to serve or revoke a notice to warn,

he requires information which another person is likely to be able to furnish, the Secretary of State may serve on the other person a notice under this section.

(2) A notice served on any person under this section may require that person—

(a) to furnish to the Secretary of State, within a period specified in the notice, such information as is so specified;
(b) to produce such records as are specified in the notice at a time and place so specified and to permit a person appointed by the Secretary of State for the purpose to take copies of the records at that time and place.

(3) A person shall be guilty of an offence if he—

(a) fails, without reasonable cause, to comply with a notice served on him under this section; or

(b) in purporting to comply with a requirement which by virtue of paragraph (a) of subsection (2) above is contained in such a notice—

(i) furnishes information which he knows is false in a material particular; or

(ii) recklessly furnishes information which is false in a material particular.

(4) A person guilty of an offence under subsection (3) above shall—

(a) in the case of an offence under paragraph (a) of that subsection, be liable on summary conviction to a fine not exceeding level 5 on the standard scale; and

(b) in the case of an offence under paragraph (b) of that subsection be liable—

(i) on conviction on indictment, to a fine;

(ii) on summary conviction, to a fine not exceeding the statutory maximum.

19.—(1) In this Part—

"controlled drug" means a controlled drug within the meaning of the Misuse of Drugs Act 1971;

"feeding stuff" and "fertiliser" have the same meanings as in Part IV of the Agriculture Act 1970;

"food" does not include anything containing tobacco but, subject to that, has the same meaning as in the Food Act 1984 or, in relation to Northern Ireland, the same meaning as in the Food and Drugs Act (Northern Ireland) 1958;

"licensed medicinal product" means—

(a) any medicinal product within the meaning of the Medicines Act 1968 in respect of which a product licence within the meaning of that Act is for the time being in force; or

(b) any other article or substance in respect of which any such licence is for the time being in force in pursuance of an order under section 104 or 105 of that Act (application of Act to other articles and substances);

"safe", in relation to any goods, means such that there is no risk, or no risk apart from one reduced to a minimum, that any of the following will (whether immediately or after a definite or indefinite period) cause the death of, or any personal injury to, any person whatsoever, that is to say—

(a) the goods;

(b) the keeping, use or consumption of the goods;

(c) the assembly of any of the goods which are, or are to be, supplied unassembled;

(d) any emission or leakage from the goods or, as a result of the keeping, use or consumption of the goods, from anything else; or

(e) reliance on the accuracy of any measurement, calculation or other reading made by or by means of the goods,

;

and "safer" and "unsafe" shall be construed accordingly;

"tobacco" includes any tobacco product within the meaning of the Tobacco Products Duty Act 1979 and any article or substance containing tobacco and intended for oral or nasal use.

(2) In the definition of "safe" in subsection (1) above, references to the keeping, use or consumption of any goods are references to—

(a) the keeping, use or consumption of the goods by the persons by whom, and in all or any of the ways or circumstances in which, they might reasonably be expected to be kept, used or consumed; and

(b) the keeping, use or consumption of the goods either alone or in conjunction with other goods in conjunction with which they might reasonably be expected to be kept, used or consumed.

* * * * *

Part V

Miscellaneous and Supplemental

36. Part I of the Health and Safety at Work etc. Act 1974 (which includes provision with respect to the safety of certain articles and substances) shall have effect with the amendments specified in Schedule 3 to this Act; and, accordingly, the general purposes of that Part of that Act shall include the purpose of protecting persons from the risks protection from which would not be afforded by virtue of that Part but for those amendments.

37.—(1) If they think it appropriate to do so for the purpose of facilitating the exercise by any person to whom subsection (2) below applies of any functions conferred on that person by or under Part II of this Act, or by or under Part IV of this Act in its application for the purposes of the safety provisions, the Commissioners of Customs and Excise may authorise the disclosure to that person of any information obtained for the purposes of the exercise by the Commissioners of their functions in relation to imported goods.

(2) This subsection applies to an enforcement authority and to any officer of an enforcement authority.

(3) A disclosure of information made to any person under subsection (1) above shall be made in such manner as may be directed by the Commissioners of Customs and Excise and may be made through such persons acting on behalf of that person as may be so directed.

(4) Information may be disclosed to a person under subsection (1) above whether or not the disclosure of the information has been requested by or on behalf of that person.

38.—(1) Subject to the following provisions of this section, a person shall be guilty of an offence if he discloses any information—

(a) which was obtained by him in consequence of its being given to any person in compliance with any requirement imposed by safety regulations or regulations under section 26 above;

(b) which consists in a secret manufacturing process or a trade secret and was obtained by him in consequence of the inclusion of the information—

(i) in written or oral representations made for the purposes of Part I or II of Schedule 2 to this Act; or

(ii) in a statement of a witness in connection with any such oral representations;

(c) which was obtained by him in consequence of the exercise by the Secretary of State of the power conferred by section 18 above;

(d) which was obtained by him in consequence of the exercise by any person of any power conferred by Part IV of this Act;

(e) which was disclosed to or through him under section 37 above.

(2) Subsection (1) above shall not apply to a disclosure of information if the information is publicised information or the disclosure is made—

(a) for the purpose of facilitating the exercise of a relevant person's functions under this Act or any enactment or subordinate legislation mentioned in subsection (3) below;
(b) for the purposes of compliance with a Community obligation; or
(c) in connection with the investigation of any criminal offence or for the purposes of any civil or criminal proceedings.

(3) The enactments and subordinate legislation referred to in subsection (2)(a) above are—

(a) the Trade Descriptions Act 1968;
(b) Parts II and III and section 125 of the Fair Trading Act 1973;
(c) the relevant statutory provisions within the meaning of Part I of the Health and Safety at Work etc. Act 1974 or within the meaning of the Health and Safety at Work (Northern Ireland) Order 1978;
(d) the Consumer Credit Act 1974;
(e) the Restrictive Trade Practices Act 1976;
(f) the Resale Prices Act 1976;
(g) the Estate Agents Act 1979;
(h) the Competition Act 1980;
(i) the Telecommunications Act 1984;
(j) the Airports Act 1986;
(k) the Gas Act 1986;
(l) any subordinate legislation made (whether before or after the passing of this Act) for the purpose of securing compliance with the Directive of the Council of the European Communities, dated 10th September 1984 (No. 84/450/EEC) on the approximation of the laws, regulations and administrative provisions of the member States concerning misleading advertising.

(4) In subsection (2)(a) above the reference to a person's functions shall include a reference to any function of making, amending or revoking any regulations or order.

(5) A person guilty of an offence under this section shall be liable—

(a) on summary conviction, to a fine not exceeding the statutory maximum;
(b) on conviction on indictment, to imprisonment for a term not exceeding two years or to a fine or to both.

(6) In this section—

"published information" means any information which has been disclosed in any civil or criminal proceedings or is or has been required to be contained in a warning published in pursuance of a notice to warn; and

"relevant person" means any of the following, that is to say—

(a) a Minister of the Crown, Government department or Northern Ireland department;

(b) the Monopolies and Mergers Commission, the Director General of Fair Trading, the Director General of Telecommunications or the Director General of Gas Supply;

(c) the Civil Aviation Authority;

(d) any weights and measures authority, any district council in Northern Ireland or any person on whom functions are conferred by regulations under section 27(2) above;

(e) any person who is an enforcing authority for the purposes of Part I of the Health and Safety at Work etc. Act 1974 or for the purposes of Part II of the Health and Safety at Work (Northern Ireland) Order 1978.

39.—(1) Subject to the following provisions of this section, in proceedings against any person for an offence to which this section applies it shall be a defence for that person to show that he took all reasonable steps and exercised all due diligence to avoid committing the offence.

(2) Where in any proceedings against any person for such an offence the defence provided by subsection (1) above involves an allegation that the commission of the offence was due—

(a) to the act or default of another; or
(b) to reliance on information given by another,

that person shall not, without the leave of the court, be entitled to rely on the defence unless, not less than seven clear days before the hearing of the proceedings, he has served a notice under subsection (3) below on the person bringing the proceedings.

(3) A notice under this subsection shall give such information identifying or assisting in the identification of the person who committed the act or default or gave the information as is in the possession of the person serving the notice at the time he serves it.

(4) It is hereby declared that a person shall not be entitled to rely on the defence provided by subsection (1) above by reason of his reliance on information supplied by another, unless he shows that it was reasonable in all the circumstances for him to have relied on the information, having regard in particular—

(a) to the steps which he took, and those which might reasonably have been taken, for the purpose of veryfing the information; and
(b) to whether he had any reason to disbelieve the information.

(5) This section shall apply to an offence under section 10, 12(1), (2) or (3), 13(4), 14(6) or 20(1) above.

40.—(1) Where the commission by any person of an offence to which section 39 above applies is due to an act or default committed by some other person in the course of any business of his, the other person shall be guilty of the offence and may be proceeded against and punished by virtue of this subsection whether or not proceedings are taken against the first-mentioned persons.

(2) Where a body corporate is guilty of an offence under this Act (including where it is so guilty by virtue of subsection (1) above) in respect of any act or default which is shown to have been committed with the consent or connivance of, or to be attributable to any neglect on the part of, any director, manager, secretary or other similar officer of the body corporate or any person who was purporting to act in any such capacity he, as well as the body corporate, shall be guilty of that offence and shall be liable to be proceeded against and punished accordingly.

(3) Where the affairs of a body corporate are managed by its members, subsection (2) above shall apply in relation to the acts and defaults of a member in connection with his functions of management as if he were a director of the body corporate.

41.—(1) An obligation imposed by safety regulations shall be a duty owed to any person who may be affected by a contravention of the obligation and, subject to any provision to the contrary in the regulations and to the defences and other incidents applying to actions for breach of statutory duty, a contravention of any such obligation shall be actionable accordingly.

(2) This Act shall not be construed as conferring any other right of action in civil proceedings, apart from the right conferred by virtue of Part I of this Act, in respect of any loss or damage suffered in consequence of a contravention of a safety provision or of a provision made by or under Part III of this Act.

(3) Subject to any provision to the contrary in the agreement itself, an agreement shall not be void or unenforceable by reason only of a contravention of a safety provision or of a provision made by or under Part III of this Act.

(4) Liability by virtue of subsection (1) above shall not be limited or excluded by any contract term, by any notice or (subject to the power contained in subsection (1) above to limit or exclude it in safety regulations) by any other provision.

(5) Nothing in subsection (1) above shall prejudice the operation of section 12 of the Nuclear Installations Act 1965 (rights to compensation for certain breaches of duties confined to rights under that Act).

(6) In this section "damage" includes personal injury and death.

42.—(1) It shall be the duty of the Secretary of State at least once in every five years to lay before each House of Parliament a report on the exercise during the period to which the report relates of the functions which under Part II of this Act, or under Part IV of this Act in its application for the purposes of the safety provisions, are exercisable by the Secretary of State, weights and measures authorities, district councils in Northern Ireland and persons on whom functions are conferred by regulations made under section 27(2) above.

(2) The Secretary of State may from time to time prepare and lay before each House of Parliament such other reports on the exercise of those functions as he considers appropriate.

(3) Every weights and measures authority, every district council in Northern Ireland and every person on whom functions are conferred by regulations under subsection (2) of section 27 above shall, whenever the Secretary of State so directs, make a report to the Secretary of State on the exercise of the functions exercisable by that authority or council under that section or by that person by virtue of any such regulations.

(4) A report under subsection (3) above shall be in such form and shall contain such particulars as are specified in the direction of the Secretary of State.

(5) The first report under subsection (1) above shall be laid before each House of Parliament not more than five years after the laying of the last report under section 8(2) of the Consumer Safety Act 1978.

43.—(1) There shall be paid out of money provided by Parliament—

(a) any expenses incurred or compensation payable by a Minister of the Crown or Government department in consequence of any provision of this Act; and
(b) any increase attributable to this Act in the sums payable out of money so provided under any other Act.

(2) Any sums received by a Minister of the Crown or Government department by virtue of this Act shall be paid into the Consolidated Fund.

44.—(1) Any document required or authorised by virtue of this Act to be served on a person may be so served—

(a) by delivering it to him or by leaving it at his proper address or by sending it by post to him at that address; or
(b) if the person is a body corporate, by serving it in accordance with paragraph (a) above on the secretary or clerk of that body; or
(c) if the person is a partnership, by serving it in accordance with that paragraph on a partner or on a person having control or management of the partnership business.

(2) For the purposes of subsection (1) above, and for the purposes of section 7 of the Interpretation Act 1978 (which relates to the service of documents by post) in its application to that subsection, the proper address of any person on whom a document is to be served by virtue of this Act shall be his last known address except that—

(a) in the case of service on a body corporate or its secretary or clerk, it shall be the address of the registered or principal office of the body corporate;
(b) in the case of service on a partnership or a partner or a person having the control or management of a partnership business, it shall be the principal office of the partnership;

and for the purposes of this subsection the principal office of a company registered outside the United Kingdom or of a partnership carrying on business outside the United Kingdom is its principal office within the United Kingdom.

(3) The Secretary of State may by regulations make provision for the manner in which any information is to be given to any person under any provision of Part IV of this Act.

(4) Without prejudice to the generality of subsection (3) above regulations made by the Secretary of State may prescribe the person, or manner of determining the person, who is to be treated for the purposes of section 28(2) or 30 above as the person from whom any goods were purchased or seized where the goods were purchased or seized from a vending machine.

(5) The power to make regulations under subsection (3) or (4) above shall be exercisable by statutory instrument subject to annulment in pursuance of a resolution of either House of Parliament and shall include power—

(a) to make different provision for different cases; and
(b) to make such supplemental, consequential and transitional provision as the Secretary of State considers appropriate.

45.—(1) In this Act, except in so far as the context otherwise requires—

"aircraft" includes gliders, balloons and hovercraft;

"business" includes a trade or profession and the activities of a professional or trade association or of a local authority or other public authority;

"conditional sale agreement", "credit—sale agreement" and "hire-purchase agreement" have the same meanings as in the Consumer Credit Act 1974 but as if in the definitions in that Act "goods" had the same meanings as in this Act;

"contravention" includes a failure to comply and cognate expressions shall be construed accordingly;

"enforcement authority" means the Secretary of State, any other Minister of the Crown in charge of a Government department, any such department and any authority, council or other person on whom functions under this Act are conferred by or under section 27 above;

"gas" has the same meaning as in Part I of the Gas Act 1986;

"goods" includes substances, growing crops and things comprised in land by virtue of being attached to it and any ship, aircraft or vehicle;

"information" includes accounts, estimates and returns;

"magistrates' court", in relation to Northern Ireland, means a court of summary jurisdiction;

"mark" and "trade mark" have the same meanings as in the Trade Marks Act 1938;

"modifications" includes additions, alterations and omission, and cognate expression shall be construed accordingly;

"motor vehicle" has the same meaning as in the Road Traffic Act 1972;

"notice" means a notice in writing;

"notice to warn" means a notice under section 13(1)(b) above;

"officer", in relation to an enforcement authority, means a person authorised in writing to assist the authority in carrying out its functions under or for the purposes of the enforcement of any of the safety provisions or of any of the provisions made by or under Part III of this Act;

"personal injury" includes any disease and any other impairment of a person's physical or mental condition;

"premises" includes any place and any ship, aircraft or vehicle;

"prohibition notice" means a notice under section 13(1)(a) above;

"records" includes any books or documents and any records in non-documentary form;

"safety provision" means the general safety requirement in section 10 above or any provision of safety regulations, a prohibition notice or a suspension notice;

"safety regulations" means regulations under section 11 above;
"ship" includes any boat and any other description of vessel used in navigation;
"subordinate legislation" has the same meaning as in the Interpretation Act 1978;
"substance" means any natural or artificial substance, whether in solid, liquid or gaseous form or in the form of a vapour, and includes substances that are comprised in or mixed with other goods;
"supply" and cognate expressions shall be construed in accordance with section 46 below;
"suspension notice" means a notice under section 14 above.

(2) Except in so far as the context otherwise requires, references in this Act to a contravention of a safety provision shall, in relation to any goods, include references to anything which would constitute such a contravention if the goods were supplied to any person.

(3) References in this Act to any goods in relation to which any safety provision has been or may have been contravened shall include references to any goods which it is not reasonably practicable to separate from any such goods.

(4) Section 68(2) of the Trade Marks Act 1938 (construction of references to use of a mark) shall apply for the purposes of this Act as it applies for the purposes of that Act.

(5) In Scotland, any reference in this Act to things comprised in land by virtue of being attached to it is a reference to moveables which have been become heritable by accession to heritable property.

46.—(1) Subject to the following provisions of this section, references in this Act to supplying goods shall be construed as references to doing any of the following, whether as principal or agent, that is to say—

(a) selling, hiring out or lending the goods;
(b) entering into a hire-purchase agreement to furnish the goods;
(c) the performance of any contract for work and materials to furnish the goods;
(d) providing the goods in exchange for any consideration (including trading stamps) other than money;
(e) providing the goods in or in connection with the performance of any statutory function; or
(f) giving the goods as a prize or otherwise making a gift of the goods;

and, in relation to gas or water, those references shall be construed as including references to providing the service by which the gas or water is made available for use.

(2) For the purposes of any reference in this Act to supplying goods, where a person ("the ostensible supplier") supplies goods to another person ("the customer") under a hire-purchase agreement, conditional sale agreement or credit-sale agreement or under an agreement for the hiring of goods (other than a hire-purchase agreement) and the ostensible supplier—

(a) carries on the business of financing the provision of goods for others by means of such agreements; and
(b) in the course of that business acquired his interest in the goods supplied to the customer as a means of financing the provision of them for the customer by a further person ("the effective supplier"),

the effective supplier and not the ostensible supplier shall be treated as supplying the goods to the customer.

(3) Subject to subsection (4) below, the performance of any contract by the erection of any building or structure on any land or by the carrying out of any

other building works shall be treated for the purposes of this Act as a supply of goods in so far as, but only in so far as, it involves the provision of any goods to any person by means of their incorporation into the building, structure or works.

(4) Except for the purposes of, and in relation to, notices to warn or any provision made by or under Part III of this Act, references in this Act to supplying goods shall not include references to supplying goods comprised in land where the supply is effected by the creation or disposal of an interest in the land.

(5) Except in Part I of this Act references in this Act to a person's supplying goods shall be confined to references to that person's supplying goods in the course of a business of his, but for the purposes of this subsection it shall be immaterial whether the business is a business of dealing in the goods.

(6) For the purposes of subsection (5) above goods shall not be treated as supplied in the course of a business if they are supplied, in pursuance of an obligation arising under or in connection with the insurance of the goods, to the person with whom they were insured.

(7) Except for the purposes of, and in relation to, prohibition notices or suspension notices, references in Parts II to IV of this Act to supplying goods shall not include—

(a) references to supplying goods where the person supplied carries on a business of buying goods of the same description as those goods and repairing or reconditioning them;
(b) references to supplying goods by a sale of articles as scrap (that is to say, for the value of materials included in the articles rather than for the value of the articles themselves).

(8) Where any goods have at any time been supplied by being hired out or lent to any person, neither a continuation or renewal of the hire or loan (whether on the same or different terms) nor any transaction for the transfer after that time of any interest in the goods to the person to whom they were hired or lent shall be treated for the purposes of this Act as a further supply of the goods to that person.

(9) A ship, aircraft or motor vehicle shall not be treated for the purposes of this Act as supplied to any person by reason only that services consisting in the carriage of goods or passengers in that ship, aircraft or vehicle, or in its use for any other purpose, are provided to that person in pursuance of an agreement relating to the use of the ship, aircraft or vehicle for a particular period or for particular voyages, flights or journeys.

47.—(1) Nothing in this Act shall be taken as requiring any person to produce any records if he would be entitled to refuse to produce those records in any proceedings in any court on the grounds that they are the subject of legal professional privilege or, in Scotland, that they contain a confidential communication made by or to an advocate or solicitor in that capacity, or as authorising any person to take possession of any records which are in the possession of a person who would be so entitled.

(2) Nothing in this Act shall be construed as requiring a person to answer any question or give any information if to do so would incriminate that person or that person's spouse.

48.—(1) The enactments mentioned in Schedule 4 to this Act shall have effect subject to the amendments specified in that Schedule (being minor amendments and amendments consequential on the provisions of this Act).

(2) The following Acts shall cease to have effect, that is to say—

(a) the Trade Descriptions Act 1972; and
(b) the Fabrics (Misdescription) Act 1913.

(3) The enactments mentioned in Schedule 5 to this Act are hereby repealed to the extent specified in the third column of that Schedule.

49.—(1) This Act shall extend to Northern Ireland with the exception of—

(a) the provisions of Parts I and III;
(b) any provision amending or repealing an enactment which does not so extend; and
(c) any other provision so far as it has effect for the purposes of, or in relation to, a provision falling within paragraph (a) or (b) above.

(2) Subject to any Order in Council made by virtue of subsection (1)(a) of section 3 of the Northern Ireland Constitution Act 1973, consumer safety shall not be a transferred matter for the purposes of that Act but shall for the purposes of subsection (2) of that section be treated as specified in Schedule 3 to that Act.

SCHEDULES

SCHEDULE 1

Limitation of Actions under Part I

Part I

England and Wales

1. After section 11 of the Limitation Act 1980 (actions in respect of personal injuries) there shall be inserted the following section—

11A.—(1) This section shall apply to an action for damages by virtue of any provision of Part I of the Consumer Protection Act 1987.
(2) None of the time limits given in the preceding provisions of this Act shall apply to an action to which this section applies.
(3) An action to which this section applies shall not be brought after the expiration of the period of ten years from the relevant time, within the meaning of section 4 of the said Act of 1987; and this subsection shall operate to extinguish a right of action and shall do so whether or not that right of action had accrued, or time under the following provisions of this Act had begun to run, at the end of the said period of ten years.
(4) Subject to subsection (5) below, an action to which this section applies in which the damages claimed by the plaintiff consist of or include damages in respect of personal injuries to the plaintiff or any other person or loss of or damage to any property, shall not be brought after the expiration of the period of three years from whichever is the later of—

(a) the date on which the cause of action accrued; and
(b) the date of knowledge of the injured person or, in the case of loss of or damage to property, the date of knowledge of the plaintiff or (if earlier) of any person in whom his cause of action was previously vested.

(5) If in a case where the damages claimed by the plaintiff consist of or include damages in respect of personal injuries to the plaintiff or any other person the injured person died before the expiration of the period mentioned in subsection (4) above, that subsection shall have effect as respects the cause of action surviving for the benefit of his estate by virtue of section 1 of the Law Reform (Miscellaneous Provisions) Act 1934 as if for the reference to that period there were substituted a reference to the period three years from whichever is the later of—

(a) the date of death; and
(b) the date of the personal representative's knowledge.

(6) For the purposes of this section "personal representative" includes any person who is or has been a personal representative of the deceased, including an executor who has not proved the will (whether or not he has renounced probate) but not anyone appointed only as a special personal representative in relation to settled land; and regard shall be had to any knowledge acquired by any such person while a personal representative or previously.

(7) If there is more than one personal representative and their dates of knowledge are different, subsection (5)(b) above shall be read as referring to the earliest of those dates.

(8) Expressions used in this section or section 14 of this Act and in Part I of the Consumer Protection Act 1987 have the same meanings in this section or that section as in that Part; and section 1(1) of that Act (Part I to be construed as enacted for the purpose of complying with the product liability Directive) shall apply for the purpose of construing this section and the following provisions of this Act so far as they relate to an action by virtue of any provision of that Part as it applies for the purpose of construing that part."

2. In section 12(1) of the said Act of 1980 (actions under the Fatal Accidents Act 1976), after the words "section 11" there shall be inserted the words "or 11A".

3. In section 14 of the said Act of 1980 (definition of date of knowledge), in subsection (1), at the beginning there shall be inserted the words "Subject to subsection (1A) below", and after that subsection there shall be inserted the following subsection—

"(1A) In section 11A of this Act and in section 12 of this Act so far as that section applies to an action by virtue of section 6(1)(a) of the Consumer Protection Act 1987 (death caused by defective product) references to a person's date of knowledge are references to the date on which he first had knowledge of the following facts—

(a) such facts about the damage caused by the defect as would lead a reasonable person who had suffered such damage to consider it sufficiently serious to justify his instituting proceedings for damages against a defendant who did not dispute liability and was able to satisfy a judgment; and
(b) that the damage was wholly or partly attributable to the facts and circumstances alleged to constitute the defect; and
(c) the identity of the defendant;

but, in determining the date on which a person first had such knowledge there shall be disregarded both the extent (if any) of that person's knowledge on any date of whether particular facts or circumstnaces would or would not, as a matter of law, constitute a defect and, in a case relating to loss of or damage to property, any knowledge which that person had on a date on which he had no right of action by virtue of Part I of that Act in respect of the loss or damage."

4. In section 28 of the said Act of 1980 (extension of limitation period in case of disability), after subsection (6) there shall be inserted the following subsection—

"(7) If the action is one to which section 11A of this Act applies or one by virtue of section 6(1)(a) of the Consumer Protection Act 1987 (death caused by defective product) subsection (1) above—

(a) shall not apply to the time limit prescribed by subsection (3) of the said section 11A or to that time limit as applied by virtue of section 12(1) of this Act; and

(b) in relation to any other time limit prescribed by this Act shall have effect as if for the words 'six years' there were substituted the words 'three years'."

5. In section 32 of the said Act of 1980 (postponement of limitation period in case of fraud, concealment or mistake)—

(a) in subsection (1) for the words "subsection (3)" there shall be substituted the words "subsections (3) and (4A)"; and
(b) after subsection (4) there shall be inserted the following subsection—

"(4A) Subsection (1) above shall not apply in relation to the time limit prescribed by section 11A(3) of this Act or in relation to that time limit as applied by virtue of section 12(1) fo this Act."

6. In section 33 of the said Act of 1980 (discretionary exclusion of time limit)—

(a) in subsection (1), after the words "section 11" there shall be inserted the words "or 11A";
(b) after the said subsection (1) there shall be inserted the following subsection—

"(1A) The court shall not under this section disapply—
(a) subsection (3) of section 11A; or
(b) where the damages claimed by the plaintiff are confined to damages for loss of or damage to any property, and other provision in its application to an action by virtue of Part I of the Consumer Protection Act 1987.";

(c) in subsections (2) and (4), after the words "section 11" there shall be inserted the words "or subsection (4) of section 11A";
(d) in subsections (3)(b), after the words "section 11" there shall be inserted the words "by section 11A"; and
(e) in subsections (8), after the words "section 11" there shall be inserted the words "or 11A".

Appendix 4: Product Safety Regulations

1. Regulations made under the Consumer Protection Act 1961, Consumer Safety Act 1978 and Consumer Protection Act 1987

Stands for Carry Cots (Safety) Regulations 1966 (S.I. 1966 No. 1610)
Electrical Appliances (Colour Code) Regulations 1969 (S.I. 1969 No. 310 as amended by S.I. 1970 No. 811 and S.I. 1977 No. 931)
Cooking Utensils (Safety) Regulations 1972 (S.I. 1972 No. 1957)
Pencils and Graphic Instruments (Safety) Regulations 1974 (S.I. 1974 No. 226)
Toys (Safety) Regulations 1964 (S.I. 1974 No. 1367)
Children's Clothing (Hood Cords) Regulations 1976 (S.I. 1976 No. 2)
Oil Heaters (Safety) Regulations 1977 (S.I. 1977 No. 167)
Perambulators and Pushchairs (Safety) Regulations 1978 (S.I. 1978 No. 1372)
Filament Lamps for Vehicles (Safety) Regulations 1982 (S.I. 1982 No. 444)
Pedal Bicycles (Safety) Regulations 1984 (S.I. 1984 No. 145 as amended by S.I. 1984 No. 1057)
Gas Catalytic Heaters (Safety) Regulations 1984 (S.I. 1984 No. 1802)
Asbestos Products (Safety) Regulations 1985 (S.I. 1985 No. 2042 as amended by S.I. 1987 No. 1979)
Nightwear (Safety) Regulations 1985 (S.I. 1985 No. 2043 as amended by S.I. 1987 No. 286)
Pushchairs (Safety) Regulations 1985 (S.I. 1985 No. 2047)
Child Resistant Packaging (Safety) Regulations 1986 (S.I. 1986 No. 758 as amended by S.I. 1990 No. 1736 and S.I. 1993 No. 1546)
Fireworks (Safety) Regulations 1986 (S.I. 1986 No. 1323 revoked by S.I. 1995 No. 415)
Plugs and Sockets (Safety) Regulations 1987 (S.I. 1987 No. 603)
Bunk Beds (Entrapment Hazards) (Safety) Regulations 1987 (S.I. 1987 No. 1377)
Furniture and Furnishings (Fire) (Safety) Regulations 1988 (S.I. 1988 No. 1324 as amended by S.I. 1989 No. 2358 and S.I. 1993 No. 207)
Ceramic Ware (Safety) Regulations 1988 (S.I. 1988 No. 1647)
Gas Cooking Appliances (Safety) Regulations 1989 (S.I. 1989 No. 149)
Low Voltage Electrical Equipment (Safety) Regulations 1989 (S.I. 1989 No. 728)
Toys (Safety) Regulations 1989 (S.I. 1989 No. 1275 as amended by S.I. 1993 No. 1547)
Food Imitations (Safety) Regulations 1989 (S.I. 1989 No. 1291)
Cosmetic Products (Safety) Regulations 1989 (S.I. 1989 No. 2233 as amended by S.I. 1990 No. 1812, S.I. 1991 No. 447, S.I. 1992 No. 1525, S.I. 1993 No. 1539, S.I. 1994 No. 1529, and S.I. 1995 No. 1478)
All-Terrain Motor Vehicles (Safety) Regulations 1989 (S.I. 1989 No. 2288)
Tobacco Products Labelling (Safety) Regulations 1991 (S.I. 1991 No. 1530 as amended by S.I. 1993 No. 1947)
Heating Appliances (Fireguards) (Safety) Regulations 1991 (S.I. 1991 No. 2693)

Gas Appliances (Safety) Regulations 1992 (S.I. 1992 No. 711)
Cigarettes (Maximum Tar Yield) (Safety) Regulations 1992 (S.I. 1992 No. 2783)
Tobacco for Oral Use (Safety) Regulations 1992 (S.I. 1992 No. 3134)
Imitation Dummies (Safety) Regulations 1992 (S.I. 1992 No. 3189)
Imitation Dummies (Safety) Regulations 1993 (S.I. 1993 No. 2923)
Plugs and Sockets etc. (Safety) Regulations 1994 (S.I. 1994 No. 1768)
Dangerous Substances and Preparations (Safety) (Consolidation) Regulations 1994 (S.I. 1994 No. 2844)
Motor Vehicle Tyres (Safety) Regulations 1994 (S.I. 1994 No. 3117)
Electrical Equipment (Safety) Regulations 1994 (S.I. 1994 No. 3260)
Toys (Safety) Regulations 1995 (S.I. 1995 No. 204)
Gas Appliances (Safety) Regulations 1995 (S.I. 1995 No. 1629)

2. Regulations made under the Health and Safety at Work Act 1974 and predecessor legislation

Agriculture (Threshers and Balers) Regulations 1960 (S.I. 1960 No. 1199 as amended by S.I. 1981 No. 1414)
Construction (General Provisions) Regulations 1961 (S.I. 1961 No. 1580)
Construction (Lifting Operations) Regulations 1961 (S.I. 1961 No. 1581 as amended by S.I. 1984 No. 1593)
Agriculture (Field Machinery) Regulations 1962 (S.I. 1962 No. 1472)
Abrasive Wheels Regulations 1970 (S.I. 1970 No. 535)
Agriculture (Tractor Cabs) Regulations 1974 (S.I. 1974 No. 2034 as amended by S.I. 1990 No. 1075)
Radioactive Substances (Carriage by Road) (Great Britain) Regulations 1974 (S.I. 1974 No. 1735 as amended by S.I. 1985 No. 1735)
Classification and Labelling of Explosives Regulations 1983 (S.I. 1983 No. 1140)
Freight Containers (Safety Convention) Regulations 1984 (S.I. 1984 No. 1890)
Ionising Radiations Regulations 1985 (S.I. 1985 No. 1333)
Dangerous Substances in Harbours Areas Regulations 1987 (S.I. 1987 No. 37)
Control of Asbestos at Work Regulations 1987 (S.I. 1987 No. 2115, as amended by S.I. 1988 No. 712, S.I. 1992 No. 2966 and S.I. 1992 No. 3068)
Road Traffic (Carriage of Explosives) Regulations 1989 (S.I. 1989 No. 615)
Electricity at Work Regulations 1989 (S.I. 1989 No. 635)
Noise at Work Regulations 1989 (S.I. 1989 No. 1790)
The Pressure Systems and Transportable Gas Containers Regulations 1989 (S.I. 1989 No. 2169)
Packaging of Explosives for Carriage Regulations 1991 (S.I. 1991 No. 2097)
Road Traffic (Carriage of Dangerous Substances in Packages etc.) Regulations 1992 (S.I. 1992 No. 742)
Road Traffic (Carriage of Dangerous Substances in Road Tankers and Tank Containers) Regulations 1992 (S.I. 1992 No. 743)
Road Traffic (Training of Drivers of Vehicles Carrying Dangerous Goods) Regulations 1992 (S.I. 1992 No. 744 as amended by S.I. 1993 No. 1122)
Health and Safety (Leasing Arrangements) Regulations 1992 (S.I. 1992 No. 1524)
Asbestos (Prohibitions) Regulations 1992 (S.I. 1992 No. 3067)
Genetically Modified Organisms (Contained Use) Regulations 1992 (S.I. 1992 No. 3217)
Placing on the Market and Supervision of Transfers of Explosives Regulations 1993 (S.I. 1993 No. 2714)
Notification of New Substances Regulations 1993 (S.I. 1993 No. 3050)
Carriage of Dangerous Goods by Road and Rail (Classification, Packaging and Labelling) Regulations 1994 (S.I. 1994 No. 669)

Carriage of Dangerous Goods by Rail Regulations 1994 (S.I. 1994 No. 670)
Notification of Existing Substances (Enforcement) Regulations 1994 (S.I. 1994 No. 1806)
Chemicals (Hazard Information and Packaging) Regulations 1994 (S.I. 1994 No. 3247)
Control of Substances Hazardous to Health Regulations 1994 (S.I. 1994 No. 3246)

3. Regulations made under the European Communities Act 1972 and other provisions

Aerosol Dispensers (EEC Requirements) Regulations 1977 (S.I. 1977 No. 1140 as amended by S.I. 1985 No. 1279)
Detergents (Composition) Regulations 1978 (S.I. 1978 No. 564 as amended by S.I. 1984 No. 1369 and S.I. 1986 No. 560)
Motor Vehicles (Type Approval) Regulations 1980 (S.I. 1980 No. 1182, as amended by S.I. 1982 No. 7, S.I. 1986 No. 1501, S.I. 1988 No. 1103, S.I. 1989 No. 2262, S.I. 1991 No. 2830 and S.I. 1992 No. 3107)
Control of Pollution (Special Waste) Regulations 1980 (S.I. 1980 No. 1709)
Motor Vehicles (Type Approval) (EEC Manufacturers) Regulations 1981 (S.I. 1981 No. 493)
Rag Flock and Other Filling Materials Regulations 1981 (S.I. 1981 No. 1218)
Constructions Plant and Equipment (Harmonisation of Noise Emission Standards) Regulations 1985 (S.I. 1985 No. 1968 as amended by S.I. 1989 No. 1127)
Control of Pollution (Supply and Use of Injurious Substances) Regulations 1986 (S.I. 1986 No. 902)
Road Vehicles (Construction and Use) Regulations 1986 (S.I. 1986 No. 1078 as amended)
Control of Pesticides Regulations 1986 (S.I. 1986 No. 1510 as amended by S.I. 1990 No. 2487)
Control of Pollution (Anglers' Lead Weights) Regulations 1986 (S.I. 1986 No. 1992 as amended by S.I. 1993 No. 49)
Gas Cylinders (Pattern Approval) Regulations 1987 (S.I. 1987 No. 116)
Control of Pollution (Anti-Fouling Paints and Treatments) Regulations 1987 (S.I. 1987 No. 783)
Materials and Articles in Contact with Food Regulations 1987 (S.I. 1987 No. 1523 as amended by S.I. 1990 No. 2487, S.I. 1991 No. 1476 and S.I. 1994 No. 979)
Construction Plant and Equipment (Harmonisation of Noise Emission Standards) Regulations 1988 (S.I. 1988 No. 361 as amended by S.I. 1992 No. 488 and S.I. 1992 No. 3043)
Falling-object Protective Structures for Construction Plant (EEC Requirements) Regulations 1988 (S.I. 1988 No. 362)
Roll-over Protective Structures for Construction Plant (EEC Requirements) Regulations 1988 (S.I. 1988 No. 363)
Pressure Vessels (Verification) Regulations 1988 (S.I. 1988 No. 896)
Agricultural or Forestry Tractors and Tractor Components (Type Approval) Regulations 1988 (S.I. 1988 No. 1567, as amended by S.I. 1989 No. 2275, S.I. 1990 No. 2336, S.I. 1992 No. 80)
Electro-Medical Equipment (EEC Requirements) Regulations 1988 (S.I. 1988 No. 1586)
Self-Propelled Industrial Trucks (EEC Requirements) Regulations 1988 (S.I. 1988 No. 1736 as amended by S.I. 1989 No. 1035)
Electrically Operated Lifts (EEC Requirements) Regulations 1989 (S.I. 1989 No. 635)

Electrical Equipment for Explosive Atmospheres (Certification) Regulations 1990 (S.I. 1990 No. 13 as amended by S.I. 1990 No. 2377, S.I. 1991 No. 2748 and S.I. 1995 No. 1186)
Household Appliances (Noise Emission) Regulations 1990 (S.I. 1990 No. 161 as amended by S.I. 1994 No. 1386)
Control of Asbestos in the Air Regulations 1990 (S.I. 1990 No. 556)
Construction Products Regulations 1991 (S.I. 1991 No. 1620 as amended by S.I. 1994 No. 3051)
Electrically, Hydraulically and Oil-Electrically Operated Lifts (Components) (EEC Requirements) Regulations 1991 (S.I. 1991 No. 2748)
Simple Pressure Vessels Regulations 1991 (S.I. 1991 No. 2749 as amended by S.I. 1994 No. 3098)
Environmental Protection (Controls of Injurious Substances) Regulations 1992 (S.I. 1992 No. 31)
Lawnmowers (Harmonisation of Noise Emissions Standards) Regulations 1992 (S.I. 1992 No. 168)
Controlled Waste Regulations 1992 (S.I. 1992 No. 588)
Non-Automatic Weighing Instruments (EEC Requirements) Regulations 1992 (S.I. 1992 No. 1579 as amended by S.I. 1995 No. 425)
Environmental Protection (Controls of Injurious Substances) (No. 2) Regulations 1992 (S.I. 1992 No. 1583)
Electromagnetic Compatibility Regulations 1992 (S.I. 1992 No. 2372 as amended by S.I. 1994 No. 3080)
Export of Dangerous Chemicals Regulations 1992 (S.I. 1992 No. 2415)
Telecommunications Terminal Equipment Regulations 1992 (S.I. 1992 No. 2423 as amended by S.I. 1994 No. 3129 and S.I. 1995 No. 144)
Supply of Machinery (Safety) Regulations 1992 (S.I. 1992 No. 3073, as amended by S.I. 1994 No. 2063)
Motor Vehicles (EC Type Approval) Regulations 1992 (S.I. 1992 No. 3107 as amended by S.I. 1993 No. 1221, S.I. 1993 No. 2198, S.I. 1994 No. 617 and S.I. 1994 No. 1570)
Personal Protective Equipment (EC Directive) Regulations 1992 (S.I. 1992 No. 3139 as amended by S.I. 1993 No. 2923 and S.I. 1994 No. 2326)
Plastic Materials and Articles in Contact with Food Regulations 1992 (S.I. 1992 No. 3145)
Active Implantable Medical Devices Regulations 1992 (S.I. 1992 No. 3146 as amended by S.I. 1995 No. 1671)
Genetically Modified Organisms (Deliberate Release) Regulations 1992 (S.I. 1992 No. 3280 as amended by S.I. 1993 No. 152)
Environmental Protection (Controls on Injurious Substances) Regulations 1993 (S.I. 1993 No. 1)
Environmental Protection (Controls on Injurious Substances) (No. 2) Regulations 1993 (S.I. 1993 No. 1643)
Clinical Thermometers (EEC Requirements) Regulations 1993 (S.I. 1993 No. 2360)
Boiler (Efficiency) Regulations 1993 (S.I. 1993 No. 3083)
Railways and Other Transport Systems (Approval of Works, Plant and Equipment) Regulations 1994 (S.I. 1994 No. 157)
Batteries and Accumulators (Containing Dangerous Substances) Regulations 1994 (S.I. 1994 No. 232)
Medicines (Homeopathic Medicinal Products for Human Use) Regulations 1994 (S.I. 1994 No. 105 as amended by S.I. 1994 No. 899)
Transfrontier Shipment of Waste Regulations 1994 (S.I. 1994 No. 1137)
General Product Safety Regulations 1994 (S.I. 1994 No. 2328 as amended by S.I. 1994 No. 3142 and S.I. 1994 No. 3144)
Medical Devices Regulations 1994 (S.I. 1994 No. 3017)
Marketing Authorisations for Veterinary Medicinal Products Regulations 1994 (S.I. 1994 No. 3142)

APPENDIX 4

Medicines for Human Use (Marketing Authorisations etc.) Regulations 1994 (S.I. 1994 No. 3144)

For lists of the very extensive regulations on food products see Halsbury's Statutory Instruments, Volume 8 (1992 Ed with supplements).

Appendix 5: Society of Motor Manufacturers and Traders' Code of Practice on Vehicle Safety Defects

1. Introduction

This "Code of Practice on Vehicle Safety Defects" (hereinafter referred to as "the Code"), which has been drawn up by the Vehicle Inspectorate representing the Secretary of State for Transport and the Society of Motor Manufacturers and Traders Limited (SMMT), concerns cases where vehicle manufacturers and concessionaires become aware of the existence of safety defects (as defined in paragraph 3 of this Introduction) in vehicles that have been sold in the U.K.

The Code deals with information to be given to the Inspectorate and to the owner/registered keeper in respect of passenger cars, commercial vehicles, passenger service vehicles and components fitted as original equipment. This document does not cover motor cycles, trailers, motor caravans or components suplied to the automotive aftermarket, or any vehicles more than ten years old.

A "safety defect" is a feature or design or construction liable to cause significant risk of personal injury or death.

2. Cases covered by the Code

The Cases covered by the Code are those where:

(a) the evidence indicates the existence of a safety defect in the vehicles; and
(b) the defect appears to be common to a number of vehicles; and
(c) some of the vehicles involved have already been sold for use in the U.K.

In some cases, it will be a matter of judgment to decide whether the number of vehicles affected by a defect is sufficient to justify invoking the Code. No fixed numerical limit can be specified because the decision must also take account of the degree of seriousness of any possible road hazard involved.

3. Recall arrangements with individual manufacturers

The Inspectorate will require a vehicle manufacturer to supply it with the names of a co-ordinator and his deputy responsible for dealig with safety recall campaigns.

4. Cases affecting components

Safety defects covered by the Code include those relating to components bought by vehicle manufacturers from other manufacturers and suppliers and sold with the vehicle as original equipment.

5. Notification of the Vehicle Inspectorate

The primary responsibility is with the vehicle manufacturer to decide when evidence of a safety defect amounts to a case notifiable under the terms of the Code. The Inspectorate will be notified as soon as the vehicle manufacturer has concluded that there is evidence of a safety defect which requires remedial action. The vehicle manufacturer shall at that stage indicate:

(a) the nature of the defect and the estimated number of vehicles involved;
(b) the nature of the safety hazard involved;
(c) the action planned at that time to remedy the defect.

In the cases where the defect appears to stem from a fault in a component produced by another manufacturer, that other manufacturer will also be notified and the Inspectorate advised accordingly.

The vehicle manufacturer will also inform the Inspectorate of all subsequent decisions on remedial action. This includes cases in which component manufacturers are involved, unless in the circumstances of the case it is agreed between the vehicle manufacturer and the appropriate component manufacturer for all remedial action to become the responsibility of the component manufacturer, in which case the latter shall keep the Inspectorate informed.

6. Initiatives by the Inspectorate in particular cases

The Inspectorate may wish to seek information from a vehicle or component manufacturer on safety defects which have been brought to the Inspectorate's notice. In these cases, the manufacturer will supply all the relevant information known to him, and co-operate so far as is reasonable with the Department in establishing whether a defect is present.

The primary responsilibity for deciding on remedial action lies with the vehicle manufacturer, but the Inspectorate may, at its discretion, put its own views on the measures proposed.

7. Notification of vehicle owners

The manufacturer will take all reasonable action to contact all owners/registered keepers and call in any affected vehicles for inspection and, if necessary, rectify components or assemblies which the manufacturer believes are safety defective. In consultation with the Inspectorate the manufacturer will arrange the despatch of a letter which will explain in layman's terms the nature of the defect and its safety significance to the owner/registered keeper. The letter will be sent directly or through the franchised dealer network. If the vehicle manufacturer or franchised dealer receives no response from the owner/registered keeper then a further letter will be sent by recorded delivery.

If requested by the manufacturer, the Driver and Vehicle Licensing Agency will, on repayment terms, and in accordance with existing procedures, either supply the vehicle manufacturer with the name and address of the owner/registered keeper shown on the Centre's records, or address and despatch a letter from the manufacturer to the owner/registered keeper.

Vehicle manufacturers will notify the Inspectorate of the response rate at three monthly intervals until the recall action is complete or it is mutually agreed that the campaign be closed as any remaining unactioned vehicles are unlikely to be traced.

8. Publication of information on vehicle defects by the Vehicle Inspectorate

The Inspectorate reserves the right, under Ministerial authority, to publish at any time any information of which it is notified, where this seems necessary in the public interest. Before doing this, the Inspectorate will consult the vehicle manufacturer, and where appropriate, the component manufacturer concerned, and will not disclose information on matters of commercial confidence to the public unless there appear to be overriding safety considerations. Subject to this proviso, the Inspectorate will also make public at regular intervals summary information on action taken on cases notified under this Code. It will normally divert to a manufacturer more specific requests on particular cases.

9. Imported vehicles

The above provisions of the Code are also to apply to imported vehicles, with the qualification that the appropriate U.K. conncessionaire will assume on behalf of his vehicle manufacturer the obligation of the latter under the Code. The Code applies to privately imported vehicles so far as the concessionaire is able to identify their presence in the U.K.

10. Exported vehicles

The Code does not cover exported vehicles. Measures to be taken in relation to these will depend upon the legal and administrative arrangements prevailing in the country of import. However, the Inspectorate and the SMMT are prepared to participate in any international discussions designed to harmonise arrangements governing notification of defects and related remedial action.

Appendix 6: British Retail Consortium — Guidelines & Checklist for Product Recall

Foreword

I am pleased to commend the British Retail Consortium's initiative in producing this valuable guidance document for retailers on the conduct of product recalls. I believe that it will provide a useful source of guidance for them whenever they may have to address this diffiicult issue. I particularly welcome the fact that it recognises that when a product needs to be recalled on safety grounds, the first priority must be the safety of the consumer.

This means that the recall must carried out quickly and efficiently. The British Retail Consortium's recognition of the importance of advance planning for achieving this objective is therefore very welcome. I hope that with their support, this guidance will enable all retailers to develop suitable arrangements for dealing promptly with recalls.

I congratulate all those involved in the development of these guidelines.

Lord Strthclyde
Minister of State for Consumer
Affairs and Small Firms

Contents

11. Traceability and batch monitoring
12. Disposal
13. Media information
14. Insurance
15. Product Recall — Important Safety Notice

1. Introduction and scope

These guidelines are intended to serve as a checklist of the measures which should be addressed by retailers in recalling products from members of the public. A variety of different approaches ae currently used in recalling products, and retailers who have not been involved in this area may find the issue complex. The retailer clearly has an important part to play in relation to product safety both before and after sale and must demonstrate due diligence in instances where products need to be recalled from members of the public.

Similar arrangements may also be necessary where an urgent repair or modification is required to ensure the safety of a product. BRC has therefore developed this general guidance of areas to be addressed. These guidelines are intended to address product recall for both large and small retailers and specific elements may need to be adjusted in that light.

The guidance is not intended to deal with the issue of the internal recall of products within the company. Nor does is address how the decision to recall is made, but rather the action to be taken from the time a decision to recall from the public has been taken and the necessity to have a plan in place before the occasion arises. The guidance is intended to apply to all product ranges including food and non-food. However, different legislative provisions apply: Primarily the Food Safety Act 1990 and the Food and Environment Protection Act 1985 apply for food, and the Consumer Protection Act 1987 applies for non-food. The General Product Safety Directive which will be implemented in the U.K. in 1994 will cover both areas.

These voluntary guidelines are not a definitive approach to product recall but may be used as a checklist or guidance on issues to be addressed. As a matter of principle, there should be no cost to the customer involved in a product recall.

2. Pre-decision to recall

This guidance does not consider in any depth the process leading up to the decision to recall a product. A number of different factors may lead to the decision to recall and each company will assess these differently. Differing timescales may apply, dependent on the product concerned, the level or risk and other factors. It is for the individual company to make its own risk assessment and to reach a decision. Similar principles to those outlined below will, however, apply: Act quickly but ensure the issue is addressed thoroughly and that information is accurate and fully verified; identify clearly who is addressing the issue. It is not possible to give guidance on the likelihood of an incident occurring but advance preparation is essential.

3. Responsibility for recall

It will be essential for the retailer to establish with the supplier (taken here to mean manufacturer or importer) where the responsibility for organising the recall lies. For proprietary branded products from a supplier where various retailers are involved, the supplier is likely to be the lead. For retailers' own-brand products, the retailer should be the focal point. However, other scenarios are less straightforward, *e.g.* products exclusive to a retailer or less well known brands. In each case it will be essential for the retailer to establish who is to initiate and take responsibility for the recall.

If the retailer is assuming responsibility for the recall, these guidelines will be very relevant. If the supplier is undertaking the recall, the retailer may nonetheless find these guidelines of assistance in dealing (albeit indirectly) with the recall. In particular, small independent retailers are unlikely to have primary responsibility for a product recall from members of the public. However, the general advice offered here may well be of assistance in ensuring a clear response to the situation.

4. Forward Planning

It is essential for each company to have a pre-arranged plan to deal with the need to recall a product from members of the public. The plan should enable a company to issue a rapid and considered response; a suggested example is as follows. It is vital that for each part of the plan it is agreed in advance who will take action and communicate with whom.

- Establish who in the company is in overall charge of the recall operation
- Agree detail of the product concerned
- Inform/discuss with supplier
- Inform/discuss with insurers and encurage supplier to do so also
- Agree the precise nature of the fault
- Indentify details of incidents which have occurred
- Agree the hazard presented, risk level and degree of urgency
- Establish the batch/code number or date of affected products and their location
- Establish the number of products affected
- Establish how the fault arose
- Confirm why only those products affected are at risk
- Establish the company's formal response
- Have available a list of key emergency telephone numbers
- Establish the format of in-store notice
- Establish the media plan
- Establish the format of advertisement
- Establish the wording of a radio/TV announcement
- Establish how to deal with media enquiries, *e.g.* nominated spokesperson
- Establish who/how to deal with customer enquiries
- Identify an independent advocate if possible
- Consider methods of communication with customers in the event of a product recall
- Inform Trade Associations
- Inform Government bodies as appropriate — *e.g.* MAFF/DoH/DTI and the Home Authority, whether Environmental Health Office or Trading Standards Office

The plan should be regularly reviewed.

Checklist

Once the decision to reall from the public has been taken and the contigency plan followed, it will be necessary to establish that all the required areas have been addressed. A checklist is given below and all appropriate action should be fully documented:

Company contact	....
Product in question	....
Batch/serial number/date	....
Location (if known)	....
Nature of fault	....
Hazard	....
Risk assessment	....
Numbers of products affected	....
Cause of fault	....
Confirmed no other products at risk	....
Action for customer	....
Nature of indicents clarified	....
Discussed with solicitor	....
Discussed with supplier and agreed action	....
Discussed with insurer	....
Discussed with local TSO/EHO	....
Discussed with responsible Government Department — DTI/ Department of Health/MAFF	....
Informed Trade Association	....
Company response agreed	....
Nominated spokesperson	....
Technical/legal support	....
Agreed refund policy	....
Statement on company response prepared	....
Response on customer enquiries prepared	....
Informed relevant staff	....
Format of recall notice agreed	....
Media plan agreed	....
Media/press pack issued	....

6. Initiating a public recall

The responsibility for organising the public recall of a product will vary between the supplier and the retailer, as described under Section 3. Large multiple retailers may take a different view to small independents. For retailers selling own brand or exclusive products, the ultimate decision will generally be for the retailer. However, in certain instances where perhaps the DTI, MAFF or DoH are involved in discussions with the supplier, it may be the supplier who makes the final decision. Moreover for independents and retailers selling branded products, the decision is likely to be taken by the supplier. It is extremely important for the supplier to discuss the issue with the retailer and to keep the retailer fully informed. The overriding question is, however, the safety of the customer.

In considering whether a product should be recalled from members of the public, the retailer should be conscious of the need to deal with the question as quickly and as openly as possible. The issue will need to be discussed with the supplier in the first instance. The issue should also be discussed with the Enforcement Authorities (local Trading Standards Departments for non-foods and some food issues, and Environmental Health Officers for food safety matters) and multiple retailers with their Home Authority. Information should also be supplied to the British Retail Consortium or other Trade Associations where appropriate to facilitate information flows to other retailers. Liaison with relevant Government Department (for food the Department of Health or Ministry of Agriculture, Fisheries and Food and for non-food the Department of Trade and Industry) may also be required.

7. Who makes the decision on whether to recall a product from the public

The decision on whether nor not to recall a product from members of the public should be made as soon as the facts are known and this should be ascertained quickly as possible. The person making the decision within a retail company should be of a sufficiently senior level and not the member of staff dealing directly with the supplier concerned (*e.g.* buying/merchandising staff) and be provided with appropriate legal and technical advice. This will assist in ensuring objectivity.

It is essential to have uniformity of approach and with a large multiple retailer or retailer selling own brand products this may well entail decisions being made by an established multidisciplinary committee. Wherever possible, relevant training should be given to persons making such important decisions.

There may be instances where product contamination is the issue and the Police are involved. In such cases there should be close liaison with the Police and any decision to recall products should be subject to their advice.

8. System of notification

Customers should be notified direct of a recall wherever possible and the retailer initiating the recall will need to advertise the recall in the national press and other media. It is suggested that advertisements should be placed in all the major national papers and where appropriate, regional papers. National or local radio, television and magazines or other media may also be used and if sufficiently important a "News Feature" sought. It may be appropriate to inform consumer magazines.

Information on the product which is being recalled should be displayed prominently on the premises, for example, in shop windows, since this is the customer's regular point of contact with the company. For some products or sectors, *e.g.* mail order, where the names and address of customers are retained and it is possible to contact the customer personally, paid advertisements may not be necessary.

9. Format of product recall notice

A recall notice will be required both for publication in advertisements and for in-store use; the notices should be similar in presentation. The notice should be headed "Product Recall — Important Safety Notice". There should be a clear, specific description together with a picture wherever possible and appropriate, which may also include an enlarged section showing the problem area of the merchandise. The notice should include the nature of the risk/reason for the recall, the specific products covered including batch or serial numbers, geographical areas affected, information on what to do with the product and whether it can still be used and the availability of help lines for further advice. An example is attached.

Where a modification to a product is required this should be stated on the recall notice and clear instructions given on the arrangements for making the modification or repair. The notice should also state whether or under what circumstances the product can be used.

10. Monitoring of response and follow up action

The level of response to a product recall should be monitored and the success rate assessed. The assessment should be undertaken in order to analyse whether an additional notice is required. The number of returns of products affected should be compared to the number of affected products sold; if substantial numbers of affected products are not accounted for, it may be necessary to undertake further action, perhaps using media e.g. local radio or magazines which were not originally employed. Guidance should be provided to staff who are sorting/assessing defective stock where personal safety may be at risk.

11. Traceability and batch monitoring

The traceability of products and information on batch or serial numbers is essential to allow a limited recall and to focus attention on any specific products covered. The use of serial and batch numbers should therefore be encouraged and their distribution monitored. In the case of foods, there is a statutory obligation under the Food (Lot Marking) Regulations 1992 for manufactured food to bear a lot mark on the label. Placing the information in a visible location, for example, on packaging or accompanying instructions should be helpful in ensuring that only the correct products are identified.

12. Disposal

Consideration should be given to the method of disposal for recalled products after their return and particularly the obligations of retailers under the Environmental Protection Act 1990, the Duty of Care Regulations and the Consumer Protection Act. The disposal of hazardous products may pose particular difficulties and should be discussed with the relevant Local Authority Environmental Health or Trading Standards Departments.

13. Media information

It is essential for retailers to be prepared to co-operate with media enquiries and to ensure that sufficient and appropriate staff are fully briefed. It may be preferable to have one nominated spokesperson to handle enquiries and for all other staff to refer queries to the spokesperson. However, other staff should also be informed; e.g. local store management and receptionists/switchboard. The spokesperson should be as open as possible, give a simple message and demonstrate concern while emphasising the positive but not promoting the company. A full knowledge of the facts is essential. Wherever possible, an independent source of advice should be given in support of the company's case. Different approaches may be used in providing information for the media, for example in preparing press packs or simply handling enquiries when they are made.

14. Insurance

Retailers may wish to consider taking out product liability insurance against the need for a major recall on a product or to discuss the issue with their suppliers. The costs of organising such a withdrawal and the effect on sales can be considerable.

15. PRODUCT RECALL — IMPORTANT SAFETY NOTICE

Description of product affected — brand, model, colour, flavour:

....
....
....

Recall by:

....

Reason for recall/Nature of the risk:

....
....

Picture of product with enlargement of affected area (if possible):

Identification of specific products covered — dates of production, serial/batch numbers, geographical area concerned:

....
....

Information on what to do with the product and whether it can still be used:

....
....

Procedures for returning the product and arrangements for replacement/repair/modification:

....
....

Helpline numbers — sources for further information:

....

Date of issue

Appendix 7: The General Product Safety Regulations 1994: Guidance for Businesses, Consumers and Enforcement Authorities

Foreword

This document provides a guide to the General Product Safety Regulations 1994*. It is for guidance only and in no way replaces the Regulations.

The guide has no legal force but is intended to help businesses, consumers and enforcement authorities understand the main features of the legislation and the circumstances in which it applies.

Those affected by the Regulations should refer to them for a full statement of the legal requirements and in case of doubt seek legal advice on questions of interpretation.

The Regulations can be obtained from Her Majesty's Stationery Office, HMSO Publications Centre, PO Box 276, London SW8 5DT, or through HMSO bookshops or from official agents for HMSO publications.

* Statutory Instrument 1994 No. 2328 HMSO, £1.95 net.

Contents

INTRODUCTION

1. The General Product Safety Regulations 1994 (referred to in this booklet as "the Regulations") came into force on 3 October, 1994. They implement into U.K. law the safety provisions of the General Product Safety Directive 92/59/EEC) (referred to in this booklet as "the GPS Directive"). The Regulations are made under section 2(2) of the European Communities Act 1972.
2. The core requirements of the Regulations follow closely the general safety requirement in Part II (section 10) of the Consumer Protection Act 1987 (referred to in this booklet as "the 1987 Act") which has been in force in the U.K. since October 1987. The Regulations call up and apply certain provisions (*e.g.* relating to enforcement powers and appeals procedures) in the 1987 Act and offences under the Regulations are analogous with those in that legislation. Enforcement practices should therefore be broadly unchanged and follow a uniform pattern. However, it should be noted that if the requirements of the Regulations apply to a product, section 10 of the 1987 Act will not apply (see para. 8).

Purpose

3. The GPS Directive (see Annex) is intended to fill gaps in European consumer safety legislation. It achieves this by:
   - specifying that products supplied to consumers, whether for a consideration or provided free of charge, must be safe;
   - defining a safe product;
   - laying down a framework for assessing safety.
4. The GPS Directive, and hence the Regulations, do *not* allow for products to be CE marked. CE marking is reserved for products covered by a New Approach Directive (see Annex), is a declaration that the product in question satisfies the particular requirements of such a directive and creates a presumption (which is rebuttable) that the product is entitled to free circulation within the Community.
5. *It should be noted that* CE marking a product which does not require to be so marked is likely to constitute an offence under section 1 of the Trade Descriptions Act 1968.

6. The Consumer Safety Unit of the Department of Trade and Industry has overall policy responsibility for the Regulations, but the Departmental sectoral responsibilites for safety matters remain unchanged. For example, where a question of food safety arises (see paras. 47–48), the responsible Departments will continue to be the Ministry of Agriculture Fisheries and Food (MAFF), the Department of Health, the Scottish Office Agriculture and Fisheries Department and the Northern Ireland Department of Health and Social Services. The Medicines Control Agency and the Veterinary Medicines Directorate have the lead on licensed medicines for human and veterinary use respectively. Similarly, the Department of Transport, which has responsibility for road safety matters, remains in the lead on the safety of motor vehicles.

Countries covered by the Directive

7. The GPS Directive applies in the European Economic Area — referred to in the Regulations (regulation 2(2)) and this guide as "the Community". As at May 1995 the Community comprised the 15 E.C. Member Countries plus Norway, Iceland and Liechtenstein.

Partial disapplication of section 10 of the Consumer Protection Act 1987

8. The Regulations largely replace section 10 (usually referred to as the general safety requirement) of the 1987 Act (regulation 5). However, section 10 will remain in being for use in certain, very limited, circumstances. For example, section 10 will continue to apply to distributors (in this sense meaning persons other than the first placer on the market) of products which are subject to specific product directives where the U.K. implementing regulations only impose obligations on the person who first places the product on the market (for example, regulations implementing the Personal Protective Equipment Directive).

PRODUCTS COVERED

9. The Regulations apply to a wide range of products but do *not* apply to service activities. Both new and secondhand products are covered. Thus in cases where specific national safety regulations apply only to new products the General Product Safety Regulations will apply when those products are supplied secondhand (but see paragraph 18). Where a specific product directive deals only with the safety of new products, the Regulations will apply to those products when supplied secondhand.

10. "Products" within the meaning of the Regulations can best be described as goods which are supplied to consumers for their private use (regulation 2(1)). Products covered include, *but are not restricted to,* clothing, medicines, primary agricultural and horticultural products, DIY tools and equipment, fireworks supplied to consumers, food and drink, household goods, nursery goods, chemicals and pesticides, and motor vehicles. Although the product coverage is wide, most will already be subject to national safety requirements. Only such goods supplied in the course of a commercial activity (see Annex) — which includes a business and a trade — are covered (private sales are outside the scope of the Regulations).

11. The Regulations do *not* apply to products used solely in the workplace (but see paragraph 12). Products which are used in the provision of a service, even if they are used for or by consumers, are also outside the scope of the

Regulations. Examples are escalators in a shopping centre, shopping trolleys provided by a supermarket for the use of consumers, or a cleaning product used as part of a car valet service and which would not otherwise be available to consumers. The safety of such products is controlled by Health and Safety at Work legislation.

12. However, if the cleaning product originally supplied for professional use, referred to in the previous paragraph, was then supplied to consumers to take away for private use it would fall within the scope of the Regulations. Similarly, the Regulations would apply to a product intended for professional use if that product was also to be supplied to a consumer for his private use. An example here is category 4 fireworks. British Standard BS7114:1988, which provides the current benchmark (see paras. 37–38 and 43) for assessing the safety of fireworks, makes it clear that only fireworks in categories 1, 2 or 3 are to be supplied for use by the general public, whereas category 4 fireworks should carry a warning that they must not be sold to, or used by, the general public.

13. In keeping with the GPS Directive, the Regulations make no provision for exemptions as such, but they do *not* apply in cases where a product is subject to specific Community legislation. Where a product is subject to specific Community legislation which is comprehensive in terms of safety (*i.e.* covers all aspects of the safety of a product) (regulation 3(c)) the Regulations are completely disapplied. However, where specific Community legislation covers only certain safety aspects of a product, the Regulations will apply to the remaining aspects of that product (regulation 4).

14. When assessing whether a directive is comprehensive in terms of safety both the intent of the particular directive and its coverage must be considered. An example of a Directive which is comprehensive is the toy safety Directive (88/378/EEC). This is clear when Article 2, which states that "toys may be placed on the market only if they do not jeopardise the safety and/or health of users or third parties when they are used as intended or in a foreseeable way, bearing in mind the normal behaviour of children", is taken with the general principles of the essential safety requirements (Annex II.I) of the Directive. Thus this Directive covers <u>all</u> aspects of the safety of toys — whether or not an aspect of safety is specifically mentioned in the later parts of Annex II or addressed by a mandated European standard is irrelevant. The same is true of other New Approach Directives (see Annex) which deal with the safety of consumer goods.

15. Also, the Regulations do *not* apply to:

- secondhand products that are antiques — regulation 3(a) (see Annex);
- products supplied for repair or reconditioning provided the purchaser is clearly informed that they are supplied for repair or reconditioning (regulation 3(b));
- products for export to a country outside the Community where the goods are exported *direct* by the U.K. manufacturer (*i.e.* the products are not placed on the Community market) and are not in circulation in the Community before being exported;
- products used *only* for display at exhibitions or trade fairs. However, such products *will* be subject to the Regulations if they are subsequently made available for supply to consumers.

16. *It should be noted* that it may not be sufficient for a trader to make or display a general statement that goods are supplied for repair or reconditioning. Purchasers should be clearly informed of this fact in each case unless, for example, the goods on sale are in a separate area of the sales premises or

trading area *and* the status of the goods is made clear in a general notice of such prominence and proportions that it cannot be overlooked by prospective purchasers.

17. In the case of specific Community legislation which includes transitional arrangements (*i.e.* a period before the requirements of a specific product directive become mandatory) the Regulations may apply in this interim period. Thus, a supplier who chooses not to adopt the requirements of that specific directive until the end of the transitional period, will be subject to requirements of the Regulations until compliance with that directive becomes mandatory. However, it is considered that it should not be the general intention that the Regulations encroach on such transitional periods and it is anticipated that recourse to the Regulations in such cases should only be necessary in exceptional circumstances where safety is jeopardised. A supplier who adopts the requirements of such a specific product directive before the mandatory date will no longer be subject to the Regulations in respect of the safety matters covered by that directive.

18. *It should be noted that* some products are subject to national safety Regulations made under the 1987 Act which require that *both new and secondhand items* must satisfy the relevant safety requirements. Examples are toys, electrical and gas cookers and heaters, upholstered furniture (flammability), and prams and pushchairs. Secondhand goods covered by regulations made under the 1987 Act which do not satisfy the relevant safey requirements set out in such regulations can be supplied to a person carrying on a business repairing or reconditioning such goods or sold as scrap but *cannot* be sold to consumers for repair or reconditioning.

SUPPLIERS AFFECTED

19. The Regulations apply to all persons in the business supply chain who are established in the U.K. and supply consumer goods in the U.K. — whether the goods are intended for consumption in the U.K. or another member State. In this context, suppliers include manufacturers, importers, wholesalers, retailers, hirers, and in certain circumstances letting agents and auctioneers.

However, auctioneers are not affected when they are merely acting under instructions to conduct the manner of the sale (*i.e.* controlling the bidding and knocking down to the highest bidder) of an item for the owner, and it is the owner who effects the sale. An auctioneer who had purchased the contents of a house on a clearance basis would be subject to the Regulations when he subsequently auctioned the contents. Similarly, an individual who buys goods to sell on a bidding basis (whether from a temporary site or established premises) will come within the ambit of the Regulations.

20. Suppliers are categorised as "producers" or "distributors". It should be noted that both terms have particular meanings for the purposes of the GPS Directive — and hence the Regulations — and do not correspond with their normal everyday usage. Thus, it should not be presumed that a wholesaler or a retailer will in every case be a "distributor" for the purpose of the Regulations, nor that "producer" refers solely to a manufacturer. For example, a retailer whose activities can affect the safety of a product (see Annex) which he supplies will be classed as a "producer" in relation to that product.

Producers

21. For practical purposes, "producer" (regulation 2(1)) is defined in two ways — either as the first placer of the product on the Community market or as someone whose activities may affect the safety of the product.

22. "Producer" in relation to a particular product means:
   (a) the manufacturer (where he is established in the Community);
   (b) an person who presents himself as the manufacturer by putting his name or trade mark on the product;
   (c) any person who repairs or reconditions the product;
   or
   (d) other professionals (see Annex) in the supply chain if their activities may affect the safety properties (see Annex) of a product after it has been supplied to them.

23. If the manufacturer is not established in the Community, the producer will be:
   - either the manufacturer's representative in the Community or,
   - where there is no Community representative, the importer of the product into the Community.

   In practice, the requirements of the Regulations, as they relate to producers, apply to any of the above persons who are established in the U.K.

24. *It should be noted* from paras. 21–23 above that it is possible for an individual product to have more than one producer for the purpose of the Regulations — *e.g.* the manufacturer who made the product and other suppliers who may affect its safety while it is in their keeping. If a supplier has affected the safety of a product he is creating a different product for the purpose of the Regulations and therefore the product is *placed on the market afresh* (the characteristics of the product he received have changed by reasons of his actions). The same considerations apply to a reconditioner of a product (see also paragraph 22(c)) who creates a different product by his actions and places it on the market anew.

Distributors

25. "Distributor" (regulation 2(1)), in contrast, is any professional in the supply chain whose activities do *not* affect the safety of a product.

RESPONSIBILITIES OF PRODUCERS AND DISTRIBUTORS

26. Both producers and distributors have responsibilities to supply only products which are safe and undertake relevant activities, including monitoring, where appropriate, to help ensure that a product remains safe throughout its reasonably foreseeable period of use.

27. The GPS Directive — and hence the Regulations — require producers and distributors to take steps to ensure that the products they supply are safe, to provide consumers with relevant information and warnings, and to keep themselves informed about the risks. However, it is accepted that the nature and extent of action necessary will vary considerably depending on the product, the risks inherent in its use, and the type of consumer at which it is aimed. In addition, the Regulations recognise that a supplier can only act within the limits of his activity. Suppliers have for a number of years been obliged to look to the safety of their products and provide the necessary information to consumers to meet customer needs or the requirements of consumer safety and product liability legislation. The practices operated by many companies have proved adequate and there should be little need to do more in the context of the Regulations.

Duties of Producers

28. A producer has a primary duty (regulation 7) to place on the market (see Annex) only safe products but he also has more specific duties, as described below.

29. A producer is also required (regulation 8), *within the limits of his activity* (see paragraph 32):

- to provide relevant information to enable consumers to assess the risks (see Annex) inherent in a product throughout the normal or reasonably foreseeable period of its use where such risks are not immediately obvious to the user. This should include information on the precautions to be taken to avoid those risks (for example, the need to wear protective gloves);
- to adopt measures commensurate with the characteristics of the products which he supplies, to enable him to be informed of the risks which these products might present and to take appropriate action, including, where necessary, withdrawing the product in question from the distribution chain.

30. Examples of such measures which *may* be appropriate are:

- marking products or product batches so that they can be identified (in many cases the manufacturer's normal quality control procedures will mean that batch marking is already in place);
- sample testing of products on the market;
- investigating complaints relating to safety;
- informing distributors of the monitoring work and the results.

31. The above are not mandatory requirements in every case and which of them will be appropriate to a particular product will be determined by the nature of the product, the group of consumers for whom it is intended and the type of activity in which the producer is engaged. In the case of producers, monitoring may, for a low risk product, consist largely of assessing complaints from consumers. More complex and higher risk products will necessitate a higher level of vigilance and attention from the producer involving an ongoing sample programme.

32. "*Within the limits of his activity*" in the context of paragraph 29 above is considered to refer to the capacity of a person, given his position in the supply chain, to influence, the safety of a product.

Duties of Distributors

33. A distributor is required (regulation 9) to act with due care to help ensure that the products he supplies are safe. In particular, he must not supply products which, as a professional (see Annex), he knows or should have presumed to be dangerous on the basis of information in his possession. In practice, the inclusion of "*he knows or should have presumed*" is likely to make available to retailers who are distributors a similar defence to that provided, in relation to the general safety requirement, in section 10(4)(b) of the 1987 Act.

Participating in Monitoring

34. A distributor is also required, *within the limits of his activity* (see paragraph 36), to:

(a) participate in monitoring the safety of products which he supplies;

(b) pass on information on the product risks, in practice this will mean:

- passing on to consumers information provided by producers about product risks;
- passing back to producers information on safety-related matters which he obtains about the experiences of customers.

(c) co-operate in action to avoid those risks.

35. The monitoring requirement placed on distributors should not be viewed in isolation. It clearly must be taken as part of the overall requirement for the distributor to supply safe products and, in general, it is anticipated that action by an enforcement authority would only be contemplated where the safety of a product is at issue. The requirement to "co-operate" in paragraph 34 may be taken to mean to co-operate with others in the supply chain — such as manufacturers, importers, wholesalers.
36. *"Within the limits of his activity"* in paragraph 34 above maybe taken to refer to the scale of the distributor's business and the facilities available to him. This does not relieve the distributor from passing to consumers all the information which the producer intended should accompany a product.

MEANING OF A SAFE PRODUCT

37. A "safe product" is any product which under normal or reasonably foreseeable conditions of use (see Annex), including duration, presents no risk or only the minimum risk compatible with the product's use and which is consistent with a high level of protection for consumers (see Annex).
38. The safety of a product will be assessed (reg. 2(1)) having regard to a number of matters and, in particular:

— the product's characteristics;
— packaging;
— instructions for assembly and maintenance, use and disposal;
— the effect on other products with which it might be used;
— labelling (see Annex) and other information provided for the consumer;
— the categories of consumers at serious risk when using the product, particularly children.

39. In practice, the above — with the exception of the reference to disposal — are closely in line with the factors set out in section 10 (the general safety duty) of the 1987 Act and will therefore be familiar to suppliers and enforcement authorities alike.

Assessing the safety of products

SPECIFIC PRODUCT DIRECTIVES

40. As noted earlier, the Regulations do *not* apply to a product that is controlled by a directive which is comprehensive in terms of safety (see paragraph 11).
41. Where no directive deals with a product, safety will be assessed by one or other of the methods specified in the Regulations (for example, see paragraphs 42–43). Where a directive deals only with certain aspects of safety, only the remaining aspects will be subject to the Regulations. In each case safety will be assessed according to a hierarchy of measures as described below.

U.K. National Law

42. Products complying with comprehensive U.K. national safety legislation (*i.e. domestic legislation which does not implement European legislation*) are safe products for the purpose of the Regulations, unless the contrary is proved (regulation 10(1)) — see also paragraphs 48 and 58. Thus, for many products coming within the scope of the Regulations there will be few or no additional safety requirements placed on suppliers.

Standards

43. Where neither a specific Directive nor national safety law applies (regulation 10(2)), safety will be assessed *taking into account:*

(i) voluntary European standards (*i.e.* harmonised standards prepared by CEN or CENELEC and which are not mandated under a directive);
(ii) Community technical specifications;
(iii) national standards (*i.e.* British Standards which are not U.K. versions of European standards);
(iv) accepted industry codes of good practice;
(v) state of the art and technology.

and the safety which consumers may reasonably expect.

44. *It should be noted that* compliance with one or other of the criteria set out in paragraph 43 will not necessarily mean that the product is a safe product if it does not provide the level of safety which consumers may reasonably expect — for example, although the product may not be inherently unsafe, it is not safe for the purpose it can reasonably be expected to perform (see also Annex definition of "*Minimum risk compatible with the product's use*"). There will be instances where, for example, a European standard exists for the product in question but does not deal with a particular aspect of safety or does so inadequately. In such cases other criteria in the list also will be applicable, *e.g.* aspects of a national standard or reference to the state of the art and technology.

Standards of the international standards organisations

45. Standards published by the ISO (International Standards Organisation) and the IEC (International Electrotechnical Commission) are given no special status in the Regulations in assessing the safety of products unless they are embodied as European or national standards. However, they should be taken as falling within the general criteria at (iii), (v) in paragraph 43.

Revocation of system of approved standards

46. It should be noted that the Regulations revoke the system of "approved standards" under section 10 of the 1987 Act (regulation 6). The approvals which had been made under that provision were cancelled by administrative act with effect from 2 August, 1994. This step was necessary because the GPS Directive does not provide for an automatic defence. The standards which previously had approved status will, of course, remain in being as standards of safety.

ENFORCEMENT

47. The responsibility for day to day enforcement of the Regulations rests with local Trading Standards Authorities in England, Wales and Scotland and in Northern Ireland the District Councils, and in the case of licensed medi-

cines the Medicines Control Agency and the Veterinary Medicines Directorate throughout the U.K. (*regulation 11*). In Scotland all food law enforcement is carried out by the District and Islands Councils. The Secretary of State has retained the powers similar to those in the 1987 Act. It is not anticipated that there will be any changes in existing enforcement practices. Enforcement powers will be those already provided for in the 1987 Act, the Food Safety Act 1990 and the Medicines Act 1968.

48. Where the safety of a product is covered by national legislation (i.e. an Act or specific regulations) that legislation will continue to provide the means for assessing safety and, accordingly, should be considered to be the appropriate vehicle for any necessary enforcement action — see also paragraphs 42 and 58. An example is food where the Food Safety Act 1990 (and regulations made under that Act) is recognised as dealing with the significant safety issues relating to food (and is enforced by Food Authorities). Thus the 1990 Act (and regulations made under that Act) will prevail in the case of food safety and food satisfying those requirements should be presumed to satisfy the requirements of the Regulations. Relevant enforcement action should be taken under the provisions of the 1990 Act (or regulations made under that Act as appropriate) and businesses should not be placed under double jeopardy by parallel action for the same matter also being taken under the Regulations. (In Northern Ireland the equivalent food safety legislation is the Food Safety (Northern Ireland) Order 1991).

The Home Authority Principle

49. The Local Authorities Co-ordinating Body on Food and Trading Standards (LACOTS) promotes the "home authority" principle which applies to all food hygiene, food safety, and trading standards matters. Under this, the local authority for the decision making place of an enterprise (usually a business's headquarters or main place of business) accepts the primary responsibility for offering advice and preventative guidance on a regular basis on safety, and other related matters, to the enterprise. Other local authorities are expected to liaise with the relevant home authority on any safety matters arising from the products supplied by that business. Businesses are therefore encouraged to make contact with, and seek advice on any particular matter from their home local authority.

50. The home authority principle is aimed at promoting uniformity of approach to trading standards matters, reducing duplication and assisting businesses to comply with the law. LACOTS monitors the effectiveness of the principle and fulfils a role in resolving any differences of interpretation in appropriate cases. A booklet describing the principle is available from LACOTS, PO Box 6, Robert Street, Croydon CR9 1LG (tel: 0181 688 1996).

Products originating from outside the United Kingdom

51. U.K. authorities will of course continue to be able to take enforcement action in the U.K. to safeguard U.K. consumers in cases where a product is first placed on the market in another Member State and is subsequently found to be unsafe when supplied in the U.K.

OFFENCES

52. It is an offence (*regulations 12 and 13*) under the Regulations for:

- a *producer* to place a product on the market unless it is safe, or offer or agree to place on the market or expose or possess for placing on the market a dangerous product (paragraphs 37–45).
- a *distributor* to supply a product unless it is safe or offer or agree to supply or expose or possess for supply a dangerous product (paragraphs 37–45).

53. Failure to comply with the respective duties described in paragraphs 34–36 is *not* a criminal offence in itself under the Regulations. Also, failure of distributors to comply with the duties described in paragraphs 34–36 will preclude a person from relying on the defence of due diligence for other offences (regulation 14(5)). It should be noted that failure by a producer to comply with the duties described in paragraphs 29–32 (regulation 8) may constitute offences under those parts of the 1987 Act applied by the Regulations.

54. *It should be noted* that a breach of the Regulations will not, of itself, constitute a failure to exercise a duty of care in relation to any civil proceedings.

Liability of persons other than the principal offender

55. Where a person (the "principal offender") has committed an offence under the Regulations and this was due to the act or default of another person, proceedings may be brought against that other person *whether or not* proceedings are also brought against the principal offender (*regulation 15(1)*).

Liability of company officers

56. Where it can be shown that an offence has been committed with the consent or connivance, or is attributable to any neglect on the part of any director, manager, secretary or other similar officer of the body corporate, such persons (in addition to the body corporate) may also be proceeded against (*regulation 15(2)–15(4)*).

Time limit for bringing prosecutions

57. The Regulations require that any prosecution for an offence under the Regulations must be brought within 12 months from the commission of that offence (*regulation 16*).

DEFENCES

Under specific legislation

58. Where the safety of a product is covered by U.K. national legislation (see paragraphs 42 and 48) and action is brought against a supplier under that legislation he will continue to have access to any defences provided therein.

Under the Regulations

59. In cases where the Regulations apply they provide a "due diligence" defence (*regulation 14(1)*) which allows a producer or distributor to argue that he took all reasonable steps and exercised all due diligence to avoid committing the alleged offence.

60. Where a producer or distributor argues that the commission of the alleged offence was due to the act or default of another person or due to reliance on information given him by another person (regulation 14(2)) he must notify this defence to the prosecution not less than seven days before the date of hearing the case. It should be noted that this is not an automatic defence and will require justification to the court. However, a distributor who has failed to comply with the requirement to participate in monitoring (as described in paragraphs 34–36) will not be able to avail himself of a defence of due diligence in respect of any contravention of the safety requirements of the Regulations with which he is charged.

Penalties

61. Offences are subject to penalties, on summary conviction, of a fine not exceeding Level 5 on the standard scale (currently £5,000) or a maximum prison term of three months, or both (*regulation 17*).

ANNEX

Definitions

Activities affecting the safety of a product placed on the market

Examples of such activities may include:

- assembly of different components, complete in themselves, received, for example, from different manufacturers;
- damage or loss of instructions when part of the supplier's operation is repackaging of the product.

Antique

In the absence of any guidance in the Directive on what constitutes an antique, the Department was not in a position to cite a definitive definition in the Regulations. However, as a working definition an antique may be taken as a product which is 100 or more years old, or which is of a type that has long gone out of circulation and as such is unlikely to be used by a consumer for its original purpose. However, if there is any doubt about whether or not the item *may* be put to use by a consumer then it *must be safe*.

Commercial Activity

This *includes* trade and business activities whether or not they are carried on for the purpose of profit. Whether, for the purpose of the Regulations, an organisation is engaging in these activities will depend on all the circumstances of its operations. There is no special exemption for charities or voluntary organisations. Such organisations which sell goods on a regular basis are for practical purposes engaged in a business activity and will be subject to the Regulations (as they are for regulations under the 1987 Act). In cases where goods covered by the Regulations are given away free, those goods may still be subject to the Regulations if other parts of the orgainsation are operating a commercial activity. Voluntary organisations which exist *solely* to provide goods free of charge to the needy are probably not engaging in a commercial activity and are not therefore subject to the Regulations.

Community

Means the European Economic Area which comprises the 15 Members of the E.C. and Norway, Iceland and Liechtenstein.

GPS Directive

Means the General Product Directive (92/59/EEC) which was adopted by the Council of Ministers on 29 June, 1992.

Labelling Information

It is not considered that products will be expected to be labelled with a warning about every conceivable potential hazard. It will be for the producer to assess the risks and hazards. Whether a warning should be given must depend on a variety of factors, including:

- the severity of the hazard;
- the risk of that hazard being realised;
- the degree to which the risk is obvious;
- the type of consumer likely to be at particular risk.

The considerations set out under 'Minimum Risk compatible with the product's use' apply also to an assessment of the labelling needs.

Member State

Means a member country of the European Economic Area (see "**Community**" above).

Minimum risk compatible with the product's use which is consistent with a high level of protection for consumers

It must be recognised that it is not possible to eliminate all risk from all products which are recognised as acceptable for use by consumers. Examples are knives and scissors which must have sharp edges to perform their function but where reasonable precautions can be taken to ensure that handles are sturdy and hands are kept away from the functional edges when such items are in use. In other cases it could be argued that consumers should be aware of the potential risks of misuse through general knowledge, acceptability, education and experience. Thus, a balanced view must be taken based on the nature of the product, its acceptance to consumers and an understanding of the characteristics which consumers may reasonably expect. The range of potential hazards which require to be drawn to the attention of consumers will depend on a number of factors (referred to in the section above on 'labelling').

New approach directive

This refers to a directive produced under the provisions of Council Resolution of 7 May, 1985 on a New Approach to Technical Harmonisation and Standards (85/C/136/01), published in the Official Journal of the European Communities (C 276) on 4 June, 1985. As at March 1995 a number of such directives had been adopted covering the safety of a wide range of consumer products — simple pressure vessels, toys, construction products, machinery, personal protective equipment, gas appliances, telecommunications equipment, medical devices. The electromagnetic compatibility Directive covers all products operated by electrical power (battery or other source). Electrical safety requirements are set out in the Low Voltage Directive (50V–1000V AC/75V–1500V DC) (although the latter is not strictly a New Approach Directive it follows a similar pattern). A number of other New Approach Directives are in the course of preparation.

Place on the Market

Means place on the *Community* market. In the context of the Regulations (*taking the definition of "producer" in regulation 2 with regulation 7*) it is clear that a product can be "placed on the market" in several ways. Examples are of when a manufacturer supplies a product to a customer or when the safety of a product has wittingly or otherwise been altered and it becomes, in effect, a new product which is thereby placed on the market anew — a particular case of the latter is when a product is reconditioned and then supplied (see paragraphs 21–24).

In the particular case of *other professionals in the supply chain, insofar as their activities may affect the safety properties of a product placed on the market* it can be taken that their responsibilities relate to any such products passing through their hands for the purpose of supply and an offence will have been committed when he has affected the safety of a product.

Products intended for sale outside the Community are not subject to the Regulations — unless the products are diverted for supply to the Community market or are subsequently imported into the Community.

Professional

In the context of paragraphs 22 and 25 of the guidance note "professional" is considered to refer to a person carrying on a commercial activity.

In the context of paragraph 33 of the guidance note "professional" is considered to refer to the knowledge and expertise which the distributor could reasonably be expected to have available to him, either alone or with others, having regard to the nature of business activity and to other relevant factors (e.g. whether he is required to have specialist education, knowledge or training in order to enter that business).

Risk (Defined in ISO/IEC Guide 51)

Risk — the probable rate of occurrence of a hazard causing harm and the degree of severity of the harm. (Hazard is defined as a potential source of harm).

APPENDIX 7

Normal or Reasonably Foreseeable Conditions of Use

Normal conditions of use can be taken to be the general usage intended by the producer without him placing unreasonable restrictions on such use by consumers.

Reasonably foreseeable use should, it is considered, where appropriate, take account of the intended and potential types of user (i.e. the elderly, the unpredictable behaviour of children) and how a reasonable person might use a product in the absence of any indications to the contrary.

APPENDIX

Further copies of this guide may be obtained from:

DTI Consumer Safety Publications

Admail 528
London SW1W 8YT
Tel: 0171-510 0151
Fax: 0171-510 0197

Enquiries about detailed application of the Regulations may be made to the normal departmental contacts for the product areas in question.

In the case of difficulty enquiries may be addressed to:

Department of Trade and Industry

Consumer Safety Unit
CA3a
4th Floor
1 Victoria Street
London SW1H 0ET
Tel: 0171-215 0359 or 0171-215 0361
Fax: 0171-215 0357

DTI General Enquiries: 0171-215 5000

TABLE OF CASES

TABLE OF CASES

European Cases

TABLE OF LEGISLATION

United Kingdom Statutes

Statutory Instruments

Statutory Instruments (Northern Ireland)

TABLE OF EUROPEAN LEGISLATION

Decisions

Directives

Recommendations

Regulations

Resolutions

Index

INDEX